HUMAN RIGHTS IN ARMED CONFLICT

It is now widely accepted that international human rights law applies in situations of armed conflict alongside international humanitarian law, but the contours and consequences of this development remain unclear. This book revisits, organizes and contextualizes the debate on human rights in armed conflict and explores the legal challenges, operational consequences and policy implications of resorting to human rights in situations of inter- and intra-state violence. It presents the benefits and the drawbacks of using international human rights law alongside humanitarian law and discusses how the idea, law and policy of human rights influence the development of the law of armed conflict. Based on legal theory, policy analysis, state practice and the work of human rights bodies it suggests a human rights-oriented reading of the law of armed conflict as feasible and necessary in response to the changing character of war.

GERD OBERLEITNER is Associate Professor of International Law and the Law of International Organisations at the Institute of International Law and International Relations, University of Graz. His publications include *Global Human Rights Institutions: Between Remedy and Ritual* (2007).

HUMAN RIGHTS IN ARMED CONFLICT: LAW, PRACTICE, POLICY

GERD OBERLEITNER

CAMBRIDGE
UNIVERSITY PRESS

CAMBRIDGE
UNIVERSITY PRESS

University Printing House, Cambridge CB2 8BS, United Kingdom

Cambridge University Press is part of the University of Cambridge.

It furthers the University's mission by disseminating knowledge in the pursuit of education, learning and research at the highest international levels of excellence.

www.cambridge.org
Information on this title: www.cambridge.org/9781107087545

First published 2015

Printed in the United Kingdom by Clays, St Ives plc

A catalogue record for this publication is available from the British Library

Library of Congress Cataloging-in-Publication Data
Oberleitner, Gerd, 1967– author.
Human rights in armed conflict : law, practice, policy / Gerd Oberleitner.
pages cm
ISBN 978-1-107-08754-5 (Hardback)
1. Humanitarian law. 2. Human rights. 3. War. 4. Violence. I. Title.
KZ6471.O24 2015
341.6′7–dc23
2014032240

ISBN 978-1-107-08754-5 Hardback

CONTENTS

ACKNOWLEDGMENTS

I am indebted to many friends and colleagues for their encouragement, advice and critique. This study was submitted as a "*Habilitationsschrift*" to the Law Faculty of the University of Graz in 2013, and my thanks go first and foremost to Wolfgang Benedek for his continuous support and inspiration and for providing the enabling environment for this research. First ideas for the book where sketched during my time as Visiting Fellow at the Centre for the Study of Human Rights at the London School of Economics and Political Science and I am grateful to Conor Gearty, Christine Chinkin, Christopher Greenwood and Chaloka Beyani for counsel and critique. I am also particularly grateful to Hans-Joachim Heintze and Daniel Thürer for their comments and for sharing their perspective on human rights in armed conflict with me. I thank my colleagues at the Institute of International Law and International Relations at the University of Graz, particularly Renate Kicker, Christian Pippan, Lisa Heschl, Matthias Kettemann, Stefan Salomon, Yvonne Karimi-Schmidt and Reinmar Nindler. I am much indebted to Kirsten Schmalenbach for her comments and advice, and I also thank Manfred Nowak, Zdislaw Kedzia, Frank Elbers, Mohammud Abdullahi, Siegfried Dohr, Paul Gragl, Astrid Reisinger-Coracini, Heike Montag, Julia Cortolezis, Markus Möstl and Kushtrim Istrefi, as well as the anonymous reviewers at Cambridge University Press. I also benefitted from discussions with my students, and my thanks go to Susanne Gölles, Gerrit Zach, Eva Ritter and Valerie Weidinger.

In the course of researching and writing this book I have been privileged to stay as a Visiting Scholar at the European Inter-University Centre in Venice and I thank Horst Fischer, Florence Benoît-Rohmer, Fabrizio Marella, George Ulrich and the staff at the Centre. I have also been warmly hosted as a Visiting Scholar at the Centre d'études des politiques étrangères et de sécurité, Université du Québec à Montréal, for which I have to thank Stéphane Roussel and Charles Létourneau. I also had the opportunity to discuss parts of the book at the Carr Centre for Human Rights Policy at the John F. Kennedy School of Government at Harvard University and I thank Charlie Clements. My thanks go also to Finola O'Sullivan at Cambridge University Press. And finally, heartfelt thanks go to my family for their constant support and encouragement.

TABLE OF CASES

Inter-American Commission on Human Rights

Bernard Coard and Others v. United States, Report No. 109/99, Case No. 10.951, OAS Doc. OEA/Ser. L/V/II.106, Doc. 3 Rev. (29 September 1999)

Ignacio Ellacuria, S.J., Segundo Montes, S-J., Armando López, S.J.; Ignacio Martin-Baró, S.J; Joaquin López y López, S.J.; Juan Ramón Moreno, S.J., Julia Elba Ramos; and Celina Mariceth Ramos v. El Salvador, Report No. 136/99, Case 10.488, OAS Doc. OEA Ser.L/V/II.106, Doc. 3 Rev. (22 December 1999)

Jose Alexis Fuentes Guerrero and Others v. Colombia, Report No. 61/99, Case 11.519, OAS Doc. OEA Ser.L/V/II.106, Doc. 7 Rev. (13 April 1999)

Lucio Parada Cea, Héctor Jaoquín Miranda Marroquín, Fausto García Funes, Andrés Hernández Carpio, Jose Catalino Meléndez and Carlos Antonio Martiínez v. El Salvador, Report No. 1/99, Case 10.480, OAS Doc. OEA Ser.L/V/II.102, Doc. 6 Rev. (27 January 1999)

Monsignor Oscar Amulfo Romero y Galdámez v. El Salvador, Report No. 37/00, Case 10.481, OAS Doc. OEA Ser.L/V/II.106, Doc. 3 Rev. (13 April 2000)

Arturo Ribón Avilán and ten others ('The Milk') v. Colombia, Report No. 26/97, Case 11.142 of 30 September 1997, OAS Doc. OEA/Ser.L/V/II.98, Doc. 6 Rev. (13 April 1998)

Disabled Peoples' International v. United States, Case 9213, Report No. 3/96, Annual Report 1986–1987, OAS Doc. OEA/Ser.L/V/II.91, Doc. 7 (22 September 1987)

Disabled Peoples' International v. United States, Case No. 9213, Decision as to the Admissibility, OAS Doc. OEA/Ser.L/V/II.71, Doc. 9 Rev. 1 (22 September 1997)

Franklin Guillermo Aisalle Molina (Ecuador v. Colombia), Report No. 112/10 Admissibility, Inter-State Petition IP-02, OAS Doc. OEA/Ser.L/V/II.140, Doc. 10 (21 October 2010)

Hugo Bustios Saavedra v. Peru, Report No. 38/97, Case No. 10.548 of 16 October 1997, OAS Doc. OEA/ Ser.L/V/II.98, Doc. 6 Rev. (13 April 1998)

Juan Carlos Abella v. Argentina, Report No. 55/97, Case No. 11.137 of 18 November 1997, OAS Doc. OEA/Ser.L/V/II.98, Doc. 6 Rev. at 161 (14 April 1998)

Marino Lopez and Others v. Colombia, Report 64/11, Case 12.573, OAS Doc. OEA/Ser.L/V/II.127, Doc. 4 Rev. 1 (31 March 2011)

Carlos Manuel Prada Gonzalez and Evelio Antonio Bolaño Castro v. Colombia, Report 63/01, Case 11.710, OAS Doc. OEA/Ser.L/V/II.111, Doc. 20 Rev. at 781 (6 April 2001)

Riofrió Massacre Colombia, Report No. 62/01, Case 11.654, OAS Doc. OEA/Ser.L/V/II.111, Doc. 20 Rev. at 758 (6 April 2001)

Inter-American Court of Human Rights

'Other Treaties' Subject to the Consultative Jurisdiction of the Court (Art. 64 American Convention on Human Rights), Advisory Opinion, OC-1/82, Ser. A, No. 1 (24 September 1982)

Las Palmeras v. Colombia, Judgment (Preliminary Objections), Ser. C, No. 67 (4 February 2000)
Mapiripán Massacre v. Colombia, Judgment (Merits, Reparations, and Costs), Ser. C, No. 134 (15 September 2005)
Plan de Sánchez Massacre v. Guatemala, Judgment (Merits), Ser. C, No. 105 (29 April 2004)
Pueblo Bello Massacre v. Colombia, Judgment (Merits, Reparations, and Costs), Ser. C, No. 140 (31 January 2006)
Serrano-Cruz Sisters v. El Salvador, Judgment (Preliminary Objections), Ser. C, No. 118 (23 November 2004)
Serrano-Cruz Sisters v. El Salvador, Judgment (Merits, Reparations and Costs), Ser. C, No. 118 (1 March 2005)
Villagrán-Morales and Others v. Guatemala (Case of the Street Children), Judgment (Merits), Series C, No. 63 (19 November 1999)

European Court of Human Rights

Ahmet Özkan and Others v. Turkey, Appl. No. 21689/93, Judgment (6 April 2004)
Akdivar and Others v. Turkey, Appl. No. 21893/93, Judgment (16 September 1996)
Akhmadov and Others v. Russia, Appl. No. 21586/02, Judgment (14 November 2008)
Akhmadova and Sadulayeva v. Russia, Appl. No. 40464/02, Judgment (10 May 2007)
Akpar and Altun v. Turkey, Appl. No. 56760/00, Judgment (27 May 2007)
Alikhadzhiyeva v. Russia, Appl. No. 68007/01, Judgment (5 July 2007)
Al-Jedda v. The United Kingdom, Appl. No. 27021/08, Judgment (7 July 2011)
Al-Skeini v. United Kingdom, Appl. No. 55721/07, Judgment (7 July 2011)
Banković and Others v. Belgium and 16 Other Contracting States, Appl. No. 52207/99, Admissibility (12 December 2001)
Baysayeva v. Russia, Appl. No. 74237/01, Judgment (5 April 2007)
Bazorkina v. Russia, Appl. No. 69481/01, Judgment (27 July 2006)
Behrami v. France, Appl. No. 71412/01, Admissibility (2 May 2007)
Bitiyeva and X v. Russia, Appl. Nos. 57953/00 and 37392/03, Judgment (21 June 2007)
Cyprus v. Turkey, Appl. Nos. 6780/74 and 6950/75, Judgment (10 July 1976)
Cyprus v. Turkey, Appl. No. 8007/77, Judgment (10 July 1978)
Cyprus v. Turkey, Appl. No. 25781/94, Judgment (10 May 2001)
Dzhabrailova v. Russia, Appl. No. 1586/05, Judgment (9 April 2009)
Engel and Others v. The Netherlands, Appl. Nos. 5100/71, 5101/71, 5102/71, 5354/72 and 5370/72, Judgment (23 November 1976)
Ergi v. Turkey, Appl. No. 23818/94, Judgment (28 July 1998)
Estamirov and Others v. Russia, Appl. No. 60272/00, Judgment (12 October 2006)
Güleç v. Turkey, Appl. No. 21593/93, Judgment (27 July 1998)
Ilaşcu and Others v. Moldova and Russia, Appl. No. 48787/99, Judgment (8 July 2004)
Imakayeva v. Russia (Appl. No. 7615/02), Judgment (9 November 2006)
Isaak and Others v. Turkey, Appl. No. 44587/98, Judgment (28 September 2006)
Isayeva v. Russia, Appl. No. 57950/00, Judgment (24 February 2005)
Isayeva, Yusupova and Bazayeva v. Russia, Appl. Nos. 57947/00, 57948/00 and 57949/00, Judgment (24 February 2005)
Issa and Others v. Turkey, Appl. No. 31821/96, Judgment (Merits) (16 November 2004)
Kaya v. Turkey, Application No. 22729/93, Judgment (28 March 2000)

Khashiyev and Akayeva v. Russia, Appl. Nos. 57942/00 and 57945/00, Judgment (24 February 2005)
Khatsiyeva and Others v. Russia, Appl. No. 5108/02, Judgment (17 January 2008)
Kononov v. Latvia, Appl. No. 35376/04, Judgment (24 July 2008)
Lawless v. Ireland (No. 3), Appl. No. 332/57, Judgment (1 July 1961)
Loizidou v. Turkey, Appl. No. 15318/89, Preliminary Objection (23 March 1995)
Loizidou v. Turkey, Appl. No. 15318/89, Judgment (18 December 1996)
McCann and Others v. The United Kingdom, Appl. No. 18984/91 Judgment (27 September 1995)
Öcalan v. Turkey, Appl. No 46221/99, Judgment (May 12, 2005)
Pad and others v. Turkey, Appl. No. 60167/00, Judgment (28 June 2007)
Saramati v. France, Germany and Norway, Appl. No. 78166/01, Admissibility (2 May 2007)
Selçuk and Asker v. Turkey, Appl. Nos. 23184/94 and 23185/94, Judgment (24 April 1998)
Trapeznikova v. Russia, Appl. No. 21539/02, Judgment (11 December 2008)
Umayeva v. Russia, Appl. No. 1200/03, Judgment (4 December 2008)
Varnava and Others v. Turkey, Appl. Nos. 16064/90, 16065/90, 16066/90, 160668/90, 160669/90, 16070/90, 16071/90, 16072/90 and 16073/90, Judgment (18 September 2009)

African Commission on Human and Peoples' Rights

African Commission on Human and Peoples' Rights, Amnesty International, Comité Loosli Bachelard, Lawyers' Committee for Human Rights, Association of Members of the Episcopal Conference of East Africa v. Sudan (48/90–50/91–52/91–89/93), Decision of 15 November 1999, 13th Activity Report 1999–2000
African Commission on Human and Peoples' Rights, Commission nationale des droits de l'homme et des libertés v. Chad (74/92), Decision of 11 October 1995, 9th Activity Report 1995–1996
African Commission on Human and Peoples' Rights, Democratic Republic of Congo v. The Republics of Burundi, Rwanda and Uganda (227/99), Decision of 29 May 2003, 20th Activity Report January to June 2006.

International Court of Justice

Armed Activities on the Territory of the Congo (Democratic Republic of the Congo v. Uganda), Judgment (19 December 2005), ICJ Reports (2006), p. 168
Corfu Channel (United Kingdom of Great Britain and Northern Ireland v. Albania), Judgment (9 April 1949), ICJ Reports (1949), p. 4
Fisheries Case (United Kingdom v. Norway), Judgment (18 December 1951), ICJ Reports, p. 116
Legal Consequences of the Construction of a Wall in the Occupied Palestinian Territory, Advisory Opinion (9 July 2004), ICJ Reports (2004), p. 136
Legality of the Threat or Use of Nuclear Weapons, Advisory Opinion (8 July 1996), ICJ Reports (1996), p. 226
Military and Paramilitary Activities in and against Nicaragua (Nicaragua v. United States of America), Judgment (27 June 1986), ICJ Reports (1986), p. 14

Other jurisprudence

International Criminal Tribunal for the Former Yugoslavia, Prosecutor v. Kunarac, Kovać and Vuković, Judgment, IT-96-23-T and IT-96-32/1-T, Judgment (22 February 2001)
International Criminal Tribunal for the Former Yugoslavia, Prosecutor v. Tadić, IT-94-1-I, Decision on Defence Motion for Interlocutory Appeal on Jurisdiction (2 October 1995)

International Criminal Tribunal for the Former Yugoslavia, Prosecutor v. Furundžija, IT-95–17/1.T, Judgment (10 December 1998)

International Military Tribunal Nuremberg, United States v. Alfried Krupp and Others, Case 10, Judgment (21 July 1948)

Landgericht Bonn (Regional Court of Bonn) Judgment, Az. 1 O 361/02 ('Varvarin case') (10 December 2003)

Permanent International Court of Justice, Case of the S.S. "Wimbledon", P.ICJ Series A., No. 1 (1923)

Special Court for Sierra Leone, Prosecutor v. Brima, Kamara and Kanu, Judgment, SCSL-2004–16-T (20 June 2007)

The Hague Court of Appeal, Mustafic v. The State of The Netherlands, Case No. 200.020.173/01 (5 July 2011)

The Hague Court of Appeal, Nehanovic v. The State of The Netherlands, Case No. 200.020.174/01 (5 July 2011)

TABLE OF LEGAL INSTRUMENTS

Additional Protocol to the American Convention on Human Rights in the Area of Economic, Social and Cultural Rights (Protocol of San Salvador), 17 November 1988, OAS Treaty Series No. 69 (1988)

African Charter on the Rights and Welfare of the Child, 11 July 1990, OAU Doc.CAB/LEG/24.9/49 (1990)

African Charter on Human and Peoples' Rights, 27 June 1981, OAU Doc. CAB/LEG/67/3 rev. 5, 21 ILM 58 (1982)

American Convention on Human Rights, 22 November 1969, OAS Treaty Series No. 36, 1144 UNTS 123

American Declaration of the Rights and Duties of Man, O.A.S. Res. XXX (1948), reprinted in OEA/Ser.L.V/II.82 Doc. 6 Rev. 1 at 17 (1992)

Charter of the United Nations, 26 June 1945, UNTS XVI

Convention (II) with Respect to the Laws and Customs of War on Land and its annex: Regulations concerning the Laws and Customs of War on Land, 29 July 1899 ('Hague Regulations 1899')

Convention (IV) respecting the Laws and Customs of War on Land and its annexed regulations, 18 October 1907 ('Hague Regulations 1907')

Convention against Torture and Other Cruel, Inhuman or Degrading Treatment, 10 December 1984, 1465 UNTS 85

Geneva Convention for the Amelioration of the Condition of the Wounded and Sick in Armies in the Field, 27 July 1929

Geneva Convention for the Amelioration of the Condition of the Wounded and Sick in Armies in the Field, 6 July 1906

Geneva Convention for the Amelioration of the Condition of the Wounded in Armies in the Field, 22 August 1864

Convention for the Protection of All Persons from Enforced Disappearance, 20 December 2006, UNTS 2715, UN Doc. A/61/448

Convention for the Protection of Cultural Property in the Event of Armed Conflict, 14 May 1954, 249 UNTS 240

Convention on Cluster Munitions, 30 May 2008, 48 ILM 357 (2009)

Convention on Prohibitions or Restrictions on the Use of Certain Conventional Weapons Which May be Deemed to be Excessively Injurious or that Have Indiscriminate Effects (with Protocols I, II and III), 10 October 1980, 1342 UNTS 137

Convention on the Elimination of All Forms of Discrimination against Women, 18 December 1979, 1249 UNTS 13

Convention on the Prohibition of the Use, Stockpiling, Production and Transfer of Anti-Personnel Mines and Their Destruction, 18 September 1997, 36 ILM 1507 (1997)

Convention on the Rights of Persons with Disabilities, 13 December 2006, 2515 UNTS 3

Convention on the Rights of the Child, 20 November 1989, 1577 UNTS 3

Convention relative to the Treatment of Prisoners of War, Geneva, 27 July 1929

Declaration Renouncing the Use, in Time of War, of Explosive Projectiles under 400 Grammes Weight, 11 December 1868 ('Declaration of St. Petersburg')

European Convention against Torture, 26 November 1987, ETS 126, 1561 UNTS 363

European Convention on Human Rights and Fundamental Freedoms, 4 November 1950, ETS 5, 213 UNTS 222

European Social Charter, 18 October 1961, ETS No. 35, 529 UNTS 89

Final Protocol and Project of an International Declaration Concerning the Laws and Customs of War, Brussels, 27 August 1874

General Order No. 100, Instructions for the Government of Armies of the United States in the Field, 24 April 1863 ('Lieber Code')

Geneva Convention (I) for the Amelioration of the Condition of the Wounded and Sick in Armed Forces in the Field, 12 August 1949, 75 UNTS 31

Geneva Convention (II) for the Amelioration of the Condition of the Wounded, Sick and Shipwrecked Members of the Armed Forces at Sea, 12 August 1949, 75 UNTS 85

Geneva Convention (III) Relative to the Treatment of Prisoners of War, 12 August 1949, 75 UNTS 135

Geneva Convention (IV) Relative to the Protection of Civilian Persons in Time of War, 12 August 1949, 75 UNTS 287

Inter-American Convention to Prevent and Punish Torture, 12 September 1985, OAS Treaty Series No. 67

International Convention on the Elimination of All Forms of Racial Discrimination, 7 March 1966, 660 UNTS 195

International Convention for the Protection of All Persons from Enforced Disappearance, 20 December 2006, 2715 UNTS, UN Doc. A/61/448

International Convention on the Protection of the Rights of All Migrant Workers and Members of Their Families, 18 December 1990, 2220 UNTS 3

International Covenant on Civil and Political Rights, 16 December 1966, 999 UNTS 171

International Covenant on Economic, Social and Cultural Rights, 16 December 1966, 993 UNTS 3

Optional Protocol to Convention on the Rights of the Child on a communications procedure, 19 December 2011, UN Doc. A/RES/66/138

Optional Protocol to Convention on the Rights of the Child on the involvement of children in armed conflict, 25 May 2000, 2173 UNTS 222

Optional Protocol to the Convention against Torture and Other Cruel, Inhuman or Degrading Treatment or Punishment, 18 December 2002, 2375 UNTS 237

Optional Protocol to the Convention on the Elimination of All Forms of Discrimination against Women, 6 October 1999, 2131 UNTS 83

Optional Protocol to the Convention on the Rights of Persons with Disabilities, 13 December 2006, UN Doc. A/61/611

Optional Protocol to the International Covenant on Civil and Political Rights, 16 December 1966, 999 UNTS 171

Optional Protocol to the International Covenant on Economic, Social and Cultural Rights, 10 December 2008, UN Doc. A/63/435

Protocol Additional to the Geneva Conventions of 12 August 1949 and relating to the protection of victims of international armed conflicts, 8 June 1977, 1125 UNTS 3

Protocol Additional to the Geneva Conventions of 12 August 1949 and relating to the protection of victims of non-international armed conflicts, 8 June 1977, 1125 UNTS 609

Protocol for the Prohibition of the Use of Asphyxiating, Poisonous or Other Gases, and of Bacteriological Methods of Warfare, 17 June 1925

Protocol to the Convention for the Protection of Cultural Property in the Event of Armed Conflict, 14 May 1954, 249 UNTS 358

Rome Statute of the International Criminal Court, 17 July 1998, 2187 UNTS 3

Second Protocol to the Hague Convention of 1954 for the Protection of Cultural Property in the Event of Armed Conflict, 26 March 1999, 2253 UNTS 172

Treaty on the Protection of Artistic and Scientific Institutions and Historic Monuments, 15 April 1935 ('Roerich Pact')

Vienna Convention on the Law of Treaties, 23 May 1969, 1155 UNTS 331

ABBREVIATIONS

ACHPR	African Charter on Human and Peoples' Rights
ACHR	American Convention on Human Rights
AP I	Protocol Additional to the Geneva Conventions of 12 August 1949 and relating to the protection of victims of international armed conflicts
AP II	Protocol Additional to the Geneva Conventions of 12 August 1949 and relating to the protection of victims of non-international armed conflicts
CAT	Convention Against Torture and Other Cruel, Inhuman or Degrading Treatment
CED	Convention for the Protection of All Persons from Enforced Disappearance
CEDAW	Convention on the Elimination of All Forms of Discrimination Against Women
CERD	International Convention on the Elimination of All Forms of Racial Discrimination
CIA	Central Intelligence Agency
CMW	International Convention on the Protection of the Rights of All Migrant Workers and Members of Their Families
CPA	Coalition Provisional Authority
CPN(M)	Communist Party of Nepal (Maoists)
CRC	Convention on the Rights of the Child
CRPD	Convention on the Rights of Persons with Disabilities
DRC	Democratic Republic of the Congo
ECHR	European Convention on Human Rights and Fundamental Freedoms
ECOSOC	Economic and Social Council
FARC	Fuerzas Armadas Revolucionarias de Colombia
FMLN	Frente Farabundo Martí para la Liberación Nacional
GC I	Geneva Convention (I) for the Amelioration of the Condition of the Wounded and Sick in Armed Forces in the Field (1949)
GC II	Geneva Convention (II) for the Amelioration of the Condition of the Wounded, Sick and Shipwrecked Members of the Armed Forces at Sea (1949)
GC III	Geneva Convention (III) Relative to the Treatment of Prisoners of War (1949)
GC IV	Geneva Convention (IV) Relative to the Protection of Civilian Persons in Time of War (1949)

HRC	Human Rights Council
HRDDP	Human Rights Due Diligence Policy
ICC	International Criminal Court
ICCPR	International Covenant on Civil and Political Rights
ICESCR	International Covenant on Economic, Social and Cultural Rights
ICJ	International Court of Justice
ICRC	International Committee of the Red Cross
ICTY	International Criminal Tribunal for the Former Yugoslavia
ILC	International Law Commission
IRA	Irish Republican Army
LTTE	Liberation Tigers of Tamil Eelam
NGO	non-governmental organization
OAS	Organization of American States
OHCHR	Office of the High Commissioner for Human Rights
OP	Optional Protocol
PKK	Partiya Karkerên Kurdistan / Kurdistan Workers' Party
PMC	private military company
RoE	Rules of Engagement
SCSL	Special Court for Sierra Leone
UDHR	Universal Declaration of Human Rights
UNDP	United Nations Development Programme
UNESCO	United Nations Educational, Scientific and Cultural Organisation
UNHCHR	United Nations High Commissioner for Human Rights
UNHCR	United Nations High Commissioner for Refugees
UNICEF	United Nations Children's Fund
UPR	Universal Periodic Review
VCLT	Vienna Convention on the Law of Treaties
VDPA	Vienna Declaration and Programme of Action

INTRODUCTION

The continued application of international human rights law in situations of armed conflict is the "new orthodoxy"[1] of our times. It is widely (although not universally) accepted that, as a matter of principle, international human rights law has a role to play in situations of armed conflict, particularly in internal armed conflicts and situations of occupation, as well as in peace support operations. Beyond the general proposition that human rights law remains applicable in armed conflicts there is, however, limited understanding of the legal, practical and political consequences of applying human rights. The crucial problem is no longer if human rights apply in armed conflicts but how they apply.[2] This is the question upon which this book is built; a question which has been lingering in the corridors of the United Nations, in courtrooms, military command centres and university lecture halls since the emergence of the international human rights regime after 1945, and is now very much present in legal writing and state practice. But notwithstanding rhetorical claims of the importance of human rights, the idea of resorting to human rights in situations of armed conflict still has the potential to divide scholars, governmental representatives, the military, judges, civil society organizations and the public.

Some may perceive the very topic of human rights in armed conflict as cynical, given that war is the antithesis and negation of everything for which human rights stand: human dignity and physical integrity, prosperity, justice, equality, peace and security – all gone when war is waged. In their view, the Universal Declaration of Human Rights of 1948 (UDHR) was meant to secure peace and prevent the recurrence of the kind of atrocities which had inspired its adoption, but should not be abused to regulate matters of warfare. Human rights, they may argue, should keep well away from this area, given that a highly specialized legal regime – the law of armed conflict or international humanitarian law – already regulates matters of armed conflict. Given that war has been assigned its own law with a formidable history of codification, there is no place for human rights on the battlefield, and there should not be, such critics may claim.

Others might wish to argue to the contrary and maintain that it is precisely in times of war when human rights are needed most, so as to protect those affected by the use of force or the abuse of power. In their opinion, human rights and humanitarian law share the common purpose of protecting individuals from threats to life, security and livelihood in

[1] Orna Ben-Naftali, "Introduction: International Humanitarian and International Human Rights Law – *Pas de Deux*" in Orna Ben-Naftali (ed.), *International Humanitarian and International Human Rights Law* (Oxford: Oxford University Press, 2011), p. 5.

[2] See Noam Lubell, "Challenges in Applying Human Rights Law to Armed Conflict" (2005) 87(860) *International Review of the Red Cross* 738.

all times of crisis, violence and abuse. When, if not in times of war, they might say, should human rights really mean something? And why should human rights with all their unlimited universal appeal not also apply on the battlefield, as they do in all other spheres of human activity?

This book sets out to explore the legal challenges, practical consequences and policy implications of resorting to international human rights law in situations of armed conflict. It is, first and foremost, a study in international law. But it is not merely meant to be an analysis of the interplay of the two legal regimes of human rights and humanitarian law as a matter of legal theory; such a task has been performed elsewhere.[3] Of course, any discussion on human rights in armed conflict is necessarily (and perhaps predominantly) about this intricate and still unresolved relationship, and sufficient space will consequently be given to explore the interface of human rights and humanitarian law. However, such legal questions need to acknowledge historical developments, connect with policy considerations and ultimately lead to operational consequences.

The study is thus based on the view that the topic of "human rights in armed conflict" is not only about the legal intricacies of reconciling human rights and humanitarian law, but comprises profound questions about the purpose, nature and scope of the whole *jus in bello* as a legal framework which governs the use of armed force in conflict scenarios of various types between, within and across states, as well as in situations of occupation (and spills over into post-conflict situations). Important as the legal questions are (in this study and beyond), the debate on human rights in armed conflict is not only about rummaging around in the legal toolbox in search for ever more sophisticated devices to fix legal loopholes.

Even though this inquiry is primarily interested in matters of international law, it asks if and how the *idea* of human rights presently informs the legal regulation of warfare and challenges the traditions, customs and perceptions of the law of war, and if the *language* of human rights can and should be used to express matters hitherto articulated in military codes and humanitarian pathos. It is an inquiry into how the *law* of human rights impacts upon, contradicts, changes or complements international humanitarian law, and it is also interested in understanding if the *policy* of human rights (understood in its broadest sense as a set of conceptions and rationale for action which guide actors and institutions towards achieving a desired result) is compatible with or opposed to the aims, purposes and objectives of regulating warfare under the law of armed conflict as it stands. And finally, this study examines if the *practice* of human rights and their international institutions, procedures and mechanisms have a role to play in matters of armed conflict.

The book takes it for granted that the debate on human rights in armed conflict is neither a fleeting trend nor a rhetorical revamp of established humanitarian discourses but poses a considerable challenge for the law as well, in practice and policy. It is interested in the conditions, consequences and implications of resorting to international human rights law in situations of armed conflict and asks which space can and should be assigned to human rights in armed conflicts – legally, politically and operationally. In particular, it examines the claim that international human rights law can support international humanitarian law in its task to humanize war; a project which enjoys widespread rhetorical support but is plagued by legal uncertainties and remains controversial in legal doctrine and state practice.

[3] See René Provost, *International Human Rights and Humanitarian Law* (Cambridge: Cambridge University Press, 2002).

For (too) long the topic of human rights in armed conflict was confined to the theorists' study rooms and was dealt with in academic discussions with little impact on policy choices in matters of warfare or on the reality of the battlefield. This has changed over the past years, and human rights in armed conflicts are now very much also a question of (national and global) politics, military practice and international jurisprudence. This trend needs to be connected with legal theory and, more importantly, embedded in broader considerations of the laws which govern the conflict and violence of various forms. And it needs to be analysed as a transformative process in which the idea of human rights exercises an impact on the way we think about war today and are likely to think about it tomorrow.

Such an analysis of the idea, law, practice and policy of human rights in armed conflicts is meant to serve various purposes: first, this study is an attempt to take stock of where we stand in explaining the role of human rights in armed conflict, and to organize, contextualize and revisit, from a contemporary perspective, the debate on human rights in armed conflict, to which a great range of scholars and practitioners have contributed over time. Secondly, the book aims at determining the prospect and limitations – in law, practice and policy – of increasingly invoking international human rights law in armed conflicts. Thirdly, it seeks to explore the potential and benefits as well as the dangers and drawbacks of increasingly referring to human rights in armed conflicts, as well as the repercussions this has on human rights and humanitarian law and on the future of warfare. And finally, the debate on human rights in armed conflict needs to be contextualized with regard to broader developments and transformation processes in international law and international relations, such as the increasing acknowledgment of the individual as a subject of international law and agent of international relations, the shifting perception of security from national to human security, and trends of a "humanization" and "constitutionalization" of international law.

It is obvious that all contributions to the debate on human rights in armed conflict reflect the (self-)perception, traditions and background of the respective communities which participate in making, shaping and applying the law applicable in armed conflicts, whether they are humanitarian professionals, governmental representatives, human rights activists, military professionals or other stakeholders. This book is no exception and approaches its topic clearly from the perspective of human rights. It is an attempt to revisit the law of armed conflict from a human rights angle and suggests a human rights-oriented reading of the law(s) which govern armed conflicts. Like every other perspective of the law of armed conflict, this is not a neutral approach. Diverging viewpoints and critique on the feasibility, practicability and possibility of resorting to human rights in armed conflicts will be considered very seriously throughout this inquiry, but its main goal is to understand and evaluate the contribution which international human rights law can make to the further humanization of war.

The study is thus critical in its methodology but open about its overall humanitarian objective, based on the guiding view that the whole law of armed conflict is, from its very origins, largely a humanitarian project which is not indifferent to human suffering: it is created to make wars less brutal, cruel and painful. This book, too, is part of century-old endeavours to "humanize" war; an antinomy in its plain meaning but a realistic reflection of the continued existence of armed conflicts and the efforts to mitigate their effects through law. While it is rooted in existing law and established legal doctrine, it is thus transformative where it argues that increased reliance on and use of international human rights law is a positive trend, notwithstanding the legal, political and practical obstacles on the way. The book's main hypothesis is that human rights impact upon and gradually change the *jus in bello* as we know it.

The book seeks to capture crucial developments, trends, experiences and expectations in the law, practice and policy of human rights in armed conflict, but it is not meant to trace the application of *all* international human rights law in *all* types of armed conflicts in detail.[4] Such a large-scale analysis is beyond its remit; indeed, it seems reminiscent of the amount of work that has gone into the study of the International Committee of the Red Cross (ICRC) on customary international humanitarian law, published in 2005, and perhaps ought to be conducted in a similar fashion.[5] Another question is also beyond the scope of this book: the human rights of members of armed forces towards their own government. The term "human rights in armed conflict" can be understood in many different ways, including as the human rights of soldiers as they carry out their duties; a field in need of further study.[6] The focus here is, however, on the way in which international human rights law protects, together with international humanitarian law, those affected by armed conflicts, first and foremost civilians.

Methodologically, the book covers the scholarly, jurisprudential and operational dimensions of the debate on human rights in armed conflicts. It builds on international legal scholarship, acknowledges the practice of states, non-state actors, international institutions and courts and international legal theory with due regard to the historic dimension of the topic. It takes into account relevant academic literature in the fields of international law, international relations and security studies, as well as military handbooks and manuals, evidence of state practice, opinions of legal advisers and international and national jurisprudence, the views and practice of international organizations as well as those of the ICRC.

Where the book traces the history of human rights in armed conflicts it is descriptive in a functional sense, as it asks why and how human rights have played a role in regulating armed conflict. Where it analyzes the law it is, necessarily, positivist in the sense of relying on established international legal doctrines of law-making and law enforcement by states as the primary actors in international law and politics. This book is, however, not only interested in *what* currently constitutes the law of armed conflict but also *why* we have the kind of law we have, and how the law might change if viewed from a human rights perspective. Given that the book is interested in exploring the historically, socially and politically contingent creation of the law of armed conflict, it ultimately builds on a constructivist view of international law and international relations and perceives and analyses the law applicable in armed conflict as a set of socially constructed agreements, influenced by an expanding range of stakeholders and shaped in processes not always under the full control of nation states.

A book which deals with international humanitarian law and armed conflicts needs a few words on terminology by way of introduction, particularly when the very notion of

[4] For a more exhaustive analysis of specific human rights norms in armed conflicts see Louise Doswald-Beck, *Human Rights in Times of Conflict and Terrorism* (Oxford: Oxford University Press, 2011).

[5] See Jean-Marie Henckaerts and Louise Doswald-Beck, *Customary International Humanitarian Law*, vol. I, *Rules* and vol. II, *Practice* (Cambridge: Cambridge University Press, 2005).

[6] See Peter Rowe, *The Impact of Human Rights Law on Armed Forces* (Cambridge: Cambridge University Press, 2006), pp. 1–162, and Gabriella Blum, "The Dispensable Lives of Soldiers" (2012) 2(1) *Journal of Legal Analysis* 70.

"humanitarianism" is part of its inquiry. The terms "international humanitarian law" and "law of armed conflict" are mostly used synonymously in textbooks and treatises. At times, the former indicates more of a "humanitarian" approach or an affiliation with the humanitarian community, while the latter sometimes suggests more of a military perspective.[7] In substance, however, both terms equally refer to the contemporary legal regime, at the core of which are the four Geneva Conventions of 1949[8] and the two Additional Protocols of 1977,[9] accompanied by over 100 treaties and other legal texts as compiled, for example, in the treaty database of the ICRC.[10] This book, too, will often use the two terms synonymously and, like many other textbooks, set them apart from the "law of war" (or the "law(s) and customs of war") which describe the law as it stood prior to 1949 before the term "humanitarian law" was coined and the notion of "war" gradually gave way to "armed conflict" in the wake of the prohibition of war under the UN Charter.[11] But given that the very term "humanitarian" will be analysed and deconstructed at various occasions in this book, greater care for terminology seems necessary.

As mentioned, it is certainly true that today all of the law of armed conflict is humanitarian in nature, and the dichotomy between "The Hague law" (with its main interest in regulating conduct on the battlefield) and "Geneva law" (with its emphasis on humanitarian protection of those *hors de combat* and civilians) is overcome, as noted by the International Court of Justice (ICJ) in its Advisory Opinion in the *Nuclear Weapons* case of 1996: "they are considered to have gradually formed one single complex system, known today as international humanitarian law."[12] Yet, not all provisions of the law are, strictly speaking, "humanitarian" by nature, as some regulate other matters of importance for the parties at war.[13] And, more importantly, the notions of "humanity" and "humanitarianism" are neither static nor are they self-evident. They have evolved dynamically and need to be read in conjunction with their counterpart, military necessity.

[7] See, for example, the textbooks by Daniel Thürer, *International Humanitarian Law: Theory, Practice, Context* (The Hague: Hague Academy of International Law, 2011) and Hans-Peter Gasser, *Humanitäres Völkerrecht: eine Einführung* (Baden-Baden: Nomos, 2007) – both authors are affiliated with the ICRC – and Gary D. Solis, *The Law of Armed Conflict* (Cambridge: Cambridge University Press, 2010), who is a (retired) member of the armed forces. Note, however, that Solis' book has the subtitle *International Humanitarian Law in Armed Conflict.* The author also refers to international humanitarian law and the law of armed conflicts as "fraternal twin[s]", p. 23.

[8] Geneva Convention (I) for the Amelioration of the Condition of the Wounded and Sick in Armed Forces in the Field, 12 August 1949, 75 UNTS 31; Geneva Convention (II) for the Amelioration of the Condition of the Wounded, Sick and Shipwrecked Members of the Armed Forces at Sea, 12 August 1949, 75 UNTS 85; Geneva Convention (III) Relative to the Treatment of Prisoners of War, 12 August 1949, 75 UNTS 135, Geneva Convention (IV) Relative to the Protection of Civilian Persons in Time of War, 12 August 1949, 75 UNTS 287.

[9] Protocol Additional to the Geneva Conventions of 12 August 1949 and relating to the Protection of Victims of International Armed Conflicts, 8 June 1977, 1125 UNTS 3, and Protocol Additional to the Geneva Conventions of 12 August 1949 and relating to the Protection of Victims of Non-international Armed Conflicts, 8 June 1977, 1125 UNTS 609.

[10] See www.icrc.org/ihl (last accessed 15 April 2014).

[11] International humanitarian law is, however, inconsistent in its reference to "war" and continues using the term, e.g., in the rules on "prisoners of war." This book, too, will occasionally refer to "war" as a generic term.

[12] *Legality of the Threat or Use of Nuclear Weapons*, International Court of Justice, Advisory Opinion of 8 July 1996 [1996] ICJ Reports 226 ("*Nuclear Weapons* case"), para. 75.

[13] Examples are norms on neutrality or on the settlement of disputes in naval warfare.

Furthermore, the notion of "humanitarian" in humanitarian law remains misleading (particularly for those not aware of its genesis and current use) for the way it seems to put humanitarian considerations above all else. Even though such considerations are ever more dominant in the law and express a certain prioritization or direction of what the law ought to be and where it ought to move, it glosses too easily over the ever-present delicate balance between military necessity and humanitarianism which allows the "collateral" killing of civilians under the rule of proportionality.[14] Strictly speaking, "humanitarian law" is thus not merely a neutral descriptor of a legal regime. Where appropriate, the present study will consequently use the term "humanitarian law" to highlight the humanitarian (i.e., "Geneva") tradition and set it apart from the "law of armed conflict." At the same time, it seems unwieldy to scrutinize every single use of the terms "law of armed conflict" and "international humanitarian law," so that the larger part of the book follows the pattern of many textbooks to use them interchangeably.

In contrast, the term *jus in bello* ("the law in/of war") is used less frequently in the literature. Where this is done it usually serves to set apart the legal rules applicable *in* wars as opposed to the norms which govern the lawfulness of going *to* war (*jus ad bellum*). The term *jus in bello* is, however, of some importance in the context of this study which argues that there is more than one legal regime (i.e., international humanitarian law / the law of armed conflict) which can govern armed conflicts. Given that the present inquiry is interested in the way human rights and humanitarian law interact to form a law *for* armed conflicts (present and future), the term *jus in bello* is perhaps closest in describing such a broader and openly structured legal frame. When the term is used in this book it thus suggests that in armed conflicts norms are at work which may come from various fields of international law, predominantly international humanitarian law but also international human rights law, refugee law, international criminal law, international environmental law, etc. For the purpose of this book the term thus covers, in a descriptive sense, norms which are (potentially) applicable regardless of their provenance or specification under a particular field of international law. Analytically, the term is meant to allow for considerations whether the law applicable in armed conflict can, might and should be more comprehensive than we imagine it today.

The book is organized in five parts. Part I considers the topic and idea of human rights in armed conflict as a matter of (political and legal) thought. This part is interested in the ideas, trends and events which have shaped the law of war throughout history and in exploring how the law connected with the emerging idea of human rights, up to and including their contemporary convergence. It accompanies the law of war as it transcends its medieval foundations rooted in faith and chivalry and leaves behind the dominant intellectual discourse of the time, the just war theory, to settle in the rational humanity of the Age of Enlightenment. It considers the codification of the law of war in the positivist and technocratic spirit of the nineteenth century as a European *mission civilicatrice*; a self-sufficient Eurocentric project of law-making which understood humanity essentially as a grace requested by humanitarian activists and extended by noble officers. It analyzes the impact of the emergence of international human rights law in 1945 on the law of armed conflict (or humanitarian law, as it was renamed with the four Geneva Conventions of 1949), and discusses how the convergence of human rights and humanitarian law turned

[14] See Adam Roberts and Richard Guelff, *Documents on the Law of War* (3rd edn., Oxford: Oxford University Press, 2000), p. 31, and Solis, *The Law of Armed Conflict* (n. 7) pp. 22–24.

from a theoretical question to a practical problem since the World Conference on Tehran of 1968.

II frames the idea of human rights in armed conflict in legal theory and examines the interplay of international human rights law and humanitarian law under the three broad paradigms of exclusivity, complementarity and integration. This is a mapping and re-ordering of the debate on human rights in armed conflict with a particularly critical focus on the doctrine of *lex specialis* as the dominant but ultimately unconvincing descriptor of the relationship between human rights and humanitarian law. This part also discusses – with reference to examples of how human rights and humanitarian law complement each other – the variegated meanings of the favoured theory of complementarity between human rights and humanitarian law and argues that complementarity cannot be understood without acknowledging the transformational pull which human rights exercises, as it becomes integrated into the law of armed conflict.

III leaves theory behind and discusses the specific legal questions, challenges and commonalities which the concurrent application of human rights and humanitarian law brings with it. This part engages with the critique that, as a matter of law and practice, human rights cannot be applied in armed conflicts, given the paradigmatic differences between human rights and humanitarian law, including the contested extra-territorial reach of human rights law and the possibility of derogating human rights in armed conflict. It also considers operational and practical obstacles which the application of human rights in armed conflict may entail.

IV discusses human rights in armed conflict as a matter of policy and as a reflection of the dynamics of war and law. This part also seeks to do justice to the way in which international humanitarian law understands armed conflicts in the different categories of international and non-international and adjusts the debate on human rights in armed conflict accordingly. More importantly, however, it suggests that the changing character of what once was termed "war" is the driving force of the whole debate on human rights in armed conflict. It claims that international human rights law is indispensable in all forms of modern types of armed conflicts between, within and across states, up to and including the use of armed force in situations beyond the clear dichotomy of international and non-international armed conflict which blur the boundaries between law enforcement and war-fighting. This part also contextualizes the dynamics of war and law in larger developments of international law, which move the law from its inter-state character towards encompassing concern for "humanity" – in all the shades which this term displays.

V considers the application and enforcement of norms of human rights and humanitarian law as "humanitarian rights." It recognizes that the application of international human rights law in armed conflicts brings with it the institutional framework of human rights law with its proliferating councils, commissions, missions, procedures, mechanisms, bodies and courts, and examines their practice and potential for ensuring respect for human rights and humanitarian law alike. Based on lessons learned from the practice of the UN Human Rights Council, UN treaty bodies and the UN High Commissioner for Human Rights, as well as the Inter-American Commission and Court of Human Rights, the European Court of Human Rights and the African Commission on Human and Peoples' Rights, this part discusses the prospects of resorting to human rights bodies and asks if they can, and should, stand in for the well-acknowledged lack of enforcement of humanitarian law, and if so, what potential pitfalls this would entail.

The concluding chapter revisits and responds to the book's central hypothesis that human rights are the main driving force and an essential component, interpretative guidance and beacon for the present and future *jus in bello*, and that an approach to international humanitarian law which is based on human rights helps to bring the law in line with the humanitarian demands of today's world.

Part I

Human rights in armed conflict: history of an idea

The law of war has a tradition which stretches back hundreds, if not thousands, of years. Regulating warfare and stipulating rules for the appropriate behaviour of warriors was a matter of concern for philosophers and priests and for politicians and military leaders since antiquity. Their views, orders and customs were refined in the European Middle Ages and codified since the late nineteenth century so as to create the law of armed conflict – or international humanitarian law – of today. The history of this law is usually presented as a linear development from its ancient roots to twenty-first century humanitarian norms which unfolded within a clearly delineated space, i.e., war. Apart from developments of the past decades, human rights have no particular place in this script. International humanitarian law and human rights, it is argued, have historically evolved along entirely different and separated lines and have "totally different origins."[1] If any relation between the two is acknowledged in a historic perspective than it is a sequential one: humanitarian law is often seen as a "precursor"[2] or "trailblazer"[3] of human rights and as one of their most important sources.

This is certainly true: international human rights law in the strict sense of the word exists only since 1945 when the UN Charter acknowledged them as a purpose of the United Nations,[4] or rather since 1948 when they were put on paper in the Universal Declaration of Human Rights.[5] Since this date, the relationship between human rights and the law of war can reasonably be discussed. Given the long history of international humanitarian law and its codification which, after all, represents one of the first efforts to create international law

[1] Louise Doswald-Beck and Sylvain Vité, "International Humanitarian Law and Human Rights Law" (1993) 33(293) *International Review of the Red Cross* 94. The 1995 edition of the *Encyclopaedia of Public International Law*, for example, argued that international humanitarian law and international human rights law developed separately and without any meaningful connection, see Karl-Josef Partsch, "Human Rights and Humanitarian Law" in Rudolf Bernhardt (ed.), *Encyclopedia of Public International Law* (Amsterdam: Elsevier, 1995), p. 911. The same argument is made in, e.g., Dietrich Schindler, "Human Rights and Humanitarian Law: Interrelationship of the Laws" (1982) 31(4) *American University Law Review* 935; and Lindsay Moir, *The Law of Internal Armed Conflict* (Cambridge: Cambridge University Press, 2002), p. 194.

[2] Roger Normand and Sarah Zaidi, *Human Rights at the UN: The Political History of Universal Justice* (Bloomington, IN: Indiana University Press, 2008), p. 30.

[3] Walter Kälin and Jörg Künzli, *The Law of International Human Rights Protection* (Oxford: Oxford University Press, 2009), p. 10.

[4] Charter of the United Nations, 26 June 1945, UNTS XVI, Art. 1(3): "The purpose of the United Nations are … to achieve international cooperation … in promoting and encouraging respect for human rights and for fundamental freedoms for all without distinction as to race, sex, language, or religion."

[5] UN General Assembly Res. 217 A (III), UN Doc. 217/A-(III) (10 December 1948).

concerned with humanitarian matters, humanitarian law seems a natural foundation and inspiration for human rights. Their broadly similar goals – protecting the lives, dignity and livelihood of humans in distress – add to this perception of humanitarian law as a forerunner of human rights.

But humanitarian law was not simply an early version of human rights, just as human rights are not a relabelled humanitarian code. Their relationship is more complex in a contemporary as well as historic perspective. They have developed largely separately, carried forward by different motivations and accelerated by different triggering events in human history.[6] Human rights were born out of struggle between the oppressed and disadvantaged against their rulers and were about justice, rights and entitlements, while humanitarian law reflected the attempt to reconcile charity and mercy with the necessities of warfare. And human rights emerged as internal matters to be translated into international law while international humanitarian law was, from the very beginning, international in the literal sense of the word as being applicable between nation states at war.

The two fields have not emerged in isolation from each other. The ideas and concepts which form the basis of today's human rights regime have influenced, and have been influenced, by the laws and customs of war. The humanitarian strand of the law of war has throughout history helped to inspire the idea of human rights, but the emerging concept of individual human rights has also affected the law of war. It has rightly been argued that:

> [i]t is not only in time of peace that the issue of human rights becomes significant, nor is it only then that it has a respectable history, despite the publicly held view that it is only since 1945 that human rights, or the denial thereof, should be a matter of concern to the law of armed conflict.[7]

The history of the law of war should thus be read in conjunction with the emergence of the idea of human rights. It is a history which reflects an ebbing and flowing of different motivations for regulating warfare which include the idea(s) of human rights as postulated before they were given a legal form in international law in 1945.

6 See Michael Bothe, "The Historical Evolution of International Humanitarian Law, International Human Rights Law, Refugee Law and International Criminal Law" in Horst Fischer, Ulrike Froissart, Wolff Heinegg von Heintschel and Christian Raap (eds.), *Krisensicherung und Humanitärer Schutz / Crisis Management and Humanitarian Protection. Festschrift für Dieter Fleck* (Berlin: Berliner Wissenschaftsverlag, 2004), p. 37.

7 Leslie C. Green, "Human Rights in Peace and War: An Historical Overview" in Horst Fischer, Ulrike Froissart, Wolff Heinegg von Heintschel and Christian Raap (eds.), *Krisensicherung und Humanitärer Schutz / Crisis Management and Humanitarian Protection. Festschrift für Dieter Fleck* (Berlin: Berliner Wissenschaftsverlag, 2004), p. 176.

1

From medieval sources to modernity

1.1 Mercy, chivalry, self-interest and justice

Rules on how to behave in war are perhaps as old as mankind.[1] Very few authors are so strict as to question the existence of rules on warfare prior to the first codifications in the 1860s.[2] Quite to the contrary, prescriptions on how warriors ought to act can be found in the earliest philosophical and religious texts of African, Asian and European origin.[3] The treatment of prisoners and the protection of the civilian population has been a concern for all of them, together with the distinction between combatants and civilians, assistance to the wounded, respect for the dead, prohibition of looting and protection of cultural property.[4]

The rules of ancient India on warfare predate their counterparts in Western and Mediterranean cultures[5] and elaborate rules on warfare can also be found in early and classical Greek history.[6] Pre-colonial Africa and Latin-America knew detailed humanitarian regulations, including the prohibition of certain types of weapons, the protection of women, children and the elderly and the setting up of ad hoc tribunals on compensation after a conflict.[7] The holy books of the main religions – the Old Testament, the Quran and the Torah – also deal with questions of warfare. The Old Testament contains a passage on feeding prisoners of war with bread and water rather than strike them dead,[8] while Islamic

[1] See David J. Bederman, "International Law in the Ancient World" in David Armstrong (ed.), *Routledge Handbook of International Law* (London: Routledge, 2009), p. 124.

[2] See Howard Levie, "History of the Law of War on Land" (2000) 82(838) *International Review of the Red Cross* 339 (who argues that no such thing as humanity in land warfare existed before the 1860s).

[3] See in greater detail Leslie C. Green, *The Contemporary Law of Armed Conflict* (Manchester: Manchester University Press, 2008), pp. 26–36.

[4] See Bertrand Ramcharan, *Contemporary Human Rights Ideas* (New York: Routledge, 2008), pp. 8–15, and Zidane Meriboute, "Humanitarian Rules and Sanctions in the Major Philosophical and Religious Traditions" in Liesbeth Lijnzaad, Johanna van Sambeek and Bahia Tahzib-Lie (eds.), *Making the Voice of Humanity Heard: Essays on Humanitarian Assistance and International Humanitarian Law in Honour of HRH Princess Margriet of the Netherlands* (Leiden: Nijhoff, 2004), pp. 379–81.

[5] See V.S. Nirmal, "International Humanitarian Law in Ancient India" in V.S. Mani (ed.), *Handbook of International Humanitarian Law* (New Delhi: Oxford University Press, 2007), pp. 37–38.

[6] See Josiah Ober, "Classic Greek Times" in Michael Howard, George J. Andreopoulos and Mark R. Shulman (eds.), *The Laws of War: Constraints on Warfare in the Western World* (New Haven, CT: Yale University Press, 1994), pp. 12–27; and Robert C. Stacey, "Age of Chivalry" in Michael Howard, George J. Andreopoulos and Mark R. Shulman (eds.), *The Laws of War: Constraints on Warfare in the Western World* (New Haven, CT: Yale University Press, 1994), pp. 27–28.

[7] See Meriboute, "Humanitarian Rules and Sanctions" (n. 4) pp. 366–68.

[8] See Ove Bring, "Hugo Grotius and the Roots of Human Rights Law" in Jonas Grimheden and Rolf Ring (eds.), *Human Rights Law: From Dissemination to Application. Essays in Honour of Göran Melander* (Leiden: Nijhoff, 2006), p. 133.

provisions on warfare speak of mercy, clemency and compassion derived from divine authority, and the Islamic legal system embodies a broad set of humanitarian rules.[9] Likewise, Deuteronomy (the fifth book of the Torah) contains rules on warfare and prohibits, for example, the destruction of trees from which the inhabitants of besieged cities gain fruits.[10] The Buddhist tradition of humanitarian principles also had decisive influence on accentuating the humanitarian duties in warfare in ancient times in South Asia.[11]

Such appeals to mercy and compassion were rooted in philosophical and moral traditions and guided by the view of humanness as a sacred value. But humanitarian law is essentially a product of the European Middle Ages. Between around 1000 AD and the mid-fifteenth century, Christian faith and the medieval ideal of chivalry became major sources of the emerging law of war. The medieval mind "regarded justice and mercy as twin attributes of kingship, as of course they were of God himself."[12] Out of such a conception the earliest expressions of the law of war would emerge and custom would guide the parties at war. Such custom was later formalized in decrees issued by European rulers, submitted by the nascent nation states to their armies, written down in bilateral pacts and agreements between warring parties and studied by the early scholars of the emerging international law. Chivalry thus followed in the footsteps of the church, sovereigns in the footsteps of chivalry, and lawyers in the footsteps of their sovereigns, all in quest for the law applicable in armed conflicts.

Christian faith provided the foundation and was deemed sufficient guidance for all matters, including when and how to use force.[13] The Council of Narbonne in 1045 is one of the earliest examples on how the church sought to restrain warfare.[14] In great detail, the Council declared unlawful attacks on clerics, monks and nuns, women, pilgrims, merchants, peasants, churches, cemeteries and cloisters, the land of the clergy, shepherds and their flocks, agricultural animals, wagons in the field and olive trees. But while the church was eager to contain warfare among Christians it was entirely in agreement with earlier concepts of Roman law that violence against outsiders – Muslims, pagans and natives – was in no need of such rules.[15] Regulating intra-Christian warfare, however, became a great concern for the church from the tenth and eleventh centuries onwards. Church councils and movements within the church paved the way for rules on warfare to protect civilians, impose limitations on warriors and protect Christian holy days from being stained by acts of

9 See Meriboute, "Humanitarian Rules and Sanctions" (n. 4) pp. 374–79; Aftab Alam, "The Islamic Concept of Humanitarian Law" in V.S. Mani (ed.), *Handbook of International Humanitarian Law* (New Delhi: Oxford University Press, 2007), pp. 44–45; and Javaid Rehman, *International Human Rights Law* (Edinburgh: Pearson, 2010), p. 767.

10 See Leslie C. Green, "Human Rights in Peace and War: An Historical Overview" in Horst Fischer, Ulrike Froissart, Wolff Heinegg von Heintschel and Christian Raap (eds.), *Krisensicherung und Humanitärer Schutz / Crisis Management and Humanitarian Protection. Festschrift für Dieter Fleck* (Berlin: Berliner Wissenschaftsverlag, 2004), pp. 176, 181.

11 See C.G. Weeramantry, "Buddhism and Humanitarian Law" in V.S. Mani (ed.), *Handbook of International Humanitarian Law* (New Delhi: Oxford University Press, 2007), pp. 12–13.

12 Theodor Meron, *Henry's Wars and Shakespeare's Laws: Perspectives on the Law of War in the Later Middle Ages* (Oxford: Clarendon Press, 1993), p. 79.

13 See Christian Tomuschat, *Human Rights between Idealism and Realism* (2nd edn., Oxford: Oxford University Press, 2008), pp. 8–9.

14 See Green, "Human Rights in Peace and War" (n. 10) p. 179.

15 See Stacey, "Age of Chivalry" (n. 6) pp. 28–29.

violence.[16] Faith was also helpful as a measuring tool for restraint in warfare: those who would convert to one's belief could be spared but not necessarily the others.

Outside the churchyard, the increasing differentiation of the European social order led to the creation of a noble class, the members of which exercised authority over the common inhabitants of peasant villages. A legal regime and cultural system emerged in which the nobility possessed horses and arms, allowing them to use organized force. While this set the nobility apart from the huddled masses, it also imposed on them a code of conduct for using such means of warfare. It has rightly been pointed out that all social classes are keen on policing themselves, and so was the war-fighting nobility.[17] And within this nobility, knights occupied a special place where military profession and social rank coincided. Such a class of noble warriors was in even greater need of rules which guided their activities because only honourable behaviour would guarantee their social status.

Consequently, an ever more elaborate code of knightly behaviour came into being and the church gradually lost its say in matters of warfare. The development of the rules applicable to the *chevaliers* became more and more a secular matter.[18] Chivalry – the duty to act honourably in war and display virtues such as justice, loyalty, courage, honour, mercy, keeping one's word and acting charitably – was exclusive to Christian knights.[19] While it provided grounds for limiting the use of force it was also a means to protect and exclusively authorize a privileged aristocratic class to fight wars and benefit from them, making the protection of civilians appear as more of a side-effect.[20] War crime trials were also not unheard of. Perhaps the most famous of them was the tribunal set up in 1474 in Breisach, Austria, by the Hanseatic League, when Peter von Hagenbach was tried for acts contrary to the laws of God and man, with looting, rape and murder figuring prominently among them. Despite his pleas that he acted upon superior orders he was executed on the grounds that he must well have realized the inhuman nature of his conduct.[21]

Chivalry and honour as sources of appropriate conduct in warfare had their roots in ancient times.[22] This professional ethic was based on fairness as the hallmark of the skilled warrior and was not necessarily in need of any further justification such as Christian faith or humanity. It was self-sufficient as an ethical commandment of a privileged class. When in 1370 captured French knights appealed to John of Gaunt and the Earl of Cambridge in the siege of Limoges to spare their lives, the fact of their knighthood sufficed to grant them humane treatment despite the English commander's order that no quarter should be given.[23] Fear of shame and dishonour remained more important incentives to obey the laws of war than appeals to Christian mercy and compassion or the prospect of punishment.

[16] Ibid. p. 29.

[17] Paul Kennedy and George J. Andreopoulos, "The Laws of War: Some Concluding Reflections" in Michael Howard, George J. Andreopoulos and Mark R. Shulman (eds.), *The Laws of War: Constraints on Warfare in the Western World* (New Haven, CT: Yale University Press, 1994), p. 215.

[18] See Stacey, "Age of Chivalry" (n. 6) pp. 29–30.

[19] See Theodor Meron, *Bloody Constraint: War and Chivalry in Shakespeare* (New York: Oxford University Press, 1998), pp. 4–5.

[20] See Chris af Jocknick and Roger Normand, "The Legitimation of Violence: A Critical History of the Laws of War" (1994) 35(1) *Harvard International Law Journal* 61.

[21] Green, *The Contemporary Law of Armed Conflict* (n. 3) p. 30. [22] Ibid. p. 29.

[23] Leslie C. Green, "Human Rights and the Law of Armed Conflict" in Leslie C. Green (ed.), *Essays on the Modern Law of War* (Ardsley, NY: Transnational, 1999), p. 436.

Neither of these sources of the law of war was necessarily informed by concerns for universal human dignity. Mercy could exceptionally be extended beyond one's own religion, and some medieval writers even argued that religious and chivalric principles were an expression of respect for the individual human person.[24] But by and large individual human dignity was measured by affiliation with religion, class or ethnicity and not universally shared: "[h]ad medieval Europeans given any serious thought to the idea of equal legal and political rights for all human beings, they would have seen them as a moral abomination, a horrid transgression against divinely ordained order."[25] European medieval "humanity" was a mixed blessing: while it introduced religious values into warfare it also defined humanity in an exclusionist manner, leaving the "barbarians" outside the realm of protection and care.[26]

1.2 Self-interest, common concern and justice

At all times high-minded humanist ideals in the law of war were also underpinned, explicitly or tacitly, by more pragmatic and utilitarian considerations. Prime among them was the idea of reciprocity: whatever you might bring about on your enemy today might be inflicted on your own troops and civilian population tomorrow. Such utilitarian considerations of self-interest would step in where faith, kindness and nobility were not in stock: "it must not be thought that these apparently humanitarian arrangements were solely the result of philanthropic sentiments of the commanders involved."[27] When hostilities were conducted by men of equal standing, reciprocity could act as a strong driving force for restraint. Killing a knight treacherously would mean exposing yourself to the revenge of his kin. In the Dutch revolt (or Eighty Years' War from 1568–1648) the initial policy of Spain was to hang all Dutch prisoners as a matter of principle but this ended when a high-ranking Spanish commander was captured by the Dutch who threatened to hang him if these executions would not stop; a proposal which Spain grudgingly accepted.[28] The downside of such high esteem for nobility was, of course, that killing folk of lower social rank would usually go unpunished and could be done without fear of retaliation, opening the gates for unrestrained violence and bloodbaths among civilians.

Tactical considerations would also fit comfortably into humanitarian demands: it is tempting to argue for the duty to care for their wounded soldiers and feed their civilians as long as this means putting financial and logistic burdens on the enemy, thus weakening his war efforts further. Humanitarian concerns were mixed with the more pragmatic need to protect civilians in order to sustain life in agricultural societies.[29]

24 Ibid. p. 65.

25 Jack Donnelly, *International Human Rights: Dilemmas in World Politics* (Boulder, CO: Westview, 2007), p. 42.

26 See Ruti G. Teitel, *Humanity's Law* (Oxford: Oxford University Press, 2011), p. 24.

27 Green, "Human Rights and the Law of Armed Conflict" (n. 23) p. 439.

28 Geoffrey Parker, "Early Modern Europe" in Michael Howard, George J. Andreopoulos and Mark R. Shulman (eds.), *The Laws of War: Constraints on Warfare in the Western World* (New Haven, CT: Yale University Press, 1994), p. 55.

29 See Leslie C. Green, "The Contemporary Law of Armed Conflict and the Protection of Human Rights" in Gerald L. Gall (ed.), *Civil Liberties in Canada: Entering the 1980s* (Toronto: Butterworths, 1982), pp. 167–68.

By the late fourteenth century a number of codes, which contained rights and duties of the privileged class of arms bearers, were formally put into existence in Italy, France and England.[30] Their impact on the ground was, however, limited and the ramblings of "free-lancing" knights (in the literal sense of the word) who felt little inclination to practice restraint against civilians added to the brutality of medieval warfare.[31] Furthermore, in all wars gentlemen soldiers had to supply their own equipment and servants and consequently depended on the profits of pillage to cover their expenses, including ransom in case of being captured. Warfare between noble men was a personal matter and legal arrangements between them were seen as more suitable to guarantee physical safety than appeals to humanity. Before going to war, contracts had to be signed, first between the prince and his captains and then between the captains and their soldiers, and the acquisition of property through looting was part of this. Captivity could also be understood as such a contractual arrangement between noblemen, and knights sought to ensure appropriate detention conditions and avert ill-treatment or death through the timely conclusion of the respective agreements.[32]

Such a view of the law of war as a set of mutually agreed contractual arrangements to secure the self-interest of the warrior class was prominent and supplemented the call of honour and the commands of God. But even though the religiously influenced strand of the law of war with its ideas of mercy and compassion and the related ideal of chivalry represented the main current of the law of war, ideas of common interest and individual dignity were not unheard of in matters of warfare.[33] Theorists such as Thomas Aquinas (1225–1274) would prove influential as they developed (influenced by the Greek philosopher Aristotle) a theory of natural law which would allow the revealing of God's will through human reasoning. The proponents of natural law stressed the right intention as the guiding principle for resorting to war as well as for the conduct of warfare. Already, Thomas Aquinas' forerunners, first and foremost St. Augustine (Augustine of Hippo, 354–430) had declared it reprehensible to fight for the sake of violence, revenge, enmity or the desire to wield power. The medieval natural law theory could build on such views and argue that the right intention, if supported by mercy and charity, is a powerful means to restrain warfare. Rules based on the right intention would apply irrespective of who the enemy would be and what the enemy would do.

This allowed the creation of rules to protect matters of common interest, such as cultural objects and sites which, in the common-oriented and cosmopolitan view of natural legal theorists, were in need of protection as a common heritage of mankind. And natural law would eventually also arrive at natural rights which, although not individual entitlements in the modern sense, were universal and inalienable rather than bestowed on a person through

30 See Maurice Hugh Keen, *The Laws of War in the Late Middle Ages* (London: Routledge and Kegan Paul, 1965), p. 19. Authors included John of Legnano, Honoré de Bonet and Christine de Pisan. Their writings would later merge with those of the "father of international law," Francisco de Vitoria, see Stephen C. Neff, *War and the Law of Nations: A General History* (Cambridge: Cambridge University Press, 2005), p. 70.

31 See Neff, *War and the Law of Nations* (n. 30) pp. 74–75.

32 See Stacey, "Age of Chivalry" (n. 6) pp. 31–32.

33 See Keen, *The Laws of War in the Late Middle Ages* (n. 30) pp. 8–12. The third source, *jus gentium*, the positive law of humans and nations, derived from the law common to everyone within the Roman Empire, would soon become of importance, too, when the rise of the nation state required a new framework for the law of war.

legal processes or relative to the adherence to specific cultures or classes.[34] Protection in war could thus be afforded irrespective of adherence to a specific culture or class but represent universal humanness.[35] This was not the dominant view of the law of war but it allowed human reasoning to separate the law from God's will and position the individual human being as an entity worthy of protection in war.

For natural law theorists, justice was another key concept: wars were either just or unjust. While the just war theory was mainly concerned with identifying the just cause for war and less with its specific conduct, it had important repercussions for the laws of war.[36] Wars were not contests between two equals which would both benefit from the protection of the law in equal measure. They were rather a means to rectify a wrong and punish a crime. As a consequence, individual unjust fighters were not considered as having the same rights and enjoying the same protection as those belonging to the just party. In such a view there was little room for elaborate rules on warfare. The only, and overriding, principle was that of necessity: whatever force necessary to bring the injustice to an end had to be tolerated, but not more.[37]

1.3 Early modern Europe: war as a public activity

When the European Middle Ages came to their end, the law of war was thus a combination of divine and natural law, ecclesiastical teaching, military custom, Christian charity and aristocratic self-interest, devised for wars that were fought for religious belief as well as feudal interests. In the sixteenth century, the law of war became more international in the sense that it would soon regulate warfare between the emerging nation states, and the laws of war began to change from governing a contest between individual knights to regulating encounters of professional armies. *Jus militare*, the law exclusively applicable to knights, was gradually replaced by international rules while the knights who now became officers in the newly established armies took with them their rules, codes and rituals which had guided them through the Age of Chivalry.[38]

At the transition from the European Middle Ages to early modern Europe, the laws of war developed with "remarkable continuity."[39] Military codes were enacted all over Europe, for example by Ferdinand of Hungary in 1526 and Maximilian II in the German-Roman Empire in 1570.[40] The "Codes of Articles and Military Laws" issued by Gustave Adolphus of Sweden in 1621 stand out as an example of the detailed regulations

[34] See Howard M. Hensel, "Theocentric Natural Law and Just War Doctrine" in Howard M. Hensel (ed.), *The Legitimate Use of Military Force: The Just War Tradition and the Customary Law of Armed Conflict* (Aldershot: Ashgate, 2008), p. 14.

[35] See Ramcharan, *Contemporary Human Rights Ideas* (n. 4) pp. 21–25. On natural law as a prerequisite for human rights see also James Griffin, *On Human Rights* (Oxford: Oxford University Press, 2008), pp. 9–11.

[36] The strict dichotomy of *jus ad bellum* (which deals with the lawfulness of a given war) and *jus in bello* (the rules on conducting war) was unknown to the scholars of the just war theory as was the respective terminology, see Robert Kolb, "Origin of the Twin Terms *Jus ad Bellum / Jus in Bello*" (1997) 37(320) *International Review of the Red Cross* 553.

[37] Ibid. 64–65. [38] See Stacey, "Age of Chivalry" (n. 6) p. 39.

[39] Parker, "Early Modern Europe" (n. 28) p. 57.

[40] See Green, "Human Rights in Peace and War" (n. 10) p. 181.

of warfare, as do the Articles of War of James II of 1688, which also included specific procedures to be followed in case of complaints and subsequent punishment of soldiers who had violated these rules.[41]

Legal doctrine bolstered the emergence of the new rules. Pierino Belli (1502–1575) published his book *De Re Militari et Bello Tractatus* (*A Treatise on Military Matters and Warfare*) in 1563 and Alberico Gentilli (1552–1608) took the ideas of an emerging humanitarian law in Belli's *Tractatus* a step further in his three books on the laws of war (*De Jure Belli Libri Tres*). The second of these books dealt with the rules of warfare and supported ideas such as sparing prisoners of war from being killed and affording protection to women and children affected by warfare.[42] Seemingly anticipating modern jurisprudence of international criminal tribunals on rape as a war crime and crimes against humanity, Gentilli even warned princes who had allowed their troops to rape women in occupied territory that such acts not only desecrated the just cause for war but were also against the law of nations and of nature.[43] In seventeenth century England, the rules on behaviour in war came together in a unique code of war (Laws and Ordinances of Warre of 1639) which was informed by religious ideas, concern for humanity and notions of chivalry.[44] While primarily devoted to military discipline and tactics, such codes began more and more to accommodate humanitarian principles, even though their impact was limited.[45]

With the Treaty of Westphalia of 1648, which terminated the Thirty Years' War and reordered the geopolitical landscape in Europe, the nation states began to establish themselves as the sovereigns within the emerging international law. As a consequence, war gradually became a contention between nation states and stopped being a personal encounter between the rulers of a feudal world. The transformed nature of statehood and the accompanying legal framework turned war into a "public activity"[46] fought by modern professional armies and for purposes which no longer required resort to just war theories. Those engaging in battle would now be less personally involved as the reasons for fighting were no longer connected to their person but rather a matter of their nation state. Armies were also no longer composed of military contractors who felt little inclination to respect any rules beyond those laid down in the contracts with their masters.

The development of new technologies and the introduction of new and more deadly weaponry on the battlefield also spurred increased interest in rules which would guide their application. Reciprocity continued to be a strong incentive and with ever more complex and costly military operations the advantages of cooperation and joint adherence to some basic rules, as well as the realistic dangers of a total collapse, became obvious. With the decline of the just war theory the search for the right cause and intention for going to war no longer mattered much, nor did religion. Sin and hate could disappear from the battlefield and were replaced by the professionalism of two trained armed forces

[41] Ibid. pp. 181–82. [42] Bring, "Hugo Grotius" (n. 8) pp. 134–35.

[43] See Theodor Meron, "Common Rights of Mankind in Gentili, Grotius and Suárez" in Theodor Meron (ed.), *War Crimes Law Comes of Age* (Oxford: Clarendon, 1998), pp. 122–29.

[44] See Green, *The Contemporary Law of Armed Conflict* (n. 3) p. 32.

[45] See Theodor Meron, "Medieval and Renaissance Ordinances of War: Codifying Discipline and Humanity" in Theodor Meron (ed.), *War Crimes Law Comes of Age* (Oxford: Clarendon, 1998), p. 1.

[46] Green, *The Contemporary Law of Armed Conflict* (n. 3) p. 30.

fighting for a predefined political outcome. As a consequence, contemporary observers felt inclined to say that:

> war is made with little animosity, and battles are fought without any personal exasperation of those who are engaged, so that parties are, almost in the very heat of a contest, ready to listen to the dictates of humanity or reason.[47]

The new Westphalian order also meant that rights and duties on the international level would only apply to nation states, which in turn forced individual persons, communities and people out of this newly emerging legal framework. What they thought no longer mattered; it was the state that took the decisions, including those on waging war. War was now one of many tools in the nation state's toolbox which could be used to conduct the political business by other means, and the law of war became nothing more than yet another such a tool for the sovereign rulers to manage the conduct of war.[48] Even so, the number and severity of atrocities committed in war seem to have declined in this period.[49] Christian compassion and humanitarianism remained incentives and bilateral treaties between warring forces on the mutual respect for hospitals and the treatment of wounded on both sides without consideration of their nationality were concluded with some frequency.[50] Between 1581 and 1864 at least 294 such treaties on wounded soldiers were concluded in Europe.[51]

Whether such constraint was attributable to a general move towards a more humane society or rather a reflection of the aristocratic values of restraint, self-control and honour which were prevalent in society at the time remains debatable.[52] But rationality certainly was a driving force for developing the laws of war.[53] Wars were now fought by nation states for limited objectives and in a series of highly formalized, even ritualistic, encounters of small, professional and disciplined armies, commanded by members of the European aristocracy, bonded together by ancestry and self-perception of superiority. Such were the rules that contemporary observers could paint peaceful scenes of wars in which "farmers were able to till between the opposing sentries and loaded wagons passed through the picket lines without being bothered."[54] War was not the total horror which earlier generations had experienced but it also meant that the threshold for going to war was lowered and Europe remained engulfed in wars within and beyond its borders.

[47] The eighteenth century Scottish philosopher and historian Adam Ferguson, quoted from Neff, *War and the Law of Nations* (n. 30) p. 90.

[48] See Teitel, *Humanity's Law* (n. 26) p. 25.

[49] See Parker, "Early Modern Europe" (n. 28) pp. 51–53.

[50] See Green, "Human Rights in Peace and War" (n. 10) pp. 182–83.

[51] See Jeremy Sarkin, "The Historical Origins, Convergence and Interrelationship of International Human Rights Law, International Humanitarian Law, International Criminal Law and Public International Law and their Application since the Nineteenth Century" (2007) 1(2) *Human Rights and International Legal Discourse* 135.

[52] See Christopher Coker, *War in an Age of Risk* (Cambridge: Polity, 2009), p. 175.

[53] See Jin Xu, "The Evolution of International Laws of War" (2008) 2 *Chinese Journal of International Politics* 177. Such rational humanitarianism did not make the world a peaceful place: between the mid-seventeenth and the end of the eighteenth centuries some sixteen wars were fought between European nations, accompanied by numerous colonial wars and revolts, see Gunther Rothenberg, "The Age of Napoleon" in Michael Howard, George J. Andreopoulos and Mark R. Shulman (eds.), *The Laws of War: Constraints on Warfare in the Western World* (New Haven, CT: Yale University Press, 1994), p. 86.

[54] Rothenberg, "The Age of Napoleon"(n. 54) p. 86.

1.4 War and peace in the emerging law of nations

For international lawyers, the ease with which states were now able to go to war presented a dilemma. Should war still be seen as the aberration and a breach of peace or as the normal state of affairs, only interrupted by short spells of tranquillity? The seventeenth century witnessed a profound intellectual struggle over the very meaning of war and peace and the associated legal frameworks. War could be perceived in different ways: as the enforcement of values against wrongdoers in pursuance of the medieval just war theory; as a contractual arrangement within which the parties could freely develop any rules they sought reasonable; or as the natural anarchical state of affairs not worthy of being tamed at all.

The latter view is inextricably linked to Thomas Hobbes (1588–1679) who turned away from the medieval view that peace was the normal state of natural law and war a deviation. To him, war was neither the exception nor a form of law enforcement as the just war theory would have it but a normal condition of inter-state affairs in an anarchic and brutal world. As a consequence, he suggested that warfare should no longer be moderated: war was a quest for survival and restraint in using force an impediment.[55] The conduct of warfare ought to depend on the success of military operations, and quite some latitude was allowed for military planners to accept collateral damage. Other (humanitarian) considerations, while in principle applicable, would need to take a step back.[56] Adherents of another school of thought, so-called "contractualists," would argue that war should neither be understood in terms of justness nor as representing anarchy but more as a contractual arrangement, a sort of contest by armed force, governed by a specially created legal framework. In such a view, the laws of peace were altogether suspended and replaced by a special legal regime of war, created by the contestants according to their needs.[57] Still, humanitarian constraints seem to have been considered largely a moral issue which ought to reside outside the sphere of contractual arrangements on warfare.[58]

Early proponents of the idea of inalienable rights would add a fourth consideration. Where Hobbes had found that free individuals were entitled to assert their natural rights limitlessly in an anarchic state of affairs, including in warfare, liberals such as John Locke (1632–1704) found that because natural law provided human beings with inalienable rights, they would in turn have the duty to respect those rights also vis-à-vis others. While Locke was not primarily concerned with matters of war and peace, his position could also be applied, in principle, to matters of warfare.[59] To him, the free and equal human nature would dictate that everyone engaged in armed conflict is entitled to the same treatment and that rules on warfare were neither useless (as they were for Hobbes) nor contingent on

55 See Neff, *War and the Law of Nations* (n. 30) pp. 135–36.

56 See Howard M. Hensel, "Anthropocentric Natural Law and Its Implications for International Relations and Armed Conflict" in Howard M. Hensel (ed.), *The Legitimate Use of Military Force: The Just War Tradition and the Customary Law of Armed Conflict* (Aldershot: Ashgate, 2008), pp. 43–44.

57 See Neff, *War and the Law of Nations* (n. 30) pp. 137–39, who points out that no single writer is clearly associated with what he terms the "contractualist" school but traces an impact of this school in the writings of Samuel Pufendorf (1632–1694).

58 Ibid. pp. 149–50.

59 Chapter III of his Second Treatise of Civil Government is entitled "Of the State of War" and deals essentially with the right to go to war and not with rules in war, see John Locke, *The Second Treatise of Civil Government* (1690, reprinted with an introduction by Joseph Carrig, New York: Barns and Noble, 2008), pp. 8–10.

considerations of justice, religious belief or charitable motivations, nor were they freely negotiable. Rather, they followed from humanity which, in turn, reflected human nature. This, above all, should be the source of exercising restraint in warfare and inform the respective rules on the lawful means and methods.[60] Samuel von Pufendorf (1632–1694), as his contemporary Locke a proponent of natural law, introduced this idea of human dignity (*dignatio*) more broadly in international law,[61] but none of the two developed a theory of the law of war based on these foundations.

Rather, it was left to Hugo Grotius (1583–1646) to rearrange the laws of war. Deploring "the lack of restraint in relation to war, such as even barbarous races should be ashamed of"[62] he wrote his *De Jure Belli ac Pacis Libri Tres*, published in Paris in 1625, which can be seen as the first attempt to systematically arrange international legal concepts.[63] Grotius moved from the medieval concept of *jus gentium* as a subset of an all-encompassing natural law which governs the relations of peoples towards *inter-national* law, i.e., a distinct set of laws applicable between the emerging nation states. In such a new system, divine orders and the belief in some form of naturally existing rules were replaced by mutual consent as the source of law-making. For the laws of war this meant replacing chivalry, honour and God's commands with contractual arrangements. It also meant that soldiers were freed from personal responsibility for their deeds as they acted on behalf of their nation state, and that killing them was justified not because they pursued an unjust cause but merely because of their status as soldiers.

Grotius' plea for restraint in warfare, although driven by his Christian faith and loathing of the brutality of war, resulted in the secularization of the just war theory and allowed extending protection to all parties in the conflict regardless of the perceived justness of their cause. With this Grotius separated peace and war more clearly than ever before. War was no longer to be seen as a series of punitive acts against wrongdoers who would disturb an eternally lasting peace but as a legal state and condition clearly set apart from peace. The whole of present international humanitarian law is built on these foundations and its three core principles reflect this approach: military necessity, i.e., the practical consideration that only acts which are necessary for military advantages are justifiable; humanity, i.e., the moral consideration that acts are unacceptable when they violate humanitarian demands; and equality, i.e., that all parties to the conflict, regardless of the actual facts and events, are entitled to equal protection by the law.[64]

Even though Grotius' call for restraint in warfare was rooted in the Christian virtue of charity[65] his treatment of the emerging international humanitarian law can also be seen as indicating "a certain element of human rights ideology with regard to civilians and prisoners

[60] See Hensel, "Anthropocentric Natural Law" (n. 56) pp. 52–53.

[61] See Christian Starck, "The Religious and Philosophical Background of Human Dignity and its Place in Modern Constitutions" in David Kretzmer and Eckart Klein (eds.), *The Concept of Human Dignity in Human Rights Discourse* (The Hague: Kluwer, 2002), p. 182.

[62] Hugo Grotius, *On the Law of War and Peace*, Prologue (1625, edited and annotated by Stephen C. Neff, Cambridge: Cambridge University Press, 2012), p. 8.

[63] See Bring, "Hugo Grotius" (n. 8) p. 136.

[64] See, e.g., Frits Kalshoven and Liesbeth Zegveld, *Constraints on the Waging of War: An Introduction to International Humanitarian Law* (4th edn., Cambridge: Cambridge University Press, 2011), p. 2. On the historic dimension see also Neff, *War and the Law of Nations* (n. 30) p. 148.

[65] See Geoffrey Best, *War and Law Since 1945* (Oxford: Clarendon Press, 1994), pp. 28–29.

of war."[66] Grotius' reference to human rights is strongest in the *Prologemina*, the introductory part of his influential publication, where he indicated to be "fully convinced . . . that there is a common law among nations, which is valid alike for war and in war"[67] and that such existing law would offer protection to individuals affected by war. But Grotius' views on the laws of war remain ambivalent, swaying between strict adherence to state practice (for example, his assessment that enslaving prisoners of war, while contrary to nature, is consistent with the law of nations) and a bold reading of the law in a human rights-friendly way (e.g., his references to freedom of thought).[68]

1.5 Enlightenment: national wars and individual rights

The rationality upon which the law of war was now built fitted comfortably in the Age of Enlightenment (the period covering the eighteenth century up to the Napoleonic wars of 1804–1815) with its "deconfessionalization"[69] of war. It was also the time when human rights began their ascent with documents such as the French Declaration of the Rights of Man and the Citizen of 1789; a prime example of a set of principles which assert popular sovereignty and individual rights against absolutist monarchies. This revolutionary intellectual and political movement was, however, first and foremost concerned with ascertaining a new place of the individual in society and had little time or ambition to reflect on warfare. The proponents of human rights were primarily concerned with the balance between liberty and security and the role of the state in securing personal freedom and economic benefit and not with questions of war and peace. Their aim was to assign a new and more prominent place for the individual human being and move it from being an anonymous part of the feudal system towards the more self-confident *citoyen* of modern Europe. The combination of (Anglo-American and French) natural rights traditions, the rise of capitalism, and ideological, industrial, scientific and military revolutions allowed the concept of inalienable individual rights to replace the predominance of divine rights and societal hierarchies.[70]

In his *Social Contract* (*Du contrat social ou principes du droit politique*) of 1762, Jean-Jacques Rousseau (1712–1778), for example, referred to the laws of war only in passing in a chapter devoted to slavery. He argued that rationality should be the source of restraint in warfare. For him, war was no longer a personal encounter of princes to whom soldiers felt loyalty but an affair entirely between nation states in which "individuals are enemies wholly by chance, not as men, not even as citizens, but only as soldiers."[71] He concluded that:

66 Bring, "Hugo Grotius" (n. 8) p. 131.

67 Grotius, *On the Law of War and Peace*, Prologue (n. 62) p. 8.

68 See Bring, "Hugo Grotius" (n. 8) pp. 139–40.

69 Parker, "Early Modern Europe" (n. 28) p. 54. See on this process Géza Herczegh, "Some Thoughts on Ideas that Gave Rise to International Humanitarian Law" in Michael N. Schmitt and Leslie C. Green (eds.), *The Law of Armed Conflict: Into the Next Millenium* (Newport, CT: Naval War College, 1998), p. 302.

70 See Roger Normand and Sarah Zaidi, *Human Rights at the UN: The Political History of Universal Justice* (Bloomington, IN: Indiana University Press, 2008), p. 11, and Donnelly, *International Human Rights Law* (n. 25) p. 43.

71 Jean-Jacques Rousseau, *The Social Contract*, Book I (translated and introduced by Maurice Cranston, London: Penguin, 1968), p. 56.

> [e]ven in real war, a just prince, while laying hands, in the enemy's country, on all that belongs to the public, respects the lives and goods of individuals: he respects rights on which his own are founded. The object of the war being the destruction of the hostile State, the other side has a right to kill its defenders, while they are bearing arms; but as soon as they lay them down and surrender, they cease to be enemies or instruments of the enemy, and become once more merely men, whose life no one has any right to take. Sometimes it is possible to kill the State without killing a single one of its members; and war gives no right which is not necessary to the gaining of its object.[72]

When the French Revolution of 1789 brought France into conflict with other European powers (which eventually led to the Revolutionary Wars from 1792–1802), the existing legal framework on warfare faced new challenges. In 1792, at the beginning of the wars (which were, after all, meant to serve the revolutionary purpose of justice and humanity) to the French government was at pains to explain that the laws of war would be followed, civilians spared and prisoners treated humanely, a proposal which they lived up only for the first year or so. The spirit of the times soon discredited military honour as un-revolutionary and the new slogan was "waging war *à l'outrance* [to the excess] or going home"; a motto which obviously did not bode well for the application of restrictive rules on the battlefield.[73]

Such revolutionary spirit was, however, short-lived, and the need for a professional and disciplined army led to a more realistic perception of the law of war as a necessary tool to wage war. This was particularly so in the Napoleonic Wars of 1803–1815 which followed the Revolutionary Wars. They ushered in an era where great nations would fight great wars. In such clashes of masses of conscripted soldiers, people were at the service of the state again rather than asserting rights against it.[74] The intensity and duration of conflicts began to rise and occasional battles fought with consideration for harvesting seasons were replaced by a continuous and coherent unleashing of all-consuming violence, projected over great space and a long time. Modern weapons technology carried destruction into the civilian population and the fight over colonies led to genocidal violence against native inhabitants without much consideration of humanity.[75] In such circumstances, attempts to moderate warfare remained largely an intellectual enterprise with limited influence on the battlefield and the fate of those *hors de combat* depended on circumstances and personalities more than on a universally accepted adherence to rules.[76]

The conservative and nationalist approach to war in the Counter-Enlightenment pushed the law of war further back. Carl von Clausewitz (1780–1831) was perhaps most influential in rejecting any universal and cosmopolitan ethos in regulating warfare and instead emphasized the role of war as a means to further the interest and policies of the nation state. Humanitarian considerations, let alone natural rights, were of little concern and war was simply an act of unlimited force to compel the enemy.[77] There was only scarce space for

[72] Ibid. p. 57. See also G.I.A.D. Draper, "Humanitarianism in the Modern Law of Armed Conflict" in Michael A. Meyer (ed.), *Armed Conflict and the New Law*, vol. I, *Aspects of the 1977 Geneva Protocols and the 1981 Weapons Convention* (London: British Institute of International and Comparative Law, 1989), p. 8.

[73] See Rothenberg, "The Age of Napoleon" (n. 54) pp. 87–88.

[74] See Normand and Zaidi, *Human Rights at the UN* (n. 70) p. 15.

[75] See Herczegh, "Some Thoughts on Ideas" (n. 69) p. 302.

[76] Rothenberg, "The Age of Napoleon" (n. 54) pp. 87–88.

[77] See Howard M. Hensel, "The Rejection of Natural Law and Its Implications for International Relations

humanitarian ideas. To Clausewitz, the law of war merely meant "certain self-imposed, imperceptible limitations hardly worth mentioning, known as international law and custom."[78] He was not alone with his views. The combination of a conservative worldview, Counter-Enlightenment and Romanticism profoundly impacted on the law of war. Any idea of universality, let alone universally shared human rights, was rejected in favour of the nationalist emphasis on one's social, cultural, economic and political heritage.[79]

and Armed Conflict" in Howard M. Hensel (ed.), *The Legitimate Use of Military Force: The Just War Tradition and the Customary Law of Armed Conflict* (Aldershot: Ashgate, 2008), p. 76.

[78] Carl von Clausewitz, *On War*, Chapter 1 (1832, edited and translated by Michael Eliot Howard and Peter Paret, Princeton, NJ: Princeton University Press, 1976), p. 75. See also Azar Gat, *The Origins of Military Thought from the Enlightenment to Clausewitz* (Oxford: Clarendon Press, 1989), p. 242.

[79] See Hensel, "The Rejection of Natural Law" (n. 77) pp. 78–79.

2

The science of warfare and the progress of civilization

2.1 The positivist nineteenth century

When the European geopolitical landscape was restructured after the Congress of Vienna of 1815, innovations in the law and policy of warfare could take hold and the law of war was resuscitated. The nineteenth century was an era of belief in human evolution and technical advances. Scientific progress was everywhere and warfare itself became a science. In terms of law, this was a positivist century in which the rules on warfare – hitherto scattered over customary principles, religious teaching, domestic laws and military manuals – could finally be consolidated under the rubric of public international law. Not only did international law provide the structure within which warfare was now regulated but the whole of international law became decisively shaped and developed by regulations for, in and around war.[1] The law of war was finally decoupled from considerations of justice and the spirit of the century also meant that the new norms on warfare turned out to be highly technical norms, informed by the technological advances of the time and created in a scientific perception of the law by nation states at the prime of their sovereignty. The positivism of this century did away with divine or "metaphysical" justifications of legal rules and sought to establish law as an objective science. At the same time, it also promoted a realist and functional view of the law as an instrument to further the interests of each individual nation state rather than any illusory international community.

The rules on warfare drafted in this spirit were state-centred, practical and technocratic rules driven by utilitarian considerations.[2] While tempered by occasional references to humanitarian considerations, neither morale and values nor the idea of any such thing as an "international community" provided guidance in the development of the law. Peace and war could also be strictly separated: "peace was a condition in which war was absent, and war a condition in which peace was absent."[3] This prevailing approach was only intermittently challenged by more liberal and cosmopolitan views which preserved the legacy of the Enlightenment, believed in individual rights and expressed empathy for non-European peoples.[4]

One of the first legal texts to be drafted in this positivist and technocratic spirit of the time, the Declaration of St. Petersburg (issued by nineteen European states in 1868),

[1] See Adam Roberts, "Land Warfare: From Hague to Nuremberg" in Michael Howard, George J. Andreopoulos and Mark R. Shulman (eds.), *The Laws of War. Constraints on Warfare in the Western World* (New Haven, CT: Yale University Press, 1994), p. 119.

[2] Ibid. pp. 167–76. [3] Ibid. p. 172.

[4] See Martti Koskenniemi, "The Legacy of the Nineteenth Century" in David Armstrong (ed.), *Routledge Handbook of International Law* (London: Routledge, 2009), p. 143.

encapsulated this "'scientific" approach when it indicated its purpose as "having by common agreement fixed the technical limits at which the necessities of war ought to yield to the requirements of humanity."[5] The treaty was a response to the emergence of a new type of weapon. Explosive rifle projectiles had recently proven their worth against enemy materiel but when used against enemy combatants they were no more useful in disabling them than any other type of bullet, yet they caused particularly heavy injuries. The drafters of the Declaration concluded that their use ought to be banned on the grounds that "the only legitimate object which states should endeavour to accomplish during war is to weaken the military forces of the enemy," that this object "would be exceeded by the employment of arms which uselessly aggravate the sufferings of disabled men, or render their death inevitable" and that the use of such weapons would be "contrary to the laws of humanity."[6] Carefully balancing military necessity with humanity, the drafters of the text introduced the dividing line of 400 grammes for such projectiles on the ground that heavier artillery shells would be primarily used against enemy materiel and would also be able to kill more than one man at a time so that their military advantage outweighed the additional suffering caused.[7]

The Declaration also proceeded from the realistic view that war cannot and should not be banned but that it was necessary to "alleviat[e] as much as possible the calamities of war,"[8] thus balancing humanitarian motives with the freedom of states to go to war. This seems unsurprising, given that these foundations of international humanitarian law were laid at a time when resort to force between states was not at all unlawful under international law.[9] In this scientific age which combined the image of war as a means of politics with mathematical calculation, "military necessity" became a key concept. It was hoped that unlike ill-defined ideas of "humanity," the idea of military necessity could be described with a degree of precision. In modern parlance, military necessity may be understood as:

> the degree and kind of force, not otherwise prohibited by the law of armed conflict, that is required in order to achieve the legitimate purpose of the conflict, namely the complete or partial submission of the enemy at the earliest possible moment with the minimum expenditure of life and resources.[10]

The term was derived from the idea of *Kriegsräson* which suggests that all means necessary to prevail over the enemy are justified. As a derivate of military necessity, humanity was understood as a principle which forbids "the infliction of suffering, injury or destruction not actually necessary for the accomplishment of legitimate military purposes."[11] This duality of military necessity and humanity – that for humanitarian reasons wars have limits which

[5] Preamble to the Declaration Renouncing the Use, in Time of War, of Explosive Projectiles under 400 Grammes Weight, 11 December 1868 ("Declaration of St. Petersburg").

[6] Preamble to the St. Petersburg Declaration.

[7] See Frits Kalshoven and Liesbeth Zegveld, *Constraints on the Waging of War: An Introduction to International Humanitarian Law* (4th edn., Cambridge: Cambridge University Press, 2011), pp. 9–10.

[8] Preamble to the St. Petersburg Declaration.

[9] Louise Doswald-Beck and Sylvain Vité, "International Humanitarian Law and Human Rights Law" (1993) 33(293) *International Review of the Red Cross* 95.

[10] UK Ministry of Defence, *The Manual of the Law of Armed Conflict* (Oxford: Oxford University Press, 2004), para. 2.2.

[11] Ibid. para. 2.4. See also International Committee of the Red Cross, *Interpretative Guidance on the Notion of Direct Participation in Hostilities under International Humanitarian Law* (Geneva: International Committee of the Red Cross, 2009), pp. 79–80.

need to be defined in a dispassionate calculation of military gain against human lives rather than by reference to justice or human dignity – informs all humanitarian instruments drafted later, even though there was disagreement on the extent to which violence would remain lawful from the very beginning.[12] Furthermore, this rational approach to humanity was challenged by two problems: first, and in a somewhat ironic twist, it often presupposed the stirring of national passions and patriotic emotions to sufficiently demonize the enemy so as to find public support for going to war; emotions which could then hardly be contained. And secondly, the advances of technology ensured that the highly specific and technical rules were often outdated and unsuitable as soon as they were agreed upon. The attempts of nineteenth-century lawyers to restrain the use of force in war have often been likened to the Lilliputians trying to enchain the Gulliver of total war.[13] Notwithstanding the humanitarian rhetoric, the premise upon which the law of war was built was thus circular: wars were limited only by the need to win, and the enemy had to endure everything necessary to that end.

2.2 Lieber Code

The mere five operative paragraphs of the Declaration of St. Petersberg regulated only a specific problem but the blueprint for the larger codification of the law of war had already been drafted five years earlier, in 1863, when the German-born professor of history and political science at Columbia University (then Columbia College) Francis Lieber (1798–1872) was asked by the United States government to compile a set of instructions to provide guidance in the American Civil War, then in its second year. The resulting text was signed by US President Lincoln on 24 April 1863 and came to be known as the Lieber Code.[14] The rationale of the Code was more utilitarian than humanitarian.[15] From the start of the war it was obvious that most American professional officers would be fighting on the Confederate side while the Union (i.e., the US government) would be left with a great number of militias and volunteers who were not only less experienced in fighting wars but also less knowledgeable in the applicable rules. Any confrontation between American soldiers would, however, have to be guided by the proper rules not only because it was going to be a contest between equals (different from fighting native Indians or Mexicans where rules and humanitarian considerations were seemingly of less of a concern for those waging military campaigns) but also because at the end of the war some form of peaceful coexistence would have to be agreed upon. Atrocities in the war ought thus to be avoided as much as possible and rules were needed to this end.

The Code contained provisions on the behaviour of armed forces, on the care for wounded and captured soldiers and regulations on the protection of civilians and civilian property. Lieber was, however, not only a utilitarian. Left without any textbook or much other guidance on the laws of war, he resorted to (in his own

[12] See Mika Nishimura Hayashi, "The Martens Clause and Military Necessity" in Howard M. Hensel (ed.), *The Legitimate Use of Military Force: The Just War Tradition and the Customary Law of Armed Conflict* (Aldershot: Ashgate, 2008), p. 137.

[13] Stephen C. Neff, *War and the Law of Nations: A General History* (Cambridge: Cambridge University Press, 2005), pp. 201–4.

[14] General Order No. 100, Instructions for the Government of Armies of the United States in the Field, 24 April 1863 ("Lieber Code").

[15] See Geoffrey Best, *War and Law Since 1945* (Oxford: Clarendon Press, 1994), pp. 40–41.

words) "[u]sage, history, reason, and conscientiousness, a sincere love of truth, justice and civilization" as foundational pillars of his work.[16] While his strict distinction between combatants and civilians and the broad protection which he accorded to the latter group speak of his humanitarian concern and has paved the way for modern humanitarian rules, he also allowed a great deal of military necessity to reign. It sounds less acceptable to today's reader when he advocates, for example, the use of intense force to shorten wars: "[t]he more vigorously wars are pursued, the better it is for humanity. Sharp wars are brief."[17] But Lieber was also influenced by the movement for the abolition of slavery and the slave-trade (he personally opposed slavery) and its spirit of emancipation. The prohibition of discrimination on the ground of class, colour or condition in the Lieber Code is a result of this.[18]

The Code was influential beyond the American Civil War and could be used to regulate international armed conflicts, too, just as Lieber had intended. After all, only 9 out of 157 articles of the Code dealt with insurrection, civil war and rebellion and even those he had added "reluctantly."[19] The use of broad and general rules, together with Lieber's friendship with Johann Caspar Bluntschli (1808–1881), Swiss professor of private and public law in Munich and later in Heidelberg, secured the Code's success across the Atlantic.[20] Different from Lieber, Bluntschli explicitly invoked human rights as essential elements of the law of armed conflict. In his textbook on international law of 1868, he stated that it must be clear that under contemporary law human rights ("*Menschenrechte*") have to be respected in war, given that humans do not cease to be human even when they are enemies.[21] He argued that the right to personal security, honour and freedom remains untouchable even in time of war.[22] For him, the rules which restrict the use of force in war and protect civilians stem from the inalienable human rights which are applicable in times of peace as well as in times of war;[23] a view which was not widely shared even in humanitarian circles and remains an important but isolated forerunner of the debate on human rights in armed conflict.

[16] Quoted from Theodor Meron, "Francis Lieber's Code and Principles of Humanity" in Jonathan I. Charney, Donald K. Anton and Mary Ellen O'Connell (eds.), *Politics, Values and Functions: International Law in the 21st Century, Essays in Honour of Professor Louis Henkin* (The Hague: Nijhoff, 1997), p. 258.

[17] Lieber Code, Art. 29.

[18] Lieber Code, Art. 57: "No belligerent has a right to declare that enemies of a certain class, color, or condition, when properly organized as soldiers, will not be treated by him as public enemies."

[19] Meron, "Francis Lieber's Code" (n. 16) p. 257.

[20] On the friendship between the two men see Dietrich Schindler, "J.C. Bluntschli's Contribution to the Law of War" in Marcelo G. Kohen (ed.), *Promoting Justice, Human Rights and Conflict Resolution through International Law, Liber Amicorum Lucius Caflisch* (Leiden: Nijhoff, 2007), p. 438.

[21] Johann Caspar Bluntschli, *Das moderne Völkerrecht der civilisierten Staaten als Rechtsbuch dargestellt* (Nördlingen: Beck, 1868), p. 31.

[22] Ibid. p. 33.

[23] See Christian Tomuschat, *Human Rights between Idealism and Realism* (2nd edn., Oxford: Oxford University Press, 2008), p. 16. Bluntschli is, however, less straightforward on this matter in his textbook on the law of war, published two years earlier, see Johann Caspar Bluntschli, *Das moderne Kriegsrecht der civilisirten Staaten als Rechtsbuch dargestellt* (Nördlingen: Beck, 1866).

2.3 Laws of war as a *mission civilisatrice*

Despite its nature as a domestic piece of legislation, the usefulness of the Lieber Code was soon discovered in Europe. The Brussels Project of an International Declaration concerning the Laws and Customs of War of 1874[24] and the *Oxford Manual on the Laws of War on Land*, drafted by the Institute of International Law in 1880,[25] were concrete results and paved the way for adoption of the conventions and declarations in the Hague Peace Conferences of 1899 and 1907. With the texts adopted in the first of these conferences, the codification of the law of war as a comprehensive legal framework began in earnest.[26] They were followed and revised by the texts adopted in the second Peace Conference of 1907.[27] These texts, later to be grouped under the notion of "Hague law," were informed by somewhat antagonistic considerations, and in their drafting humanitarian and utilitarian motivations coincided.[28] On the one hand, warring nations wanted to know with some certainty how they could lawfully conduct military campaigns and avoid critique and contempt from various quarters, a matter which had plagued them in past conflicts. The emerging peace movement of the nineteenth century proved most troublesome for those advocating wars as a means of politics as it questioned the right of states to go to war in general and the conduct of warfare in particular. The *Oxford Manual* of 1880 is frank in this respect when it states in the Preamble that:

> so long as the demands of opinion remain indeterminate, belligerents are exposed to painful uncertainty and to endless accusations. A positive set of rules, on the contrary, if they are judicious, serves the interests of belligerents and is far from hindering them.[29]

On the other hand, humanitarian considerations could not be brushed aside completely. The 1899 and 1907 Hague Conventions were, after all, "animated by the desire to serve . . . the interests of humanity."[30] The vision embodied in these instruments was to reduce unnecessary suffering and inhumane treatment by prohibiting certain kinds of weapons or methods of warfare as a balancing act between military necessity and humanitarian

24 Final Protocol and Project to an International Declaration Concerning the Laws and Customs of War, Brussels, 27 August 1874.

25 Institute of International Law, *The Laws of War on Land* (Oxford: Institute of International Law, 9 September 1880) ("Oxford Manual").

26 The conference adopted Hague Convention (II) with respect to the Laws and Customs of War on Land and its Annex: Regulations concerning the Laws and Customs of War on Land, 20 July 1899 ("Hague Regulations 1899"), together with texts on maritime warfare, asphyxiating gases, expanding bullets and warfare with the use of balloons. See on the drafting history in greater detail Jean-Marie Henckaerts, "The Development of International Humanitarian Law and the Continued Relevance of Custom" in Howard M. Hensel (ed.), *The Legitimate Use of Military Force: The Just War Tradition and the Customary Law of Armed Conflict* (Aldershot: Ashgate, 2008), pp. 117–20.

27 Hague Convention (IV) with respect to the Laws and Customs of War on Land and its annexed Regulations, 18 October 1907 ("Hague Regulations 1907") were accompanied by texts on neutrality, the status of merchant ships, submarine mines and other matters of naval warfare.

28 See Dietrich Schindler, "International Humanitarian Law: Its Remarkable Development and Its Persistent Violation" (2003) 5(2) *Journal of the History of International Law* 166.

29 Oxford Manual (n. 25) Preface.

30 Preambles to Hague Convention (II) with respect to the Laws and Customs of War on Land of 1899 and Convention (IV) with respect to the Laws and Customs of War on Land of 1907.

concern.[31] They contained humanitarian rules on prisoners of war and the protection of the wounded and sick and persons under belligerent occupation.

But it needs to be recalled that the Hague Peace Conferences devised rules on warfare on land nearly as a byproduct. The main aim of the 1899 Peace Conference (which it failed to achieve) was to prevent future wars by introducing a system of inter-state arbitration.[32] Many governments had been sceptical about the whole idea of convening the conference from the start but civil society organizations – first and foremost religious peace movements such as the Quakers – enthusiastically embraced the humanitarian message in which the Russian government had veiled its proposal to convene the conference.[33] And indeed, what the conference failed to achieve in the area of disarmament and peace it made up for in the revision of the laws of war: it produced the first multilateral codification on the laws of land warfare, a Convention on maritime warfare, and prohibited the discharge of explosives from balloons and the use of asphyxiating gases.[34] It also prohibited the use of so-called "dum-dum" bullets which expand upon impact and increase the amount of injuries. The drafting history of this document is, however, also an example that considerations of universal human dignity were not on the conference agenda when the British delegate to the conference argued that such bullets should still be allowed in fighting against natives in colonial uprisings in Africa because ordinary bullets would not work against such savages.[35]

In light of the outcome of the 1899 Peace Conference, the expectations for the second Hague Peace Conference of 1907 were muted, and like eight years earlier its results were disappointing with regard to peace and disarmament. But again the conference adopted a number of legal texts on the laws of war, the most important being Convention IV and its annexed Regulations (the "Hague Regulations"). Out of the thirteen texts on the law of war adopted at the conference, ten dealt with the laws of war (with a special focus on naval warfare to which eight of those ten conventions were devoted). A third Peace Conference, scheduled to be held within eight years of the second, never materialized as the First World War broke out.

It is somewhat ironic that the Hague Peace Conferences did not bring about peace but instead produced rules for the improvement of fighting. And even these rules have been judged as having little immediate influence on the battlefield.[36] But perhaps the two conferences should not be assessed in light of what they actually achieved but by the very ideas expressed in them. The texts resulting from the conferences had finally made it clear that the law of war could be negotiated as multilateral legal instruments rather than being extracted from divine commands or customary behaviour of noble warriors: "[m]ultilateral politics bleached the great ideas of honour and chivalry out of its legal instruments along with 'the Supreme Being.'"[37] They had also established the consensus that belligerents are

[31] Hague Regulations 1907, Art. 22: "The right of belligerents to adopt means of injuring the enemy is not unlimited." Article 23(e) especially forbids "[t]o employ arms, projectiles, or material calculated to cause unnecessary suffering."

[32] See Kalshoven and Zegveld, *Constraints on the Waging of War* (n. 7) p. 11.

[33] See Roger Normand and Sarah Zaidi, *Human Rights at the UN: The Political History of Universal Justice* (Bloomington, IN: Indiana University Press, 2008), pp. 37–39.

[34] See Roberts, "Land Warfare" (n. 1) p. 121.

[35] See Normand and Zaidi, *Human Rights at the UN* (n. 33) p. 40.

[36] Best, *War and Law Since 1945* (n. 15) p. 46. [37] Ibid. p. 409.

not entitled to unlimited discretion as to the means of warfare they employ and that those *hors de combat* (and civilians in particular) should be spared as much as possible from the consequences of war. And they had introduced the idea that the fate of individual human beings should matter in international law, marking "the birth of global efforts to inscribe the rights and interests of human beings into international law. The birth was premature but not stillborn."[38]

It has been argued that in the 1899 Hague Peace Conference "the seeds of what would become the international human rights system were planted"[39] in as far as cardinal human rights principles such as protecting individuals from state abuse, breaking through the sovereign prerogative of states and separating the interests of the citizens from their governments were first acknowledged in an international treaty-making process. Indeed, the humanitarians and war critics engaged in this process were partly successful in pushing for the inclusion of humanitarian considerations and their work can be seen as early human rights advocacy.[40] Elements of the human rights language did appear in the respective texts, such as in Article 46 of the Hague Regulations 1907.[41]

But provisions clearly designed to protect civilians in armed conflicts remained scarce in the text, and the ambiguous references to "rights and honours" (such as in the provision just quoted) reflect uncertainty on whether the individual's entitlement to human dignity or the *chevaliers*' obligation to act honourably would form the basis of protecting war victims.[42] The Hague Conventions of 1899 and 1907 were obviously not human rights documents but sought to balance military needs and humanitarian demands: "[i]t is only in an incidental fashion, and if one interprets the concept in the broadest sense, that one is able to say that, apart from the relations between the armed forces, the Hague Regulations dealt with human rights."[43] And yet, these texts foreshadowed the possibility of directly protecting individuals through international treaty law and cut back on states' absolute sovereign prerogative under international law.

Another feature which set the development of international humanitarian law in the nineteenth century apart from earlier periods of history was the drafters' self-perception of being on a *mission civilisatrice*. Now, restraint in warfare no longer reflected God's will or a chivalric attitude, nor was it only a rational calculation or, alternatively, an expression of natural law. It was, on top of this, meant to demonstrate Europe's desire to advance civilization. Many of the texts adopted since the Declaration of St. Petersburg of 1868 explicitly refer to this civilizing force of law, including the Declaration itself.[44] The Hague Conventions of 1899 and 1907 echoed this language when they presented themselves

[38] Normand and Zaidi, *Human Rights at the UN* (n. 33) p. 42. [39] Ibid. p. 35.

[40] See Schindler, "International Humanitarian Law" (n. 28) 166; and Normand and Zaidi, *Human Rights at the UN* (n. 33) p. 35.

[41] Hague Regulations 1907, Art. 46: "Family honour and rights, the lives of persons, and private property, as well as religious convictions and practice, must be respected."

[42] See Tomuschat, *Human Rights between Idealism and Realism* (n. 23) p. 16; and George H. Aldrich, "The Laws of War on Land" (2000) 94(1) *American Journal of International Law* 31.

[43] Leslie C. Green, "Human Rights and the Law of Armed Conflict" in Leslie C. Green (ed.), *Essays on the Modern Law of War* (Ardsley, NY: Transnational, 1999), p. 442.

[44] The Preamble to the Declaration of St. Petersburg declares that "[t]he progress of civilization should have the effect of alleviating as much as possible the calamities of war."

as animated not only by the desire to serve the interests of humanity but also "the ever increasing requirements of civilization."[45]

Civilization was seen as the hallmark of industrialized Europe with its professional armies and thus, like medieval references to humanity, exclusive. It did not necessarily reflect a commitment to universal human dignity. As a consequence, any religiously or ideologically inspired racist and intolerant worldview could dehumanize their opponents as being outside "civilization" and unworthy of protection by the law. The objective of wars against such opponents was mostly unlimited and often geared towards eradication and the means and methods applied in such wars followed suit, up to and including the Second World War and the Holocaust.[46]

2.4 Martens Clause and the dictates of public conscience

Another element in the Hague Conventions speaks more audibly of a human rights-oriented perspective on the laws of war than the scattered reference to individual rights and honours and the pompous invocation of the law's civilizing force. In the 1899 Hague Peace Conference, Fedor Fedorovich (Frédéric) Martens (1845–1909), a German-speaking Estonian employed to represent Russia, drafted an ambiguous clause later to be named after him. Martens had been entrusted with negotiations over the status of civilians who had taken up arms against an occupying force. Some conference delegates wanted them to be treated as *francs-tireurs* (and thus subject to execution) while others saw them as lawful combatants.[47] In the absence of an agreement Martens thought that, as a minimum, they should be entitled to basic protection and proposed a text vague enough to be acceptable to the delegates. The resulting clause was adopted by unanimous vote as part of the Hague Convention 1899 and the text was repeated in the 1907 Hague Convention where it read:

> Until a more complete code of the laws of war has been issued, the High Contracting Parties deem it expedient to declare that, in cases not included in the Regulations adopted by them, the inhabitants and the belligerents remain under the protection and the rule of the principles of the law of nations, as they result from the usages established among civilized peoples, from the laws of humanity, and the dictates of the public conscience.[48]

The clause has since become "one of the legal myths of the international community,"[49] and the opaque text lends itself to a number of interpretations. In the most restricted sense it is seen as a reminder that customary law continues to play a role in the area of international humanitarian law, but on numerous occasions it has also been acknowledged that the clause

[45] Preambles to Hague Convention (II) with respect to the Laws and Customs of War on Land of 1899 and Convention (IV) with respect to the Laws and Customs of War on Land of 1907.

[46] See Howard M. Hensel, "The Rejection of Natural Law and Its Implications for International Relations and Armed Conflict" in Howard M. Hensel (ed.), *The Legitimate Use of Military Force: The Just War Tradition and the Customary Law of Armed Conflict* (Aldershot: Ashgate, 2008), pp. 85–88.

[47] Kalshoven and Zegveld, *Constraints on the Waging of War* (n. 7) p. 11.

[48] Preamble to the Hague Convention 1907, see Kalshoven and Zegveld, *Constraints on the Waging of War* (n. 7) p. 11.

[49] Antonio Cassese, "The Martens Clause: Half a Loaf or Simply Pie in the Sky?" (2000) 11(1) *European Journal of International Law* 188.

goes beyond that.[50] Martens had obviously not sought to introduce the laws of humanity and the dictates of public conscience as new sources of international law but had rather employed "loose language for the purpose merely of solving a diplomatic problem."[51] Indeed, the clause is not the carefully negotiated answer to the question of what makes the essence of international humanitarian law nor does it speak the language of individual human rights. It acknowledges, however, that no international treaty can ever fully regulate all possible circumstances and prohibits certain acts which may have slipped through the treaty's regulatory net and stipulates that all acts in war, whether mentioned in a treaty or not, are subject to the laws of humanity. It thus provides a yardstick to judge the conduct of hostilities by general principles beyond those enshrined in international treaties. It can also be seen as a tool to interpret specific obligations in humanitarian law and a guiding principle to which any newly developed norm must stand up. It echoes natural law and indicates that the laws of armed conflict are not only legal texts but also a "moral code."[52] The clause seems to suggest that humanitarian law should thus develop not only by means of treaty and customary law but also by constant reference to natural law as an equally important source which complements and corrects a predominantly technocratic and positivist approach to humanitarian law.

The clause is also based on the realization that international humanitarian law as it stands at any given moment does not, and never will, regulate the conduct of hostilities once and for all, and that the law can and must be further developed. This was confirmed by the International Court of Justice (ICJ) in the *Nuclear Weapons* case when the Court rejected the position of the Russian government that the Martens Clause had become redundant with the adoption of the Geneva Conventions which would, in the government's view, be the "complete code" the Clause had asked for.[53] Humanitarian law is thus open for further development on the basis of legal principles beyond and separate from international humanitarian treaty law. With this, international humanitarian law could become an expression of the world community rather than an expression of the practice of powerful states.[54] And more than that: the law of armed conflict would not solely be the prerogative of states but reflect community interests and values beyond positive law and even irrespective of the will of states.[55]

Although the debates over the clause were largely academic and restricted to a small circle of international jurists, the clause has been invoked on various occasions.[56] After it lay dormant for a long time the Nuremberg and Tokyo war crimes trials, set up to deal with the crimes committed in the Second World War, reignited interest in the "laws of humanity" as

50 See for the varying views Cassese, ibid. 189–92, and Rupert Ticehurst, "The Martens Clause and the Laws of Armed Conflict" in Naorem Sanajaoba (ed.), *A Manual of International Humanitarian Laws* (New Delhi: Regency, 2004), pp. 312–13.

51 Cassese, "The Martens Clause" (n. 49) 202. More sceptical commentators such as Geoffrey Best see it as "not much more than a swallow announcing a summer still some way off," Best, *War and Law Since 1945* (n. 15) p. 250.

52 Ticehurst, "The Martens Clause" (n. 50) p. 319.

53 *Legality of the Threat or Use of Nuclear Weapons*, International Court of Justice, Advisory Opinion of 8 July 1996 [1996] ICJ Reports 226 ("*Nuclear Weapons* case"), para. 226. In his Dissenting Opinion to the Advisory Opinion, Judge Weeramantry argued that the clause demonstrates that the entire philosophy of the law of war was humanitarian, see para. 486. See also Ticehurst, "The Martens Clause" (n. 50) pp. 313–14.

54 See Ticehurst, "The Martens Clause" (n. 50) p. 319.

55 See Hayashi, "The Martens Clause" (n. 12) p. 151.

56 Normand and Zaidi, *Human Rights at the UN* (n. 33) p. 41.

embodied in the clause. The Nuremberg Tribunal, for example, referred to the clause in the *Krupp* case of 1948, a case which involved war crimes, crimes against humanity, exploitation of occupied territory and forced labour by executives of the Friedrich Krupp armament and ship construction company.[57] A year after the *Krupp* trial, the ICJ referred to "elementary considerations of humanity" in the *Corfu Channel* case, arguing that the duty of Albania to warn passing vessels of the United Kingdom of mines laid in the Corfu Channel would flow from such considerations.[58] In the *Nicaragua* case, the Court argued that the "considerations of humanity" of the Martens Clause had found its way into Common Article 3 of the Geneva Conventions.[59] The International Criminal Tribunal for the Former Yugoslavia (ICTY) used the clause in several of its judgments.[60] The clause, or parts of it, are also quoted in various places in the Geneva Conventions of 1949 and the Additional Protocols of 1977 (e.g., Geneva Convention I, Article 63 Geneva Convention II, Article 62, Geneva Convention III, Article 142 and Geneva Convention IV, Article 158 and in Article 1(2) of Additional Protocol I and the Preamble to Additional Protocol II).[61] The UN's International Law Commission (ILC) held that the clause:

> provides that even in cases not covered by the specific international agreements, civilians and combatants remain under the protection and authority of the principles of international law derived from established custom, from the principles of humanity and from the dictates of public conscience.[62]

Notions similar to those used in the Martens Clause appear in other international humanitarian law texts, such as the 1925 Geneva Protocol on Gas and Bacteriological Warfare ("conscience of nations")[63] and in the provisions on denunciation of the four Geneva Conventions of 1949 (which make clear that even if states parties withdraw from one of the treaties, they remain bound by the Martens Clause, which is quoted *verbatim*).[64] The 1976 UN Convention on Certain Conventional Weapons and the 1997 Ottawa Treaty on antipersonnel landmines also quote the Martens Clause in their Preambles.[65] In a similar

[57] *United States* v. *Alfried Krupp and others*, Case 10, International Military Tribunal Nuremberg, Judgment of 21 July 1948; see Theodor Meron, "On Custom and the Antecedents of the Marten's Clause in Medieval and Renaissance Ordinances of War" in Ulrich Beyerlin (ed.), *Recht zwischen Umbruch und Bewahrung. Festschrift für Rudolf Bernhardt* (Berlin: Springer, 1995), pp. 173–74.

[58] *Corfu Channel* (*United Kingdom of Great Britain and Northern Ireland* v. *Albania*), International Court of Justice, Judgment of 9 April 1949 [1949] ICJ Reports 4, para. 22.

[59] *Military and Paramilitary Activities in and against Nicaragua* (*Nicaragua* v. *United States of America*), International Court of Justice, Judgment of 27 June 1986 [1986] ICJ Reports 14, paras. 113–14.

[60] See Theodor Meron, "The Martens Clause, Principles of Humanity, and Dictates of Public Conscience" (2000) 94(1) *American Journal of International Law* 82.

[61] Additional Protocol I, Art. 1(2), for example, reads: "In cases not covered by this Protocol or by other international agreements, civilians and combatants remain under the protection and authority of the principles of international law derived from established custom, from the principles of humanity and from the dictates of public conscience."

[62] Report of the International Law Commission on the Work of its Forty-Sixth Session (2 May–22 July 1994), UN Doc. A/49/10 (1994), p. 131. See also Ticehurst, "The Martens Clause" (n. 50) p. 315.

[63] Preamble to the Protocol for the Prohibition of the Use of Asphyxiating, Poisonous or Other Gases, and of Bacteriological Methods of Warfare, 17 June 1925.

[64] Geneva Convention I, Art. 63(4); Geneva Convention II, Art. 62(4); Geneva Convention III, Art. 142(4); and Geneva Convention IV, Art. 158(4).

[65] Convention on Prohibitions or Restrictions on the Use of Certain Conventional Weapons which may be Deemed to be Excessively Injurious or that have Indiscriminate Effects, 10 October 1980, 1342 UNTS

way, the Universal Declaration of Human Rights and the Rome Statute of the International Criminal Court use the term "conscience of mankind" and "conscience of humanity" in their respective Preambles.[66]

When the clause is read within the current debate on the role of human rights in armed conflict, it seems indeed "an exceptional early statement"[67] on the idea that humanitarian law can be complemented by human rights.[68] Some have gone as far as to suggest that the clause is indeed the "origin of international human rights law in the positivistic sense."[69] In light of the clause's broad and general wording and drafting history, this seems questionable. Martens had obviously not had the intention to resort to human rights when suggesting his compromise formula to overcome the deadlock in the negotiations. But the clause does open up the law of armed conflict to considerations beyond an axiomatic and schematic balancing of humanitarian concerns and military necessity and allows other sources to inform the law, and it certainly points towards the existence of humanitarian principles which exist outside and prior to the codification of international humanitarian law.[70]

The principles mentioned in the clauses – "usages established among civilized peoples", "the laws of humanity" and the "dictates of the public conscience" – may well be seen as a "common denominator"[71] of international humanitarian law and international human rights law. Historically and in a contemporary perspective, the terms can be understood as references to human rights.[72] This is what, for example, the Conseil de guerre de Bruxelles did, when it decided in a case involving the maltreatment of interned civilians during the German occupation of Belgium in 1950. It found that the duty to respect the lives of persons under the law of occupation needed to be substantiated by reference to Article 5 of the Universal Declaration of Human Rights.[73] The tribunal reasoned that because such acts of inhuman treatment were not specifically prohibited under the Hague Regulations one must resort to the Martens Clause to fill this gap. This, in turn, necessitates drawing on international human rights law to give meaning to the "principles of humanity" and "dictates of public conscience" mentioned in the clause.[74] In the *Nuclear Weapons* case, the ICJ

137, and Convention on the Prohibition of the Use, Stockpiling, Production and Transfer of Anti-Personnel Mines and Their Destruction, 18 September 1997 (1997) 36 ILM 1507.

66 Preamble to the Universal Declaration of Human Rights, UN General Assembly Res. 217 A (III), UN Doc. 217/A-(III) (10 December 1948), and Preamble to the Rome Statute of the International Criminal Court, 17 July 1998, 2187 UNTS 3.

67 Best, *War and Law Since 1945* (n. 15) p. 250.

68 See Hans-Joachim Heintze, "On the Relationship between Human Rights Law Protection and International Humanitarian Law (2004) 86(856) *International Review of the Red Cross* 797.

69 Jeremy Sarkin, "The Historical Origins, Convergence and Interrelationship of International Human Rights Law, International Humanitarian Law, International Criminal Law and Public International Law and their Application since the Nineteenth Century" (2007) 1(2) *Human Rights and International Legal Discourse* 128.

70 See Ticehurst, "The Martens Clause" (n. 50) p. 319.

71 Hans-Peter Gasser, "International Humanitarian Law and Human Rights Law in Non-International Armed Conflict: Joint Venture or Mutual Exclusion?" (2002) 45 *German Yearbook of International Law* 155.

72 See Cassese, "The Martens Clause" (n. 49) 212; and Heintze, "On the Relationship" (n. 68) 797–98.

73 Hague Regulations 1907, Art. 46: "Family honour and rights, the lives of persons, and private property, as well as religious convictions and practice, must be respected"; Universal Declaration of Human Rights, Art. 5: "No one shall be subjected to torture or to cruel, inhuman or degrading treatment or punishment."

74 See Cassese, "The Martens Clause" (n. 49) 207.

similarly viewed the "dictates of public conscience" as expressing UN General Assembly resolutions as well as global public opinion and the views of the international human rights movement.[75] From an international legal perspective, the Martens Clause thus incorporates natural law concepts which embody common values among all peoples and civilizations in a combination of spiritual values, humanitarian principles and professional ethics which are linked to the survival of humankind and individual human dignity.[76] It stipulates that the existing law of war is never the final regulation of warfare but needs to be supplemented by principles which, in turn, today cannot be understood in any other way than as a reflection of international human rights law.

2.5 *Inter arma caritas*: Henri Dunant and the Red Cross

Hague law was primarily meant to inform those active in battle on the appropriate professional behaviour, regulate the conduct of hostilities and prohibit means and methods of warfare deemed unacceptable. Humanity figured in these texts as much as reasonably possible – from the perspective of the military. It was left to practical humanitarians to advocate more effectively for humanity on the battlefield and to create what later came to be known as "Geneva law," which emphasized humanitarian concerns and, rather than regulating combat, sought to protect the victims of armed conflicts: civilians and their property, those not or no longer engaged in combat ("non-combatants" such as medical and religious personnel) and those *hors de combat*, i.e., the wounded and sick, the shipwrecked and those which had surrendered). While the two branches of international humanitarian law have never been strictly separated and their division has long become obsolete, this dichotomy of a Hague and a Geneva strand of the law of war nevertheless influenced, and continues to influence, the perception of the very purpose of the law of war as a tool in the hands of the military or a practical shield for humanitarian protection.

Henri Dunant (1818–1910) represents this pragmatic humanitarian approach. Different from the governmental consultant Lieber and academic theorists on the law of war, he was a non-governmental organization (NGO) activist and "idea entrepreneur."[77] Dunant's motivation to assist war victims was humanitarian and practical at the same time. Appalled by the wounded and dying soldiers left unattended on the battlefield of Solferino in 1859, he sought to set up a private agency to care for wounded and sick soldiers. While the fate of the wounded in military hospitals had improved considerably since the middle of the nineteenth century, the ad hoc agreements which were often put in place to transfer wounded from the battlefield to such hospitals were notoriously ineffective, leading Dunant to push for a simple and stable international arrangement.[78] He succeeded, and

[75] ICJ, *Nuclear Weapons* case (n. 53), Dissenting Opinion of Judge Weeramantry, para. 490. See also Theodor Meron, *The Humanization of International Law* (Leiden: Nijhoff, 2006), p. 24.

[76] See Michel Veuthey, "Public Conscience in International Humanitarian Law Today" in Horst Fischer, Ulrike Froissart, Wolff Heinegg von Heintschel and Christian Raap (eds.), *Krisensicherung und Humanitärer Schutz / Crisis Management and Humanitarian Protection. Festschrift für Dieter Fleck* (Berlin: Berliner Wissenschaftsverlag, 2004), p. 614.

[77] David Forsythe, *The Humanitarians: The International Committee of the Red Cross* (Cambridge: Cambridge University Press, 2005), p. 15. On the perception of Dunant by his contemporaries see François Bugnion, "Henry Dunant" in David Forsythe (ed.), *Encyclopedia of Human Rights* (Oxford: Oxford University Press, 2009), pp. 70–72.

[78] See Best, *War and Law Since 1945* (n. 15) p. 42.

in 1863 the International Committee of the Red Cross was established.[79] A year later, the first Geneva Convention was adopted, obliging states to offer basic protection to the wounded and sick.[80] The text was revised in 1906 and 1929.[81] With them, the fate of individuals had found its way into treaty law and the Geneva Convention of 1864 was indeed the first instance that "human values as such"[82] were protected under international law.

Dunant's concern for humanitarian matters has been convincingly explained by his religious background and his affiliation with the European humanist movement.[83] His approach is characteristic of the mix of Christianity, humanism and a practical sense for social change which drove the development of humanitarian law in these times. But Dunant and his followers were not primarily inspired by the idea of human rights as universal entitlements; this was seemingly too lofty an objective for a Swiss businessman. In Dunant's tradition "humanity" was still more a grace then a right. Despite their humanitarian ethos, the Geneva Conventions of 1864, 1906 and 1929 were not informed by inalienable individual human rights but by charity. *Inter arma caritas* ("in war, charity") was thus chosen as, and remains, the motto of the ICRC.[84] The organization was essentially founded to substitute what the state would not deliver: care for the human beings who had served this state in war. It was meant to remedy the irresponsibility of states which would provide more veterinarians for horses used in warfare than doctors to care for wounded soldiers.[85]

As a private charity organization and as guardian of humanitarian law the ICRC considered itself as a neutral, confidential and impartial relief organization, broker and mediator; "more the expert drafting secretariat than the vociferous advocate prepared to duel publicly with states."[86] The ICRC's activities eventually came to rest on three pillars: pragmatic (and mostly confidential) action; working towards a protective legal framework; and a cooperative attitude towards governments which were seen as partners and not adversaries despite the fact that their behaviour in war had necessitated the very creation of the ICRC as a humanitarian counter-weight.[87] Unlike the anti-slavery movement, which around the same time pressed for what later became a human right, the ICRC's emphasis on charity allowed little space for the emerging idea of individual human rights. The organization was also specific because of its close ties with the Swiss Confederation (just like the

[79] The other founding members of the International Committee of the Red Cross were Henri Dufour, Gustav Moynier, Louis Appia and Théodore Maunoir, see Alain Sigg, *International Human Rights Law, International Humanitarian Law, Refugee Law: Geneva from Early Origins to the 21st Century* (Berne: Swiss Federal Department of Foreign Affairs, 2003), p. 71.

[80] Geneva Convention (I) for the Amelioration of the Condition of the Wounded in Armies in the Field, 22 August 1864.

[81] Geneva Convention (I) for the Amelioration of the Condition of the Wounded and Sick in Armies in the Field, 6 July 1906, and Geneva Convention (I) for the Amelioration of the Condition of the Wounded and Sick in Armies in the Field, 27 July 1929.

[82] Daniel Thürer, *International Humanitarian Law: Theory, Practice, Context* (The Hague: Hague Academy of International Law, 2011), pp. 197–98.

[83] Jean Guillermand, "The Historical Foundations of Humanitarian Action" in Naorem Sanajaoba (ed.), *A Manual of International Humanitarian Laws* (New Delhi: Regency, 2004), p. 4 and pp. 15–16.

[84] Preamble to the Statutes of the International Committee of the Red Cross, adopted at the 15th International Conference of the Red Cross (Geneva, 1986), amended in 1995 (Resolution 7 of the 26th International Conference of the Red Cross and Red Crescent) and 2006 (Resolution 1 of the 29th International Conference of the Red Cross and Red Crescent).

[85] Forsythe, *The Humanitarians* (n. 77) p. 15. [86] Ibid. p. 261. [87] Ibid. p. 19.

National Red Cross Societies were, and continue to be, more or less closely associated with their respective governments), which occasionally led to sceptical remarks on the independence and neutrality of the organization right from the start.[88]

While the ICRC thus shared the liberal and moralistic attitudes of the forerunners of the human rights movements, such as the Anti-Slavery Society, it was not driven by the radical and egalitarian spirit which fuelled the anti-slavery movement. The ICRC's inherently conservative and state-oriented attitude made it search discreetly for cooperation, refrain from openly naming and shaming violators of the law and resort to publicity only as a last resort. Another conservative element was soon added to this, namely, that of being well-known, respected and predictable. States were soon aware of the limited mandate and minimalist approach of the ICRC. It has thus been argued that from the start, the organization would seek to achieve liberal ends with conservative means, i.e., by activating the military code of honour of its governments and their military apparatus.[89] On the other hand, the organization found itself soon tasked with safeguarding the basic dignity and welfare of individuals in conflict situations (what would soon be called human rights). This tension may explain the ICRC's continuously cautious approach to human rights which lasts until today: it shares the liberal and moral impetus of human rights without approving of its radical egalitarian spirit and partisan approach.[90]

[88] Ibid. pp. 20–22.
[89] Ibid. pp. 166–71. The author uses the expression "minimalist social liberalism in action", see p. 167.
[90] Ibid. pp. 169–71.

3

1945: whither war?

3.1 1914–1945: war as trauma and war as crime

In this blend of legal positivism, civilizing spirit, military necessity and charitable impetus the law of war was codified at the turn of the nineteenth to the twentieth century. The hope that this evolving legal framework with the more than twenty general and specific conventions and declarations in place back then would make a difference in the protection of those affected by war was high: "[t]he nineteenth century formulated the laws of war; the twentieth century was expected to apply them."[1] Such expectations were shattered in the First (1914–1918) and Second World Wars (1939–1945). As all wars, they had to be fought in the framework of the existing law of armed conflict but twentieth century wars proved to be an altogether different matter. For the world as much as for the established law of war, the two wars were traumatic experiences, which would eventually lead to a rebranding of the law as international humanitarian law and would see the birth of international human rights law.

The First World War saw established laws and customs of war violated widely. New means of warfare ridiculed the treaties and declarations so pompously celebrated only a few years ago, and the technocratic rules of the law of war could easily be circumvented. The first use of poison gas by the Germans in 1915, for example, was justified with reference to the 1899 Declaration on Asphyxiating Gases which prohibited the use of such gases when diffused by projectiles while in fact it was released from thousands of cylinders stationed along six kilometres of frontline.[2] On the other hand, even respecting the laws of war meant unspeakable horror: the hundreds of thousands of soldiers slain by new technology such as machine-guns and far-ranging artillery were not necessarily killed in violation of the laws of war which (to paraphrase the words of the 1868 Declaration of St. Petersburg) saw as the legitimate object of warfare the weakening of enemy armed forces without superfluous injuries. The mass slaughter at the Western Front and elsewhere gave excellent examples thereof. For many contemporaries, such mass-killings of conscript teenage soldiers, driven by a powerful military-industrial machinery, separated law from morality and shattered an idea held so dearly in the nineteenth century: that civilized nations could fight civilized wars and that those wars could be regulated so as to constitute an acceptable element of politics.[3]

Many came to be convinced that wars could not be regulated at all but needed to be abolished. This was not a climate conducive to revising the law of war. After the First World

[1] A.J.P. Taylor, "War and Peace" (1980) 2(19) *London Review of Books* 5.

[2] See Adam Roberts, "Land Warfare: From Hague to Nuremberg" in Michael Howard, George J. Andreopoulos and Mark R. Shulman (eds.), *The Laws of War. Constraints on Warfare in the Western World* (New Haven, CT: Yale University Press, 1994), p. 123.

[3] Ibid. pp. 125–27.

War, the ICRC prepared a number of drafts for a revised Geneva Convention with a view to strengthening the protection of civilians but governments were reluctant to engage in such discussions. A conference scheduled in 1940 to discuss these suggestions was prevented from taking place by the outbreak of the Second World War.[4] The 1923 Hague Rules on Air Warfare, drafted by a group of experts, were also never adopted by states.[5] Some new codifications were brought on their way, among them a Protocol prohibiting poison gas.[6] Like the Hague Convention of 1899 it was the result of a conference which had pursued a grander goal, namely, complete disarmament, but had failed.[7] The document prioritized humanitarian needs over military necessity and outlawed the use of poison gas completely and regardless of its potential military value and the way it was used.[8]

But overall the interwar period 1918–1939 brought no appropriate responses to the failures of the law of armed conflict. The "intellectual aridity"[9] of this time with regard to the role of humanitarian rules for war as well as peace helped to prepare the ground for the horrors to come. Individual human beings dissolved into armies comprising millions of men, melted into the crowds rallying around the swastika in national-socialist Germany and vanished in the concentration camps as unrecognizable mass. Exceptional events, such as the drafting of the "Déclaration des droits internationaux de l'homme" by the Institute of International Law in 1929, which focused essentially on governmental responsibilities rather than individual rights, went unnoticed.[10] Workers' rights (as protected by the newly established International Labour Organisation) and protective regimes for national minorities (in the League of Nations) remained exceptions.[11]

The Second World War brought the final blow to the positivist concept of war as a morally indifferent affair. With its 50 million victims the war changed the fundamental conception upon which the laws of war rested "away from a focus on fairness and mutuality as between the warring states, to a primary concern with relieving the suffering of victims of war."[12] Such a victim's perspective emphasized human dignity rather than humanitarianism. The extent to which the civilian population had been deliberately targeted, including and culminating in the near extinction of the European Jewish population in the Holocaust, made it clear that established principles of international humanitarian law were insufficient. In the First World War, 5 per cent of all victims had been civilians, a number which rose to

4 See Dietrich Schindler, "International Humanitarian Law: Its Remarkable Development and Its Persistent Violation" (2003) 5(2) *Journal of the History of International Law* 166.

5 See Leslie C. Green, "Human Rights and the Law of Armed Conflict" in Leslie C. Green (ed.), *Essays on the Modern Law of War* (Ardsley, NY: Transnational, 1999), p. 444.

6 See, e.g., the Protocol on the Prohibition of the Use of Asphyxiating, Poisonous or Other Gases, and of Bacteriological Methods of Warfare, 17 June 1925, and the Treaty on the Protection of Artistic and Scientific Institutions and Historic Monuments, 15 April 1935, the so-called "Roerich Pact."

7 See Frits Kalshoven and Liesbeth Zegveld, *Constraints on the Waging of War: An Introduction to International Humanitarian Law* (4th edn., Cambridge: Cambridge University Press, 2011), p. 14.

8 Green, "Human Rights and the Law of Armed Conflict" (n. 5) p. 445.

9 Christian Tomuschat, *Human Rights between Idealism and Realism* (2nd edn., Oxford: Oxford University Press, 2008), p. 21.

10 Ibid. p. 21.

11 See Roger Normand and Sarah Zaidi, *Human Rights at the UN: The Political History of Universal Justice* (Bloomington, IN: Indiana University Press, 2008), pp. 43–57.

12 C. Neff, *War and the Law of Nations: A General History* (Cambridge: Cambridge University Press, 2005), p. 315.

50 per cent in the Second World War.[13] At the same time, the casualties of soldiers were lower in the Second World War than in the First World War: the progressively refined rules seemingly worked for soldiers but failed to protect civilians.[14] It was thus considered necessary to abandon "the ethos of the duellist, in favour of the more tender outlook of the physician"[15] when drafting new rules for warfare.

The consequences of the Second World War also instituted the idea that war as such should be a crime in the emerging new world order. It was seen as possible and necessary to criminalize wars of aggression as well as certain behaviour in war. The invention of crimes against humanity fused the ideas and principles on which the law of armed conflict and international human rights law (soon to emerge) rested and the difference between unlawful conduct in warfare and outrages against human dignity became blurred, even though there was disagreement on whether individual criminal responsibility would mean creating new law or could build on established custom.[16] In the criminal trials in Nuremberg (International Military Tribunal from 1945–1946) and Tokyo (International Military Tribunal for the Far East from 1946–1948) the three strands of international humanitarian law, international human rights law (in the form of crimes against humanity) and international criminal law converged for the first time.[17]

3.2 United Nations and the despicable laws of war

The new world order, created in 1945, was built on two cornerstones; the prohibition of war and the creation of the international human rights regime. The Charter of the United Nations contained provisions on both matters.[18] This posed some problems for the further development of humanitarian law: how should war be regulated now that war was practically outlawed, and how would the law of war relate to the emerging international human rights regime? The UN's response to the first question was simple: in order to avoid the dilemma of being in charge of a regulatory framework for an activity now deemed illegal, the organization turned its back on the law of war.[19] The law of war was not mentioned in the Charter at all and the International Law Commission, the UN body tasked with the development and codification of international law, struck the law of war from its agenda out of fear that any work on it would show "lack of confidence in the efficiency of the means at the disposal of the United Nations for maintaining peace."[20]

[13] See Schindler, "International Humanitarian Law" (n. 4) 170.

[14] See Roberts, "Land Warfare" (n. 2) p. 128–31. [15] Neff, *War and the Law of Nations* (n. 12) p. 340.

[16] See, e.g., Green, "Human Rights and the Law of Armed Conflict" (n. 5) p. 446.

[17] On the history of international criminal law see Antonio Cassesse, *International Criminal Law* (2nd edn., Oxford: Oxford University Press, 2008), pp. 3–31.

[18] UN Charter, Art. 2(4): "All Members shall refrain in their international relations from the threat or use of force against the territorial integrity or political independence of any state, or in any other manner inconsistent with the Purposes of the United Nations"; and Art. 1(3) which mandates the UN to achieve international cooperation in promoting and encouraging respect for human rights and fundamental freedoms for all. Article 55 takes this general purpose of the UN into the operational part of the Charter and allows the organization to promote universal respect for, and observance of, human rights and fundamental freedoms for all without distinction as to race, sex, language or religion.

[19] See Kalshoven and Zegveld, *Constraints on the Waging of War* (n. 7) pp. 21–22.

[20] Summary Records of the First Session, 12 April–9 June 1949, UN Doc. A/CN.4/SER.A/1949, (1949) 1 *Yearbook of the International Law Commission* 281.

The reasons why the UN abstained from developing the laws of war were manifold. First, the organization feared that any involvement in developing the law of armed conflict would contradict the prohibition of the use of force in the UN Charter and strain the carefully negotiated political balance on this question in the organization.[21] Secondly, there was concern that working on the development of the law of war would induce a lack of confidence by the public in the UN's ability to prevent future wars and damage its reputation before it had even time to prove its worth.[22] Thirdly, and with a utopian touch, it was argued that the lessons had been learned anyway and war was now illegal and unlikely to occur. This was seemingly also the view of the International Law Commission when it boldly stated that with "[w]ar having been outlawed, the regulation of its conduct has ceased to be relevant."[23] Fourthly, the UN found it difficult to reconcile the idea of the impartiality of the law of war which applied to both sides, regardless of their reasons for resorting to force, with the illegality of wars of aggression under the UN Charter.[24] And fifthly, the UN felt uneasy about the relationship between the established law of war and the emerging international human rights law. How could an organization legitimately stand for the value of every human being while accepting principles enshrined in international humanitarian law which allowed for mass slaughter of soldiers and collateral damage of civilians?[25] As a consequence, the law of war was not given a place in the newly created UN system.

Reality soon kicked in, however, and already in the Korean War (1950–1953) the UN General Assembly condemned the treatment of prisoners of war by the North Korean and Chinese Communist armies as a violation of international humanitarian law,[26] thus acknowledging the continued importance of international humanitarian law and the UN's interest in it. In the same resolution, the Assembly also said that such incidents were not only a matter of international humanitarian law but also affronted "human rights and the dignity and worth of the human person."[27] This argument rested on the other important response to the atrocities of the first half of the twentieth century: the creation of the international human rights regime. Its relationship to the law of armed conflict had yet to be settled.

21 See Iqbal al-Fallouji, "Pour une thèse plus humaniste de 'tous les droits de l'homme'" in Christophe Swinarski (ed.), *Studies and Essays on International Humanitarian Law and Red Cross Principles in Honour of Jean Pictet* (The Hague: Nijhoff, 1984), p. 626.

22 See Schindler, "International Humanitarian Law" (n. 4) 170.

23 Summary Records of the First Session (n. 20) 281. See also Hans-Peter Gasser, "International Humanitarian Law and Human Rights Law in Non-International Armed Conflict: Joint Venture or Mutual Exclusion?" (2002) 45 *German Yearbook of International Law* 149.

24 See Dietrich Schindler, "The International Committee of the Red Cross and Human Rights" (1979) 19 *International Review of the Red Cross* 7.

25 A sixth concern came to the attention of the UN only later, when the practice of peace-keeping began to stand in for the dysfunctional system of collective security: what about the application of the law of war to military forces acting under the command of the UN, as envisaged in Art. 43 of the UN Charter? See Anne Ryniker, "Respect du droit international humanitaire par les forces des Nations Unies" (1999) 81 (836) *Revue International de la Croix-Rouge* 795–97.

26 UN General Assembly Res. A804 (VIII), Question of atrocities committed by the North Korean and Chinese Communist Forces against United Nations prisoners of war in Korea, UN Doc. A804 (VIII) (3 December 1953), Preamble, para. 2.

27 Ibid. para. 2.

3.3 Universal Declaration of Human Rights: human rights for peace

The events prior to 1945 had reinforced the conviction that the protection and promotion of human dignity must be part of any endeavour to build a safer world. Consequently, human rights played a role in the San Francisco Conference of 1945 in which the UN Charter was adopted. The Atlantic Charter drafted a few years earlier, in 1941 (which laid down the war aims of the Allies), had not referred to human rights and had been criticized for it.[28] The UN Charter, however, affirmed the UN's "faith in fundamental human rights, in the dignity and worth of the human person, in the equal rights of men and women"[29] and included the above-mentioned provisions on human rights. Despite the double standards applied even by the major proponents of human rights in their domestic and international politics, human rights were now firmly on the international agenda.[30]

In order to clarify the meaning of the Charter's human rights provisions, the UN General Assembly adopted the Universal Declaration of Human Rights in 1948. Like the Hague and Geneva Conventions, the Declaration was a response to a previous war, but while the experiences of two World Wars provided the backdrop against which the document was created, it was not drafted in a humanitarian spirit. It was informed by the idea of universally shared inalienable rights rather than motivated by charitable impulses, and it was created in the belief that war should be eradicated. Guaranteeing human dignity was seen as essential to achieve this goal.[31]

The Declaration was also inspired by the peace movement of the late nineteenth and early twentieth centuries. It renounced war and postulated human rights as a means to secure peace as a counter-weight against the war movement, i.e., the socio-political tendency of the majority of Europeans who had accepted or even embraced war as a means of politics in the first half of the century.[32] The Declaration reflected a radically different vision of the role of (international) law as a means against war rather than a regulatory tool for war. With this, it presented a profound critique of the very foundations of the law of war, which was accused of being an accomplice of the war movement for the way it had allowed wars to be waged. The law of war was accused of conveying, since its codification in the 1860s, the idea that:

> war need not be as nasty as the anti-war party said it was, and that in any case non-combatants and their private property could largely be kept out of it. Thus was generated the germ of the tragic illusion that has boomed *pari passu* with the "progressive development" of international humanitarian law: the two-faced illusion whose active aspect invites civilian war-lovers to imagine that they can have their belligerent cake and eat it, and whose passive aspect encourages war-haters to hope that when war happens, civilians will not be hurt.[33]

The Universal Declaration of Human Rights was meant to be different and its Preamble reflected this difference, first and foremost the genuine respect for the value of human dignity as a pre-legal concept, i.e., the "recognition of the inherent dignity and of the equal and inalienable rights of all members of the human family."[34] On this basis, the Declaration

[28] See Normand and Zaidi, *Human Rights at the UN* (n. 11) pp. 91–92.
[29] Preamble to the UN Charter.
[30] The United Kingdom had no intention to allow self-determination for its colonies and the United States was yet to recognize racism as a problem; see Normand and Zaidi, *Human Rights at the UN* (n. 11) p. 94.
[31] See Geoffrey Best, *War and Law Since 1945* (Oxford: Clarendon Press, 1994), p. 55. [32] Ibid. p. 45.
[33] Ibid. [34] Preamble to the Universal Declaration of Human Rights.

pursued three interlinked aims:[35] securing peace (the Preamble speaks of human rights as "the foundation of freedom, justice and peace in the world"); guaranteeing prosperity ("promote social progress and better standards of life in larger freedom," in the words of the Preamble); and allowing stability in international relations (i.e., "promote the development of friendly relations between nations").[36] The denial of human rights as a root cause and implicit element of aggressive war was acknowledged.[37]

As a reference to the preceding war, the Declaration emphasized that "disregard and contempt for human rights have resulted in barbarous acts which have outraged the conscience of mankind."[38] The text had originally included specific reference to the two World Wars but this was removed when the Third Committee of the General Assembly discussed the draft as submitted by the [then] Commission of Human Rights, a decision which René Cassin (who had written this section of the Declaration) later embraced on the grounds that the text should be seen as oriented towards the future and not as resenting the past.[39] The term "war" or "armed conflict" does not appear in the operational part of the Declaration. Most of the drafters seem to have assumed that the enjoyment of human rights would presuppose a state of peace, and only a few argued for the application of the Declaration also in times of war.[40] While the drafters had obviously gone back to the experience of the war as the "epistemic foundation of the particular rights in question,"[41] there was no open discussion on this matter.

The new human rights regime was also deeply (and for many states troublingly) intrusive in their internal affairs in comparison to the law of war. In the absence of any meaningful regulations for civil wars, insurgencies and other forms of internal violence, the law of war had so far only obliged states to protect enemy soldiers *hors de combat* and enemy civilians, but not their own. In contrast, the Declaration's Preamble made one thing clear: "whereas it is essential, if man is not to be compelled to have recourse, as a last resort, to rebellion against tyranny and oppression, . . . human rights should be protected by the rule of law."[42] So far, international law had shown little interest to outlaw such "tyranny and oppression" but now things had changed: "[h]umanitarian law evolved as a result of humanity's concern for the victims of war, whereas human rights law evolved as a result of humanity's concern for the victims of a new kind of internal war – the victims of the Nazi death camps."[43]

[35] See Best, *War and Law Since 1945* (n. 31) p. 70.

[36] Preamble to the Universal Declaration of Human Rights.

[37] Medard R. Rwelamira, "Human Rights and International Humanitarian Law: The Link or Common Ground Revisited" (1992) 3(3) *Stellenbosch Law Review* 339.

[38] Preamble to the Universal Declaration of Human Rights.

[39] See Mary Ann Glendon, *A World Made New: Eleanor Roosevelt and the Universal Declaration of Human Rights* (New York: Random House, 2002), p. 176.

[40] Kolb refers to the delegate of Lebanon to the Third Committee of the UN General Assembly as the only source in this respect, see Robert Kolb, "The Relationship between International Humanitarian Law and International Human Rights Law: A Brief History of the 1948 Universal Declaration of Human Rights and the 1949 Geneva Conventions" (1998) 38(324) *International Review of the Red Cross* 409.

[41] Johannes Morsink, "World War Two and the Universal Declaration" (1993) 15(2) *Human Rights Quarterly* 358.

[42] Preamble to the Universal Declaration of Human Rights.

[43] Christina Cerna, "Human Rights in Armed Conflict: Implementation of International Humanitarian Law Norms by Regional Intergovernmental Human Rights Bodies" in Frits Kalshoven and Yves Sandoz (eds.), *Implementation of International Humanitarian Law* (Dordrecht: Nijhoff, 1989), p. 34.

3.4 "International humanitarian law": what's in a name?

Less than a year after the Universal Declaration of Human Rights, the four Geneva Conventions of 1949 (for the wounded and sick in armed forces in the field; the wounded, sick and shipwrecked members of the armed forces at sea; for prisoners of war; and for the protection of civilian persons in time of war) were adopted. They were modestly presented as a revision of the law of war but effectively confirmed the idea that the whole of the law of war is humanitarian by nature. From now on, this branch of law would also be called "international humanitarian law." It was one of three terminological moves. The two others were the clear separation of *jus ad bellum* (on the lawfulness of the use of force under the UN Charter) and *jus in bello* (on the conduct of warfare), and the transition from the "law of war" to the "law of armed conflict." Those changes in terminology were interlinked and none of them was merely semantic. None of them, however, was entirely convincing, either.

The distinction between *jus ad bellum* in the UN Charter (which is effectively a *jus contra bellum*) and *jus in bello* is today firmly embedded in international legal theory and practice. The legal Latin conveys the impression that this distinction is age-old but it has been pointed out that they were created only at the time of the League of Nations and extensively used only after the Second World War, even though the respective ideas had been expressed earlier, e.g., in Grotius' writing and by Immanuel Kant (1724–1804), who referred to "*Recht zum Kriege*" (law for war) and "*Recht im Kriege*" (law in war).[44] But within the just war theory the rights and duties of warriors depended on the justness of their cause and there was a clear separation of the two spheres. When the just war theory lost its dominance and gave way to war as a means of politics, there was not much need to discuss the lawfulness of war. All that was needed were formal rules for fighting. Likewise, the specific term *jus in bello* was rarely, if ever, used before the 1930s, not even in the 1899 and 1907 Peace Conferences in the Hague. It seems that the Vienna School of international law made the term popular. Josef Kunz is at times credited with its invention and Alfred Verdross used it as synonymous with the term *Kriegsrecht* (laws of war) in his handbook of international law of 1937, although he found few scholars who would follow suit, so that it seemingly became a widely accepted notion only after the Second World War.[45]

The term "law of armed conflict" was introduced to replace the "law of war," so as to capture the new realities of warfare, given that openly declared wars between nation states were replaced by the use of force between states in various forms. In response to this development, the four Geneva Conventions of 1949 were made applicable "to all cases of declared war or of any other armed conflict which may arise between two or more of the High Contracting Parties, even if the state of war is not recognized by one of them."[46] In marked difference to earlier text, their drafters had sought to extend their protective force to all types of armed violence between states regardless of any characterization by states.[47] At

[44] Robert Kolb, "Origin of the Twin Terms *Jus ad Bellum / Jus in Bello*" (1997) 37(320) *International Review of the Red Cross* 553.

[45] Ibid. 553–62. The author lists the abundance of legal terms that had come and gone instead: *usus in bello*, *modus belli gerendi*, *lex armorum*, *jus militare*, *jura at usus armorum*, *droit d'armes*, *usance de guerre*, *Kriegsmanier*, laws of war and *lois de la guerre*.

[46] Geneva Conventions, Common Art. 2.

[47] See Tomuschat, *Human Rights between Idealism and Realism* (n. 9) p. 304.

the same time, "war" as a term of art continues to figure prominently in humanitarian law, e.g., in the notion of "prisoner of war" to which Geneva Convention III is devoted.

The qualification of the law of war as "humanitarian" in its totality (and not only comprising the "Geneva" strand of the law of war) has a more ambiguous history. There is considerable uncertainty as to how the very term "international humanitarian law" came into existence and some argue that it had never been used before 1949.[48] It is usually said to have been coined by the influential jurist Jean Pictet, who had joined the International Committee of the Red Cross (ICRC) in 1937 and became the organization's Director in 1946, Director-General in 1966 and Vice-President in 1971 and was instrumental in drafting the 1949 Geneva Conventions. The reasons for introducing this term remain disputed. Some suggest that Pictet used it deliberately so as to emphasize the humanitarian goals of the Geneva law over the legacy of the Hague rules and also to set humanitarian law clearly apart from the newly emerging human rights.[49] Others argue to the contrary and attribute the creation of the term to the human rights movement which sought to break the law of war away from its roots in the Hague law.[50]

While the new term was soon widely used, not all were convinced of it, as the new term "somewhat blurs the distinction between the law of armed conflicts and human rights and gives rise to occasional confusion between these two branches of international law."[51] Different from the "law of war" which describes the boundaries and context within which the law operates, "humanitarian law" is about the law's goal. And indeed, the meaning of "humanitarian" in humanitarian law remains ambiguous. To some, humanitarian law is still a subset of the broader law of armed conflict which protects individuals *hors de combat* and those who do not take part in hostilities.[52] Other parts of humanitarian law are then not necessarily humanitarian, e.g., rules on neutrality, or of a merely technical nature. On the other hand, the ICJ made it clear that the Geneva and the Hague traditions in the law of armed conflict "have become so closely interrelated that they are considered to have gradually formed one single complex system, known today as international humanitarian law."[53] Even so, the humanitarian character of the law of armed conflict can only be understood in relation to military necessity which allows acts which by their very nature can hardly be seen as "humanitarian."[54]

The rise of human rights complicated matters, and the semantic closeness of "humanitarian" (law) and "human" (rights) may have given rise to some confusion, given that "humanitarian" conveys the idea of "humanity," i.e., the compassionate sentiment for the fate of other humans, whereas human rights refer to the inalienable and inherent character of legal rights as being grounded in human nature. But then again, "humanity" also has different meanings which are derived from the antique *humanitas*: apart from the factual

[48] See Schindler, "International Humanitarian Law" (n. 4) 171.

[49] See, e.g., Karl-Josef Partsch, "Human Rights and Humanitarian Law" in Rudolf Bernhardt (ed.), *Encyclopedia of Public International Law* (Amsterdam: Elsevier, 1995), p. 910.

[50] See Schindler, "The International Committee of the Red Cross and Human Rights" (n. 24) 8.

[51] Schindler, "International Humanitarian Law" (n. 4) 171.

[52] See, e.g., Rwelamira, "Human Rights and International Humanitarian Law" (n. 37) 332.

[53] *Legality of the Threat or Use of Nuclear Weapons*, International Court of Justice, Advisory Opinion of 8 July 1996 [1996] ICJ Reports 226 ("*Nuclear Weapons* case"), para. 75.

[54] See Theodor Meron, "Convergence of International Humanitarian and Human Rights Law" in Daniel Warner (ed.), *Human Rights and Humanitarian Law: The Quest for Universality* (The Hague: Nijhoff, 1997), p. 99.

description of the whole of humankind it can mean a moral impetus to act with due regard for the well-being of others. It may be used as equal to "humanism," i.e., the ethical ideal in which humans and their values, needs and dignity are at the centre of attention and the guiding principles (whether this is expressed as a general idea or as the worldview of the European Renaissance). In the idea of humanism, human rights and humanitarian law can meet, as both demonstrate concern for protecting and ensuring individuals' value, needs and dignity. Such ideas can also be expressed as "humanitarianism," i.e., the idea to care for one another and the more practical and operational concern for effectively guaranteeing people's survival and welfare and alleviating their suffering. Depending on the language used, the terms "humanity / humanitarianism" can thus be open textured.

3.5 Geneva Conventions of 1949 and human rights

In the signing ceremony of the Geneva Conventions, Max Petitpierre, the President of the Conference, drew parallels between the Universal Declaration of Human Rights and the Geneva Conventions. He reminded the delegates that:

> our texts are based on certain of the fundamental rights proclaimed in [the Universal Declaration of Human Rights] – respect for the human person, protection against torture and against cruel, inhuman or degrading punishments or treatment ... The Universal Declaration of the Rights of Man [*sic*!] and the Geneva Conventions are both derived from one and the same ideal.[55]

The role of human rights in the drafting of the Geneva Conventions is, however, more ambiguous than such statements make believe; indeed, many contemporaries might have disagreed with comments such as this. There remains a marked disagreement on the role of human rights in the drafting of humanitarian law after 1945. Some emphasize the independence of the two drafting exercises and the deep gap which separated their respective communities when they conclude that "[a]fter saluting the flag of principles each camp tackled its subject-matter on the basis of its own rules and methods."[56] The experiences of the previous wars obviously united them but beyond war as the "epistemic foundation"[57] of both documents there were few connections between the two communities of humanitarian law and human rights.

The reason for such separation was, however, less a fundamental incompatibility between the two fields but the deliberate choice not to enter each other's turf for political reasons. The legal communities and institutional frameworks of humanitarian law and the emerging human rights law were not only distinct to the extent that they did not take note of each other but had different views and perceptions of the link between war and law.[58] The separation of international humanitarian law and international human rights law after 1945 was thus driven by policy considerations which resulted in different law-making processes in separate forums and communities and was not so much the result of any legal, logical or dogmatic reason. UN bodies, first and foremost the International Law Commission, were

[55] Quoted from Kolb, "The Relationship" (n. 40) 414. [56] Ibid. 415.

[57] Morsink, "World War Two" (n. 41) p. 358.

[58] See Robert Kolb, "Human Rights Law and International Humanitarian Law between 1945 and the Aftermath of the Teheran Conference of 1968" in Robert Kolb and Gloria Gaggioli (eds.), *Research Handbook on Human Rights and Humanitarian Law* (Cheltenham: Edward Elgar, 2013), pp. 42–43.

concerned that dealing with international humanitarian law would question the prohibition on the use of force just enshrined in the Charter while the ICRC did not want to get entangled in the "political" aspects of the emerging human rights regime as this might have endangered its independence.[59]

But the drafting of the Universal Declaration of Human Rights and the Geneva Convention, respectively, were not completely disconnected, either.[60] Human rights did influence the Geneva Conventions, and the attention paid to human rights allowed for a gradual transformation of the law of armed conflict to a humanitarian law which was oriented alongside human rights, at least in certain aspects.[61] Human rights were mentioned occasionally in the proceedings and official reports of the conference which drafted the Geneva Conventions. Only the Danish delegation seemed to have used human rights language more consistently (which, as historians claim, was considered as a slightly eccentric attitude by other delegations).[62] "The military men and diplomatic officials of those delegations," one commentator summed up the mood of the conference, "found no need to complicate discussions of the rugged issues before them by opening doors to a conference chamber where war and its problems were only reluctantly admitted to exist." The delegations to the conferences tasked with drafting the Geneva Conventions and the Universal Declaration of Human Rights were also composed of different persons and only a few delegates participated personally in the drafting of both texts, such as the Australian and Mexican ambassadors to the UN.[63]

While no formal connections between the two parallel drafting processes were established, the drafters of both documents still kept an eye on each other, particularly when it came to discussing the fourth Convention on the protection of civilians and the rules on internal armed conflicts common to all four Conventions. The general tendency was to keep away from rules on how governments should treat persons subject to their jurisdiction on their own territory and leave such matters to the emerging human rights documents.[64] Even so, some delegations suggested an explicit reference to human rights language in Geneva Convention III on prisoners of war, arguing that even persons not benefiting from the convention should enjoy the rights derived from other sources, including human rights. The Mexican delegation suggested that a reference should be made to human rights when dealing with the law of occupation so that changes in the law of occupied territories would not be allowed to violate the Universal Declaration of Human Rights.[65] The question on how to treat rebels also led some to invoke human rights as minimum protective rules.[66]

And had there not been a disagreement on the conceptual basis of human rights among the delegates to the conference which drafted the Geneva Conventions, the document might well have had a common Preamble emphasizing that "respect for the personality and

[59] See Michael Bothe, "Humanitäres Völkerrecht und Schutz der Menschenrechte: Auf der Suche nach Synergien und Schutzlücken" in Pierre-Marie Dupuy, Bardo Fassbender, Malcolm N. Shaw and Karl-Peter Sommermann (eds.), *Common Values in International Law, Essays in Honour of Christian Tomuschat* (Kehl: Engel, 2006), p. 66.

[60] Such a completely unrelated drafting history seems to be suggested by Gasser, "International Humanitarian Law and Human Rights Law" (n. 23) 152–53.

[61] See Schindler, "International Humanitarian Law" (n. 4) 170.

[62] Best, *War and Law Since 1945* (n. 31) p. 145. [63] Kolb, "The Relationship" (n. 40) 413.

[64] See Best, *War and Law Since 1945* (n. 31) p. 144. [65] Kolb, "The Relationship" (n. 40) 413.

[66] Green, "Human Rights and the Law of Armed Conflict" (n. 5) p. 448.

dignity of human beings constitutes a universal principle which is binding even in the absence of any contractual undertaking."[67] Even the position of the US delegation was not as critical of the link between human rights and humanitarian law as it is today, with military lawyers expressing the view (in the American Society of International Law in 1949) that the Geneva Conventions are "human rights operating on the wartime scene."[68]

More importantly than such general professions, however, was the direct impact of human rights on the text of the Conventions. In some places, the documents cover the spirit or contain the explicit language of "rights" of protected persons instead of imposing obligations on the belligerents. The rules on non-renunciation of entitlements to protection are an example. Under the Geneva Conventions, the wounded and sick, prisoners of war, civilians and other specifically protected persons may in no circumstances renounce their rights under the Conventions.[69] Attempts of some delegations to steer away from such a rights-based approach in the drafting of the Conventions were not successful: a proposal to change the suggested reference to rights "secured to" individuals in Common Article 7 of the Geneva Conventions (which is Article 8 in Geneva Convention IV) to "stipulated on their behalf" was rejected. The same happened in Common Article 6 of the Geneva Conventions (which is Article 7 in Geneva Convention IV) which allowed for special agreements to be concluded in addition to the Conventions.[70]

The Commentary on Geneva Convention IV notes in this respect that the wording finally chosen was "doubtless under the influence of the theoretical trends which also resulted in the Universal Declaration of Human Rights."[71] The principle of non-discrimination is also present in the Geneva Conventions, e.g., in Article 12 of Geneva Convention I which states that the wounded and sick "shall be treated humanely and cared for by the Party to the conflict in whose power they may be, without any adverse distinction founded on sex, race, nationality, religion, political opinions, or any other similar criteria."[72] And the whole of Geneva Convention III on prisoners of war is rightly said to be informed by the idea that humane treatment is a right and not a favour.[73] It also worked the other way round: the prohibition of the death penalty for juvenile offenders, for example, emerged as a norm of international humanitarian law in Geneva Convention IV in 1949 and was transposed to the International Covenant on Civil and Political Rights (ICCPR) in the drafting process in 1957.[74]

67 See Jean Pictet (ed.), *Commentary on the First Geneva Convention for the Amelioration of the Condition of the Wounded and Sick in Armed Forces in the Field* (Geneva: International Committee on the Red Cross, 1952), p. 21. See also Sergey Sayapin, "The International Committee of the Red Cross and International Human Rights Law" (2009) 9(1) *Human Rights Law Review* 97.

68 Best, *War and Law Since 1945* (n. 31) p. 72.

69 Geneva Conventions I, II and III, Art. 7 and Geneva Convention IV, Art. 8; see Schindler, "International Humanitarian Law" (n. 4) 170.

70 These articles now contain the phrase "no special agreement shall adversely affect the situation of the wounded and sick, of members of the medical personnel or of chaplains, as defined by the present Convention, nor restrict the rights which it confers upon them." See also Theodor Meron, *The Humanization of International Law* (Leiden: Nijhoff, 2006), p. 39.

71 See Jean Pictet (ed.), *Commentary to the Fourth Geneva Convention Relative to the Protection of Civilian Persons in Time of War* (Geneva: International Committee of the Red Cross, 1952), p. 77.

72 Geneva Convention I, Art. 12. 73 See Best, *War and Law Since 1945* (n. 31) p. 145.

74 See William Schabas, "*Lex specialis*? Belts and Suspenders? The Parallel Operation of Human Rights Law and the Law of Armed Conflict, and the Conundrum of Jus ad Bellum" (2007) 40(2) *Israel Law Review* 598.

Human rights are, however, most visible in three areas in which the Geneva Conventions broke new ground: the minimum rules of Common Article 3 for armed conflicts not of an international character; the detailed rules on the protection of civilians in Geneva Convention IV; and the provisions on grave breaches of the Geneva Conventions, which are, in essence, a list of individual human rights as contained also in the Universal Declaration of Human Rights. Richard Quentin-Baxter, who was present at the negotiations of the Geneva Conventions as the delegate of New Zealand, remarked that Common Article 3 of the four Geneva Conventions was the first time that states had accepted in treaty form that they were accountable for how they treated their own citizens, well before the human rights Covenants did the same upon their adoption in 1966. Prior to the 1949 Geneva Conventions, the law of armed conflict had not dealt with internal armed conflicts, although the International Red Cross Movement had been arguing for a provision along the lines of Common Article 3 since at least 1912.[75]

Common Article 3 to the Geneva Conventions, with its prohibition of discrimination, murder, torture, degrading and humiliating treatment, mutilation, hostage-taking and emphasis on judicial guarantees, does indeed read like a human rights code *en miniature* within a humanitarian law document.[76] The provision departs from the hitherto well-established principle that international humanitarian law should not be concerned with the relation between a state and its nationals.[77] It goes beyond the strict approach of the established law of war which assigned rights and duties on the basis of status (as combatant or civilian) and allows a progressive acknowledgment that certain basic humanitarian norms apply irrespective of status.[78] It enables international humanitarian law to spread downwards, into the domestic sphere, while at the same time international human rights law had spread upwards, from constitutional arrangements into international law. In Common Article 3 the two met, starting to "rub together like two huge tectonic plates."[79]

The protection of civilians was deemed worthy of a new convention altogether. As a direct response to the suffering of civilians in the Second World War who had been subjected "to every form of indignity and cruelty known to man,"[80] Geneva Convention IV extended its protection not only to those involved in hostilities but also to those who found themselves in the hands of the adversary armed forces. In light of its objective, the text

[75] See, e.g., Jeremy Sarkin, "The Historical Origins, Convergence and Interrelationship of International Human Rights Law, International Humanitarian Law, International Criminal Law and Public International Law and their Application since the Nineteenth Century" (2007) 1(2) *Human Rights and International Legal Discourse* 134; and Best, *War and Law Since 1945* (n. 31) p. 208.

[76] See, e.g., Cordula Droege, "Elective Affinities? Human Rights and Humanitarian Law" (2008) 90(871) *International Review of the Red Cross* 504.

[77] See Louise Doswald-Beck and Sylvain Vité, "International Humanitarian Law and Human Rights Law" (1993) 33(293) *International Review of the Red Cross* 112.

[78] Paul Kennedy and George J. Andreopoulos, "The Laws of War: Some Concluding Reflections" in Michael Howard, George J. Andreopoulos and Mark R. Shulman (eds.), *The Laws of War: Constraints on Warfare in the Western World* (New Haven, CT: Yale University Press, 1994), p. 220. There was considerable dispute about whether or not Common Art. 3 represented customary law at the time of its drafting, see Theo van Boven, "Reliance on Norms of Humanitarian Law by United Nations' Organs" in Astrid J.M. Delissen and Gerard J. Tanja (eds.), *Humanitarian Law of Armed Conflict: Challenges Ahead, Essays in Honour of Frits Kalshoven* (Dordrecht: Nijhoff, 1991), p. 502.

[79] Charles H.B. Garraway, "'To Kill or not to Kill': Dilemmas in the Use of Force" (2010) 14(3) *Journal of Conflict and Security Law* 501.

[80] See, e.g., Green, "Human Rights and the Law of Armed Conflict" (n. 5) p. 449.

was soon hailed, perhaps somewhat too optimistically, as a "manifesto of human rights for civilians during armed conflict."[81] For some delegations to the drafting process, the link between human rights and the Convention was so evident that they suggested bringing the text together with the Universal Declaration of Human Rights in a more formal manner.[82]

When the Preamble to the Fourth Geneva Convention was drafted, it was suggested to use human rights language and insert references to "divine principle," "respect for suffering humanity" or "universal human law."[83] The ICRC proposed to use one and the same Preamble for all four Conventions which would have read "[r]espect for the personality and dignity of human beings constitute a universal principle which is binding even in the absence of any contractual undertaking."[84] But the emerging consensus on this – and indeed on any Preamble – broke down in a squabble over whether there should be a reference to God (on the suggestion of the Holy See) or to the Nuremberg Principles (as pushed for by the Soviet Union). Both suggestions proved divisive, while reference to human rights had already been accepted by all parties "to the point even of being taken for granted,"[85] only to be left out at the last moment.

And finally, the provisions on grave breaches of Article 147 of Geneva Convention IV are, in essence, a list of human rights violations.[86] They include acts of wilful killing, torture or inhuman treatment, biological experiments, wilfully causing great suffering or serious injury to body or health, unlawful deportation or transfer, unlawful confinement of a protected person, violations of fair trial and hostage-taking. So obvious was the impact of human rights that some argued that "[a]s early as 1949, the Fourth Geneva Convention did indeed establish a body of law which may be called 'human rights in armed conflict,' the terminology used by the Tehran International Conference on Human Rights."[87]

Not all were satisfied, though, with the inclusion of human rights language in the operative part of Geneva Convention IV. While there was no opposition to enhancing the protection of the enemy population, many states objected to the idea that the Convention should tell them how to run their own hospitals and care for their own wounded and sick. The reluctance to engage with human rights was fuelled by the consideration that in comparison to human rights, humanitarian law was established, mature and tested, supervised by the independent and impartial ICRC, practical, realistic, operational and known to military practitioners; these were rules from which no derogation was possible and the violation of which could be sanctioned in military and penal law. The emerging legal regime of human rights had none of this: there was only the Universal Declaration of Human Rights with its visionary appeal to human dignity. It comes as little surprise that human rights were not greeted with much enthusiasm in humanitarian circles at the time.[88]

But even so, human rights began to inform the development of the laws of war and changed their character: "humanitarian" in the Geneva Conventions was no longer meant to refer to the kind of humanity which had previously driven international humanitarian

81 Leslie C. Green, *The Contemporary Law of Armed Conflict* (Manchester: Manchester University Press, 2008), p. 179.
82 Ibid. 83 Kolb, "The Relationship" (n. 40) 412–14.
84 Best, *War and Law Since 1945* (n. 31) pp. 70–71. 85 Ibid. p. 72.
86 See, e.g., Green, "Human Rights and the Law of Armed Conflict" (n. 5) p. 450.
87 Gasser, "International Humanitarian Law and Human Rights Law" (n. 23) 156. The author refers to the Tehran World Conference on Human Rights of 1968.
88 Robert Quentin-Baxter, "Human Rights and Humanitarian Law: Confluence of Conflict?" (1985) 9 *Australian Yearbook of International Law* 103.

law. The idea of humanity in warfare had undergone yet another transformation. What used to be perceived as a grace extended by noble chevaliers, pious officers and kind-hearted businessmen changed to a set of individual entitlements as laid down in the growing international human rights law. Not many contemporaries would have subscribed to such a view, though. Well into the 1970s, "humanitarian" in international humanitarian law was seen as clashing and incompatible with the idea of human rights.[89] But since 1945, "humanitarian" cannot be understood in any other way than as a reference to the emerging and ever refined international human rights regime. Where the law of armed conflict prior to 1949 necessitated adherence to religious faith, chivalry, a charitable impulse or the belief to civilize men and nations, international human rights law introduced, in 1948, the idea of an inclusive, rights-based, universal approach to humanity and humanitarian matters. Now there were two fields with a very similar goal: protecting individual human dignity, lives and livelihood. Seemingly, the tacit consensus was that one was meant for times of peace and the other for times of war and that both would operate independently. Still, they would have to coexist: human rights had not absorbed humanitarian law and human rights were not a revision of humanitarian law. For a while, they would go their separate ways until the Tehran World Conference of 1968 suggested otherwise.

[89] See, e.g., Karl-Josef Partsch, "Menschenrechte und Rotkreuz-Grundsätze. Justitiartagung 1973" in Wolfgang Voit (ed.), *Völkerrechtliche Beiträge der Tagungen der Justitiare und Konventionsbeauftragten des deutschen Roten Kreuzes 1957–1989* (Bochum: Universitätsverlag Dr. N. Brockmeyer, 1995), pp. 201–2.

4

Human rights in armed conflict

4.1 Geneva, New York, Tehran: World Conference of Human Rights 1968

In the years following the adoption of the Geneva Convention and the Universal Declaration of Human Rights, the "tacit acceptance"[1] of two separate legal regimes persisted. The one notable exception to the United Nations' lack of interest in the laws of war was the concern which the United Nations Educational, Scientific and Cultural Organisation (UNESCO) showed for the protection of cultural values in armed conflicts in the 1954 Hague Convention on Cultural Property and its two Protocols.[2] The International Committee of the Red Cross (ICRC) also remained sceptical of human rights for various reasons. First, the organization's approach to any law, including international humanitarian law, was a pragmatic one: it sought to provide relief rather than pursue justice.[3] The ICRC was concerned that human rights would not deliver what they promised, and the lack of binding treaty obligations on human rights on the universal level until the two UN Covenants (on civil and political rights and on social, economic and cultural rights) entered into force in 1976,[4] together with the absence of any meaningful monitoring mechanism led the organization to question the potential of human rights. The ICRC thought of the growing human rights movement as a somewhat utopian project, striving for the perfect world but achieving nothing. In comparison, it considered international humanitarian law as capable of protecting concrete persons in real life.[5]

The ICRC also realized how different its approach was, even in areas where human rights were at stake, for example in situations of detention.[6] The organization had started to visit detained persons already in 1919, and it visited not only prisoners of war and those detained

[1] Charles H.B. Garraway, "Occupation Responsibilities and Constraints" in Howard M. Hensel (ed.), *The Legitimate Use of Force: The Just War Tradition and the Customary Law of Armed Conflict* (Aldershot: Ashgate, 2008), p. 268.

[2] Convention for the Protection of Cultural Property in the Event of Armed Conflict, 14 May 1954, 249 UNTS 240, Protocol to the Convention for the Protection of Cultural Property in the Event of Armed Conflict, 14 May 1954, 249 UNTS 358, and Second Protocol to the Hague Convention of 1954 for the Protection of Cultural Property in the Event of Armed Conflict, 26 March 1999, 2253 UNTS 172.

[3] David Forsythe, *The Humanitarians: The International Committee of the Red Cross* (Cambridge: Cambridge University Press, 2005), p. 244, where he also remarks on the irony that as a consequence the ICRC develops international humanitarian law primarily for others.

[4] International Covenant on Economic, Social and Cultural Rights, 16 December 1966, 993 UNTS 3, entered into force on 3 January 1976 and International Covenant on Civil and Political Rights, 16 December 1966, 999 UNTS 171, entered into force on 23 March 1976.

[5] Forsythe, *The Humanitarians* (n. 3) pp. 164–65.

[6] See David P. Forsythe, "Human Rights and Internal Conflicts: Trends and Recent Developments" (1982) 12 *California Western International Law Journal* 299.

in internal conflicts but also persons detained "by reasons of events," a phrase invented by the ICRC to overcome the reluctance of states to allow humanitarian action in situations of domestic tensions. In human rights parlance, many of those persons were political prisoners. With such visits the ICRC transcended its conflict-related mandate and was way ahead of the international human rights regime.[7] The ICRC also sought to protect refugees but found itself overwhelmed by the masses of refugees and their demands, so that eventually refugee protection became a separate field of law and operations were entrusted first to private refugee associations and later to the Nansen Refugee Office of the League of Nations and finally the UN High Commissioner for Refugees, thus set apart from international humanitarian law and humanitarian assistance (the prerogatives of the ICRC) as well the emerging human rights law.[8]

When Amnesty International kick-started activism on political prisoners in the 1960s, the ICRC concluded that the organization and the ICRC were obviously not pushing for quite the same outcome: while the ICRC was concerned with making conditions of detention bearable for the prisoner, Amnesty International denounced detention as such a human rights violation and demanded immediate and unconditional release of the persons concerned.[9] And even where the ICRC invoked human rights, it relied on their ethos more than on their legal character.[10] The organization was constantly concerned with its impartiality and sought to "fashion a human rights policy built on ethical choice"[11] rather than directly use international human rights law.

The separation between human rights and humanitarian law was challenged when the World Conference on Human Rights, convened in Tehran from 22 April to 13 May 1968 on the occasion of the twentieth anniversary of the Universal Declaration of Human Rights, was tasked with drawing up a human rights agenda for the UN in light of achievements and future challenges. With the Vietnam War (1964–1973) in its fourth year, war was a topic very much on the mind of the delegates. For many of them the ever-rising number of civilian casualties in this war, transmitted live on television, demonstrated the inadequacy of the existing rules for warfare. Civilian deaths had continued to rise for decades, from 50 per cent in the Second World War to 60 per cent in the Korean War to 70 per cent in the Vietnam War, and international humanitarian law seemed unable to halt this development.[12]

The conference proved to be a deciding event in bringing together international humanitarian law and international human rights law.[13] It adopted Resolution No. XXIII entitled "Human rights in armed conflict."[14] The text was adopted without much debate and with near consensus (fifty-three states voted in favour and only Switzerland abstained, driven by the concern that this new approach might infringe the ICRC's mandate and position, and

[7] In the Cold War period, Forsythe found the ICRC to have visited sixty or seventy countries each year, which is equivalent to the number of countries in which Amnesty International took an interest; see Forsythe, *The Humanitarians* (n. 3) p. 87 and pp. 94–95.

[8] Forsythe, *The Humanitarians* (n. 3) p. 34. [9] Ibid. p. 164.

[10] David P. Forsythe, "Choices More Ethical than Legal: The International Committee of the Red Cross and Human Rights" (1993) 7(1) *Ethics and International Affairs* 134.

[11] Ibid. 151. [12] Geoffrey Best, *War and Law Since 1945* (Oxford: Clarendon Press, 1994), p. 412.

[13] See John Dugard, "Bridging the Gap between Human Rights and Humanitarian Law" (1998) 38(324) *International Review of the Red Cross* 445.

[14] World Conference on Human Rights, Resolution XXIII on human rights in armed conflict, UN Doc. A/CONF/32/41 (12 May 1968), 18.

annoyed that the ICRC had not been consulted on the terms of the resolution).[15] The then Secretary-General of the International Commission of Jurists, Sean MacBride, is usually seen as the mastermind behind the resolution.[16] He could build on earlier meetings and draft texts, including the "Montreal Statement" adopted by a group of individual human rights proponents, which had expressed concern that the law of armed conflict was in urgent need of revision.[17] The resolution was thus a response to the failures of humanitarian law to provide effective protection and to the law's inability to effectively cover all types of armed conflicts.

The text had little substance; all it did was to invite the UN General Assembly to study "steps which could be taken to assure the better application of existing humanitarian international conventions and rules in all armed conflicts"[18] as well as "the need for new conventions or possible revision of existing conventions to ensure the better protection of civilians, prisoners and combatants in all armed conflicts and the prohibition and limitation of the use of certain methods and means of warfare."[19] It also requested the UN Secretary-General, in consultation with the ICRC:

> to draw the attention of all member States of the United Nations system to the existing rules of international law on the subject and urge them, pending the adoption of new rules of international law relating to armed conflicts, to ensure that in all armed conflicts the inhabitants and belligerents are protected in accordance with the principles of the law among nations derived from the usages established among civilized peoples, from the laws of humanity and from the dictates of the public conscience.[20]

The value as well as the precise aim of the resolution remain disputed.[21] Despite its title, the resolution did not refer to human rights at all, except for a general reference to the importance of the Universal Declaration of Human Rights, and rather resorted to the language of the Martens Clause. The complete absence of the UN human rights Covenants in the resolution, adopted only two years earlier, in 1966, is even more striking. Even its very title – "human rights in armed conflict" – is somewhat opaque and confusing. The term was not explained in the resolution nor used anywhere else in the text. At first sight, it appears as if twenty years after its emergence international humanitarian law would be turned into a branch of human rights law and be renamed "human rights in armed conflicts." Consequently, some accused the drafters of having wrongly equated "human rights in armed conflict" with "international humanitarian law."[22]

The resolution was criticized as an unreasonable attempt to merge humanitarian law and human rights law and rejected on the grounds that it "disregards the fact that wars negate human rights, that the latter actually do not exist in times of armed conflicts, and

[15] Only Vietnam joined Switzerland in the subsequent plenary vote which resulted in 67 votes in favour, 9 against and 2 abstentions, see W.E. Hewitt, "Respect for Human Rights in Armed Conflicts" (1971) 4 *New York University Journal of International Law and Politics* 43.

[16] See Christina Cerna, "Human Rights in Armed Conflict: Implementation of International Humanitarian Law Norms by Regional Intergovernmental Human Rights Bodies" in Frits Kalshoven and Yves Sandoz (eds.), *Implementation of International Humanitarian Law* (Dordrecht: Nijhoff, 1989), pp. 39–40.

[17] See Hewitt, "Respect for Human Rights in Armed Conflicts" (n. 15) 43.

[18] Resolution XXIII (n. 14) para. 1(a). [19] Ibid. para. 1(b).

[20] Ibid. para. 2, the latter part of which quotes the Martens Clause.

[21] Cerna, "Human Rights in Armed Conflict" (n. 16) p. 40.

[22] See Keith D. Suter, "An Enquiry into the Meaning of the Phrase 'Human Rights in Armed Conflict'" (1976) 15(3–4) *Revue de droit pénal militaire et de droit de la guerre* 397.

that their function is then taken over by the humanitarian law but only in regard to certain individuals and under certain conditions."[23] Given the lack of any substantial reference to international human rights law in the text it was suggested that the resolution should more appropriately have been named "humanitarian principles in armed conflicts."[24]

Others, however, found the term a natural and fitting reflection of the "close intimacy"[25] of the two regimes. The majority of contemporary and later commentators were favourable towards the resolution, even though their views on its meaning differed. Some argued that the idea of "human rights in armed conflict" was meant to comprise the law on victims of armed conflicts (traditionally the Geneva law) and the law on the conduct of hostilities (traditionally the Hague law) with no more distinction to be made between the two.[26] Others saw the resolution as merely recognizing an unspecified link between these two bodies of law, while again others acknowledged it as expressing a systematic convergence of international humanitarian law and international human rights law and emphasized the growing impact of human rights law on international humanitarian law.[27] Some argued that in Tehran the two bodies of law were fusing, or that human rights would revise the law of armed conflict, and that the conference had torn down the distinction between the laws of war and the laws of peace as established in international legal doctrine since Grotius' *De jure belli ac pacis*.[28]

It seems perhaps more realistic to argue that the Tehran Conference merely used human rights, or the rubric of human rights, to legitimize international humanitarian law when it found itself in a time of crisis.[29] In this sense, the resolution was part and parcel of attempts to revitalize, reaffirm and develop humanitarian law and constitutes one of many steps which would eventually lead to the adoption of the 1977 Additional Protocols.[30] But even if that was the primary goal of the resolution, it had the effect of positioning humanitarian law in a new light: as an instrument which could ultimately be meant to secure human rights in armed conflict.[31] And it also ended the "benign neglect"[32] which international humanitarian law and international human rights law had shown towards each other and allowed the

23 Suter, "An Enquiry into the Meaning of the Phrase" (n. 22) 400. 24 Ibid. 422.

25 See G.I.A.D. Draper, "Humanitarianism in the Modern Law of Armed Conflict" in Michael A. Meyer (ed.), *Armed Conflict and the New Law*, vol. I, *Aspects of the 1977 Geneva Protocols and the 1981 Weapons Convention* (London: British Institute of International and Comparative Law, 1989), p. 4.

26 Karl-Josef Partsch, "Human Rights and Humanitarian Law" in Rudolf Bernhardt (ed.), *Encyclopedia of Public International Law* (Amsterdam: Elsevier, 1995), p. 910.

27 See Arthur Henry Robertson, "Humanitarian Law and Human Rights" in Christophe Swinarski (ed.), *Studies and Essays on International Humanitarian Law and Red Cross Principles in Honour of Jean Pictet* (The Hague: Nijhoff, 1984), p. 796.

28 Cerna, "Human Rights in Armed Conflict" (n. 16) p. 40.

29 See Michael Bothe, "Die Anwendung der Europäischen Menschenrechtskonvention in bewaffneten Konflikten – eine Überforderung?" (2005) 65 *Zeitschrift für ausländisches öffentliches Recht und Völkerrecht* 621.

30 Hans-Peter Gasser, "International Humanitarian Law and Human Rights Law in Non-International Armed Conflict: Joint Venture or Mutual Exclusion?" (2002) 45 *German Yearbook of International Law* 154.

31 See Stefanie Schmahl, "Der Menschenrechtsschutz in Friedenszeiten im Vergleich zum Menschenrechtsschutz im Krieg" in Jana Hasse, Erwin Müller and Patricia Schneider (eds.), *Humanitäres Völkerrecht: politische, rechtliche und strafgerichtliche Dimensionen* (Baden-Baden: Nomos, 2001), p. 71.

32 Gasser, "International Humanitarian Law and Human Rights Law" (n. 30) p. 154.

UN to break away from its self-imposed distance from humanitarian law, thus opening the possibility to consider the relationship between the two legal regimes afresh.[33]

The UN General Assembly endorsed this particular outcome of the Tehran Conference with Resolution 2444 (XXIII) of 1968, entitled "Respect for human rights in armed conflict." With this resolution, the General Assembly invited the UN Secretary General, in consultation with the ICRC, to undertake the studies requested by the conference.[34] With this rather modest demand it endorsed also the start of a process which, in the words of one commentator, ultimately "brought the three currents of The Hague, Geneva and New York together into one main stream."[35] The General Assembly subsequently adopted Resolution 2597 (XXIV) of 16 December 1969 (also entitled "Respect for human rights in armed conflict") and Resolution 2675 (XXV) of 9 December 1970 which affirmed that "fundamental human rights, as accepted in international law and laid down in international instruments, continue to apply fully in situations of armed conflict."[36] More resolutions on this matter followed.[37]

In the following years, the UN Secretary-General issued altogether nine reports in response to the request formulated in General Assembly Resolution 2444, starting with the first one in 1969 which was prepared by the (then) UN Human Rights Division.[38] The report had "a decidedly human rights bias."[39] In it, the UN Secretary-General suggested that intergovernmental organizations ought to play a more prominent role in monitoring compliance with international humanitarian law. The suggestion was based on Common Article 8 of the Geneva Conventions (which is Article 9 in Geneva Convention IV), which states that "[t]he present Convention shall be applied with the cooperation and under the scrutiny of the Protecting Powers whose duty it is to safeguard the interests of the Parties to the conflict," as well as Common Article 10 of the Geneva Conventions (which is Article 11 in Geneva Convention IV), which states that:

33 See René Provost, *International Human Rights and Humanitarian Law* (Cambridge: Cambridge University Press, 2002), pp. 3–4.

34 Resolution 2444 (XXIII), para. 2. See in greater detail on the drafting history and the negotiations Hewitt, "Respect for Human Rights in Armed Conflict" (n. 15) 47–50.

35 Frits Kalshoven and Liesbeth Zegveld, *Constraints on the Waging of War: An Introduction to International Humanitarian Law* (4th edn., Cambridge: Cambridge University Press, 2011), p. 25. The term "New York law," coined by Kalshoven and Zegveld, is meant to denote the influence of the UN and human rights on international humanitarian law, but is not widely used; see ibid. p. 20.

36 Basic Principles for the Protection of Civilian Populations in Armed Conflicts, UN Doc. GA/Res. 2675 (XXV) (9 December 1970), para. 1.

37 UN General Assembly Res. 2852 on respect for human rights in armed conflict, UN Doc. A/2852 (XXVI) (20 December 1971); UN General Assembly Res. 2853 on respect for human rights in armed conflict, UN Doc. A/2853 (XXVI) (20 December 1971); UN General Assembly Res. 3032 on respect for human rights in armed conflict, UN Doc. A/3032 (XXVII) (18 December 1972); UN General Assembly Res. 3102 on respect for human rights in armed conflict, UN Doc. A/3102 (XXVII) (12 December 1973); UN General Assembly Res. 3319 on respect for human rights in armed conflict, UN Doc. A/3319 (XXIX) (14 December 1974); UN General Assembly Res. 3500 on respect for human rights in armed conflict, UN Doc. A/3500 (XXX) (15 December 1975); UN General Assembly Res. 31/19 on respect for human rights in armed conflict, UN Doc. A/RES/31/19 (24 November 1976); UN General Assembly Res. 32/44 on respect for human rights in armed conflict, UN Doc. A/RES/32/44 (8 December 1977).

38 *Report of the Secretary General on Respect for Human Rights in Armed Conflict*, UN Doc. A/7720 (20 November 1969).

39 Cerna, "Human Rights in Armed Conflict" (n. 16) p. 41.

> [t]he High Contracting Parties may at any time agree to entrust to an organization which offers all guarantees of impartiality and efficacy the duties incumbent on the Protecting Powers by virtue of the present Convention ... If protection cannot be arranged accordingly, the Detaining Power shall request or shall accept, subject to the provisions of this Article, the offer of the services of a humanitarian organization, such as the International Committee of the Red Cross, to assume the humanitarian functions performed by Protecting Powers under the present Convention.[40]

In the Secretary-General's opinion this could be any impartial and effective organization which undertakes the humanitarian functions of Protecting Powers. This was meant to remedy the fact that the institution of Protecting Powers was hardly ever used and that the ICRC, when acting as Protecting Power, could be perceived as a less effective supervisory procedure for violations of humanitarian law because of its principles of neutrality and confidentiality.[41] The report saw the need for a more effective supervision of humanitarian norms and suggested entrusting intergovernmental organizations with this task. The General Assembly, however, would have none of this and instructed the Secretary-General to focus on wars of liberation instead.[42]

This is what the second report did.[43] Having studied conflicts arising from the struggle of peoples under colonial and foreign rules for liberation and self-determination and their place in the Geneva Conventions, the report suggested setting up a mechanism for determining the nature of a conflict, i.e., whether it would meet the requirements of Common Article 3 of the Geneva Conventions or not. It was suggested that the ICRC or an intergovernmental organization could be this mechanism or, alternatively, that states should be obliged to formally declare a state of emergency under human rights treaties, such as the recently adopted International Covenant on Civil and Political Rights (ICCPR), when an internal armed conflict broke out.[44] In addition, the report proposed setting up a new UN agency mandated to contribute to the application of the Geneva Conventions and UN human rights instruments alike, including qualifying the nature of a conflict and occupation, assessing prisoner of war status, deciding on combatant status, creating and administering safe havens for civilians, and coordinating relief efforts in conflict situations.[45]

When this second report was issued, a vivid debate on human rights in armed conflict arose in the 25th session of the General Assembly in 1970. The two reports had made a strong link between human rights and humanitarian law in all situations of violence and had assigned a more prominent role to human rights instruments, but governments had different views on this.[46] Six draft resolutions were debated over four weeks in the Assembly's Third Committee (the committee entrusted with, *inter alia*, human rights and humanitarian matters). One proposal for a resolution (by France) was meant to ask the (then) UN Human Rights Commission to prepare an international treaty on the protection of journalists in armed conflicts. One (by the United States) was concerned with prisoners of

[40] Geneva Convention IV, Art. 11. [41] Cerna, "Human Rights in Armed Conflict" (n. 16) p. 42.

[42] UN General Assembly Res. 2597 (XXIV), UN Doc. A/2597 (16 December 1969), para. 1; see also Cerna, "Human Rights in Armed Conflict" (n. 16) p. 43.

[43] *Report of the Secretary-General on Respect for Human Rights in Armed Conflicts*, UN Doc. A/8052 (18 September 1970).

[44] See Cerna, "Human Rights in Armed Conflict" (n. 16) pp. 43–44.

[45] *Report of the Secretary-General* (n. 43) para. 247.

[46] See Cordula Droege, "The Interplay between International Humanitarian Law and International Human Rights Law in Situations of Armed Conflict" (2007) 40(2) *Israel Law Review* 315.

war. Two resolutions (by Norway and Greece) asked for the compilation of basic principles or minimum rules regarding the protection of civilians in armed conflict, while the United Kingdom, together with twelve co-sponsors, sought to ensure that the ICRC and not the UN would further develop humanitarian rules.[47] All resolutions were adopted but only the United Kingdom's proposal to leave everything related to humanitarian law to the ICRC became a reality. The French idea of asking a UN human rights body to develop international humanitarian law rules went nowhere, while the Norwegian and Greek proposals for minimum standards lay dormant until they were (unsuccessfully) put on the agenda again in the 1980s. None of the other proposals made in the first two reports of the Secretary-General were ever realized.

After 1970, the General Assembly went silent on international humanitarian law and indeed left it all to the ICRC. The Secretary-General's subsequent reports changed into mere summaries of the ICRC's Diplomatic Conferences and the last report was issued in 1979. The notion of "human rights in armed conflict" survived, however, as the terminology preferred by the UN to describe its involvement in matters of armed conflict, as evidenced by the recent publication of the UN Office of the High Commissioner for Human Rights (OHCHR) on *International Legal Protection of Human Rights in Armed Conflict*.[48] And, perhaps more importantly, the Tehran Conference and the subsequent developments had triggered a vivid academic debate on the role of human rights in armed conflict, as the number of contributions to edited books and academic journals on this topic in the late 1960s and in the 1970s demonstrated.[49]

[47] See Hewitt, "Respect for Human Rights in Armed Conflicts" (n. 15) 59–64.

[48] United Nations Office of the High Commissioner for Human Rights, *International Legal Protection of Human Rights in Armed Conflict* (New York and Geneva: United Nations, 2011).

[49] See, e.g., and in addition to writings already quoted above, Dietrich Schindler, "Das humanitäre Kriegsrecht im Rahmen der internationalen Garantie der Menschenrechte" in Deutsche Gesellschaft für die Vereinten Nationen (ed.), *Internationales Kolloquium über Menschenrechte* (Berlin: Deutsche Gesellschaft für die Vereinten Nationen, 1968), pp. 40–54; Sean MacBride, "Human Rights in Armed Conflicts: The Inter-Relationship between the Humanitarian Laws and the Law of Human Rights" (1970) 9(2) *Review of Penal Military Law and the Law of Armed Conflict* 373; Arthur Henry Robertson, "Human Rights as the Basis of International Humanitarian Law" in Institute of International Humanitarian Law (ed.), *Proceedings of the International Conference on Humanitarian Law* (Sanremo: Institute of International Humanitarian Law, 1970), pp. 55–76; Igor P. Blischchenko, "Armed Conflict and Protection of Human Rights" (1971) 18 *Review of Contemporary Law* 23; G.I.A.D. Draper, "The Relationship between the Human Rights Regime and the Law of Armed Conflict" (1971) 1 *Israel Yearbook of Human Rights* 191; Gerhard von Glahn, "The Protection of Human Rights in Time of Armed Conflict" (1971) 1 *Israel Yearbook of Human Rights* 208; G.I.A.D. Draper, "Human Rights and the Law of War" (1972) 12 *Virginia Journal of International Law* 326; Henri Meyrowitz, "Le droit de la guerre et les droits de l'homme" (1972) 88 *Revue de droit militaire et de droit de la guerre* 1059; George H. Aldrich, "Human Rights and Armed Conflict: Conflicting Views" (1973) 67 *American Journal of International Law Proceedings* 141; George H. Aldrich, "Human Rights in Armed Conflict: Development of the Law" (1973) 68 *Department of State Bulletin* 876; D.W. Greig, "Human Rights and Armed Conflict: Conflicting Views" (1973) *Proceedings of the American Society of International Law* 141; Geouffre de la Pradelle, "Human Rights and Armed Conflicts: On the 500th Anniversary of the Birth of Las Casas (1474–1874-1974)" (1977) 17(199) *International Review of the Red Cross* 402; Yoram Dinstein, "The International Law of Inter-State Wars and Human Rights" (1977) 7 *Israel Yearbook of Human Rights* 139; R.R. Baxter, "Human Rights in War" (1977) 31(4) *Bulletin of the American Academy of Arts and Sciences* 4; G.I.A.D. Draper, "Humanitarian Law and Human Rights" (1979) *Acta Juridica* 193; and G.I. A.D. Draper, "Humanitarian Law and Human Rights" in C.F. Forsythe and J.E. Schiller (eds.), *Human Rights: The Cape Town Conference* (Cape Town: Juta, 1979), pp. 193–206.

4.2 International Committee of the Red Cross and human rights

With the Secretary-General's suggestions having gone nowhere and with the blessing of the UN, the ICRC invigorated its work to reaffirm and develop international humanitarian law. The 21st International Conference of the Red Cross, held in Istanbul from 6 to 13 September 1969, adopted (as one of more than thirty resolutions) Resolution XIII on the "Reaffirmation and development of the laws and customs applicable in armed conflicts." It sought to put the genie back into the bottle and argued that attempts to develop humanitarian rules for all types of armed conflicts as an important means to strengthen fundamental human rights needed to be kept well within the boundaries of humanitarian law.

The ICRC was given the explicit mandate to work, in cooperation with the UN, towards proposing new rules to supplement existing international humanitarian law and convene, as desirable, diplomatic conferences to pursue this goal.[50] The result was the Conference of Government Experts on the Reaffirmation and Development of International Humanitarian Law applicable to Armed Conflicts, which took place in Geneva from 24 May to 12 June 1971 and paved the way for Diplomatic Conferences, held in four annual sessions from 1974 to 1977, which in turn led to the adoption of the Additional Protocols to the Geneva Conventions in 1977.

After the Tehran World Conference, the rift between the ICRC as the guardian of international humanitarian law and the world of human rights thus persisted; the ICRC upheld its position as the prime actor in the field and saw no need to move closer towards human rights. Quite to the contrary, the organization emphasized the differences between the two regimes on the grounds that the detailed rules of international humanitarian law must not be replaced by the overly general guarantees and politically sensitive content of international human rights law. It would only gradually take a more permissive approach during the negotiations of the Protocols from 1974–1977, even though it still rejected any direct reference to human rights.[51]

This gradual change of attitude was also a response to the growing critique of the organization's approach and operational culture. It was obvious that the ICRC had no intention to be a pacifist or justice organization which would judge the phenomenon of war morally, comment on states' decision to resort to the use of armed force, or go public with many of its findings on violations of the law, and rightly so, as this is what makes the organization unique.[52] But the organizational culture of the ICRC was exposed to the public in the Tansley Report of 1975, which criticized the secrecy prevailing in the ICRC and an arrogant attitude towards other humanitarian actors as well as towards the human rights movement.[53] The report ultimately led to a more open attitude within the ICRC and towards the outside world and other actors, including the human rights movement. But even so, the organization had no intention to openly advocate human rights. Where it

[50] See Hewitt, "Respect for Human Rights in Armed Conflicts" (n. 15) 51–52.

[51] See Partsch, "Human Rights and Humanitarian Law" (n. 26) p. 911; and Suter, "An Enquiry into the Meaning of the Phrase" (n. 22) 408–9.

[52] Even though some dismissively referred to this attitude as "very Swiss," see Michael Ignatieff, *The Warrior's Honor: Ethnic War and the Modern Conscience* (New York: Henry Hold, 1998), p. 121.

[53] See Forsythe, *The Humanitarians* (n. 3) pp. 88–92. The report is the outcome of an evaluation of the ICRC and other components of the Red Cross Movement from 1973–1975, headed by the Canadian Donald Tansley.

resorted to human rights it translated their content in humanitarian terms, speaking, for example, of the "dissemination" rather than the "promotion" (the term used by the human rights movement) of human rights.[54]

At the same time, the ICRC has, in effect, always promoted respect for human rights in its operational activities, and does so today: wherever the ICRC engages with parties to a conflict with the aim of ensuring adherence to international humanitarian law it effectively asks those parties to live up to their human rights obligations in so far as international humanitarian law and international human rights law obligations overlap.[55] And where the ICRC provides material assistance in relief operations, it effectively secures the right to food, water and shelter without saying so.[56] In conflict situations it remains obviously cautious not to directly mention human rights "although the occasional reference to human rights instruments is not ruled out."[57] The organization also engages in situations outside armed conflicts, where international humanitarian law is inapplicable, provided the ICRC Statute allows such activities and the respective government agrees. Examples are visits to detainees, providing material assistance, restoring family links after conflicts, aiding displaced persons or acting on behalf of persons affected by internal violence – actions which the ICRC seems to perceive as safeguarding human rights.

Even so, the ICRC continued to invoke the ethical value of human dignity rather than international human rights law, an attitude which can be explained in different ways: the ICRC's concern about the effectiveness of actions undertaken in the absence of the clear legal obligations of humanitarian law; the fact that it would require the organization to depart from well-established methods and experiences; and fear of endangering the organization's principles of humanity, neutrality and impartiality.[58] After all, the ICRC wants to be measured by immediate practical success which it finds difficult to achieve through invoking human rights.[59] It is thus no surprise that the organization has repeatedly been called upon to "resist the temptation of being drawn into associations or working relationships that might damage its ability to fulfil its humanitarian mission."[60]

In 1983, the ICRC sought to clarify matters in its report on *The Red Cross and Human Rights*, prepared by the International Committee and the Secretariat of the League of Red Cross Societies. The report showed the obvious, namely, how deeply the ICRC was operationally involved in securing the human rights of displaced persons, refugees, hostages, separated families and unaccompanied children. More than a dozen human rights provisions were listed in the report to the respect for which the ICRC directly contributed. The report confirmed the complementarity of human rights and humanitarian law even

[54] Cornelio Sommaruga, "Humanitarian Law and Human Rights in the Legal Arsenal of the ICRC" in Daniel Warner (ed.), *Human Rights and Humanitarian Law: The Quest for Universality* (The Hague: Nijhoff, 1997), p. 128.

[55] Ibid.

[56] See François Bugnion, "International Red Cross and Red Crescent Movement" in David P. Forsythe, *Encyclopedia of Human Rights* (Oxford: Oxford University Press, 2009), p. 177.

[57] Sommaruga, "Humanitarian Law and Human Rights" (n. 54) p. 129. [58] Ibid. p. 132.

[59] Dunant's activities have set the standard in this respect: while in the Crimean War of 1854–1856 (i.e., before the adoption of the First Geneva Convention) 60 per cent of the wounded soldiers died for lack of medical care, only 7.5 per cent died for the same reason in the First World War, see Dietrich Schindler, "International Humanitarian Law: Its Remarkable Development and Its Persistent Violation" (2003) 5(2) *Journal of the History of International Law* 169.

[60] Daniel Thürer, *International Humanitarian Law: Theory, Practice, Context* (The Hague: Hague Academy of International Law, 2011), p. 154.

though it rejected any further integration or merger of the two regimes. It also stressed the distinct character and role of the ICRC which would not allow it to become any further involved with the protection and promotion of human rights, but at the same time suggested the study of how the organization's possibilities, priorities and limits could be brought in line with international human rights law.[61]

4.3 Additional Protocols of 1977

The Diplomatic Conference on the Reaffirmation and Development of International Humanitarian Law applicable in Armed Conflicts of 1974–1977, held in Geneva under the auspices of the International Committee of the Red Cross in Geneva, resulted in the two Additional Protocols to the Geneva Conventions on international and non-international armed conflicts. The ICRC was, however, not enthusiastic about convening the conference (nor was the Swiss Confederation) as in their view it was motivated more by political and strategic interests, particularly of the states which had recently emerged from colonialism, than by humanitarian considerations.[62] These states had never been content with being bound by a set of laws on armed conflict in the development of which they had had nothing to say. Any revision of humanitarian law would thus have to consider their claim for a more representative, equitable and just international order, and issues such as neo-colonialism, imperialism and racism, which already figured prominently on the agenda of the UN, could be expected to be part of negotiations on humanitarian law. And, to make matters worse for those who had already been critical of the Tehran World Conference in 1968, the same could be expected with regard to human rights. The Western states also played along in preparing the Diplomatic Conference reluctantly, out of a sense of defensiveness, if not guilt, about the suffering caused by the Vietnam War, as George Aldrich, head of the US delegation in the Diplomatic Conference 1974–1977, remarked.[63] The whole process seemed unhelpful for narrowing the rift between the ICRC and the UN.

In a more positive spirit, the drafting of the Protocols could, however, also be seen as a first "multicultural"[64] effort in the making of humanitarian law, and as "de-westernizing" this legal regime. The number of participating states had increased compared to previous humanitarian conferences, and the conference was expected to "generate texts in the making of which every political and racial region of the world could be said to have had a hand."[65] Finally, the work yielded some acceptable results, given the political and ideological divisions which had to be overcome.[66] The conference ended with the adoption of two Protocols to the Geneva Conventions, one on international and one on non-international armed conflicts.

[61] See Robertson, "Humanitarian Law and Human Rights" (n. 27) pp. 800–1.
[62] See Partsch, "Human Rights and Humanitarian Law" (n. 26) p. 911.
[63] See Forsythe, *The Humanitarians* (n. 3) p. 261.
[64] René Kosirnik, "The 1977 Protocols: A Landmark in the Development of International Humanitarian Law" in Naorem Sanajaoba (ed.), *A Manual of International Humanitarian Laws* (New Delhi: Regency, 2004), p. 75.
[65] Best, *War and Law Since 1945* (n. 12) p. 416.
[66] See Schindler, "International Humanitarian Law" (n. 59) 173.

The idea to create one single text which would cover all sorts of armed conflicts regardless of their character had found no support.[67]

As could be expected, the texts confirmed that the Hague and Geneva law had finally merged and the whole of the law was humanitarian in nature.[68] Additional Protocol I repeated the basic principles of international humanitarian law such as the prohibition of unnecessary suffering,[69] the distinction between civilians and combatants[70] and the protection of civilians.[71] It also introduced new norms such as the presumption of civilian status in case of doubt;[72] the protection of medical personnel;[73] the obligation to determine if a new weapon is prohibited by international humanitarian law;[74] the prohibition of starvation as a means of warfare;[75] and the protection of the environment.[76] It also added precautionary principles for lawful targeting[77] and provided for new implementation mechanisms, such as the duty of military commanders to suppress and to report to competent authorities breaches of the Conventions and of the Protocol,[78] and the Humanitarian Fact-Finding Commission.[79]

Many of the provisions of Additional Protocol I drew heavily and visibly on international human rights law.[80] The Fundamental Guarantees of Article 75 of the Protocol, for example, are essentially a list of human rights provisions carried over from the ICCPR, particularly ICCPR, Article 14. They comprise the prohibition of violence to the life, health, physical or mental well-being of persons, including acts such as murder, torture, corporal punishment, mutilation, humiliating and degrading treatment, enforced prostitution, indecent assaults, hostage-taking and collective punishments, and lay down the right to information on the causes of arrest, detention and internment and to penal sentencing by a regularly constituted court in respect of generally recognized principles of regular judicial procedure.

The explicit prohibition of reprisals as incompatible with a human-rights oriented view of the law of armed conflict is another example.[81] Additional Protocol I also carried over the Martens Clause, although slightly rephrased,[82] and made some derogable human rights non-derogable humanitarian obligations, including medical care and the rights of prisoners to correspond with their families.[83] It also contained detailed provisions for persons

[67] Best, *War and Law Since 1945* (n. 12) p. 346.

[68] See, e.g., George H. Aldrich, "Some Reflections on the Origins of the 1977 Geneva Protocols" in Christophe Swinarski (ed.), *Studies and Essays on International Humanitarian Law and Red Cross Principles in Honour of Jean Pictet* (The Hague: Nijhoff, 1984), p. 130.

[69] Additional Protocol I, Art. 35(2). [70] Ibid. Art. 48. [71] Ibid. Art. 51(1). [72] Ibid. Art. 50(1).

[73] Ibid. Art. 15. [74] Ibid. Art. 36. [75] Ibid. Art. 54. [76] Ibid. Art. 55. [77] Ibid. Arts. 57 and 58.

[78] Ibid. Art. 87. [79] Ibid. Art. 90.

[80] See Louise Doswald-Beck and Sylvain Vité, "International Humanitarian Law and Human Rights Law" (1993) 33(293) *International Review of the Red Cross* 113.

[81] The respective provisions are Geneva Convention I, Art. 46; Geneva Convention II, Art. 47; Geneva Convention III, Art. 13(3); Geneva Convention IV, Art. 33(3); Additional Protocol II, Arts. 20, 51(6), 53 (c), 54(4) and 55(2); see also Schindler, "International Humanitarian Law" (n. 59) 183.

[82] Additional Protocol I, Art. 1(2): "In cases not covered by this Protocol or by other international agreements, civilians and combatants remain under the protection and authority of the principles of international law derived from established custom, from the principles of humanity and from the dictates of public conscience."

[83] See Droege, "The Interplay" (n. 46) 316.

deprived of their liberty.[84] In light of these developments, the Protocol was welcomed as filling important gaps in the protection of civilians.[85]

Drafting Additional Protocol II on internal armed conflicts was less of a success. Its most innovative feature is indeed "that at least it exists."[86] The text was severely cut back in the last round of negotiations, when a privileged status for combatants in internal armed conflicts was dropped and rules on the conduct of hostilities and implementation mechanisms were deleted from the draft.[87] But this text, too, relied on human rights. The part on humane treatment (Articles 4–6) reproduces to a large extent language used in the ICCPR.[88] It includes respect for person, honour, convictions and religious practices; the right to be treated humanely and without discrimination; the prohibition of violence to the life, health and physical or mental well-being of persons; murder; torture, cruel treatment or mutilation; corporal punishment; collective punishment; taking of hostages; humiliating and degrading treatment; rape, enforced prostitution and indecent assaults; and slavery and the slave trade.

So obvious is the link to the language of human rights that Part II on "Human Treatment" has been called a "human rights instrument."[89] The provisions stipulate that children shall be provided with the necessary care including education, shall be reunited with their families and not be recruited into the armed forces under the age of fifteen years. Additional Protocol II also relates directly to international human rights treaties and argues that "international instruments relating to human rights offer a basic protection to the human person."[90] The Commentary on Additional Protocol II goes as far as to say that Protocol II "contains virtually all the irreducible rights of the Covenant on Civil and Political Rights."[91]

To many, the impact of human rights on the Protocols was so obvious that they viewed their adoption as having "moved the dichotomy between the two legal regimes [i.e., international humanitarian law and international human rights law] to a vanishing point."[92] With the Protocols the complementarity of human rights and humanitarian law has become obvious and also largely accepted by states, and the ICRC, too, began to reconsider its position.[93] The drafting history of the Geneva Conventions and the Additional Protocols confirms the view that indeed "[t]he undeniable humanitarian texture

[84] Additional Protocol, Art. 4(5) provides for the treatment of the wounded and sick; food and drinking water; health and hygiene; medical assistance; relief; the right to practise one's religion and receive spiritual assistance; safe working conditions; separate quarters for women; correspondence; protection from the effects of hostilities; fair trial guarantees; and the prohibition of the death penalty for minors, pregnant women and mothers of young children.

[85] See Schindler, "International Humanitarian Law" (n. 59) 172.

[86] Kosirnik, "The 1977 Protocols" (n. 64) p. 74. [87] Ibid. p. 74.

[88] See Additional Protocol II, Arts. 4, 5 and 6 on fundamental guarantees, penal prosecutions and protection and care.

[89] Michael Bothe, Karl-Josef Partsch and Waldemar A. Solf, *New Rules for Victims of Armed Conflicts: Commentary on the Two 1977 Protocols Additional to the Geneva Conventions of 1949* (The Hague: Nijhoff, 1982), p. 619.

[90] Additional Protocol II, Preamble, para. 2.

[91] Yves Sandoz, Christophe Swinarski and Bruno Zimmermann (eds.), *Commentary on the Additional Protocols of 8 June 1977 to the Geneva Conventions of 12 August 1949* (Geneva: Nijhoff, 1987), para. 4430.

[92] Medard R. Rwelamira, "Human Rights and International Humanitarian Law: The Link or Common Ground Revisited" (1992) 3(3) *Stellenbosch Law Review* 339.

[93] See Droege, "The Interplay" (n. 46) 316.

of the post-1945 law of war drew to it, with magnetic force, the inexorable progress of the regimes of human rights."[94]

4.4 Fundamental standards of humanity

While the Additional Protocols of 1977 enhanced the protection of civilians in armed conflict and introduced protective rules in internal armed conflicts, they also further compartmentalized international humanitarian law with their distinctions between non-international armed conflicts under Common Article 3 of the Geneva Conventions and Additional Protocol II, as well as the special rules for wars of national liberation under Additional Protocol I, not to mention the unclear threshold between internal tensions, riots and disturbances, on the one hand, and armed conflicts, on the other. Ambiguous situations of "internationalized" or "transnational" violent post-conflict scenarios and the use of force in UN mandated peace operations added to the complexity. Gaps in the protection became particularly visible in situations which did not reach the threshold of an armed conflict and in which states declared a state of emergency and derogated from human rights provisions.[95]

Two suggestions were on the table to remedy this heterogeneous scenario of protective rules. The first one – to apply all rules for international armed conflicts to internal ones – proved to be unacceptable for states. The ICRC had made such a suggestion in the drafting of the Additional Protocols but had not found sufficient support.[96] The second suggestion – to agree on core protective rules for all conflict scenarios – enjoyed some support under the rubric of "Fundamental Standards of Humanity" between the beginning of the 1980s and the mid-1990s. This latter suggestion drew heavily on human rights.

The creation of a single legal instrument with minimum protective norms for all situations had already been proposed in different forms. Several, partly overlapping discussions and drafting exercises had engaged with this problem.[97] Theodor Meron's call for a new instrument with rules on internal strife proved to be influential.[98] It was followed by a study undertaken by the (then) Sub-Commission for the Promotion and Protection of

[94] Draper, "Humanitarian Law and Human Rights" (n. 49) 194.

[95] See Theodor Meron, "Contemporary Conflicts and Minimum Humanitarian Standards" in Karel Wellens (ed.), *International Law: Theory and Practice. Essays in Honour of Eric Suy* (The Hague: Nijhoff, 1998), p. 624.

[96] See Walter Kälin and Jörg Künzli, *The Law of International Human Rights Protection* (Oxford: Oxford University Press, 2009), p. 145.

[97] See, e.g., Theodor Meron, "On the Inadequate Reach of Humanitarian and Human Rights Law and the Need for a New Instrument" (1983) 77(3) *American Journal of International Law* 604; and Tom Hadden and Colin Harvey, "The Law of Internal Crisis and Conflict: An Outline Prospectus for the Merger of International Human Rights Law, the Law of Armed Conflict, Refugee Law, and the Law on Humanitarian Intervention" (1999) 81(833) *International Review of the Red Cross* 121. Towards the end of the Cold War, an even larger project of creating a New International Humanitarian Order (parallel to the New International Economic Order and the New International Information Order) enjoyed a short-lived existence, with an Independent Commission on International Humanitarian Issues and an Independent Bureau for Humanitarian Issues being set up, see Forsythe, *The Humanitarians* (n. 3) p. 94.

[98] See Theodor Meron, "Towards a Humanitarian Declaration on Internal Strife" (1984) 78(4) *American Journal of International Law* 859; and Theodor Meron, "Draft Model Declaration on Internal Strife" (1988) 28(262) *International Review of the Red Cross* 59.

Human Rights (the precursor of the Advisory Committee of the UN Human Rights Council),[99] a study by the International Commission of Jurists,[100] the adoption of minimum standards by the International Law Association,[101] and the ICRC's Draft Code of Conduct in the Event of Internal Disturbances and Tensions.[102]

None of these suggestions solicited sufficient support, even though they were only meant to bring together existing rules, principles and customs rather than create new norms.[103] Such standards needed to be both humanitarian and fundamental: humanitarian in the sense of protecting individuals regardless of their legal classification as humanitarian law, human rights law or refugee law; and fundamental as they would ensure basic physical protection of individuals. They should apply in "situations where fighting and conflict, of whatever intensity, is taking place inside countries, and without prejudice to any legal characterisation of the fighting for the purpose of applying international humanitarian law."[104]

With these conditions in mind, a group of experts assembled at the Åbo Akademi University Institute for Human Rights in Turku/Åbo in Finland and adopted in 1990 what later came to be known as the Draft Declaration of Minimum Humanitarian Standards. The declaration was based on a draft by Theodor Meron and Allan Rosas and was first published in 1991.[105] The drafters' explanatory comments echo the fears of a gap in the protection of individuals in situations of violence. They speak of:

[99] Study of Implications for Human Rights of Recent Developments Concerning Situations Known as States of Siege or Emergency, UN Doc. E/CN.4/Sub.2/1982/15 (27 July 1982).

[100] International Commission of Jurists, *States of Emergency: Their Impact on Human Rights* (Geneva: International Commission of Jurists, 1983).

[101] International Law Association, "The Paris Minimum Standards of Human Rights Norms in a State of Emergency", reprinted in (1985) 79(4) *American Journal of International Law* 1072.

[102] The ICRC had already drafted a short document entitled "Fundamental Rules of International Humanitarian Law Applicable in Armed Conflicts" in 1978, see ICRC Conference of Government Experts (1971) No. V, 86; reprinted in Rosemary Abi-Saab, M. El Kouhene and Z. Vivi (eds.), *Modern Wars: The Humanitarian Challenge, Report for the Independent Commission on International Humanitarian Issues* (London: ZED Books, 1986), pp. 180–81. For the text of the Draft Code of Conduct in the Event of Internal Disturbances and Tensions see Hans-Peter Gasser, "A Measure of Humanity in Internal Disturbances and Tensions: Proposal for a Code of Conduct" (1988) 28(262) *International Review of the Red Cross* 38. The Siracusa Principles on derogation from human rights obligations in times of emergency also deal with parts of this problem, see Siracusa Principles on the Limitation and Derogation of Provisions in the International Covenant on Civil and Political Rights, UN Doc. E/CN.4/1984/4 (28 September 1984), Annex.

[103] See Heinrich B. Reimann, "Menschenrechtsstandards in bewaffneten Konflikten" in Christophe Swinarski (ed.), *Studies and Essays on International Humanitarian Law and Red Cross Principles in Honour of Jean Pictet* (The Hague: Nijhoff, 1984), p. 776.

[104] See, e.g., *Analytical Report of the UN Secretary-General to the UN Human Rights Commission on Minimum Humanitarian Standards*, UN Doc. C/E.4/1998/87 (7 January 1998), para. 6.

[105] Declaration of Minimum Humanitarian Standards, UN Doc. E/CN.4/Sub.2/1991/55, reprinted in (1991) 31(282) *International Review of the Red Cross* 330. See also the introductory remarks by Hans-Peter Gasser, "Internal Disturbances and Tensions: New Draft Declaration of Minimum Humanitarian Standards" (1991) 31(282) *International Review of the Red Cross* 328. On the drafting history see Allan Rosas, "Human Rights at Risk in Situations of Internal Violence and Public Emergency" in Asbjorn Eide and Jan Helgesen (eds.), *The Future of Human Rights Protection in a Changing World: Fifty Years since the Four Freedoms Address, Essays in Honour of Torkel Opsahl* (Oslo: Norwegian University Press, 1991), p. 167; and Asbjorn Eide, Theodor Meron and Allan Rosas, "Combating Lawlessness in Gray Zone Conflicts Through Minimum Humanitarian Standards" (1995) 89(1) *American Journal of International Law* 216.

> the difficulties experienced in protecting human dignity in situations of internal violence that fall below the thresholds of applicability of international humanitarian instruments but with the margin of public emergency, . . . compounded by the inadequacy of the non-derogable provisions of human rights instruments, the weakness of international monitoring and control procedures, and the need to define the character of the conflict situations.[106]

The Declaration postulated an irreducible core of non-derogable humanitarian norms and human rights which are to be respected in all situations and at all times and which would weave a safety net based on the fundamental principle of humanity.[107] There was, however, no agreement on the legal nature of such norms, i.e., whether they are customary law (as most states thought), non-binding principles or altogether new rights.[108] After some debate, the term "fundamental" was chosen instead of the term "minimum," as the latter could have induced states to apply only the minimum of protection even where higher levels of protection would be legally warranted.[109] "Humanitarian standards applicable in all situations"[110] and "Universal Declaration of Humanitarian Law"[111] had been other suggestions for naming such a text. As for their content, the standards bridged human rights and humanitarian law.[112] The drafters had drawn on both bodies of law without necessarily giving preference to either of them or deciding on their relationship.[113]

The idea was to have the UN General Assembly formally adopt the Declaration, but the text never made it further up the UN hierarchy than the UN Commission on Human Rights, which, in 1995, recognized the need to address principles applicable to situations of internal and related violence, disturbance, tension and public emergency, but refrained from formally adopting the text.[114] Based on a recommendation made in a seminar on the standards in Cape Town in 1996, the Commission then asked the Secretary-General to seek

[106] Theodor Meron and Allan Rosas, "A Declaration of Minimum Humanitarian Standards" (1991) 85(2) *American Journal of International Law* 375.

[107] See Art. 1 of the Declaration: "This Declaration affirms minimum humanitarian standards which are applicable in all situations, including internal violence, disturbances, tensions, and public emergency, and which cannot be derogated from under any circumstances. These standards must be respected whether or not a state of emergency has been proclaimed."

[108] See Marco Odello, "Fundamental Standards of Humanity: A Common Language of International Humanitarian and Human Rights Law" in Roberta Arnold and Noelle Quénivet (eds.), *International Humanitarian Law and Human Rights Law: Towards a Merger in International Law* (Leiden: Nijhoff, 2008), p. 50.

[109] See ibid. p. 31.

[110] See *Report of the Sub-Commission on Prevention of Discrimination and Protection of Minorities*, UN Doc. E/CN.4/1997/77/Add.1 (28 January 1997), para. 47.

[111] Ibid. para. 77.

[112] Gasser, "International Humanitarian Law and Human Rights Law" (n. 30) 159. See also *Report of the Sub-Commission on Prevention of Discrimination and Protection of Minorities*, UN Doc. E/CN.4/1997/77/Add.1 (28 January 1997), para. 38.

[113] Odello, "Fundamental Standards of Humanity" (n. 108) pp. 21 and 55.

[114] With Commission on Human Rights Res. 1995/29, UN Doc. E/CN.4/RES/29 (3 March 1995), para. 1. See Martin Scheinin, *Turku/Abo Declaration of Minimum Humanitarian Standards (1990)*, International Council on Human Rights Policy Working Paper (2006), available at www.ichrp.org/files/papers/91/120B_-_Turku-Abo_Declaration_of_Minimum_Humanitarian_Standards_Scheinin__Martin__2005.pdf (last accessed 15 April 2014).

the views of states and submit a report to it on the matter.[115] In this report, the Secretary-General identified applicable international humanitarian law and international human rights law standards, discussed the advantages and disadvantages of what was now called "Fundamental Standards of Humanity" and commented on the possible nature and content of a respective legal instrument.[116]

The Secretary-General continued, on request of the Commission on Human Rights, to report regularly on this topic.[117] The most recent reports are compilations of developments in the area of protection of individuals affected by violence, and record the main rules and principles applicable in such situations.[118] They clearly recognize the interplay between international human rights law, international humanitarian law, international criminal law, international refugee law and other relevant bodies of law.[119] Yet, their only (repeated) conclusion is that there is no need for the adoption of new standards but rather for ensuring respect for existing standards.[120] Today, the notion of "fundamental standards of humanity" in the reports seems to have become a catchword for the interplay of human rights and humanitarian law.[121]

At the end, the whole project failed because it had come under attack from different sides: many governments felt uncomfortable (to say the least) to take on any new obligations in politically precarious situations such as internal strife or riots, while human rights organizations feared that existing human rights obligations might be watered down, and the ICRC was (again) concerned about blurring the lines between international humanitarian law and international human rights law obligations and feared for its mandate.[122] The process of seeking formal adoption in the UN has now seemingly come to a standstill, and the future of the Declaration is uncertain. The text could serve as an educational tool to alert parties to the conflict, in an accessible way, to the minimum norms they are bound to respect,[123] or it may be taken entirely from the UN's agenda and placed into the hands of interested non-governmental organizations (NGOs) in the hope of developing the text into a code of conduct akin to the Montreux

[115] Commission on Human Rights Res. 1997/21, UN Doc. E/CN.4/RES/1997/21 (11 April 1997); see also Odello, "Fundamental Standards of Humanity" (n. 108) p. 32.

[116] See *Analytical Report of the Secretary-General on Fundamental Standards of Humanity*, UN Doc. E/CN.4/1998/87 and Add 1 (5 January 1998).

[117] *Analytical Report of the Secretary-General on Fundamental Standards of Humanity*, UN Doc. E/CN.4/1999/92 (18 December 1999); UN Doc. E/CN.4/2000/94 (27 December 2000); UN Doc. E/CN.4/2001/91, UN Doc. E/CN.4/2002/103, UN Doc. E/CN.4/2004/90 (27 December 2000); UN Doc. E/CN.4/2006/87 (3 March 2006); UN Doc. A/HRC/7/62 (12 March 2008) (the report postpones the now biannual report to the eighth session of the Human Rights Council); UN Doc. A/HRC/8/14 (28 May 2008). No report has been submitted since.

[118] Odello, "Fundamental Standards of Humanity" (n. 108) p. 54.

[119] *Analytical Report of the Secretary-General on Fundamental Standards of Humanity*, UN Doc. E/CN.4/2006/87, para. 3.

[120] See, e.g., *Report of the Secretary-General on Fundamental Standards of Humanity*, UN Doc. A/HRC/8/14, para. 38.

[121] See Anna-Lena Svensson-McCarthy, "Minimum Humanitarian Standards: From Cape Town Towards the Future" (1994) 53 *Review of the International Commission of Jurists* 27.

[122] See Scheinin, "Turku/Abo Declaration" (n. 114) p. 3.

[123] See Jean-Daniel Vigny and Cecilia Thompson, "Fundamental Standards of Humanity: What Future?" (2002) 20(2) *Netherlands Quarterly of Human Rights* 198; and Scheinin, "Turku/Abo Declaration" (n. 114) 5.

Document on private military companies.[124] The gaps in the protection of civilians which had originally spurred the work on the Declaration have also narrowed, making further work in this area seem less pressing.[125] With the universal ratification of the Geneva Conventions and rising ratifications of the ICCPR and other human rights treaties, more states than ever are bound by humanitarian norms and the "ratification gap" in the protection of civilians has narrowed. In addition, the ICRC study on customary humanitarian law of 2005 has brought more clarity on customary law. The "derogation gap" has also narrowed through an increased understanding and acceptance of the limits of derogation, the agreement that even where human rights are derogated in situations of emergency their core content may remain applicable, and the acknowledgment that corollary procedural rights of derogated rights continue to apply. The gap in protective rules for internal conflicts has also been filled by the jurisprudence of ad hoc criminal tribunals which has made clear that many rules of international armed conflict apply to internal conflicts, while the rise of international criminal law has added a means of enforcing humanitarian norms in a way not imagined in the early stages of the project of Fundamental Standards of Humanity.

4.5 "Humanitarian rights": humanitarian law in human rights documents

The integration of human rights language and principles into humanitarian law documents, in particular in the Fourth Geneva Convention and in the Additional Protocols, had already demonstrated the potential compatibility of the two legal regimes. This development was mirrored with the adoption of the Convention on the Rights of the Child (CRC) in 1989, which started a process of integrating humanitarian norms into human rights documents. Article 38 of the Convention obliges states parties to respect and ensure respect for international humanitarian law and to take all feasible measures to ensure that persons under the age of fifteen do not directly take part in hostilities.[126] The expression "respect and ensure respect" is borrowed from Common Article 1 to the four Geneva Conventions.[127] Even though the provision was rightly criticized for not expressing the best interests of the

[124] See Emily Crawford, *Road to Nowhere? The Future for the Declaration on Fundamental Standards of Humanity*, Sydney Law School Legal Studies Research Paper No. 12/02 (2012), available at http://works.bepress.com/emily_crawford/2 (last accessed 15 April 2014); and Montreux Document on Pertinent International Legal Obligations and Good Practices for States related to Operations of Private and Security Military Companies during Armed Conflict, UN Doc. A/63/467 and S/2008/636 (6 October 2008), Annex.

[125] See Martin Scheinin, *Fundamental Standards of Humanity*, Background Paper to the International Expert Meeting, Stockholm, 22–24 February 2000, UN Doc. A/CN.4/2000/145, pp. 56–57.

[126] Convention on the Rights of the Child, 20 November 1989, 1577 UNTS 3, Art. 38: "1. States Parties undertake to respect and to ensure respect for rules of international humanitarian law applicable to them in armed conflicts which are relevant to the child. 2. States Parties shall take all feasible measures to ensure that persons who have not attained the age of fifteen years do not take a direct part in hostilities. 3. States Parties shall refrain from recruiting any person who has not attained the age of fifteen years into their armed forces. In recruiting among those persons who have attained the age of fifteen years but who have not attained the age of eighteen years, States Parties shall endeavour to give priority to those who are oldest. 4. In accordance with their obligations under international humanitarian law to protect the civilian population in armed conflicts, States Parties shall take all feasible measures to ensure protection and care of children who are affected by an armed conflict."

[127] See Sharon Detrick, *A Commentary on the United Nations Convention on the Rights of the Child* (The Hague: Nijhoff, 1999), pp. 650– 51.

child as the age limit should have been eighteen,[128] it became clear that the dichotomy between human rights as peace-time treaties and humanitarian law as war-time treaties was no longer tenable.[129]

The provision regulates a matter which concerns both international human rights law and international humanitarian law and effectively carries over Article 77(2) of Additional Protocol I.[130] Specific as the provision is, it nevertheless demonstrates that obligations of states in armed conflict can no longer be measured by international humanitarian law alone but that international human rights law needs to be taken into account and can potentially also supersede or replace international humanitarian law obligations.[131] In the same spirit, the Commentary to Article 77 of Additional Protocol I had already argued that this provision is about human rights as it:

> serves as a development of both the fourth Geneva Convention and of other rules of international law which govern the protection of fundamental human rights in time of armed conflict, particularly the International Covenant of 1966 on Civil and Political Rights and the Declaration on the Rights of the Child.[132]

The Optional Protocol to the Convention on the Rights of the Child on the involvement of children in armed conflict repeats this provision of the CRC with a higher age limit.[133] It obliges states parties to take measures to ensure that children below the age of eighteen do not directly participate in hostilities (Article 1) and are not recruited for military service (Article 2), and it asks states to raise the minimum limit of fifteen years for voluntary recruitment (except for military academies, Article 3). This provision also applies to non-state armed groups and obliges them not to recruit or use children under eighteen, and obliges states parties to prohibit and criminalize such acts of non-state armed groups (Article 4). For states parties to the Protocol, the lower standard of international humanitarian law is thus replaced by the higher standard of international human rights law; another example of the complementarity of the two legal regimes.[134]

In addition, the Optional Protocol's Preamble requires all states to abide by the provisions of international humanitarian law,[135] while Article 5 contains another reference to

128 See, e.g., Hans-Joachim Heintze, "Die völkerrechtliche Stellung des Kindes im bewaffneten Konflikt" (1991) 3 *Journal of International Law of Peace and Armed Conflict* 92; and Matthew Happold, "The Optional Protocol to the Convention on the Rights of Children on the Involvement of Children in Armed Conflict" (2000) 3 *Yearbook of International Humanitarian Law* 227.

129 See Hans-Joachim Heintze, "Konsequenzen der Konvergenz von Menschenrechtsschutz und humanitärem Völkerrecht" in Horst Fischer, Ulrike Froissart, Wolff Heinegg von Heintschel and Christian Raap (eds.), *Krisensicherung und humanitärer Schutz / Crisis Management and Humanitarian Protection. Festschrift für Dieter Fleck* (Berlin: Berliner Wissenschaftsverlag, 2004), p. 245.

130 Additional Protocol I, Art. 77: "Protection of children: 1. Children shall be the object of special respect and shall be protected against any form of indecent assault. The Parties to the conflict shall provide them with the care and aid they require, whether because of their age or for any other reason."

131 See Hans-Joachim Heintze, "Theories on the Relationship between International Humanitarian Law and Human Rights Law" in Robert Kolb and Gloria Gaggioli (eds.), *Research Handbook on Human Rights and Humanitarian Law* (Cheltenham: Edward Elgar, 2013), p. 62.

132 Sandoz, Swinarski and Zimmermann, *Commentary on the Additional Protocols* (n. 91) para. 3176.

133 Optional Protocol to Convention on the Rights of the Child on the Involvement of Children in Armed Conflict, 25 May 2000, 2173 UNTS 222.

134 See Heintze, "Konsequenzen der Konvergenz" (n. 129) pp. 246–47.

135 Optional Protocol to the CRC on the Involvement of Children in Armed Conflict, Preamble.

humanitarian law.[136] In light of such provisions and subsequent developments in law and practice, it has thus been argued that in the field of children's rights in armed conflict, international humanitarian law and international human rights law are largely congruent.[137] It should also be noted that the 26th International Conference of the Red Cross in 1995, which followed the entry into force of the CRC, supported the Optional Protocol to the CRC in this respect.[138]

It has occasionally been argued that this is only the exception which proves the rule that human rights and humanitarian law are incompatible.[139] This seems hardly tenable, given the explicit will of the drafters and of states to allow precisely for such a complementarity. There is also a range of other legal texts adopted later which likewise transcend the distinction between international humanitarian law and international human rights law.[140] The African Charter on the Rights and Welfare of the Child obliges states to "respect and ensure respect for rules of international humanitarian law applicable in armed conflicts which affect the child."[141] In particular, states have to take all measures to ensure that children do not directly participate in hostilities, are not recruited in the armed forces and are generally protected and cared for in all situations of conflict, whether international or internal, and in internal tension and strife.[142] The Convention on the Rights of Persons with Disabilities (CRPD) obliges states parties "under international law, including international humanitarian law and international human rights law, all necessary measures to ensure the protection and safety of persons with disabilities in situations of risk, including situations of armed conflict, humanitarian emergencies and the occurrence of natural disasters."[143] The Cluster Munitions Convention mirrors this with a reference to the Convention on the Rights of Persons with Disabilities in its Preamble (and to human rights law in its provision on victim assistance).[144]

The Convention for the Protection of All Persons from Enforced Disappearance (CED) has also taken on board the right to know the whereabouts of disappeared persons as

[136] Optional Protocol to the CRC, Art. 5: "Nothing in the present Protocol shall be construed as precluding provisions in the law of a State Party or in international instruments and international humanitarian law that are more conducive to the realization of the rights of the child."

[137] See, e.g., Vesselin Popovski, "Protection of Children in International Humanitarian Law and Human Rights Law" in Roberta Arnold and Noelle Quénivet (eds.), *International Humanitarian Law and Human Rights Law: Towards a Merger in International Law* (Leiden: Nijhoff, 2008), p. 420.

[138] See Kalshoven and Zegveld, *Constraints on the Waging of War* (n. 35) p. 216.

[139] See Michael J. Dennis, "Application of Civil and Political Rights Treaties Extraterritorially during Times of Armed Conflict" (2007) 40(2) *Israel Law Review* 501.

[140] See Darryl Robinson and Valerie Oosterveld, "The Evolution of Humanitarian Law" in Rob McRae and Don Hubert (eds.), *Human Security and the New Diplomacy: Protecting People, Promoting Peace* (Montreal: McGill-Queen's University Press, 2001), pp. 164–66.

[141] African Charter on the Rights and Welfare of the Child, 11 July 1990, OAU Doc.CAB/LEG/24.9/49 (1990), Art. 22.

[142] Ibid.

[143] Convention on the Rights of Persons with Disabilities, 13 December 2006, 2515 UNTS 3, Art. 11.

[144] Cluster Munition Convention, Preamble and Art. 5(1): "Each State Party with respect to cluster munition victims in areas under its jurisdiction shall, in accordance with applicable international humanitarian and human rights law, adequately provide age- and gender-sensitive assistance, including medical care, rehabilitation and psychological support, as well as provide for their social and economic inclusion."

stipulated in Additional Protocol I and Geneva Convention IV in its Article 18.[145] Article 33 of Additional Protocol I obliges states to search for missing persons of the adverse party and provides for detailed procedural steps to be taken as a legal obligation of all parties concerned for such searches, and similar but more extensive provisions can be found in CED, Article 18 which extends the protective reach of Article 33 of Additional Protocol I. Geneva Convention IV, Article 106 is even more specific as it obliges states to allow interned persons to send an internment card with information on the location of detention and health conditions to the detained person's family and to the ICRC Central Tracing Agency.[146] The right to know the facts surrounding human rights violations is also part of the Basic Principles and Guidelines on the Right to a Remedy and Reparations for Victims of Gross Violations of International Human Rights Law and Serious Violations of International Humanitarian Law, which clearly combine both legal regimes.[147]

The Guiding Principles on Internal Displacement also link international humanitarian law and international human rights law and join them together with refugee law.[148] The Islamic Declaration of Human Rights, adopted by the Islamic Conference of Ministers of Foreign Affairs in April 1990, reads in parts like an international humanitarian law document. While the text is rightly criticized for its ambiguous language which departs from the universal character of human rights, it applies to persons who do not participate in fighting and provides protection for the aged, women and children, the wounded, sick and prisoners, as well as rules on the means of combat.[149]

The Vienna Declaration and Programme of Action of 1993 (the outcome of the World Conference on Human Rights in Vienna in 1993) also explicitly mentions international humanitarian law and highlights the role of Geneva Convention IV in securing respect for human rights, particularly in situations of occupation and with regard to children and humanitarian access, calls upon the UN advisory services and technical assistance to include international humanitarian law, and emphasizes the importance of the Additional Protocols and the role of the UN in ensuring adherence to international humanitarian law.[150]

4.6 International Committee of the Red Cross and "Fundamental Guarantees"

On 16 October 1990, the UN General Assembly decided to invite the ICRC as an observer at the UN.[151] This was the first time that observer status was granted to a non-governmental

[145] Convention for the Protection of All Persons from Enforced Disappearance, UN Doc. A/61/448, UNTS 2715.

[146] Geneva Convention IV, Art. 106; see also Droege, "The Interplay" (n. 46) 343.

[147] Basic Principles and Guidelines on the Right to a Remedy and Reparation for Victims of Gross Violations of International Human Rights Law and Serious Violations of International Humanitarian Law, General Assembly Res. 60/147, UN Doc. GA/Res/60/147 (16 December 2005).

[148] On the interconnectedness of these legal regimes in the Guiding Principles see Antônio Augusto, *Cançado Trindade, International Law of Humankind: Towards a New Jus Gentium* (Leiden: Nijhoff, 2010), pp. 518–20.

[149] Cairo Declaration on Human Rights in Islam (5 August 1990), UN Doc. A/CONF.157/PC/62/Add.18 (1993), Art. 3.

[150] See Vienna Declaration and Programme of Action, UN Doc. A/CONF.157/23 (12 July 1993), paras. 3, 23, 29, 38, 50, 56, 79, 82 and 96. See also Roman Jasica, "Internationales humanitäres Recht und Menschenrechte" (1994) 1 *Journal of International Law of Peace and Armed Conflict* 5.

[151] See General Assembly Res. 45/6, UN Doc. A/RES/45/6 (16 October 1990).

organization, a decision which was explained by the special nature of the ICRC.[152] The Explanatory Report annexed to the resolution notes that "the tasks of ICRC and the United Nations increasingly complement one another and cooperation between the two institutions is closer, both in their field activities and in their efforts to enhance respect for international humanitarian law."[153] The ICRC began to seek closer cooperation with UN agencies such as UNICEF, the United Nations Children's Fund and the UN High Commissioner for Refugees (UNHCR), and the UN and the ICRC began to cooperate in the field.[154] It was another step towards closing the rift between the ICRC and the UN, and with it came a new interest of the ICRC in human rights.

The 1998 *Avenir* Statement of the ICRC confirmed this approach by adding the goal of strengthening dialogue with other players to three other strategic goals (restoring respect for humanitarian values, bringing humanitarian action close to the victims and increasing efficiency).[155] Inevitably, this provided new opportunities to reconsider the ICRC's diffident attitude towards human rights.[156] Then ICRC President Cornelio Sommaruga considered this growing emphasis on human rights to have a positive effect on the organization.[157] The *Avenir* Statement also called for strengthening the relationship between international humanitarian law and international human rights law as a way to ensure that the Geneva Conventions and Additional Protocols remain relevant.[158]

Already in the 1980s, the ICRC had adopted Doctrines (internal documents which provide guidance to staff on various matters) on issues of human rights, even though without using human rights terminology.[159] In more recent Doctrines, such as Doctrine DOCT/63-2006/1 of 2006, a range of human rights are explicitly identified, to which the ICRC might want to refer in its activities, although the organization is careful to emphasize its distinctiveness.[160] Even so, over the years, the link between the ICRC and the UN human

152 See Wilfried Remans, "The Granting of Observer Status by the General Assembly of the United Nations to the International Federation of the Red Cross and Red Crescent Societies" in Karel Wellens (ed.), *International Law: Theory and Practice, Essays in Honour of Eric Suy* (The Hague: Nijhoff, 1998), pp. 347–62.

153 Explanatory Report, Annex to General Assembly Res. 45/6, UN Doc. A/RES/45/6 (16 October 1990), para. 12.

154 See Bertrand Ramcharan, *The United Nations High Commissioner for Human Rights and International Humanitarian Law*, Program on Humanitarian Policy and Conflict Research, Harvard University, Occasional Paper Series No. 3 (2005), p. 22.

155 See David P. Forsythe, "1949 and 1999: Making the Geneva Conventions Relevant after the Cold War" (1999) 81(834) *International Review of the Red Cross* 272.

156 See David P. Forsythe, "Human Rights and the International Committee of the Red Cross" (1990) 12(2) *Human Rights Quarterly* 288.

157 Cornelio Sommaruga, "Respect for International Humanitarian Law: ICRC Review of Five Years of Activity (1987–1991)" (1992) 32(286) *International Review of the Red Cross* 77.

158 Forsythe, "1949 and 1999" (n. 155) 270–71.

159 See, e.g., DOCT/34-1985/5 (8 July 1985) on judicial guarantees; DOCT/50-1988/5 (1 May 1993) on detention conditions; DOCT /4-1993/1 (1 May 1993) on situations of internal violence; DOCT/56-1996/1 (29 May 1996) on judicial proceedings in situations of detention and imprisonment; DOCT/28-2003/5 (8 May 2003) on disappeared persons; and DOCT/15-2005/10 (11 April 2005) on *demarches* in case of violations of international humanitarian law and other fundamental protective rules; see Sergey Sayapin, "The International Committee of the Red Cross and International Human Rights Law" (2009) 9(1) *Human Rights Law Review* 98.

160 *The Invocation of International Human Rights Law by the International Committee of the Red Cross*, DOCT/63-2006/1 (25 August 2006), see Sayapin, "The International Committee of the Red Cross" (n. 159) 98.

rights system has become closer, and the ICRC President and the UN High Commissioner for Human Rights now meet regularly.[161]

Today, the organization considers issues such as non-discrimination; violence against life, physical and psychological integrity; torture and inhuman or degrading treatment or punishment; inhumane detention conditions; slavery and forced labour; children's right to education; arbitrary arrest and detention; judicial guarantees; family rights; enforced disappearance; deportation and arbitrary exile; and deprivation of property, as situations which require resort to international human rights law in addition to international humanitarian law.[162] But when it comes to applying the law, the ICRC applies either international humanitarian law or no law at all (and instead offers its humanitarian services). Despite arguing for the complementarity of human rights and humanitarian law, the organization continues to emphasize the differences between international humanitarian law and international human rights and the *lex specialis* nature of humanitarian law which it sees as "indispensable"[163] for determining their relationship. And it points out that "[b]eyond this general approach the organisation sees many intricate questions open which can only be identified and answered on a case-by-case basis."[164]

On the other hand, human rights figure prominently in a range of recent studies conducted under the auspices of the ICRC and published by the organization. The most important of them is arguably the study on customary humanitarian law, published in 2005.[165] In 1996, the ICRC initiated a process to identify existing customary humanitarian law and present it in the form of simple rules. The document is a response to the increased interest in customary humanitarian law to regulate internal armed conflicts.[166] It brings together 161 rules which have been identified as a reflection of state practice and *opinio juris*.[167]

Chapter 32 of the study, entitled "Fundamental Guarantees," identifies nineteen such rules: humane treatment of civilians and persons *hors de combat* (Rule 87) and prohibition of the following acts: discrimination on the grounds of race, colour, sex, language, religion or belief, political or other opinion, national or social origin, birth or other status, or any other similar criteria (Rule 88); murder (Rule 89); torture, cruel or inhuman treatment and

161 See Ramcharan, *The United Nations High Commissioner* (n. 154) pp. 38–39.

162 See in greater detail Sayapin, "The International Committee of the Red Cross" (n. 159) 99–126.

163 International Committee of the Red Cross, *International Humanitarian Law and the Challenges of Contemporary Armed Conflicts, Report to the 31st International Conference of the Red Cross and Red Crescent* (2011), p. 14. See also Jakob Kellenberger, "Protection Through Complementarity of the Law" in International Institute of Humanitarian Law (ed.), *International Humanitarian Law and Other Legal Regimes: Interplay in Situations of Violence. Challenges and Prospects. 27th Round Table on Current Problems of International Humanitarian Law, Sanremo, 4–6 September 2003* (Sanremo: International Institute of Humanitarian Law, 2003), p. 22.

164 ICRC, *International Humanitarian Law and the Challenges of Contemporary Armed Conflicts* (n. 163) p. 14.

165 Jean-Marie Henckaerts and Louise Doswald-Beck, *Customary International Humanitarian Law*, vol. I, *Rules* and vol. II, *Practice* (Cambridge: Cambridge University Press, 2005).

166 See Schindler, "International Humanitarian Law" (n. 59) 178.

167 It must be noted that despite support of studies from states and academic circles, some states have criticized the study as not necessarily representing the consent of all states as to its methodology and result. The United States had particular concern that not all rules would indeed reflect customary law, see Walter Kälin, "The ICRC's Compilation of the Customary Rules of Humanitarian Law" in Thomas Giegerich (ed.), *A Wiser Century? Judicial Dispute Settlement, Disarmament and the Laws of War 100 Years after the Second Hague Peace Conference* (Berlin: Duncker&Humblot, 2009), pp. 419–21.

outrages upon personal dignity, in particular humiliation and degrading treatment (Rule 90); corporal punishment (Rule 91); mutilation, medical or scientific experiments or any other medical procedure not indicated by the state of health of the person concerned and not consistent with generally accepted medical standards (Rule 92); rape and other forms of sexual violence (Rule 93); slavery and the slave trade in all their forms (Rule 94); uncompensated or abusive forced labour (Rule 95); hostage-taking (Rule 96); use of human shields (Rule 97); enforced disappearance (Rule 98); arbitrary deprivation of liberty (Rule 99); conviction or sentence without a fair trial affording all essential judicial guarantees (Rule 100); *nulla poena sine lege* (accusation or conviction of a criminal offence on account of any omission which did not constitute a criminal offence under national or international law at the time it was committed) and imposition of heavier penalties than that which was applicable at the time the criminal offence was committed (Rule 101); conviction of an offence not on the basis of individual criminal responsibility (Rule 102); and collective punishment (Rule 103). The study also asks for respect for the convictions and religious practices of civilians and persons *hors de combat* (Rule 104) and respect for family life as far as possible (Rule 105).[168]

The term "Fundamental Guarantees" used in the study is not a legal term of art (although it appears in the titles of Article 75 of Additional Protocol I and Article 4 of Additional Protocol II) but is rather used as "a label and a way of bringing together certain rules which have something in common."[169] The Guarantees are, in the words of the study's main authors, "overarching rules that apply to all persons at all times."[170] While the study presents the Fundamental Guarantees as part of international humanitarian law applicable in international and non-international armed conflicts, it often resorts to international human rights law (i.e., human rights treaties and other instruments as well as human rights case law) to define their respective content.[171] The authors highlight that the Fundamental Guarantees stem from "extensive State practice to the effect that human rights law must be applied during armed conflicts."[172] The study takes it for granted that international human rights law continues to apply in armed conflict and emphasizes that since UN General Assembly Resolution 2625 of 1970,[173] it has become accepted practice for the General Assembly, the Security Council and the Commission on Human Rights to condemn human rights violations taking place during armed conflicts. The study refers to the jurisprudence of the European Court of Human Rights[174] and resolutions on human rights of the General Assembly, the Security Council, the Commission on Human Rights and the Human Rights Council in respect of Afghanistan, Iraq, Sudan, the Russian Federation, the former

[168] Henckaerts and Doswald-Beck, *Customary International Humanitarian Law* (n. 165) vol. I, pp. 299–383.

[169] Françoise Hampson, "Fundamental Guarantees" in Elizabeth Wilmshurst and Susan Breau (eds.), *Perspectives on the ICRC Study on Customary International Humanitarian Law* (Cambridge: Cambridge University Press, 2007), p. 282.

[170] Henckaerts and Doswald-Beck, *Customary International Humanitarian Law* (n. 165) vol. I, p. 299.

[171] Henckaerts and Doswald-Beck, *Customary International Humanitarian Law* (n. 165) vol. II, pp. 1986–2536.

[172] Henckaerts and Doswald-Beck, *Customary International Humanitarian Law* (n. 165) vol. I, p. 303.

[173] General Assembly Res. 2675 (XXV), UN Doc. GA/Res. 2675 (XXV) (9 December 1970), entitled "Basic principles for the protection of civilian populations in armed conflicts."

[174] For examples see Heike Krieger, "A Conflict of Norms: The Relationship between Humanitarian Law and Human Rights Law in the ICRC Customary Law Study" (2006) 11(2) *Journal of Conflict and Security Law* 278.

Yugoslavia, Uganda, Liberia, Sierra Leone, the Occupied Palestinian Territory and Kuwait.[175]

The use of human rights language in the ICRC study is obvious, and it has been highlighted that the use of international human rights law to interpret international humanitarian law works well with regard to concepts firmly rooted in international humanitarian law, such as respect for religious convictions and practices or human rights concepts such as the right to family life.[176] The study is somewhat ambiguous towards the principle of *lex specialis*: on the one hand, it argues for resorting to the principle so as to shield important principles of humanitarian law, such as the rules on precautions in attack or the right to life, from an interpretation solely through the lens of human rights. On the other hand, the study seems to backtrack from the *lex specialis* rule and the idea that international humanitarian law dominates over international human rights law and instead suggests that international human rights law impacts on and influences international humanitarian law and the two are largely congruent, in particular in situations of occupation.[177]

The 2009 ICRC Interpretative Guidance on Direct Participation in Hostilities (the outcome of an expert consultation process convened by the TMC Asser Institute which resulted in three reports without an agreed outcome) also sees human rights as governing the use of force in armed conflicts in addition to international humanitarian law.[178] In a controversial recommendation on "Restraints in the Use of Force" the Interpretative Guidance argued that "the absence of an unfettered 'right' to kill does not necessarily imply a legal obligation to capture rather than kill regardless of circumstances."[179] This suggestion has been criticized heavily on the grounds that it introduces an (unacceptable) human rights standard in the way in which international humanitarian law governs the use of force.[180]

In its study on *Strengthening the Legal Protection of Victims of Armed Conflict*, submitted to the 31st International Conference of the Red Cross and Red Crescent Societies in October 2011, the ICRC identified the protection of persons deprived of their liberty and monitoring compliance of international humanitarian law as the main challenges ahead.[181] In both areas human rights play an important, albeit contentious role, as the ICRC admits.[182] Even so, the ICRC was anxious to maintain its position that:

> international human rights law cannot entirely make up for the deficiencies that may exist in international humanitarian law, and the ICRC remains convinced that the latter,

[175] See Henckaerts and Doswald-Beck, *Customary International Humanitarian Law* (n. 165) vol. I, pp. 303–4.

[176] See Krieger, "A Conflict of Norms" (n. 174) 278. [177] Ibid. 277.

[178] See ICRC, Interpretative Guidance on the Notion of Direct Participation in Hostilities (2009). For a critical view see Charles H.B. Garraway, "'To Kill or not to Kill': Dilemmas in the Use of Force" (2010) 14 (3) *Journal of Conflict and Security Law* 504.

[179] See ICRC, Interpretative Guidance on the Notion of Direct Participation in Hostilities (2009), p. 78.

[180] See, e.g., W. Hays Parks, "Part IX of the ICRC 'Direct Participation in Hostilities' Study: No Mandate, No Expertise, and Legally Incorrect" (2010) 42(3) *New York University Journal of International Law and Politics* 769.

[181] International Committee of the Red Cross, *Strengthening Legal Protection for Victims of Armed Conflict, International Conference of the Red Cross and Red Crescent Societies (28 November–1 December 2011)*, ICRC Doc. 31IC/11/5.1.1 (October 2011), pp. 8–16. Environmental protection in armed conflicts and protection of displaced persons were two other areas identified as such challenges in the document but unlike the former two issues were not accepted by states as primary areas for future development, see pp. 16–24.

[182] ICRC, *Strengthening Legal Protection for Victims of Armed Conflict* (n. 181) p. 7.

as a universal legal regime that is binding on all the parties to a conflict and from which there can be no derogation, must be adapted as such to meet the challenges of contemporary armed conflicts.[183]

4.7 Role of civil society

Despite the involvement of the ICRC, the law of armed conflict was and still is predominantly a law "made by the military for the military of established military powers."[184] But as in other fields of international law, global civil society organizations, activist movements, NGO coalitions and networks of states and non-state actors play an increasingly important role in law-making on humanitarian issues.[185] The drafting processes of the Conventions on landmines and cluster munitions are examples of such multi-stakeholder law-making processes. Beyond law-making, human rights NGOs also actively and regularly resort to humanitarian law when criticizing states' behaviour in situations of violence. Unlike the ICRC, the guardian of humanitarian law, on the one hand, and human rights bodies with their human rights-based mandate on the other hand, NGOs need not necessarily worry about using human rights and humanitarian language interchangeably to denounce violations of human dignity, at least as long as their constituencies do not disagree.[186] Such combined reference to obligations and violations of human rights and humanitarian law has indeed become commonplace in many NGO statements on conflict situations, since NGOs began to issue reports on human rights and humanitarian law violations in conflicts all over the world in the 1970s.[187]

Human Rights Watch was at the forefront of this development, and today the organization considers itself competent and able to monitor violations not only of human rights but also of international humanitarian law.[188] Not all human rights NGOs followed suit immediately: Amnesty International and the International Commission of Jurists, for example, kept well away from international humanitarian law, refused to report on international humanitarian law violations and decided not to participate in the ICRC's preparatory work for the Additional Protocols.[189] This has changed over time, and many human rights NGOs have now developed substantial expertise in international humanitarian law, publicly demand respect for it, and refer to it when alerting international human rights monitoring bodies and criminal courts and tribunals to situations in which civilians are under threat.[190]

[183] Ibid. p. 25.

[184] Michael Bothe, "Durchsetzung der Menschenrechte und des humanitären Völkerrechts – ein Paradigmenwechsel?" in Thilo Marauhn (ed.), *Die Rechtsstellung des Menschen im Völkerrecht* (Tübingen: Mohr, 2003), p. 126 (translated from German).

[185] See Forsythe, *The Humanitarians* (n. 3) pp. 263–64.

[186] See Rachel Brett, "The Role of NGOs" in International Institute of Humanitarian Law (ed.), *Strengthening Measures for the Respect and Implementation of International Humanitarian Law and Other Rules Protecting Human Dignity in Armed Conflict*, 28th Round Table on Current Problems of International Humanitarian Law, Sanremo, 2–4 September 2004 (Sanremo: International Institute of Humanitarian Law, 2004), p. 40.

[187] See David Weissbrodt, "The Role of International Organizations in the Implementation of Human Rights and Humanitarian Law in Situations of Armed Conflict" (1988) 21 *Vanderbilt Journal of Transnational Law* 318.

[188] See Best, *War and Law Since 1945* (n. 12) p. 383. [189] Ibid. p. 385.

[190] See Habib Slim, "Les moyens de mise en oeuvre du droit international humanitaire: rôle des organisations non gouvernementales" in International Institute of Humanitarian Law (ed.),

The approach of NGOs to international humanitarian law, as well as their role in securing adherence to the law and exposing violations, has changed considerably over the past decades. Their methodologies of fact-finding were refined through the use of technology such as satellite imagery and GPS devices, social networking and the application of social-science based analytical methods to gather information in conflict areas. Increased legal and technical expertise in international humanitarian law is now available in many NGOs and regular contacts with military analysts and theorists, including the integration of military experts into human rights NGOs, allow more accurate damage assessment and calculations of the number of victims. This has, in turn, increased the pressure on NGOs to ensure accuracy, independence, impartiality and accountability for their reports.[191]

The way in which human rights NGOs have established themselves as new players in a field so far exclusively occupied by the institutions and communities of international humanitarian law was, however, not warmly welcomed by everybody. The intrusion of human rights NGOs into hitherto closed circles of military experts, in particular, has met with scepticism and suspicion from all sides: when NGOs cooperate with the military (perhaps in the hope of exercising beneficial influence on the protection of civilians) they are likely to put themselves up for critique by their own constituency, while humanitarian circles may view their activities with as much scepticism as the military.[192] In practice, NGOs still have a long way to go to become fully accepted dinner guests at high-level international humanitarian law events, as their repeated complaints demonstrate.[193] But their growing importance in monitoring violations and shaping the law is another step in bringing human rights and humanitarian law closer together.

4.8 Humanity as grace and humanity as right

The foundational considerations and values upon which the rules for warfare rested throughout history are not static, as has been demonstrated in this chapter. They have changed and evolved over time, and the ideas which informed the law of war and the law of peace were not isolated but communicated with each other. The medieval rules on the conduct of hostilities, on the lawful means and methods of warfare and on the protection of civilians were derived from Christian faith, based on considerations of mercy and compassion and carried by the ethical code of chivalry. Limits on the use of force were accepted more for the sake of one's own soul than out of concern for universal human dignity.

Strengthening Measures for the Respect and Implementation of International Humanitarian Law and Other Rules Protecting Human Dignity in Armed Conflict, 28th Round Table on Current Problems of International Humanitarian Law, Sanremo, 2–4 September 2004 (Sanremo: International Institute of Humanitarian Law, 2004), pp. 75–80.

191 See Dinah Pokempner, "Recognizing and Furthering the Role of NGOs in International Humanitarian Law" in International Institute of Humanitarian Law (ed.), *Strengthening Measures for the Respect and Implementation of International Humanitarian Law and Other Rules Protecting Human Dignity in Armed Conflict*, 28th Round Table on Current Problems of International Humanitarian Law, Sanremo, 2–4 September 2004 (Sanremo: International Institute of Humanitarian Law, 2004), p. 47.

192 See Arne Willy Dahl, "The Role of Non-Governmental Organizations in Strengthening the Respect of International Humanitarian Law" in International Institute of Humanitarian Law (ed.), *Strengthening Measures for the Respect and Implementation of International Humanitarian Law and Other Rules Protecting Human Dignity in Armed Conflict*, 28th Round Table on Current Problems of International Humanitarian Law, Sanremo, 2–4 September 2004 (Sanremo: International Institute of Humanitarian Law, 2004), p. 53.

193 See Pokempner, "Recognizing and Furthering the Role of NGOs" (n. 191) pp. 49–50.

Humanity was a religious duty as much as it was the privilege of a noble class of warriors, and rules on warfare were derived from faith and mercy as much as they were a pragmatic means at the disposal of professional soldiers. War was the norm and not the exception, driven by a chivalric elite which thrived by keeping wars going. Concern for human rights in a modern sense as universal individual entitlements had no place in a medieval worldview.[194]

When the law of war was codified from the 1860s onwards within a rational humanitarian worldview, humanity was understood as the progress of civilization. One may see this as "the idea of human rights, though perhaps not under that name."[195] But effectively the idea of human rights and their expression in the European Enlightenment had only limited influence on the development of the laws of war and their codification. But occasionally, the emerging idea of human rights – as natural law, common interest and universally shared human dignity, advocated by cosmopolitan and liberal thinkers – influenced and challenged the emerging law of war to go beyond orchestrating the honourable duelling of warring parties and facilitating the orchestration of battles. These early ideas of human rights could swirl the waters of the legal mainstream of the law of war but not really alter its course. Still, there were areas in which the two emerging legal regimes would meet.

Humanitarian law was ahead of human rights as the only international legal framework which accommodated the fate of individuals. Its legal force and practical impact was unmatched by the still utopian ideas and academic debates on human rights. At the same time, humanitarian law was not a blueprint for human rights as the two ideas differed in their objectives: human rights wanted to change society while humanitarian law wanted to change war. But in doing so, humanitarian law had to deal with matters which later would be expressed in the language of human rights. It concerned itself with the place of individuals affected by state-conducted violence, their natural right to security, dignity and well-being, the boundaries of state sovereignty and the protective obligations of states towards individuals in distress. Humanitarian law demonstrated to the forerunners of the human rights movement that individual needs could be put on the international agenda and formulated as international law.

With the emergence of the human rights regime after 1945, the newly crafted humanitarian law was steered away from its medieval roots of charity and chivalry as well as its self-perception as a tool for regulating warfare as a means of politics in the nineteenth century. For the founding fathers of the law of armed conflict (or at least its humanitarian strand), charity had been the main impulse to restrain the use of force, and for the military, humanity in war could only be understood as professional ethos and corollary to military necessity. Humanitarian law consisted, and for many still consists, of "good deeds carried out for reasons of humanity, not pursuant to any categorical legal imperative."[196] The

[194] See Suter, "An Enquiry into the Meaning of the Phrase" (n. 22) 405–14.

[195] Frits Kalshoven, "Human Rights, the Law of Armed Conflicts and Reprisals" (1975) 11(121) *International Review of the Red Cross* 183. For similar arguments see W.A. Solf, "Human Rights in Armed Conflict: Some Observations on the Relationship of Human Rights Law to the Law of Armed Conflict" in Henry Hyunwook Han (ed.), *World in Transition: Challenges to Human Rights, Development and World Order* (Washington, DC: University Press of America, 1979), p. 43, who sees an overlap of those ideas.

[196] Christina Cerna, "The History of the Inter-American System's Jurisprudence as Regards Situations of Armed Conflict" (2011) 2(1) *Journal of International Humanitarian Legal Studies* 4.

protection of civilians still contains such historic remnants of humanity perceived as grace and fairness in combat. The very notion "innocent," so often attached to civilians injured in warfare, is a reminder of this legacy: from a moral-philosophical point of view an "innocent" civilian has to be protected not because he or she has any entitlement, right or claim to be left unharmed, but because it would be disreputable for the ethical warrior to injury anyone else than the rightful opponent in a fair and honourable fight.[197]

Human rights introduced the idea of an individual entitlement to dignity into these considerations. From the start, international human rights law was "claiming rights rather than asking for grace."[198] As a consequence, the very idea of humanity and humanitarianism began to move away from a grace extended by the powerful to a right being demanded by the self-conscious citizen. Today, such universal human dignity is undoubtedly the foundation of humanity in war.[199] As today's "hegemonic moral discourse,"[200] human rights inform also the very idea of humanity in warfare and the rules resulting from it, locating them no longer in ethical considerations such as chivalry and honour and in the virtues of mercy and charity but in human dignity as an inalienable right of humans.

The separation of the two fields after 1945 soon gave way to the recognition of their complementarity and interaction, and since then, the development has indeed gone "from mutual suspicion and disinterest to ... mutual cooperation and progressive inter-penetration of international humanitarian law and international human rights law."[201] This can already be traced in the Geneva Conventions of 1949 and certainly in the Additional Protocols of 1977. Subsequent developments in law, policy, jurisprudence and practice confirm this complementarity. The development took a while to be realized:

> [b]ecause the two legal streams had such different sources, protagonists, and preoccupations, their community of interest took some years to be realized and generally admitted; but by the turn of the 1980s it was becoming popularly admitted to such effect that careful people found it desirable to recall the differences as well as the similarities.[202]

The ethos, language and law of human rights thus exercises considerable pull on established concepts and norms of international humanitarian law. This is all the more important as there is no formal revision of international humanitarian law to be expected anytime soon. Indeed, it remains doubtful if a formal revision of international humanitarian law in line with historic law-making events is necessary and beneficial, as such a reform may weaken

[197] See Gabriella Blum, "The Dispensable Lives of Soldiers" (2012) 2(1) *Journal of Legal Analysis* 91, with reference to the Hobbesian view that honour is the only law applicable in war.

[198] Partsch, "Human Rights and Humanitarian Law" (n. 26) p. 912.

[199] See, e.g., *Prosecutor* v. *Anto Furundžija*, IT-95_17/1.T, International Criminal Tribunal for the Former Yugoslavia, Judgment of 10 December 1998, para. 183, where the Court emphasized that the principle of human dignity is the "basic underpinning" of international human rights and international humanitarian law.

[200] See Roger Normand and Sarah Zaidi, *Human Rights at the UN: The Political History of Universal Justice* (Bloomington, IN: Indiana University Press, 2008), p. 8.

[201] Robert Kolb and Richard Hyde, *An Introduction to the International Law of Armed Conflict* (Oxford: Hart, 2008), p. 274.

[202] Best, *War and Law Since 1945* (n. 12) p. 69.

rather than strengthen protection.[203] As a result of the developments described in this chapter, *jus in bello* has become increasingly human rights-oriented, and international human rights law now seems to provide "the beacons within which the law of war continues to develop."[204] The scope and depth of such a human rights-oriented humanitarian law is, however, only beginning to emerge. Its legal challenges, policy implications and operational consequences will be analyzed in the following chapters.

[203] See, e.g., Kenneth Watkin, "21st Century Conflict and International Humanitarian Law: Status Quo or Change?" in Michael N. Schmitt and Jelena Pejic (eds.), *International Law and Armed Conflict: Exploring the Faultlines* (Leiden: Nijhoff, 2007), p. 296; Marco Sassolì, "Use and Abuse of the Laws of War in 'The War on Terrorism'" (2004) 22(2) *Law and Inequality: A Journal of Theory and Practice* 220; and Roy S. Schöndorf, "Extra-State Armed Conflicts: Is there a Need for a New Legal Regime?" (2004) 37 (1) *New York University Journal of International Law and Politics* 1.

[204] Rwelamira, "Human Rights and International Humanitarian Law" (n. 92) 330.

Part II

Human rights and humanitarian law: theory

With the adoption of the Universal Declaration of Human Rights in 1948 and the Geneva Conventions in 1949, the relationship between the emerging international human rights law and the law of armed conflict (now rebranded as international humanitarian law) had become a matter of interest. But right from the start, different theoretical conceptualizations of this relationship were put forward in the debate on the role of human rights in armed conflict and metaphorical rhetoric was mixed with legal analysis and policy considerations in attempts to clarify the interplay of human rights and humanitarian law. There was no shortage of concepts to this end; quite to the contrary: every contributor added a new nuance and soon, views ranged from the unquestioned primacy of humanitarian law and the subsequent complete exclusion of human rights from the theatre of war to various forms of concurrence and complementarity, only to be challenged by theories of integration and incorporation of human rights into humanitarian law and their cross-fertilization, up to a merger, fusion or even the identity of the two regimes. It seems there was hardly a theory which was not tested.[1]

In order to retrospectively organize this debate, the various approaches to describing the relationship between human rights and humanitarian law will be grouped under three broad headings: exclusivity, complementarity and integration.[2] Even though the boundaries between them are blurred, these three clusters allow tracing of the main arguments advanced by each theory: proponents of the idea of exclusivity see human rights and humanitarian law as either completely separate regimes for peace and war with not even a potential overlap between them, or they argue that, alternatively, where a concurrent application of human rights and humanitarian law exists, the latter is exclusively applicable under the doctrine of *lex specialis*. Both arguments lead effectively to the inapplicability of human rights in situations of armed conflict. In contrast, "complementarists" consider human rights and humanitarian law not as mutually exclusive but as two sets of law which,

[1] For a succinct overview of the debate see Noelle Quénivet, "Introduction: The History of the Relationship between International Humanitarian Law and Human Rights Law" in Roberta Arnold and Noelle Quénivet (eds.), *International Humanitarian Law and Human Rights Law: Towards a Merger in International Law* (Leiden: Nijhoff, 2008), pp. 1–12.

[2] See the similar approaches taken by Bernhard Schäfer, *Zum Verhältnis Menschenrechte und humanitäres Völkerrecht. Zugleich ein Beitrag zur extraterritorialen Geltung von Menschenrechtsverträgen* (Potsdam: Universitätsverlag Potsdam, 2006), p. 35, who divides the theories into separation, integration and complementarity; and Costas Kombos and Maria Hadjisolomou, "Human Rights and Humanitarian Law: A Dichotomy Transcended?" (2006) 10(1) *Mediterranean Journal of Human Rights* 127, who argue for distinguishing between a cumulative effect, an interpretative function and the speciality of humanitarian law.

despite their differences, can apply jointly in situations of armed conflict. For them, overlaps and similarities in the values, goals, functions and structure of the two regimes necessitate at least some communication and perhaps even cooperation between the two, while the idea of *lex specialis* can or must still be invoked to understand the limits of complementarity. Finally, "integrationists" claim that human rights and humanitarian law, rather than merely coexisting and occasionally coinciding, gradually converge or may even fuse at some point. For proponents of this theory, the integration of human rights into the established law of armed conflict is about more than merely delimiting the respective spheres of application, but rather indicates that the law of armed conflict is undergoing a transformation under the influence of human rights.

While it seems necessary to trace this debate and its conceptual ramifications in their historical and contemporary forms as a prequel to discussing the actual application of human rights in armed conflicts, it is also suggested that theorizing human rights in armed conflict as a problem of regime fragmentation in international law is ultimately of limited value. As the International Law Commission concluded in its study in 2006 on the fragmentation of international law: "[t]he whole complex of inter-regime relations is presently a legal black hole."[3] In light of this verdict, and taking into account that operational clarity and practical acceptability are important for any type of rule in situations of armed conflict, legal theory may be of limited help in settling the relationship between human rights and humanitarian law. Commentators have therefore rightly cautioned that the role of human rights in armed conflict will finally be decided not through abstract application of broad determinative principles but rather in a pragmatic analysis of individual situations.[4]

[3] Report of the Study Group of the International Law Commission, finalized by Martii Koskenniemi, *Fragmentation of International Law: Difficulties Arising from the Diversification and Expansion of International Law*, UN Doc. A/CN.4/L.682 (13 April 2006), para. 485. The aim of the study was to evaluate the phenomenon of fragmentation as a characteristic feature of international law and to study the effects of processes of fragmentation for international law.

[4] See Iain Scobbie, "Principle or Pragmatics? The Relationship between Human Rights Law and the Law of Armed Conflict" (2009) 14(3) *Journal of Conflict and Security Law* 457.

5

Exclusivity: the misconceived idea of *lex specialis*

5.1 Separation and self-contained regimes

From a strictly separatist position, human rights and humanitarian law are fundamentally different and irreconcilable to the extent that there can be no meaningful debate on human rights in armed conflict. The different historic development of the two systems, the dissimilar nature of their respective norms and the different goals they pursue in law and policy keep them apart and prevents any discussion on their simultaneous applicability for theoretical as well as practical reasons. It was asserted that the law of armed conflict is so radically different from international human rights law in its origin, foundation, nature, object and content that the two are not only diametrically opposed but that neither can be derived from the other.[1]

Such a position maintains that international humanitarian law and international human rights law neither share a common history nor common goals but have a fundamentally different legal structure and "no over-reaching axiology, no value system that unifies the objectives of these fields of international law."[2] They are mutually exclusive.[3] Such a complete separation of international humanitarian law and international human rights law has been suggested only rarely. Where a separation was argued for, metaphorical concepts such as presenting international humanitarian law and international human rights law as "two curtains"[4] were introduced instead. Each of these curtains was meant to shield

[1] "Nous avons constaté que le droit des conflits armés et la notion des droits de l'homme sont, par leur origine, leur fondament, leur nature, leur object, leur contenu, radicalement différents, s'ils ne sont pas diamétralement opposés, et qu'ils sont irréductible l'un à l'autre." Henri Meyrowitz, "Le droit de la guerre et les droits de l'homme" (1972) 88 *Revue de droit pénal militaire et de droit de la guerre* 1104. It has been pointed out that the author was less concerned with legal theory but that his arguments were part of a larger assault on the way in which the UN sought to participate in the development of international humanitarian law, a move which he found to be inspired by what he considered propagandist ideas arising from the conflict in the Middle East, see Karl-Josef Partsch, "Menschenrechte und Rotkreuz-Grundsätze. Justitiartagung 1973" in Wolfgang Voit (ed.),*Völkerrechtliche Beiträge der Tagungen der Justitiare und Konventionsbeauftragten des deutschen Roten Kreuzes 1957–1989* (Bochum: Universitätsverlag Dr. N. Brockmeyer, 1995), pp. 201–2.

[2] Iain Scobbie, "Principle or Pragmatics? The Relationship between Human Rights Law and the Law of Armed Conflict" (2009) 14(3) *Journal of Conflict and Security Law* 457, who nevertheless sees potential for complementarity.

[3] Barry Feinstein, "The Applicability of the Regime of Human Rights in Times of Armed Conflict and Particularly to Occupied Territories: The Case of Israel's Security Barrier" (2005) 4(2) *Northwestern Journal of International Human Rights* 301.

[4] Keith D. Suter, "An Enquiry into the Meaning of the Phrase 'Human Rights in Armed Conflict'" (1976) 15 (3–4) *Revue de droit pénal militaire et de droit de la guerre* 422.

the individual from threats in different moments: international humanitarian law in times of war and international humanitarian law in times of peace. But even this suggestion was mitigated by the argument that during armed conflicts the curtain of international human rights law (i.e., the two UN human rights Covenants) would not be drawn back completely but only "largely."[5]

Few authors insist today on the complete separation of the two bodies of law on the grounds of their entirely irreconcilable nature. Where they do (as Bill Bowring seemingly does in his analysis of the European Court of Human Rights' case law on Chechnya) they admit to hold "in all probability a heretical view."[6] And indeed, the author's claim that presenting international humanitarian law and international human rights law as complementary, even if only potentially, would be "[c]halk … being compared with, or even substituted by, cheese"[7] seems over the top. His main supportive arguments – that the two fields of law have a different history, that international humanitarian law is conservative while international human rights law is revolutionary, and that international human rights law provides a standing for victims in individual complaints procedures as opposed to the ICRC's intermediary role[8] – are (partly) correct but ultimately unpersuasive (as will be discussed in the following chapters), and the claim that there is consequently not even a discussion to be had on the role of human rights in armed conflict is misplaced. Quite to the contrary, such arguments should rather inspire a careful analysis of the place for human rights in armed conflict and the interplay of human rights and humanitarian law, bearing in mind Geoffrey Best's dictum that "[t]he judgment of persons who from the beginning understood their shared sources and discerned the extent of their overlap has been more vindicated than that of persons who strove to deny their affinity and to keep them apart."[9]

In terms of international law, arguments for a complete separation of international human rights and humanitarian law necessarily invoke the idea of them being 'self-contained regimes" under international law. It is disputed to which extent regimes (defined as "set[s] of implicit or explicit principles, norms, rules and decision-making procedures around which actors' expectations converge in a given area of international relations")[10] are autonomous or self-contained. The notion of self-contained regimes was coined in the *S.S. Wimbledon* case before the Permanent International Court of Justice in 1923.[11] The subsequent interpretation and expansion of the Court's views in international legal scholarship gave rise to the idea that a legal subsystem which contains a full, exhaustive and definitive set of (secondary) rules is a self-contained regime independent from general law, an idea which has rightly attracted considerable criticism.[12]

[5] Ibid. 322.

[6] Bill Bowring, "Fragmentation, *Lex Specialis* and the Tensions in the Jurisprudence of the European Court of Human Rights" (2010) 14(3) *Journal of Conflict and Security Law* 485.

[7] Ibid. 486. [8] Ibid. 487–89.

[9] See Geoffrey Best, *War and Law Since 1945* (Oxford: Clarendon Press, 1994), p. 75.

[10] Stephen D. Krasner, "Structural Causes and Regime Consequences: Regimes as Intervening Variables" in Stephen D. Krasner (ed.), *International Regimes* (Ithaca, NY: Cornell University Press, 1983), p. 2.

[11] See *S.S. Wimbledon Case*, Permanent International Court of Justice, P.I.C.J. Series A., No. 1 (1923). In the case, the Court found that the status of the Kiel Canal in Germany, guaranteed by the Treaty of Versailles of 1919, constituted a self-contained regime with regard to the public international law on waterways.

[12] See Bruno Simma and Dirk Pulkowski, "Of Planets and the Universe: Self-Contained Regimes in International Law" (2003) 17(3) *European Journal of International Law* 491, with reference to those critical voices.

While it is obvious that there exist distinct functional fields of international law, usually established by a treaty or treaties, guided by specific principles and bolstered with implementing bodies, the self-contained character of such fields of law must be questioned. They may well be comprised of a highly specific set of norms and characterized by the formal or informal activities of scholars, diplomats and civil society actors with a legal culture of their own, but they are not completely isolated from general public international law.[13] Indeed, the term "'self-contained regime" is a misnomer: no regime is entirely self-contained, as general international law always serves at least as the normative background against which the regime has to be measured, supplements it and provides fall-back provisions in case of regime failure.[14] If human rights and humanitarian law were to be constructed as such self-contained regimes, they would need to have sufficiently clear boundaries, so that questions of exceptionality, speciality or interpretation cannot even arise. This is obviously not the case, as demonstrated by the dominant discourse on the *lex specialis* nature of humanitarian law in relation to human rights law.[15]

5.2 Special regimes and the fragmentation of international law

In light of the misconceptions surrounding the idea of self-contained regimes, it has been suggested to replace the term by "special regime" to better describe fields such as international humanitarian law or international human rights law.[16] Unlike self-contained regimes, such regimes have, as the International Law Commission (ILC) made clear, "neither clear boundaries nor a strictly determined normative force."[17] In other words, they are neither mutually exclusive nor isolated from general international law but simply cover an issue of concern (e.g., "human rights" or "humanitarian matters"). This characteristic has been summed up in the dictum that while special regimes can, in theory, opt out of all rules of international law (with the exception of *jus cogens*) they cannot opt out of the system of international law.[18] Even supporters of a particularistic view, who see international law as nothing more than an assortment of regimes, agree that such regimes do not exist in isolation but communicate with each other.[19] International humanitarian law and international human rights law are thus "no watertight compartments"[20] within international law, as some separatists seem to argue. That they exist as special regimes says *a priori* nothing about their relationship but merely demonstrates the fragmentation of international law.

[13] See Report of the Study Group of the International Law Commission, finalized by Martii Koskenniemi, *Fragmentation of International Law: Difficulties Arising from the Diversification and Expansion of International Law*, UN Doc. A/CN.4/L.682 (13 April 2006) ("ILC Study on Fragmentation"), paras. 152 and 156–57.

[14] Ibid. para. 192.

[15] On the relevant jurisprudence of the European Court of Human Rights see ILC Study on Fragmentation (n. 13) paras. 161–64.

[16] See ibid. para. 152(5). [17] Ibid. para. 173.

[18] See Joost Pauwelyn, *Conflict of Norms in Public International Law: How WTO Rules Relate to Other Rules of International Law* (Cambridge: Cambridge University Press, 2003), p. 37.

[19] See Simma and Pulkowski, "Of Planets and the Universe" (n. 12) 502–3, with reference to international legal, international relations and sociological scholarship.

[20] Christopher Greenwood, "Rights at the Frontier: Protection of the Individual in Time of War" in Barry A.K. Rider (ed.), *Law at the Centre: The Institute of Advanced Legal Studies at Fifty* (Dordrecht: Kluwer, 1999), p. 278.

This fragmentation describes the diversity and proliferation of instruments, regulations and subjects of international law as a segmented legal order with independent and autonomous branches, sections or regimes. The existence of the two regimes of international human rights law and international humanitarian law is an example thereof. There are different reasons for and different manifestations of such a fragmentation, depending on the legal character, political objectives, functions, as well as the legal culture, communities and institutions associated with specific regimes.[21] Fragmentation is essentially a functional diversification of international law, often driven by the process of globalization, where vague general provisions of international law are substituted by ever more nuanced legal rules in response to new trends, threats and technologies.[22] Trade law, investment law and environmental law, for example, regulate matters of trade, investment and environment "better" than general public international law in the sense of a heightened clarity of the law, a more effective enforcement or a more context-sensitive approach, while general law remains a fall-back position in case of regime failure.[23]

The existence of the two regimes of human rights and humanitarian law may reflect such a functional fragmentation of international law as a deliberate division of labour. After 1945, international humanitarian law continued to provide protection to those affected by armed conflicts, while human rights law had the purpose of organizing states and societies along the new coordinates of individual human dignity as an international concern and was tasked with preventing the re-occurrence of the atrocities of the past. Humanitarian law also undoubtedly "humanized" not only war but also international law as a whole (by putting the individual human being at its centre) but it never claimed to organize the state and peacetime societal structures in the way human rights did.

At the same time, there are specific features of fragmentation seemingly unique to the dichotomy of human rights and humanitarian law, which go beyond a functional division of labour and have also historical and contextual connotations. The tacit agreement between human rights and humanitarian law not to tread on each other's toes in the period after 1945 was an uneasy case of fragmentation, as the two fields were not clearly functionally different in terms of the issues they covered (such as, for example, human rights law and international trade law), but were rather heading in the same general direction of humanization, albeit in different circumstances. Given that, in some sense, humanitarian law was a forerunner of such a humanization when compared to human rights, humanitarian law was now confronted with a new legal regime which took on board concerns hitherto exclusive to the former. This gives their fragmentation an historic or temporal connotation with an "older" humanitarian law and a "modern" human rights law. And the differentiation of the two fields is also contextual because the two regimes were created not so much for two radically different subject matters or areas as (to use the example just mentioned) human rights and trade law. Rather, the application of human rights and humanitarian law is (or was originally) meant to be intrinsically linked to temporal and spatial circumstances: only the existence of an armed conflict can trigger the debate on the relationship between human rights and humanitarian law as the latter (with exceptions) does not apply outside this context. No similar triggering mechanism exists in other areas of fragmentation. For human

[21] See Simma and Pulkowski, "Of Planets and the Universe" (n. 12) 504.

[22] See Gunther Teubner and Andreas Fischer-Lescano, "Regime-Collisions: The Vain Search for Legal Unity in the Fragmentation of Global Law" (2004) 25(4) *Michigan Journal of International Law* 1004.

[23] See ILC Study on Fragmentation (n. 13) paras. 186–90.

rights and humanitarian law, the question of fragmentation thus arises only within, and is intimately tied to, armed conflict as a legal phenomenon, and hinges on the very perception of "war" and "peace," as well as on the categorization of armed conflicts. This dichotomy between a law of war and a law of peace is, however, disintegrating, and the changing character of "war" in its modern manifestations erodes the claim that the law of war is special and, in a functional sense, better suited to regulate matters within this context. As the perception of and the boundaries between war and peace shift, so does the relationship between human rights and humanitarian law.

It may still be argued that the application of international human rights law in armed conflict and the associated discussion on the relationship between humanitarian law and human rights law is only a variation of what has been called the "*and* problem":[24] human rights *and* trade, human rights *and* environment, human rights *and* business, and so on. While this is partly correct, the debate is not simply about "human rights *and* war" as two different subject maters. Historically and contemporarily, the law of armed conflict is driven by much of the same concerns, values and objectives which guide human rights law, albeit differently calibrated and tuned to the necessities of warfare. The debate on human rights and humanitarian law is thus a debate on different layers of fragmentation.

5.3 *Lex specialis* in international law

Diverging views exist on how to deal with this fragmentation of international law. Regardless of whether one is more interested in preserving the unity of international law or is in favour of specialization, the creation and growth of special regimes and their institutions and community usually "take[s] place with relative ignorance of legislative and institutional activities in the adjoining fields and of general principles and practices of international law."[25] Norm collision is thus likely, norm conflicts may occur, and norm coordination becomes an issue of concern. The prime legal technique suggested for clarifying the relationship between human rights and humanitarian law is the principle of *lex specialis derogat legi generali*. As a widely recognized principle of domestic as well as international law, it describes the relationship between norms of a special character in relation to norms of a general character with a view towards ensuring the application of the more appropriate norm in a given situation. The principle stipulates that when a matter is regulated by a general norm (*lex generalis*) and a more specific norm (*lex specialis*), the latter prevails. This idea became firmly embedded in international legal reasoning very early on.[26]

And indeed, a number of assumptions seem to speak for resorting to the principle of *lex specialis* in certain situations. A special rule may better reflect the will of the parties and, as a consequence, may be considered more binding by them and induce compliance more easily than a general rule. A special rule is also likely to have greater clarity and power to define

[24] Michael Bothe, "Die Anwendung der Europäischen Menschenrechtskonvention in bewaffneten Konflikten - eine Überforderung?" (2005) 65 *Zeitschrift für ausländisches öffentliches Recht und Völkerrecht* 615.

[25] Ibid. para. 8.

[26] See Conor McCarthy, "Legal Conclusion or Interpretative Process? *Lex Specialis* and the Application of International Human Rights Standards" in Roberta Arnold and Noelle Quénivet (eds.), *International Humanitarian Law and Human Rights Law: Towards a Merger in International Law* (Leiden: Nijhoff, 2008), pp. 103–4.

problems and solutions and may consequently prove to be better suited to the particular circumstances and thus more effective in providing a suitable solution to the problem at hand. In light of such expectations, the value and utility of the principle of *lex specialis* has, by and large, been accepted without much ado since the classic writers in international law, including Hugo Grotius.[27]

But the principle of *lex specialis* is problematic. What seems at first glance to be a simple exercise in logical reasoning – discerning the special from the general – poses considerable problems in theory and practice. Consequently, the precise legal status of the principle has never been fully and convincingly clarified. In the view of the majority of legal commentators, *lex specialis* is not an element of customary law but rather an intrinsic part of international law.[28] The principle did not make it into the Vienna Convention on the Law of Treaties (VCLT), unlike the principle *lex posterior derogat legi priori* (that newer law derogates older law), which is laid down in VCLT, Article 30.[29] The precise meaning of *lex specialis*, the relationship it has with other and similar principles, such as *lex posterior*, and the legal consequences resulting from its application remain uncertain. Authors have identified at least ten partially overlapping or contradictory perceptions of *lex specialis*. They comprise, *inter alia*, *lex specialis* as a logical principle, a general principle of law, an interpretative device or as merely an expression of common sense or grammatical usage of legal texts; some denounce the principle as merely a legal proverb or reject its validity altogether.[30]

In domestic law, *lex specialis* can be used with greater ease as a tool for determining the relation between norms whose place is predetermined in a hierarchical national normative system with a central legislator. But when transposed to international law its suitability to determine the relationship of norms diminishes.[31] International obligations of a "soft-law" character with their fluid legal quality contribute to this problem.[32] And where international courts and tribunals have used the *lex specialis* doctrine they have done so mostly incoherently, and their mechanical application of the principle in disregard of its variegated meanings has not contributed to more clarity.[33] The verdict that *lex specialis* (and similar principles) can claim only limited standing, are complicated to apply, may collide with each other and offer, at best, fragmentary solutions, still holds true.[34]

When the ILC studied the fragmentation of international law, it found *lex specialis* to be a balancing act of reconciling the need to unravel the purpose of a norm and ensure its practical relevance and effectiveness with an otherwise hierarchical and mechanical perception of legal interpretation, but the ILC was not able to dispel convincingly the

[27] See ILC Study on Fragmentation (n. 13) para. 60.

[28] See Erich Vranes, "*Lex superior, lex specialis, lex posterior* – zur Rechtsnatur der "Konfliktlösungsregeln" (2005) 65 *Zeitschrift für ausländisches öffentliches Recht und Völkerrecht* 403.

[29] Vienna Convention on the Law of Treaties, 23 May 1969, 1155 UNTS 331.

[30] See on the following views Vranes, "*Lex superior, lex specialis, lex posterior*" (n. 28) 392–93.

[31] See Anja Lindroos, "Addressing Norm Conflicts in a Fragmented Legal System: The Doctrine of *Lex Specialis*" (2005) 74 *Nordic Journal of International Law* 39.

[32] See Pauwelyn, *Conflict of Norms* (n. 18) p. 90.

[33] See Lindroos, "Addressing Norm Conflicts" (n. 31) 48; and ILC Study on Fragmentation (n. 13) para. 68.

[34] See Vranes, "*Lex superior, lex specialis, lex posterior*" (n. 28) 393, with reference to the works of earlier legal scholars such as Karl Englisch.

critics' doubts on the principle.[35] In light of these uncertainties it suggested using *lex specialis* law restrictively and only for clarifying the relationship between norms within a single treaty or between closely related treaties, and not for assessing the relationship of norms in different international instruments or legal frameworks.[36]

5.4 International Court of Justice and *lex specialis*

Despite such reservations and warnings, *lex specialis* continues to enjoy a high reputation as the most appropriate or even as the only way to explain the relationship between international humanitarian law and international human rights law.[37] Given that treaties in both regimes contain no clauses on solving norm conflicts with respect to each other, any such conflict needs to be resolved by interpretation or other legal techniques, and *lex specialis* seems to offer an elegant way to do so.

The International Court of Justice (ICJ) introduced the principle to clarify the relationship between human rights and humanitarian law in its *Nuclear Weapons* case in 1996, as mentioned earlier. It repeated and refined its position in the 2004 Advisory Opinion on the *Legal Consequences of the Construction of a Wall in the Occupied Palestinian Territory*,[38] while the third case on the concurrent application of human rights and humanitarian law, the decision in *Democratic Republic of Congo* v. *Uganda*, refrains from invoking the principle.[39] Despite critique on the Court's reasoning (or lack thereof) as to why and how the principle performs its task, the vast majority of scholarly voices followed suit, as did the International Committee of the Red Cross (ICRC). In contrast, international human rights bodies (the Inter-American Commission and Court of Human Rights, the European Court of Human Rights, the African Commission on Human and People's Rights and the UN human rights treaty bodies) have taken different approaches, as will be discussed later.

Despite the support which the ICJ's views on *lex specialis* enjoyed since 1996 and the repeated reference to its decisions in scholarly writings and state practice, the Court's use of the principle of *lex specialis* to clarify the interplay of human rights and humanitarian law in the Advisory Opinion in the *Nuclear Weapons* case and the Advisory Opinion in the *Wall* case remains ultimately unconvincing. In the first case on the legality of nuclear weapons, the Court was faced with the question brought before it by the World Health Organization and the UN General Assembly whether the use of nuclear weapons would violate Article 6 of the International Covenant on Civil and Political Rights (ICCPR) on the right to life or their use would be lawful under international humanitarian law.[40] In determining the

35 See ILC Study on Fragmentation (n. 13) para. 67, and (for a critique on the principle) Nancy Prud'homme, "*Lex specialis*: Oversimplifying a More Complex and Multifaceted Relationship?" (2007), 40(2) *Israel Law Review* 379.

36 See ILC Study on Fragmentation (n. 13) para. 68. See also Heike Krieger, "A Conflict of Norms: The Relationship between Humanitarian Law and Human Rights Law in the ICRC Customary Law Study" (2006) 11(2) *Journal of Conflict and Security Law* 280.

37 See, e.g., René Provost, *International Human Rights and Humanitarian Law* (Cambridge: Cambridge University Press, 2002), p. 277; and Krieger, "A Conflict of Norms" (n. 36) 271.

38 *Legal Consequences of the Construction of a Wall in the Occupied Palestinian Territory*, International Court of Justice, Advisory Opinion of 9 July 2004 [2004] ICJ Reports, para. 136 ("*Wall* case").

39 *Armed Activities on the Territory of the Congo (Democratic Republic of the Congo* v. *Uganda)*, International Court of Justice, Judgment of 19 December 2005 [2006] ICJ Reports, para. 168.

40 Request for an Advisory Opinion, UN Doc. GA/Res ES-10/14 (8 December 2003).

relationship between ICCPR, Article 6(2) on the right not to be arbitrarily deprived of one's life and the respective rules of international humanitarian law, which allow for the lawful killing of combatants, the Court observed that:

> the protection of the International Covenant of Civil and Political Rights does not cease in times of war, except by operation of Article 4 of the Covenant whereby certain provisions may be derogated from in a time of national emergency. Respect for the right to life is not, however, such a provision. In principle, the right not arbitrarily to be deprived of one's life applies also in hostilities. The test of what is an arbitrary deprivation of life, however, then falls to be determined by the applicable *lex specialis*, namely, the law applicable in armed conflict which is designed to regulate the conduct of hostilities. Thus whether a particular loss of life, through the use of a certain weapon in warfare, is to be considered an arbitrary deprivation of life contrary to Article 6 of the Covenant, can only be decided by reference to the law applicable in armed conflict and not deduced from the terms of the Covenant itself.[41]

This statement has been interpreted very differently.[42] Some concluded that the Court saw international humanitarian law in armed conflict as the only applicable regime, which displaces international human rights law, regardless of the facts or norms in question.[43] Others understood the Court as arguing for the complementary application of human rights law,[44] as if human rights and humanitarian law would apply "side-by-side, the *lex specialis* playing the greater role of the two."[45] Again others found the Court in favour of a unity of international humanitarian law and international human rights law.[46] The ILC study on fragmentation argued that in the Advisory Opinion:

> *[l]ex specialis* did hardly more than indicate that though it might have been desirable to apply only human rights, such a solution would have been too idealistic, bearing in mind the speciality and persistence of armed conflict. So the Court created a systemic view of the law in which the two sets of rules related to each other as today's reality and tomorrow's promise, with a view to the overriding need to ensure the "survival of a State."[47]

What the Court certainly did suggest was a duty to interpret a specific norm of international human rights law in light of the special norm of humanitarian law, given that the latter contains specific provisions on this question. In the Court's view, the arbitrariness of the deprivation of life as stipulated in ICCPR, Article 6 needs to be measured against the demands of the respective principles of humanitarian law. But the application of the *lex*

[41] *Legality of the Threat or Use of Nuclear Weapons*, International Court of Justice, Advisory Opinion of 8 July 1996 [1996] ICJ Reports 226 ("*Nuclear Weapons* case"), para. 25.

[42] See Prud'homme, "*Lex specialis*" (n. 35) 372.

[43] This seems to be inferred by Michael J. Dennis, "Application of Human Rights Treaties Extraterritorially in Times of Armed Conflict and Military Occupation" (2005) 99(1) *American Journal of International Law* 141; but see the critique by Prud'homme, "*Lex specialis*" (n. 35) 372–73.

[44] See United Nations Office of the High Commissioner for Human Rights, *International Legal Protection of Human Rights in Armed Conflict* (New York and Geneva: United Nations, 2011), p. 61.

[45] Pauwelyn, *Conflict of Norms* (n. 18) p. 410.

[46] See Hans-Joachim Heintze, "Konsequenzen der Konvergenz von Menschenrechtsschutz und humanitärem Völkerrecht" in Horst Fischer, Ulrike Froissart, Wolff Heinegg von Heintschel and Christian Raap (eds.), *Krisensicherung und humanitärer Schutz / Crisis Management and Humanitarian Protection. Festschrift für Dieter Fleck* (Berlin: Berliner Wissenschaftsverlag, 2004), p. 250.

[47] ILC Study on Fragmentation (n. 13) para. 104.

specialis principle was merely claimed in the Advisory Opinion rather than explained or substantiated.[48] The ILC Study on the Fragmentation of International Law was consequently particularly critical of the way in which the Court, without further explanation, set aside what in the ILC's view was effectively the more special standard of international human rights law in favour of the more relaxed standard of international humanitarian law on permissible killing in armed conflicts.[49] It also needs to be mentioned that the Court's views were limited to an (imagined) international armed conflict in which nuclear weapons would be used by one state against another. The Advisory Opinion says nothing about the role of human rights in internal armed conflicts or situations of occupation.[50]

The Court referred again to *lex specialis* in the Advisory Opinion in the *Wall* case when it was asked by the UN General Assembly to consider the legal consequences of the construction of the barrier stretching over 670 kilometers between Israel and the Occupied Palestinian Territory.[51] While Israel saw international humanitarian law as not applicable to this situation, the Court found the construction of the wall to be a violation of the applicable international human rights *and* international humanitarian law. The Court rejected Israel's argument of self-defence and necessity and asked for the immediate dismantling of the wall and for reparations to the victims.[52]

With regard to human rights, the Court repeated in this Advisory Opinion its position on their continued application during armed conflict, which can be seen as a clarification that human rights as such continue to apply and not merely the right to life, which had been at stake in the *Nuclear Weapons* case.[53] Unlike the *Nuclear Weapons* case, the *Wall* case was not about a hypothetical question but an actual and imminent situation of occupation.[54] The ICJ took the view that there are three options in which this relationship between human rights and humanitarian law can be presented:

> some rights may be exclusively matters of international humanitarian law; others may be exclusively matters of human rights law; yet others may be matters of both these branches of international law. In order to answer the question put to it, the Court will have to take into consideration both these branches of international law, namely human rights law and, as *lex specialis*, international humanitarian law.[55]

This obviously suggests that human rights and humanitarian law can overlap but other than that, the statement remains opaque.[56] The Advisory Opinion has consequently been

48 See Vera Gowlland-Debbas, "The Right to Life and Genocide: The Court and International Public Policy" in Laurence Boisson de Chazournes and Philippe Sands (eds.), *International Law, the International Court of Justice and Nuclear Weapons* (Cambridge: Cambridge University Press, 1999), pp. 321–26, who deplores the scarcity of human rights arguments in the Advisory Opinion.

49 See ILC Study on Fragmentation (n. 13) paras. 96 and 118.

50 See Philip Alston, Jason Morgan-Foster and William Abresch, "The Competence of the UN Human Rights Council and Its Special Procedures in Relation to Armed Conflicts: Extrajudicial Executions in the 'War on Terror'" (2008) 19 *European Journal of International Law* 191.

51 Request for an Advisory Opinion, UN. Doc GA/Res ES-10/14 (8 December 2003).

52 See Ardi Imseis, "Critical Reflections on the International Humanitarian Law Aspects" (2005) 99(1) *American Journal of International Law* 102, and Prud'homme, "*Lex specialis*" (n. 35) 376.

53 ICJ, *Wall* case (n. 38) para. 106.

54 Hans-Joachim Heintze, "On the Relationship between Human Rights Law Protection and International Humanitarian Law (2004) 86(856) *International Review of the Red Cross* 797.

55 ICJ, *Wall* case (n. 38) para. 106.

56 See in greater detail Alexander Orakhelashvili, "Legal Consequences of the Construction of a Wall in the Occupied Palestinian Territory: Opinion and Reaction" (2006) 11(1) *Journal of Conflict and Security Law* 119.

criticized as "didactically correct, albeit not materially helpful in the absence of further elaboration",[57] as offering no guidance whatsoever,[58] and as an "almost comically uninformative statement."[59] In a more positive spirit, some saw it as an altogether novel approach when compared to the earlier Advisory Opinion in the *Nuclear Weapons* case, and as introducing the idea of complementarity of human rights and humanitarian law while at the same time retaining the idea of *lex specialis.*[60] The Court also seemed to suggest that the two must be interpreted in light of each other rather than one simply prevailing over the other.[61] But ultimately the statement provides no useful guidance on the three situations it imagines.[62]

While both Advisory Opinions, on the *Wall* and on *Nuclear Weapons*, are indeed "the most authoritative determination that human rights provisions continue to apply in times of armed conflict,"[63] they seem to create more confusion than clarity as to how the *lex specialis* principle is meant to explain the relationship between international humanitarian law and international human rights law. In both cases, the Court referred to *lex specialis* only in abstract terms and did not effectively *apply* humanitarian law as *lex specialis*, even when it examined the freedom of movement in the West Bank as a human right guaranteed in the ICCPR (which it found Israel to have violated).[64] It is somewhat surprising that despite this lack of analytical clarity and guidance in the two Advisory Opinions, they have allowed the principle of *lex specialis* to take such a firm grip on the debate on the relationship between human rights and humanitarian law.[65]

In *Democratic Republic of the Congo* v. *Uganda* in 2005, the Court was again confronted with the application of human rights in a situation of occupation.[66] The Court was asked to decide on violations of human rights and humanitarian law allegedly perpetrated by Ugandan armed forces in the occupied parts of the Congo. This is the first and so far only binding decision on such a matter and thus *res judicata.*[67] The Court again accepted the application of human rights in belligerent occupation and held that Uganda had violated

57 See Yoram Dinstein, *The International Law of Belligerent Occupation* (Cambridge: Cambridge University Press, 2009), p. 87.

58 See Dennis, "Application of Human Rights Treaties Extraterritorially" (n. 43) 133.

59 Roger O'Keefe, "Legal Consequences of the Construction of a Wall in the Occupied Palestinian Territory: A Commentary" (2004) 37 *Revue Belge de Droit International* 135.

60 See Prud'homme, "*Lex specialis*" (n. 35) 377; and William Schabas, "*Lex specialis*? Belts and Suspenders? The Parallel Operation of Human Rights Law and the Law of Armed Conflict, and the Conundrum of Jus ad Bellum" (2007) 40(2) *Israel Law Review* 597.

61 Françoise Hampson and Ibrahim Salama, *Working Paper of the UN Sub-commission on the Promotion and Protection of Human Rights on the Relationship between Human Rights Law and International Humanitarian Law*, UN Doc. E/CN.4/2005/14 (21 June 2005), para. 57.

62 See Marko Milanovic, "Norm Conflicts, International Humanitarian Law and Human Rights Law" in Orna Ben-Naftali (ed.), *International Humanitarian and International Human Rights Law* (Oxford: Oxford University Press, 2011), p. 100. Some seem to understand that *lex specialis* applies in all scenarios but this is not what the Court said, see Schabas, "*Lex specialis?*" (n. 60) 597.

63 Theodor Meron, *The Humanization of International Law* (Leiden: Nijhoff, 2006), p. 266.

64 See Dinstein, *The International Law of Belligerent Occupation* (n. 57) p. 87.

65 See also Prud'homme, "*Lex specialis*" (n. 35) 378.

66 ICJ, *DRC* v. *Congo* (n. 39) para. 168. See on the case in greater detail Alexander Orakhelashvili, "Legal Stability and Claims of Change: The International Court's Treatment of *Jus Ad Bellum* and *Jus in Bello*" (2006) 75(3–4) *Nordic Journal of International Law* 371.

67 Alston, Morgan-Foster and Abresch, "The Competence of the UN Human Rights Council" (n. 50) 194.

its obligations under international human rights law *and* international humanitarian law. The argument that whatever the Court said on this matter in the Advisory Opinion in the *Wall* case was only due to the special and prolonged nature of the occupation could now no longer be made. In the Court's view any occupation creates positive and negative obligations of the occupant under international humanitarian law for acts of a state's armed forces as well as for acts of private individuals which the state failed to prevent; a view with potentially far-reaching consequences, as has rightly been pointed out.[68]

Apart from this, however, the Court did not specify the interplay between international humanitarian law and international human rights law any further than it had done previously. Instead, the Court refrained from explicitly referring to the *lex specialis* nature of humanitarian law, leaving it thus open whether it wished to follow its approach in the previous two cases or refrained from invoking this principle deliberately. The three pronouncements of the Court seem to speak for a move away from the principle of *lex specialis*: while the Court had seemingly argued for the primacy of humanitarian law in the *Nuclear Weapons* case, it had established a more equal relationship between the two in the *Wall* case, only to remain silent in the third and so far final case on human rights in armed conflict. In light of the explanatory scarcity of the three texts, the Court's intentions remain, however, uncertain.

5.5 Exclusivist position of the United States

The United States and, to some extent, also Israel are most outspoken in their insistence on the exclusive nature of humanitarian law as *lex specialis*.[69] In its response to the Inter-American Commission on Human Rights on precautionary measures to be taken in the situation in Guantánamo Bay, for example, the US government argued that human rights and humanitarian law are separate and distinct, international human rights law is not applicable to the conduct of hostilities or the capture and detention of enemy combatants, which are governed by the more specific laws of armed conflict, and where humanitarian law is applicable, it operates to exclude human rights law.[70] The United States considers that historically and functionally human rights and humanitarian law were not meant to regulate the same subject matter, i.e., warfare, that human rights law is not sufficiently clear in comparison to international humanitarian law, and that it thus cannot replace the latter.[71] Such arguments are supported by policy considerations, particularly the fear that

[68] See Tim Ruys and Sten Verhoeven, "DRC v. Uganda: The Applicability of International Humanitarian Law and Human Rights Law in Occupied Territories" in Roberta Arnold and Noelle Quénivet (eds.), *International Humanitarian Law and Human Rights Law: Towards a Merger in International Law* (Leiden: Nijhoff, 2008), p. 195.

[69] See (critical) Gary D. Solis, *The Law of Armed Conflict* (Cambridge: Cambridge University Press, 2010), p. 24.

[70] See Response of the United States to Request for Precautionary Measures, Detainees in Guantanamo Bay, Cuba (15 April 2002) (2002) 41 ILM 1025. See also Dirk Lorenz, *Der territoriale Anwendungsbereich der Grund- und Menschenrechte. Zugleich ein Beitrag zum Individualschutz in bewaffneten Konflikten* (Vienna: Neuer Wissenschaftlicher Verlag, 2005), p. 212. Similar arguments were made before the UN Committee Against Torture, see Opening Remarks by John R. Bellinger III, Legal Adviser, US Department of State, before the UN Committee Against Torture (5 May 2006), available at www.state.gov/g/drl/rls/68557.htm (last accessed 15 April 2014).

[71] See Dennis, "Application of Human Rights Treaties Extraterritorially" (n. 43) 139.

the application of human rights is likely to restrain the United States' freedom to act in armed conflicts and in situations of occupation beyond what humanitarian law allows, which would put additional and unacceptable burdens on military decision-making and on the armed forces, create uncertainties in military planning and operational practice as to the applicable rules, and lead to criminal prosecution or other forms of accountability of the armed forces.[72] In addition, there is concern that replacing humanitarian law with human rights law will ultimately result in reducing the protective scope of the former or nullify it altogether.[73]

The United States is particularly critical of what they consider an unacceptably progressive jurisprudence of human rights bodies with regard to human rights in armed conflict. This jurisprudence is seen as partly exceeding the treaty bodies' mandates, and is perceived, together with liberal human rights scholarship in favour of the application of human rights in armed conflicts, as seeking to trump established state practice and *opinio juris* on the non-applicability of human rights in armed conflict.[74] Such arguments ignore, however, that in light of the overwhelming support for the application of international human rights law in armed conflict, the United States is increasingly isolated; some would even refer to its position as "anachronistic."[75] A lack of state consent on the application of human rights in armed conflict cannot be discerned, contrary to such claims being made.[76] The state practice to which the United States refers is largely the position of the United States and Israel. Other states, such as the Netherlands and Belgium, have at times rejected the extra-territorial application of human rights treaty law, but acknowledge the complementary nature of human rights and humanitarian law. Only Ecuador and Colombia have argued in cases before the Inter-American Commission and Court of Human Rights, albeit somewhat inconsistently, that humanitarian law prevails as a regime over human rights law.[77] It has thus been said that:

> [t]he United States' position … is noteworthy in that the United States offers no legal authority in support of its exclusionist thesis. It would presumably be hard pressed to do this without at least contradicting the positions that it has taken clearly and unequivocally in a variety of contexts outside the current framework of the Human Rights Council where its own conduct is potentially being impugned.[78]

The United States also seemingly does not deny the application of human rights principles and customary human rights law in armed conflicts, and when commenting on the work of the Special Rapporteur of the International Law Commission on the effect of armed conflict on treaties, the United States explicitly stated that "certain human rights and environmental

[72] See Michelle Hansen, "Preventing the Emasculation of Warfare: Halting the Expansion of Human Rights Law into Armed Conflict" (2007) 194 *Military Law Review* 65.

[73] Ibid.

[74] See Dennis, "Application of Human Rights Treaties Extraterritorially" (n. 43) 139. The second argument which the United States regularly presents against the application of human rights in armed conflict and defends with reference to state practice, the lack of extra-territorial reach of human rights treaty law, will be dealt with later.

[75] Nils Melzer, *Targeted Killing in International Law* (Oxford: Oxford University Press, 2008), p. 79.

[76] Hansen, "Preventing the Emasculation of Warfare" (n. 72) 65.

[77] Their arguments will be considered later, together with the responses of the Inter-American Commission and Court.

[78] Alston, Morgan-Foster and Abresch, "The Competence of the UN Human Rights Council" (n. 50) 197.

principles did not cease to apply in time of armed conflict."[79] And when being reviewed under the Universal Periodic Review (UPR) before the Human Rights Council in 2011, the United States argued in a more nuanced way that:

> [t]o the extent that human rights law may apply in armed conflict or national actions taken in self-defence, in all cases, the United States works to ensure that its actions are lawful. The delegation noted first, that international human rights law and international humanitarian law are complementary, reinforcing, and animated by humanitarian principles designed to protect innocent life. Second, while the United States complied with human rights law wherever applicable, the applicable rules for the protection of individuals and the conduct of hostilities in armed conflict outside a nation's territory are typically found in international humanitarian law, which apply to government and non-government actors. Third, determining which international law rules apply to any particular government action during an armed conflict is highly fact-specific.[80]

It is also not obvious that the United States and Israel could claim the status of a persistent objector to the formulation of an emerging customary international law on the application of human rights in armed conflict (and it is also not clear whether they would want to argue for such a status). As has been noted, claiming the status of a persistent objector under international law on this particular matter is difficult, given that the objections against the application of human rights law in armed conflict are seemingly not raised against a substantive norm but rather against the relationship between two sets of rules.[81] Any such objection would also need to be consistent; whether this can be demonstrated in light of some of the more ambiguous statements on the applicability of human rights in armed conflicts is an open question. One could also add that at least where *jus cogens* norms are concerned, the status of a persistent objector may not be claimed at all.

5.6 *Lex specialis*: an inadequate device

(a) Distinguishing "general" and "special"

The principle of *lex specialis*, as formulated by the ICJ and applied by many states, is particularly problematic when used with regard to the relationship between human rights and humanitarian law for three main reasons: first, distinguishing a special norm from a general norm is less a matter of legal logic than a purposive decision; secondly, it remains unclear whether the principle is meant to interpret norms in light of each other or serve as a conflict-solving tool; and thirdly, *lex specialis* is – quite contrary to how it is perceived – bi-directional, because speciality and generality are not static but changeable, depending on the context, and humanitarian law can be as much *lex specialis* as human rights. *Lex specialis*

[79] United Nations General Assembly, Sixth Committee, Summary Record of the 20th meeting of 3 November 2005, statement of the United States, UN Doc. A/C.6/60/SR.20 (29 November 2005), para. 33, quoted from Alston, Morgan-Foster and Abresch, "The Competence of the UN Human Rights Council" (n. 50) 195.

[80] *Report of the Working Group of the Universal Periodic Review: United States of America*, UN Doc. A/HRC/16/11 (4 January 2011), para. 53.

[81] See Françoise Hampson, "The Relationship between International Humanitarian Law and Human Rights Law from the Perspective of a Human Rights Treaty Body" (2008) 90(871) *International Review of the Red Cross* 551 (with reference to the ICJ's pronouncements in the *Fisheries* case (*United Kingdom* v. *Norway*), Judgment of 18 December 1951 [1951] ICJ Reports 116).

is thus an inadequate device to describe the relationship between human rights and humanitarian law.

First and foremost, the Advisory Opinion of the ICJ in the *Nuclear Weapons* case must not be read so as to suggest that international humanitarian law prevails as a regime over international human rights law. The Court had examined only a specific rule (the right not to be arbitrarily deprived of one's life as in ICCPR, Article 6) in light of humanitarian law. An "*en bloc*" application of international humanitarian law, which "switches off" human rights must be rejected, as it confuses the existence of specialized legal regimes with the principle of *lex specialis*: the principle is about identifying the relationship between two specific norms and not between legal regimes.[82] The idea that humanitarian law mechanically replaces other law may have resonated favourably in times when declarations of war and peace treaties started and ended wars, but such a view can no longer be sustained. It presupposes that the regime of humanitarian law is internally coherent and consistent, as a single treaty would be, which is not the case with regard to the multitude of treaties and customary standards which make up international humanitarian law.[83]

But even if applied only to a specific norm, the juxtaposition of "general" and "special" remains troublesome. Invoking the *lex specialis* nature of humanitarian law suggests that a norm of human rights law is "general" while one of humanitarian law is "special." There is, however, no justification for considering human rights law as "general" law. As legal regimes, both human rights and humanitarian law are "special" laws against the backdrop of general public international law, and their relationship is one between two special regimes, or between specific norms within these regimes. Where two special regimes exist, *lex specialis* is not applicable, as it needs a background-foreground relationship. It is not a means to decide on the relationship between two norms of two different "subsets" of international law which are in potential conflict.[84] And if it is used in such a situation, it can become next to meaningless, as each subsystem, in its self-perception as a special regime, may claim that its rules are *lex specialis*.[85] The relationship between human rights and humanitarian law can thus be perceived in all sorts of ways – as contradictory, complementary, cumulative or otherwise – but not as "speciality" in the sense which the application of the *lex specialis* principle requires.

It seems that the way in which *lex specialis* is used confuses "generality vs. speciality" with "normality vs. exception": the "general" law of human rights is the one applying in "normal," i.e., peace-time conditions, whereas the "special" law replaces the "general" law in the exceptional situation of war. And because peace and war are opposite phenomena, so

[82] See Christopher Greenwood, "Historical Development and Legal Basis" in Dieter Fleck (ed.), *The Handbook of International Humanitarian Law* (Oxford: Oxford University Press, 2008), p. 75; Paul Eden and Matthew Happold, "Symposium: The Relationship between International Humanitarian Law and International Human Rights Law" (2010) 14(3) *Journal of Conflict and Security Law* 446; Marko Milanovic, "A Norm Conflict Perspective on the Relationship between International Humanitarian Law and Human Rights Law" (2009) 14(3) *Journal of Conflict and Security Law* 462; and Danio Campanelli, "The Law of Military Occupation Put to the Test" (2008) 90(871) *International Review of the Red Cross* 657.

[83] See McCarthy, "Legal Conclusion or Interpretative Process?" (n. 26) pp. 105–10.

[84] See Lindroos, "Addressing Norm Conflicts" (n. 31) 42.

[85] See Gerald Hafner, *Risks Ensuing from Fragmentation of International Law, Report of the International Law Commission*, Annex 321, UN GAOR, 55th Session, Supplement No. 10, UN Doc. A/55/10 (27 September 2000).

their respective legal regimes are said to exclude each other. This is, however, not only a superficial and unsubstantiated dichotomy of "peace" and "war," but also a misappropriation of the principle of *lex specialis*.[86] Juxtaposing the "special" law of international humanitarian law against the "general" law of human rights mistakenly equates "general" with "normal." It has rightly been said that the idea that humanitarian law as *lex specialis* totally pre-empts all other international law, including human rights law, "originated at a time when strict compartmentalization between conditions of peace and of war were possible, [which] is no longer tenable today."[87]

Such a view would also ignore that some rules of international humanitarian law apply in peace-time (e.g., the rules on the use of the ICRC emblem or on the dissemination of international humanitarian law),[88] stretch beyond the end of an armed conflict (e.g., on the repatriation of prisoners of war),[89] or apply to states which are not party to a conflict (e.g., the duty to search for and persecute or extradite persons suspected of war crimes).[90] While these may be minor questions compared to the application of international human rights law in armed conflict, it nevertheless confirms that a strict separation of war and peace is not even contemplated by international humanitarian law.

Deriving the speciality of humanitarian law only from the context of "war" is thus not helpful. "General" could indeed be understood in the sense that international human rights law applies at all times, while the "special" international humanitarian law applies only in "special times," i.e., in war. But using the temporal scope of application of international humanitarian law ("in times of armed conflict") as a framework of reference for deciding on the speciality of norms is not what "general" means in the *lex specialis* principle. For the purposes of the principles, "general" refers to a broader, non-specific rule as opposed to a more specific one. It does not carry a temporal meaning. The argument that humanitarian law is specially made for armed conflicts says nothing else than precisely that: humanitarian law applies in armed conflict. But it says nothing about its relationship with other legal regimes in such a situation.

The fact that humanitarian law itself identifies the conditions in which it applies does give it the presumption to be special, but the speciality needs to be measured on the basis of concrete circumstances and does not derive from the fact that humanitarian law is meant to apply in armed conflicts. Special facts must lead to a deviation from the general law and make the special law seem more appropriate and valid than the general rule: "the special nature of the facts justifies a deviation from what would otherwise be the 'normal' course of action."[91] Such facts may then call for the application of the special, i.e., most appropriate norm, regardless of the legal regime in which it resides. As a consequence, human rights law may be the special law in a given situation, too, and *lex specialis* becomes a bi-directional principle.

86 See for a similar argument Krieger, "A Conflict of Norms" (n. 36) 271.

87 Gowlland-Debbas, "The Right to Life and Genocide" (n. 48) p. 325.

88 On the misuse of the emblem see Geneva Convention I, Arts. 53 and 54 and Geneva Convention II, Arts. 41–45; and on dissemination see Geneva Convention I, Art. 47; Geneva Convention II, Art. 48; Geneva Convention III, Art. 127; and Geneva Convention IV, Art. 144.

89 See Geneva Convention III, Part IV.

90 See Geneva Convention I, Art. 49; Geneva Convention II, Art. 50; Geneva Convention III, Art. 129 and Geneva Convention IV, Art. 146.

91 ILC Study on Fragmentation (n. 13) paras. 104–5.

Even if a relationship of speciality could be established between human rights and humanitarian law, one remains faced with the problem that the application of the principle of *lex specialis* presupposes that the general and special norms deal with the same subject matter.[92] It is widely accepted that if this is not the case a conflict of norms cannot occur.[93] "Subject matter" is, however, a vague term.[94] Identifying a "subject matter" requires labelling a matter as, for example, a "human rights problem," a "security issue" or an "environmental question," none of which is a clear legal qualification. "Human rights" and "humanitarian law" could be such different subject matters, or they could not, depending on how the interested parties interpret the term.[95] Some have suggested that norms of human rights and humanitarian law are not necessarily dealing with the same subject matter but merely "cohabit in the same factual space."[96]

Any decision on the speciality of a norm is furthermore purposive. The aim as well as the prerequisite of applying the principle of *lex specialis* is to identify the correct meaning, as opposed to the incorrect meaning of conflicting norms.[97] But how is one to know which norm is the correct one to apply and which one is the false one? Preference could be given, for example, to the norm which can best be argued for, or the norm which is most likely to produce a certain outcome, or the norm which is least conflicting with the general norm. The principle of *lex specialis* is purposive because ultimately one has to take into account the intentions of the parties to decide which norm takes precedence. This, however, means that what presents itself as an exercise in legal logic functions only when additional extra-legal considerations are factored into the equation to decide what is "special."[98] As all other acts of legal interpretation, the application of *lex specialis* does not (only) follow the internal logic of the law but is driven by extraneous factors.[99]

Determining the "speciality" of a norm thus ultimately depends on the intentions of the parties in question, which in turn reflect their priorities, values and interests. Deciding on how relevant a norm is for regulating a situation depends on the outcome one seeks to achieve: "special *for what*?" is the question. What is special depends entirely on the objective: "whether a rule is seen as an 'application,' 'modification' or 'exception' to another rule, depends on how we view those rules in the environment in which they are applied, including what we see as their object and purpose."[100] The principle of *lex specialis* thus leaves much discretion to the decision-makers, who can cloak all sorts of objectives under

[92] Ibid. para. 112, and Simma and Pulkowski, "Of Planets and the Universe" (n. 12) 488. See on the difference between *lex specialis ratione materiae* and *lex specialis ratione personae* Andrea Bianchi, "Dismantling the Wall: The ICJ's Advisory Opinion and its Likely Impact on International Law" (2004) 47 *German Yearbook of International Law* 371.

[93] See ILC Study on Fragmentation (n. 13) para. 117, and Pauwelyn, *Conflict of Norms* (n. 18) p. 389.

[94] VCLT, Art. 30, for example, uses the term "same subject matter" as a wide concept which comprises incompatible as well as compatible treaties, an approach which led to considerable controversies in the drafting process; see Kirsten Schmalenbach, "Application of Successive Treaties in relation to the Same Subject Matter" in Oliver Dörr and Kirsten Schmalenbach (eds.), *The Vienna Convention on the Law of Treaties, A Commentary* (Heidelberg: Springer, 2012), p. 510.

[95] See ILC Study on Fragmentation (n. 13) paras. 117–118.

[96] See McCarthy, "Legal Conclusion or Interpretative Process?" (n. 26) p. 117.

[97] See Vranes, "*Lex superior, lex specialis, lex posterior*" (n. 28) 400.

[98] See Prud'homme, "*Lex specialis*" (n. 35) 368; and McCarthy, "Legal Conclusion or Interpretative Process?" (n. 26) p. 104.

[99] See Simma and Pulkowski, "Of Planets and the Universe" (n. 12) 490.

[100] ILC Study on Fragmentation (n. 13) para. 97.

the pretence of legal reasoning.[101] As a matter of fact, in practice decision-makers first decide which rule does more justice to the situation, and then characterize it as *lex specialis*.[102] It has rightly been warned that as a consequence the principle allows manipulation of the law to support diametrically opposed arguments for and against the separation of international humanitarian law and international human rights law.[103] Indeed, its practical application demonstrates that it has been used to switch international human rights law off and on, depending on when it becomes morally intolerable rather than legally required.[104]

Different ways to overcome the vagueness of "speciality" have been suggested, but none of them seems convincing. It has been proposed to measure the speciality of humanitarian law by the dichotomy of "close" and "far": the norm which applies more closely is the special one.[105] This replaces the special character of a "speciality" of a norm with its "proximity" to the subject matter. In a similar way the idea of the greater "contact surface area"[106] of special rules (as opposed to general rules) has been suggested as a way to decide on the speciality of a norm. But the respective terminology of "battlefields" and "surface areas" leaves it open how to measure such areas and distances, and such approaches may help to identify a situation for what it is, but otherwise remain "only a rule of thumb."[107]

(b) Norm conflict or norm interpretation?

To date, it remains unclear whether *lex specialis* is a tool for interpreting norms or for solving norm conflicts.[108] Some argue fervently that the principle has historically and genuinely always been understood as a mechanism to solve norm conflicts,[109] while others are equally convinced that the principle is primarily or solely an interpretative device.[110] The ILC Study on the Fragmentation of International Law presented the two options in the following way:

> One is the case where the specific rule should be read and understood within the confines or against the background of the general standard, typically as an elaboration, updating or a technical specification of the latter. The specific and the general point, as it were, in the same direction. Sometimes *lex specialis* is, however, understood more narrowly to

[101] See Lindroos, "Addressing Norm Conflicts" (n. 31) 42.

[102] Marco Sassòli and Laura M. Olson, "The Relationship between International Humanitarian Law and Human Rights Law Where it Matters: Admissible Killing and Internment of Fighters in Non-international Armed Conflicts" (2008) 90(871) *International Review of the Red Cross* 603.

[103] See Prud'homme, "*Lex specialis*" (n. 35).

[104] See Milanovic, "Norm Conflicts, International Humanitarian Law and Human Rights Law" (n. 62) pp. 124–25.

[105] Lindroos, "Addressing Norm Conflicts" (n. 31) 36.

[106] Marco Sassòli, "The Role of Human Rights and International Humanitarian Law in New Types of Armed Conflicts" in Orna Ben-Naftali (ed.), *International Humanitarian and International Human Rights Law* (Oxford: Oxford University Press, 2011), p. 71.

[107] Daniel Thürer, *International Humanitarian Law: Theory, Practice, Context* (The Hague: Hague Academy of International Law, 2011), p. 130.

[108] See Milanovic, "Norm Conflicts, International Humanitarian Law and Human Rights Law" (n. 62) pp. 113–16.

[109] See ILC Study on Fragmentation (n. 13) para. 88.

[110] Ibid. para. 56. See also Vranes, "*Lex superior, lex specialis, lex posterior*" (n. 28) 391; Pauwelyn, *Conflict of Norms* (n. 18) p. 385; and Gowlland-Debbas, "The Right to Life and Genocide" (n. 48) pp. 138–39.

> cover the case where two legal provisions that are both valid and applicable, are in no hierarchical relationship, and provide incompatible direction on how to deal with the same set of facts. In such case, *lex specialis* appears as a conflict-solution technique.[111]

A norm conflict is a situation "where two norms that are both valid and applicable point to incompatible decisions so that a choice must be made between them."[112] The ILC Study on the Fragmentation of International Law identified three types of such conflicts: those between general law and a particular, unorthodox interpretation of general law; those between general law and a particular rule that claims to be an exception to it; and those between two types of special law.[113] Such conflicts can be "narrow," i.e., when two norms impose mutually exclusive obligations, or "broad" in the sense that they lead to diverging but not necessarily mutually exclusive outcomes.[114]

If, on the other hand, *lex specialis* is seen as a means of norm interpretation, then the special norm elaborates, updates or specifies the general norm. In this case, both the special and the general norm point towards the same direction, with the special norm clarifying the general one.[115] The general rule can also be seen as articulating a rationale or purpose of the special rule, provide the background to its application, or govern and control the application of the special rule.[116] In such a case priority must be given to the norm which describes and addresses the situation of concern in a more precise and accurate way, as compared to the other norm in question, which could nevertheless be applied, albeit with a less appropriate outcome.[117] Some would even assert that in such a situation the general and special rules effectively "accumulate."[118] In this case, there is no conflict of norms and no diverging outcome, and the principle of *lex specialis* functions like an instruction guide which allows the determination of how the general rule was meant to function.[119] The general rule thus remains as an interpretive guideline which outlines the principles and purposes of the special rules, or, as the ILC's Study on the Fragmentation of International Law put it, "[e]ven as [the *lex specialis* test] works so as to justify recourse to an exception, what is being set aside does not vanish altogether."[120]

The difference between the purpose of *lex specialis* to solve norm conflicts and to interpret norms is, however, only gradual, as the ILC acknowledged. It found that it is difficult to distinguish when a rule is merely adapted or modified and when it is overruled by an exceptional rule.[121] And given that in all likelihood an act of interpretation is needed to clarify the content of a rule before a conflict can be identified, interpretation and conflict resolution can hardly be distinguished from each other.[122] It comes thus as little surprise that the ILC Study on Fragmentation concluded that "[t]he relation of general and particular may often be complex and two-sided so that even as the particular sets aside the general, the latter . . . will continue to provide interpretative direction to the former."[123]

These two approaches – norm conflict and norm interpretation – can also be rephrased as elaboration and exception: *lex specialis* as elaboration means that the special law adapts general law to specific circumstances, while *lex specialis* as exception means that the special

[111] ILC Study on Fragmentation (n. 13) para. 58. [112] Ibid. para. 24. [113] Ibid. para. 47.
[114] See Erich Vranes, "The Definition of 'Norm-Conflict' in International Law and Legal Theory" (2006) 17(2) *European Journal of International Law* 399.
[115] See ILC Study on Fragmentation (n. 13) para. 28. [116] Ibid. paras. 29 and 31. [117] Ibid. para. 58.
[118] Pauwelyn, *Conflict of Norms* (n. 18) p. 410. [119] See Krieger, "A Conflict of Norms" (n. 36) 275.
[120] ILC Study on Fragmentation (n. 13) para. 104. [121] Ibid. paras. 92 and 95. [122] Ibid. para. 412.
[123] Ibid. para. 94.

rule overrules a general norm.[124] These two different approaches – *lex specialis* as norm conflict or norm interpretation – have also been referred to as *lex specialis complementa* and *lex specialis derogato*, although this terminology has not taken hold in scholarly writing or jurisprudence.[125] If this is the case, however, one needs to bear in mind that as a general principle of law any exceptionally applied special rule needs to be construed and interpreted narrowly, so as not to unduly displace the general rule on which it hinges: broad general laws necessitate specific and limited exceptions.[126] One may consequently argue that if a norm of international humanitarian law is *lex specialis* as an exception from the general rule of human rights, then its content has to be read so as not to deviate too much from the general norm.[127]

There is thus considerable disagreement on what actually happens when *lex specialis* is applied. But the argument that *lex specialis* allows for the complementarity and, even more problematic, a cumulative application of two rules, is questionable.[128] The precondition for the use of the principle of *lex specialis* is that at least some discernible potential inconsistency between two norms exists, and the consequence of its application is that the special law prevails over the general norm, whether as the solution of a norm conflict or by way of interpretation. When *lex specialis* is applied, it must consequently lead to preferring one norm over the other, even if the other norm remains applicable, otherwise two norms complement each other: complementarity and *lex specialis derogat legi generali* therefore cannot mean the same.

(c) A bi-directional relationship

It is now widely accepted that, as the UN High Commissioner for Human Rights puts it, "in situations of conflict of norms, the most detailed and specific rule should be chosen over the more general rule, on the basis of a case-by-case analysis, irrespective of whether it was a human rights or a humanitarian norm."[129] International humanitarian law and international human rights law may thus both be *lex specialis*, depending on the situation, as mentioned above.[130] The ICJ has argued similarly in its Advisory Opinion in the *Wall* case. As a consequence, whenever human rights law provides a more special norm, it needs to be given priority over international humanitarian law.[131] After all, international human rights norms can be at least as specific as international humanitarian law

124 See Krieger, "A Conflict of Norms" (n. 36) 269–70.

125 See Andrea Gioia, "The Role of the European Court of Human Rights in Monitoring Compliance with Humanitarian Law in Armed Conflict" in Orna Ben-Naftali (ed.), *International Humanitarian Law and International Human Rights Law* (Oxford: Oxford University Press, 2011), p. 214.

126 See in greater detail Natasha Balendra, "Defining Armed Conflict" (2008) 29(6) *Cardozo Law Review* 2490.

127 See ibid. 2491.

128 This has been done, see Bothe, "Die Anwendung der Europäischen Menschenrechtskonvention" (n. 24) 620.

129 Office of the United Nations High Commissioner for Human Rights, *Report on the Outcome of the Expert Consultation on the Issue of Protecting the Human Rights of Civilians in Armed Conflict*, UN Doc. A/HRC/11/31 (4 June 2009), para. 13.

130 See Natasha Balendra, "International Human Rights Law and International Humanitarian Law: Alternative Frameworks for Interaction" in Christoffer C. Eriksen and Marius Emberland (eds.), *The New International Law* (The Hague: Nijhoff, 2010), p. 133.

131 See Krieger, "A Conflict of Norms" (n. 36) 273–74.

norms.[132] With regard to the right to life, for example, international humanitarian law may be *lex specialis* in situations of armed conflict (as the ICJ said in its *Nuclear Weapons* case), whereas for judicial guarantees international human rights law may be the *lex specialis*. The way in which international human rights law has helped the development of humanitarian law in this area is well acknowledged, even by those otherwise critical of the role of human rights in situations of armed conflict.[133] And the situation may even be more fluid: Common Article 3 of the Geneva Conventions, for example, can be seen as both "special" and "general":[134] it is special in a contextual and purposive sense because it is particularly geared towards providing minimum humanitarian protection in the situations it seeks to regulate. But when compared to human rights law it is by no means special as to its content: the "outrages on personal dignity" and the "humiliating and degrading treatment" which it seeks to prevent become clear when read in the language of human rights.[135] But at the same time, it is special again for its prohibition of hostage-taking, which has no counterpart in international human rights law.

A similar situation may arise for some socio-economic rights which are worded in a broad programmatic fashion, as opposed to detailed humanitarian norms (for example, in the law of occupation) which one might prefer as *lex specialis*.[136] Yet, if one draws on the often detailed concluding observations of human rights treaty bodies on socio-economic rights, then human rights may be more special than humanitarian law.[137] Geneva

[132] See David S. Koller, "The Moral Imperative: Toward a Human-Rights Based Law of War" (2005) 46(1) *Harvard International Law Journal* 263.

[133] Cornelio Sommaruga, "Humanitarian Law and Human Rights in the Legal Arsenal of the ICRC" in Daniel Warner (ed.), *Human Rights and Humanitarian Law: The Quest for Universality* (The Hague: Nijhoff, 1997), p. 127.

[134] Geneva Conventions, Common Art. 3: "In the case of armed conflict not of an international character occurring in the territory of one of the High Contracting Parties, each Party to the conflict shall be bound to apply, as a minimum, the following provisions: 1.) Persons taking no active part in the hostilities, including members of armed forces who have laid down their arms and those placed 'hors de combat' by sickness, wounds, detention, or any other cause, shall in all circumstances be treated humanely, without any adverse distinction founded on race, colour, religion or faith, sex, birth or wealth, or any other similar criteria. To this end, the following acts are and shall remain prohibited at any time and in any place whatsoever with respect to the above-mentioned persons: (a) violence to life and person, in particular murder of all kinds, mutilation, cruel treatment and torture; (b) taking of hostages; (c) outrages upon personal dignity, in particular humiliating and degrading treatment; (d) the passing of sentences and the carrying out of executions without previous judgment pronounced by a regularly constituted court, affording all the judicial guarantees which are recognized as indispensable by civilized peoples."

[135] See also Krieger, "A Conflict of Norms" (n. 36) 275–76.

[136] Compare, e.g., International Covenant on Economic, Social and Cultural Rights (ICESCR), Art. 11(1) on the right to food ("The States Parties to the present Covenant recognize the right of everyone to an adequate standard of living for himself and his family, including adequate food") ... and Geneva Convention IV, Art. 89 on the nutrition of interned persons ("Daily food rations for internees shall be sufficient in quantity, quality and variety to keep internees in a good state of health and prevent the development of nutritional deficiencies. Account shall also be taken of the customary diet of the internees. Internees shall also be given the means by which they can prepare for themselves any additional food in their possession. Sufficient drinking water shall be supplied to internees. The use of tobacco shall be permitted. Internees who work shall receive additional rations in proportion to the kind of labour which they perform. Expectant and nursing mothers and children under fifteen years of age, shall be given additional food, in proportion to their physiological needs.").

[137] See Noam Lubell, "Challenges in Applying Human Rights Law to Armed Conflict" (2005) 87(860) *International Review of the Red Cross* 751.

Convention III is another example, as it is a highly specialized treaty on the treatment of prisoners of war and thus *lex specialis* which prevails over human rights law which has no specific rules on prisoners of war. While many thus see no space whatsoever for human rights law given the regulatory density of Geneva Convention III,[138] others argue that humanitarian law guarantees for prisoners of war such as on fair trial can only meaningfully be derived from human rights law, because the latter are more detailed and thus more "special" than the norms of Geneva Convention III.[139] *Lex specialis* is thus not a means to guarantee the perpetual dominance of humanitarian law and exclude human rights during armed conflicts but, if applied, necessitates searching for the most special norm, whatever its provenance.

(d) *Abandoning* lex specialis: *from dogma to pragmatism*

The reason why *lex specialis* continues to enjoy support is twofold: first, there is a seductive force in its seeming simplicity as a tool of legal logic, which has led many to cling on to it for more than a quarter of a century, even though they have little to show in return.[140] Secondly, the principle can be used to pay lip-service to the universality of human rights and their continued application in times of armed conflict, while at the same time effectively excluding human rights from such situations. This way, one can have one's cake and eat it: human rights are applicable in theory but do not need to be applied in practice. There have rightly been warnings that "the sweeping application of *lex specialis* as an exclusionary device"[141] would allow states to evade international obligations by choosing norms more to their liking under the cover of an allegedly mechanical logical legal device rather than having to reveal a policy choice.

But contrary to such attempts to evade international obligations, *lex specialis* is also seen by many as a bulwark against watering down the protection offered in armed conflicts. The fear is that when international humanitarian law loses its status as *lex specialis*, there is no substitute for ensuring effective operational protection in armed conflicts. Adherents of this view usually acknowledge that human rights continue to apply in a complementary fashion with humanitarian law, but are driven by the (understandable) concern that the carefully crafted system of humanitarian law needs to be preserved and the (less plausible) conclusion that *lex specialis* is the right tool for the job. This consideration is obviously bolstering arguments for human rights law not to be inserted into armed conflict in an "unqualified manner" but rather in a "sensitive way."[142] It is doubtful, however, if the vagueness of *lex*

[138] See Michael Bothe, "Humanitäres Völkerrecht und Schutz der Menschenrechte: Auf der Suche nach Synergien und Schutzlücken" in Pierre-Marie Dupuy, Bardo Fassbender, Malcolm N. Shaw and Karl-Peter Sommermann (eds.), *Common Values in International Law, Essays in Honour of Christian Tomuschat* (Kehl: Engel, 2006), pp. 83–85.

[139] See Greenwood, "Rights at the Frontier" (n. 20) p. 287. Geneva Convention III, Art. 84 calls for a court which offers "the essential guarantees of independence and impartiality, as generally recognised." Art. 105 on the rights and means of defence provides some clarity, but Additional Protocol I, Art. 75(4) is equally general when it states that a sentence has to be "pronounced by an impartial and regularly constituted court respecting the generally recognized principles of regular judicial procedure." The jurisprudence of human rights treaty bodies and courts discusses these principles in great detail.

[140] See Prud'homme, "*Lex specialis*" (n. 35) 394.

[141] See Orna Ben-Naftali and Yuval Shany, "Living in Denial: The Application of Human Rights in the Occupied Territories" (2004) 1(37) *Israel Law Review* 56.

[142] Heintze, "On the Relationship" (n. 54) 797.

specialis makes it the right means to achieve this goal. Even though *lex specialis* continues to be the overriding principle to inform the relationship between international human rights and humanitarian law, its role in describing and prescribing the role of human rights in armed conflicts is increasingly challenged for its theoretical soundness and practical usefulness, and rightly so.[143] The principle simply is not the coherent framework for clarifying the interplay of international humanitarian law and international human rights law as which it has been presented for so long, and it does not do justice to the complexity of this interplay.[144] Stating that only international humanitarian law as *lex specialis* can reasonably govern armed conflicts is not legal reasoning, "it is dogma."[145]

The continued reliance on the principle is not justified as it has not meaningfully, consistently and predictably clarified the relationship between international humanitarian law and international human rights law since it has been invoked by the ICJ. The very foundations of *lex specialis* remain questionable in abstract terms, as well as in their practical application, and it has rightly been said that "[a]s is often the case with legalese Latin, *lex specialis* is descriptively misleading, vague in meaning, and of little practical use in application."[146]

Other approaches outside the *lex specialis* principle which allow for a complementary application of human rights and humanitarian law without considerations of "speciality" are being advocated (and will be discussed in following chapters), but their contours and implications remain uncertain.[147] The arguments has been made that because *lex specialis* is unhelpful in solving conflicts between human rights and humanitarian law, their relationship should be construed as competition rather than conflict.[148] It seems, however, that rather than constructing competitive or conflictive theories, the overall goal should be to allow the mutual interpretation of human rights and humanitarian law with a view to ensuring maximum protection as the guiding principle, while at the same time preserving the consistency of international law and guaranteeing operational clarity.

143 See McCarthy, "Legal Conclusion or Interpretative Process?" (n. 26) p. 101.

144 See Prud'homme, "*Lex specialis*" (n. 35) 359 and 382.

145 Louise Doswald-Beck, "The Right to Life in Armed Conflict: Does International Humanitarian Law Provide All the Answers?" (2007) 88(864) *International Review of the Red Cross* 903.

146 Milanovic, "Norm Conflicts, International Humanitarian Law and Human Rights Law" (n. 62) p. 124.

147 See Balendra, "International Human Rights Law and International Humanitarian Law" (n. 130) p. 118.

148 See Jean d'Aspremont and Elodie Tranchez, "The Quest for a Non-Conflictual Coexistence of International Human Rights Law and Humanitarian Law: Which Role for the *Lex Specialis* Principle?" in Robert Kolb and Gloria Gaggioli (eds.), *Research Handbook on Human Rights and Humanitarian Law* (Cheltenham: Edward Elgar, 2013), p. 242.

6

Complementarity: maximizing protection

6.1 A variegated approach

Proponents of the idea of the complementarity of human rights and humanitarian law argue that the two are distinct but related and overlapping.[1] For them, the two regimes complement each other "in a manner that no other two branches of law do,"[2] despite historic and functional differences. This position now enjoys widespread support. It is the view taken by human rights bodies, for example by the UN Human Rights Committee which in General Comment No. 31 stated that international humanitarian law and human rights law are complementary branches of international law.[3] The International Committee of the Red Cross (ICRC), too, argues for protection through complementarity,[4] and the International Court of Justice (ICJ)'s Advisory Opinion in the *Wall* case can be seen as advocating complementarity, too.[5] Case studies of situations of armed conflict also seem to reveal that in practice the complementary application of international humanitarian law and international human rights law can be observed.[6] The situation in Kuwait after the occupation by Iraq has been subjected to a particularly thorough analysis, and the fear that the joint application of human rights and humanitarian law would lead to a lower protective standard could not be confirmed.[7] And even the father of the Geneva

[1] See, e.g., Hans-Peter Gasser, "International Humanitarian Law and Human Rights Law in Non-International Armed Conflict: Joint Venture or Mutual Exclusion?" (2002) 45 *German Yearbook of International Law* 162; and Goran Melander, "International Humanitarian Law and Human Rights" (1985) 29 *Scandinavian Studies in Law* 137.

[2] Medard R. Rwelamira, "Human Rights and International Humanitarian Law: The Link or Common Ground Revisited" (1992) 3(3) *Stellenbosch Law Review* 346.

[3] Human Rights Committee, *General Comment No. 31 (Article 2) on the Nature of the General Legal Obligation Imposed on States Parties to the Covenant*, UN Doc. E/CCPR/C/21/Rev.1/Add.3 (26 May 2004), para. 11.

[4] See, e.g., Jakob Kellenberger, "Protection Through Complementarity of the Law" in International Institute of Humanitarian Law (ed.), *International Humanitarian Law and Other Legal Regimes: Interplay in Situations of Violence. Challenges and Prospects. 27th Round Table on Current Problems of International Humanitarian Law, Sanremo, 4–6 September 2003* (Sanremo: International Institute of Humanitarian Law, 2003), pp. 9–16.

[5] See Bernhard Schäfer, *Zum Verhältnis Menschenrechte und humanitäres Völkerrecht. Zugleich ein Beitrag zur extraterritorialen Geltung von Menschenrechtsverträgen* (Potsdam: Universitätsverlag Potsdam, 2006), p. 42.

[6] See M.A. Babiker, *Application of International Humanitarian and Human Rights Law to the Armed Conflict of the Sudan: Complementary or Mutually Exclusive Regimes?* (Antwerp: Intersentia, 2007), p. 276.

[7] See Walter Kälin, *Report on the Situation of Human Rights in Kuwait under Iraqi Occupation*, UN Doc. E/CN.4/1992/26 (16 January 1992); and Walter Kälin, "Die Interdependenz von Menschenrechtsschutz und humanitärem Völkerrecht: Lehren aus der Kuwait-Krise" (1993) 3(3) *Schweizerische Zeitschrift für*

Conventions, Jean Pictet, had already argued that human rights and humanitarian law are "mutually complementary, and admirably so."[8]

But even though this view dominates, "complementarity" is often used more as a catchword which leaves the precise nature of the interplay of human rights and humanitarian law open.[9] Complementarity is a variegated approach, and opinions differ considerably as to what it means. It obviously rejects the separatist position and instead suggests some connection between human rights and humanitarian law and it also does not advocate an integration or fusion of human rights and humanitarian law.[10] Complementarity describes how two entities come together to connect or interact without losing their respective form or identity.

Complementarity is often equated with convergence and a cumulative application of norms.[11] Convergence should, however, correctly be understood as a process which leads towards complementarity, while the cumulative application of two norms is, strictly speaking, less than complementarity. It merely describes a (temporal) coexistence or parallelism of human rights and humanitarian law as two applicable but otherwise isolated sets of norms which are uninterested in the outcome of their co-application and, more importantly, not geared towards any cooperative or mutually supportive effort, as complementarity seems to suggest.[12] The European Union Guidelines on Promoting Compliance with International Humanitarian Law, for example, remain ambiguous in this respect when they say that:

> international humanitarian law is applicable in time of armed conflict and occupation. Conversely, human rights law is applicable to everyone within the jurisdiction of the State concerned in time of peace as well as in time of armed conflict. Thus while distinct, the two sets of rules may both be applicable to a particular situation and it is therefore sometimes necessary to consider the relationship between them.[13]

These may be subtle differences and ultimately not very important. But they beg the question whether complementarity is understood more as a static parallelism of unconnected norms, or as an active interplay, communication and mutual influence of norms. If complementarity means the latter (as it should), then it means that human rights and humanitarian law effectively work together to achieve a common goal or purpose. In light of

internationales und europäisches Recht 236 and 238–42. The UN Security Council and the Commission on Human Rights both referred to international humanitarian law and the UN human rights Covenants as applicable to the situation, see UN Security Council Res. 666, UN Doc. S/RES/666 (14 September 1990) and Commission on Human Rights Res. 1991/67, UN Doc. E/CN.4/RES/1991/67 (6 March 1991).

8 Jean Pictet, *Development and Principles of International Humanitarian Law* (Dordrecht: Nijhoff, 1985), p. 3.

9 See Hilaire McCoubrey, *International Humanitarian Law: Modern Developments in the Limitation of Warfare* (Aldershot: Ashgate, 1998), p. 5.

10 See, e.g., Aristides Calogeropoulos-Stratis, "Droit humanitaire – droits de l'homme et victimes des conflits armés" in Christophe Swinarski (ed.), *Studies and Essays on International Humanitarian Law and Red Cross Principles in Honour of Jean Pictet* (The Hague: Nijhoff, 1984), p. 661.

11 See, e.g., Walter Kälin, *Human Rights in Times of Occupation: The Case of Kuwait* (Bern: Stämpfli, 1994), p. 27; and Hilaire McCoubrey, *International Humanitarian Law: Modern Developments in the Limitation of Warfare* (Aldershot: Ashgate, 1998), p. 5.

12 This seems to be suggested by Gasser, "International Humanitarian Law and Human Rights Law" (n. 1) 150.

13 Updated European Union Guidelines on Promoting Compliance with International Humanitarian Law (IHL) [2009] OJ C303/12, para. 12.

the common purpose of human rights and humanitarian law, it can be assumed that this goal is the protection of the individual.

Complementarity can also be viewed as an instrument or, more specifically, as a legal principle for achieving such a political goal.[14] This seems to be reflected in Vienna Convention on the Law of Treaties (VCLT), Article 31(3)(c) which allows the taking into account of "any relevant rules of international law applicable in the relations between the parties"[15] when interpreting treaties. If it is necessary to resort to other norms in order to understand the meaning of a given norm in a specific context, this other norm can be said to be invoked in a "complementary" manner. Complementarity thus becomes an interpretative principle: two norms on a given subject matter are being used in a complementary fashion to identify what the law means.

Obviously, this brings the idea of complementarity closer to the principle of *lex specialis*, and as a consequence commentators on the ICJ's Advisory Opinion in the *Nuclear Weapons* case were confused as to whether the Court meant to prefer humanitarian law over human rights law and exclude the latter, or rather apply the two in a complementary fashion. And indeed, complementarity has been associated or even equated with the principle of *lex specialis.*[16] This is, however, a misappropriation of the term: unlike *lex specialis*, complementarity is less about establishing prevalence than it is about securing consistency, filling gaps and achieving broader normative coverage.[17] The terms "cross-pollination"[18] and "cross-fertilization"[19] have been used to describe this fact. Others prefer to call such an interpretative approach to complementarity a *renvoi*, in analogy to private law.[20] Unlike the principle of *lex specialis* which purports to act as a stringent exercise in legal logic leading to the exclusion of a norm, *renvoi* is about the more pragmatic choice of law. Given that the principle of *renvoi* is a challenging and ill-defined concept even in private law from where it is borrowed, its use may be of limited value.[21] Still, it does support the idea that the relationship between human rights and humanitarian law is about norm coordination rather than norm exclusion. As has been argued elsewhere:

> [i]n times of armed conflict, human rights law applies simultaneously to international humanitarian law. The latter should not be considered as a *lex specialis* derogating from human rights law in its entirety. It should rather be considered as a complementary body

[14] See Cordula Droege, "Elective Affinities? Human Rights and Humanitarian Law" (2008) 90(871) *International Review of the Red Cross* 521.

[15] VCLT, Art. 31(3)(c).

[16] See United Nations Office of the High Commissioner for Human Rights, *International Legal Protection of Human Rights in Armed Conflict* (New York and Geneva: United Nations, 2011), p. 54.

[17] See Cordula Droege, "The Interplay between International Humanitarian Law and International Human Rights Law in Situations of Armed Conflict" (2007) 40(2) *Israel Law Review* 341.

[18] René Provost, *International Human Rights and Humanitarian Law* (Cambridge: Cambridge University Press, 2002), p. 350.

[19] Droege, "The Interplay" (n. 17) 342.

[20] See Robert Kolb and Richard Hyde, *An Introduction to the International Law of Armed Conflict* (Oxford: Hart, 2008), pp. 270–74. The authors argue for the existence of three specific constellations with regard to the relationship between international humanitarian law and international human rights law: subsidiarity, *renvoi* and merger.

[21] See on the principle in private international law Berlingher Remus Daniel, "The *Renvoi* in Private International Law" (2013) 3(1) *International Journal of Social Science and Humanity* 66.

of law allowing in many cases the strengthening of the general protections offered by human rights law.[22]

6.2 Interpretation, cumulative application and filling gaps

(a) Systematic coherence

In more concrete terms, the complementarity of human rights and humanitarian norms allows the use of norms of human rights law to fill gaps in humanitarian law, to apply norms of both regimes cumulatively so as to heighten the level of protection, or to interpret norms in light of each other.[23] This is what the ICRC Study on Customary International Humanitarian Law obviously means when it advocates (in the section on "Fundamental Guarantees") the use of human rights instruments, documents and case law "in order to support, strengthen and clarify analogous principles of humanitarian law."[24] When complementarity is understood in such a way, it is geared towards harmonizing norms of human rights and humanitarian law in light of their common goals.[25]

Obviously, similar arguments have been made for the principle of *lex specialis* as far as interpretation is concerned. The difference is that *lex specialis* ultimately seeks to identify the "correct" (i.e., special) norm at the expense of the inappropriate general norm, whereas in a complementary approach the aim is to achieve systemic coherence in light of shared underlying principles. This acknowledges that a sharp demarcation of "special" legal regimes is not envisaged in international law, particularly when their subject matter bears similarities:

> even though international human rights law, international criminal law and international humanitarian law are not identical, they can be "fuzzier" sets than is sometimes thought, and are certainly not autopoietic systems. Therefore, they ought not to be treated as such, but like many things, with due respect for context, human rights law and humanitarian law can end up playing in harmony if not unity.[26]

The idea of a harmonious interpretation is challenged where the norms in question are very ambiguous or irreconcilable.[27] It has thus been suggested to distinguish between genuine

[22] Gloria Gaggioli and Robert Kolb, "A Right to Life in Armed Conflict? The Contribution of the European Court of Human Rights" (2007) 37 *Israel Yearbook on Human Rights* 163.

[23] See, e.g., Héctor Gros Espiell, "Humanitarian Law and Human Rights" in Janusz Symonides (ed.), *Human Rights: Concepts and Standards* (Aldershot and Paris: Ashgate and UNESCO, 2000), p. 3. The filling of gaps has occasionally and somewhat ambiguously also been termed subsidiarity, see Kolb and Hyde, *An Introduction to the International Law of Armed Conflict* (n. 20), pp. 270–74. See the respective calls to use human rights, humanitarian law and refugee law in a cumulative fashion in *Report of the Secretary General on the Protection of Civilians in Armed Conflict*, UN Doc. S/1999/957 (8 December 1999), para. 36.

[24] Jean-Marie Henckaerts and Louise Doswald-Beck, *Customary International Humanitarian Law*, vol. I, *Rules* (Cambridge: Cambridge University Press, 2005), p. 299.

[25] See Ruona Iguyovwe, "The Interplay between International Humanitarian Law and International Human Rights Law" in Aldo Zammit Borda (ed.), *International Humanitarian Law and the International Red Cross and Red Crescent Movement* (London: Routledge, 2010), p. 41.

[26] Robert Cryer, "The Interplay of Human Rights and Humanitarian Law: The Approach of the ICTY" (2009) 14(3) *Journal of Conflict and Security Law* 527.

[27] See Natasha Balendra, "International Human Rights Law and International Humanitarian Law: Alternative Frameworks for Interaction" in Christoffer C. Eriksen and Marius Emberland (eds.), *The New International Law* (The Hague: Nijhoff, 2010), pp. 133–36.

and apparent norm conflicts: while the latter can be solved by interpretative techniques because the application of the two norms may lead to a diverging but not necessarily diametrically opposed outcome, the former situation cannot be solved within the law at all and needs extra-legal solutions.[28] Where international humanitarian law and international human rights law cannot be read in harmony there is need for legislation rather than interpretation, and states would need to agree on new rules for armed conflict.[29] But few, if any, such contradictory cases have, however, yet been identified and such contradictions seem to be more a fear than evidenced in practice. Particular problems may arise when the use of human rights law in situations of occupation does not conform to the demand of humanitarian law to leave the law of the land unmodified, a question which will be dealt with in greater detail in Part 4. The most vivid debates on contradictory regulations arise with regard to the right to life and the way in which human rights and humanitarian law regulate the use of deadly force (a matter which will be dealt with later).

(b) Civil and political rights

That such a mutual interpretation, cumulative application and filling of gaps is possible, has been repeatedly demonstrated.[30] Even though an exhaustive, article-by-article analysis of the potential (and pitfalls) of such mutual interpretation, cumulative application and filling of gaps has yet to be undertaken, there are sufficient examples which demonstrate the feasibility of this approach.[31] Some principles such as non-discriminatory treatment, for example, are of equal importance for human rights and humanitarian law.[32] The open-worded references to the principle of fair trial in humanitarian law can also benefit from an interpretation in light of human rights norms.[33] It is an area where international human

[28] See Marko Milanovic, "Norm Conflicts, International Humanitarian Law and Human Rights Law" in Orna Ben-Naftali (ed.), *International Humanitarian and International Human Rights Law* (Oxford: Oxford University Press, 2011), pp. 102 and 108.

[29] See Paul Eden and Matthew Happold, "Symposium: The Relationship between International Humanitarian Law and International Human Rights Law" (2010) 14(3) *Journal of Conflict and Security Law* 447.

[30] See, e.g., Hans-Joachim Heintze, "On the Relationship between Human Rights Law Protection and International Humanitarian Law (2004) 86(856) *International Review of the Red Cross* 793; and UN OHCHR, *International Legal Protection of Human Rights in Armed Conflict* (n. 16) p. 57. For a comparison of specific norms of human rights law and humanitarian law in table form see Kälin, *Human Rights in Times of Occupation* (n. 11) pp. 64–67; and Christian Johann, *Menschenrechte im bewaffneten Konflikt. Zur Anwendbarkeit der Europäischen Menschenrechtskonvention und des Internationalen Pakts über bürgerliche und politische Rechte auf Kriegshandlungen* (Berlin: Berliner Wissenschaftsverlag, 2012), pp. 32–35.

[31] See also Orna Ben-Naftali, "Introduction: International Humanitarian and International Human Rights Law – *Pas de Deux*" in Orna Ben-Naftali (ed.), *International Humanitarian and International Human Rights Law* (Oxford: Oxford University Press, 2011), pp. 5–6; and Noelle Quénivet, "Introduction: The History of the Relationship between International Humanitarian Law and Human Rights Law" in Roberta Arnold and Noelle Quénivet (eds.), *International Humanitarian Law and Human Rights Law: Towards a Merger in International Law* (Leiden: Nijhoff, 2008), pp. 9–11.

[32] See Geneva Convention I, Art. 12; Geneva Convention II, Art. 12; Geneva Convention III, Art. 16; Additional Protocol I, Art. 9(1); Geneva Convention IV, Art. 13; see also Jelena Pejic, "Non-discrimination in Armed Conflict" (2001) 83(841) *International Review of the Red Cross* 183.

[33] See Peter Rowe, *The Impact of Human Rights Law on Armed Forces* (Cambridge: Cambridge University Press, 2006), pp. 153–56; and International Committee of the Red Cross, *International Humanitarian*

rights law offers greater regulatory density and clarity compared to international humanitarian law. Common Article 3 to the Geneva Conventions, for example, prohibits "the passing of sentences and the carrying out of executions without previous judgment pronounced by a regularly constituted court, affording all the judicial guarantees which are recognized as indispensable by civilized peoples."[34] ICCPR, Article 14 specifies that such a court needs to be "a competent, independent and impartial tribunal established by law,"[35] and extensive case law of human rights treaty bodies on the meaning of these terms exists.[36] Similar arguments can be made with respect to the judicial guarantees for prisoners of war (in Geneva Convention III, Articles 96, 99 and 108) and for persons in occupied territories (in Geneva Convention IV, Articles 54, 64–74 and 117–126).[37]

The important question of detention in conflict situations is particularly susceptible to accommodating human rights law.[38] The interplay of international human rights and international humanitarian law in situations of detention is, with the exception of the United States, widely acknowledged.[39] Despite many rules on detention and internment in all four Geneva Conventions and in the Additional Protocols, it is commonly accepted that the level of protection is insufficient and in need of being supplemented by international human rights law, particularly in internal armed conflicts where Common Article 3 of the Geneva Conventions and Additional Protocol II provide only rudimentary protection.[40] The same can be said for review procedures in situations of detention and internment.[41] Persons deprived of their liberty have been identified by the ICRC as posing regulatory challenges, and women, children and vulnerable groups in armed conflict, including the elderly and disabled, are insufficiently protected under international humanitarian law.[42] The ICRC thus sees the rules on detention conditions in international humanitarian law and international human rights law as largely congruent.[43] The different regulations for international and non-international armed conflicts complicate the matter so that the ICRC suggested clarifying the interplay between international humanitarian law and international

Law and the Challenges of Contemporary Armed Conflicts, Report to the 31st International Conference of the Red Cross and Red Crescent (2011), p. 16.

34 Geneva Conventions, Common Art. 3(1)(d). 35 ICCPR, Art. 14(1).

36 See also Kolb and Hyde, *An Introduction to the International Law of Armed Conflict* (n. 20), p. 271.

37 See Fionnuala Ní Aoláin, "The Individual Rights of Access to Justice in Times of Crisis: Emergencies, Armed Conflict and Terrorism" in Francesco Francioni (ed.), *Access to Justice as a Human Right* (Oxford: Oxford University Press, 2007), pp. 79–86.

38 See Rowe, *The Impact of Human Rights Law on Armed Forces* (n. 33) pp. 148–153.

39 See, e.g., Jelena Pejic, "Procedural Principles and Safeguards for Internment/Administrative Detention in Armed Conflict and Other Situations of Violence" in Larry Maybee and Benarji Chakka (eds.), *Custom as a Source of International Humanitarian Law* (Geneva: International Committee of the Red Cross and Asian African Legal Consultative Organisation, 2005), p. 378. On the US misconceptions of international humanitarian law standards of persons detained in the "War on Terrorism" see Ryan Goodman, "Editorial Comment: The Detention of Civilians in Armed Conflict" (2009) 103(1) *American Journal of International Law* 48.

40 See Pejic, "Procedural Principles and Safeguards" (n. 39) p. 377.

41 See, e.g., University Centre for International Humanitarian Law, *Report of the Expert Meeting on the Supervision of the Lawfulness of Detention during Armed Conflict* (2004), pp. 16–19.

42 See International Committee of the Red Cross, *Strengthening Legal Protection for Victims of Armed Conflict, International Conference of the Red Cross and Red Crescent Societies (28 November–1 December 2011)*, ICRC Doc. 31IC/11/5.1.1 (October 2011), pp. 9–10.

43 See International Committee of the Red Cross, *International Humanitarian Law and the Challenges of Contemporary Armed Conflicts* (n. 33) p. 16

human rights law on a case-by-case basis.[44] The internment of individuals in non-international armed conflicts lacks specific rules in humanitarian law beyond Common Article 3 of the Geneva Conventions, and benefits from reference to more special human rights provisions on judicial and procedural guarantees, review and remedy, detention conditions, and personal security and integrity.[45]

The Copenhagen Process on the Handling of Detainees in International Military Operations was initiated by Denmark in 2007 and concluded in 2012 with the adoption of the Copenhagen Principles on the Handling of Detainees in International Military Operations, a set of non-binding recommendations which identify best practices in handling detainees.[46] It can be seen as a response to such concerns for the way it seeks to meet the challenges of multinational operations in detaining persons. In the process, human rights and humanitarian law were seen as complementary so as to allow identifying standards for handling detainees. It was driven by the recognition that the uncertainty about *which* law applies *when* (human rights, humanitarian law or domestic law in situations of international or non-international conflict, occupations, multinational military and peace operations, internal tensions or other situations of violence) has reached a level which makes conduct in accordance with the law extremely difficult for the military, and reflects the quest for reaching a higher degree of protection and a greater level of operational clarity in a pragmatic manner.[47]

The prohibition of torture is defined more narrowly under human rights law as "an act committed by or at the instigation of or with the consent or acquiescence of a public official or other person acting in an official capacity,"[48] than it is under humanitarian law which places obligations on governmental and non-governmental actors. The International Criminal Tribunal for the Former Yugoslavia (ICTY) has thus adapted the definition of torture to include such groups by interpreting Article 2 of the Convention Against Torture and Other Cruel, Inhuman or Degrading Treatment (CAT) in light of the requirements of humanitarian law, so as to allow for the most favourable protection.[49] The reference to "inhuman treatment" of prisoners of war in Geneva Convention III, Article 130 and Geneva Convention IV, Article 147 can be read in light of the norms and the extensive case law of human rights bodies.

The prohibition of medical experiments is found in Article 11 of Additional Protocol I as well as in ICCPR, Article 7.[50] It has also been suggested to read, where appropriate, Geneva Convention III, Article 13 on the general protection of prisoners of war ("Prisoners of war must at all times be humanely treated")[51] and Geneva Convention III, Article 12 on their transfer ("Prisoners of war may only be transferred by the Detaining Power to a Power

[44] Ibid. pp. 16–17.

[45] See Daniel Thürer, *International Humanitarian Law: Theory, Practice, Context* (The Hague: Hague Academy of International Law, 2011), pp. 142–44.

[46] See Ministry of Foreign Affairs of Denmark, available at http://um.dk/en/politics-and-diplomacy/copenhagen-process-on-the-handling-of-detainees-in-international-military-operations (last accessed 15 April 2014).

[47] See Craig A. Brannagan, "The Copenhagen Process on the Handling of Detainees in International Military Operations: A Canadian Perspective on the Challenges and Goals of Warfare" (2010) 15(3) *Journal of Conflict and Security Law* 504 and 517.

[48] CAT, Art. 2(1). [49] See Droege, "The Interplay" (n. 17) 342.

[50] See Schäfer, "Zum Verhältnis Menschenrechte und humanitäres Völkerrecht" (n. 5) p. 45.

[51] Geneva Convention III, Art. 13.

which is a party to the Convention and after the Detaining Power has satisfied itself of the willingness and ability of such transferee Power to apply the Convention")[52] in light of Article 3 of the European Convention on Human Rights (ECHR) on inhuman or degrading treatment or punishment,[53] so as to conclude that transferring a prisoner of war held by a state party to the ECHR to a state in which the prisoner faces the death penalty amounts in effect to a violation of Geneva Convention III, Article 13, given that the death penalty is an inhuman punishment under the ECHR.[54] Internal displacement is another area where international humanitarian law, international human rights law and refugee law are widely considered as jointly applicable, and the Guiding Principles on Internal Displacement of 1998 draw on these different legal sources.[55]

(c) Economic, social and cultural rights

The close nexus and growing convergence of cultural rights in international humanitarian law and international human rights law has been highlighted with regard to the protection of cultural heritage in armed conflicts.[56] In particular, it has been argued that an analysis of the respective rules under international humanitarian law, such as in the 1954 Hague Convention and its Protocols, demonstrates that such protection is not only afforded to material representations of cultural heritage, but is meant to ensure the enjoyment of and access to cultural heritage as a human right.[57] The right to take part in cultural life, as stipulated, for example, in ICESCR, Article 15(1),[58] is interpreted by the Committee on Economic, Social and Cultural Rights as encompassing not only the preservation and presentation of mankind's cultural heritage and the duty to preserve cultural property, but also the prohibition of their wilful destruction by force.[59]

52 Geneva Convention III, Art. 12: "Prisoners of war may only be transferred by the Detaining Power to a Power which is a party to the Convention and after the Detaining Power has satisfied itself of the willingness and ability of such transferee Power to apply the Convention."

53 European Convention on Human Rights and Fundamental Freedoms, 4 November 1950, ETS 5, 213 UNTS 222, Art. 3: "No one shall be subjected to torture or to inhuman or degrading treatment or punishment."

54 See Heike Krieger, "Die Verantwortlichkeit Deutschlands nach der EMRK für seine Streitkräfte im Auslandseinsatz" (2002) 62 *Zeitschrift für ausländisches öffentliches Recht und Völkerrecht* 695.

55 UN Guiding Principles on Internal Displacement, UN Doc. E/CN.4/1998/53, Add. 2 (17 April 1998), and Sadako Ogata, "Human Rights, Humanitarian Law and Refugee Protection" in Daniel Warner (ed.), *Human Rights and Humanitarian Law: The Quest for Universality* (The Hague: Nijhoff, 1997), pp. 138–39; and Thürer, *International Humanitarian Law* (n. 45), p. 146.

56 See, e.g., Howard M. Hensel, "The Protection of Cultural Objects during Armed Conflicts" in Howard M. Hensel (ed.), *The Law of Armed Conflict: Constraints on the Contemporary Use of Military Force* (Aldershot: Ashgate, 2006), pp. 49–103; and Erika J. Techera, "Protection of Cultural Heritage in Times of Armed Conflict: The International Legal Framework Revisited" (2007) 4(1) *Macquarie Journal of International and Comparative Environmental Law* 1, neither of whom, however, mention human rights.

57 See Ana Filipa Vrdoljak, "Cultural Heritage in Human Rights and Humanitarian Law" in Orna Ben-Naftali (ed.), *International Humanitarian and International Human Rights Law* (Oxford: Oxford University Press, 2011), p. 302.

58 ICESCR, Art. 15(1): "The States Parties to the present Covenant recognize the right of everyone: (a) to take part in cultural life."

59 See Roger O'Keefe, *The Protection of Cultural Property in Armed Conflict* (Cambridge: Cambridge University Press, 2006), p. 305.

Freedom of religion, i.e., the right to choose, have and practise a religious belief, is often side-lined as less important in armed conflicts where "core" rights such as life, liberty and subsistence are at stake. But religious matters are well covered by international humanitarian law which contains the prohibition of discrimination on religious grounds.[60] Prisoners of war are entitled to practise their religion freely within the boundaries of disciplinary routine.[61] But the terms used in Article 34 ("complete latitude" of belief, constraints of "disciplinary routine" and "adequate premises" for worship) lend themselves to an interpretation by human rights law and jurisprudence.[62]

Economic, social and cultural rights are more elaborate in humanitarian (occupation) law, which knows detailed regulations on education, health care, food and supply with relief goods, whereas under human rights law detailed guidelines and case law have emerged to clarify the programmatic provisions of human rights treaties in this area.[63] They form an important part of the law of occupation.[64] The right to health is perhaps most intrinsically woven into the fabric of international humanitarian law, the very development of which started with Henry Dunant's concern for the wounded soldiers on the battlefield of Solferino and their need for medical assistance. The first two Geneva Conventions are concerned with this matter, as is reflected in their very titles.[65] Additional Protocol I also entitles the wounded, sick and shipwrecked of whatever party and without any discrimination to "receive, to the fullest extent practicable and with the least possible delay, the medical care and attention required by their condition."[66] The protection of medical infrastructure, personnel and equipment is central to the rules of international armed conflict,[67] and Occupying Powers have the duty to ensure food and medical supplies and maintain public health and hygiene facilities and services.[68] Still, human rights law can strengthen these provisions where they are more exact.[69]

The right to food is expressed in different ways under international humanitarian law: as part of humanitarian relief, with regard to the food security of detained and interned

60 See Geneva Convention I, Art. 12; Geneva Convention II, Art. 12; Geneva Convention III, Art. 16; Additional Protocol I, Art. 9(1); Geneva Convention IV, Art. 13; and Additional Protocol I, Art. 75. See also Hilaire McCoubrey, "The Protection of Creed and Opinion in the Laws of Armed Conflict" (2000) 5 (2) *Journal of Conflict and Security Law* 139.

61 Geneva Convention III, Art. 34: "Prisoners of war shall enjoy complete latitude in the exercise of their religious duties, including attendance at the service of their faith, on condition that they comply with the disciplinary routine prescribed by the military authorities. Adequate premises shall be provided where religious services may be held."

62 See on religious rights under humanitarian law in greater detail McCoubrey, "The Protection of Creed" (n. 60) 142–45; and Heintze, "On the Relationship" (n. 30) 795.

63 See, e.g., Food and Agricultural Organisation, Voluntary Guidelines to support the progressive realization of the right to adequate food in the context of national food security (23 November 2004), available at ftp://ftp.fao.org/docrep/fao/009/y7937e/y7937e00.pdf (last accessed 15 April 2014).

64 See Noam Lubell, "Challenges in Applying Human Rights Law to Armed Conflict" (2005) 87(860) *International Review of the Red Cross* 751.

65 Geneva Convention I for the Amelioration of the Condition of the Wounded and Sick in Armed Forces in the Field and Geneva Convention II for the Amelioration of the Condition of the Wounded, Sick and Shipwrecked Members of Armed Forces at Sea.

66 Additional Protocol I, Art. 10.

67 See in greater detail Pierre Perrin, "The Right to Health in Armed Conflict" in Andrew Clapham and Mary Robinson (eds.), *Realizing the Right to Health* (Zurich: Rüffer & Rub, 2009), pp. 160–62.

68 See Geneva Convention IV, Arts. 55 and 56.

69 See Perrin, "The Right to Health in Armed Conflict" (n. 67) p. 169.

persons, and in situations of occupation. Prisoners of war, for example, and civilian internees are entitled to basic daily food rations,[70] and Occupying Powers are obliged to ensure the supply of food to the population to the fullest extent possible, which includes the duty to bring additional foodstuffs, if necessary.[71] The Occupying Power must not requisition food other than for use by occupation forces and administrative personnel, and only when the requirements of the civilian population are taken into account.[72] International humanitarian law is general and specific at the same time with regard to these issues. It is specific as it introduces limits to the right to food not provided for under international humanitarian law (i.e., the needs of occupation forces) and as far as humanitarian relief is concerned, and general as it does not specify what "necessary" foodstuffs are, so that recourse to human rights law may be helpful.[73] Unlike rules on the protection of and supply with food, the right to water is not very obvious in international humanitarian law. An exception is the prohibition of contaminating water, a remnant of medieval rules on warfare.[74] Often, the right to water is provided as equivalent to the right to food[75] or is covered by rules which protect means indispensable for the survival of the civilian population.[76]

Linking the human right to education and armed conflict is also a relatively recent phenomenon despite the many provisions of international humanitarian law on the

[70] See Geneva Convention III, Art. 26: "The basic daily food rations shall be sufficient in quantity, quality and variety to keep prisoners of war in good health and to prevent loss of weight or the development of nutritional deficiencies." This article also contains provisions for the habitual diet of prisoners, additional rates for working prisoners, drinking water and tobacco, and adequate premises for eating. Geneva Convention IV, Art. 89 on civilian internees uses similar wording and extends the protection to nursing mothers and children.

[71] See Geneva Convention IV, Art. 55.

[72] Geneva Convention IV, Art. 55: "The Occupying Power may not requisition foodstuffs, articles or medical supplies available in the occupied territory, except for use by the occupation forces and administration personnel, and then only if the requirements of the civilian population have been taken into account. Subject to the provisions of other international Conventions, the Occupying Power shall make arrangements to ensure that fair value is paid for any requisitioned goods."

[73] See on the right to food and the obligation to provide relief in greater detail Uwe Kracht, "Human Rights and Humanitarian Norms: The Right to Food in Armed Conflict" in Morten Bergsmo (ed.), *Human Rights and Criminal Justice for the Downtrodden, Essays in Honour of Asbjorn Eide* (Leiden: Nijhoff, 2003), pp. 267–68; and Jelena Pejic, "The Right to Food in Situations of Armed Conflict: The Legal Framework" (2001) 83(84) *International Review of the Red Cross* 1109.

[74] See Ameur Zemmali, "The Right to Water in Times of Armed Conflict" in Liesbeth Lijnzaad, Johanna van Sambeek and Bahia Tahzib-Lie (eds.), *Making the Voice of Humanity Heard, Essays on Humanitarian Assistance and International Humanitarian Law in Honour of HRH Princess Margriet of the Netherlands* (Leiden: Nijhoff, 2004), p. 311.

[75] E.g. in Geneva Convention III, Arts. 26 and 89 on the daily food rations of prisoners of war or in Geneva Convention III, Arts. 20 and 46 on the care for prisoners of war while they are being evacuated or transferred.

[76] E.g. Additional Protocol I, Art. 54(2): "It is prohibited to attack, destroy, remove or render useless objects indispensable to the survival of the civilian population, such as foodstuffs, agricultural areas for the production of foodstuffs, crops, livestock, drinking water installations and supplies and irrigation works, for the specific purpose of denying them for their sustenance value to the civilian population or to the adverse Party, whatever the motive, whether in order to starve out civilians, to cause them to move away, or for any other motive." See Théo Boutruche, "Le statut de l'eau en droit international humanitaire" (2000) 82(840) *International Review of the Red Cross* 891.

protection of educational institutions.[77] International humanitarian law takes into account the educational needs of children in international[78] and non-international armed conflicts[79] and situations of occupation,[80] as well as those of particularly vulnerable groups such as orphans and unaccompanied children.[81] Such general obligations of "ensuring education" can be interpreted in light of international human rights law, which not only contain more specific provisions on the right to education, but has also refined and operationalized the substance and content of the right to education, e.g., through the General Comments of treaty bodies.[82] General Comment No. 13 of the Committee on Economic, Social and Cultural Rights, together with the reports of the UN Special Rapporteur on the right to education, for example, defines the right to education in terms of its availability, accessibility, acceptability and adaptability,[83] a method of direct relevance for discerning the obligations of Occupying Powers.[84]

(d) *Indivisibility of human rights*

It is often assumed that only certain human rights apply in situations of armed conflicts. They are often referred to as "core" human rights which have particular importance in situations of armed conflict because they regulate matters similar, or equivalent, to international humanitarian law, or contribute otherwise in a meaningful way. Sometimes they are equated with non-derogable human rights or *jus cogens* norms.[85] Such claims

77 See Sobhi Tawil, "International Humanitarian Law and Basic Education" (2000) 82(840) *International Review of the Red Cross* 583. On the protection of educational institutions under international humanitarian law see generally David A.G. Lewis, "The Protection of Civilian Educational Institutions during the Active Hostilities of International Armed Conflict in International Humanitarian Law" in Jonas Grimheden and Rolf Ring (eds.), *Human Rights Law: From Dissemination to Application, Essays in Honour of Göran Melander* (Leiden: Nijhoff, 2006), pp. 99–118.

78 See, e.g., Geneva Convention IV, Art. 94 on interned children: "The education of children and young people shall be ensured; they shall be allowed to attend schools within their place of internment or outside."

79 See, e.g., Additional Protocol II, Art. 4(3)(a): "Children . . . shall receive an education, including religious and moral education."

80 See, e.g., Geneva Convention IV, Art. 59: "The Occupying Power shall, with the cooperation of the national and local authorities, facilitate the proper working of all institutions devoted to the care and education of children."

81 Geneva Convention IV, Art. 50: "The Parties to the conflict shall take the necessary measures to ensure that children under fifteen, who are orphaned or are separated from their families as a result of the war, are not left to their own resources, and that their maintenance, the exercise of their religion and their education are facilitated in all circumstances."

82 See in greater detail and with reference to the sources of the right to education in international human rights law Jonathan T. Horowitz, "The Right to Education in Occupied Territories: Making More Room for Human Rights in Occupation Law" (2004) 7 *Yearbook of International Humanitarian Law* 249.

83 See Committe on Economic, Social and Cultural Rights, *General Comment No. 13 ICESCR on the Right to Education*, UN Doc. E/C.12/1999/10 (8 December 1999), para. 6; and *Report of the Special Rapporteur on the Right to Education*, E/CN.4/2002/60, paras. 27–29. See also the *Report of the Special Rapporteur on the Right to Education in Emergency Situations*, UN Doc. A/HRC/8/10 (20 May 2008).

84 See Jonathan Horowitz, "The Right to Education in Occupied Territories: Making More Room for Human Rights in Occupation Law" (2004) 7 *Yearbook of International Humanitarian Law* 253.

85 See Stefanie Schmahl, "Der Menschenrechtsschutz in Friedenszeiten im Vergleich zum Menschenrechtsschutz im Krieg" in Jana Hasse, Erwin Müller and Patricia Schneider (eds.), *Humanitäres Völkerrecht: politische, rechtliche und strafgerichtliche Dimensionen* (Baden-Baden: Nomos, 2001), p. 62.

which single out certain human rights provisions as applicable on the grounds of their alleged character as "core" rights stand, however, in opposition to the widely accepted indivisibility of human rights and challenge the doctrinal unity and universality of international human rights law.[86] There is no authoritative or accepted categorization within international human rights law into "core" and "non-core" rights. Singling out rights on the grounds of their alleged "importance" or "relevance" for armed conflict is a subjective approach unsupported by international human rights law.

While there may be pragmatic reasons for focusing on human rights norms of the greatest practical importance in a given situation, including only "core" rights and ignoring others is no more than an anecdotal version of the *lex specialis* principle. It substitutes the principle's legal logic with subjective experiences and reflections on what could be relevant in armed conflict and what not. The diverging views on what constitutes such a "core" reflect the inadequacy of this subjective approach, and often such suggestions to exclude human rights on the basis of their irrelevance seem not to have been put to the test.

Not so long ago, for example, it had been argued that human rights such as the freedom of the press, association and expression have no importance whatsoever in armed conflict,[87] an argument hardly tenable in light of the role of mass media and journalists in situations of armed conflict and with a view towards the respective provisions of humanitarian law which can be read in conjunction with human rights norms. The human right to form and join trade unions may also seem to be a classic peace-time right only.[88] At the same time, the operation of trade unions and the associated rights of their members may be of concern in occupied territories, even though trade unions are not mentioned in the 1907 Hague Regulations or in the 1949 Geneva Conventions and Additional Protocols.[89] But it has been inferred from the general provision of Article 43 of the Hague Regulations that where a right to form trade unions existed prior to the occupation, the occupant must respect, maintain and ensure this right's exercise as a "law in force" in the sense of Article 43.[90] In the absence of any further rules on trade unions in humanitarian law, human rights law is likely to be invoked.

Similarly, the rights of children to be heard in judicial and administrative proceedings may be seen as superfluous in situations of armed conflict as another classic "peace-time" right.[91] However, the reference to "all matters affecting the child" has been interpreted by

[86] See UN OHCHR, *International Legal Protection of Human Rights in Armed Conflict* (n. 16) p. 14; and Iain Scobbie, "Principle or Pragmatics? The Relationship between Human Rights Law and the Law of Armed Conflict" (2009) 14(3) *Journal of Conflict and Security Law* 454.

[87] See Dietrich Schindler, "The International Committee of the Red Cross and Human Rights" (1979) 19 *International Review of the Red Cross* 11.

[88] See Schmahl, "Der Menschenrechtsschutz in Friedenszeiten" (n. 85) p. 62.

[89] See, e.g., John Quigley, "Trade Unions and War: The Right to Organize under Belligerent Occupation" (1990) 13(2) *Hastings International and Comparative Law Review* 243 and 262–65 (on Israel's restrictions of trade union rights in the Occupied Palestinian Territories). See for the respective provisions in human rights law, e.g., ICCPR, Art. 22(1): "Everyone shall have the right to freedom of association with others, including the right to form and join trade unions for the protection of his interests" and ICESCR, Art. 8(1): "The States Parties to the present Covenant undertake to ensure: (a) The right of everyone to form trade unions and join the trade union of his choice, subject only to the rules of the organization concerned, for the promotion and protection of his economic and social interests."

[90] See Quigley, "Trade Unions and War" (n. 89) 244 and 254–58 (with regard to the continued applicability of the Labour Conventions of the International Labour Organisation).

[91] CRC, Art. 12: "1. States Parties shall assure to the child who is capable of forming his or her own views the right to express those views freely in all matters affecting the child, the views of the child being given due

the Committee on the Rights of the Child to encompass also matters arising in situations of emergency, including armed conflict, on the grounds that:

> [t]here is a growing body of evidence of the significant contribution that children are able to make in conflict situations, post-conflict resolution and reconstruction processes following emergencies. Thus, the Committee emphasized in its recommendation after the day of general discussion in 2008 that children affected by emergencies should be encouraged and enabled to participate in analyzing their situation and future prospects.[92]

6.3 Maximum protection or graduated approach?

Reliance on the principle of most favourable protection – a *lex favorabilis*[93] – to understand the relationship between human rights and humanitarian law seems consistent with the overarching goal of preserving the consistency of international law through the harmonious interpretation of fragmented norms, which is well acknowledged.[94]

It has been argued above that the principle of *lex specialis* is not suitable to ensure a harmonious interpretation of human rights and humanitarian law with a view towards ensuring systemic unity rather than fragmentation. While the principle purports to work along these lines, it cannot convince, as the decision on the speciality of a norm is not a reflection of legal logic but needs to have a direction: special to achieve what? In light of the demands of complementarity as a joint effort of human rights and humanitarian law, this direction could, in general terms, be defined as providing the highest possible level of protection of individuals in situations of armed conflict.

Two particular suggestions have been made, which are meant to allow reading human rights and humanitarian law in a harmonious way and with a view towards providing such protection, without ignoring the different frameworks of human rights and humanitarian law. One focuses more on the ultimate humanitarian goals which the two share, and relies on the idea of employing the norm most favourable for the individual, while the other is more concerned with preserving the integrity and operability of humanitarian law and proposes a graduated approach. The two suggestions proceed from different assumptions. The first one emphasizes the convergence of human rights and humanitarian law in terms of goals and values and terminology and concludes that, if read together, the two regimes call for the maximum protection to be achieved by that norm, or the interpretation of that

weight in accordance with the age and maturity of the child. 2. For this purpose, the child shall in particular be provided the opportunity to be heard in any judicial and administrative proceedings affecting the child, either directly, or through a representative or an appropriate body, in a manner consistent with the procedural rules of national law."

92 Committee on the Rights of the Child, *General Comment No. 12 on the Right of the Child to be Heard*, UN Doc. CRC/C/GC/12 (20 July 2009), para. 125.

93 See Anne Laurence Graf-Brugère, "A *Lex Favorabilis*? Resolving Norm Conflicts between Human Rights Law and Humanitarian Law" in Robert Kolb and Gloria Gaggioli (eds.), *Research Handbook on Human Rights and Humanitarian Law* (Cheltenham: Edward Elgar, 2013), p. 251.

94 See Guglielmo Verdirame, "Human Rights in Wartime: A Framework for Analysis" (2008) 6 *European Human Rights Law Review* 703. Some compare this to the idea of *interprétation conforme* (consistent interpretation), a term borrowed from constitutional law and law of the European Union, which again can be transposed to international law only with difficulties, see, e.g., the cursory reference to this principle in UN OHCHR, *International Legal Protection of Human Rights in Armed Conflict* (n. 16) p. 58.

norm, which is most favourable to the concerned individual(s).[95] The other seeks to respect and retain the functional demands of humanitarian law and its ability to regulate the use of force in accordance with the intentions of states parties to the Geneva Conventions in a more conservative interpretation of humanitarian law and sees human rights as appropriate in some, but not all, situations.[96]

The idea of maximum protection calls for the application of the norm which provides (or for interpreting norms in light of each other so as to provide) the highest level of protection regardless of the source from which the respective norms flow. It presumes that it is the intent of states parties of instruments of humanitarian law and human rights law to be bound by the highest possible standard with regard to the protection of individuals in times of armed conflicts.[97] Both humanitarian law and human rights law can provide this protection in a specific situation. The argument resembles the principle of *lex specialis* for the way the principle seems to suggest a similar approach: the norm with the highest level of protection is the "special" norm. But under *lex specialis*, the special norm is not necessarily the norm which provides the highest level of protection.[98]

The most favourable protection clauses, or savings clauses, contained in international human rights treaties, and similar provisions in humanitarian law instruments, support such an idea of a harmonious interpretation in light of the overarching objective of the highest possible protection. Article 5(2) common to the ICCPR and ICESCR provides that:

> (t)here shall be no restriction upon or derogation from any of the fundamental human rights recognized or existing in any State Party to the present Covenant pursuant to law, conventions, regulations or custom on the pretext that the present Covenant does not recognize such rights or that it recognizes them to a lesser extent.[99]

ECHR, Article 53[100] and Article 29(2) of the American Convention on Human Rights (ACHR)[101] are worded similarly, while Articles 60 and 61 of the African Charter on Human and Peoples' Rights (ACHPR) are broader clauses to a comparable effect.[102] Strictly

[95] *Prosecutor* v. *Kunarac, Kovać and Vuković*, International Criminal Tribunal for the Former Yugoslavia, IT-96-23-T and IT-96-32/1-T, Judgment of 22 February 2001, para. 467.

[96] See Geoffrey Corn, "Mixing Apples and Hand Grenades: The Logical Limit of Applying Human Rights Norms to Armed Conflicts" (2010) 1(1) *International Humanitarian Legal Studies* 55.

[97] See Balendra, "International Human Rights Law and International Humanitarian Law" (n. 27) p. 127.

[98] See Milanovic, "Norm Conflicts, International Humanitarian Law and Human Rights Law" (n. 28) p. 459.

[99] ICCPR, Art. 5(2) and ICESCR, Art. 5(2).

[100] ECHR, Art. 53: "Nothing in this Convention shall be construed as limiting or derogating from any of the human rights and fundamental freedoms which may be ensured under the laws of any High Contracting Party or under any other agreement to which it is a Party."

[101] American Convention on Human Rights, 22 November 1969, OAS Treaty Series No. 36, 1144 UNTS 123, Art. 29(2): "No provision of this Convention shall be interpreted as . . . restricting the enjoyment or exercise of any right or freedom recognized by virtue of the laws of any State Party or by virtue of another convention to which one of the said states is a party." See also Douglas Cassel, "Extraterritorial Application of Inter-American Convention Human Rights Instruments" in Fons Coomans and Menno T. Kamminga (eds.), *Extraterritorial Application of Human Rights Treaties* (Antwerp: Intersentia, 2004), p. 179.

[102] African Charter on Human and Peoples' Rights, 27 June 1981, OAU Doc. CAB/LEG/67/3 rev. 5 (1982) 21 ILM 58, Art. 60: "The Commission shall draw inspiration from international law on human and peoples' rights, particularly from the provisions of various African instruments on Human and Peoples'

speaking, such clauses are collision clauses, but it may well be argued that the idea of most favourable protection expressed in them can be used to determine the relationship between human rights and humanitarian law.[103]

Humanitarian law knows a similar clause in Article 75(8) of Additional Protocol I,[104] and the way in which the Martens Clause opens humanitarian law to allow for greater protection beyond existing positive law (including by invoking human rights law) support the view that humanitarian law, too, seeks to provide the highest positive level of protection. One should also not forget that with the adoption of the Additional Protocols in 1977, international humanitarian law has issued a kind of "standing invitation" to human rights law to supplement it and apply complementarily: Article 72 of Additional Protocol I allows space for "other applicable rules of international law relating to the protection of fundamental human rights during armed conflict."[105] Such an approach would effectively replace the *lex specialis* doctrine and require instead the use of the most favourable norm for the individual (s) concerned to provide maximum protection.[106]

There is, however, concern that such an idea means losing sight of the way in which humanitarian law balances humanitarian concerns with considerations of military necessity.[107] A graduated approach has thus been suggested, which is meant to do justice to the specific functional demands of humanitarian law to use armed force within humanitarian limits and reflect the will of the states parties to the Geneva Conventions and Additional Protocols, while still avoiding the exclusivist rhetoric of the *lex specialis* principle.[108] In this

Rights, the Charter of the United Nations, the Charter of the Organisation of African Unity, the Universal Declaration of Human Rights, other instruments adopted by the United Nations and by African countries in the field of Human and Peoples' Rights, as well as from the provisions of various instruments adopted within the Specialised Agencies of the United Nations of which the Parties to the present Charter are members." ACHPR, Art. 61: "The Commission shall also take into consideration, as subsidiary measures to determine the principles of law, other general or special international conventions, laying down rules expressly recognised by Member States of the Organisation of African Unity, African practices consistent with international norms on Human and Peoples' Rights, customs generally accepted as law, general principles of law recognised by African States as well as legal precedents and doctrine."

103 See Walter Kälin, "Die Interdependenz " (n. 7) 242; and Krieger, "Die Verantwortlichkeit Deutschlands" (n. 54) 693.

104 Geneva Convention IV, Art. 75(8): "No provision of this Article may be construed as limiting or infringing any other more favourable provision granting greater protection, under any applicable rules of international law, to persons covered by paragraph 12"; see in greater detail Pejic, "Procedural Principles and Safeguards for Internment/Administrative Detention" (n. 39) p. 378.

105 Additional Protocol I, Art. 72: "The provisions of this Section are additional to the rules concerning humanitarian protection of civilians and civilian objects in the power of a Party to the conflict contained in the Fourth Convention, particularly Parts I and III thereof, as well as to other applicable rules of international law relating to the protection of fundamental human rights during international armed conflict."

106 See Heike Krieger, "A Conflict of Norms: The Relationship between Humanitarian Law and Human Rights Law in the ICRC Customary Law Study" (2006) 11(2) *Journal of Conflict and Security Law* 274. For a similar argument see Michael Bothe, "Humanitäres Völkerrecht und Schutz der Menschenrechte: Auf der Suche nach Synergien und Schutzlücken" in Pierre-Marie Dupuy, Bardo Fassbender, Malcolm N. Shaw and Karl-Peter Sommermann (eds.), *Common Values in International Law, Essays in Honour of Christian Tomuschat* (Kehl: Engel, 2006), pp. 88–89.

107 See Balendra, "International Human Rights Law and International Humanitarian Law" (n. 27) p. 127; and Corn, "Mixing Apples and Hand Grenades" (n. 96) 55.

108 See ibid. 52–57.

approach, human rights law is allowed into armed conflict only gradually: the application of humanitarian law is associated with the use of armed force in war and war-like situations, while human rights are associated with (comparably peaceful) law enforcement operations. But unlike the outdated dichotomy of war and peace, this approach acknowledges the fluid nature of modern conflicts with their legal grey zones. The more "war" there is, the argument goes, the more humanitarian law should apply, the less "war," the more space should be made for human rights. In other words:

> where the situation is remote from the battlefield and state authorities have enough control over a situation to be able to carry out law enforcement operations, human rights law provides the most appropriate framework.[109]

The full range of humanitarian law applicable in international armed conflicts would thus largely exclude human rights in such conflicts on the grounds that they are superfluous (given the regulatory density of humanitarian law for international armed conflicts) and unsuitable (given that no law enforcement paradigm exists upon which human rights law is said to be based). In internal armed conflicts, less humanitarian law and more human rights law would apply because of the scarcity of humanitarian law for such situations and the suitability of human rights to govern the relationship between the state and those under its jurisdiction. The same would be the case for situations of occupation, where hostilities are the exception and ensuring law and order the norm.

It has also been suggested that one should shield core areas of warfare, including considerations of military necessity and proportionality in attacks involving civilians, completely from any application of human rights law.[110] This would effectively create a *cordon sanitaire* to preserve the health of humanitarian law. Similarly, it has been argued that one should apply (more) humanitarian law when only combatants are involved in a given situation and (more) human rights law when civilians are involved.[111] Obviously, such an approach is particularly pertinent when it comes to the way in which human rights and humanitarian law regulate the use of deadly force; the problem (and with it the idea of a graduated approach) will therefore be examined again in greater detail later, when the right to life in armed conflict will be discussed. The obvious problem with this graduated approach as a general interpretative yardstick is that the "far/close" dichotomy is overly imprecise, builds upon the problematic notion of the "battlefield" or constructs artificially clear situations where "only" war or "only" law enforcement exist. Ultimately, it cannot convince because it seems little more than a revamped theory of exclusion which shields, if not all of armed conflict, at least some areas from the application of human rights law.

On the basis of such ideas the search for practical and pragmatic ways to reconcile human rights and humanitarian law continues. Given that suggestions such as creating

109 Droege, "The Interplay" (n. 17) 347.

110 See, e.g., Rob McLaughlin, "The Law of Armed Conflict and International Human Rights Law: Some Paradigmatic Differences and Operational Implications" (2010) 13 *Yearbook of International Humanitarian Law* 242.

111 Nancy Prud'homme, "*Lex specialis*: Oversimplifying a More Complex and Multifaceted Relationship?" (2007) 40(2) *Israel Law Review* 391.

appropriate conflict clauses in treaty law which establish clear priorities and coordinate the simultaneous application of international humanitarian law and international human rights law have not met with a positive response by states, it is left to state practice to clarify the interplay of human rights and humanitarian law on a case-by-case basis for the time being.[112]

[112] Balendra, "International Human Rights Law and International Humanitarian Law" (n. 27) p. 136. See on the critique on searching for overarching theories and the need for practical solutions also John Tobin, "Seeking Clarity in relation to the Principle of Complementarity: Reflections on the Recent Contributions of Some International Bodies" (2007) 8(2) *Melbourne Journal of International Law* 359.

7

Integration: the transformative influence of human rights

7.1 Neither *genus* nor *species*

"Exclusivists" and "complementarists" may differ in their arguments: while the former argue for the precedence of humanitarian law, the latter seek to reconcile differences in the application of norms by way of interpretative techniques to achieve a coherent legal framework for armed conflicts which still acknowledges the primacy of humanitarian law, at least in certain circumstances. But both schools of thought agree that the distinctiveness of the two legal regimes needs to be preserved, and deny and reject any further integration of human rights into humanitarian law. From 1945 onwards, however, there was precisely this third view which argued that human rights and humanitarian law need to be seen as an integrated legal regime. Again, the boundaries between these different concepts are fluid and somewhat artificial: if one sees complementarity as a static phenomenon, one is likely to argue for keeping human rights and humanitarian law separate; if one sees complementarity as a process, one may agree that eventually the two fields may merge.

As in the other two theoretical approaches, there is no shortage of variations of the general theme of "integration." Obviously, the idea of a (formal) complete identity of the two legal regimes is as incorrect as the strictly separatist view.[1] Sometimes the common heritage of human rights and humanitarian law is emphasized and they are presented as two branches growing from a common stem.[2] At times the relationship between international humanitarian law and international human rights law is also described in analogy to that between *genus* and *species*, which, in analogy to biological taxonomy, allows seeing one legal regime as a subset of another. Usually human rights are considered as "the genus of which humanitarian law is a species."[3] In such a view, international humanitarian law only adds specific, conflict-related rights to international human rights law so as to expand the protective scope of international human rights law in response to the specific threats and risks of armed conflict.[4] The argument has been made, for example, that:

[1] As rightly made clear by Yoram Dinstein, *The Conduct of Hostilities under the Law of International Armed Conflict* (2nd edn., Cambridge: Cambridge University Press, 2010), p. 19.

[2] Héctor Gros Espiell, "Humanitarian Law and Human Rights" in Janusz Symonides (ed.), *Human Rights: Concepts and Standards* (Aldershot and Paris: Ashgate and UNESCO, 2000), p. 345.

[3] Arthur Henry Robertson, "Humanitarian Law and Human Rights" in Christophe Swinarski (ed.), *Studies and Essays on International Humanitarian Law and Red Cross Principles in Honour of Jean Pictet* (The Hague: Nijhoff, 1984), p. 797. This is how others understood the term "human rights in armed conflict", e.g., Bernhard Schäfer, *Zum Verhältnis Menschenrechte und humanitäres Völkerrecht. Zugleich ein Beitrag zur extraterritorialen Geltung von Menschenrechtsverträgen* (Potsdam: Universitätsverlag Potsdam, 2006), p. 37.

[4] See Robertson, "Humanitarian Law and Human Rights" (n. 3) p. 798.

> [t]here is no doubt that specific international humanitarian law is aimed at protecting human rights in certain situations, by means of special procedures and for certain categories of persons. Thus it is part of what could be called international human rights law in the broad sense.[5]

Similarly, it has been argued that "[s]ince international humanitarian law aims to maintain a modicum of civilization amid the worst of all cataclysms human communities can experience, namely, war, it may be classified as one of the branches of international human rights law."[6] Others have argued that international humanitarian law is human rights law for application in the most extreme situations[7] and that "the law of Geneva may be seen, either as a poor relation of human rights law, or as an outstandingly successful example of a specialised branch of human rights law at work."[8]

Such biological analogies are, however, also construed rather at will and as a result some see international humanitarian law as a *species* of the *genus* international human rights law, while others claim the exact opposite. Already Jean Pictet was ambiguous in this regard. He seemingly understood, in 1949, humanitarian law as comprising the law of armed conflict and the emerging international human rights law and argued that "[i]nternational humanitarian law, in the broad sense, is constituted by all the international legal provisions, whether of statute or common law, ensuring respect for the individual and promoting his development."[9] At the same time, he concluded elsewhere that "[i]n fact, Human Rights [*sic*!] represent the most generous principles in humanitarian law, whose laws of war are only one particular and exceptional case, which appears precisely at times when war restricts or harms the exercising of human rights."[10] Others have gone as far as putting all international norms relating to human beings (international human rights law, refugee law, international labour law, and more) under the umbrella of international humanitarian law.[11] Or it has been suggested that humanitarian law should be used as an umbrella term to cover laws with the objective of humanizing warfare, primarily international humanitarian law and international human rights law.[12]

Historically, systematically and *de lege lata* these variations of a *genus/species* relationship are, however, problematic. International humanitarian law is not a specialized branch of

5 Gros Espiell, "Humanitarian Law and Human Rights" (n. 2) p. 347. Similar arguments have been made by Hansjoachim Linde, "Überlegungen zu den Menschenrechten und zum humanitären Völkerrecht" (1996) 2 *Journal of International Law of Peace and Armed Conflict* 96; and Nagendra Singh, *Enforcement of Human Rights in Peace and War and the Future of Humanity* (Dordrecht: Nijhoff, 1986), p. 136.

6 Christian Tomuschat, *Human Rights between Idealism and Realism* (2nd edn., Oxford: Oxford University Press, 2008), p. 292.

7 Rhona K. Smith, *Textbook on International Human Rights* (4th edn., Oxford: Oxford University Press, 2010), p. 14.

8 Robert Quentin-Baxter, "Human Rights and Humanitarian Law: Confluence of Conflict?" (1985) 9 *Australian Yearbook of International Law* 103.

9 Jean Pictet, *Humanitarian Law and the Protection of War Victims* (Leiden/Geneva: Henry Dunant Institute, 1975), p. 13.

10 Jean Pictet, *The Principles of International Humanitarian Law* (Geneva: International Committee of the Red Cross, 1967), p. 12.

11 Enrique P. Syquia, "Dr Jean Pictet and International Humanitarian Law" in Christophe Swinarski (ed.), *Studies and Essays on International Humanitarian Law and Red Cross Principles in Honour of Jean Pictet* (The Hague: Nijhoff, 1984), p. 556.

12 Gary D. Solis, *The Law of Armed Conflict* (Cambridge: Cambridge University Press, 2010), p. 22.

human rights law and human rights law is not a rebranded modern humanitarian code. Such views do not do justice to the way in which human rights influenced the development of humanitarian law after 1945, and disregard the historic development and contemporary contextual and functional fragmentation. Humanitarian law is also not an early version of human rights law and was not replaced by international human rights law in 1948 nor was it merged with human rights law, and as a *terminus technicus* "international humanitarian law" should not be used as an umbrella for different legal regimes of a broadly "humanitarian" outlook. Such references tend to obscure rather than contribute to clarifying the interplay of human rights and humanitarian law.

7.2 Towards a human rights-based *jus in bello*

Rather than employing misleading biological taxonomies and creating formal classifications, it seems more important to consider the influence which the idea, language, law and policy of human rights, as expressed in the international human rights law devised after 1945, exercises on international humanitarian law, because this is what the debate on human rights in armed conflicts is in essence: a debate on the possible transformation of the law of armed conflict as we know it. Positioning the two regimes in a static way against each other or as part of each other does not sufficiently explain their interaction. A static understanding of complementarity as concurrence of norms disregards this transformative process.[13]

If one understands the convergence of human rights and humanitarian law as such a process, their relationship becomes more fluid and can be positioned on a trajectory from competition (i.e., the struggle about which norm is more special and should thus prevail and replace the other) to the quest of coherence (i.e., reconciling distinct frameworks in light of shared underlying concerns in a complementary way). Arguing for such a transformative process as part or result of complementarity suggests that international humanitarian law and international human rights form together (potentially with other fields of law) a full and complete *jus in bello*, which responds to the underlying goals and values of humanity in armed conflicts which were hitherto expressed in humanitarian law.

This process may be referred to as "intersection"[14] or as a "confluence"[15] of human rights and humanitarian law, or perhaps, somewhat misleadingly, as their "fusing"[16] or "meshing."[17] The Office of the UN High Commissioner for Human Rights argues, in its Fact Sheet on international humanitarian law and human rights, that international humanitarian law, international human rights law and international criminal law have "merged to form one

[13] Daniel Thürer has juxtaposed the two approaches as static rule-exception vs. mutual influence and oscillation, see Daniel Thürer, *International Humanitarian Law: Theory, Practice, Context* (The Hague: Hague Academy of International Law, 2011), p. 125.

[14] Paul Kennedy and George J. Andreopoulos, "The Laws of War: Some Concluding Reflections" in Michael Howard, George J. Andreopoulos and Mark R. Shulman (eds.), *The Laws of War: Constraints on Warfare in the Western World* (New Haven, CT: Yale University Press, 1994), p. 225.

[15] Quentin-Baxter, "Human Rights and Humanitarian Law" (n. 8) 94.

[16] Felicity Rogers, "Australia's Human Rights Obligations and Australian Defence Force Operations" (1999) 18 *University of Tasmania Law Review* 1–2.

[17] Theodor Meron, "On the Inadequate Reach of Humanitarian and Human Rights Law and the Need for a New Instrument" (1983) 77(3) *American Journal of International Law* 589.

stream of action."[18] The International Criminal Tribunal for the Former Yugoslavia (ICTY) argued that "[w]ith regard to certain of its aspects, international humanitarian law can be said to have fused with human rights law,"[19] and many observers of this development agree that since the 1968 Tehran Conference on Human Rights such a partial merger has already occurred and that "the degree of merger could be reinforced by future evolution."[20] Earlier on, Theodor Meron had argued for one unified complex of rights under different institutional umbrellas[21] while Alan Rosas saw human rights and humanitarian law belonging to the "same family"[22] of international standards. Such an "integrationist" view has recently taken a firmer hold in the debate on human rights in armed conflict and seems on the rise, yet it remains disputed.[23] Some embrace it for the way it goes beyond complementarity,[24] while others caution that it is difficult or impossible to blend the rules of humanitarian law and human rights law, and warn that:

> while there is indeed space for enlightened cross-pollination and better integration of human rights and humanitarian law, each performs a task for which it is better suited than the other, and the fundamentals of each system remain partly incompatible with each other.[25]

A formal merger of the two regimes is widely considered undesirable.[26] Even those who think that such a merger has already happened concede that it has ended "with not

[18] Office of the High Commissioner for Human Rights, *International Humanitarian Law and Human Rights Law*, Fact Sheet No. 13 (Geneva: United Nations, 1991).

[19] *Prosecutor* v. *Kunarac, Kovać and Vuković*, International Criminal Tribunal for the Former Yugoslavia, IT-96-23-T and IT-96-32/1-T, Judgment of 22 February 2001, para. 467.

[20] Robert Kolb and Richard Hyde, *An Introduction to the International Law of Armed Conflict* (Oxford: Hart, 2008), p. 273.

[21] Theodor Meron, *Human Rights in Internal Strife: Their International Protection* (Cambridge: Grotius, 1987), p. 28.

[22] Alan Rosas, "The Interrelationship between Human Rights and International Humanitarian Law" in College of Europe and International Committee of the Red Cross (eds.), *Current Challenges in International Humanitarian Law, Proceedings of the Bruges Colloquium, 27–28 October 2000* (Bruges: College of Europe and International Committee of the Red Cross, 2001), p. 95.

[23] See Dirk Lorenz, *Der territoriale Anwendungsbereich der Grund- und Menschenrechte. Zugleich ein Beitrag zum Individualschutz in bewaffneten Konflikten* (Vienna: Neuer Wissenschaftlicher Verlag, 2005), p. 205; critical e.g., Schäfer, *Zum Verhältnis Menschenrechte und humanitäres Völkerrecht* (n. 3) 39. See also Hans-Joachim Heintze, "Convergence between Human Rights Law and International Humanitarian Law and the Consequences for the Implementation" in Hans-Joachim Heintze and Andrej Zwitter (eds.), *International Humanitarian Law and Humanitarian Assistance: A Crosscut through Legal Issues Pertaining to Humanitarianism* (Berlin: Springer, 2011), pp. 84–85.

[24] See Hans-Joachim Heintze, "On the Relationship between Human Rights Law Protection and International Humanitarian Law (2004) 86(856) *International Review of the Red Cross* 794.

[25] René Provost, *International Human Rights and Humanitarian Law* (Cambridge: Cambridge University Press, 2002), pp. 349–50.

[26] See Kolb and Hyde, *An Introduction to the International Law of Armed Conflict* (n. 26), pp. 272–74; Cordula Droege, "Elective Affinities? Human Rights and Humanitarian Law" (2008) 90(871) *International Review of the Red Cross* 521; Noelle Quénivet and Roberta Arnold, "Conclusions" in Noelle Quénivet and Roberta Arnold (eds.), *International Humanitarian Law and Human Rights Law: Towards a Merger in International Law*" (Leiden: Nijhoff, 2008), pp. 591–92; Thürer, *International Humanitarian Law* (n. 13) p. 126; and Hans-Peter Gasser, "International Humanitarian Law and Human Rights Law in Non-International Armed Conflict: Joint Venture or Mutual Exclusion?" (2002) 45 *German Yearbook of International Law* 162.

altogether satisfactory results."[27] The underlying fear is that such a development might be to the detriment of international humanitarian law. The situation reminded one commentator of the joke on the joint venture between the pig and the chicken: when opening a breakfast café together the chicken promised to contribute the egg, while asking the pig to supply the bacon.[28] One need not be so fearful of human rights nor go as far as arguing that such a merger would be a "genetically modified mutation."[29] But the view that such a merger might cost humanitarian law its competitive advantage to provide protection in armed conflict is widely held:

> [i]t is true that the antagonism which formerly existed between the two concepts has faded away. This does not justify the merging of both concepts into one, the result of which might be a rather low level of protection and a loss of the merits which they each separately possess.[30]

A technical merger of human rights and humanitarian law is not only broadly rejected, it is also difficult to imagine in practical legal terms. But what happens is in fact the integration or incorporation of human rights (as idea, law and policy) in the existing law(s) which govern situations of armed conflict.[31] One may consider this a "human rights infused approach"[32] to humanitarian law or call it, in analogy to the human rights-based approach in development and other fields, the development of a human rights-based law of armed conflict. Given that the term "law of armed conflict" may be understood wrongly by some as a reference to the Hague law (as opposed to Geneva law), it might be preferable to speak of a human rights-based *jus in bello*: a legal framework which governs all questions of armed conflicts in their various forms, which is constituted at its core of international humanitarian law, and where international human rights law is applied in a complementary or cumulative fashion while at the same time providing the foundational normative value and operational direction.

Such a human rights-based approach to war goes beyond reconciling norms of international human rights law and international humanitarian law. Human rights are not only an add-on to humanitarian law but rather provide "the value oriented foundation of the specific rules evolved for armed conflict."[33] While the aim is primarily to ensure the highest

[27] Charles H.B. Garraway, "'To Kill or not to Kill': Dilemmas in the Use of Force" (2010) 14(3) *Journal of Conflict and Security Law* 499.

[28] Torsten Stein, "Comment to Hans-Peter Gasser, International Humanitarian Law and Human Rights Law in Non-international Armed Conflict: Joint Venture or Mutual Exclusion" (2002) 45 *German Yearbook of International Law* 163.

[29] Noam Lubell, "Parallel Application of International Humanitarian Law and International Human Rights Law: An Examination of the Debate" (2007) 40(2) *Israel Yearbook of Human Rights* 655.

[30] Karl-Josef Partsch, "Human Rights and Humanitarian Law" in Rudolf Bernhardt (ed.), *Encyclopedia of Public International Law* (Amsterdam: Elsevier, 1995), p. 912.

[31] Also referred to as a "mixed model", see David Kretzmer, "Targeted Killing of Suspected Terrorists: Extra-Judicial Execution or Legitimate Means of Defence?" (2005) 16(2) *European Journal of International Law* 174; see also Thürer, *International Humanitarian Law* (n. 13) 151.

[32] Christine Byron, "A Blurring of the Boundaries: the Application of International Humanitarian Law by Human Rights Bodies" (2007) 47(4) *Virginia Journal of International Law* 892.

[33] Tomuschat, *Human Rights between Idealism and Realism* (n. 6) p. 292. Some also use the idea of human rights as a prism through which the laws of armed conflict can be seen, see Conor McCarthy, "Legal Conclusion or Interpretative Process? *Lex Specialis* and the Application of International Human Rights Standards" in Roberta Arnold and Noelle Quénivet (eds.), *International Humanitarian Law and Human Rights Law: Towards a Merger in International Law* (Leiden: Nijhoff, 2008), p. 115.

possible level of protection by interpreting humanitarian law from a human rights perspective, such an approach also poses fundamental questions as to what the law of armed conflict ultimately seeks to achieve. Among those questions are the ease with which humanitarian law accepts the mass killing of (largely male) adolescents and young adults which have been conscripted into armed forces, sometimes compulsorily and without having a choice to deny military service or doing so with negative effects on their personal and professional future; the remaining notion of collateral damage of civilians; the long-term societal, economic and environmental impact of war; the terrorization and traumatization of civilians as well as soldiers in otherwise lawful acts of warfare; and the continued and often growing militarization of societies and local and global economies.[34] A human rights-based approach is thus no quick-fix to ensure the complementarity or harmony of human rights and humanitarian law as a matter of law but a long-term challenge for the ever-shifting perceptions of war and law.

[34] See Karima Bennoune, "Toward a Human Rights Approach to Armed Conflict: Iraq 2003" (2004) 11(1) *University of California Davis Journal of International Law and Policy* 174.

Part III

Human rights and humanitarian law: challenges and commonalities

The complementarity of human rights and humanitarian law and the way in which human rights informs the interpretation and development of humanitarian law cannot themselves overcome existing differences between the two legal regimes, nor should they be an invitation to gloss over possible obstacles to a proposed human rights-based *jus in bello* in law and practice. Theodor Meron's warning, that despite the convergence of human rights and humanitarian law any such obstacles and objections to the application of human rights in armed conflicts need to be considered carefully, remains valid.[1] This Part of the study will examine some crucial arguments which question the applicability of human rights in armed conflicts, and the respective questions of law and practice which result from the complementarity of human rights and humanitarian law, loosely around the legal concepts of *ratione temporis, loci, materiae* and *personae*.

One particularly important objection to the application of human rights in armed conflicts is the argument that *ratione loci* international human rights treaty law cannot apply extra-territorially. The idea that armed forces carry with them human rights obligations when acting abroad remains divisive, less so when they operate under a UN Security Council mandate in peace support operations, but very much so in situations of international armed conflicts and occupation. Another objection *ratione materiae* is that the broad and general individual entitlements under international human rights law cannot be matched with international humanitarian law's paradigm of specific and pragmatic state obligations. The most vivid debate is on one particular right which was deliberately omitted in the previous chapters because it deserves greater attention: the right to life. The way in which human rights law and humanitarian law approach the use of deadly force demonstrate for many the limits of applying human rights in armed conflict.

A related objection *ratione personae* is that humanitarian law cannot capture the individualistic approach of international human rights law, because it is concerned with distinct groups which are usually juxtaposed: combatants and civilians, friends and enemies, lawful and unlawful participants in armed conflicts, and so on. The question is how the universal and individualistic approach of human rights can be reconciled with this characteristic of humanitarian law without damaging the latter's important protective principle of distinction between combatants and civilians. The reach of human rights and humanitarian law *ratione personae* is perhaps of greatest importance when it comes to non-state armed groups. While they can figure under humanitarian law as a party to the conflict,

[1] See the warning by Theodor Meron, *The Humanization of International Law* (Leiden: Nijhoff, 2006), p. 240.

assigning human rights obligations to non-state armed groups remains a problem and another reason for critics to caution against the use of human rights law in armed conflict.

Ratione temporis, the debate on human rights in armed conflicts is about their application "in times of war." Regardless of its technical reduction to "armed conflict" under humanitarian law, the phenomenon of war remains multi-layered in its character, image and objective. The term "human rights in armed conflict" is used here and elsewhere as a euphemism for dealing with different forms of armed conflicts, which in turn necessitates engaging with the changing character of war and its different images and manifestations in law and reality. The sweeping proposal to apply human rights in such situations needs to be reconciled with international humanitarian law's problematic categorization of armed conflicts as either international or non-international and needs to capture (allegedly) new types of conflicts.

Beyond such legal categories lie different perceptions of war as a phenomenon. It makes a difference (also for the application of human rights) if one sees "war" as an emergency; a means of politics; a contest between nation states; a crime; a means of law enforcement and international community policing; or as simply managing violence; not to speak of the use of force in situations of occupation, peace support operations and post-conflict scenarios. Some of the problems associated with applying human rights in these various situations are legal (and will be dealt with in this Part of the study), while others are problems of policy, to be considered in the next Part on the changing character of war and its repercussions on the debate regarding human rights in armed conflict. As will be argued there, it is the changing character of war which drives and, at the same time, is informed by the ever closer nexus of human rights and humanitarian law.

And finally, even if obstacles in theory and law can be overcome, the application of human rights in armed conflict remains to be translated into workable rules on the ground. This process has not even started yet in earnest, so that the debate on human rights in armed conflict is seen with concern by those who ultimately need to apply rules in armed conflict.

8

The right to life: the limits of human rights in armed conflict?

8.1 Paradigmatic differences: war-fighting and law enforcement

Like many others, the International Committee of the Red Cross (ICRC) sees "the greatest differences"[1] between international humanitarian law and international human rights law in the right to life. In the eyes of many commentators, the way in which human rights and humanitarian law think about the use of deadly force – the central element of armed conflicts – reflects paradigmatic differences so profound that there can be no complementarity in this matter. Humanitarian law can be seen as a permissive regime which grants positive authorization to use force in order to achieve military aims. In a seemingly paradox way, it facilitates and, at the same time, limits killing and destruction, whereas international human rights law is restrictive and accepts lethal force only as last resort. For humanitarian law, the use of force is an integral part of the law, while killing is antithetical to the very idea of human rights.[2] In light of these considerations it has been suggested that the two regimes need to be kept "distinct as far as possible"[3] – but how far is as far as possible? Are the differences between human rights and humanitarian law on this question so fundamental that (at least) this very core of humanitarian law must be preserved uninfluenced by human rights law even if their application might be accepted in other areas of armed conflict? Or is the difference merely a gradual one, and a complementary application of human rights and humanitarian law is possible? There is profound disagreement on this question, compounded by the fact that, somewhat surprisingly and despite the importance of this matter, the links between the human right to life and humanitarian law have only rather recently been subjected to a more thorough analysis beyond blanket statements of their incompatibility.[4]

[1] ICRC, *International Humanitarian Law and the Challenges of Contemporary Armed Conflicts, Report to the 31st International Conference of the Red Cross and Red Crescent* (2011), pp. 18–20.

[2] See Rob McLaughlin, "The Law of Armed Conflict and International Human Rights Law: Some Paradigmatic Differences and Operational Implications" (2010) 13 *Yearbook of International Humanitarian Law* 219 and 223.

[3] See, e.g., Andreas Paulus, "The Use of Force in Occupied Territories: The Applicable Legal Framework" in *Appendix to the Expert Meeting: Occupation and Other Forms of Administration of Foreign Territory* (Geneva: International Committee of the Red Cross, 2012), p. 144.

[4] See Christian Tomuschat, "The Right to Life: Legal and Political Foundations" in Christian Tomuschat, Evelyne Lagrange and Stefan Oeter (eds.), *The Right to Life* (Leiden: Nijhoff, 2010), p. 15. It should be noted that the right to life in armed conflict has many facets which cannot be considered here. They include, for example, deaths not resulting from the direct use of lethal force, the question of the death penalty in armed conflicts, and the question whether members of the armed forces are violated in their

Since the International Court of Justice (ICJ)'s Advisory Opinion in the *Nuclear Weapons* case it is widely held that with regard to the right to life humanitarian law prevails as *lex specialis*. As mentioned earlier, the Court said that while in principle, the right not arbitrarily to be deprived of one's life applies also in hostilities, the test of what is an arbitrary deprivation of life is determined by the applicable *lex specialis* humanitarian law.[5] This was widely understood as a confirmation that humanitarian law is exclusive as well as exhaustive on this particular matter. Accordingly, it has been argued that "the right to life adds nothing at the substantive level to the provisions of the laws of war."[6] In light of the *lex specialis* character of humanitarian law, killing in armed conflict is thus permissible as long as it conforms to the requirements of humanitarian law, and humanitarian law only.[7] But in both legal regimes things are not as straightforward as they seem.

International human rights law assigns a high status to the right to life, but even though it is a non-derogable right under international human rights treaty law it is not absolute: the right to life merely protects from being killed arbitrarily.[8] The International Covenant on Civil and Political Rights (ICCPR), European Convention on Human Rights (ECHR), American Convention on Human Rights (ACHR) and African Charter on Human and Peoples' Rights (ACHPR) all use similar language to this end.[9] Apart from the death penalty, these treaties allow the use of deadly force by government agents only under stringent conditions, usually in law enforcement operations.[10] The use of deadly force can be lawful in self-defence and in the defence of others from unlawful acts, against resistance to attempts to arrest a person or prevent their escape, and in similar acts of law enforcement.

right to life by their own government when sent to war and killed in combat in "friendly fire" or in other incidents, see Peter Rowe, *The Impact of Human Rights Law on Armed Forces* (Cambridge: Cambridge University Press, 2006), pp. 137–47. See in greater detail Noelle Quénivet, "The Right to Life in International Humanitarian Law and Human Rights Law" in Roberta Arnold and Noelle Quénivet (eds.), *International Humanitarian Law and Human Rights Law: Towards a Merger in International Law* (Leiden: Nijhoff, 2008), pp. 331–53.

5 ICRC, *International Humanitarian Law and the Challenges of Contemporary Armed Conflicts* (n. 1) pp. 19–20.

6 Christopher Greenwood, "Rights at the Frontier: Protection of the Individual in Time of War" in Barry A.K. Rider (ed.), *Law at the Centre: The Institute of Advanced Legal Studies at Fifty* (Dordrecht: Kluwer, 1999), p. 287.

7 See Walter Kälin and Jörg Künzli, *The Law of International Human Rights Protection* (Oxford: Oxford University Press, 2009), p. 273.

8 See Nigel S. Rodley, "Integrity of the Person" in Daniel Moeckli, Sangeeta Shah and Sandesh Sivakumaran (eds.), *International Human Rights Law* (Oxford: Oxford University Press, 2010), p. 221.

9 ICCPR, Art. 6(1): "Every human being has the inherent right to life. This right shall be protected by law. No one shall be arbitrarily deprived of his life." ECHR, Art. 2: "1. Everyone's right to life shall be protected by law. No one shall be deprived of his life intentionally save in the execution of a sentence of a court following his conviction of a crime for which this penalty is provided by law. 2. Deprivation of life shall not be regarded as inflicted in contravention of this article when it results from the use of force which is no more than absolutely necessary: (a) in defence of any person from unlawful violence; (b) in order to effect a lawful arrest or to prevent the escape of a person lawfully detained; (c) in action lawfully taken for the purpose of quelling a riot or insurrection." ACHR, Art. 4(1): "Every person has the right to have his life respected. This right shall be protected by law and, in general, from the moment of conception. No one shall be arbitrarily deprived of his life." ACHPR, Art. 4: "Human beings are inviolable. Every human being shall be entitled to respect for his life and the integrity of his person. No one may be arbitrarily deprived of this right."

10 On the conditions and consequences of the use of force by law enforcement agents see Paul Tavernier, "Le recours á la force par la police" in Christian Tomuschat, Evelyne Lagrange and Stefan Oeter (eds.), *The Right to Life* (Leiden: Nijhoff, 2010), pp. 41–66.

In such situations, the use of force must be absolutely necessary and proportionate to the aim pursued, so that it constitutes a means of last resort.[11] With the exception of the ECHR, no human rights treaty explicitly covers the right to life in the context of an armed conflict. The ECHR connects both in its provision on derogation: ECHR, Article 15(2) allows derogating the right to life "in respect of deaths resulting from lawful acts of war."[12] In pursuance of the ICJ's Advisory Opinion quoted earlier, the argument can thus be made that where force is used in conformity with humanitarian law, it is not used arbitrarily under human rights treaties.

Different from the protection of the right to life against arbitrary killings, the objective of international humanitarian law, it has been said, is to inform us on "[h]ow to kill your fellow human beings in a nice way."[13] Less ironically, the balancing of military necessity and humanitarian concerns is central to international humanitarian law, but is unknown to international human rights law. In both legal regimes, the use of force is limited, and both refer to "necessity" and "proportionality" for this purpose, but they mean different things. And different from human rights law, humanitarian law distinguishes between the use of force against a lawful military target and the protection of civilians. The fundamental principle of distinction between combatants and civilians leads to different regulatory frameworks within humanitarian law, which do not mirror the approach taken by human rights law.[14]

Under humanitarian law, enemy soldiers may be killed as a first resort on the basis of their status: the mere presumption of hostility manifest in their status as combatant or armed fighter is sufficient. The essence of this approach is summed up in the ICRC Commentary to Additional Protocol II: "Those who belong to armed forces or armed groups may be attacked at any time."[15] In other words, international humanitarian law allows the most efficient means to disable the enemy to secure a military advantage, while international human rights law allows the degree of force necessary to counter a specific threat and restore the *status quo ante*.[16] Under humanitarian law, enemy soldiers are not viewed in light of their threat level: as long as they have not surrendered or are otherwise *hors de combat*, they are a lawful target, irrespective of their conduct.[17] On the other hand, the use of force is not unlimited under humanitarian law; indeed, this is the very essence of

[11] See Kälin and Künzli, *The Law of International Human Rights Protection* (n. 7) pp. 276–79, with reference to the respective case law of human rights bodies.

[12] ECHR, Art. 15(2).

[13] G.I.A.D. Draper, "The Relationship between the Human Rights Regime and the Law of Armed Conflict" (1971) 1 *Israel Yearbook of Human Rights* 191.

[14] See Additional Protocol I, Art. 48: "In order to ensure respect for and protection of the civilian population and civilian objects, the Parties to the conflict shall at all times distinguish between the civilian population and combatants and between civilian objects and military objectives and accordingly shall direct their operations only against military objectives."

[15] Yves Sandoz, Christophe Swinarski and Bruno Zimmermann (eds.), *Commentary on the Additional Protocols of 8 June 1977 to the Geneva Conventions of 12 August 1949* (Geneva: Nijhoff, 1987), para. 4789. On the rules of targeting see, e.g., Yoram Dinstein, *The Conduct of Hostilities under the Law of International Armed Conflict* (2nd edn., Cambridge: Cambridge University Press, 2010), pp. 27–29.

[16] See Geoffrey Corn, "Mixing Apples and Hand Grenades: The Logical Limit of Applying Human Rights Norms to Armed Conflicts" (2010) 1(1) *International Humanitarian Legal Studies* 76.

[17] Ibid. 85.

humanitarian law.[18] But the use of force against enemy combatants is limited only by the requirement that it must lead to some discernible military advantage and does not induce unnecessary suffering.[19]

International human rights law, in contrast, is not status-based but conduct- or cause-based: unless it is determined that an imminent threat is caused by the conduct of a person, deadly force must not be used in law enforcement operations.[20] And human rights law is not only concerned with minimizing the damage to possible bystanders (as does humanitarian law with regard to civilians) but also allows harming the target of violence only proportional to the threat it poses: where capture or lesser means of force are possible against the target they must be used before deadly force is applied as a last resort. In human rights law the very term "proportionality" is part of the necessity test for limitations of human rights: where states seek to limit the application of human rights in pursuance of an allegedly legitimate aim, the respective measure must be proportionate to the goal sought to be achieved.[21] It has thus been said that in contrast to human rights law, which prohibits a "'shoot to kill" policy, humanitarian law simply manages such a policy.[22] The latter seems to demonstrate an "overbreadth"[23] in the application of deadly force compared to human rights law.

Where bystanders are likely to be affected, the yardstick under human rights law is to minimize the harm done to them in law enforcement operations as far as possible. The standard formulation used, for example, by the European Court of Human Rights in this respect is to require states to plan and conduct their operations "in such a way as to avoid or minimize, to the greatest extent possible, any risk."[24] In armed conflict, the use of force under humanitarian law is limited by the principle of proportionality where civilians are likely to be affected. This means that force must not be excessive to the anticipated military advantage and an attack is unlawful when it:

> may be expected to cause incidental loss of civilian life, injury to civilians, damage to civilian objects, or a combination thereof, which would be excessive in relation to the concrete and direct military advantage anticipated.[25]

[18] See Additional Protocol I, Art. 35(1): "In any armed conflict the right of the Parties to the conflict to choose methods and means of warfare is not unlimited."

[19] See the Preamble to the Declaration of St. Petersburg 1868: "Considering that the progress of civilization should have the effect of alleviating as much as possible the calamities of war; that the only legitimate object which States should endeavour to accomplish during war is to weaken the military forces of the enemy; that for this purpose it is sufficient to disable the greatest possible number of men; that this object would be exceeded by the employment of arms which uselessly aggravate the sufferings of disabled men, or render their death inevitable; that the employment of such arms would, therefore, be contrary to the laws of humanity." See also Dinstein, *The Conduct of Hostilities under the Law of International Armed Conflict* (n. 15) pp. 4–8.

[20] See Corn, "Mixing Apples and Hand Grenades" (n. 16) 76.

[21] See Frédéric Mégret, "Nature of Obligations" in Daniel Moeckli, Sangeeta Shah and Sandesh Sivakumaran (eds.), *International Human Rights Law* (Oxford: Oxford University Press, 2010), p. 142.

[22] See Kenneth Watkin, "Assessing Proportionality: Moral Complexity and Legal Rules" (2005) 8 *Yearbook of International Humanitarian Law* 36.

[23] Corn, "Mixing Apples and Hand Grenades" (n. 16) 77.

[24] *Ergi* v. *Turkey*, European Court of Human Rights, Appl. No. 23818/94, Judgment of 28 July 1998, para. 79.

[25] Additional Protocol I, Art. 51(5)(b). The precautionary principles for targeting as codified in Additional Protocol I, Arts. 57 and 58 support this provision and provide specific guidance to military commanders;

This idea of proportionality is said to be rooted in the medieval Christian doctrine of "double effect," which allows reconciling the absolute prohibition of attacking civilians with the need to conduct warfare against military targets and, as a compromise, considers unintended but foreseeable civilian casualties as acceptable under certain conditions.[26] This moral component of the principle of proportionality was later supplemented by a more mechanical approach of calculating the acceptable "collateral damage" of military actions, which in the realities of modern warfare may have to be reconciled with political considerations of targeting in light of war objectives and public pressure; all of which turns the application of the proportionality principle into a complex and morally and emotionally charged matter.[27] The genesis of proportionality in international humanitarian law also reflects that in its modern form it was accepted only rather recently. Despite being (at least implicitly) mentioned for the first time in the 1924 Hague Air Warfare Rules, it was seemingly not accepted by states as customary law until the 1970s.[28]

Both legal regimes thus resort to the principles of "necessity" and "proportionality," but the terms carry different meanings.[29] The objectives of humanitarian law – managing the use of force as a first resort against military targets and weighing military advantage and "collateral damage" when civilians are concerned – are seen as incompatible with the necessity and proportionality test under human rights law.[30] Mixing the two is perceived as problematic, if not impossible, in theory as well as in practice, and the stakes are seemingly high: "[t]here is perhaps no other area of potential conflict where the infusion of international humanitarian law with international human rights law could lead to a greater slide into utopia, and a consequent slide into irrelevance."[31]

The underlying argument is that war-fighting is simply not law enforcement. Observers of the US armed forces' struggle to control the occupied Iraqi town of Fallujah in November 2004, for example, have pointed out that with 540 air strikes and 14,000 artillery and mortar shells and 2,500 tank main gun rounds fired "[t]his was not a 'law enforcement' operation easily subjected to a human rights based normative regime."[32] If this is true in such situations, it is the more so in international armed conflicts. The rationale for using force under international human rights law, it has been pointed out, is to re-establish security and law and order in society, while the rationale for using force

see in greater detail Dinstein, *The Conduct of Hostilities under the Law of International Armed Conflict* (n. 15) pp. 138–45.

26 See Watkin, "Assessing Proportionality" (n. 22) 26. 27 Ibid. 30–31.

28 See A.P.V. Rogers, "The Principle of Proportionality" in Howard M. Hensel (ed.), *The Legitimate Use of Military Force: The Just War Tradition and the Customary Law of Armed Conflict* (Aldershot: Ashgate, 2008), p. 209.

29 See McLaughlin, "The Law of Armed Conflict and International Human Rights Law" (n. 2) 231–35, and Andreas Paulus and Mindia Vashakmadze, "Asymmetrical War and the Notion of Armed Conflict: A Tentative Conceptualization" (2009) 91(873) *International Review of the Red Cross* 120. On proportionality in the jurisprudence of the European Court of Human Rights, see also Enzo Cannizzaro and Francesco de Vittor, "Proportionality in the European Convention on Human Rights" in Robert Kolb and Gloria Gaggioli (eds.), *Research Handbook on Human Rights and Humanitarian Law* (Cheltenham: Edward Elgar, 2013), pp. 125–45.

30 See Watkin, "Assessing Proportionality" (n. 22) 37.

31 Marko Milanovic, "Norm Conflicts, International Humanitarian Law and Human Rights Law" in Orna Ben-Naftali (ed.), *International Humanitarian and International Human Rights Law* (Oxford: Oxford University Press, 2011), p. 121.

32 See, e.g., Watkin, "Assessing Proportionality" (n. 22) 37.

under international humanitarian law is the submission of the enemy as promptly and efficiently as possible.[33]

Those denying a place for human rights considerations in targeting decisions are concerned that "the paradigmatic functionality of the [law of armed conflict] concept of proportionality remains clear."[34] Introducing international human rights law into the historically developed balance of humanitarian considerations and military necessity, it is argued, would inevitably be perceived as operationally illogical by armed forces and lead to disregard of or resistance to any such new rules.[35] The main fear which results from a conflation of law enforcement and war-fighting is that this would expose military forces to unacceptably high risks of being targeted without the ability to respond swiftly and effectively.[36] From a military perspective, it has been argued, this "borders on the absurd."[37] It is also feared that including a human rights proportionality assessment would meet with considerable problems in training and mission preparation,[38] and that applying a human rights proportionality principle to every military attack would be too time-consuming and complex.[39]

8.2 Proportionality revisited

This may reflect the dominant view of the irreconcilable nature of human rights and humanitarian law on this question, but there are a number of caveats. One is about the suggested dichotomy of war-fighting and law enforcement, and the other about the different perception of proportionality. First, the separatist arguments very much assume an image of war akin to Oppenheim's classic definition of war as "a contention between two or more states through their armed forces for the purpose of overpowering each other and imposing such conditions as the victor pleases."[40] As will be discussed in greater detail later, the character of war is changing, and the majority of military operations are conducted in different settings than Oppenheim may have anticipated. This is not meant to question the fact that where an armed conflict exists, humanitarian law applies, but suggests that where operations are conducted in a way that analogies to law enforcement operations can be made, the exclusivity and exhaustiveness of humanitarian law may be questionable.

The problem is compounded by the well-known difficulties in determining the existence of an armed conflict and the problem of the threshold between internal disturbances and internal armed conflicts. The fact that in situations of heavy fighting combat weapons, fighter jets and artillery were being used led, for example, the European Court of Human Rights to conclude in 2005 in *Isayeva* v. *Russia* on the situation in Chechnya that the use of such means and methods does not detract from the law enforcement nature of the operation.[41] And just as there is no single image of "war," there is no standard model of law enforcement operations with universally applicable levels of acceptable armed force. International human rights law can accommodate different contexts of law enforcement

[33] See Corn, "Mixing Apples and Hand Grenades" (n. 16) 86.

[34] McLaughlin, "The Law of Armed Conflict and International Human Rights Law" (n. 2) 241.

[35] Corn, "Mixing Apples and Hand Grenades" (n. 16) 56. [36] Ibid. 88–90. [37] Ibid. 91.

[38] Ibid. 56. [39] See Watkin, "Assessing Proportionality" (n. 22) 39.

[40] L. Oppenheim in Hersch Lauterpacht, *International Law* (7th edn., 1952), p. 202, quoted in Yoram Dinstein, *War, Aggression and Self-Defence* (5th edn., Cambridge: Cambridge University Press, 2011), p. 5.

[41] See *Isayeva* v. *Russia*, European Court of Human Rights, Appl. No. 57950/00, Judgment of 24 February 2005, para. 191. The argument is problematic for the way in which the Court, at the same time, excluded humanitarian law from its considerations.

with varying means and methods. As has rightly been said, a law enforcement operation in a peaceful Swiss village may be judged differently from the conduct of law enforcement officers operating against heavily armed Mexican drug cartels in Veracruz.[42]

Arguing for a strict separation of law enforcement and war-fighting are thus variations of the peace/war dichotomy and, while often correct, may equally often miss the fluid character of the use of force. It has thus been suggested that a human rights proportionality assessment may be possible only in internal conflicts or small-scale conflicts but certainly not in large international conflicts, as this would alter the normative framework of armed conflicts in a way which was never intended.[43] Such a graduated approach seems to better accommodate the character of many armed conflicts. But then again, excluding international armed conflicts is built more upon the image of war as either "real" wars (in which a human rights proportionality assessment has no place) and "'small-scale" "quasi-law enforcement operations" (which are susceptible to human rights law) than on clear criteria on the level of violence necessary to exclude human rights law. It also does not acknowledge armed conflicts which are both international and internal at the same time.

Secondly, it seems that the differences between human rights and humanitarian law are not as paradigmatic as many believe when it comes to limiting the use of force through the idea of proportionality. As far as the unintended and collateral consequences of the use of force are concerned, the principle of proportionality conveys in both legal regimes the idea that harming those not the object of the lawful use of force needs to be prevented, even though different high thresholds are applied.[44] The difference could be described as the absolute necessity of human rights law and the contingent necessity of humanitarian law: the former requires restraint to the maximum possible while the latter requires restraint to the maximum possible in light of additional, i.e., military, considerations.

If the complementarity of human rights and humanitarian law is understood as allowing human rights to provide the direction for the development of humanitarian law, it follows that the principle of proportionality under humanitarian law could be modified and assimilated to the way it is perceived in international human rights law.[45] A human rights-based principle of proportionality would not do away with the corresponding idea of military necessity but suggests that the "excessive use of force" in humanitarian law is understood not just as disproportionate to the military aims likely to be achieved, but as entailing the obligation to use the least damaging means and methods, together with an overall weighing of values and interests informed by international human rights law.[46] In effect, it would lead to further restrictions being read into the principle of military necessity, where reasonable.

[42] See for similar arguments Nils Melzer, "Bolstering the Protection of Civilians in Armed Conflict" in Antonio Cassesse (ed.), *Realizing Utopia: The Future of International Law* (Oxford: Oxford University Press, 2012), p. 512.

[43] See Watkin, "Assessing Proportionality" (n. 22) 41.

[44] See Melzer, "Bolstering the Protection of Civilians in Armed Conflict" (n. 42) p. 512–13.

[45] Abandoning proportionality altogether is certainly not an option and not seriously suggested anywhere, see Christian Tomuschat, "Human Rights and International Humanitarian Law" (2010) 21(1) *European Journal of International Law* 20.

[46] See Daniel Thürer, *International Humanitarian Law: Theory, Practice, Context* (The Hague: Hague Academy of International Law, 2011), p. 76.

This is usually rejected with the argument that such reliance on human rights is superfluous because if the outcome is a refined targeting process which enables greater precision and lower numbers of civilian casualties, this can be achieved under existing humanitarian law, by using modern weapons technology, and on the basis of military-ethical considerations through appeals to "the hearts of men."[47] This, however, stands very much in the nineteenth century tradition of humanity being granted as a reflection of honour and charity.

Suggestions for such an approach to invoke human rights come, essentially, from recent counter-insurgency operations, where international human rights law may effectively clarify obligations under international humanitarian law and, as a result, heighten the level of protection offered.[48] The prohibition of attacks on civilians and the civilian population,[49] for example, is usually understood as allowing attacks on individual enemy soldiers hiding in a crowd of civilians regardless of the conduct of those soldiers. The death of civilians is acceptable as long as (humanitarian law) proportionality guarantees that the damage done is not excessive in relation to the anticipated results of the attack. A stricter reading of this provision could allow such attacks only when enemy soldiers pose an immediate danger. A similar effect could occur with regard to Additional Protocol I, Article 57(2)(c) on effective warning.[50] It is commonly assumed that issuing such a warning to civilians in danger of being affected by an attack on a lawful military target is sufficient to comply with this provision. Whether or not they choose to ignore this warning or find it impossible to follow it is not a matter of concern for the attacker. A human rights-based approach might require an additional verification of the situation, where appropriate, e.g., to establish whether civilians can effectively and reasonably leave the area and find shelter elsewhere. This seems to have been suggested by the European Court of Human Rights when it found Russia to be in violation of the ECHR (in *Isayeva* v. *Russia*, concerning attacks of the Russian armed forces on Chechen fighters in the village of Katyr-Yurt), because the government had not taken into consideration that, despite warnings having been given, there was effectively no safe place for civilians to go.[51]

Such proposals may already have been made or implemented in individual circumstances by military planners and decision-makers in counter-insurgency operations, and be reflected in Rules of Engagement (RoE). But the rationale for devising such rules is usually the acknowledgment that under certain circumstances such an approach is necessary from a utilitarian point of view, i.e., that saving lives of civilians in such situations helps in winning the hearts and minds of local people, facilitates their operation and may effectively protect their own troops. Turning such considerations into universally applicable binding law would be another step.[52] The arguments made above – that such a human rights

[47] See Watkin, "Assessing Proportionality" (n. 22) 52.

[48] On the following scenarios see Federico Sperotto, "Counter-Insurgency, Human Rights, and the Law of Armed Conflict" (2009) 17(1) *Human Rights Brief* 21, available at www.wcl.american.edu/hrbrief/17/1 sperotto.pdf (last accessed 15 April 2014), who draws on his experiences as legal military advisor in Afghanistan.

[49] Additional Protocol I, Art. 51(2): "The civilian population as such, as well as individual civilians, shall not be the object of attack."

[50] Ibid. Art. 57(2): "With respect to attacks, the following precautions shall be taken: ... (c) effective advance warning shall be given of attacks which may affect the civilian population, unless circumstances do not permit."

[51] *Isayeva* v. *Russia* (n. 41) para. 187.

[52] See Sperotto, "Counter-Insurgency" (n. 48) 21–22.

proportionality assessment is too complex, time-consuming and not part of military training – are practical concerns to be taken seriously, but they are not objections as a matter of principle.

It also seems questionable to suggest that under human rights law there is always time and space for carefully weighing the options, while under humanitarian law this is never the case.[53] This would be rather a blanket statement: depending on the circumstances, proportionality under humanitarian law can be no less complex than under human rights law. On the other hand, targeting decisions under humanitarian law may be a long process, while peace-time law operations may sometimes need split-second decisions on the use of armed force, depending on the circumstances. The example of a (peace-time) terrorist hijacking of a large civilian airliner carrying hundreds of passengers is an example that under international human rights law matters of proportionality quantitatively and qualitatively similar to those in armed conflicts may arise.[54]

8.3 Lawful killing or duty to capture?

The situation is more difficult with regard to the (lawful) killing of enemy combatants as a first resort based on their status. Introducing the concept of the human right to life would mean that their killing is only acceptable when no less damaging means are available, different from the present interpretation of the principle of military necessity which allows the killing of enemy combatants *qua* their status at any time.[55] Can it be argued that "killing must be a last resort, even in war?"[56] Such views are sharply rejected as a mistaken interpretation of the prohibition of unnecessary suffering and as operationally impossible, given that the strength of international humanitarian law lies in the simplicity with which it presumes that all members of the enemy armed forces are lawful targets regardless of the threat they pose.[57] At present, such suggestions are not supported by state practice and *opinio juris*.[58]

The "capture/kill debate" (on whether there exists a duty to use the least damaging means and capture enemy combatants rather than kill them) is as yet undecided. Even so, such a duty can be argued for. First, the argument that humanitarian law is permissive in the way it allows the lawful killing of enemy combatants at will (save the prohibition of unnecessary suffering) is tied to achieving a military advantage. The identification of the opponent as a lawful target is not merely a question of status, but connects with the presumption of hostility and thus entails an implicit threat analysis: the potential threat which enemy combatants pose makes them a lawful target and not their mere existence.[59] This is a low threshold but nevertheless includes at least implicit considerations of proportionality in

[53] See for this argument McLaughlin, "The Law of Armed Conflict and International Human Rights Law" (n. 2) 237–38.

[54] See Watkin, "Assessing Proportionality" (n. 22) 40.

[55] See Thürer, *International Humanitarian Law* (n. 46) p. 80.

[56] Philip Alston, *Report of the Special Rapporteur on Extrajudicial, Summary or Arbitrary Executions, Addendum – Mission to Sri Lanka*, UN Doc. E/CN.4/2006/53/Add.5 (27 March 2006), para. 29.

[57] See Corn, "Mixing Apples and Hand Grenades" (n. 16) 75, with reference to other authors.

[58] Ibid. 81.

[59] See David S. Koller, "The Moral Imperative: Toward a Human-Rights Based Law of War" (2005) 46(1) *Harvard International Law Journal* 254.

killing enemy combatants: only to the extent that such a threat can reasonably be discerned (the removal of which provides a military advantage) is killing permissible.

Secondly, it seems at least not impossible to infer the duty of such a "least harmful means" test historically from international humanitarian law, given the ambiguity of the drafting history of the respective provisions and the different approaches of the humanitarian and military communities.[60]

Thirdly, such a duty to capture rather than kill may be discerned from humanitarian law in certain situations, particularly in internal armed conflicts, the often quoted example being that of a rebel fighter caught shopping in the supermarket where capture rather than killing is a reasonable option.[61] The latter case is, however, usually argued with the problematic idea of the distance from the "battlefield," and not with a human rights-based duty to apply minimum force.[62] Some see such a principle at work in all situations except international armed conflicts and where civilians directly participate in hostilities.[63] The prohibition under humanitarian law to shoot aircrews parachuting in distress also points towards the possibility that international humanitarian law does make exceptions from the rule that the status of combatants alone is a sufficient ground for attacking them lawfully.[64] It is, however, unclear whether this rule is motivated by humanitarian concerns or rather reflects the chivalry among pilots, who historically were perceived as elite warriors with an ethos of their own.[65]

Fourthly, such a duty to capture rather than kill seems to reflect wider trends, such as the changing image of the soldier from warrior to professional security provider, the growing civilianization of the armed forces, and advances in target techniques and technology, all of which cast doubts on the necessity of killing all enemy soldiers indiscriminately.[66]

And fifthly, it can be argued that such a move from a "shoot to kill" policy to a "kill when necessary"[67] policy would not be an innovation, but would transform the discretion of military commanders to capture rather than kill into a legal duty not to kill when capture is possible.[68] Such examples seem to demonstrate that the idea of a human rights-based approach to the use of force should not be ruled out as a matter of principle, but that it is rather about analyzing its feasibility under operational, tactical and resource constraints to find out when it is legally sound and realistically applicable.[69] The fears expressed in this

60 See in greater detail Ryan Goodman, "The Power to Kill or Capture Enemy Combatants" (2013) 24(3) *European Journal of International Law* 819, and the critique by Jens David Ohlin, *The Capture-Kill Debate: Lost Legislative History or Revisionist History?*, Cornell Legal Studies Research Paper (8 March 2013), available at http://papers.ssrn.com/sol3/papers.cfm?abstract_id=2230486 (last accessed 15 April 2014).

61 Marco Sassòli and Laura M. Olson, "The Relationship between International Humanitarian Law and Human Rights Law Where it Matters: Admissible Killing and Internment of Fighters in Non-international Armed Conflicts" (2008) 90(871) *International Review of the Red Cross* 613–16.

62 Ibid. 626–27.

63 See Louise Doswald-Beck, "The Right to Life in Armed Conflict: Does International Humanitarian Law Provide All the Answers?" (2007) 88(864) *International Review of the Red Cross* 904.

64 Additional Protocol I, Art. 41(1): "No person parachuting from an aircraft in distress shall be made the object of attack during his descent."

65 See Gabriella Blum, "The Dispensable Lives of Soldiers" (2012) 2(1) *Journal of Legal Analysis* 80.

66 Ibid. 72–74. 67 Ibid. 114. 68 See Corn, "Mixing Apples and Hand Grenades" (n. 16) 80–81.

69 See Blum, "The Dispensable Lives of Soldiers" (n. 65) 115. Similarly Corn, "Mixing Apples and Hand Grenades" (n. 16) 56; and Theodor Meron, *The Humanization of International Law* (Leiden: Nijhoff, 2006), p. 276.

regard, namely, that a human rights-based approach will limit the autonomy of military forces and create higher risks, will be discussed later.

8.4 A unified use of force regime?

Whether such changes would, and should, ultimately lead to a unified use of force regime for all situations from peace-time law enforcement operations to international armed conflicts is an open question.[70] From the point of legal theory this might be welcome, as it would remedy the current segmentation of different types of proportionality, which, as has rightly been argued, disregards "the integrity, coherence, and equilibrium of the international normative framework as a whole."[71] It has been suggested to preserve this central element of humanitarian law from being modified by human rights which, it is feared, "confuses battlefield operations."[72] In such a model, the complementary application of international human rights and international humanitarian law is acknowledged, but the central element which international humanitarian law seeks to regulate, "the application of combat power,"[73] would remain exclusively governed by international humanitarian law as the one and only appropriate law. This graduated approach has been discussed (and rejected) as a general interpretative yardstick for clarifying the interplay of human rights and humanitarian law, above.

With regard to the use of deadly force, this approach suggests that all other military activities outside "combat," perhaps also including the use of force in peace operations, could still be governed by international human rights law jointly with international humanitarian law, but that the application of deadly force would not.[74] Such a model can be accompanied by considerations based on a distinction between operational opponents (i.e., enemy soldiers) and other individuals over which, for whatever reason and in whatever form, authority is being exercised (or who are, in the words of international humanitarian law, "in the hands of the enemy").[75] The argument is that whenever such individuals are exposed to measures such as physical violence, arrest, detention or any other act outside combat, they are, in effect, confronted with law enforcement-like practices to which international human rights law can suitably be applied by way of analogy. Where there is no such nexus, only humanitarian law would apply.[76]

Such a "pre- and post-submission"[77] treatment of opponents would effectively create two groups: "operational opponents" to which only international humanitarian law would apply, and combatants *hors de combat* and civilians, who would in addition enjoy human rights protection.[78] In a way, it is a reinterpretation of the notion of "enemy": civilians and combatants *hors de combat* are no longer the enemy, whereas active combatants are. The former can be seen as persons under the jurisdiction of a government, whereas the latter cannot.[79] In a similar way it has been argued that "where international humanitarian law is

[70] See Melzer, "Bolstering the Protection of Civilians in Armed Conflict", p. 514; and Francisco Forrest Martin, "Using International Human Rights Law for Establishing a Unified Use of Force Rule in the Law of Armed Conflict" (2001) 64 *Sasketchewan Law Review* 395.

[71] See Melzer, "Bolstering the Protection of Civilians in Armed Conflict" (n. 42) p. 511.

[72] Corn, "Mixing Apples and Hand Grenades" (n. 16) 66. [73] Ibid. 59. [74] Ibid. 59–60.

[75] Geneva Convention IV, Art. 4. [76] See Corn, "Mixing Apples and Hand Grenades" (n. 16) 60–62.

[77] Ibid. 68. [78] Ibid. 71. [79] Ibid. 73.

lex specialis – such as during 'hot' conflict – human rights law is not applicable."[80] The crux lies, of course, in introducing such new terminology: "operational opponents," "combat" and "hot conflicts" are imprecise terms or unknown to the law.[81] The confusion on the battlefield, it must be feared, will thus likely increase rather than be reduced.

Alternatively, and in acknowledgment that the boundaries of war-fighting and law enforcement cannot be kept so tightly guarded as to allow humanitarian law to govern the former and human rights the latter, a mixed model can be imagined.[82] It is based on the view that in most modern conflicts neither a law enforcement model nor an armed conflict model appropriately reflects the reality. It seeks, in particular, to respond to the practice of targeted killings as increasingly resorted to by the United States in its "War on Terror" which pose multiple problems with regard to the use of force.[83]

The lawfulness of these targeted killings hinges on the determination of an armed conflict (as a non-international armed conflict, a transnational law enforcement operation, or a new type of "extra-state" armed conflict); on the classification of the targets (as terrorists, civilians directly participating in hostilities, non-state armed fighters or unlawful enemy combatants); and on the targeting process which draws, depending on the former classifications, on humanitarian law's principles of distinction, proportionality, necessity and precaution; or on criteria under human rights law; or a combination thereof.[84] The increased reliance on remote-controlled drones to deliver precision strikes against persons identified as international terrorists adds to the complexity.[85]

It has been suggested that a law enforcement approach to international terrorism cannot adequately capture situations where transnational terrorist activities are connected to non-international armed conflicts, while a war-fighting model allows states to use unacceptably unlimited powers to target persons identified as enemy fighters at will, so that both need to be used. Again, this model does not provide ultimately convincing answers and suffers, particularly, from the way it seeks to deal with the fall-out of the controversial "War on

80 Paulus, "The Use of Force in Occupied Territories" (n. 3) p. 144.

81 The definition of "operational opponents" as "objects of deliberate violence" helps little to clarify the matter, see Corn, "Mixing Apples and Hand Grenades" (n. 16) 67.

82 See David Kretzmer, "Targeted Killing of Suspected Terrorists: Extra-Judicial Execution or Legitimate Means of Defence?" (2005) 16(2) *European Journal of International Law* 201–4.

83 An exhaustive treatment of this question is impossible here; see instead Nils Melzer, *Targeted Killing in International Law* (Oxford: Oxford University Press, 2008).

84 On the widely diverging views, see in greater detail Kirsten Schmalenbach, "Der Rechtsstaat und sein Henker: Gezieltes Töten als Mittel der Terrorbekämpfung (2012) 60 *Jahrbuch des Öffentlichen Rechts der Gegenwart* 251; Peter M. Cullen, "The Role of Targeted Killings in the Campaign Against Terror" (2008) 48(1) "*Joint Force Quarterly* 22; Amos Guiora, "Targeted Killing as Active Self-Defense" (2005) 36(2–3) *Case Western Reserve University Journal of International Law* 319; Afsheen Radsan and Richard Murphy, "Measure Twice, Shoot Once: Higher Care for CIA Targeted Killing" (2011) 4 *University of Illinois Law Review* 1201; Marko Milanovic, "Lessons for Human Rights and Humanitarian Law in the War on Terror: Comparing Hamdan and the Israeli *Targeted Killings* Case" (2007) 89(866) *International Review of the Red Cross* 373; and Michael N. Schmitt, "Targeted Killings and International Law: Law Enforcement, Self-defense and Armed Conflict" in Roberta Arnold and Noelle Quénivet (eds.), *International Humanitarian Law and Human Rights Law: Towards a Merger in International Law* (Leiden: Nijhoff, 2008), pp. 525–53.

85 See, e.g., Chris Downes, "'Targeted Killings' in an Age of Terror: The Legality of the Yemen Strike" (2004) 9(2) *Journal of Conflict and Security Law* 277, on the first lethal drone strike outside Afghanistan on 3 November 2002 in Yemen.

Terror," rather than reconciling the demands of international human rights law with the logic of humanitarian law. While the right to life in armed conflict remains thus an unresolved and divisive issue, it is also obvious that, ultimately, differences between human rights and humanitarian law are gradual rather than paradigmatic, and that a blanket rejection of human rights law in armed conflicts on this critical question is not supported by state practice and legal theory.

9

The extra-territorial application of human rights: functional universality

9.1 Reach of human rights

Whenever states engage in military operations beyond their borders, the extra-territorial application of human rights becomes an issue. It remains a vividly debated question in international legal scholarship as well as a matter of great practical relevance. At its centre is the notion of jurisdiction and the way in which states are duty-bound and responsible for acts abroad. In human rights law, the application of human rights norms depends on a state's jurisdiction. It rests on the idea that human rights govern the relationship between the government (and its agents) and those over which the government has jurisdiction, so that a state party to a human rights treaty has obligations towards individuals only in as far as such a jurisdictional link can be established. "Jurisdiction" is, however, an ambiguous term with multiple meanings and no treaty-based legal definition, and there is disagreement on how to confine it with regard to related but different concepts such as attribution, the scope of obligation and the responsibility for wrongful acts.[1] Under general public international law it describes the ability as well as the limits of the legal competence of states to regulate the conduct of (natural and legal) persons by means of its domestic law, and may cover jurisdiction to prescribe, adjudicate and enforce. Such jurisdiction flows from the equal sovereignty of states and describes the extent of each state's right to regulate such conduct, whether prescriptive (as law-making) or executive (as law enforcement). Jurisdiction is essentially territorial for the way it describes a state's prerogative to regulate matters on its territory; where it is exercised extra-territorially it is likely to infringe the rights of other states if not expressly consented to.[2]

Jurisdiction under international human rights law differs, however, from this meaning of jurisdiction. It is not about a state's ability to legislate and enforce law abroad but may describe the factual exercise of power or control or authority over territory and/or persons.[3] It is also about the extent of duties owed towards an individual, and it delimits a state's obligation to

[1] See Michal Gondek, "Extraterritorial Application of the European Convention on Human Rights: Territorial Focus in the Age of Globalization?" (2005) 52(3) *Netherlands International Law Review* 364; Marko Milanovic, *Extraterritorial Application of Human Rights Treaties* (Oxford: Oxford University Press 2011), pp. 21–41; and John Cerone, *Out of Bounds? Considering the Reach of International Human Rights Law*, New York University School of Law Centre for Human Rights and Global Justice Working Paper No. 5 (2006), pp. 26–32, available at www.chrgj.org/publications/docs/wp/WPS_NYU_CHRGJ_Cerone_Final.pdf (last accessed 15 April 2014).

[2] See Malcolm Shaw, *International Law* (6th edn., Cambridge: Cambridge University Press, 2008), pp. 645–47; and Jerzy Kranz, "Die völkerrechtliche Verantwortlichkeit für die Anwendung militärischer Gewalt" (2010) 48(3) *Zeitschrift für ausländisches öffentliches Recht und Völkerrecht* 308.

[3] See Milanovic, *Extraterritorial Application of Human Rights Treaties* (n. 1) pp. 39–41.

respect, protect and fulfil human rights.[4] Such power or control or authority, is normally exercised within a state's territory. But when a state acts outside its territory, as is the case in international armed conflicts, situations of occupations, when intervening in internal armed violence on territory other than its own or in multi-national peace operations, problems arise.[5]

The idea that armed forces acting abroad potentially carry with them the whole array of human rights obligations which a state has assumed under international law is an alarming prospect for many states engaged, or likely to be engaged, in military operations abroad, and the ensuing potential legal and political problems have led many states to advocate strongly against such extra-territorial application of international human rights law. In conflicts which do not conform to humanitarian law's dichotomy of international and internal armed conflict, such as "internationalized" conflicts (where states intervene in internal conflicts) and in "extra-territorial" conflicts (where states are engaged in hostilities with non-state actors outside their own territory), the question of extra-territorial application of human rights may be equally troublesome.

A strict territorial jurisdiction would make human rights obligations end at a state's borders. Together with an exclusivist understanding of the principle *lex specialis*, this would effectively leave no space for human rights in armed conflicts beyond a state's territory at all. If the applicability of international humanitarian law were indeed to be understood as strictly territorial, i.e., confined to the territory of states parties to human rights treaties, extra-territorial action of states would not be covered by international human rights law, leaving humanitarian law as the only applicable legal regime, or would possibly create a legal black hole, where neither human rights nor humanitarian law apply. On the other hand, the suggestion that states are obliged to guarantee everywhere a human rights standard akin to that which it has to ensure within its own territory is seen as utopian by many. The UK Law Lords obviously took this view in *Al-Skeini* v. *United Kingdom* (which will be discussed below) when, confronted with the prospect that the UK government might have to guarantee all rights under the European Convention on Human Rights (ECHR) in occupied Iraq, they found this "manifestly absurd"[6] and "utterly unreal."[7]

The question whether or not, and to which extent, international human rights law applies extra-territorially is thus central to the debate on human rights in armed conflict. Scholarly views, state practice and the jurisprudence of human rights bodies on this question differ considerably.[8] The dispute is essentially about human rights treaty law (which also varies in its approach to jurisdiction); customary law seems not to face the same problems as human rights treaty law given that there are no clauses limiting its territorial reach.[9] Yet, similar theoretical and practical problems may well occur but have not yet been analyzed.[10]

4 See Sarah Joseph, "Scope of Obligations" in Daniel Moeckli, Sangeeta Shah and Sandesh Svikumaran (eds.), *International Human Rights Law* (Oxford: Oxford University Press, 2010), p. 160; and Walter Kälin and Jörg Künzli, *The Law of International Human Rights Protection* (Oxford: Oxford University Press, 2009), p. 129.

5 As is the case when state agents operate outside a state's territory in situations not involving an armed conflict, a question which cannot be pursued here.

6 *Al-Skeini* v. *United Kingdom*, European Court of Human Rights, Appl. No. 55721/07, Judgment of 7 July 2011, para.78.

7 Ibid. para. 124.

8 See Joseph, "Scope of Obligations" (n. 4) p. 161.

9 See Noam Lubell, *Extraterritorial Use of Force against Non-State Actors* (Oxford: Oxford University Press, 2010), pp. 232–35.

10 See Milanovic, *Extraterritorial Application of Human Rights Treaties* (n. 1) p. 3.

9.2 Legal basis of the extra-territorial application of human rights

(a) International Covenant on Civil and Political Rights

Given that there are no overarching rules in public international law in favour of or against the extra-territorial application of treaty provisions, the only guidance can be found in the respective treaty.[11] But not all human rights treaties contain jurisdictional clauses, and where they do, these clauses read considerably differently. In particular, there is no common approach to the link between jurisdiction and territory, and this systemic shortcoming is matched by an equally incoherent jurisprudence on jurisdiction. The arguably strictest rule on jurisdiction is found in the International Covenant on Civil and Political Rights (ICCPR), Article 2: "Each State Party to the present Covenant undertakes to respect and to ensure to all individuals within its territory and subject to its jurisdiction the rights recognized in the present Covenant."[12] The duality of "territory" and "jurisdiction" seems to constitute, in a literal reading, a cumulative demand, so that only persons who reside in the territory *and* fall under the jurisdiction of a state party are protected by the Covenant.[13]

Given that the ICCPR is the only treaty with such a dual requirement, the logic and validity of this provision has been questioned. The Human Rights Committee, in *Sergio Ruben Lopez Burgos* v. *Uruguay* (on the abduction and detention of two Uruguayan citizens abroad and their subsequent forcible transfer home by Uruguayan state agents) argued for the extra-territorial application of the Covenant despite the requirement of "territory." In its decision the Committee effectively rejected a literal interpretation of this provision and found that ICCPR, Article 2(1):

> does not imply that the State . . . cannot be held accountable for violations of rights under the Covenant which its agents commit upon the territory of another State, whether with acquiescence of the Government of that State or in opposition to it.[14]

Moreover, and with reference to ICCPR, Article 5(1),[15] the Committee found that:

> it would be unconscionable to so interpret the responsibility under Article 2 of the Covenant as to permit a state party to perpetrate violations of the Covenant on the territory of another State, which violations it could not perpetrate on its own territory.[16]

[11] Ibid. p. 10, with reference to the drafting of the Vienna Convention on the Law of Treaties and ICJ jurisprudence.

[12] On the extra-territorial application of the ICCPR in general see Dominic McGoldrick, "Extraterritorial Application of the International Covenant on Civil and Political Rights" in Fons Coomans and Menno T. Kamminga (eds.), *Extraterritorial Application of Human Rights Treaties* (Antwerp: Intersentia, 2004), pp. 41–72; and Martin Scheinin, "Extraterritorial Effect of the International Covenant on Civil and Political Rights" in Fons Coomans and Menno T. Kamminga (eds.), *Extraterritorial Application of Human Rights Treaties* (Antwerp: Intersentia, 2004), pp. 73–81.

[13] See McGoldrick, "The Extraterritorial Application of the International Covenant" (n. 12) p. 48.

[14] *Sergio Ruben Lopez Burgos* v. *Uruguay*, Human Rights Committee, Communication No. 52/1979, UN Doc. A/36/40 (29 July 1981), para. 12(3).

[15] ICCPR, Art. 5(1): "Nothing in the present Covenant may be interpreted as implying for any State, group or person any right to engage in any activity or perform any act aimed at the destruction of any of the rights and freedoms recognized herein or at their limitation to a greater extent than is provided for in the present Covenant."

[16] *Sergio Ruben Lopez Burgos* v. *Uruguay* (n. 14) para. 12(3).

This has remained a central argument in favour of the extra-territorial application of human rights law beyond the ICCPR: that a double standard must be avoided, under which states can do abroad what they are prohibited from doing at home.[17] It does not, however, clarify the conditions and consequences of such extra-territorial application. The Committee has repeated this position on various occasions, particularly with regard to situations of occupation[18] and peace-keeping.[19] It has also picked up on it in its General Comment No. 31, where it found that:

> the enjoyment of Covenant rights is not limited to citizens of States Parties but must also be available to all individuals . . . who may find themselves in the territory or subject to the jurisdiction of the State Party. This principle also applies to those within the power or effective control of the forces of a State Party acting outside its territory, regardless of the circumstances in which such power or effective control was obtained, such as forces constituting a national contingent of a State Party assigned to an international peace-keeping or peace-enforcement operation.[20]

The Committee continued by clarifying the interplay of human rights and humanitarian law in situations where the former applies extra-territorially and said that:

> the Covenant applies also in situations of armed conflict to which the rules of international humanitarian law are applicable. While, in respect to certain Covenant rights, more specific rules of international humanitarian law may be specially relevant for the purposes of the interpretation of Covenant rights, both spheres of law are complementary, not mutually exclusive.[21]

State practice with regard to the extra-territorial application of the ICCPR is inconsistent. The Netherlands, for example, responded to the ICCPR (when confronted with allegations that its peace-keeping forces had failed to secure the safe haven of Srebrenica in Bosnia-Herzegovina and thus allowed Serb forces to execute thousands of Bosnians) that "the citizens of Srebrenica, vis-à-vis the Netherlands, do not come within the scope" of ICCPR, Article 2(1).[22] Belgium argued similarly.[23] Australia approached the question in a more nuanced way when it said that:

[17] See Ralphe Wilde, "Legal 'Black Hole'? Extraterritorial State Action and International Treaty Law on Civil and Political Rights" (2005) 26 *Michigan Journal of International Law* 791.

[18] See Human Rights Committee, *Concluding Observations on Cyprus*, UN Doc. CCPR/C/79/Add.39 (21 September 1994), para. 3; and Human Rights Committee, *Concluding Observations on Israel*, UN Doc. CCPR/C/79/Add.93 (18 August 1998), para. 10.

[19] See Human Rights Committee, *Concluding Observations on Belgium*, UN Doc. CCPR/CO/81/BEL (12 August 2004), para. 6; and Human Rights Committee, *Concluding Observations on Netherlands*, CCPR/CO/72/NET (27 August 2001) para. 8.

[20] Human Rights Committee, *General Comment No. 31 on the Nature of the General Legal Obligation Imposed on States Parties to the Covenant*, UN Doc. CCPR/C/21/Rev.1/Add.13 (26 May 2004), para. 10. The ICJ confirmed the Committee's views, see *Legal Consequences of the Construction of a Wall in the Occupied Palestinian Territory*, International Court of Justice, Advisory Opinion of 9 July 2004 [2004] ICJ Reports, paras. 108–11 ("*Wall* case").

[21] Human Rights Committee, *General Comment No. 31* (n. 20), para. 11.

[22] Human Rights Committee, *Concluding Observations on the Netherlands*, UN Doc. CCPR/CO/72/NET/Add.1 (29 April 2003), para. 19.

[23] See the concern expressed by the Human Rights Committee, *Concluding Observations on Belgium*, UN Doc. CCPR/CO/81/BEL (12 August 2004), para. 6.

> [t]he only circumstances in which Australia would be in a position to afford all the rights and freedoms under the Covenant extraterritorially would be where it was exercising all of the powers normally exercised by a sovereign State, such as having the power to prescribe and enforce laws, as a consequence of an occupation, a consensual deployment, or a United Nations mandated mission. In no other circumstances could it be said that Australia was in a position to give effect to *all* of the rights in the Covenant.[24]

The strictest view is held by the United States, which has repeatedly made clear that it does not consider the ICCPR applicable extra-territorially in any circumstances.[25] In its view, arguments for the extra-territorial application of the Covenant are not supported by the text, objectives and drafting history of the Covenant; ignore the primacy of humanitarian law; lead to legal and operational confusion; and increase the gap between legal theory (which supports the extra-territorial application of human rights law in armed conflicts) and state practice (which points towards the contrary).[26] With regard to the Covenant's application in armed conflicts, the US Department of Defence stated in 2003 that it "does not apply outside the United States or its special maritime and territorial jurisdiction, and ... does not apply to operations of the military during an international armed conflict."[27] Before UN human rights treaty bodies the United States argued as follows:

> The United States recalls its longstanding position ... that the obligations assumed by the United States under the Covenant apply only within the territory of the United States. In that regard, the United States respectfully submits that this Committee request for information is outside the purview of the Committee. The United States also notes the legal status and treatment of [persons detained in Guantanamo Bay, Iraq and other places of detention outside the United States] is governed by the law of war.[28]

[24] Australia, *Replies to the List of Issues to be Taken Up in connection with the Consideration of the Fifth Periodic Report of the Government of Australia*, UN Doc. CCPR/C/AUS/Q/5/Add.1 (5 February 2009), para. 18 (emphasis in the original).

[25] See Bernhard Schäfer, *Zum Verhältnis Menschenrechte und humanitäres Völkerrecht. Zugleich ein Beitrag zur extraterritorialen Geltung von Menschenrechtsverträgen* (Potsdam: Universitätsverlag Potsdam, 2006), p. 24.

[26] See Michael J. Dennis, "Application of Human Rights Treaties Extraterritorially in Times of Armed Conflict and Military Occupation" (2005) 99(1) *American Journal of International Law* 141.

[27] United States Defence Department, *Working Group Report on Detainee Interrogations in the Global War on Terrorism: Assessment of Legal Historical, Policy, and Operational Considerations* (6 March 2003), p. 6, available at www.antiwar.com/news/?articleid=2776. The US Army, however, seems to take no official position on this question, see Gary D. Solis, *The Law of Armed Conflict* (Cambridge: Cambridge University Press, 2010), p. 25.

[28] Human Rights Committee, *Third Periodic Report - United States*, UN Doc. CCPR/C/USA/3 (26 November 2005), para. 130. See also Annex I to the document. See also an earlier exchange of views on this matter in Human Rights Committee, *Summary Record of the 1405th Meeting: United States of America*, UN Doc. CCPR/C/SR.1405 (24 April 1995), para. 20: "Mr. Klein had asked whether the United States took the view that the Covenant did not apply to government actions outside the United States. The Covenant was not regarded as having extraterritorial application. In general, where the scope of application of a treaty was not specified, it was presumed to apply only within a party's territory. Article 2 of the Covenant expressly stated that each State party undertook to respect and ensure the rights recognized 'to all individuals within its territory and subject to its jurisdiction.' That dual requirement restricted the scope of the Covenant to persons under United States jurisdiction and within United States territory. During the negotiating history, the words 'within its territory' had been debated and were added by vote, with the clear understanding that such wording would limit the obligations to within a Party's territory."

The main arguments of the United States were developed in the context of the detention facilities operated by the United States abroad in Guantánamo Bay, Cuba and in Iraq and in Afghanistan in the "War on Terror."[29] In response to allegations of human rights violations in Guantánamo Bay the United States confirmed their view that the ICCPR is inapplicable extra-territorially.[30] The same argument could not be made by the United States with regard to the Convention Against Torture (CAT), which applies to *any* territory under the jurisdiction of a state party, so that the United States resorted to the *lex specialis* argument instead, and found the application of human rights law was precluded by humanitarian law, while for all other treaties one would need to identify those rights which could potentially be applied extra-territorially.[31] Israel similarly argues that the ICCPR and the International Covenant on Economic, Social and Cultural Rights (ICESCR), particularly, are not applicable in the West Bank and the Gaza Strip, as these territories are not subject to its sovereign territory and jurisdiction, and as a reflection of the well-established distinction between human rights and humanitarian law.[32]

[29] See, e.g., Opening Remarks by John Bellinger III, Legal Adviser, US Department of State, US Meeting with UN Committee Against Torture (5 May 2006), available at www.state.gov/j/drl/rls/68557.htm (last accessed 15 April 2014).

[30] See Letter dated 31 January 2006 addressed to the Office of the High Commissioner for Human Rights, by the Permanent Representative of the United States of America to the United Nations and other International Organizations in Geneva, Commission on Human Rights, Report of the Chairperson of the Working Group on Arbitrary Detention, Leila Zerrougui; the Special Rapporteur on the independence of judges and lawyers, Leandro Despouy; the Special Rapporteur on torture and other cruel, inhuman or degrading treatment of punishment, Manfred Nowak; the Special Rapporteur on freedom of religion or belief, Asma Jahangi; and the Special Rapporteur on the right of everyone to the enjoyment of the highest attainable standard of physical and mental health, Paul Hunt, UN Doc. E/CN.4/2006/120 (27 February 2006), Annex II; and Reply of the Government of the United States of America to the Report of the Five UN Special Rapporteurs on Detainees in Guantanamo Bay, Cuba (10 March 2006). See also Opening Statement to the Human Rights Committee by Matthew Waxman, Head of US Delegation, on the Report Concerning the International Covenant on Civil and Political Rights (17 July 2006), available at http://2001-2009.state.gov/g/drl/rls/70392.htm (last accessed 15 April 2014); Human Rights Committee, *Concluding Observations on United States of America*, UN Doc. CCPR/C/USA/CO/3 (15 September 2006), para. 3.

[31] See Opening Remarks by John R. Bellinger III, Legal Adviser, US Department of State, before the UN Committee Against Torture (5 May 2006), available at www.state.gov/g/drl/rls/68557.htm. In response, the Committee Against Torture urged the United States to "recognize and ensure that the Convention applies at all times, whether in peace, war or armed conflict, in any territory under its jurisdiction," see Committee Against Torture and Other Cruel, Inhuman or Degrading Treatment of Punishment, *Concluding Observations: United States of America*, UN Doc. CAT/C/USA/CO/2 (25 July 2006), para. 14. See also Conor McCarthy, "Legal Conclusion or Interpretative Process? *Lex Specialis* and the Application of International Human Rights Standards" in Roberta Arnold and Noelle Quénivet (eds.), *International Humanitarian Law and Human Rights Law: Towards a Merger in International Law* (Leiden: Nijhoff, 2008), p. 107; and Dirk Lorenz, *Der territoriale Anwendungsbereich der Grund- und Menschenrechte. Zugleich ein Beitrag zum Individualschutz in bewaffneten Konflikten* (Vienna: Neuer Wissenschaftlicher Verlag, 2005), p. 212.

[32] See Human Rights Committee, *Second Periodic Report of Israel*, UN Doc. CCPR/C/ISR/2001/2 (4 December 2001), para. 8; and Committee on Economic, Social and Cultural Rights, *Second Periodic Report of Israel*, UN Doc. E/1990/6/Add.32 (16 October 2001), para. 5. In its Concluding Observations on Israel's report under the ICCPR, the Human Rights Committee reiterated its contrary opinion that the Covenant does apply, see Human Rights Committee, *Concluding Observations on Israel*, UN Doc. CCPR/CO/78/ISR (5 August 2003), para. 11.

In the view of the United States, the plain reading of the ICCPR supports its position,[33] and the drafting history of the ICCPR also shows beyond doubt that the Covenant was, and is, meant to be understood literally ("in the territory") and was never meant to apply extra-territorially, in contrast to the views held by the Human Rights Committee.[34] Moreover, the United States suggests that the extra-territorial application of international humanitarian law is merely an invention of legal theory and finds no support in state practice.[35] Where the ICCPR was applied extra-territorially, the United States argues, it was only in exceptional circumstances and outside situations of armed conflict or occupations.[36] The United States also points out that, in its view, the derogation clause in the ICCPR reflects the intention not to allow extra-territorial application of its provisions,[37] and that the International Court of Justice (ICJ) has not openly supported the ideas contained in General Comment No. 31 of the Human Rights Committee when it gave the Advisory Opinion in the *Wall* case and in its judgment in *Democratic Republic of Congo* v. *Uganda*.[38] And finally, whatever state practice and *opinio juris* may, or may not, exist on this question, the United States claims that its objection is a persistent one and cannot be overruled or changed: whatever other states may do, no extra-territorial obligations under the ICCPR can arise for the United States.[39]

Fervently as the United States argues its case, it rests on fragile grounds. The literal reading of the ICCPR does indeed speak for the US position, and the approach of the Human Rights Committee effectively to turn "territory *and* jurisdiction" in the text of the ICCPR to "territory *or* jurisdiction" in its General Comment No. 31 by suggesting that the text speaks of disjunctive conjunction, seems indeed unpersuasive.[40] But given that the ICCPR differs in its terminology from all other treaties, the decision on whether or not it applies extra-territorially should not primarily rest on a literal reading of the text, but on a consideration of the object and purpose of international human rights treaties as a whole. In light of the jurisprudence and (inconsistent) state practice, such a literal reading is at least questionable. The way in which the United States understands the Covenant's *travaux préparatoires* also differs considerably from that of other states and commentators (and the Human Rights Committee). It has been pointed out that reference to "jurisdiction" was inserted in the text on the insistence of the United States and against the wishes of many delegations, so as to exclude a duty to legislate in occupied territories such as Germany, Austria and Japan, as well as territories leased by the United States (including Guantánamo), and not as an objection against extra-territorial obligations as a matter of principle.[41] The ICJ confirmed the views of the Human Rights Committee in this respect when it argued that "in adopting the wording chosen, the drafters of the Covenant did not

[33] Michael J. Dennis and Andre M. Surena, "Application of the International Covenant on Civil and Political Rights in Times of Armed Conflict and Military Occupation: The Gap between Legal Theory and State Practice" (2008) 6 *European Human Rights Law Review* 719.

[34] See Dennis and Surena, "Application of the International Covenant" (n. 33) 726–27; and Dennis, "Application of Human Rights Treaties Extraterritorially" (n. 26) 123–24 and 127.

[35] Dennis and Surena, "Application of the International Covenant" (n. 33) 715–17 and 731.

[36] Ibid. 720. [37] Ibid. 727–31. [38] Ibid. 721–22.

[39] See Michael J. Dennis, "Application of Civil and Political Rights Treaties Extraterritorially during Times of Armed Conflict" (2007) 40(2) *Israel Law Review* 501–2.

[40] See Dennis and Surena, "Application of the International Covenant" (n. 33) 720, with reference to the respective authors. See also Manfred Nowak, *UN Covenant on Civil and Political Rights: CCPR Commentary* (2nd edn., Kehl: Engel, 2005), pp. 43–44.

[41] See Milanovic, *Extraterritorial Application of Human Rights Treaties* (n. 1) p. 224.

intend to allow States to escape from their obligations when they exercise jurisdiction outside their national territory."[42] It also seems that the United States has never made a specific reservation on this question.

The reasons for the strong opposition of the United States and some other states to the extra-territorial application of the ICCPR mirror those put forward in defence of the exclusive nature of humanitarian law as *lex specialis* discussed above. An added concern seems to be that the extra-territorial application of human rights treaties will increase the accountability for the consequences of military actions; will negatively affect the right to self-defence; and will discourage states from participating in peace operations:

> military action by any of the 162 states parties anywhere in the world, including actions taken in exercise of the inherent right of self-defence recognised in Article 51 of the United Nations Charter, in the context of UN enforcement actions or other forms of peacekeeping would bring all those affected by such operations (including enemy combatants) within the scope of the protections provided by the Covenant ... It would also appear to include liability for any lack of vigilance by the state in preventing violations of human rights and international humanitarian law by other actors present in areas under military occupation, including rebel groups acting on their own account. The resulting monetary exposure would risk undermining significantly the states' participation in such missions.[43]

Such fears are even greater in situations of occupation, where the Occupying Power might have to guarantee the full range of ICCPR rights. This, it is argued, would be contradictory to the non-transformative nature of occupation law as prescribed by international humanitarian law and in disregard of the effective level of control the Occupying Power has.[44]

In contrast, states such as France, Sweden, Switzerland and member states of the Arab League have explicitly argued in favour of the extra-territorial application of the ICCPR (and the ICESCR and Convention on the Rights of the Child (CRC)) in their submission in the *Wall* case to the ICJ.[45] Poland and Italy have also accepted the applicability of the ICCPR for their troops abroad.[46] Germany, somewhat more cautiously, has stated that it guarantees the ICCPR rights in such situations without explicitly accepting the extra-territorial reach of the Covenant:

> Pursuant to Article 2, paragraph 1, Germany ensures the rights recognized in the Covenant to all individuals within its territory and subject to its jurisdiction. Wherever its police or armed forces are deployed abroad, in particular when participating in peace missions, Germany ensures to all persons that they will be granted the rights recognized in the Covenant, insofar as they are subject to its jurisdiction. Germany's

42 ICJ, *Wall* case (n. 20) para. 109, see also Milanovic, *Extraterritorial Application of Human Rights Treaties* (n. 1) p. 226.

43 Dennis and Surena, "Application of the International Covenant" (n. 33) 724–25.

44 Ibid. 725.

45 For details see Schäfer, *Zum Verhältnis Menschenrechte und humanitäres Völkerrecht* (n. 25) 24.

46 Human Rights Committee, *Concluding Observations on Poland*, UN Doc. CCPR/CO/82/POL (2 December 2004), para. 3: "The Committee welcomes the commitment of the State party to respect the rights recognized in the Covenant for all individuals subject to its jurisdiction in situations where its troops operate abroad, particularly in the context of peacekeeping and peace-restoration missions." Human Rights Committee, *Concluding Observations on Italy*, UN Doc. CCPR/C/ITA/CO/5 (24 April 2006), para. 3: "The Committee welcomes the State party's position that the guarantees of the Covenant apply to the acts of Italian troops or police officers who are stationed abroad, whether in a context of peace or armed conflict."

> international duties and obligations, in particular those assumed in fulfilment of obligations stemming from the Charter of the United Nations, remain unaffected. The training it gives its security forces for international missions includes tailor-made instruction in the provisions of the Covenant.[47]

(b) Jurisdiction in human rights treaties

The approach of other UN human rights treaties to jurisdiction clauses is incoherent.[48] In marked difference, both Optional Protocols to the ICCPR contain jurisdiction clauses without any reference to territory.[49] The Convention on the Protection of the Rights of All Migrant Workers (CMW) replaces the word "and" used in the ICCPR by "or," so as to read "within their territory or subject to their jurisdiction,"[50] thus rejecting the cumulative demand of territory and jurisdiction in the ICCPR. CAT links territory and jurisdiction in yet another way by adding the word "any," so that each state party is to take effective legislative, administrative, judicial or other measures to prevent acts of torture in any territory under its jurisdiction.[51] In the drafting of CAT, the United States had pointed out that in their view the Convention was not meant to apply to armed conflicts or supersede international humanitarian law, and had found the support of Switzerland, Norway and Israel.[52] The text also refers to jurisdiction in more specific provisions.[53] The Optional Protocol to the CAT on a system of regular visits uses jurisdiction in yet another sense, replaces reference to territory by the word "places," and also adds the notion of "control" to jurisdiction:

> Each State Party shall allow visits, in accordance with the present Protocol, by the mechanisms referred to in articles 2 and 3 to any place under its jurisdiction and control where persons are or may be deprived of their liberty.[54]

[47] Human Rights Committee, *Comments by the Government of Germany to the Concluding Observations on of the Human Rights Committee*, UN Doc. CCPR/CO/80/DEU/Add.1 (11 April 2005). See also Schäfer, *Zum Verhältnis Menschenrechte und humanitäres Völkerrecht* (n. 25) p. 24.

[48] See Milanovic, *Extraterritorial Application of Human Rights Treaties* (n. 1) p. 12.

[49] Second Optional Protocol to the ICCPR, Art. 1 on the abolition of the death penalty ("1. No one within the jurisdiction of a State Party to the present Protocol shall be executed. 2. Each State Party shall take all necessary measures to abolish the death penalty within its jurisdiction"); and Optional Protocol to CRC, Art. 1 on a communications procedure ("A State Party to the Covenant that becomes a Party to the present Protocol recognizes the competence of the Committee to receive and consider communications from individuals subject to its jurisdiction who claim to be victims of a violation by that State Party of any of the rights set forth in the Covenant.").

[50] CMW, Art. 7: "States Parties undertake, in accordance with the international instruments concerning human rights, to respect and to ensure to all migrant workers and members of their families within their territory or subject to their jurisdiction the rights provided for in the present Convention without distinction of any kind such as to sex, race, colour, language, religion or conviction, political or other opinion, national, ethnic or social origin, nationality, age, economic position, property, marital status, birth or other status."

[51] CAT, Art. 2(1).

[52] See Dennis, "Application of Civil and Political Rights Treaties Extraterritorially" (n. 39) 483, with reference to Committee on Human Rights, *Report of the Working Group on a Draft Convention Against Torture*, UN Doc. ECN.4/1984/72 (9 March 1984), para. 5.

[53] CAT, Art. 6 on the intention to exercise jurisdiction over persons accused of having committed torture; Arts. 7 and 8 on extradition; Art. 11 on review of interrogation rules, methods and practices; Art. 12 on investigation; Art. 13 on remedies; and Art. 16 on cruel, inhuman or degrading treatment

[54] CAT, Art 4(1).

The CRC refers to jurisdiction without mentioning territory at all.[55] Its Optional Protocol on the involvement of children in armed conflict contains a general jurisdiction clause,[56] while the Optional Protocol on the sale of children, child prostitution and child pornography does not.[57] In its General Comment on Article 38, the Committee on the Rights of the Child has made clear that this provision, as well as the Optional Protocol on children in armed conflict, "entail extraterritorial effects."[58] Again the United States took a different position and argued that CRC, Article 2 can only be read in conjunction with Article 38, so that no provision of the Covenant other than Article 38 applies extra-territorially.[59]

The Convention for the Protection of All Persons from Enforced Disappearance (CED) speaks of "the territory under the jurisdiction of a State party,"[60] and the Convention on the Elimination of All Forms of Racial Discrimination (CERD) refers to jurisdiction only with regard to racial segregation and apartheid[61] and the right to effective remedies.[62] No other provision of CERD is limited by a jurisdiction clause, nor is there a general jurisdiction clause covering the whole text. The ICESCR, the Convention on the Elimination of All Forms of Discrimination Against Women (CEDAW) and the Convention on the Rights of Persons with Disabilities (CRPD) contain no general jurisdiction clause.[63] The extra-

[55] CRC, Art. 2(1): "States Parties shall respect and ensure the rights set forth in the present Convention to each child within their jurisdiction without discrimination of any kind, irrespective of the child's or his or her parent's or legal guardian's race, colour, sex, language, religion, political or other opinion, national, ethnic or social origin, property, disability, birth or other status."

[56] Optional Protocol to the CRC, Art. 6(1) on involvement of children in armed conflict: "Each State Party shall take all necessary legal, administrative and other measures to ensure the effective implementation and enforcement of the provisions of the present Protocol within its jurisdiction" and Art. 6(3): "States Parties shall take all feasible measures to ensure that persons within their jurisdiction recruited or used in hostilities contrary to the present Protocol are demobilized or otherwise released from service. States Parties shall, when necessary, accord to such persons all appropriate assistance for their physical and psychological recovery and their social reintegration."

[57] Although it refers to jurisdiction with regard to extradition of offenders, see Optional Protocol CRC, Art. 5 on the sale of children, child prostitution and child pornography.

[58] CRC, *General Comment No. 6 on the Treatment of Unaccompanied and Separated Children Outside Their Country of Origin*, UN Doc. CRC/GC/2005/6 (1 September 2005), para. 28.

[59] See Dennis, "Application of Human Rights Treaties Extraterritorially" (n. 26) 129.

[60] CED, Art. 34: "If the Committee receives information which appears to it to contain well-founded indications that enforced disappearance is being practised on a widespread or systematic basis in the territory under the jurisdiction of a State Party, it may, after seeking from the State Party concerned all relevant information on the situation, urgently bring the matter to the attention of the General Assembly of the United Nations, through the Secretary-General of the United Nations."

[61] CERD, Art. 3: "States Parties particularly condemn racial segregation and apartheid and undertake to prevent, prohibit and eradicate all practices of this nature in territories under their jurisdiction."

[62] CERD, Art. 6: "States Parties shall assure to everyone within their jurisdiction effective protection and remedies, through the competent national tribunals and other State institutions, against any acts of racial discrimination which violate his human rights and fundamental freedoms contrary to this Convention, as well as the right to seek from such tribunals just and adequate reparation or satisfaction for any damage suffered as a result of such discrimination."

[63] ICESCR has a jurisdiction clause with respect to one of its provisions, namely, on primary education, in ICESCR, Art. 14: "Each State Party to the present Covenant which, at the time of becoming a Party, has not been able to secure in its metropolitan territory or other territories under its jurisdiction compulsory primary education, free of charge, undertakes, within two years, to work out and adopt a detailed plan of action for the progressive implementation, within a reasonable number of years, to be fixed in the plan, of the principle of compulsory education free of charge for all." The Optional Protocol to ICESCR on individual complaints also mentions jurisdiction in Art. 13: "A State Party shall take all appropriate

territorial reach of the ICESCR remains disputed, and a systemic and widely accepted theory of its respective obligations has yet to be formulated.[64] The Committee on Economic, Social and Cultural Rights understands the treaty as broadly applicable with regard to a state's obligations to respect, protect and fulfil its obligations, while others take a more nuanced approach.[65] The United States argues that no extra-territorial application can be read into the treaty and that, in addition, the absence of a derogation provision in the ICESCR means that (in light of Vienna Convention on the Law of Treaties (VCLT), Article 62, which applies unless a different intention can be discerned in the treaty or is otherwise established), the ICESCR is binding only in respect of a state party's territory.[66]

In the view of the United States, the drafting history of the ICESCR also indicates that an initial proposal for a jurisdiction clause was deleted on request of several states; that the treaty mentions territorial jurisdiction otherwise only with regard to territories over which states parties exercised unquestioned sovereignty; and that any pronouncements by the Committee on Economic, Social and Cultural Rights in support of an extra-territorial application of the treaty have no validity, as the Committee (unlike other human rights treaty bodies) is not mandated to decide authoritatively on individual cases and was not set up as a monitoring body, but as an auxiliary body for the UN Economic and Social Council (ECOSOC), which was the original monitoring body of the Covenant.[67]

Unlike the ICCPR, the ECHR does not mention territory. It obliges states parties to "secure to everyone within their jurisdiction"[68] the rights and freedoms of the Convention. The drafting history of the Convention shows that the inclusion of the word "jurisdiction" in the ECHR was obviously not driven by concern for the principle of jurisdiction as understood in general public international law. The term simply replaced the original suggestion to refer to "all persons residing within the territory" of a state party, which was seen as too restrictive (as the concept of residence might have been interpreted in a narrow legal sense under domestic law), so that "within their jurisdiction" was chosen as a compromise formula.[69] Otherwise, the Convention's *travaux préparatoires* are not conclusive as to the exact meaning of jurisdiction in the ECHR.[70]

Today, jurisdiction under the Convention is understood as covering also extra-territorial activities on the territory of other states, but the European Court of Human Rights has produced ambiguous jurisprudence on the contours of the extra-territorial reach of the

measures to ensure that individuals under its jurisdiction are not subjected to any form of ill-treatment or intimidation as a consequence of communicating with the Committee pursuant to the present Protocol."

64 See Fons Coomans, "Some Remarks on the Extraterritorial Application of the International Covenant on Economic, Social and Cultural Rights" in Fons Coomans and Menno T. Kamminga (eds.), *Extraterritorial Application of Human Rights Treaties* (Antwerp: Intersentia, 2004), p. 185; and Rolf Künnemann, "Extraterritorial Application of the International Covenant on Economic, Social and Cultural Rights" in Fons Coomans and Menno T. Kamminga (eds.), *Extraterritorial Application of Human Rights Treaties* (Antwerp: Intersentia, 2004), pp. 212–31.

65 See Joseph, "Scope of Obligations" (n. 4) pp. 165–67, with reference to the Committee's jurisprudence.

66 See Dennis, "Application of Human Rights Treaties Extraterritorially" (n. 26) 127.

67 Ibid. 127–28. With the entry into force of the individual complaints Protocol to the ICESCR, the argument on the limited mandate of the Committee has lost its validity.

68 ECHR, Art. 1.

69 See Milanovic, *Extraterritorial Application of Human Rights Treaties* (n. 1) p. 38, with reference to the *travaux préparatoires* of the ECHR.

70 See Marten Peschardt Pedersen, "Territorial Jurisdiction in Article 1 of the European Convention on Human Rights" (2004) 73(3) *Nordic Journal of International Law* 283.

Convention.[71] Calls for the extra-territorial application of the Convention include statements by the Parliamentary Assembly of the Council of Europe, which has urged all states to accept the applicability of the ECHR for European troops in Iraq.[72] The UK *Manual of the Law of Armed Conflict* also considers the ECHR applicable in the occupied territory, depending on the circumstances.[73]

The European Social Charter[74] does not contain a jurisdiction clause, while the European Convention for the Prevention of Torture and Inhuman or Degrading Treatment or Punishment uses language similar to, but slightly different from, CAT with regard to visits of the European Committee for the Prevention of Torture and Inhuman or Degrading Treatment or Punishment: "Each Party shall permit visits, in accordance with this Convention, to any place within its jurisdiction where persons are deprived of their liberty by a public authority."[75]

The Inter-American Convention on Human Rights uses language similar to the ECHR in establishing jurisdiction without reference to territory,[76] as does the Inter-American Convention to Prevent and Punish Torture.[77] The Protocol of San Salvador to the American Convention on Human Rights refers to jurisdiction only with respect to the right of health.[78] The Inter-American Convention on Forced Disappearance of Persons refers to jurisdiction in various different contexts such as criminal prosecution of persons in a state party's jurisdiction,[79] with regard to extradition[80] and the delineation of criminal and military jurisdiction.[81] The Inter-American Convention on the Prevention, Punishment and Eradication of Violence Against Women contains no jurisdiction clause, and the

[71] See Sarah Miller, "Revisiting Extraterritorial Jurisdiction: A Territorial Justification for Extraterritorial Jurisdiction under the European Convention" (2009) 20(4) *European Journal of International Law* 1224.

[72] Parliamentary Assembly of the Council of Europe, Resolution 1386 (24 June 2004), para. 18. See also Schäfer, *Zum Verhältnis Menschenrechte und humanitäres Völkerrecht* (n. 25) 25.

[73] See UK Ministry of Defence, *The Manual of the Law of Armed Conflict* (Oxford: Oxford University Press, 2004), p. 282.

[74] European Social Charter, 18 October 1961, ETS No. 35, 529 UNTS 89.

[75] European Convention Against Torture, 26 November 1987, ETS No. 126, 1561 UNTS 363, Art. 1.

[76] ACHR, Art. 1: "The States Parties to this Convention undertake to respect the rights and freedoms recognized herein and to ensure to all persons subject to their jurisdiction the free and full exercise of those rights and freedoms, without any discrimination for reasons of race, color, sex, language, religion, political or other opinion, national or social origin, economic status, birth, or any other social condition."

[77] Inter-American Convention on Torture, Art. 6: "In accordance with the terms of Article 1, the States Parties shall take effective measures to prevent and punish torture within their jurisdiction . . . The States Parties likewise shall take effective measures to prevent and punish other cruel, inhuman, or degrading treatment or punishment within their jurisdiction."

[78] Additional Protocol to the American Convention on Human Rights in the area of Economic, Social and Cultural Rights (Protocol of San Salvador), 17 November 1988, OAS Treaty Series No. 69 (1988), Art. 10(2): "In order to ensure the exercise of the right to health, the States Parties agree to recognize health as a public good and, particularly, to adopt the following measures to ensure that right: . . . (b) Extension of the benefits of health services to all individuals subject to the State's jurisdiction."

[79] Inter-American Convention on Forced Disappearance of Persons, Art. I: "The States Parties to this Convention undertake: . . . (b) To punish within their jurisdictions, those persons who commit or attempt to commit the crime of forced disappearance of persons and their accomplices and accessories" and Art. IV: "The acts constituting the forced disappearance of persons shall be considered offenses in every State Party. Consequently, each State Party shall take measures to establish its jurisdiction over such cases in the following instances: (a) When the forced disappearance of persons or any act constituting such offense was committed within its jurisdiction."

[80] Ibid. Art. VI. [81] Ibid. Arts. IX and X.

African Charter on Human and Peoples' Rights and its Protocol on the Rights of Women, as well as the African Charter on the Rights and Welfare of the Child, also do not refer to jurisdiction.

With the exception of the ICCPR no treaty thus ties jurisdiction clearly to territory. Understanding the jurisdiction of the ICCPR as limited within the territory of states parties is consequently inconsistent, at least where the same obligations are contained in other treaties which contain no such limits. Given that all of these treaties (with the exception of CERD) were adopted after the ICCPR, the principle of *lex posterior* could also be used to support the idea that a literal reading of the ICCPR is out of tune with current human rights law-making which is characterized by an obvious move away from invoking territory as a limiting factor for human rights obligations.

As for treaties without jurisdiction clauses, it would seem implausible to understand their absence so as to strictly limit these treaties to the territory of the states parties, given that such provisions have been inserted in other treaties. It seems thus appropriate to argue that all human rights treaties allow for the extra-territorial application of their obligations, including in situations of armed conflict.[82] This view is also shared by the ICRC even though it cautions that the precise extent of the extra-territorial application of international human rights has yet to be fully discerned.[83]

(c) *Case law: territorial and personal jurisdiction*

The jurisprudence of human rights bodies and courts is only partly helpful in delineating the contours of the extra-territorial application of human rights treaty law. It supports, as a matter of principle, the idea that such extra-territorial application of human rights in situations of armed conflict is possible, but the human rights bodies differ in the way they understand jurisdiction as control over territory and/or persons. The ICJ, for its part, has found in *DRC* v. *Uganda* that "international human rights instruments are applicable 'in respect of acts done by a state in the exercise of its jurisdiction outside its own territory,' particularly in occupied territories."[84] In its decision, the Court combined human rights and humanitarian law obligations when it said that:

> the Republic of Uganda, by the conduct of its armed forces, which committed acts of killing, torture and other forms of inhumane treatment of the Congolese civilian population, destroyed villages and civilian buildings, failed to distinguish between civilian and military targets and to protect the civilian population in fighting with other combatants, trained child soldiers, incited ethnic conflict and failed to take measures to put an end to such conflict; as well as by its failure, as an Occupying Power, to take measures to respect and ensure respect for human rights and

[82] Andreas Zimmermann, "Extraterritorial Application of Human Rights Treaties: The Case of Israel and the Palestinian Territories Revisited" in Isabelle Buffard, James Crawford, Alain Pellet and Stefan Wittich (eds.), *International Law between Universalism and Fragmentation, Essays in Honour of Gerhard Hafner* (Leiden: Nijhoff, 2008), p. 764.

[83] See International Committee of the Red Cross, *International Humanitarian Law and the Challenges of Contemporary Armed Conflicts, Report to the 31st International Conference of the Red Cross and Red Crescent* (2011), p. 15.

[84] See *Armed Activities on the Territory of the Congo (Democratic Republic of the Congo* v. *Uganda)*, International Court of Justice, Judgment of 19 December 2005 [2006] ICJ Reports, para. 216.

> international humanitarian law in Ituri district, violated its obligations under international human rights law and international humanitarian law.[85]

Earlier, the Inter-American Commission on Human Rights had considered the Inter-American human rights instruments as extra-territorially applicable, and has done so ever since.[86] When dealing with petitions filed after the United States' invasion of Panama in 1989 and confronted with the US objections to its competence in this matter, it merely glossed over the question by arguing that:

> [i]n the context of the present case, the guarantees set forth in the American Declaration are implicated. This case set forth allegations cognizable within the framework of the Declaration. Thus the Commission is authorized to consider the subject matter of the case.[87]

But a decade later, in the *Coard* case (on the detention and ill-treatment of applicants from Grenada by US authorities following the overthrow of the government of Grenada by US armed forces), the Commission turned to the question of the extra-territorial application of the American Declaration on its own and found that:

> under certain circumstances, the exercise of [the Commission's] jurisdiction over acts with an extraterritorial locus will not only be consistent with but required by the norms which pertain. The fundamental rights of the individual are proclaimed in the Americas on the basis of the principles of equality and non-discrimination – "without distinction as to race, nationality, creed or sex." Given that individual rights inhere simply by virtue of a person's humanity, each American State is obliged to uphold the protected rights of any person subject to its jurisdiction. While this most commonly refers to persons within a state's territory, it may, under given circumstances, refer to conduct with an extra-territorial locus where the person concerned is present in the territory of one state, but subject to the control of another state – usually through the acts of the latter's agents abroad. In principle, the inquiry turns not on the presumed victim's nationality or presence within a particular geographic area, but on whether, under the specific circumstances, the State observed the rights of a person subject to its authority and control.[88]

The Commission repeated this understanding of jurisdiction as an expression of a state's authority and control over a person rather than a territorial matter in *Armando Alejandra, Jr. and others* v. *Cuba*. Alejandra and three other members of an activist organization opposed to the Cuban government were shot down by a Cuban fighter jet when travelling in their light airplane in international airspace, following repeated violations of Cuban airspace as a protest against the Cuban government. The Commission considered the

[85] Ibid. para. 345. Some commentators conclude from this passage, however, that the Court sees international humanitarian law and international humanitarian law applying "differently," Yoram Dinstein, *The International Law of Belligerent Occupation* (Cambridge: Cambridge University Press, 2009), p. 88.

[86] See Christina Cerna, "Extraterritorial Application of the Human Rights Instruments of the Inter-American System" in Fons Coomans and Menno T. Kamminga (eds.), *Extraterritorial Application of Human Rights Treaties* (Antwerp: Intersentia, 2004), pp. 141–74.

[87] *Salas and others* v. *United States*, Inter-American Commission on Human Rights, Report. No. 31/93, Case No. 10573, Decision on Admissibility of 14 October 1993, para. 6.

[88] *Bernard Coard and others* v. *United States*, Inter-American Commission on Human Rights, Report No. 109/99, Case No. 10.951, OAS Doc. OEA/Ser.L/V/II.106 Doc. 3 rev., Decision of 29 September 1999, para. 37.

application admissible, as it saw the individuals under the authority and control of Cuba regardless of where the act took place, whether in the territory of a state party, in the territory of another state party or in international airspace.[89] More recently, the Commission justified its decision on the request for precautionary measures in the Guantánamo case with reference to the "authority and control" argument it had used earlier.[90] It has thus consistently viewed jurisdiction as personal and not territorial in nature.[91] At the same time, it needs to be mentioned that it had never decided on a situation outside the Inter-American human rights system.[92]

The European Court of Human Rights, too, understood jurisdiction primarily as tied to control exercised by the state in its early case law, first and foremost in *Louizidou* v. *Turkey* in 1995 on the obligations of Turkey in occupied Northern Cyprus. In this case it recalled that jurisdiction is not restricted to the territory of a state. The Court argued that:

> the responsibility of a Contracting Party may also arise when as a consequence of military action – whether lawful or unlawful – it exercises effective control of an area outside its national territory. The obligation to secure, in such an area, the rights and freedoms set out in the Convention derives from the fact of such control whether it be exercised directly, through its armed forces, or through a subordinate local administration.[93]

In *Cyprus* v. *Turkey* in 2001, the European Court clarified its position:

> Having effective overall control over northern Cyprus, [Turkey's] responsibility cannot be confined to the acts of its own soldiers or officials in northern Cyprus but must also be engaged by virtue of the acts of the local administration which survives by virtue of Turkish military and other support. It follows that, in terms of Article 1 of the Convention, Turkey's "jurisdiction" must be considered to extend to securing the entire range of substantive rights set out in the Convention and those additional Protocols which she has ratified, and that violations of those rights are imputable to Turkey.[94]

The European Court changed its tune in the much criticized decision in *Banković and others* v. *Belgium and 16 Other Contracting States* of 2001, where it had to decide on the

[89] *Armando Alejandra, Jr. and others* v. *Cuba*, Inter-American Commission on Human Rights, Report No. 86/99, Case No. 11.589, Decision of 29 September 1999, para. 23. See for more cases Cerna, "Extraterritorial Application" (n. 86) pp. 143–52.

[90] "OAS member states have charged the Commission with supervising member states' observance of human rights in the Hemisphere. These rights include those prescribed under the American Declaration of the Rights and Duties of Man, which constitutes a source of legal obligation for all OAS member states in respect of persons subject to their authority and control," *Detainees at Guantanamo Bay, Cuba*, Inter-American Commission on Human Rights, Request for Precautionary Measures of 12 March 2002.

[91] See Douglas Cassel, "Extraterritorial Application of Inter-American Convention Human Rights Instruments" in Fons Coomans and Menno T. Kamminga (eds.), *Extraterritorial Application of Human Rights Treaties* (Antwerp: Intersentia, 2004), p. 177.

[92] Cerna, "Extraterritorial Application" (n. 86) pp. 170–73.

[93] *Loizidou* v. *Turkey*, European Court of Human Rights, Appl. No. 40/1993(435/514), Preliminary Objection of 23 February 1995, para. 62. On extra-territorial application in the jurisprudence of the European Court of Human Rights, see also Rick Lawson, "Life After Banković: On the Extraterritorial Application of the European Convention on Human Rights" in Fons Coomans and Menno T. Kamminga (eds.), *Extraterritorial Application of Human Rights Treaties* (Antwerp: Intersentia, 2004), pp. 90–103.

[94] *Cyprus* v. *Turkey*, European Court of Human Rights, Appl. No. 25781/94, Judgment of 10 May 2001, para. 77.

applicability of the Convention to the victims of the NATO bombs which had hit the radio and television station RTS in Belgrade in 1999.[95] The applicants considered the dead and injured to have been under the respondent states' jurisdiction with regard to the high-altitude bomb attack. In light of the facts – the projection of armed force over a great distance, the absence of any NATO troops on the ground, and the attribution of the operation to NATO which as an international organization was not a state party to the ECHR – the Court declared the application inadmissible on the grounds that even though NATO member states were states parties to the Convention, the victims had not been under their jurisdiction within the meaning of ECHR, Article 1.[96] By way of justification, the Court stated that the territory in question was not covered by the Convention, which is generally not designed "to be applied throughout the world."[97] The Court said that:

> [h]ad the drafters of the Convention wished to ensure jurisdiction as extensive as that advocated by the applicants, they could have adopted a text the same as or similar to the contemporaneous Articles 1 of the four Geneva Conventions of 1949.[98]

In the European Court's view, effective control meant exercising "some of the public powers normally to be exercised"[99] by the local government. The way in which the Court seemingly considered jurisdiction, different from earlier cases, as a primarily territorial concept, and constructed its extra-territorial exercise as merely exceptional, has led to critique. It was widely thought that the Court confused normative jurisdiction, as understood in general public international law, with the factual exercise of control as required under human rights law.[100] The Court was accused of relying, in an unduly restrictive manner, on an historic-subjective interpretation of Article 1 without acknowledging the provision's object and purpose.[101]

Others supported the European Court's view that no jurisdictional link in the form of any prolonged structured relationship and authority or control over the targeted persons in the RTS building had been established. In their opinion, human rights law was inapplicable, more so as international humanitarian law could have been invoked, albeit not before the European Court of Human Rights.[102] The decision was also defended as reflecting state practice and scholarly writings. The main argument here was that any other interpretation

[95] *Banković and others* v. *Belgium and 16 Other Contracting States*, European Court of Human Rights, Appl. No. 52207/99, Decision on Admissibility of 12 December 2001.

[96] Gondek, "Extraterritorial Application" (n. 1) 353.

[97] *Banković and others* v. *Belgium and others* (n. 95) para. 80. [98] Ibid. para. 75. [99] Ibid. para. 71.

[100] Gondek, "Extraterritorial Application" (n. 1) 353.

[101] For this critique see Kerem Altiparmak, "Banković: An Obstacle to the Application of the European Convention on Human Rights in Iraq?" (2004) 9(2) *Journal of Conflict and Security Law* 223; Ralphe Wilde, "Triggering State Obligations Extraterritorially: The Spatial Test in Certain Human Rights Treaties" (2007) 40(2) *Israel Law Review* 503; and Marko Milanovic, "From Compromise to Principle: Clarifying the Concept of State Jurisdiction in Human Rights Treaties" (2008) 8 *Human Rights Law Review* 411.

[102] See *Banković and others* v. *Belgium and others* (n. 95) para. 75; and Matthew Happold, "Banković v. Belgium and the Territorial Scope of the European Convention on Human Rights" (2003) 3(1) *Human Rights Law Review* 90. Whether or not humanitarian law would have played a role in the case remains a speculation.

of the Convention would have meant to wrongly equate the question of jurisdiction with analyzing the cause and effect of the action taken.[103]

The Court also found that the Convention rights in situations such as these could not be "divided and tailored."[104] The applicants had claimed that the respondent states were bound to secure the provisions of the Convention proportionate to the degree of control they exercised of the airspace. The Court was not willing to follow this argument on the grounds that each state party is bound to secure the entire range of Convention rights and not parts of it.

What is certainly obvious is that, seen in larger political context, the European Court of Human Rights was afraid of opening the floodgates for complaints of victims of all sorts of military operations, being drawn into questions of international humanitarian law, and eventually finding itself unable to cope with such complaints.[105] Although the judgment created considerable confusion, it seems at least that *Banković* can be read as a confirmation that even though extra-territorial jurisdiction of international human rights law cannot be rejected as a matter of principle, it has limits in situations where combat activities in international armed conflicts are at stake. For the European Court, the jurisdiction clause of the ECHR seems to cover only situations where control over territory or persons within military operations is established, which is not the case in combat operations in international armed conflicts.[106]

Between the lines, the Court also seems to have considered humanitarian law as *lex specialis* which renders the Convention inapplicable.[107] The Court's arguments were compounded by its reference to the concept of a European *espace juridique* which allows the Convention to be applied only "in an essentially regional context and notably in the legal space (*espace juridique*) of the Contracting States."[108] In the absence of clarity on what this concept means, its use has rightly been criticized as an unacceptably Eurocentric view unsupported by legal doctrine.[109]

Subsequent cases qualified this strict approach to jurisdiction taken in *Banković* somewhat, even though they were not decided with regard to international armed conflicts.[110] In

[103] *Banković and others* v. *Belgium and others* (n. 95) para. 75. See also Heike Krieger, "Die Verantwortlichkeit Deutschlands nach der EMRK für seine Streitkräfte im Auslandseinsatz" (2002) 62 *Zeitschrift für ausländisches öffentliches Recht und Völkerrecht* 672.

[104] *Banković and others* v. *Belgium and others* (n. 95) para. 71.

[105] See Michael O'Boyle, "The European Convention on Human Rights and Extraterritorial Jurisdiction: A Comment on 'Life After Banković'" in Fons Coomans and Menno T. Kamminga (eds.), *Extraterritorial Application of Human Rights Treaties* (Antwerp: Intersentia, 2004), pp. 125 and 135.

[106] See Krieger, "Die Verantwortlichkeit Deutschlands" (n. 103) 697. [107] Ibid. 698.

[108] *Banković and others* v. *Belgium and others* (n. 95) para. 80.

[109] See, e.g., Luigi Condorelli, "La protection des droits de l'homme lors d'actions militaires menées à l'étranger" in College d'Europe (ed.), *The Need for Justice and Requirements for Peace and Security, Proceedings of the Bruges Colloquium, 9–10 September 2004* (Bruges: College d'Europe, 2005), pp. 99–101; John Cerone, "Human Rights on the Battlefield" in Stéphanie Lagoutte, Hans-Otto Sano and Peter Scharff Smit (eds.), *Human Rights in Turmoil: Facing Threats, Consolidating Achievements* (Leiden: Nijhoff, 2007), p. 121; and Cordula Droege, "The Interplay between International Humanitarian Law and International Human Rights Law in Situations of Armed Conflict" (2007) 40(2) *Israel Law Review* 315, 328–29. For similar problems with regard to the inter-American human rights system see Cerna, "Extraterritorial Application" (n. 86) p. 170.

[110] See in greater detail Tarik Abdel-Monem, "How Far Do the Lawless Areas of Europe Extend? Extraterritorial Application of the European Convention on Human Rights" (2005) 14(2) *Journal of Transnational Law and Policy* 179.

Ilaşcu and others v. *Moldova and Russia* in 2004, the European Court saw the effective control which the Russian Federation exercised over Transnistria (the region in Moldova where the human rights violations were alleged) as entailing jurisdiction under ECHR, Article 1 (with residual responsibilities left to the state which had partly lost control over its territory).[111] The *Öcalan* case contradicted (and, for some commentators even reversed) *Banković*. When the Court found Turkey responsible for detaining the leader of the Kurdistan Workers' Party (PKK), Abdullah Öcalan, in Kenya, it considered such extra-territorial actions of state agents as within the jurisdiction of Turkey.[112]

In *Issa* v. *Turkey*, the European Court refused to apply the Convention on the grounds that the Turkish military had not established a presence within northern Iraq that would amount to the threshold of overall control over a certain territory and thus jurisdiction within the meaning of the ECHR.[113] In *Pad and others* v. *Turkey*, Iranian nationals living close to the Turkish border were killed when a Turkish army helicopter opened fire. It was disputed on which side of the border the killing took place but the Court opted for a personal model of jurisdiction in disregard of any question of territory, seemingly in contrast to *Banković*.[114] And in *Isaak and others* v. *Turkey*, the Court accepted the application of the ECHR for incidents in a UN controlled buffer zone in northern Cyprus over which the Turkish police (which had beaten the victims to death) could not have been said to have effective overall control.[115]

In the *Behrami* and *Saramati* cases the European Court, in a rightly much criticized move, declared the application inadmissible on the grounds that the acts could not be attributed to anyone. Unexploded cluster bombs (relics of 1999 NATO airstrikes in the territory of the former Yugoslavia) were found by children, resulting in the death of a boy, while another was badly injured. The Court concluded that even though the actions of peace-keeping forces in Kosovo were led by NATO, such acts were neither attributable to NATO nor to its member states, but only to the UN (as it had authorized the presence of peace-keepers), but given that the UN was not a state party to the ECHR no jurisdictional link could be established.[116]

111 *Ilaşcu and others* v. *Moldova and Russia*, European Court of Human Rights, Appl. No. 48787/99, Judgment of 8 July 2004, para 313. The Court did not, however, rely on international humanitarian law on the respective duties of the Occupying Power nor did it resort to Geneva Conventions, Common Art. 1 which requires that states respect and ensure respect of international humanitarian law which would have supported the argument that both the Russian Federation and Moldova have responsibilities in Transnistria.

112 *Öcalan* v. *Turkey*, European Court of Human Rights, Appl. No. 46221/99, Judgment of 12 May 2005, para. 71; see Wilde, "Legal 'Black Hole'?" (n. 17) 795.

113 *Issa and others* v. *Turkey*, European Court of Human Rights, Appl. No. 31821/96, Judgment of 11 November 2004, para. 61.

114 *Pad and others* v. *Turkey*, European Court of Human Rights, Appl. No. 60167/00, Judgment of 28 June 2007.

115 *Isaak and others* v. *Turkey*, European Court of Human Rights, Appl. No. 44587/98, Judgment of 28 September 2006.

116 *Behrami* v. *France* and *Saramati* v. *France, Germany and Norway*, European Court of Human Rights, Appl. Nos. 71412/01 and 78166/01, Decision on Admissibility of 2 May 2007, para. 152; for a critique see Marko Milanovic and Tatjana Papić, "As Bad as it Gets: The European Court of Human Rights' Behrami and Saramati Decision and General International Law" (2008) 58(2) *International and Comparative Law Quarterly* 267.

With its decision in *Al-Skeini* v. *United Kingdom*, mentioned earlier, the European Court positioned itself anew on the extra-territorial application of the ECHR, at least as far as situations of occupations are concerned. The judgment seemed to overturn *Banković*, at least in some aspects.[117] The case involved the death of Iraqi citizens in British-occupied Basra in Iraq. Three of the applicants were killed by the UK armed forces in the streets of Basra, one when British forces exchanged fire with unknown persons, one drowned after being beaten by UK soldiers, and one died in custody on a UK military base after having been tortured.[118] The applicants claimed a violation of ECHR, Article 2 (right to life) for the lack of effective investigations into the events. The United Kingdom rejected the application of the ECHR to the situation in line with the Court's reasoning in *Banković* and argued that, with the exception of the person killed in British custody, there was no jurisdiction under ECHR, Article 1. Such jurisdiction, it was said, must be understood as essentially territorial and as within the *espace juridique* of the Convention; alternatively, there was no effective control by the United Kingdom over the territory anyway due to the unstable security situation at the time.[119] The government also argued that such a jurisdictional link also could not be established by invoking the United Kingdom's obligations under international humanitarian law (i.e., to ensure public order and safety as demanded by Hague Regulations, Article 43), as the Convention was autonomous and distinct from international humanitarian law and that only the latter would regulate the acts of the United Kingdom.[120]

The UK courts largely followed the government's arguments and accepted that the state had not had the necessary forces to deal adequately with the insurgency and thus exercised no effective (spatial) control, so that it could guarantee the rights enshrined in the ECHR. Furthermore, with the exception of individuals in UK custody, there was no (personal) control over the persons shot at long distance in the streets of Basra.[121] The European Court of Human Rights, however, found a violation of the procedural element of Article 2 with regard to five of the six applicants.[122] It rejected the government's views and held that:

> [i]t can be seen, therefore, that following the removal from power of the Ba'ath regime and until the accession of the Interim Government, the United Kingdom (together with the United States) assumed in Iraq the exercise of some of the public powers normally to be exercised by a sovereign government. In particular, the United Kingdom assumed authority and responsibility for the maintenance of security in South East Iraq. In these exceptional circumstances, the Court considers that the United Kingdom, through its soldiers engaged in security operations in Basrah during the period in question, exercised authority and control over individuals killed in the course of such security operations, so as to establish a jurisdictional link between the deceased and the United Kingdom for the purposes of Article 1 of the Convention[123] . . . It follows that in all these cases there was a

[117] See Anna Cowan, "A New Watershed: Re-evaluating *Banković* in Light of Al-Skeini" (2012) 1(1) *Cambridge Journal of International and Comparative Law* 214; and Christine Chinkin, "International Humanitarian Law, Human Rights and the UK Courts" in Laurence Boisson de Chazournes and Marcelo G. Kohen, *International Law and the Quest for its Implementation* (Leiden: Nijhoff, 2010), pp. 252–64.

[118] *Al-Skeini* v. *United Kingdom* (n. 6) paras. 33–71. [119] Ibid. paras. 109–19.

[120] Ibid. paras. 117 and 119.

[121] See in greater detail Cowan, "A New Watershed" (n. 117) 217–19, and for a critical view Marko Milanovic, "Al-Skeini and Al-Jedda in Strasbourg" (2012) 23 *European Journal of International Law* 126.

[122] *Al-Skeini* v. *United Kingdom* (n. 6) para. 177. See in greater detail Abdel-Monem, "How Far Do the Lawless Areas of Europe Extend?" (n. 110) 200–2.

[123] *Al-Skeini* v. *United Kingdom* (n. 6) para. 149.

> jurisdictional link for the purposes of Article 1 of the Convention between the United Kingdom and the deceased ... since the death occurred in the course of a United Kingdom security operation, when British soldiers carried out a patrol in the vicinity of the applicant's home and joined in the fatal exchange of fire, there was a jurisdictional link between the United Kingdom and this deceased also.[124]

The Court thus emphasized the exercise of physical power and control over the persons in question as the trigger for jurisdiction[125] and concluded that "whenever the State through its agents exercises control and authority over an individual, and thus jurisdiction, the State is under an obligation under Article 1."[126] Indeed, in his dissenting opinion in the decision of the UK House of Lords, Lord Justice Sedley had already argued that even though the United Kingdom had no control over executive, legislative or judicial matters it still had full control over the killing of the civilians:

> it sits ill in the mouth of a state which has helped to displace and dismantle by force another nation's civil authority to plead that, as an occupying power, it has so little control that it cannot be responsible for securing the population's basic rights. On the other hand, it cannot: the invasion brought in its wake a vacuum of civil authority which British forces were and still are unable to fill.[127]

But while the European Court's decision seems to move away from the reasoning in *Banković* and connect with the Court's earlier case law, it leaves the core arguments of *Banković* intact: where there is no public power but merely the projection of force (as was the case in *Banković*) there is no jurisdiction.[128] The killing of the applicants is within the jurisdiction of the United Kingdom because the United Kingdom exceptionally exercised public power with regard to them. This "state agent authority exception to territorial jurisdiction"[129] allows jurisdiction to be exercised where physical control or power over a person can be observed in specific cases. At the same time the Court relied on the fact that the United Kingdom exercised "public powers," which is a "nebulous"[130] concept. It seems to mix a personal and spatial model of jurisdiction: jurisdiction exists where control over a person is exercised within the public powers over a territory. How exactly this relates to its earlier case law is unclear.

Even so (and although the case is only about the procedural duties to investigate cases of torture and killings), the potential implications are far-reaching, and it has rightly been said that the decision should be read carefully by legal advisors and decision-makers in Europe.[131] The case is also important for two other aspects: first, the European Court departed from its earlier view that the Convention rights cannot be divided and tailored.[132] In essence this seems to allow for a flexible interpretation of the Convention in light of circumstances and capacities so as not to impose an undue standard.[133] The Court said that:

> [i]t is clear that, whenever the State through its agents exercises control and authority over an individual, and thus jurisdiction, the State is under an obligation under Article 1 to

[124] Ibid. para. 150. [125] Ibid. para. 136. [126] Ibid. para. 137.
[127] Ibid. para 194. See also paras. 195–97.
[128] See also Milanovic, "Al-Skeini and Al-Jedda in Strasbourg" (n. 121) 130.
[129] Cowan, "A New Watershed" (n. 117) 220.
[130] Milanovic, "Al-Skeini and Al-Jedda in Strasbourg" (n. 121) 139. [131] Ibid. 131.
[132] See Cowan, "A New Watershed" (n. 117) 219.
[133] See *Al-Skeini* v. *United Kingdom* (n. 6) paras. 168–77.

> secure to that individual the rights and freedoms under Section 1 of the Convention that are relevant to the situation of that individual. In this sense, therefore, the Convention rights can be "divided and tailored" (compare *Banković*, cited above, § 75).[134]

And secondly, the Court also effectively debunked the idea of *espace juridique* when it found that:

> where the territory of one Convention State is occupied by the armed forces of another, the occupying State should in principle be held accountable under the Convention for breaches of human rights within the occupied territory, because to hold otherwise would be to deprive the population of that territory of the rights and freedoms hitherto enjoyed and would result in a "vacuum" of protection within the "Convention legal space" (see *Loizidou* (merits), cited above, § 78; *Banković*, cited above, § 80). However, the importance of establishing the occupying State's jurisdiction in such cases does not imply, *a contrario*, that jurisdiction under Article 1 of the Convention can never exist outside the territory covered by the Council of Europe Member States.[135]

Al-Skeini is thus, by all means, a significant departure from *Banković*.[136] But it does not convincingly clarify the extra-territorial application of the Convention in situations of armed conflict.[137] The concurring opinion of Judge Bonello is instructive in this regard. Bonello, who chastised the European Court harshly for its inconsistent approach to jurisdiction, argued that the majority view constituted merely a pretext to change the benchmarks of jurisdiction from case to case, depending on the desired outcome, leading to ever more complex and incoherent theories of jurisdiction.[138] Indeed, the way in which the Court relied on a personal model of jurisdiction up to *Banković* and switched back to it afterwards, depending on whether the results of the respective model led to acceptable results or not, does not demonstrate theoretical consistency.[139] In Judge Bonnello's view, a functional approach to jurisdiction would avoid this:

> In my view, the one honest test, in all circumstances (including extra-territoriality), is the following: did it depend on the agents of the State whether the alleged violation would be committed or would not be committed? Was it within the power of the State to punish the perpetrators and to compensate the victims? If the answer is yes, self-evidently the facts fall squarely within the jurisdiction of the State. All the rest seems to me clumsy, self-serving alibi hunting, unworthy of any State that has grandiosely undertaken to secure the "universal" observance of human rights whenever and wherever it is within its power to secure them, and, may I add, of courts whose only *raison d'etre* should be to ensure that those obligations are not avoided or evaded.[140]

He also reduced the "public power" construct to an interpretation of control compatible with obligations under humanitarian law when he argued that:

[134] Ibid. para. 137. Note that there is not much to "compare" with *Banković* given that the Court had said the exact opposite in the paragraph it quotes.

[135] Ibid. para. 142, see also Cowan, "A New Watershed" (n. 117) 219.

[136] Even though the Court pretended that its earlier jurisprudence is entirely compatible despite it being contradictory, as Judge Bonello remarked in his dissenting opinion in the case, see *Al-Skeini* v. *United Kingdom* (n. 6) Concurring Opinion of Judge Bonello, paras. 4–8.

[137] See Cowan, "A New Watershed" (n. 117) 225–26.

[138] *Al-Skeini* v. *United Kingdom* (n. 6) Concurring Opinion of Judge Bonello, paras. 4–7.

[139] Milanovic, *Extraterritorial Application of Human Rights Treaties* (n. 1) pp. 186–87.

[140] *Al-Skeini* v. *United Kingdom* (n. 6) Concurring Opinion of Judge Bonnello, para. 16.

> [o]nce a State is acknowledged by international law to be "an occupying power," a rebuttable presumption ought to arise that the occupying power has "authority and control" over the occupied territory, over what goes on there and over those who happen to be in it – with all the consequences that flow from a legal presumption. It will then be incumbent on the occupying power to prove that such was the state of anarchy and impotence prevailing, that it suffered a deficit of effective authority and control. It will no longer be for the victim of wartime atrocities to prove that the occupying power actually exercised authority and control. It will be for the occupying power to rebut it.[141]

9.3 A capability approach: towards functional universality

Notwithstanding these different approaches to control over person and territory, there is obviously a "progressive unhinging of international human rights obligations from territoriality, which has removed one of the main obstacles to the application of human rights law to international armed conflicts."[142] It seems widely accepted that international human rights law applies without territorial restrictions when a state exercises effective and factual control over territory or persons.[143] But the different approaches to qualifying such control or power need to be reconciled.[144] It makes a difference if control is understood as factual presence and the capability and potential to exercise some form of (physical) power, or as exercising authority and (public) power which presupposes or creates a special, prolonged relationship or legal bond which cannot be found in single acts but needs a certain continuity characterized by a certain degree of organization.[145]

Both the spatial and personal models of jurisdiction are problematic in this regard. The difficulty with the spatial model is, put simply, size. If control is exercised over space (i.e., territory) it seems to cover substantial and clearly defined areas such as "the nation state" but there is no reason to limit the size of the area in ever-diminishing cycles, from geographic regions and areas (such as occupied territories) down to villages, military camps and prison cells. The attempts by the United States to argue, for example, that persons held in secret detention facilities outside the United States are not under the jurisdiction of the United States (and thus not covered by CAT, Article 16)[146] as they were held in "places" rather than "territories" (although the "places", i.e., buildings used by the CIA, were themselves located in such "territories," namely, in European countries) "brings the spatial conception of state

[141] Ibid. para. 24.

[142] Guglielmo Verdirame, "Human Rights in Wartime: A Framework for Analysis" (2008) 6 *European Human Rights Law Review* 703.

[143] See Lorenz, *Der territoriale Anwendungsbereich der Grund- und Menschenrechte* (n. 31) p. 199; Milanovic, *Extraterritorial Application of Human Rights Treaties* (n. 1) 58–61; and Michael Bothe, "Humanitäres Völkerrecht und Schutz der Menschenrechte: Auf der Suche nach Synergien und Schutzlücken" in Pierre-Marie Dupuy, Bardo Fassbender, Malcolm N. Shaw and Karl-Peter Sommermann (eds.), *Common Values in International Law, Essays in Honour of Christian Tomuschat* (Kehl: Engel, 2006), p. 73 (who seems to restrict jurisdiction to territory).

[144] See Wilde, "Legal 'Black Hole'?" (n. 17) 804.

[145] See Krieger, "Die Verantwortlichkeit Deutschlands" (n. 103) 671.

[146] CAT, Art. 16 obliges states to prevent cruel, inhuman or degrading treatment "in any territory under its jurisdiction."

jurisdiction to a breaking point."[147] There is nothing that puts an end to the ever-shrinking space over which jurisdiction can extend.[148]

Personal jurisdiction avoids such problems and is thus the favoured model to describe jurisdiction under human rights law.[149] It corresponds better with the universality of human rights and avoids double standards, as obligations cannot be evaded simply on the grounds of the location where a human rights violation happens, even though the state may have full control. But just as the spatial model cannot be prevented from shrinking to infinity, the personal model cannot be prevented from expanding. The idea that physical control is necessary to exercise jurisdiction means that certain situations can easily be captured, first and foremost situations of detention and acts committed when physical force is applied. For the European Court in *Al-Skeini*, this meant that torture and death in a military detention facility was unquestionably covered by the ECHR. But it also meant that when an individual was shot at close range by a military patrol in the street, such control was exercised. On the other hand, those killed by high-altitude bombing in Belgrade were not, hence the *Banković* case was declared inadmissible.

Somewhere in between must seemingly be the threshold of exercising jurisdiction. For the European Court of Human Rights, the answer seems to lie in the context: situations of security operations in situations of occupation with their mixed model of spatial and personal control (if this is what the Court meant by "public power") differ from international armed conflicts.[150] But it seems that this contextual argument does not solve the question of control convincingly.[151] At the same time, a purely personal model of control will eventually collapse because it must not and cannot be arbitrarily limited.[152]

It has thus been suggested to apply another model across the spatial and territorial jurisdiction and distinguish between positive and negative obligations. Based on the consideration that state agents can always refrain from certain acts (and thus respect human rights obligations) they do not always have the capabilities to secure or ensure these obligations and protect against violations by third parties. As a consequence, only the former type of obligations can meaningfully be placed on a state acting extra-territorially. It is meant to reconcile universality and effectiveness in the extra-territorial application of

[147] Milanovic, *Extraterritorial Application of Human Rights Treaties* (n. 1) p. 130, with reference to the Memorandum for John A. Rizo re Application of United States Obligations under Article 16 of the Convention Against Torture to Certain Techniques that May be Used in the Interrogation of High Value al Qaeda Detainees (30 May 2005), available at www.fas.org/irp/agency/doj/olc/article16.pdf (last accessed 15 April 2014).

[148] See Milanovic, *Extraterritorial Application of Human Rights Treaties* (n. 1) p. 134.

[149] See, e.g., Wilde, "Triggering State Obligations Extraterritorially" (n. 101) 524; Lawson, "Life After Banković" (n. 93) p. 83; and Joseph, "Scope of Obligations" (n. 4) p. 167. For a contrasting view see Miller, "Revisiting Extraterritorial Jurisdiction" (n. 71) 1236–46, who argues that every case of extra-territorial application of international human rights law necessitates some significant connection between the territory of the state party and that of the state where the extra-territorial act takes place, and supports – with a view towards the ECHR's specific regional reach – the revival of the territorial model.

[150] See Cowan, "A New Watershed" (n. 117) 224.

[151] Françoise Hampson, "The Relationship between International Humanitarian Law and Human Rights Law from the Perspective of a Human Rights Treaty Body" (2008) 90(871) *International Review of the Red Cross* 570.

[152] See Milanovic, *Extraterritorial Application of Human Rights Treaties* (n. 1) pp. 207–8.

human rights.[153] While it remains to be tested whether a strict dichotomy of positive and negative obligations is adequate to capture the indivisibility of human rights or may unduly exclude human rights in certain situations, the idea to use the functionality test suggested by Judge Bonnello in a way that limits the obligations of states acting extra-territorially by the degree to which a state can reasonably be said to exercise control seems the most appropriate way forward.[154]

Such a "capability approach" needs to reconcile the demand of the universal reach of human rights to avoid double standards (i.e., accepting a higher standard at home while arguing for a lower standard, or no obligation at all, abroad) and the indivisibility of human rights (i.e., accepting positive as well as negative obligations) with the capacity of a state to adhere to such obligations in the variegated contexts of armed conflict and occupation in a complementary fashion with international humanitarian law and in an operationally feasible manner. The scope of international human rights law obligations then depends on a state's capacity to guarantee international human rights law: "[t]o say that states must respect human rights in times of war is thus believed to entail the proposition that they can do so."[155] This reflects a core idea of international humanitarian law, as already expressed in the drafting of the Additional Protocols of 1977, that no one is compelled to do the impossible.[156] It also seeks to avoid what was feared by the European Court of Human Rights in *Banković*, namely, that:

> the applicants' submission is tantamount to arguing that anyone adversely affected by an act imputable to a Contracting State, wherever in the world that act may have been committed or its consequences felt, is thereby brought within the jurisdiction of the State for the purpose of Article 1 of the Convention.[157]

At present, the inchoate jurisprudence of human rights bodies seems to help little in identifying the contours of such a capability approach. A few benchmarks may be discerned, however. The overall objective must be to avoid double standards with regard to human rights obligations. Extra-territorial jurisdiction thus exists wherever situations obviously lead to or are manifestly created to avoid obligations under human rights treaties which would undoubtedly arise for acts within a state's territory. It has rightly been argued that there must not be legal black hole: human rights obligations can neither be evaded because acts are carried out outside the territory of a state party to a human rights treaty nor because the rhetoric of war is invoked in the anticipation that this renders international human rights law inapplicable.[158]

In light of state practice and case law it seems that at present the extra-territorial application of human rights in armed conflicts are accepted where "public powers" are exercised in situations of occupation in a combination of territorial and personal control. Whether this is always the case in situations of occupation is not yet finally settled, even though there is a strong presumption for it: every occupation can be said to result in the

[153] Ibid. pp. 209–22. [154] See, e.g., Cerone, "Human Rights on the Battlefield" (n. 109) pp. 130–31.

[155] Verdirame, "Human Rights in Wartime" (n. 142) 692.

[156] As maintained by the Official Records of the 1974–1977 Diplomatic Conference, see Sandesh Sivakumaran, "Re-envisaging the International Law of Armed Conflict" (2001) 22(1) *European Journal of International Law* 258.

[157] *Banković and others* v. *Belgium and others* (n. 95) para. 75.

[158] See Wilde, "Legal 'Black Hole'?" (n. 17) 805.

exercise of jurisdiction,[159] and when the occupant is so weak as not to sustain the occupation (and thus jurisdiction), it is no longer an occupation.[160] "Effective control" (under international humanitarian law) and "authority" (under international human rights law) are thus seen as synonymous and allow for the application of human rights law in situations of occupation.[161] Problems remain with regard to the residual authority and capacity of the local government.[162] Where states (through international organizations) administer territory other than their own, such as in Kosovo, the question of jurisdiction is furthermore compounded by the unclear sharing of responsibilities between states and international organizations, as demonstrated by the much criticized decision of the European Court of Human Rights in the *Behrami* and *Saramati* cases mentioned earlier.

Effective control is also exercised where physical control over a person is obvious, such as in detention and similar situations, and where analogies to these situations can be found.[163] To avoid that personal control is understood to be limitless, criteria may need to be introduced. They may, or may not, mirror the difference between positive and negative obligations but certainly need to exclude indirect effects which cannot be attributed to a state. The first of such criteria have been suggested: a degree of flexibility must ensure that obligations are not considered unrealistic and impractical while such flexibility must at the same time not render obligations meaningless as to their impact; and the obligations must be sufficiently clear and predictable for states to be able to comply with them.[164]

The core problem is to adjust human rights obligations in such a way that they are not "watered down"[165] to an unacceptable extent. And they need to be read as complementary to obligations arising under humanitarian law. A graduated approach has been suggested under which more effective control would also lead to the application of more international human rights and less control would call for more international humanitarian law.[166] In light of cases such as *Al-Skeini*, effective control would be exercised beyond doubt in military camps and detention facilities, whereas less or no effective control could exist in military operations in the field. But the dichotomy "inside/outside detention facilities" is hardly convincing, just as the idea of measuring the "distance to the battlefield" has been rejected earlier as equally unhelpful. The UN expert consultation on human rights in armed conflict consequently concluded that such a "battlefield" test raises complex legal questions.[167]

[159] See Milanovic, *Extraterritorial Application of Human Rights Treaties* (n. 1) p. 147.

[160] Dinstein, *The International Law of Belligerent Occupation* (n. 85) pp. 42–45.

[161] Hampson, "The Relationship between International Humanitarian Law and Human Rights Law" (n. 151) 567.

[162] See Milanovic, *Extraterritorial Application of Human Rights Treaties* (n. 1) pp. 147–51.

[163] See Schäfer, *Zum Verhältnis Menschenrechte und humanitäres Völkerrecht* (n. 25) 34. It seems that substantive and procedural rights are equally covered.

[164] Milanovic, Extraterritorial Application of Human Rights Treaties (n. 1) pp. 106–17. [165] Ibid. 114.

[166] Advocated also in UN OHCHR, *International Legal Protection of Human Rights in Armed Conflict* (2011), p. 63, with reference to Office of the United Nations High Commissioner for Human Rights, *Report on the Outcome of the Expert Consultation on the Issue of Protecting the Human Rights of Civilians in Armed Conflict*, UN Doc. A/HRC/11/31 (4 June 2009), para. 14.

[167] Ibid. para. 14.

10

War as emergency: derogation

10.1 The idea and law of derogation

Under international human rights law, derogation allows certain human rights to be temporarily suspended in light of national emergency situations which may include armed conflicts. Such derogation provisions can be found in the International Covenant on Civil and Political Rights (ICCPR),[1] the European Convention on Human Rights (ECHR)[2] and the American Convention on Human Rights (ACHR).[3] They seem to reflect the idea of a defence of necessity in international law and transpose it into human rights law.[4] They are escape clauses which allow states, in an allegedly "realistic" perspective, to suspend human rights so as not to be unduly restricted in defending their very existence. Their message is that, when things really go wrong, there is still a way out, as states are not bound to adhere to human rights obligations if this means committing "state suicide."

What seems to reflect common sense is, however, difficult to capture as a legal phenomenon. Derogation clauses, as well as the whole idea of derogation remain opaque in international legal and international relations scholarship.[5] They function in a complex matrix of concerns to guarantee human rights as inherent entitlements and protect citizens and domestic institutions effectively in situations of violence, while at the same

[1] ICCPR, Art. 4(1): "In time of public emergency which threatens the life of the nation and the existence of which is officially proclaimed, the States Parties to the present Covenant may take measures derogating from their obligations under the present Covenant to the extent strictly required by the exigencies of the situation, provided that such measures are not inconsistent with their other obligations under international law and do not involve discrimination solely on the ground of race, colour, sex, language, religion or social origin."

[2] ECHR, Art. 15(1): "In time of war or other public emergency threatening the life of the nation any High Contracting Party may take measures derogating from its obligations under this Convention to the extent strictly required by the exigencies of the situation, provided that such measures are not inconsistent with its other obligations under international law."

[3] ACHR, Art. 27(1): "In time of war, public danger, or other emergency that threatens the independence or security of a State Party, it may take measures derogating from its obligations under the present Convention to the extent and for the period of time strictly required by the exigencies of the situation, provided that such measures are not inconsistent with its other obligations under international law and do not involve discrimination on the ground of race, color, sex, language, religion, or social origin."

[4] See Frédéric Mégret, "Nature of Obligations" in Daniel Moeckli, Sangeeta Shah and Sandesh Sivakumaran (eds.), *International Human Rights Law* (Oxford: Oxford University Press, 2010), p. 143.

[5] See Emilie M. Hafner-Burton, Laurence R. Helfer and Christopher J. Fariss, "Emergency and Escape: Explaining Derogations from Human Rights Treaties" (2011) 65 *International Organization* 674.

time securing the stability and existence of the state and its institutions. Infringements of certain rights, particularly civil liberties as understood in domestic legal systems, were seen as acceptable under strict limits so as to ensure the overall functioning and survival of state and society. "Fundamental" liberties, such as the prohibition of torture and the right to life, were deemed as sacrosanct while other, seemingly less important, rights could be derogated.[6] Derogation remains a paradox for the way it allows the suspension of rights precisely in times when they are most needed. The way in which states deal with the human rights obligations in situations of crisis can be seen as the acid test for their commitment, given that it is precisely in such situations where human rights protection against abusive and overreacting security forces in defence of a state apparatus under threat becomes important.[7]

The idea of derogation becomes more perplexing when seen in the context of armed conflict. The fact that (certain) human rights can be derogated on the grounds of an armed conflict presuppose two considerations: first, war needs to be seen as an emergency which threatens the nation state, and secondly, it echoes the idea that there is a law of peace which can (partly) be suspended as the laws of war kick in. This seems connected to the exclusivist understanding of *lex specialis* and seems to suggest that (some) human rights have no place on the battlefield.

But, somewhat paradoxically, the very fact that some human rights (under some human rights treaties) can be derogated in times of armed conflict serves to confirm the view that, logically, the other human rights continue to apply in armed conflict, contrary to any separatist theory: "the inclusion of derogation provisions in human rights instruments actually serves to underline that human rights continue to apply in times of armed conflict."[8] Indeed, the International Court of Justice (ICJ) has based its view that human rights continue to apply in armed conflict on the existence of derogation provisions when it said that "the protection of the ICCPR does not cease in times of war, except by operation of Article 4 of the Covenant whereby provisions may be derogated from in a time of national emergency."[9] Similar to *lex specialis*, derogation is thus no blanket rejection of human rights in situations of armed conflict.

[6] See Hafner-Burton, Helfer and Fariss, "Emergency and Escape" (n. 5) pp. 676–78.

[7] See Dominic McGoldrick, "The Interface between Public Emergency Powers and International Law" (2004) 2(2) *International Journal of Constitutional Law* 388.

[8] Cordula Droege, "The Interplay between International Humanitarian Law and International Human Rights Law in Situations of Armed Conflict" (2007) 40(2) *Israel Law Review* 314; Lindsay Moir, *The Law of Internal Armed Conflict* (Cambridge: Cambridge University Press, 2002), p. 196; and Andrea Gioia, "The Role of the European Court of Human Rights in Monitoring Compliance with Humanitarian Law in Armed Conflict" in Orna Ben-Naftali (ed.), *International Humanitarian Law and International Human Rights Law* (Oxford: Oxford University Press, 2011), p. 204.

[9] *Legality of the Threat or Use of Nuclear Weapons*, International Court of Justice, Advisory Opinion of 8 July 1996 [1996] ICJ Reports 226 ("*Nuclear Weapons* case"), para. 25. The Court repeated this statement in the Wall Advisory Opinion: "the protection offered by human rights convention does not cease in case of armed conflicts, save through the effect of provisions for derogation of the kind to be found in Article 3 of the International Covenant on Civil and Political Rights," *Legal Consequences of the Construction of a Wall in the Occupied Palestinian Territory*, International Court of Justice, Advisory Opinion of 9 July 2004 [2004] ICJ Reports, para. 106. There is no statement similar to that of the ICJ by the European Court of Human Rights as to the continued application of the ECHR in times of armed conflict.

10.2 "A threat to the life of the nation": war as a state of emergency

Under human rights law, a number of conditions for and limitations of derogation need to be examined.[10] Their cumulative effect makes derogation an ambiguous and overrated, practically under-utilized and theoretically ill-understood device. To start with, the notion of a "state of emergency" which allows for derogations is an "eminently indeterminate notion,"[11] particularly when applied to armed conflicts. The ICCPR, for example, does not mention "war" or "armed conflict." In the drafting process of the text, the United Kingdom proposed to include the words "in time of war or other national emergency." This was rejected by other delegations in light of the recent prohibition of the use of armed force in the UN Charter. The idea that a state would invoke war as a lawful state of affairs seemed incompatible with the Charter.[12] As a compromise, the notion "public emergency" was used to cover emergencies including armed conflicts.[13] The ECHR also uses the term "war" as one example of a public emergency ("war or other public emergencies").[14]

Not every armed conflict qualifies as an emergency, as the UN Human Rights Committee made clear when it said that "[t]he Covenant [on Civil and Political Rights] requires that even during an armed conflict measures derogating from the Covenant are allowed only if and to the extent that the situation constitutes a threat to the life of the nation."[15] Similarly, the European Court of Human Rights has qualified a public emergency as "an exceptional situation of crisis or emergency which affects the whole population and constitutes a threat to the organized life of the community of which the State is composed."[16] While a situation of emergency must obviously have an impact on the community, the opaque and metaphoric notion of a "nation's life" has led to considerable uncertainties.[17] The respective chapter on emergencies and humanitarian law in Gross and Ni Aoláin's exhaustive study on emergency powers in theory and practice thus opens with the observation that the relationship between war and emergency is under-explored theoretically.[18] Not only is there uncertainty as to how to qualify the various types of conflicts, but the very idea that emergencies (including armed conflicts) are the exception of otherwise peaceful states of

[10] See, e.g., Venkat Iyer, "States of Emergency, Human Rights, and International Humanitarian Law" in V.S. Mani (ed.), *Handbook of International Humanitarian Law in South Asia* (New Delhi: Oxford University Press, 2007), p. 196.

[11] René Provost, *International Human Rights and Humanitarian Law* (Cambridge: Cambridge University Press, 2002), p. 273.

[12] Christina Cerna, "Human Rights in Armed Conflict: Implementation of International Humanitarian Law Norms by Regional Intergovernmental Human Rights Bodies" in Frits Kalshoven and Yves Sandoz (eds.), *Implementation of International Humanitarian Law* (Dordrecht: Nijhoff, 1989), p. 46.

[13] See Droege, "The Interplay" (n. 8) 319, with reference to the *travaux préparatoires* of the Covenant.

[14] ECHR, Art. 15.

[15] Human Rights Committee, *General Comment No. 29*, UN Doc. CCPR/C/21/Rev.1/Add.11 (31 August 2001), para. 3.

[16] *Lawless* v. *Ireland (No. 3)*, European Court of Human Rights, Appl. No. 332/57, Judgment of 1 July 1961, para. 28. In the first draft, the provision was meant to read "threatening the interests of the people," see Cerna, "Human Rights in Armed Conflict" (n. 12) p. 47.

[17] See Iyer, "States of Emergency" (n. 10) pp. 199–200.

[18] See Oren Gross and Fionnuala Ní Aoláin, *Law in Times of Crisis: Emergency Powers in Theory and Practice* (Cambridge: Cambridge University Press, 2006) p. 326.

affairs needs to be questioned in light of continuous and prolonged situations of intra-state fragility and insecurity.

In addition, the respective treaty provisions quoted earlier make clear that such emergency has to be formally proclaimed and other states parties notified of this declaration. But the usual approach of states is to ignore the derogation provision and, in the case of an internal armed conflict, deny the existence of such a conflict altogether. There is thus no state practice of proclaiming the existence of an international armed conflict and only a mixed state practice in non-international armed conflicts, and derogations under international human rights law are rare.[19] In the conflicts in which ECHR member states were involved, for example, such as the Falklands conflict, the Gulf War of 1990–1991, the former Yugoslavia and Iraq in 2003, no derogation was made.[20]

The requirement of proclaiming a public emergency leads to another question which, in another ironic twist, brings the institutions of international human rights into an area which is usually seen as the prerogative of humanitarian law, namely, the determination of the existence of an armed conflict. Given that human rights bodies or courts can examine the validity of a declaration of emergency under the respective treaty, they may be faced with the need to determine whether an armed conflict is indeed a state of emergency. With this, they enter unchartered waters: are human rights bodies and courts entitled to assess the existence of an armed conflict? Some would answer this affirmatively and argue that the derogation clauses of human rights treaties provide a window of opportunity for the supervision of international humanitarian law by human rights bodies.[21]

10.3 Derogation gap and the limits of derogation

Derogation may also lead straight into what may be termed the derogation gap: when a state lawfully derogates from provisions of a human rights treaty but at the same time does not recognize the existence of an armed conflict and thus denies the application of humanitarian law, neither law applies. It has rightly been said that "[t]here is no logical justification for this state of affairs."[22] The Human Rights Committee sought to rectify this by arguing that "[e]ven when derogating from international human rights law, the rules of international humanitarian law remain in force and provide the bottom-line below which states' actions must never fall."[23]

This is not the case for non-derogable rights which always apply. Under the ICCPR, non-derogable rights are the right to life; the prohibition of torture and cruel, inhuman or

19 See Droege, "The Interplay" (n. 8) 319, with reference to Turkey's proclamation in the Kurdish conflict and Russia's non-proclamation in the situation in Chechnya.

20 See Peter Rowe, "The Application of the European Convention on Human Rights During an Armed Conflict" in Richard Burchill, Nigel D. White and Justin Morris (eds.), *International Conflict and Security Law, Essays in Memory of Hilaire McCoubrey* (Cambridge: Cambridge University Press, 2005), p. 187. On the European Court of Human Rights' approach to this matter see Andreas Paulus, "The Protection of Human Rights in Internal Armed Conflict in Europe, Remarks on the Isayeva Decisions of the European Court of Human Rights" (2006) *Uppsala Yearbook of East European Law* 68.

21 See, e.g., Cerna, "Human Rights in Armed Conflict" (n. 12) pp. 47–48.

22 Christopher Greenwood, "Rights at the Frontier: Protection of the Individual in Time of War" in Barry A.K. Rider (ed.), *Law at the Centre: The Institute of Advanced Legal Studies at Fifty* (Dordrecht: Kluwer, 1999), p. 291.

23 See Human Rights Committee, *General Comment No. 29* (n. 15) para. 11.

degrading punishment and medical or scientific experimentation without consent; the prohibition of slavery, slave trade and servitude; the prohibition of imprisonment because of the inability to fulfil a contractual obligation; the principle of legality in the field of criminal law (the requirement for clear and precise criminal legal provisions which were in place and applicable at the time the criminalized act took place); the recognition of everyone as a person before the law; and freedom of thought, conscience and religion.[24]

To this list, the Human Rights Committee has added, in General Comment No. 29, four types of rights: first, *jus cogens* (peremptory) norms of international law (which the Committee said extend beyond the list of non-derogable rights under the Covenant); secondly, the human rights principle of non-discrimination and, more specifically, the associated prohibition of incitement to discrimination, hostility or violence through advocating national, racial or religious hatred; thirdly, norms derived from international humanitarian law (i.e., the prohibition of taking hostages; abductions or unacknowledged detention; deportation or forced transfer of minorities; collective punishment; arbitrary deprivations of liberty; and fundamental principles of fair trial); and fourthly, human rights violations expressed as crimes against humanity.[25]

Non-derogable rights under the ECHR are the right to life, the prohibition of torture, slavery and servitude and the prohibition of punishment without law.[26] With regard to the right to life, Article 15(2) makes it clear that deaths resulting from lawful acts of war are not covered by the protection offered under Article 1. ACHR, Article 27(2) stipulates that no suspension is possible of the right to juridical personality (Article 3); life (Article 4); humane treatment (Article 5); freedom of slavery (Article 6); the right not to be convicted for an act which was not criminalized at the time it was committed (Article 9); freedom of conscience and religion (Article 12); rights of the family (Article 17); right to a name (Article 18); rights of the child (Article 19); right to a nationality (Article 20); the right to participate in public affairs and public service, and the right to vote (Article 23); as well as judicial guarantees essential for the protection of these rights. CAT is also clear about the non-derogable nature of the prohibition of torture.[27]

These lists suffer from serious shortcomings from the way they were drawn up in the drafting process of the respective treaties. It has been pointed out that there was no exhaustive examination and justification for the list of non-derogable rights and for the reasons to include rights in these lists and exclude others.[28] The division between derogable and non-derogable rights – a mantra in all debates on derogation – is thus highly questionable from a systematic, historic and teleological perspective. It also needs to be pointed out that even when derogable rights are derogated (on the basis of a proclamation of a state of emergency), not all such rights (or parts thereof) are necessarily suspended automatically. It is widely accepted that even derogated rights must, in a functional interpretation, be

[24] ICCPR, Art. 4(2): "No derogation from articles 6, 7, 8 (paragraphs 1 and 2), 11, 15, 16 and 18 may be made under this provision."

[25] Human Rights Committee, *General Comment No. 29* (n. 15) paras. 11 and 12.

[26] ECHR, Art. 15(2): "No derogation from Article 2, except in respect of deaths resulting from lawful acts of war, or from Articles 3, 4 (paragraph 1) and 7 shall be made under this provision."

[27] CAT, Art. 2(2): "No exceptional circumstances whatsoever, whether a state of war or a threat of war, internal political instability or any other public emergency, may be invoked as a justification of torture."

[28] See Jaime Oraá, *Human Rights in States of Emergency in International Law* (Oxford: Clarendon Press, 1992), p. 124.

respected "in so far as this is possible in the circumstances."[29] Derogation thus means that even derogated human rights may continue to apply, albeit in a modified manner.[30] Furthermore, the procedural and judicial guarantees which are essential in order to give effect to the protected non-derogable rights may never be subject to measures which would, in effect, circumvent the protection of such non-derogable rights.[31]

Not all human rights treaties contain derogation clauses; in fact, derogation provisions are the exception.[32] It can hardly be argued that the absence of a derogation provision in human rights treaties expresses the will of the states parties that all those rights are derogable. The correct view, which seems to be confirmed by state practice, is that all such treaties continue to apply in armed conflict.[33] This is also what the ICJ said in its Advisory Opinion in the *Nuclear Weapons* case: "the protection offered by human rights conventions does not cease in case of armed conflict, save through the effect of provisions for derogation of the kind to be found in Article 4 of the International Covenant on Civil and Political Rights."[34] The Committee on the Rights of the Child has argued specifically that in the absence of a derogation clause, the Convention on the Rights of the Child (CRC) remains applicable in armed conflict.[35] The African Commission on Human and Peoples' Rights has done the same with regard to the African Convention on Human and Peoples' Rights (ACHPR).[36] Given that no derogation clauses were included in any human rights treaty drafted since the two Covenants of 1966, derogation can be seen as a remnant of the early years of the international human rights regime.[37]

Even if rights are lawfully derogated, further limitations apply. Every derogation is limited in time and must be lifted as soon as the public emergency (or armed conflict equivalent to a public emergency) ends. Any measure taken during such a time must be necessary and proportional, i.e., strictly required by the emergency, and none other than the least intrusive means may be applied. Derogations must also be consistent with other international obligations which include, in particular, obligations under international humanitarian law.[38] The interplay between the two is obvious. ICCPR, Article 24, for

[29] Louise Doswald-Beck and Sylvain Vité, "International Humanitarian Law and Human Rights Law" (1993) 33 *International Review of the Red Cross* 106.

[30] See Droege, "The Interplay" (n. 8) 320.

[31] Human Rights Committee, *General Comment No. 29* (n. 15) para. 3. Only ACHR, Art. 27(2) lists such rights as specifically protected: "[t]he foregoing provision does not authorize any suspension of . . . the judicial guarantees essential for the protection of such rights."

[32] There is also no derogation from the Universal Declaration of Human Rights, given its legal nature as a General Assembly Resolution, just as there is no derogation from customary international human rights law.

[33] See Gioia, "The Role of the European Court of Human Rights" (n. 8) p. 205; and Report of the Special Rapporteur on the Situation of Human Rights in Occupied Kuwait, UN Doc. E/CN.4/1992/26 (16 January 1992), paras. 50–54.

[34] ICJ, *Nuclear Weapons* case (n. 9) para. 106.

[35] See Committee on the Rights of the Child, *Day of General Discussion ("Children in Armed Conflict"), Report on Second Session (28 September–9 October 1992)*, UN Doc. CRC/C/10 (19 October 1992), p. 67; and Jenny Kuper, *International Law Concerning Child Civilians in Armed Conflict* (Oxford: Clarendon Press, 1997), p. 46.

[36] African Commission on Human and Peoples' Rights, Commission Nationale des Droits de l'Homme et des Libertés, *Ninth Activity Report* (1995), para. 22.

[37] See UN Secretary General, *Report of the UN Secretary General, Fundamental Standards of Humanity*, UN Doc. E/CN.4/1999/92, para. 20.

[38] See Mégret, "Nature of Obligations" (n. 4) p. 144.

example, protects children in a general way.[39] If a derogation was invoked in an armed conflict with the intention to suspend such protection, Additional Protocol I, Article 77, which is formulated in a similar way, would then apply.[40] In the case of derogating from ICCPR, Article 8(3)(a), which prohibits forced labour in general terms,[41] Geneva Convention IV, Article 51, with ten cumulative conditions on the prohibition of forced labour, would then apply.[42]

The Human Rights Committee has thus argued that "during armed conflict, whether international or non-international, rules of international humanitarian law become applicable and help ... to prevent abuse of a State's emergency powers."[43] This, again, puts international human rights bodies in a position to consider international humanitarian norms.[44] In light of all these considerations, derogation is not the strong argument for excluding human rights law from applying in armed conflicts which it is often presented as.

[39] ICCPR, Art. 24(1): "Every child shall have, without any discrimination as to race, colour, sex, language, religion, national or social origin, property or birth, the right to such measures of protection as are required by his status as a minor, on the part of his family, society and the State."

[40] Additional Protocol I, Art. 77(1): "Children shall be the object of special respect and shall be protected against any form of indecent assault. The Parties to the conflict shall provide them with the care and aid they require, whether because of their age or for any other reason."

[41] ICCPR, Art. 8(3)(a): "3. No one shall be required to perform forced or compulsory labour."

[42] Geneva Convention IV, Art. 51.

[43] Human Rights Committee, *General Comment No. 29* (n. 15) para. 3.

[44] See Hans-Joachim Heintze, "Konsequenzen der Konvergenz von Menschenrechtsschutz und humanitärem Völkerrecht" in Horst Fischer, Ulrike Froissart, Wolff Heinegg von Heintschel and Christian Raap (eds.), *Krisensicherung und humanitärer Schutz / Crisis Management and Humanitarian Protection. Festschrift für Dieter Fleck* (Berlin: Berliner Wissenschaftsverlag, 2004), p. 258.

11

Human rights and humanitarian obligations

11.1 Reframing rights and obligations: respect, protect, fulfil

"Human rights law is centred, indeed built, on the granting of rights to the individual, while humanitarian law is focused on the direct imposition of obligations on the individual."[1] This view of the nature of the norms of the law of armed conflict – that international humanitarian law is about obligations and international human rights law about rights – is still widely used as an argument against their complementarity.[2] As legal terms, "rights" and "obligations" differ, as does the corresponding terminology of "human rights" and "humanitarian law." It has thus been argued that:

> [t]he term "rights" in the expression "human rights" refers to subjective rights, powers or faculties which human beings possess in virtue of their recognition by national law and/ or international law. The term "law" in "international humanitarian law" refers to an objective set of principles and rules which, in international law, govern the protection of individuals in international or internal armed conflict.[3]

The difference can also be described with regard to rights-holders and duty-bearers: "international humanitarian law indicates how a party to a conflict is to behave in relation to people at its mercy, whereas human rights law concentrates on the rights of the recipients of a certain treatment."[4]

A great deal has been made of this difference which seems to preclude too close a relationship between human rights and humanitarian law. René Provost's exhaustive study of the relationship between human rights and humanitarian law, for example, devotes a large section to the difference between human rights and humanitarian obligations which he considers to be a marked one. "The emphasis of human rights law," he argues, "is on granting positive rights to the individual, while humanitarian law protects the interests of the individual through means other than the granting of rights."[5] The main difference described in his study, though, lies in the procedural capacity of claiming rights as opposed to the states' obligations to act in certain ways and less in the substance of rights and

[1] René Provost, *International Human Rights and Humanitarian Law* (Cambridge: Cambridge University Press, 2002), p. 13.

[2] See, e.g., Dominic McGoldrick, "Human Rights and Humanitarian Law in the UK Courts" (2007) 40(2) *Israel Law Review* 533; and Provost, *International Human Rights and Humanitarian Law*, p. 13.

[3] Héctor Gros Espiell, "Humanitarian Law and Human Rights" in Janusz Symonides (ed.), *Human Rights: Concepts and Standards* (Aldershot and Paris: Ashgate and UNESCO, 2000), p. 348.

[4] See Louise Doswald-Beck and Sylvain Vité, "International Humanitarian Law and Human Rights Law" (1993) 33 *International Review of the Red Cross* 101.

[5] Provost, *International Human Rights and Humanitarian Law* (n. 1) p. 16.

obligations. There is no doubt that this procedural capacity along with the institutional framework for remedies differs, but other than that the claim that human rights and humanitarian law are categorically different in terms of their legal nature is exaggerated; in fact it is a mistaken view.[6] It certainly cannot be used to claim that the complementary application of human rights and humanitarian law in armed conflict is altogether impossible.

First, juxtaposing "rights" and "law" is partly a semantic issue. It has rightly been observed that, different from the English language, "in Latin, Spanish, French, Italian, German and the Slavonic languages . . . the same word (ius, derecho, droit, diritto, recht [*sic!*], pravo), derived from the objective concept of law, has both meanings."[7] Secondly, and more importantly, human rights (as individual entitlements) can, and are, also expressed as obligations.[8] Granted by international treaty law as they are, they express the exchange of rights and duties between states to the benefit of individual human beings under the jurisdiction of these very states, as much as they have a special character as *erga omnes* norms with a high normative worth, given that they flow from, and reflect, the inherent human dignity which is not at the disposal of states.[9] Human rights are individual entitlements which are mirrored by the obligation of states to respect, protect and fulfil human rights towards persons under their jurisdiction. They are thus not always phrased as individual entitlements but also as state obligations: "[h]uman rights norms operate on three levels – as the rights of individuals, as obligations assumed by states, and as legitimate expectations of the international community."[10]

And just as human rights are not only about "rights," humanitarian law is not only about "obligations." It has rightly been argued that the simple formula according to which international humanitarian law is about obligations of the parties to a conflict whereas international human rights law is about individual rights falls short of explaining the complexity of both regimes.[11] Both contain rights and corresponding duties and prohibitive, preventive and protective norms as well as norms which require state action.[12]

The framing of humanitarian law as states' obligations and not individual rights in humanitarian treaties reflects, first and foremost, the law's history: when international humanitarian law was codified 150 years ago as a first attempt to secure humanitarian

6 See Walter Kälin and Jörg Künzli, *The Law of International Human Rights Protection* (Oxford: Oxford University Press, 2009), p. 153.

7 Gros Espiell, "Humanitarian Law and Human Rights" (n. 3) p. 348.

8 See, e.g., Frédéric Mégret, "Nature of Obligations" in Daniel Moeckli, Sangeeta Shah and Sandesh Sivakumaran (eds.), *International Human Rights Law* (Oxford: Oxford University Press, 2010), pp. 124–49, who consistently refers to "human rights obligations" when discussing human rights law.

9 Ibid. pp. 127–32.

10 Philip Alston, *Report of the Special Rapporteur on Extrajudicial, Summary or Arbitrary Executions, Addendum – Mission to Sri Lanka*, UN Doc. E/CN:4/2006/53/Add.5 (27 March 2006), para. 25.

11 See Jeremy Sarkin, "The Historical Origins, Convergence and Interrelationship of International Human Rights Law, International Humanitarian Law, International Criminal Law and Public International Law and their Application since the Nineteenth Century" (2007) 1(2) *Human Rights and International Legal Discourse* 133.

12 See Jovan Patrnogic, "Human Rights, Humanitarian Law and Refugee Law: Interdependence and Harmonization" in Fernando Ainsa (ed.), *Human Rights at the Dawn of the of the Twenty-First Century, Karel Vasak Amicorum Liber* (Bruxelles: Bruylant, 1999), pp. 1109–10.

concerns and (albeit to a lesser extent) concern with individual human dignity, the only framework available was that of the language of international law as it then stood. The language of states' "obligations" and "duties" rather than that of individual "rights" echoes the legal as well as the social and philosophical origins of international humanitarian law and its roots in Christian charity and European upper-class notions of morality.[13] With the drafting of the Geneva Conventions after 1945, a rethinking of international humanitarian law along new lines took place which allowed accommodating conceptual changes such as the idea of the universal application of international humanitarian law instead of a reciprocal relationship between states parties.[14] An increasing number of rules of international humanitarian law, in particular those providing for fundamental guarantees of all persons in the power of a party to the conflict and in non-international armed conflict, were thus formulated as subjective rights, and deliberately so.[15] This "amazing parallelism"[16] of the language of human rights and humanitarian law has repeatedly been highlighted as a particular characteristic of humanitarian law-making after 1945. While "traditional" international humanitarian law contained almost exclusively inter-state rights and obligations, contemporary international humanitarian law also recognizes individual rights.

One may mention Common Articles 6/6/6/7 and 7/7/7/8 of the Geneva Conventions which are aimed at preventing the renunciation of the individual rights of protected persons.[17] Additional Protocol I, Article 75, to consider another example, transfers rights

[13] David Forsythe, *The Humanitarians: The International Committee of the Red Cross* (Cambridge: Cambridge University Press, 2005), p. 251.

[14] See Geneva Conventions, Common Art. 1, which requires international humanitarian law to be respected "in all circumstances" and Geneva Conventions, Common Art. 2, which contains a "*si omnes*" clause for conflicts with non-state parties to the Convention. See Georges Abi-Saab, "The Specificities of Humanitarian Law" in Christophe Swinarski (ed.), *Studies and Essays on International Humanitarian Law and Red Cross Principles in Honour of Jean Pictet* (The Hague: Nijhoff, 1984), p. 266.

[15] See United Nations Office of the High Commissioner for Human Rights, *International Legal Protection of Human Rights in Armed Conflict* (New York and Geneva: United Nations, 2011), p. 15; and Cordula Droege, "The Interplay between International Humanitarian Law and International Human Rights Law in Situations of Armed Conflict" (2007) 40(2) *Israel Law Review* 349.

[16] Theodor Meron, "Convergence of International Humanitarian and Human Rights Law" in Daniel Warner (ed.), *Human Rights and Humanitarian Law: The Quest for Universality* (The Hague: Nijhoff, 1997), p. 101.

[17] Geneva Convention I, Art. 6 and Geneva Convention II, Art. 6: "No special agreement shall adversely affect the situation of the wounded and sick, of members of the medical personnel or of chaplains, as defined by the present Convention, nor restrict the rights which it confers upon them"; Geneva Convention II, Art. 6: "No special agreement shall adversely affect the situation of wounded, sick and shipwrecked persons, of members of the medical personnel or of chaplains, as defined by the present Convention, nor restrict the rights which it confers upon them"; Geneva Convention III, Art. 6: "No special agreement shall adversely affect the situation of prisoners of war, as defined by the present Convention, nor restrict the rights which it confers upon them"; Geneva Convention IV, Art. 7: "No special agreement shall adversely affect the situation of protected persons, as defined by the present Convention, nor restrict the rights which it confers upon them"; and Geneva Convention IV, Art. 8: "Protected persons may in no circumstances renounce in part or in entirety the rights secured to them by the present Convention"; Geneva Convention I, Art. 7 and Geneva Convention II, Art. 7: "Wounded and sick, as well as members of the medical personnel and chaplains, may in no circumstances renounce in part or in entirety the rights secured to them by the present Convention, and by the special agreements referred to in the foregoing Article, if such there be"; Geneva Convention III, Art. 7: "Prisoners of war may in no circumstances renounce in part or in entirety the rights secured to them by the present

contained in human rights treaties into the text of the Protocol, as does Common Article 3 of the Geneva Conventions, which is deliberately worded in rights terminology so as to emphasize the character of the rights granted as subjective rights.[18] Other rules of humanitarian law, too, are phrased as "rights," "entitlements" or "benefits," including Geneva Convention III, Article 14 on respect for the person of prisoners;[19] Geneva Convention III, Article 84 on fair trial guarantees;[20] Geneva Convention III, Article 105 on the rights and means of defence;[21] Geneva Convention III, Article 109 on repatriation;[22] Geneva Convention IV, Article 27 on protected persons;[23] Geneva Convention IV, Article 38 on the status and treatment of protected persons;[24] Geneva Convention IV, Article 78 on the procedural aspects of security detention;[25] Geneva Convention IV, Article 80 on internees;[26] Geneva Convention IV, Article 146 on the executions of convictions;[27] Additional Protocol I, Article 11 on medical experiments on the wounded, sick and shipwrecked;[28] Additional Protocol I, Article 45 on the protection of persons who have taken part in hostilities;[29]

Convention, and by the special agreements referred to in the foregoing Article, if such there be"; and Geneva Convention IV, Art. 8: "Protected persons may in no circumstances renounce in part or in entirety the rights secured to them by the present Convention, and by the special agreements referred to in the foregoing Article, if such there be."

[18] See Kälin and Künzli, *The Law of International Human Rights Protection* (n. 6) p. 153, with reference to Commentary on Geneva Conventions III and IV.

[19] Geneva Convention III, Art. 14: "Prisoners of war are entitled in all circumstances to respect for their persons and their honour."

[20] Ibid. Art. 84: "In no circumstances whatever shall a prisoner of war be tried by a court of any kind which does not offer the essential guarantees of independence and impartiality as generally recognized, and, in particular, the procedure of which does not afford the accused the rights and means of defence provided for in Article 105."

[21] Ibid. Art. 105: "The prisoner of war shall be entitled to assistance by one of his prisoner comrades, to defence by a qualified advocate or counsel of his own choice, to the calling of witnesses and, if he deems necessary, to the services of a competent interpreter. He shall be advised of these rights by the Detaining Power in due time before the trial."

[22] Ibid. Art. 109: "No sick or injured prisoner of war who is eligible for repatriation under the first paragraph of this Article, may be repatriated against his will during hostilities."

[23] Geneva Convention IV, Art. 27: "Protected persons are entitled, in all circumstances, to respect for their persons, their honour, their family rights, their religious convictions and practices, and their manners and customs."

[24] Ibid. Art. 38: "In any case, the following rights shall be granted to them: (1) They shall be enabled to receive the individual or collective relief that may be sent to them; (2) They shall, if their state of health so requires, receive medical attention and hospital treatment to the same extent as the nationals of the State concerned; (3) They shall be allowed to practise their religion and to receive spiritual assistance from ministers of their faith; (4) If they reside in an area particularly exposed to the dangers of war, they shall be authorized to move from that area to the same extent as the nationals of the State concerned."

[25] Ibid. Art. 78: "This procedure shall include the right of appeal for the parties concerned."

[26] Ibid. Art. 80: "Internees shall retain their full civil capacity and shall exercise such attendant rights as may be compatible with their status."

[27] Ibid. Art. 146: "In all circumstances, the accused persons shall benefit by safeguards of proper trial and defence."

[28] Additional Protocol I, Art. 11(5): "The persons described in paragraph 1 [on the prohibition of medical experiments] have the right to refuse any surgical operation."

[29] Ibid. Art. 45(3): "Any person who has taken part in hostilities, who is not entitled to prisoner-of-war status and who does not benefit from more favourable treatment in accordance with the Fourth Convention shall have the right at all times to the protection of Article 75 of this Protocol. In occupied territory, any such person, unless he is held as a spy, shall also be entitled, notwithstanding Article 5 of the Fourth Convention, to his rights of communication under that Convention."

Additional Protocol II, Article 4 on fundamental guarantees;[30] and Additional Protocol II, Article 6 on fair trial guarantees.[31]

Geneva Convention III, Article 118 has also been highlighted for the way it has changed its meaning under the influence of human rights. When the provision that prisoners of war must be released and repatriated without delay after the end of hostilities was inserted into the Geneva Conventions in 1949 it was informed by the delay in repatriations of German and Japanese prisoners of war after the Second World War by the Soviet Union (with the last German prisoner of war being repatriated thirteen years after the end of the war).[32] It was not foreseen in Geneva Convention III that prisoners might not wish to return home. A debate arose as to whether the provision should be understood as a strict obligation by a state party to repatriate prisoners of war regardless of the circumstances and their expressed intent, or if repatriation is an individual right conferred upon the prisoner. The matter was resolved along the latter interpretation of Geneva Convention III, so that by the time of the Gulf War of 1990–1991 repatriation was seen as a right of prisoners and a forceful repatriation as a violation of this individual right.[33]

Not only is there sufficient evidence *de lege lata* that international humanitarian law recognizes individual rights and international human rights law imposes obligations, there is, *de lege ferenda*, a re-orientation in the matrix of individual rights, obligations and responsibilities. The three are increasingly seen as intertwined: the assertion of individual human rights vis-à-vis the state is accompanied by the rise of individual criminal responsibility for grave violations of obligations in international humanitarian law and international human rights law, so that the whole construction of "rights" and "responsibilities" in international law is moving.[34] This rights-based character of humanitarian law is also acknowledged in state practice, as the above example of prisoners of war demonstrates, as does the reference to "rights" in the UK *Manual of the Law of Armed Conflict* which

[30] Additional Protocol II, Art. 4(1): "All persons who do not take a direct part or who have ceased to take part in hostilities, whether or not their liberty has been restricted, are entitled to respect for their person, honour and convictions and religious practices."

[31] Ibid. Art. 6(2): "No sentence shall be passed and no penalty shall be executed on a person found guilty of an offence except pursuant to a conviction pronounced by a court offering the essential guarantees of independence and impartiality. In particular: (a) the procedure shall provide for an accused to be informed without delay of the particulars of the offence alleged against him and shall afford the accused before and during his trial all necessary rights and means of defence; (b) no one shall be convicted of an offence except on the basis of individual penal responsibility; (c) no one shall be held guilty of any criminal offence on account of any act or omission which did not constitute a criminal offence, under the law, at the time when it was committed; nor shall a heavier penalty be imposed than that which was applicable at the time when the criminal offence was committed; if, after the commission of the offence, provision is made by law for the imposition of a lighter penalty, the offender shall benefit thereby; (d) anyone charged with an offence is presumed innocent until proved guilty according to law; (e) anyone charged with an offence shall have the right to be tried in his presence; (f) no one shall be compelled to testify against himself or to confess guilt."

[32] See Christopher Greenwood, "Rights at the Frontier: Protection of the Individual in Time of War" in Barry A.K. Rider (ed.), *Law at the Centre: The Institute of Advanced Legal Studies at Fifty* (Dordrecht: Kluwer, 1999), p. 282.

[33] Ibid. p. 283.

[34] See Andrew Clapham, "Rights and Responsibilities: A Legal Perspective" in Oliver Jütersonke and Keith Krause (eds.), *From Rights to Responsibilities: Rethinking Interventions for Humanitarian Purposes*, PSIS Special Study No. 7 (Geneva: Programme for Strategic and International Security Studies, 2006), pp. 63–85.

considers it the objective of humanitarian law "to safeguard the fundamental human rights of persons who are not, or no longer, taking part in the conflict (such as prisoners of war, the wounded, sick, and shipwrecked) and of civilians."[35]

In support of the view that the legal frameworks of human rights and humanitarian law are incompatible, it has also been argued that international humanitarian law's reliance on reciprocity is at odds with human rights' invocation of the common interest and *erga omnes* character. However, it has long been acknowledged that reciprocity has lost much of its importance in international humanitarian law, a development which went hand in hand with the rising importance of international human rights law and the influence it exercised on the development of international humanitarian law. The prohibition of reprisals, in particular, has been traced back to the influence of human rights, leading to erosion, if not prohibition of reprisals in international humanitarian law as it currently stands.[36] Already the Commentaries to the Geneva Conventions of 1952 affirmed that:

> the Conventions are coming to be regarded less and less as contracts on a basis of reciprocity concluded in the national interest of each of the parties, and more and more as solemn affirmations of principles respected for their own sake, and as a series of unconditional engagements on the part of each of the Contracting Parties' vis-à-vis the others.[37]

More specifically, Geneva Convention III can also be seen not merely as an engagement concluded on the basis of reciprocity but as unilateral engagements towards other states parties with regard to the protection of prisoners of war.[38]

Similar to international human rights law, the obligations of states to respect international humanitarian law under Common Article 1 of the Geneva Conventions[39] can be clustered as obligations to protect, respect and fulfil.[40] International humanitarian law carries with it positive and negative obligations, as does international human rights law.[41] Respect for human rights means that states must not take measures that infringe human rights, and similarly international humanitarian law requires states to abstain from physical violence against protected persons and prisoners of war[42] or the

[35] UK Ministry of Defence, *The Manual of the Law of Armed Conflict* (Oxford: Oxford University Press, 2004), p. 3.

[36] See Theodor Meron, *The Humanization of International Law* (Leiden: Nijhoff, 2006), p. 15.

[37] Jean Pictet (ed.), *Commentary on the First Geneva Convention for the Amelioration of the Condition of the Wounded and Sick in Armed Forces in the Field* (Geneva: International Committee on the Red Cross, 1952), p. 28.

[38] Jean Pictet (ed.), *Commentary on the Third Geneva Convention Relative to the Treatment of Prisoners of War* (Geneva: International Committee on the Red Cross, 1951), pp. 17–18.

[39] Geneva Conventions, Common Art. 1: "The High Contracting Parties undertake to respect and to ensure respect for the present Convention in all circumstances."

[40] See Kälin and Künzli, *The Law of International Human Rights Protection* (n. 6) pp. 156–57.

[41] UN OHCHR, *International Legal Protection of Human Rights in Armed Conflict* (n. 15) pp. 17–18.

[42] See, e.g., Geneva Convention IV, Art. 31: "No physical or moral coercion shall be exercised against protected persons, in particular to obtain information from them or from third parties"; and ibid. Art. 32: "The High Contracting Parties specifically agree that each of them is prohibited from taking any measure of such a character as to cause the physical suffering or extermination of protected persons in their hands. This prohibition applies not only to murder, torture, corporal punishment, mutilation and medical or scientific experiments not necessitated by the medical treatment of a protected person, but also to any other measures of brutality whether applied by civilian or military agents"; and ibid. Art. 34: "The taking of hostages is prohibited."

taking of hostages.[43] International humanitarian law obliges states to protect prisoners of war from public curiosity,[44] maintain law and order in occupied territories[45] and protect vulnerable groups, for example, women from rape and children from recruitment into the armed forces.[46] The provisions on the protection of the wounded and sick;[47] on protected persons;[48] on the protection of objects indispensable to the survival of the civilian population;[49] on the safety of prisoners of war;[50] on detention conditions;[51] and on the protection of women against sexual violence,[52] are examples for the imposition of a duty to protect from any infringement of their rights, including by third parties. The protective force of international humanitarian law against violations by third parties is also expressed in the states' duty to prevent, investigate, punish and ensure redress for human rights violations by non-state actors.[53]

Finally, states are required under international humanitarian law to fulfil certain rights, i.e., to take legislative, administrative, budgetary, judicial and other steps towards fully realizing human rights; in the case of economic, social and cultural rights this has to happen progressively.[54] This corresponds to provisions under humanitarian law which require states to supply food, shelter and health care, to organise medical supplies and to ensure

43 Ibid. Art. 34: "The taking of hostages is prohibited."

44 See Geneva Convention III, Art. 13; and also Gordon Risius and Michael A. Meyer, "The Protection of Prisoners of War Against Insults and Public Curiosity" (1993) 33(295) *International Review of the Red Cross* 288.

45 See Hague Regulations 1907, Art. 43: "The authority of the legitimate power having actually passed into the hands of the occupant, the latter shall take all steps in his power to re-establish and insure, as far as possible, public order and safety."

46 Geneva Convention IV, Art. 27: "Women shall be especially protected against any attack on their honour, in particular against rape, enforced prostitution, or any form of indecent assault"; and Additional Protocol I, Art. 77(2): "The Parties to the conflict shall take all feasible measures in order that children who have not attained the age of fifteen years do not take a direct part in hostilities and, in particular, they shall refrain from recruiting them into their armed forces."

47 Geneva Convention IV, Art. 16: "The wounded and sick, as well as the infirm, and expectant mothers, shall be the object of particular protection and respect."

48 Ibid. GC IV: "Protected persons ... shall at all times be humanely treated, and shall be protected especially against all acts of violence or threats thereof and against insults and public curiosity. Women shall be especially protected against any attack on their honour, in particular against rape, enforced prostitution, or any form of indecent assault."

49 Additional Protocol I, Art. 54: "(1) Starvation of civilians as a method of warfare is prohibited. (2) It is prohibited to attack, destroy, remove or render useless objects indispensable to the survival of the civilian population, such as foodstuffs, agricultural areas for the production of foodstuffs, crops, livestock, drinking water installations and supplies and irrigation works, for the specific purpose of denying them for their sustenance value to the civilian population or to the adverse Party, whatever the motive, whether in order to starve out civilians, to cause them to move away, or for any other motive."

50 Geneva Convention III, Art. 19: "Prisoners of war shall not be unnecessarily exposed to danger while awaiting evacuation from a fighting zone."

51 Additional Protocol I, Art. 75(5): "Women whose liberty has been restricted for reasons related to the armed conflict shall be held in quarters separated from men's quarters."

52 Ibid. Art. 76(1): "Women shall be the object of special respect and shall be protected in particular against rape, forced prostitution and any other form of indecent assault."

53 See Human Rights Committee, *General Comment No. 31 (Article 2) on the Nature of the General Legal Obligation Imposed on States Parties to the Covenant*, UN Doc. E/CCPR/C/21/Rev.1/Add.3 (26 May 2004), para. 8.

54 See Committee on Economic, Social and Cultural Rights, *General Comment No. 3 on the Nature of State Obligations*, UN Doc. E/1991/23, Annex III (14 December 1990), para. 2.

public health and hygiene in occupied territories,[55] as well as to provide medical treatment to prisoners of war,[56] and care and aid for children.[57] These all represent obligations which need to be fulfilled by states as social rights, including through the provision of adequate resources.[58]

11.2 The individual in humanitarian law

Unlike human rights law, status matters greatly in humanitarian law, which recognizes individual persons as combatants, those *hors de combat*, those who are assigned a special status (such as religious or medical personnel), civilians, and more. This is different from the universal and individualistic approach upon which international human rights law is built. "The [Geneva] Conventions' universe is a curious one," it has been said, "utterly unlike the human rights one. People become real only in certain situations or when they are doing certain things."[59] Distinguishing between these groups is at the very core of humanitarian law and enables it to assign protection where needed; indeed, for some, creating such groups is its very *raison d'être:* "the prime objective of [the law of armed conflict] is to make sure they remain separate, and are always treated differently."[60] Under humanitarian law, individuals "necessarily become identified with a community."[61] The distinction between different groups, particularly between combatants and civilians, is the main organizing principle of the law.[62] The norms of international humanitarian law have thus a double function (at least in international armed conflicts) for the way in which they protect the individual *per se* and as a member of the (political) community to which it belongs (i.e., the "enemy state" or the "party to the conflict").[63]

In contrast, the main driving force for applying human rights in armed conflict, regardless of the legal problems associated, is the simple fact that all humans have human rights: "[i]f human rights are inherent in human beings, they cannot also be

[55] See Geneva Convention IV, Part III, for example, on public health in occupied territories, on which ibid. Art. 56 states: "To the fullest extent of the means available to it, the Occupying Power has the duty of ensuring and maintaining, with the cooperation of national and local authorities, the medical and hospital establishments and services, public health and hygiene in the occupied territory, with particular reference to the adoption and application of the prophylactic and preventive measures necessary to combat the spread of contagious diseases and epidemics."

[56] Geneva Convention III, Art. 15: "The Power detaining prisoners of war shall be bound to provide free of charge for their maintenance and for the medical attention required by their state of health."

[57] Additional Protocol I, Art. 77(1): "Children shall be the object of special respect and shall be protected against any form of indecent assault. The Parties to the conflict shall provide them with the care and aid they require, whether because of their age or for any other reason."

[58] See Kälin and Künzli, *The Law of International Human Rights Protection* (n. 6) p. 157.

[59] Geoffrey Best, *War and Law Since 1945* (Oxford: Clarendon Press, 1994), p. 144.

[60] Rob McLaughlin, "The Law of Armed Conflict and International Human Rights Law: Some Paradigmatic Differences and Operational Implications" (2010) 13 *Yearbook of International Humanitarian Law* 224.

[61] Provost, *International Human Rights and Humanitarian Law* (n. 1) p. 344.

[62] See Yoram Dinstein, *The Conduct of Hostilities under the Law of International Armed Conflict* (2nd edn., Cambridge: Cambridge University Press, 2010), p. 8; and Paul Kennedy and George J. Andreopoulos, "The Laws of War: Some Concluding Reflections" in Michael Howard, George J. Andreopoulos and Mark R. Shulman (eds.), *The Laws of War: Constraints on Warfare in the Western World* (New Haven, CT: Yale University Press, 1994), p. 215.

[63] See Kälin and Künzli, *The Law of International Human Rights Protection* (n. 6) p. 140.

contingent – unless one believes that during war both soldiers and victims cease to be human beings."[64] But this seeming contradiction should not lead to the conclusion that humanitarian law is only about groups and cannot accommodate the individual human being (and with it human rights), and that it is thus "broadly futile to empower individuals by granting them rights upon which they will be unable to act."[65] There is a gradual shift from a reciprocity-based understanding of international humanitarian law in which individuals figure only as protected enemy persons towards a human rights-oriented understanding which allows for individuals to claim rights against the government under the jurisdiction of which they find themselves; a development which can be discerned already in the Geneva Conventions of 1949.[66] International humanitarian law itself has undergone a change away from the enemy/friend dichotomy as soon as it acknowledged the protected status of civilians which may, in some instances, not at all support their own state but even be oppressed by it.[67]

The history of humanitarian law is also about broadening the scope of protected persons and providing ever more specific protection to those most vulnerable. What started merely with concern for wounded soldiers in Solferino now covers the entire civilian population and is directed towards specific groups such as children affected by war. Common Article 12 of Geneva Conventions I and II applies to all wounded and sick regardless of their nationality and Common Article 3 of the Geneva Conventions is also usually understood as applying regardless of nationality, as is Additional Protocol II.[68] Additional Protocol I, Article 75 also contains no restrictions based on nationality and applies to persons "affected by a situation referred to in Article 1."[69] Child soldiers are protected under humanitarian law and human rights not against the enemy but against their own army and state.[70]

A particular characteristic of humanitarian law, which follows from the law's differentiation between different groups, is perceived more and more as a challenge: the way in which humanitarian law assigns different values to different lives.[71] This hierarchy of lives plays out on many levels, from the lack of a diligent "body count" of insurgents and the very lack of clear provisions in humanitarian law for such investigative measures, as opposed to listing and honouring every soldier killed. It is obvious with regard to the inequality of civilian and military casualties in remote-controlled wars, as well as the inadequacy or lack of litigation and claims procedures for war-related damage, which leads to casually handing out a couple of hundred dollars in hasty negotiations as compensation for a child killed in Afghanistan or elsewhere. The debate on balancing force protection with humanitarian (and human rights) obligations and the discussion on how many risks armed forces need to take compared with the potential collateral damage their

64 Daniel Thürer, *International Humanitarian Law: Theory, Practice, Context* (The Hague: Hague Academy of International Law, 2011), p. 133.

65 Provost, *International Human Rights and Humanitarian Law* (n. 1) p. 344.

66 See Meron, *The Humanization of International Law* (n. 36) p. 34.

67 Sandesh Sivakumaran, "Re-envisaging the International Law of Armed Conflict: A Rejoinder to Gabriella Blum" (2011) 22(1) *European Journal of International Law* 274.

68 Theodor Meron, "Human Rights in Time of Peace and in Time of Armed Strife: Selected Problems" in Thomas Buergenthal (ed.), *Contemporary Issues in International Law* (Kehl: Engel, 1984), p. 14.

69 Additional Protocol I, Art. 75(1).

70 Sivakumaran, "Re-envisaging the International Law of Armed Conflict" (n. 67) pp. 274–75.

71 See Mary Kaldor, *Human Security. Reflections on Globalization and Intervention* (Cambridge: Polity, 2007), p. 170.

operations entail – from high-altitude bombing to search operations on the ground – is also part of this problem.[72] It is suggested that this, too, is about the role of human rights in armed conflicts, as it seems that a strictly status-based approach of humanitarian law gradually gives way to a universalized human rights discourse with yet unclear contours.[73] These are concerns which lead directly to operationalizing the call for human rights in armed conflict.

[72] Ibid. p. 180. [73] See Ruti G. Teitel, *Humanity's Law* (Oxford: Oxford University Press, 2011), p. 164.

12

Operationalizing human rights in armed conflict

12.1 The idea of human rights and the image of the warrior

It is one thing to argue for the complementarity of human rights and humanitarian law and advocate the increased integration of the language, law and policy of human rights into the law of armed conflict; effectively putting it in practice is a different challenge. "The difficult task, for both theory and practice," it has rightly been said, "is to develop – case by case and within a more general scheme – criteria for deciding how the two regimes relate to each other when they overlap."[1] Calls to move beyond debating the applicability of human rights in armed conflict to effectively apply them resound ever louder.[2] What has been considered at length from a theoretical point of view has only partly been translated to operational realities: "[w]hilst all this is of great interest to academics, it does not assist the soldier on the ground."[3] Even those who accept, as a matter of principle, that human rights apply extra-territorially and complementarily with humanitarian law (whether within or without the principle of *lex specialis*), fear that this may fail in the operationalization.[4]

A closer analysis of these concerns reveals two main sets of arguments: one is related to the perceived incompatibility of human rights with the ethos of the warrior and his self-perception, knowledge and training, while the other has to do with the fear that more human rights in armed conflict may equal more protection for civilians as well as more risks for the soldiers on the battlefield, as well as in subsequent court proceedings for alleged violations of the law.

The first of these two concerns is that the lack of clarity and agreement over the exact relationship between human rights and humanitarian law is likely to lead to confusion among those called upon actually to implement the law in situations of armed conflict. There is particular concern that the specific and detailed rules of international humanitarian law would somehow be "trumped"[5] or watered down by the more generally worded

[1] Daniel Thürer, *International Humanitarian Law: Theory, Practice, Context* (The Hague: Hague Academy of International Law, 2011), p. 132.

[2] Sandesh Sivakumaran, "International Humanitarian Law" in Daniel Moeckli, Sangeeta Shah and Sandesh Sivakumaran (eds.), *International Human Rights Law* (Oxford: Oxford University Press, 2010), p. 538.

[3] Charles H.B. Garraway, "'To Kill or not to Kill': Dilemmas in the Use of Force" (2010) 14(3) *Journal of Conflict and Security Law* 502.

[4] See, e.g., Rob McLaughlin, "The Law of Armed Conflict and International Human Rights Law: Some Paradigmatic Differences and Operational Implications" (2010) 13 *Yearbook of International Humanitarian Law* 218.

[5] Christopher Greenwood, "Rights at the Frontier: Protection of the Individual in Time of War" in Barry A.K. Rider (ed.), *Law at the Centre: The Institute of Advanced Legal Studies at Fifty* (Dordrecht: Kluwer, 1999), p. 285.

provisions of international human rights law. The latter is rejected because it seems drafted in general terms suited to be applied by courts, whereas international humanitarian law is a specific and detailed code for military personnel.[6] Given the importance of clear, simple and practical rules for military personnel it has been warned that "[i]n an era of an already complex and often confused battle space, there can be little tolerance for adding complexity and confusion to the rules that war-fighters must apply in the execution of their missions. Instead, clarity is essential to aid them in navigating this complexity."[7]

Different ways to respond to this concern could be imagined. One would be to set aside the theoretical concerns expressed over the intricate relationship of human rights and humanitarian law and link them to specific contexts in a more straightforward way:[8] where there is no conflict, international human rights law should apply; in international armed conflicts international humanitarian law should apply; in internal conflicts and occupation international human rights law should apply when sufficient authority and control is available to hold the state to account for its actions and/or where actions have a law enforcement character rather than a war character; in non-international armed conflicts one would need to distinguish between low-intensity conflicts where non-state parties do not control territory and international human rights law applies everywhere, and high-intensity conflicts where territory is controlled by non-state parties and international humanitarian law would take the lead. Remaining doubts should be sorted out by dedicated Rules of Engagement in specific operations. While this is a straightforward solution from a practical point of view, it may suffer from disagreements over the qualification of the conflict as a prerequisite to decide which law should apply.

Another suggestion hinges on the idea of a *cordon sanitaire* for core humanitarian rules and would mean keeping this core clear from human rights so that it can remain operational. It has been suggested that such an approach would be of particular importance in light of operational demands (as opposed to academic debate) and that "[d]eciding what is non-negotiably [the law of armed conflict] is thus the missing critical step in identifying how to manage those issues which might conceivably sit astride both [international human rights law] and [the law of armed conflict] paradigms, and be subject to productive, meaningful, and defensible [international human rights law] infusion."[9] Again, however, this seems like a variation of the position of an exclusivity of humanitarian law and it needs to be seen critically for the way it draws artificial boundaries around self-defined "red lines."

Finally, one could pragmatically reduce the complexity of the legal frameworks and translate them into workable rules for practice, as is done for international humanitarian law in the form of distilled rules and manuals, guidelines and instructions for the individual soldier.[10] In light of the difficulties which the quest for "Fundamental Standards of Humanity" has entailed, this seems easier to suggest than implement but could be done

[6] Ibid. p. 283.

[7] Geoffrey Corn, "Mixing Apples and Hand Grenades: The Logical Limit of Applying Human Rights Norms to Armed Conflicts" (2010) 1(1) *International Humanitarian Legal Studies* 54. Similarly, Louise Doswald-Beck and Sylvain Vité, "International Humanitarian Law and Human Rights Law" (1993) 33(293) *International Review of the Red Cross* 118; and Michael J. Kelly, "Critical Analysis of the International Court of Justice Ruling on Israel's Security Barrier" (2005) 29(1) *Fordham International Law Journal* 188.

[8] On the following suggestions see Garraway, "To Kill or not to Kill" (n. 3) 509–10.

[9] McLaughlin, "The Law of Armed Conflict and International Human Rights Law" (n. 4) 242.

[10] Geoffrey Best, *War and Law Since 1945* (Oxford: Clarendon Press, 1994), p. 419.

in selected fields in which states find agreement possible, such as was the case with the Copenhagen Principles on handling detainees, mentioned above.

This would also mean introducing human rights into training for military personal. It has been cautioned that the lack of human rights knowledge among military staff is a problem.[11] At the same time, the consequences which potentially flow from decisions such as *Al-Skeini* with their call for respecting human rights in situations of occupation or armed conflict for the training, planning and coordination of combat operations, as well as for military doctrine in general, are obvious. This is, however, not as novel a problem as it may seem. The European Court of Human Rights has on various occasions established benchmarks for the training and planning of law enforcement and the training of military forces where they are involved in such operations,[12] and such training in human rights is already part and parcel of peace support operations.[13]

An associated concern is that armed forces may not be receptive to the message of human rights because it deviates from the paradigmatic approach of humanitarian law, particularly when it comes to the use of deadly force as part and parcel of the professional self-perception of the armed forces.[14] The motivation of reciprocity as a driving force for adhering to the law, it could be argued, is lacking under human rights law: ensuring respect for humanitarian law and the way in which it protects the enemy armed forces (to which soldiers may even feel a professional bond) is one thing; appreciating the universal human rights of all opponents may be quite another. The basic tenet of their universal application may break down in a scenario where destroying the enemy is the whole point of the exercise. Soldiers may simply find human rights unrealistic in the context they find themselves in, different from the rationale of humanitarian law which is clear to them.

As a consequence, armed forces may not only lack the knowledge of human rights law, they may also fail to understand its underlying rationale and ultimately reject it, given that the killing of enemy combatants as a first resort "is an essential component for developing a warrior ethos [and] asking them to operate under such a framework during armed conflict is inconsistent with their fundamental purpose: to be ready, willing and able to kill on demand."[15] This, however, seems to suggest that the self-perception of soldiers excludes concern for human rights, particularly for those of their opponents and relies on medieval codes of honour, which saw humanity as merciful acts by respectable commanders and not as rights which are endowed on everyone. But in our times of post-heroic wars, honour and chivalry as motivating forces to implement humanitarian rules can no longer be seen as driving forces (or as the only driving forces) for restraint in combat, at least in armies of democratic countries or armies which consider their members as citizens in uniform,

[11] See Peter Rowe, *The Impact of Human Rights Law on Armed Forces* (Cambridge: Cambridge University Press, 2006), pp. 114–17.

[12] See McLaughlin, "The Law of Armed Conflict and International Human Rights Law" (n. 4) 229, with reference to a number of cases.

[13] The United Nations Training School Ireland, to name one example, for best practice in human rights training for military forces, see www.military.ie/education-hq/military-college/united-nations-training-school-ireland (last accessed 15 April 2014).

[14] See on this and the following arguments Rowe, *The Impact of Human Rights Law on Armed Forces* (n. 11) p. 115.

[15] Corn, "Mixing Apples and Hand Grenades" (n. 7) 83.

equipped with all human rights, as they are.[16] But it is true that a human rights-based approach to the law of war might require a significant shift in the mind-sets of political and military actors.[17] This is, however, not an impediment but should be seen as a timely requirement and demand. How else can it be explained that in a recent volume on "new wars and new soldiers," there is abundant reference to the professional ethic of soldiers as the constituting paradigm of behaviour in situations of armed conflict, but a remarkably complete absence of human rights?[18]

12.2 Rights and risks

The second set of arguments against human rights in armed conflict from an operational perspective deals with the concern that they will lead to an increased legal and operational burden placed on armed forces and will force the military to take higher risks in operations. This would mean a burden "in terms of resource allocation, decision-making systems, and the balance to be struck between caution and risk."[19] The co-application of human rights law, it is warned, would overstretch the capacity of armed forces to effectively apply the law: "[i]f [armed forces] were obliged to also comply with human rights, applicable law would become rather complicated and, in many cases, inoperable."[20] Particularly in operations carried out by coalition forces (or in situations where such forces are in charge of occupied territory), human rights law may create differential obligations when states are not parties to the same treaties.[21] Again, and in line with the suggestion made above, one would thus have to create guiding rules, for example in Rules of Engagement, to counter this problem and include human rights law in an appropriate way.[22]

An associated fear is that when human rights are applied, the freedom to act according to military requirements and successfully accomplish military missions will be lost, and that military operations will fail or not be undertaken at all, when they cannot be carried out under the (permissive) humanitarian law, as opposed to the restrictive human rights law. It is argued that "[i]f we expect our soldiers to conduct operations, we must provide a legitimate means by which they can do so."[23] It is correct that under a human rights paradigm the use of force may be regulated differently and further restrictions beyond humanitarian law could apply. This is a matter to be discussed with great care. But if the argument assumes that humanitarian law is permissive to the extent that ultimately military necessity trumps humanitarian considerations, it boils down to different interpretations of the role of humanitarian law. One may respond with Hersch Lauterpacht that:

[16] See Christopher Coker, *War in an Age of Risk* (Cambridge: Polity, 2009), p. 177.

[17] See David S. Koller, "The Moral Imperative: Toward a Human-Rights Based Law of War" (2005) 46(1) *Harvard International Law Journal* 263.

[18] See Paolo Tripodi and Jessica Wolfendale, "Introduction" in Paolo Tripodi and Jessica Wolfendale (eds.), *New Wars and New Soldiers* (Aldershot: Ashgate, 2011), pp. 1–12.

[19] McLaughlin, "The Law of Armed Conflict and International Human Rights Law" (n. 4) 226–30 and 242.

[20] Wolff Heinegg von Heintschel, "Symposium: The Rule of Law in Conflict and Post-Conflict Situations: Factors in War to Peace Transitions" (2004) 27(3) *Harvard Journal of Law and Public Policy* 872.

[21] Sivakumaran, "International Humanitarian Law" (n. 2) p. 537.

[22] See Federico Sperotto, "Counter-Insurgency, Human Rights, and the Law of Armed Conflict" (2009) 17(1) *Human Rights Brief* 21.

[23] Garraway, "To Kill or not to Kill" (n. 3) 509.

> we shall entirely fail to understand the true character of the law of war unless we realise that its purpose is almost entirely humanitarian in the literal sense of the word, namely, to prevent or mitigate suffering and in some cases, life, from the savagery of battle and passion. This, and not the regulation of hostilities is its essential purpose. Rules of Warfare are not primarily rules governing the technicalities and artifices of a game. They have evolved or have been expressly enacted for the protection of actual or potential victims of war.[24]

The concern that, beyond resources and rules, adhering to human rights law means accepting a higher risk to suffer damage, injury or death in operations, is of particular importance. It is also a divisive question: "for some this outcome will be one to be applauded. For some, this outcome will be one to be guarded against."[25] Military operations, it is argued, must not be unduly overburdened with risk to the life of the soldiers to accommodate concern for civilians' lives, let alone when attacking enemy combatants.[26] But even where such arguments are supported by the current understanding of international humanitarian law, they nevertheless effectively suggest externalizing such risks to a sometimes unacceptable degree to the civilian population, as does the whole construction of the principle of proportionality under humanitarian law as it stands. This, however, seems less and less tenable in light of the requirements of humanity understood as a right to which those affected by armed conflicts are entitled under a human rights-based perception of humanitarian protection. At the same time, the warning that it would be idealist and utopian to allow the primacy of protection to be absolute in disregard of the implicit logic of military operations needs to be taken into account.[27]

The final concern is that the increased involvement of human rights bodies and courts in monitoring and litigating violations of the law in armed conflicts will lead to "a flood of litigation from soldiers' families and, perhaps worse, ... commanding officers will become reluctant to commit troops to anything too risky."[28] In light of already existing disciplinary and (national and international) criminal accountability for grave violations of humanitarian law such fears seem, however, misplaced as far as individual criminal prosecution is concerned – human rights law has nothing on offer in this respect. The argument that, in addition to criminal responsibility, bodies such as the European Court of Human Rights will necessarily consider military operations through a human rights lens is correct, and will find support from many and face opposition from others. Both these arguments will be examined in greater detail in light of the practice of treaty bodies in the final chapter of this study. Before that, the idea of human rights in armed conflict will be put in the larger context of developments in law and war.

[24] Hersch Lauterpacht, "The Problem of the Revision of the Law of War" (1952) 29 *British Yearbook of International Law* 382.

[25] See McLaughlin, "The Law of Armed Conflict and International Human Rights Law" (n. 4) 242.

[26] See Kenneth Watkin, "Assessing Proportionality: Moral Complexity and Legal Rules" (2005) 8(36) *Yearbook of International Humanitarian Law* 37–38.

[27] See Stefan Oeter, "Collateral Damages: Military Necessity and the Right to Life" in Christian Tomuschat, Evelyne Lagrange and Stefan Oeter (eds.), *The Right to Life* (Leiden: Nijhoff, 2010), p. 193.

[28] "Soldiers' Human Rights: The Charge of the Legal Brigade," *The Economist*, May 2009, p. 52.

Part IV

The dynamics of war and law

The phrase "human rights in armed conflict" is somewhat misleading for the way it glosses over the categorization of armed conflicts under humanitarian law as either international or non-international, with additional special norms for situations of occupation.[1] The exceptional rules for wars of national liberation "in which peoples are fighting against colonial domination and alien occupation and against racist régimes in the exercise of their right of self-determination,"[2] which are assimilated to international conflicts solely for the purpose of extending the protective regime of the Geneva Conventions and the division between non-international armed conflicts under either Common Article 3, on the one hand, or Additional Protocol II, on the other hand (which requires higher thresholds to be reached by non-state armed groups, particularly with regard to exercising control over territory) complicates matters.[3] The debate on human rights in armed conflicts needs to be matched with this typology.

At the same time, this established dichotomy of international and non-international armed conflicts is today being challenged as increasingly irrelevant in light of the multitude of situations which fall in between or outside this classic scheme. Among them are "internationalized" conflicts (i.e., internal conflicts with various forms of third-party intervention), conflicts which spill over into the territory of other states and "extra-state" or "transnational" armed conflicts, fought between nation states and non-state armed groups with no clear delineation within national borders, including the so-called "War on Terror." To this one may add the use of armed force in UN mandated peace support operations situations.

The problems resulting from the heterogeneity of conflict situations for the application of international humanitarian law have been discussed at length elsewhere and need not be repeated here.[4] As far as human rights are concerned, this poses a challenge, as their

[1] Geneva Conventions, Common Art. 2, makes them applicable to all cases of declared war or of any other armed conflict which may arise between two or more of the High Contracting Parties, even if the state of war is not recognized by one of them.

[2] Additional Protocol I, Art. 1(4).

[3] Geneva Conventions, Common Art. 3: "In the case of armed conflict not of an international character occurring in the territory of one of the High Contracting Parties"; Additional Protocol II, Art. 1(1): "This Protocol . . . shall apply to all armed conflicts . . . which take place in the territory of a High Contracting Party between its armed forces and dissident armed forces or other organized armed groups which, under responsible command, exercise such control over a part of its territory as to enable them to carry out sustained and concerted military operations and to implement this Protocol."

[4] See generally Sylvain Vité, "Typology of Armed Conflicts in International Humanitarian Law: Legal Concepts and Actual Situations" (2009) 91(873) *International Review of the Red Cross* 69.

application in different situations has different preconditions and consequences. At the same time, there is also an obvious correlation between the existence of these different types of armed conflicts and the application of human rights. The blurring of the boundaries between war and peace in the classical sense and the emergence of conflict situations other than wars between nation states are a driving force for the debate on human rights in armed conflict:

> [t]he convergence of international humanitarian law and human rights shows that war and peace, civil wars and international conflicts, international law and internal law, all have increasingly overlapping areas. It follows that the law of war and the law of peace, international law and internal law, the scopes of which were at first clearly distinct, are today often applicable at the same time side by side. Thus, the Geneva Conventions and the human rights conventions may often be applied in cumulative fashion.[5]

This correlation works both ways: the existence of different types of armed conflicts calls for the application of human rights, just as the integration of human rights into situations of armed conflict challenges and changes the image of "war" in its various facets. War and law are both dynamic, and changes in one of them interact with the other: the changing character of war necessitates the application of international human rights law, and the application of human rights law changes the image of war.

[5] Dietrich Schindler, "The International Committee of the Red Cross and Human Rights" (1979) 19 *International Review of the Red Cross* 9.

13

The changing character of war

13.1 War as risk management

While the application of international humanitarian law in internal armed conflicts, situations of occupation and peace support operations is usually well acknowledged (as will be discussed below), doubts are raised with regard to the (full) applicability of international human rights law in international armed conflicts.[1] While internal armed conflicts are characterized by a (hostile) relationship between the government and those being governed akin to (peace-time) law enforcement scenarios and are thus obviously susceptible to the application of human rights law, in international armed conflicts the *lex specialis* principle is seen as overriding international human rights law on the grounds that humanitarian law is both exclusive and exhaustive. In such situations, it is argued, human rights *cannot* apply on the grounds of irreconcilable paradigmatic differences and legal obstacles, and they *need not* apply as they have nothing to contribute in terms of regulation above and beyond international humanitarian law.[2] It is certainly correct that international humanitarian law, with its history of codification which stretches back 150 years, regulates international armed conflicts extensively and in great detail. At the same time, the breadth of humanitarian law for international armed conflicts does not *per se* exclude the complementary application of human rights in international armed conflicts. While many of the examples provided for such a complementary application in the previous chapters related to internal armed conflicts or situations of occupation, human rights in armed conflict should not be understood as exclusively a matter for such situations.

"War" is not a static phenomenon, and the way in which war has changed and continues to change its character questions the exclusive reliance on humanitarian law on legal grounds as well as for reasons of policy.[3] "Since war – the province of humanitarian law – has changed so much," it has rightly been asked, "how can we be confident that rules established in the nineteenth and twentieth centuries will continue to be effective or pertinent in the twenty-first?"[4] Even those otherwise critical of applying human rights in

[1] See, e.g., Kenneth Watkin, "Controlling the Use of Force: A Role for Human Rights Norms in Contemporary Conflicts" (2004) 98(1) *American Journal of International Law* 2.

[2] Ibid. 22 and 30.

[3] See on the changing character of war and the role of law in general Mary Kaldor, *New and Old Wars: Organized Violence in a Global Era* (3rd edn., Cambridge: Polity, 2012); David Kennedy, *Of War and Law* (Princeton, NJ: Princeton University Press, 2006); and Michael Byers, *War Law* (New York: Grove Press, 2005).

[4] Daniel Thürer, *International Humanitarian Law: Theory, Practice, Context* (The Hague: Hague Academy of International Law, 2011), p. 378.

armed conflict acknowledge such concerns and consider that the nature of modern conflicts transcends the age-old image of war as a contention between states, and makes the application of human rights law not only possible but necessary.[5] It has rightly been argued that this, and not the writings of progressive human rights scholars and overly ambitious human rights commissions and courts, is the "momentum behind the complementarity trend ... too powerful to reverse."[6]

In Oppenheim's classic definition of war as a means for overpowering the enemy so as to impose "such conditions of peace the victor pleases,"[7] there may indeed have been little space for human rights. But such wars hardly exist any longer. As Rupert Smith, one of the UK's most experienced military leaders and thinkers said, "[w]ar is no longer a massive deciding event in a dispute in international affairs."[8] Conditions may still be imposed on those defeated but (with exceptions) modern wars are no longer about territorial conquest. The use of armed force abroad has become a tool for managing insecurity in inter-state relations and within states. Christopher Coker has convincingly argued that even though modern states were created through wars, "today's states wage wars which have no political or social function. For us war has become risk management in all but name."[9] National interests have not vanished but they are no longer the sole or ultimate legitimization for war. They have been replaced by the use of force as a tool for social engineering, whether this means securing economic liberalism, democratization or nation-building, and armed force is used to confront instability, restore security and contain failing states and fragile societies.[10]

The traditional objective of military campaigns was victory achieved through decisive acts on the battlefield, but with these changes, victory in war has also become elusive. When war is about managing global disorder, there is little success to be had in defeating the enemy. And even though the view of war as a contest is still deeply entrenched in military theory, today's armed conflicts no longer deliver clear victories. Already during the Cold War the US military saw the necessity of redefining "winning" in other terms, and since then the notion of victory has become tainted.[11] And yet, humanitarian law with its nineteenth century ideas of victory and defeat is largely built around such an image of war as a contest. But the goals, conduct and constraints of modern wars have become complex to an extent that the decisive moment of victory and defeat can hardly be pinned down, and those reporting "mission accomplished" at some point during military campaigns seem often detached from the reality on the ground.[12] This inconclusiveness of war, together with the demands of modern warfare, have led to arguments that the idea of

[5] See Geoffrey Corn, "Mixing Apples and Hand Grenades: The Logical Limit of Applying Human Rights Norms to Armed Conflicts" (2010) 1(1) *International Humanitarian Legal Studies* 71.

[6] Ibid. 56.

[7] See Lassa Oppenheim in Hersch Lauterpacht (ed.), *International Law* (7th edn., 1952), vol. II, quoted in Yoram Dinstein, *War, Aggression and Self-Defence* (5th edn., Cambridge: Cambridge University Press, 2011), p. 5: "War is a contention between two or more States through their armed forces, for the purpose of overpowering each other and imposing such conditions as the victor pleases."

[8] Rupert Smith, *The Utility of Force: The Art of War in the Modern World* (London: Allen Lane, 2005), p. 1.

[9] Christopher Coker, *War in an Age of Risk* (Cambridge: Polity, 2009), p. 150. [10] Ibid. p. 35.

[11] US President Dwight D. Eisenhower (1953–1961) reportedly said that the only thing that frightened him more than losing the Cold War was winning it, see Coker, *War in an Age of Risks* (n. 9) p. 122.

[12] Ibid. pp. 177 and 121, where the author uses the example of the Israeli military operations against Lebanon in 2006, where despite Israel's "victory" of eliminating 25 per cent of Hezbollah's front-line

achieving victory in war is dead and ought to be replaced by promoting greater security or, more modestly, "reducing insecurity to more acceptable levels."[13]

And just as there is no longer unquestioned victory, there is also no clear defeat. The long-term engagement with small networked or even isolated "enemies" can create unpredictable costs for nation states, and the minor means and methods applied by such groups can be in stark contrast to their impact. The defeat of states in their wars against networked opponents may thus come not on the battlefield but as a gradual wasting away of military, economic and political power in such asymmetric encounters. Calculations such as in the case of one Iraqi insurgent group which invested US$2,000 in explosive devices to destroy an oil pipeline that cost the Iraqi government US$500 million in lost revenue (a "return on investment" of 25 million per cent) are instructive in this regard.[14] Iraq is a case study at hand where coalition forces could only secure themselves basic infrastructure and oil exports but could not achieve any significant victory in the classic sense.[15]

But if today victory means achieving regional or global security as well as reconstituting human security, then the idea, language and law of human rights necessarily comes into play: "[w]ar seems to have escaped the narrow parameters that it was given in the course of the twentieth century – deterrence and defence. Its principle theme is now security in its various, often mutually exclusive forms."[16] And if war is about risk management, then the law of war should be a law of risk management, too. In the traditional image of war the attacker cannot be blamed for overpowering and destroying the enemy, but in risk management operations there seems to be a legal and moral obligation to anticipate the consequences of military action. It is questionable if the paradigm of humanitarian law is sufficient in this respect or if human rights law would not provide an altogether different and more appropriate compass.

13.2 New wars, old laws

States have lost their monopoly of warfare. Yet, this monopoly was the central premise of the law of war since its codification in the late nineteenth century. Back then, the law was created to regulate the wars of nation states which could mobilize standing armies to operate on clearly marked battlefields isolated from the rest of society. Today, violence is asymmetric, "civilianized," criminal, commercial and networked. Such "new wars" are often fought by private actors, from warlords to criminal organizations and from terrorist networks to private military and security contractors. Weapon bearers (labelled, often interchangeably, as insurgents, terrorists, criminals and mercenaries) plan (and occasionally carry out) their operations in cyber-space, act jointly in mutually supportive infinite loops and finance their equipment with the exploitation of natural resources or organized crime. And wars are economic opportunities with no incentive to bring them to an end, which makes war the norm and not the exception in many regions of the world and mocks the sequence of peace giving way to war to be followed by peace again.[17] The resulting violence blurs the distinction between peace and war and cares little for what international law has to say on all this.[18]

strength with comparatively low Israeli casualties and a considerable subsequent reduction of Hezbollah's activities against Israel, nothing conclusive has been achieved in the long run.

[13] Ibid. p. 121, with reference to statements by EU Defence Ministers. [14] Ibid. p. 166.

[15] Ibid. pp. 125–26. [16] Ibid. p. 63. [17] See Kaldor, *New and Old Wars* (n. 3) pp. 71–118.

[18] See Thürer, *International Humanitarian Law* (n. 4) pp. 246–48.

Such new wars are characterized by a "civilianization" in the sense that civilians are being disproportionately affected and, at the same time, motivated to take up arms and participate in hostilities.[19] Today's wars are removed from the archetype of war as a conflict between states of equal legal and political standing, carried out by their well organized armed forces in a symmetrical way. They are fought between unequal parties and across boundaries by those not conforming to the dichotomy of civilians and combatants. This, in turn, entails a broader delimitation and loss of boundaries, geographically as well as with regard to the acceptable means and methods. The use of modern technology, from drones to automated weapons systems and information technology, is a facet and driving force of these wars.[20] It has rightly been observed that:

> the existing definitions of the traditional subjects of international humanitarian law, namely authorities and individuals, and the implementing mechanisms offered by international treaties and institutions are no longer appropriate when it comes to the protagonists of new types of conflict – especially unstructured groups – or to the new power bases represented by private economic and financial giants.[21]

The European wars between nation states (which have led to the creation of humanitarian law) and the twentieth century wars of industrialized nations in Europe and Asia (which further shaped it) have given way to such new forms of violence. Common Article 3 of the Geneva Conventions had archetypical civil wars such as the Spanish Civil War in mind, but today's conflicts no longer follow such blueprints.[22] Yet, the old laws still govern such new wars.[23] Even though the idea of "new wars" needs to be read with some caution – it has rightly been said that "the claim that some situations are genuinely completely new never survives critical historical analysis"[24] – the existence of such conflicts in a grey zone between international and non-international armed conflicts and the associated question of the legal status of those participating in such conflicts are more than obvious. These are "post-modern wars," to which established categories of nationality, territory and politics can be applied only with great difficulties,[25] and they are "hybrid wars" in the way in which they cut through conventional criteria of public and private space, state and non-state regulation and formal and informal responses to violence.[26]

What sets such new wars apart from the traditional encounter between nation states and historic civil wars is that their illegitimate character triggers a cosmopolitan response in a

[19] See Daniel Thürer, "International Humanitarian Law: Essence and Perspectives" (2007) 2 *Schweizerische Zeitschrift für internationales und öffentliches Recht* 6.

[20] See, e.g., Eric Talbot Jensen, "The Future of the Law of Armed Conflict: Ostriches, Butterflies, and Nanobots," available at http://ssrn.com/abstract=2237509 (last accessed 15 April 2014).

[21] René Kosirnik, "The 1977 Protocols: A Landmark in the Development of International Humanitarian Law" in Naorem Sanajaoba (ed.), *A Manual of International Humanitarian Laws* (New Delhi: Regency, 2004), p. 84.

[22] See Marco Sassòli, "The Role of Human Rights and International Humanitarian Law in New Types of Armed Conflicts" in Orna Ben-Naftali (ed.), *International Humanitarian and International Human Rights Law* (Oxford: Oxford University Press, 2011), p. 46.

[23] See Thürer, *International Humanitarian Law* (n. 4) p. 248.

[24] Sassòli, "The Role of Human Rights and International Humanitarian Law" (n. 22) p. 34.

[25] See Christopher Coker, "The Collision of Modern and Post-Modern War" in Julian Lindley-French and Yves Boyer (eds.), *The Oxford Handbook of War* (Oxford: Oxford University Press, 2012), pp. 57–68.

[26] See Rob de Wijk, "Hybrid Conflict and the Changing Nature of Actors" in Julian Lindley-French and Yves Boyer (eds.), *The Oxford Handbook of War* (Oxford: Oxford University Press, 2012), pp. 358–72.

globalized environment.[27] The forms of such responses, from the idea of humanitarian intervention to the "Responsibility to Protect," remain divisive.[28] Whether one sees them as misguided military humanitarianism or as redefining state sovereignty they are, or should be, informed by the three *topoi* of legitimacy, accountability and respect for universal human dignity.[29] Seen in light of the law of armed conflict, such a view necessitates the complementary application of cosmopolitan norms as currently expressed in international humanitarian law, human rights law and international criminal law in a complementary way, so that any debate on new wars is at the same time also a debate on human rights in such wars.

13.3 Terrorism and "trans-national" conflicts

Including the "Global War on Terrorism" (or "War on Terror"), as propagated by the United States after the terrorist attacks of 11 September 2001 on US soil, under the rubric "new wars in need of new rules" necessitates some qualifications. Most importantly, one needs to remember that the reasons for the Bush administration to argue for this type of war was not so much the legitimate demand for self-defence but turned out to be a means of exploiting alleged loopholes in the law, so as to conduct operations of a kind and in a way which were, and remain, to a large extent blatantly unlawful under international law.[30] Advocating such a war was not meant to thoughtfully adjust the existing normative framework to the fight against terrorism or to advocate the creation of new cosmopolitan rules. Quite to the contrary, the Bush administration's attitude was a far cry from any serious invocation of the law, took away protection from potential victims and exposed inferior military ranks acting upon (allegedly inadequate) rules to accountability for their actions.[31] The damage brought about by this perception of the law and its subsequent distortion has been widely debated and need not be recalled here.[32]

The view that action against internationally operating terrorists outside a clearly established nexus to an armed conflict – as understood by humanitarian law – would constitute a war in the legal sense has rightly and consistently been rejected by the International Committee of the Red Cross (ICRC) and a broad range of scholarly voices.[33] They can rely

[27] See Kaldor, *New and Old Wars* (n. 3) p. 3.

[28] See for this debate and examples in greater detail Thomas G. Weiss, *Humanitarian Intervention* (Cambridge: Polity, 2013), pp. 66–96.

[29] See Kaldor, *New and Old Wars* (n. 3) pp. 120–21.

[30] See for this critique also Sassòli, "The Role of Human Rights and International Humanitarian Law" (n. 22) p. 49, with regard to the arguments made by the proponents of the "War on Terrorism."

[31] Ibid. p. 49, where the author quotes a US defence attorney acting on behalf of a US private accused of torture with the following statement: "The President of the United States doesn't know what the rules are! The Secretary of Defense doesn't know what the rules are. But the government expects this [Private First Class] to know what the rules are?"

[32] See, e.g., Peter G. Danchin, "Human Rights, Humanitarian Law and the "War on Terrorism" in Afghanistan" in Dennis Dijkzeul (ed.), *Between Force and Mercy: Military Action and Humanitarian Aid* (Berlin: Berliner Wissenschaftsverlag, 2004), pp. 109–45.

[33] See, e.g., Gabor Rona, "Interesting Times for International Humanitarian Law: Challenges from the 'War on Terror'" (2003) 2 *Fletcher Forum of World Affairs* 55; and Roberta Arnold, "The New War on Terror: Legal Implications under International Humanitarian Law" in Susan C. Breau and Agnieszka Jachec-Neale, *Testing the Boundaries of International Humanitarian Law* (London: British Institute of International and Comparative Law, 2006), pp. 85–112. For the contrasting view see John B. Bellinger

on the fact that before the "War on Terror" terrorist acts were viewed in state practice and scholarly writing as problems of criminal law and law enforcement and not as constituting an armed conflict.[34] In contrast, the military action against Afghanistan after the attacks of 11 September 2001 and continuing operations against Al-Qaida in Afghanistan and elsewhere were judged by the United States as constituting one single worldwide armed conflict which will continue as appropriate.[35] In 2010, the Legal Adviser in the US State Department, Harold Hongju Koh, confirmed that the United States is still at war with Al-Qaida and associates.[36]

The Bush administration saw international humanitarian law as in principle applicable to this conflict, but denied that terrorists qualify as lawful enemy fighters while at the same time rejecting their civilian status, which resulted in a lack of protection under humanitarian law as well as under human rights law. The latter was not considered applicable to this armed conflict on the grounds of the *lex specialis* nature of humanitarian law and the lack of the extra-territorial reach of the ICCPR. The resulting status of largely unprotected "unlawful enemy combatants" was not accepted in legal doctrine and state practice outside the United States.[37] These are not premises upon which a discussion of terrorism and international law should build. Nor should the rhetoric of war and the constant invocation of a state of emergency in the Western World, which has been introduced in the debate on terrorism after 9/11, be accepted, regardless of how firmly entrenched it has become in politics, scholarship and everyday life.[38] Confronting terrorism remains essentially a matter of criminal law and for law enforcement agents and courts.[39]

Still, the way in which terrorist groups operate across borders has indeed introduced a novel way of violence, and countering this threat may blur the boundaries of law enforcement and war-fighting further in legal theory as well as in practice. Activities in pursuit of terrorist organizations within complex contexts, such as the French military operation in Mali against jihadist non-state armed groups affiliated with terrorist networks in 2013 – "a harbinger of post-modern conflict"[40] – can seemingly not be conducted under a law enforcement paradigm alone, but are also not fully compatible with existing international humanitarian law for international and internal conflicts.

III, "Legal Issues in the War on Terrorism: A Reply to Silja N. Vöneky" (2007) 8(9) *German Yearbook of International Law* 871.

34 See Sassòli, "The Role of Human Rights and International Humanitarian Law" (n. 22) pp. 54–55.

35 For references to various US sources on this matter, including the White House, Memorandum of 7 February 2002, Appendix C to Independent Panel to Review DoD Detention Operations (24 August 2004), see Sassóli, "The Role of Human Rights and International Humanitarian Law" (n. 22) pp. 39–40.

36 See Harold Honju Koh, Speech at the Annual Meeting of the American Society of International Law, Washington DC, 25 March 2010, available at www.state.gov/s/l/releases/remarks/139119.htm (last accessed 15 April 2014).

37 See, e.g., Knut Dörmann, "The Legal Situation of 'Unlawful/Unprivileged Combatants'" (2003) 85(849) *International Review of the Red Cross* 45. In greater detail see also Gabriella Blum and Philip B. Heymann, *Laws, Outlaws, and Terrorists: Lessons from the War on Terrorism* (Cambridge MA: MIT Press, 2010).

38 See the critique by Conor Gearty, "The Superpatriotic Fervour of the Moment" (2008) 28(1) *Oxford Journal of Legal Studies* 183.

39 See Marco Sassòli, "Terrorism and War" (2006) 4(5) *Journal of International Criminal Justice* 956; and Roberta Arnold, "Terrorism in International Humanitarian Law and Human Rights Law" in Roberta Arnold and Noelle Quénivet (eds.), *International Humanitarian Law and Human Rights Law: Towards a Merger in International Law* (Leiden: Nijhoff, 2008), pp. 475–97.

40 See Françoise Heisbourg, "A Surprising Little War: First Lessons of Mali" (2013) 55(2) *Survival: Global Politics and Strategy* 7.

Such "transnational" conflict scenarios have led to suggestions for a new legal regime to capture such situations.[41]

The contours of such a regime remain unclear but the argument that "when a situation of extra-state violence exists, the laws of peace arguably become irrelevant"[42] shows the direction in which some would wish to steer such a potentially emerging legal regime. But the view that conducting anti-terrorist operations under the laws of peace – to which human rights law seemingly belongs – is a "utopian aspiration"[43] mistakenly builds on the view of the exceptional nature of the US approach to international terrorism and ignores that many other states (and, as of late, also the United States) apply precisely such "laws of peace" (i.e., national and international criminal law in conjunction with international and national human rights law) to countering terrorist threats and responding to terrorist attacks. Actions taken against terrorist threats by the United Kingdom and Spanish authorities before and after 9/11, for example, were not qualified as constituting an armed conflict.[44]

Rather, if such a new legal framework against terrorism as a "transnational" conflict were to emerge, it would not only have to include but build on a joint application of human rights and humanitarian law. It would have to work on the presumption that human rights law is the main applicable law to which, if necessary, rules of humanitarian law could be added, depending on the circumstances. This new law should contain, as has rightly been suggested, more stringent rules on targeting, which curtail the collateral damage done to civilians in such regulations, and thus needs to be modelled along law enforcement operations.[45] This makes the predominant position of international human rights law indispensible.

13.4 War-fighting and law enforcement

The paradigmatic differences between war-fighting and law enforcement have already been discussed with regard to the right to life, but it is obvious that they run through the debate on human rights in armed conflict like a red thread. The way in which the UN Charter has prohibited war – apart from self-defence and under a mandate of the UN Security Council – has changed the image of war altogether. The Charter conveyed the idea that a war can be lawful only against a law-breaker. Consequently, international policing and human security missions have begun to replace what used to be seen as a contest of nation states. This challenges the legal framework of war: "[a]s the character of armed conflict changes into one characterized best as law enforcement actions, so too should the law governing the conduct of armed conflict."[46]

The debate on human rights in armed conflict is thus not only a matter of legal theory but a confrontation between advocates of a human rights-oriented law enforcement paradigm

41 See Roy S. Schöndorf, "Extra-State Armed Conflicts: Is there a Need for a New Legal Regime?" (2004) 37(1) *New York University Journal of International Law and Politics* 1, 61–62; and Geoffrey S. Corn and Eric Talbot Jensen, "Transnational Armed Conflict: A 'Principled' Approach to the Regulation of Counter-Terror Combat Operations" (2009) 42(1) *Israel Law Review* 46.

42 Schöndorf, "Extra-State Armed Conflict" (n. 41) 21. 43 Ibid. 28.

44 See Hilaire McCoubrey and Nigel D. White, *International Law and Armed Conflict* (Aldershot: Ashgate, 1992), p. 318.

45 Schöndorf, "Extra-State Armed Conflict" (n. 41) 62–68.

46 Francisco Forrest Martin, "Using International Human Rights Law for Establishing a Unified Use of Force Rule in the Law of Armed Conflict" (2001) 64 *Sasketchewan Law Review* 353.

and a security-oriented armed conflict paradigm.[47] They find it hard to agree: while proponents of the human-rights oriented view accuse the other side of clinging to yesterday's concepts of war as a means of politics, supporters of a security-oriented view accuse their opponents of distorting and hijacking established legal concepts to argue a cause unsupported by state practice and *opinio juris*. But the variegated ways in which the ideas of law enforcement and war-fighting conflate are not created by those arguing for a greater role of human rights in armed conflict. Nor can such new types of conflicts be put back into the conventional storage spaces of humanitarian law by even the staunchest defenders of its purity. They reflect larger processes which the law needs to take into account so as not to slide into irrelevance, a concern upon which both sides of the debate will easily agree.

The boundary between law enforcement and military action with their respective frameworks of human rights and humanitarian law seems, for better or worse, "ever less tenable."[48] A range of complex war situations exist and more may well be added as geopolitical forces are reshaped, societies change and technologies develop. They include complex situations such as in the Great Lakes region in central Africa with its mix of international armed conflicts, civil war, ethnic conflict and internal violence, international organized criminal activities and the exploitation of natural resources by non-state armed actors in fragile and collapsing states.[49] Situations such as in Iraq also demonstrate the often ignored link between war and organized crime. The dissolution of the Iraqi army in 2003, for example, had allowed the existing criminal structures of Iraq to open up, and those wielding power as a consequence could hire criminals and jobless young people with no prospects and hook up with organized terrorist networks to finance and sustain their activities against the occupying forces with oil-smuggling and kidnapping of foreigners (a crime which rose from 1 per cent of all recorded crimes to 70 per cent in 2004 and which insurgents often outsourced to independent criminals).[50] Other cases of blurring law enforcement and war-fighting are the anti-piracy operations off the coast of Somalia,[51] the internal violence in the Mexican "drug war,"[52] and the mix of military force and community policing in the clearing of Brazilian *favelas*.[53] They are, at least in some aspects,

[47] See Yuval Shany, "Human Rights and Humanitarian Law as Competing Legal Paradigms for Fighting Against Terror" in Orna Ben-Naftali (ed.), *International Humanitarian and International Human Rights Law* (Oxford: Oxford University Press, 2011), pp. 14–24 and 33, where the author argues for a mixed paradigm comprising elements of armed conflict and law enforcement to read, as much as possible, elements of human rights law into the laws of war.

[48] Kennedy, *On Law and War* (n. 3) p. 113.

[49] See Filip Reyntjens, *The Great African War: Congo and Regional Geopolitics, 1996–2006* (Cambridge: Cambridge University Press, 2011); and René Lemarchand, *The Dynamics of Violence in Central Africa* (Philadelphia, PA: University of Pennsylvania Press, 2009).

[50] See Coker, *War in an Age of Risks* (n. 9) p. 124.

[51] See, e.g., Douglas Guilfoyle, "The Legal Challenges in Fighting Piracy" in Bibi van Ginkel and Frans-Paul van der Putten (eds.), *The International Response to Somali Piracy: Challenges and Opportunities* (Leiden: Nijhoff, 2010), pp. 127–52.

[52] See Patrick Gallahue, "Mexico's 'War on Drugs': Real or Rhetorical Armed Conflict?" (2011) 24(1) *Journal of International Law of Peace and Armed Conflict* 39; and Carina Bergal, "The Mexican Drug War: The Case for a Non-International Armed Conflict Classification" (2011) 34(4) *Fordham International Law Journal* 1042.

[53] See Richard Bennett, *Asserting the Presence of the State, One Step at a Time: Rio de Janeiro, Brazil, 2008–2010*, Innovations for Successful Societies Policy Note (Princeton, NJ: Princeton University Press, 2011), available at www.princeton.edu/successfulsocieties/content/focusareas/PL/policynotes/view.xml?id=139 (last accessed 15 April 2014) and Carlos Iván Fuentes, *The Applicability of International Humanitarian Law to Situations of Urban Violence: Are Cities Turning into War Zones?*, McGill University Centre for Human Rights and Legal

less than war but more than law enforcement, if not under the law than at least in public perception.

The idea of law enforcement is also penetrating "traditional" means and methods of warfare. In some situations the military is being restructured operationally along a policing model altogether. The US military, for example, has adopted policing-style models of operations where special forces replace large infantry battalions, which includes the use of infestation tactics to deploy personnel deeper and longer into the field so as to establish links with the population, and a redirection of weapons technique from grand weapons system to means which provide security on the ground, such as hand-held reconnaissance drones, individual electronic shields and remote-controlled bomb-disposal robots.[54]

The emergence of international criminal responsibility and the subsequent need to bring accused to criminal tribunals such as the International Criminal Tribunal for the Former Yugoslavia (ICTY), has led to setting up "'snatch squads" – military units which, in all but name, act like police forces in bringing alleged perpetrators of crimes to justice. Where this happens outside the agreed jurisdictional reach of international criminal justice for war crimes, genocide and crimes against humanity (as provided in the Statutes of ad hoc criminal tribunals and in the ICC Statute), the boundaries between war-fighting and law enforcement are blurred. Examples are the ways in which coalition armed forces (and in particular their military police units) and local police cooperate to capture criminals who are unconnected to any insurgency and do not pose a threat to the armed forces or an Occupying Power, but still play a role in the larger criminal war economy of drug or arms trade.[55]

All such policing-style methods of warfare and innovative counter-insurgency campaigns, as advocated and implemented, for example, by the United States in Afghanistan, stress the importance of understanding, emphasizing with and exploiting local conditions and, as an operational consequence, accepting and adapting to local culture. Indeed, "cultural competence" is the buzzword in the US counter-insurgency strategy in Afghanistan, and the very word "culture" is mentioned 187 times in the US army's counter-insurgency field manual of 2007.[56] In contrast, the term "human rights" is mentioned only eighteen times in the publication (and where it is, without any substantial reference to international human rights law), and is omitted altogether in the index. It is obvious that while some paradigmatic characteristics of human rights are seen as useful, the language and law of human rights is still difficult to accept.

13.5 Armed force in peace support operations

In contrast, the role of human rights in peace support operations has attracted widespread interest since the first UN mandated peace-keeping operations, and their importance in such operations is widely acknowledged.[57] While they obviously cannot be considered

Pluralism Working Paper (26 February 2008), available at http://ssrn.com/abstract=1134123 (last accessed 15 April 2014).

54 See Coker, *War in an Age of Risks* (n. 9) pp. 160–64. 55 Ibid. p. 162.

56 See US Army Marine Corps, *Counterinsurgency Field Manual* (Chicago, IL: University of Chicago Press, 2007). See also Coker, *War in an Age of Risks* (n. 9) p. 163.

57 See Mary Katanayagi, *Human Rights Functions of United Nations Peacekeeping Operations* (The Hague: Nijhoff, 2002); and Sylvia Maus, "Human Rights in Peacekeeping Missions: A Framework for Humanitarian Obligations?" in Hans-Joachim Heintze and Andrej Zwitter (eds.), *International*

armed conflicts, given the consent of states in their creation, the interplay of human rights and humanitarian law may arise even in such missions, when armed force is being used in a way or to an extent that keeping the peace gives way to enforcing this very peace. First and foremost, respect for human rights in peace-keeping operations is not an add-on but reflects the very nature and rationale of such operations. The rights of civilians become the direct obligation of the members of the armed force operating under UN mandate.[58] The Capstone Doctrine on UN Peacekeeping Operations, a core document in this area, refers to human rights and international humanitarian law as constituent elements in the legal framework which governs such operations. Understanding human rights, training in human rights, recognizing and responding to human rights violations, respecting human rights and acting in accordance with human rights are seen as intrinsic elements of peace-keeping operations.[59]

Human rights are part of practically all recent peace operations mandated by the UN Security Council. They are institutionalized, in a joint effort by the UN Office of the High Commissioner and the UN Department of Peacekeeping Operations, in human rights components of peace operations which are tasked with monitoring the human rights situation, preventing and redressing human rights violations, reporting on human rights issues and assisting in building national capacities to address human rights problems.[60]

But the legal framework of such operations remains a patchwork. Since the first peace-keeping operations it was particularly contested if humanitarian law would be applicable to military activities carried out by peace-keeping troops.[61] While classic peace-keeping operations required the consent of the state concerned and allowed the use of force only in self-defence and were thus unlikely to result in hostilities to which humanitarian law would apply, this has changed with the creation of ever more robust peace operations. Today, broader concepts such as crisis management operations, peace enforcement and peace support and stabilization operations have supplemented or replaced peace-keeping operations with their traditional mandate of keeping a fragile truce between parties to a conflict.[62] Their purpose includes the use of force beyond self-defence and thus mirrors the idea of law enforcement operation. But in a fragile environment such operations may easily be confronted with a blurring of the lines between a law enforcement paradigm and

Humanitarian Law and Humanitarian Assistance: A Crosscut through Legal Issues Pertaining to Humanitarianism (Berlin: Springer, 2011), pp. 104–28.

58 See Peter Rowe, *The Impact of Human Rights Law on Armed Forces* (Cambridge: Cambridge University Press, 2006), pp. 224 and 232.

59 See *United Nations Peacekeeping Operations: Principles and Guidelines* (New York, United Nations, 2008), pp. 13–16. See also Wolfgang Benedek, "Mainstreaming Human Security in United Nations and European Union Peace and Crisis Management Operations: Policies and Practice" in Wolfgang Benedek, Matthias C. Kettemann and Markus Möstl (eds.), *Mainstreaming Human Security in Peace Operations and Crisis Management: Policies, Problems, Potential* (London: Routledge, 2010), pp. 13–31.

60 For details on the human rights components of UN peace-keeping operations see Office of the High Commissioner for Human Rights, Strategic Management Plan, pp. 63–123, available at www.ohchr.org/Documents/Press/SMP2010-2011.pdf (last accessed 15 April 2014).

61 See Daphne Shraga, "UN Peacekeeping Operations: Applicability of International Humanitarian Law and Responsibility for Operations-Related Damage" (2000) 94(2) *American Journal of International Law* 406; and Satish Nambiar, "Applicability of International Humanitarian Law to United Nations Peace Operations" in V.S. Mani (ed.), *Handbook of International Humanitarian Law* (New Delhi: Oxford University Press, 2007), pp. 217–30.

62 See Gert-Jan F. van Hegelsom, "The Law of Armed Conflict and UN Peace-Keeping and Peace-Enforcing Operations" (1993) 6 *Hague Yearbook of International Law* 45.

war-fighting within their overall mandate to provide human security and guarantee human rights.[63]

Security Council Resolution 2098 on the Democratic Republic of the Congo (DRC), adopted in March 2013, for example, breathes the spirit of such robust peace-making and adds to the legal and political complexity of UN peace operations. In fact, it seems to introduce an altogether new type of peace operation as it sets up the first-ever UN "Intervention Brigade" with an offensive combat mandate to "neutraliz[e] armed groups"[64] in the DRC. The Brigade is meant to operate in a:

> robust, highly mobile and versatile manner and in strict compliance with international law, including international humanitarian law and with the human rights due diligence policy on UN-support to non-UN forces (HRDDP), to prevent the expansion of all armed groups, neutralize these groups, and to disarm them in order to contribute to the objective of reducing the threat posed by armed groups on state authority and civilian security in eastern DRC.[65]

This brings robust peace-keeping to a new level but does little to remedy the resulting uneasy *mélange* of norms, which is a problem of profound practical significance.[66] International human rights law is obviously the appropriate legal framework when troops are engaged in crowd and riot control, ensuring public order and safety and confronting criminal activities. But humanitarian law may come into play whenever troops go beyond defending themselves and/or assist one party to the conflict, in which case they may be seen as engaging in hostilities governed by international humanitarian law without, however, being able to renounce their human rights-based mandate.[67]

But given that the multi-national forces deployed effectively act as law enforcement agents of the international community, they cannot be bound by the same rules as their opponents who are, by definition, law-breakers. Troop-contributing states are obviously also interested in not seeing members of their armed forces as combatants, given that this would possibly allow enemy armed forces to lawfully attack them. As a consequence, they usually seek to distinguish the application of humanitarian law for protective purposes from the question of combatant status, which is a problem, given that the two are logically intertwined.[68] In practice, the UN has accepted international humanitarian law as applicable to UN peace-keeping forces but details on this application have been left

[63] On the way this combines *jus in bello* and *jus ad bellum* considerations, see Sassòli, "The Role of Human Rights and International Humanitarian Law" (n. 22) p. 43.

[64] Security Council Res. 2098, UN Doc. S/RES/2098 (28 March 2013), para. 9, which reads in full "Decides ... that MONUSCO [United Nations Organization Stabilization Mission in the Democratic Republic of the Congo] shall ... on an exceptional basis and without creating a precedent or any prejudice to the agreed principles of peacekeeping, include an 'Intervention Brigade' consisting *inter alia* of three infantry battalions, one artillery and one Special Force and Reconnaissance company ... with the responsibility of neutralizing armed groups."

[65] Security Council Res. 2098, UN Doc. S/RES/2098 (28 March 2013), para. 12(b).

[66] Sassòli, "The Role of Human Rights and International Humanitarian Law" (n. 22) p. 43.

[67] See Sylvain Vité, "Typology of Armed Conflicts in International Humanitarian Law: Legal Concepts and Actual Situations" (2009) 91(873) *International Review of the Red Cross* 87.

[68] See in support of this view and for this unsettled question in general Sassòli, "The Role of Human Rights and International Humanitarian Law" (n. 22) pp. 43–45.

open.[69] The UN Secretary-General's Bulletin of 1999 remains the guideline.[70] It clarifies that:

> [t]he fundamental principles and rules of international humanitarian law set out in the present bulletin are applicable to United Nations forces when in situations of armed conflict they are actively engaged therein as combatants, to the extent and for the duration of their engagement.[71]

But the Bulletin does not give a full list of such applicable humanitarian rules, whether as treaty or customary law, nor does it clarify the legal basis for such application of humanitarian law. It is thus usually seen as a reaffirmation of general principles and as a teaching tool, but not as a unilateral legal act of the UN.[72] It also remains unclear if the "active engagement" in combat relates to any acts taken without the consent of the host state, or when force is used regularly, or when a conflict reaches a certain threshold of violence. It also leaves open which mechanism should be used to ensure the accountability of UN forces for violations of humanitarian law.[73]

There is thus little clarity on the incorporation of international humanitarian law in peace support operations, even though virtually all such recent operations seem to accept the complementarity or even fusion of human rights and humanitarian law in mission planning, preparation, training and conduct.[74] This obviously includes the extra-territorial application of human rights in such situations.[75] But the so-called "Mogadishu line,"[76] i.e., the question when peace operations need to be guided by a humanitarian law-driven approach to establish supremacy and security before engaging in peace-building measures, or whether a human rights-based approach of conflict-solving and capacity-building should prevail in unstable post-conflict situations, remains a problem.

In reality, the constant shift between the two approaches ("hunting a Taliban IED [improvised explosive device] layer one day, ... assisting in building a school the next day")[77] is an operational issue as much as a challenge for the mind-set of members of armed

[69] See Walter Kälin and Jörg Künzli, *The Law of International Human Rights Protection* (Oxford: Oxford University Press, 2009), pp. 150–51.

[70] United Nations Secretary General's Bulletin, Observance by United Nations Forces of International Humanitarian Law, UN Doc. ST/SGB/1999/13 (6 August 1999). The Brahimi Report does not specifically refer to humanitarian law, see *Report of the Panel on United Nations Peace Operations*, UN Doc. A/55/305 and S/2000/809 (21 August 2000); and Peter F. Chapman, "Ensuring Respect: United Nations Compliance with International Humanitarian Law" (2009) 17 *Human Rights Brief* 1, 3, available at www.wcl.american.edu/hrbrief/17/1chapman.pdf (last accessed 15 April 2014).

[71] UN Secretary General's Bulletin, Art. 1(1).

[72] See Marten Zwanenburg, *Accountability of Peace Support Operations* (Leiden: Nijhoff, 2005), pp. 173–74.

[73] See Chapman, "Ensuring Respect" (n. 70) p. 4.

[74] See Katarina Mansson, "Implementing the Concept of Protection of Civilians in the Light of International Humanitarian Law and Human Rights Law: The Case of MONUC" in Roberta Arnold and Noelle Quénivet, *International Humanitarian Law and Human Rights Law: Towards a Merger in International Law* (Leiden: Nijhoff, 2008), pp. 589–90.

[75] See Kälin and Künzli, *The Law of International Human Rights Protection* (n. 69) p. 150.

[76] See Rob McLaughlin, "The Law of Armed Conflict and International Human Rights Law: Some Paradigmatic Differences and Operational Implications" (2010) 13 *Yearbook of International Humanitarian Law* 229, with reference to General Sir Michael Rose's description of the dividing line between peace-keeping and war-fighting in UN mandated peace operations.

[77] Ibid. 230.

forces engaged in peace support operations. The associated question of the attribution of responsibility is equally unsettled in law and practice: can violations of (human rights and humanitarian) law be attributed to the troop contributing state(s) or to the United Nations? In situations where the United Nations effectively administers post-conflict territory, as was the case in East Timor or Kosovo, the balance is likely to tilt further towards human rights law, as the absence of conflict or occupation leaves no space for humanitarian law.[78]

[78] See Tobias H. Irmscher, "The Legal Framework for the Activities of the United Nations Administration Mission in Kosovo: The Charter, Human Rights, and the Law of Occupation" (2001) 44 *German Yearbook of International Law* 375. See also (more critical) Marco Sassòli, "Legislation and Maintenance of Public Order and Civil Life by Occupying Powers" (2005) 16(4) *European Journal of International Law* 691–93.

14

Governing internal armed violence

14.1 Towards a human rights law of internal armed conflicts?

As discussed earlier, the law of non-international armed conflicts, as laid down in Common Article 3 of the Geneva Conventions and later in Additional Protocol II of 1977, and as still largely expressed in customary law, is strongly influenced by human rights law and borrows from its language. This seems comprehensible, because such conflicts usually occur on the territory of a state and involve questions of how a government relates to those under its jurisdiction, albeit in hostilities. Given that an internal armed conflict is (at least mostly) confined to the territory of a given state, the extra-territorial application of human rights is also less of a problem ("internationalized" conflicts which spill across borders or involve non-state actors on various territories notwithstanding).

And because the law of non-international armed conflict provides only for minimum guarantees, the argument that it is *lex specialis* is also less tenable than in international armed conflicts. At the same time, it has repeatedly been highlighted that the lower level of protection under humanitarian law is legally illogical as well as morally reprehensible: "[w]hat is inhumane, and consequently proscribed, in international wars, cannot but be inhumane and inadmissible in civil strife."[1] This leaves potentially more space for human rights to fill gaps.[2]

The reluctance of states to grant any legal status to rebels or to recognize non-state armed groups as legitimate participants in armed conflicts, their treatment as criminals under domestic law and their unclear status under international law, together with the fragile legal construct of belligerency as well as the concern that external intervention in internal conflicts would adversely affect the territorial integrity and sovereignty of states affected by civil wars, worked together to prevent a clear legal framework for internal armed conflicts.[3] At the same time, the humanitarian problems created by such conflicts were all too obvious and called for regulation in a way comparable to international armed conflicts. But only in 1921 did the Tenth International Conference of the Red Cross adopt a resolution

[1] *Prosecutor* v. *Tadić*, International Criminal Tribunal for the Former Yugoslavia, IT-94-1-I, Decision on Defence Motion for Interlocutory Appeal on Jurisdiction of 2 October 1995, para. 119.

[2] See Noam Lubell, "Challenges in Applying Human Rights Law to Armed Conflict" (2005) 87(860) *International Review of the Red Cross* 738, 746; and Lindsay Moir, *The Law of Internal Armed Conflict* (Cambridge: Cambridge University Press, 2002), pp. 193–231.

[3] On the historic development of the law of internal armed conflict and the foundational values and considerations see Rosemary Abi-Saab, "Humanitarian Law and Internal Conflicts: The Evolution of Legal Concern" in Astrid J.M. Delissen and Gerard J. Tanja (eds.), *Humanitarian Law of Armed Conflict: Challenges Ahead, Essays in Honour of Frits Kalshoven* (Dordrecht: Nijhoff, 1991), pp. 209–23.

to deal with this matter, and only in 1949 was a first international regulation (Common Article 3 of the Geneva Conventions) adopted, as a single paragraph for internal armed conflicts. Additional Protocol II of 1977 more or less successfully sought to increase the level of protection available in such situations but, as a consequence, the existence of different legal frameworks poses problems for the systemic coherence of the law.[4]

Over the past decades, the law of non-international armed conflicts has undergone dramatic changes. Some saw it (in a paraphrasing of Hersch Lauterpacht's famous dictum of international humanitarian law as being at the vanishing point of international law) as the "vanishing point of international humanitarian law."[5] But gradually the uncertainty over the applicable rules gave way to a more solid corpus of treaty and customary law which governs internal conflicts.[6] Three intertwined developments have led to this situation:[7] first, the assimilation of internal and international conflicts in terms of the protection of civilians through the identification of customary rules applicable in internal conflicts. The fact that 149 of the 161 rules of the ICRC study on customary humanitarian law are applicable in non-international conflicts speaks a clear language in this regard.[8] Secondly, the rise of international criminal law and the emergence of international criminal jurisprudence, particularly through the ICTY, also contributed to fill this gap.[9] The third factor (which is of interest here) is the increased reliance on international human rights law. Over a relatively short period of time an "international law of internal armed conflict"[10] has thus emerged. This is all the more important because non-international armed conflicts (and their derivates "internationalized" and "transnational" armed conflicts) have increased dramatically, and in the near absence of traditional international armed conflicts represent today's standard type of armed conflict. This makes their regulation, and with it the question of the role of human rights in such situation, an ever more pressing issue.[11]

How the two paradigmatic approaches – assimilating the law of internal armed conflicts with the law of international armed conflicts or drawing on international human rights law – can be reconciled, is not clear. The first approach (borrowing from humanitarian law for international armed conflicts) is informed by the idea that what is prohibited in international armed conflicts should not be allowed in internal armed conflicts. It has led to an ever greater rapprochement of the law of international and non-international armed

[4] See Frits Kalshoven, "Applicability of Customary International Law to Non-International Armed Conflicts" in Antonio Cassese (ed.), *Current Problems of International Law, Essays on U.N. Law and on the Law of Armed Conflict* (Milano: Giuffrè, 1975), pp. 276–85.

[5] David Turns, "At the 'Vanishing Point' of International Humanitarian Law: Methods and Means of Warfare in Non-International Armed Conflicts" (2002) 45 *German Yearbook of International Law* 115.

[6] See International Institute of Humanitarian Law, *The Manual on the Law of Non-International Armed Conflicts* (Sanremo: International Institute of Humanitarian Law, 2006).

[7] See Sandesh Sivakumaran, "Re-envisaging the International Law of Armed Conflict" (2001) 22(1) *European Journal of International Law* 220.

[8] See *Magazine of the Red Cross and Red Crescent Movement*, available at www.redcross.int/EN/mag/magazine2005_2/24-25.htm (last accessed 15 April 2014).

[9] See, e.g., Christopher Greenwood, "The Development of International Humanitarian Law by the International Criminal Tribunal for the Former Yugoslavia" (1998) 2 *Max Planck Yearbook of United Nations Law* 97.

[10] Sivakumaran, "Re-envisaging the International Law of Armed Conflict" (n. 7) 220.

[11] See Robert Kolb and Richard Hyde, *An Introduction to International Law of Armed Conflict* (Oxford: Hart, 2008), p. 269.

conflict immediately after the Additional Protocols of 1977.[12] The distinction between international and non-international armed conflicts is becoming ever more blurred and gradually waning, as confirmed by the jurisprudence of the ad hoc international criminal tribunals, the view of the International Committee of the Red Cross (ICRC), the approach of the Security Council and the Statute of the International Criminal Court (ICC). In other words, more (customary) humanitarian law (of international armed conflict) is inserted into the law of internal armed conflicts and core rules for international armed conflicts are now routinely applied to non-international ones, be it in state practice, jurisprudence or legal writing.[13]

The alternative approach (to rely on international human rights law to fill in the gaps in the law of non-international armed conflict) effectively allows human rights law to regulate such situations directly. While the inclusion of rules of international armed conflicts assimilates internal violence with wars between states (and introduces problems of its own), the use of human rights law introduces a law enforcement paradigm into the confrontation between the government and non-state actors (or re-enforces it). It also means that the co-application of human rights norms in such situations is a more pressing issue than in international armed conflicts.[14] The emergence of such a "human rights law of internal armed conflict"[15] which effectively competes with the idea of relying on customary humanitarian law remains disputed, and state practice and jurisprudence are not conclusive on this question.

The idea of such a human rights law of internal armed conflict can be presented in two forms: one can imagine a fusing of all rules for all internal violence regardless of its qualification under humanitarian law. Such a unified use of force framework would cover all forms of violence, from peace-time disorder to civil wars, regardless of their intensity.[16] It would, however, do away with the boundary between internal violence and internal armed conflict, which is not only recognized in humanitarian treaty law but also an essential component of triggering the very application of humanitarian law.[17] Alternatively, a threshold approach suggests using the intensity of internal violence as the benchmark:

[12] W.A. Solf, "Problems with the Application of Norms Governing Interstate Armed Conflicts to Non-International Armed Conflicts" (1983) 13 *Georgia Journal of International and Comparative Law* 291.

[13] See Lubell, "Challenges in Applying Human Rights Law" (n. 2) 747; and Theodor Meron, *The Humanization of International Law* (Leiden: Nijhoff, 2006), pp. 31–33.

[14] See, e.g., Marco Sassòli and Laura M. Olson, "The Relationship between International Humanitarian Law and Human Rights Law Where it Matters: Admissible Killing and Internment of Fighters in Non-international Armed Conflicts" (2008) 90(871) *International Review of the Red Cross* 603; Heike Krieger, "A Conflict of Norms: The Relationship between Humanitarian Law and Human Rights Law in the ICRC Customary Law Study" (2006) 11(2) *Journal of Conflict and Security Law* 273; and Cordula Droege, "Elective Affinities? Human Rights and Humanitarian Law" (2008) 90(871) *International Review of the Red Cross* 527.

[15] See William Abresch, "A Human Rights Law of Internal Armed Conflict: The European Court of Human Rights in Chechnya" (2005) 16(4) *European Journal of International Law* 749. The term will be of interest again with regard to the approach of the European Court of Human Rights discussed later.

[16] See Abresch, "A Human Rights Law of Internal Armed Conflict" (n. 15) 752–57; and Francisco Forrest Martin, "Using International Human Rights Law for Establishing a Unified Use of Force Rule in the Law of Armed Conflict" (2001) 64 *Sasketchewan Law Review* 372.

[17] See Additional Protocol II, Art. 1(2): "This Protocol shall not apply to situations of internal disturbances and tensions, such as riots, isolated and sporadic acts of violence and other acts of a similar nature, as not being armed conflicts."

low-intensity conflicts would be governed (more) by human rights law and high-intensity conflicts (more) by humanitarian law.[18]

While this would do (more) justice to the intent of states and reflect state practice, it introduces artificial dividing lines along the intensity of a conflict which lack sufficient clarity in (humanitarian) customary and treaty law. Additional Protocol II, Article 1(2) may remain a guiding beacon in this respect, but state practice is not encouraging so that in reality the boundaries remain blurred.

Both the unified and threshold approach would be fundamental shifts in regulating non-international armed conflicts.[19] But the grey zone between violence below and above that threshold which results from the respective provision of humanitarian law[20] is notorious, as is the tendency of states to deny the existence of an internal armed conflict altogether without much legal justification. The "threshold approach" is thus confronted with particular problems in practice.[21]

A further approach – to distil only principles from human rights and humanitarian law and identify fundamental norms applicable in all situations of violence in a non-binding document which provides operational guidance – has been tried in the Turku Declaration on Minimum Humanitarian Standards and has failed to attract sufficient support, as discussed above. In light of the reluctance of states to put their faith in such an approach, and given that state practice has already filled some of the gaps which were the initial driving force for the whole process, the Declaration no longer serves as a model.

In light of the difficulty, if not impossibility, of clearly discerning low-level intensity emergencies from high-level intensity conflicts, it remains questionable whether the applicable legal regimes can be neatly separated into international human rights law for the former category and international humanitarian law for the latter. It is also unclear what would be gained if human rights law alone would be regulating an internal armed conflict, given that the gaps in customary law which were still apparent in the years after 1977 have largely been closed.[22] Again, it seems more appropriate to apply human rights and humanitarian law concurrently and as a continuum so as to acknowledge and appropriately respond to the fluidity of such conflict situations and avoid legal gaps in the protection.[23] Such a "smooth passage from the law guaranteeing respect for human rights in peacetime to the rules established to protect humanitarian concerns in time of internal violence"[24] seems to reflect the complementarity of human rights and humanitarian law even though it would, once more, trade in doctrinal stringency for a case-by-case assessment of the applicable law.

[18] See Gloria Gaggioli and Robert Kolb, "A Right to Life in Armed Conflict? The Contribution of the European Court of Human Rights" (2007) 37 *Israel Yearbook on Human Rights* 158.

[19] See Sandesh Sivakumaran, *The Law of Non-International Armed Conflict* (Oxford: Oxford University Press, 2012), p. 94.

[20] Additional Protocol II, Art. 1(2): "1(2). This Protocol shall not apply to situations of internal disturbances and tensions, such as riots, isolated and sporadic acts of violence and other acts of a similar nature, as not being armed conflicts."

[21] See Sivakumaran, *The Law of Non-International Armed Conflict* (n. 19) p. 98. [22] Ibid. pp. 98–99.

[23] See Oren Gross and Fionnuala Ní Aoláin, *Law in Times of Crisis: Emergency Powers in Theory and Practice* (Cambridge: Cambridge University Press, 2006), pp. 363–64.

[24] Hans-Peter Gasser, "International Humanitarian Law and Human Rights Law in Non-International Armed Conflict: Joint Venture or Mutual Exclusion?" (2002) 45 *German Yearbook of International Law* 158.

14.2 Role of non-state actors

(a) Legal obligations of non-state actors in armed conflicts

In contrast to human rights law which confers obligations only on states parties to human rights treaties, international humanitarian law imposes obligations on all parties to a conflict, including non-state armed groups.[25] Under humanitarian law, conferring rights and duties on non-state actors was originally informed by the idea of belligerency. Under this legal doctrine, insurgents were entitled to a degree of recognition and subsequent entitlements under international law once they were formally recognized as belligerents. This doctrine of formal recognition has fallen into desuetude, so that today non-state actors are directly obliged under international humanitarian law without the requirement of being recognized as belligerents.[26] In non-international armed conflicts, international humanitarian law applies to all parties to the conflict,[27] and national liberation movements can accept the application of the Geneva Conventions and Additional Protocols under Additional Protocol I, Article 96(3).[28] The Protocol does not explicitly refer to the "parties to the conflict," unlike Common Article 3 of the Geneva Conventions. These words have been deleted in the drafting process for fear of elevating the legal status of insurgents. But the rules of the Protocol "grant the same rights and impose the same duties on both the established government and the insurgent party."[29] The capacity of non-state actors to adhere to the provisions of Additional Protocol II is also a requirement for its application.[30]

Such direct conferral of international obligations is not meant to turn non-state actors into subjects of international law, as the final sentence of Common Article 3 of the Geneva Conventions makes clear.[31] While this accommodates the states' view that insurgencies, rebellions and other attempts to overthrow the government in power remain unlawful acts under domestic law and anyone participating in such acts is liable to criminal prosecution, it

[25] See in detail Jann K. Kleffner, "The Applicability of International Humanitarian Law to Organized Armed Groups" (2011) 93(882) *International Review of the Red Cross* 443; and Sandesh Sivakumaran, "Binding Armed Opposition Groups" (2006) 55 *International and Comparative Law Quarterly* 369.

[26] See, e.g., Ingrid Detter, *The Law of War* (Cambridge: Cambridge University Press, 2000), p. 43.

[27] Geneva Conventions, Common Art. 3: "In the case of armed conflict not of an international character occurring in the territory of one of the High Contracting Parties, each Party to the conflict shall be bound to apply, as a minimum, the following provisions." Article 19 of the 1954 Hague Convention on the Protection of Cultural Property repeats these words and also applies to non-state actors in non-international armed conflicts.

[28] Additional Protocol I, Art. 96(3): "The authority representing a people engaged against a High Contracting Party in an armed conflict of the type referred to in Article 1, paragraph 4, may undertake to apply the Conventions and this Protocol in relation to that conflict by means of a unilateral declaration addressed to the depositary."

[29] Yves Sandoz, Christophe Swinarski and Bruno Zimmermann (eds.), *Commentary on the Additional Protocols of 8 June 1977 to the Geneva Conventions of 12 August 1949* (Geneva: Nijhoff, 1987), para. 4442.

[30] Additional Protocol II, Art. 1(1): "This Protocol . . . shall apply to all armed conflicts . . . which take place in the territory of a High Contracting Party between its armed forces and dissident armed forces or other organized armed groups which, under responsible command, exercise such control over a part of its territory as to enable them to carry out sustained and concerted military operations and to implement this Protocol."

[31] Geneva Conventions, Common Art. 3: "The application of the preceding provisions shall not affect the legal status of the parties to the conflict."

does confer "a curious sort of recognition"[32] to non-state actors. The legal justification for such a conferral of rights on non-state actors, which is otherwise not foreseen under international law, has been explained by different theories: that private individuals are bound by the legal commitments of states of which they are a national; that they (or some of them) are the de facto government; that the effectiveness of the treaty requires the conferral of such obligations; or (most convincingly) that states have specifically consented in international humanitarian law treaties to confer such obligations on non-state actors.[33]

The fact that international humanitarian law directly obliges non-state actors, while human rights law contains no such provisions or doctrinal instructions, leads to fears that applying human rights in armed conflict will effectively reduce the level of protection, as non-state actors can evade such complementary or additional obligations. The ICRC, in particular, is concerned that the increasing application of international human rights law to armed conflicts might be detrimental because it does not bind such actors, who have neither the legal status nor the will nor the capacity to adhere to international human rights law (with the possible exception of some such actors which exercise sufficient control over territory).[34]

These concerns are accurate and serious but the argument of the comparative advantage of humanitarian law on this matter seems nevertheless exaggerated. It assumes that humanitarian law is easily applicable to all parties to the conflict, which is obviously not the case in any asymmetrical armed conflict (as the ICRC is well aware, of course, and to which it responds by taking great efforts to reach out to non-state armed groups.)[35] The stronger and the weaker side in such asymmetrical conflicts are likely to take different approaches towards their obligations under humanitarian law and the inferior side, in particular, may be inclined to violate humanitarian law to make up for its weaker status and counter the omnipotence of the enemy. And where states with overwhelming military power are involved, every conflict is likely to be asymmetrical.[36] The basic tenets of humanitarian law simply do not work well in asymmetric conflicts: regular armed forces have no equivalent counterpart and conduct "warfare without the possibility of chivalry."[37]

Non-state armed groups often lack the necessary structures, and the absence of discipline, hierarchy, communication procedures and organization can make it difficult to adhere to

[32] Andrew Clapham, "Human Rights Obligations of Non-State Actors in Conflict Situations" (2006) 88(863) *International Review of the Red Cross* 496.

[33] See on the various views and their representatives Clapham, "Human Rights Obligations of Non-State Actors in Conflict Situations" (n. 32) 498–99. On the latter theory see, in particular, Liesbeth Zegveld, *Accountability of Armed Opposition Groups in International Law* (Cambridge: Cambridge University Press, 2002), p. 17.

[34] See International Committee of the Red Cross, *International Humanitarian Law and the Challenges of Contemporary Armed Conflicts, Report to the 31st International Conference of the Red Cross and Red Crescent* (2011), pp. 14–15.

[35] See Vincent Bernard, "Editorial: Engaging Armed Groups" (2011) 93(883) *International Review of the Red Cross* 581, and the contributions contained in that issue.

[36] Indeed, the (unacceptable) argument has already been made that the United States cannot adhere fully to international humanitarian law in such asymmetrical conflicts if it wants to defeat the enemy. On this proposal see (dismissive) Marco Sassòli, "The Role of Human Rights and International Humanitarian Law in New Types of Armed Conflicts" in Orna Ben-Naftali (ed.), *International Humanitarian and International Human Rights Law* (Oxford: Oxford University Press, 2011), p. 36.

[37] Paul Kahn, "The Paradox of Riskless Warfare" (2002) 22(3) *Philosophy and Public Policy Quarterly* 4.

humanitarian law.[38] And when such conflicts are perceived as law enforcement or policing operations against a morally or legally "guilty" party, any equality of the parties is lost for good.[39] The situation is complicated by the fact that more and more customary rules of international armed conflicts are deemed applicable in non-international conflicts, which also expands the range of rules which non-state groups need to be able to uphold. At the same time, this raises the demands with regard to their internal organization, so that less and less groups qualify as parties to the conflict under humanitarian law.[40] The binding force of humanitarian law on non-state groups is thus neither straightforward in theory nor easily secured in practice; a deplorable fact which, however, mitigates the perceived advantage of humanitarian law over human rights law.

Whether and to which extent non-state actors are bound by human rights obligations remains disputed. Some authors fervently reject the idea that non-state armed groups have human rights obligations. To quote one voice: "Human rights obligations are binding on governments only and the law has not yet reached the stage whereby, during internal armed conflict, insurgents are bound to observe the human rights of government forces, let alone of opposing insurgents."[41] At present, the direct applicability of international human rights law to non-state actors is indeed not fully supported by state practice and legal doctrine.[42] But it seems equally fair to say that the view that only international humanitarian law and not international human rights law applies to non-state actors is "no longer a universally shared assumption."[43] Claims that they have human rights obligations are made by a considerable number of scholars.[44] There is growing awareness that both bodies of law increasingly impose obligations on state and non-state actors, albeit in different contexts and degrees.[45]

The legal grounds for establishing such human rights obligations vary. Where a non-state armed group controls territory or otherwise takes over governmental functions, it may be seen as a government in an embryonic stage which can only claim legitimacy when it shoulders the burden of respecting international norms.[46] This view enjoys the greatest support among the explanations as to why non-state actors should be bound by human

38 See Sassòli, "The Role of Human Rights and International Humanitarian Law" (n. 36) p. 38.

39 See Kahn, "The Paradox of Riskless Warfare" (n. 37) 4.

40 See Sassòli, "The Role of Human Rights and International Humanitarian Law" (n. 36) pp. 58–59.

41 Moir, *The Law of Internal Armed Conflict* (n. 2) p. 194; and similarly Zegveld, *Accountability of Armed Opposition Groups in International Law* (n. 33) p. 53.

42 Sivakumaran, "Re-envisaging the International Law of Armed Conflict" (n. 7) 242.

43 Clapham, "Human Rights Obligations of Non-State Actors in Conflict Situations" (n. 32) 508.

44 See, e.g., Clapham, "Human Rights Obligations of Non-State Actors in Conflict Situations" (n. 32) 491–523; and Jean-Marie Henckaerts and Cornelius Wiesener, "Human Rights Obligations of Non-State Armed Groups: A Possible Contribution from Customary International Law?" in Robert Kolb and Gloria Gaggioli (eds.), *Research Handbook on Human Rights and Humanitarian Law* (Cheltenham: Edward Elgar, 2013), p. 161.

45 United Nations Office of the High Commissioner for Human Rights, *International Legal Protection of Human Rights in Armed Conflict* (New York and Geneva: United Nations, 2011), p. 21. For a similar argument see Dieter Fleck, "Humanitarian Protection against Non-State Actors" in Jochen Abr. Frowein, Klaus Scharioth, Ingo Winkelmann and Rüdiger Wolfrum, *Verhandeln für den Frieden – Negotiating for Peace, Liber Amicorum Tono Eitel* (Berlin: Springer, 2003), p. 79.

46 Christian Tomuschat, "The Applicability of Human Rights Law to Insurgent Movements" in Horst Fischer, Ulrike Froissart, Wolff Heinegg von Heintschel and Christian Raap, *Krisensicherung und humanitärer Schutz / Crisis Management and Humanitarian Protection. Festschrift für Dieter Fleck* (Berlin: Berliner Wissenschaftsverlag, 2004), p. 587.

rights law.[47] Special procedures of the UN Human Rights Council have repeatedly argued that non-state actors who exercise control over territory and have a political structure can be expected to comply with human rights standards.[48]

But it remains disputed whether or not the actual exercise of quasi-governmental powers is an additional prerequisite for their ability to take on obligations under human rights law. Such explanations also do not function where no territorial control exists or where the taking over of governmental functions is not envisaged, i.e., where non-state armed groups are exploiting natural resources, engaging in organized crime or conducting terrorist operations with no intention to become a government or behave as such. There are additional variations of this theme, for example, where the state remains bound by human rights law jointly with a non-state armed group when the latter exercises governmental authority in a certain territory with the authorization of government, or acts de facto on the instructions or control of the government.[49]

Alternatively, one may see the human rights obligations of non-state actors as a correlative to the human rights which they, or rather their individual members, enjoy, and as "no different from the obligations insurgents have under international humanitarian law."[50] Given that equality of obligation is an important characteristic for protective laws in situations of armed conflict, the insertion of human rights law into this context necessitates accepting that, where one party is bound by a protective norm, so must the other be, regardless of the source of this norm.[51] And finally, one may simply focus on the capability of non-state actors to adhere to international human rights law. Whether or not a non-state armed group is capable of complying with international human rights law needs to be decided on a case-by-case basis.[52] The stakes may be too high for many groups who will not be able to ensure, for example, an appropriate legal and institutional framework, including courts and other independent bodies or relevant expertise, and cannot convincingly demonstrate appropriate standards of investigation and court proceedings. On the other hand, in some cases such capacities may be available. Frente Farabundo Martí para la Liberación Nacional (FMLN) of El Salvador, for example, even had a Secretariat for the Promotion and Protection of Human Rights.[53] This may say little about the effective capacity and willingness to comply with human rights standards, but that is a problem which can also be observed with regard to human rights commitments made by states.

(b) Developments in practice

Calls on non-state actors to respect human rights and humanitarian law in situations of armed conflict have now become a catch-phrase and non-state parties to armed conflicts are

[47] See Fleck, "Humanitarian Protection Against Non-State Actors" (n. 45) p. 79.

[48] Sivakumaran, "Re-envisaging the International Law of Armed Conflict" (n. 7) 244, with particular reference to Special Rapporteur, *Report on Extra-judicial, Summary or Arbitrary Executions in Sri Lanka*, E/CN.4/2005/7 (22 December 2004), para. 76.

[49] See UN OHCHR, *International Legal Protection of Human Rights in Armed Conflict* (n. 45) 27.

[50] Fleck, "Humanitarian Protection against Non-State Actors" (n. 45) p. 79, and similarly Sivakumaran, "Re-envisaging the International Law of Armed Conflict" (n. 7) 252 (with reference to subsequent reports of Special Rapporteurs and scholarly literature).

[51] Tomuschat, "The Applicability of Human Rights Law to Insurgent Movements" (n. 46) p. 576.

[52] See Sivakumaran, "Re-envisaging the International Law of Armed Conflict" (n. 7) 255–56.

[53] Ibid. 256.

habitually urged "to respect international humanitarian law as well as fundamental human rights,"[54] irrespective of their legal status. The Security Council regularly calls upon non-state armed actors in situations of non-international armed conflict to comply with international humanitarian law and international human rights law simultaneously. In the former Yugoslavia, Afghanistan, Angola, Guinea-Bissau, Côte d'Ivoire, Liberia, Angola, Somalia, Sierra Leone, Sudan, Somalia and the Democratic Republic of Congo, the Council called on all parties to the conflicts to end human rights violations and respect their obligations under international humanitarian law.[55] In Resolution 1564 of 2004 (to quote one example), the Council called upon Sudanese rebel groups to "take all necessary steps to respect international humanitarian law and international human rights law."[56] More specifically, the Security Council demands respect by all parties to a conflict for the treatment of women and girls, the use of child soldiers, access to humanitarian assistance and the protection of the civilian population under both international humanitarian law and international human rights law.[57]

Never did the Council invoke any idea of belligerency of non-state actors,[58] nor did it create any new norms not hitherto known to international law in its resolutions.[59] Rather, the Council presumed in all those situations that non-state actors have obligations under both international humanitarian law and international human rights law.[60] The UN Security Council and the (then) Human Rights Commission have applied international humanitarian law to non-state armed groups even in situations as chaotic as in Somalia.[61] In Resolution 1894 of 2009 on the protection of civilians in armed conflict the Council acknowledged also, in general terms, the primary responsibility of states to protect civilians in armed conflicts, but demanded that all parties to the conflict respect international humanitarian law, international human rights law and refugee law.[62] The Special Rapporteurs of the Human Rights Council have also frequently called upon non-state actors, such as the Special Rapporteur on extra-judicial, summary or arbitrary executions in his report on Sri Lanka, who said that:

> the LTTE [Liberation Tigers of Tamil Eelam] does not have legal obligations under [the International Covenant on Civil and Political Rights], but it remains subject to the demand of the international community, first expressed in the Universal Declaration of Human Rights, that every organ of society respect and promote human rights.[63]

The Special Rapporteur considered that the claimed aspiration of the LTTE to legitimately represent the people of Sri Lanka provided the grounds for such

[54] Institute of International Law, Resolution on the Application of International Humanitarian Law and Fundamental Human Rights in Armed Conflicts in which Non-State Entities are Parties (1999), Art. II.
[55] See on the various resolutions Clapham, "Human Rights Obligations of Non-State Actors in Conflict Situations" (n. 32) 499–501.
[56] Security Council Res. 1564, UN Doc. S/RES/1564 (18 September 2004), Preamble.
[57] See Clapham, "Human Rights Obligations of Non-State Actors in Conflict Situations" (n. 32) 496.
[58] See Rüdiger Wolfrum and Christiane E. Philipp, "The Status of the Taliban: Their Obligations and Rights under International Law" (2002) 6(1) *Max Planck Yearbook of United Nations Law* 583.
[59] See Tomuschat, "The Applicability of Human Rights Law to Insurgent Movements" (n. 46) 586.
[60] See Clapham, "Human Rights Obligations of Non-State Actors in Conflict Situations" (n. 32) 501 and 504.
[61] Zegveld, *Accountability of Armed Opposition Groups in International Law* (n. 33) pp. 138–41.
[62] Security Council Res. 1894, UN Doc. S/RES/1894 (11 November 2009), para. 1.
[63] UN Doc. E/CN.4/2006/53/Add.5, para. 25.

responsibilities.[64] Both arguments were repeated with regard to Hezbollah (and the argument of Hezbollah's territorial control was added) in the joint report of special procedures of the UN Commission on Human Rights on Lebanon and Israel.[65] This report also recalled the long-standing practice of the Security Council to urge non-state armed groups to respect human rights despite their lack of legal standing akin to a state, particularly those which exercise significant control over territory and population and have an identifiable political structure.[66]

The Convention on the Rights of the Child (CRC) has (once more) a special position, as its Optional Protocol on children in armed conflict provides that "[a]rmed groups that are distinct from the armed forces of a State should not, under any circumstances, recruit or use in hostilities persons under the age of eighteen years."[67] The majority of commentators seem to understand this provision as binding only states but this view is not universally shared.[68] The Committee on the Rights of the Child also regularly monitors the compliance of non-state armed groups and expresses its concern over violations of the Convention by these groups. It also issues recommendations directly to them, although not very consistently. In its Concluding Observations on the Democratic Republic of the Congo in 2012, for example, the Committee expressed concern regarding the recruitment of children by non-state armed groups, but addressed recommendations in this respect only to the state.[69] With regard to Nepal, the Committee directly urged the Communist Party of Nepal (Maoists) (CPN(M)) "to respect child rights within the areas in which they operate."[70] Its Concluding Observations on Sri Lanka were addressed only to the government, including on the matter of recruitment of children by non-state armed groups.[71] In its Concluding Observations on Sudan, however, it extended its recommendations to "as far as possible, other relevant actors."[72]

In light of existing state practice it is yet unsettled whether assigning human rights obligations to non-state armed groups indeed expresses the will of the international

[64] See *Report of the Special Rapporteur*, UN Doc. E/CN.4/2006/53/Add.5 (27 March 2006), paras. 25 and 27. The respective obligation is, however, only in the Preamble to the Declaration which itself is not legally binding as a resolution of the UN General Assembly.

[65] See Special Rapporteur on extra-judicial, summary or arbitrary executions, Philip Alston; Special Rapporteur on the right of everyone to the enjoyment of the highest attainable standard of physical and mental health, Paul Hunt; Representative of the Secretary-General on human rights of internally displaced persons, Walter Kälin; and Special Rapporteur on adequate housing as a component of the right to an adequate standard of living, Miloon Kothari, *Report on the Mission to Lebanon and Israel*, UN Doc. A/HRC/2/7 (2 October 2006), para. 19. See also Clapham, "Human Rights Obligations of Non-State Actors in Conflict Situations" (n. 32) 507.

[66] See *Report on the Mission to Lebanon and Israel*, UN Doc. A/HRC/2/7 (n. 65) para. 19.

[67] Optional Protocol to the Convention on the Rights of the Child, Art. 4(1) on the involvement of children in armed conflict.

[68] See Sivakumaran, "Re-envisaging the International Law of Armed Conflict" (n. 7) 249, with reference to the respective authors.

[69] See Committee on the Rights of the Child, *Concluding Observations on the Democratic Republic of the Congo*, UN Doc. CRC/C/OPAC/COD/CO/1 (7 March 2012), paras. 32–33.

[70] See Committee on the Rights of the Child, *Concluding Observations on Nepal*, UN Doc. CRC/C/15/Add.261 (21 September 2005), para. 12.

[71] See Committee on the Rights of the Child, *Concluding Observations on Sri Lanka*, UN Doc. CRC/C/OPAC/LKA/CO/1 (1 October 2010), paras. 16–17.

[72] See Committee on the Rights of the Child, *Concluding Observations on Sudan*, UN Doc. CRC/C/121 (11 December 2002), para. 279.

community,[73] is an expectation rather than a binding legal obligation,[74] or constitutes simply a pragmatic recognition of the realities of conflict that some non-state actors can, and should, respect human rights.[75] There is evidence that non-state actors may, in principle, be interested in respecting human rights for utilitarian or legitimacy reasons. Some have adopted and concluded commitments, declarations, codes of conduct, guidelines or memoranda of understandings on human rights.[76] There are also instances where non-state actors have accepted obligations under international human rights law publicly, such as the CPN(M) in 2004 (when the group issued a statement in which it welcomed UN human rights field operations and committed itself to human rights standards)[77] or by written agreements, such as the Agreement on Human Rights between El Salvador and the FMLN.[78] The reasons to do so seem to mirror those for adhering to international humanitarian law.[79]

Even if one accepts the applicability of international humanitarian law to non-state actors in legal theory and believes in such appeals, agreements and self-proclaimed responsibilities, practical problems remain with regard to the willingness and capability of non-state actors to effectively respect and ensure respect for human rights. Assigning rights to them in theory is not matched by the practical realization of such claims. The difficulties lie in the degree of organization (or lack thereof) of non-state armed groups, as has just been mentioned, but also in the way they approach human rights, a law in the formation of which they had no say. And there is also the problem of how to deal with non-state actors whose very purpose is to violate human rights, such as criminal and terrorist organizations.[80]

Identifying with greater clarity and more convincingly the legal grounds for such obligations, the specific human rights obligations at stake, and the protective gaps which need to be filled, is a challenge ahead. And providing incentives for non-state armed groups to adhere to human rights law is a challenge in which little has been invested, compared to humanitarian law.[81] Monitoring and engaging with non-state actors is necessary. Again, this is not exclusively a problem with regard to their human rights obligations, but also with regard to obligations under humanitarian law. Initiatives such as Geneva Call and UN

[73] Tomuschat, "The Applicability of Human Rights Law to Insurgent Movements" (n. 46) pp. 586–87.

[74] It has been pointed out that apart from the Security Council such calls come primarily from UN (human rights) bodies and Truth and Reconciliation Commissions, see Sivakumaran, "Re-envisaging the International Law of Armed Conflict" (n. 7) 252.

[75] UN OHCHR, International Legal Protection of Human Rights in Armed Conflict (n. 45) p. 25.

[76] See Clapham, "Human Rights Obligations of Non-State Actors in Conflict Situations" (n. 32) 510–12, with reference to studies undertaken in Burundi, Liberia, Somalia, Sierra Leone, Afghanistan, Sudan, Democratic Republic of the Congo, Angola, East Timor, Democratic Peoples' Republic of Korea and the Russian Federation.

[77] See Sivakumaran, *The Law of Non-International Armed Conflict* (n. 19) p. 122.

[78] Agreement on Human Rights between the Government of El Salvador and the Frente Farabundo Martí para la Liberación Nacional, UN Doc. A/44/971-S/21541 (26 July 1990), Annex, available at www.usip.org/publications/peace-agreements-el-salvador (last accessed 15 April 2014).

[79] See on the reasons to comply with humanitarian law Olivier Bangerter, "Reasons Why Armed Groups Choose to Respect International Humanitarian Law or Not" (2011) 93(882) *International Review of the Red Cross* 353.

[80] See Clapham, "Human Rights Obligations of Non-State Actors in Conflict Situations" (n. 32) 511.

[81] See on these efforts Marco Sassòli, "Taking Armed Groups Seriously: Ways to Improve Their Compliance with International Humanitarian Law" (2010) 1(1) *International Journal of Humanitarian Legal Studies* 5.

bodies, e.g., the UN Secretary-General's Special Representative for Children in Armed Conflict, are active in this field, mostly with regard to the recruitment of child soldiers.[82]

It may be necessary to include new modes of law-making and devise implementation and monitoring tools.[83] One may also have to translate the essence of human rights norms rather than their detailed and often state-specific content to the realities of non-state actors. International humanitarian law has developed clauses which take into account the circumstances and which can be used for translating such state-centred obligations to non-state actors.[84] Such modifications of state-based norms to fit non-state actors has already been done in the jurisprudence of the ICTY.[85] The Special Court for Sierra Leone also found, for example, that imposing liability for committing the crime of recruiting child soldiers is not hindered by the fact that non-state armed groups resort to this practice.[86]

The danger of watering down human rights obligations in this process of "shaping"[87] international human rights law norms so that non-state armed groups can comply with them is, however, real and must be countered. If the standard for, say "due process" is not the one applicable to states under international humanitarian law, is it then a self-defined standard set by the non-state armed group? In other words, can state law simply and generally be substituted by the self-created "law" of a given armed group, or by agreement among groups and governments? Moreover, the next step would then be to include non-state armed groups in the creation of norms to make sure they – like states – feel bound by them. Some argue, for pragmatic as well as historic reasons, that this should be the case. Pragmatically, because utilizing existing and emerging unilateral declarations, codes of conduct or agreements adopted by non-state armed groups may induce the likelihood that they feel bound by such texts. Historically, because even one of the founding documents of international humanitarian law, the Lieber Code, may legally be qualified as a unilateral declaration of a party to the conflict, i.e., President Lincoln in the American Civil War.[88] None of this is easy and all of it will meet with scepticism and critique by governments and civil society organizations, but outright rejection of any role for non-state actors in matters of human rights is not only unsupported by law and practice, it ultimately also fails the victims of their acts.[89]

The dramatic increase of outsourcing military tasks to private military companies (PMCs) is another feature of modern wars and begs the question as to which legal framework(s) should appropriately regulate the conduct of those involved in situations of armed conflict. The importance of PMCs today is significant and has come to the attention of the public in the Iraq war, where the unwillingness to provide sufficient security on the US side and the inability to do so on the Iraqi side let to a transfer of a variety of tasks to

[82] See Clapham, "Human Rights Obligations of Non-State Actors in Conflict Situations" (n. 32) 512. For Geneva Call see www.genevacall.org (last accessed 15 April 2014).

[83] See Sophie Rondeau, "Participation of Armed Groups in the Development of the Law Applicable to Armed Conflicts" (2011) 93(883) *International Review of the Red Cross* 649.

[84] See, e.g., Additional Protocol II, Art. 5(2): "within the limits of their capabilities"; ibid. Art. 4(3)(b): "all appropriate steps"; ibid. Art. 7(2): "to the fullest extent possible"; and ibid. Art. 8: "all possible measures."

[85] Sivakumaran, "Re-envisaging the International Law of Armed Conflict" (n. 7) 257, with reference to ICTY, *Prosecutor* v. *Tadić* (n. 1) para. 126.

[86] *Prosecutor* v. *Brima, Kamara and Kanu*, Special Court for Sierra Leone, SCSL-2004-16-T, Judgment of 20 June 2007, para. 734.

[87] Sivakumaran, "Re-envisaging the International Law of Armed Conflict" (n. 7) 259. [88] Ibid. 260–61.

[89] See Clapham, "Human Rights Obligations of Non-State Actors in Conflict Situations" (n. 32) 523.

private actors, including core military activities.[90] The regular (US and Iraqi) armed forces, together with the regular police force soon found themselves working with other arms bearers and various US contractors, totalling in the hundreds of thousands of personnel organized along commercial (as well as ethnic and religious orientations) rather than reflecting governmental authority.[91]

The ability of PMCs to violate norms of both legal regimes has been demonstrated on various occasions, together with the inadequate means to hold them to account.[92] While many see PMCs as mercenaries and their activities as blatantly illegal under international law,[93] there is a tendency to understand their activities as a matter of corporate responsibility and thus in need of regulation and capable of being regulated.[94] If such a regulatory framework is envisaged, it would necessarily have to contain, *inter alia*, humanitarian law and human rights law in a complementary manner. The Montreux Document, adopted in 2008, reflects this consensus that international humanitarian law and human rights law need to be applied jointly to regulate PMCs.[95] Suggestions to regulate PMCs also include setting them apart from other non-state armed actors, treating their case under the rubric of "business and human rights" and applying, for example, the Norms on the Responsibilities of Transnational Corporations and Other Business Enterprises with regard to Human Rights to their activities.[96]

As with non-state armed groups, their ability to be bound by human rights law, adhere to human rights law and be accountable for violations of human rights law poses a range of problems in law, practice and policy.[97] Among them is the question whether they might be

[90] See in greater detail David Isenberg, *Shadow Force: Private Security Contractors in Iraq* (Westport: Praeger, 2009).

[91] See Christopher Coker, *War in an Age of Risk* (Cambridge: Polity, 2009), p. 126.

[92] See Avril McDonald, "Ghosts in the Machine: Some Legal Issues concerning US Military Contractors in Iraq" in Michael N. Schmitt and Jelena Pejic (eds.), *International Law and Armed Conflict: Exploring the Faultlines* (Leiden: Nijhoff, 2007), pp. 357–402; and David Kassebaum, "A Question of Facts: The Legal Use of Private Security Firms in Bosnia" (2000) 38 *Columbia Journal of Transnational Law* 581.

[93] For an overview of their arguments see Sarah Percy, "Morality and Regulation" in Simon Chesterman (ed.), *From Mercenaries to Market: The Rise and Regulation of Private Military Companies* (Oxford: Oxford University Press, 2009), pp. 11–28.

[94] For an in-depth analysis of the attribution of responsibility see, e.g., Lindsey Cameron and Vincent Chetail, *Privatizing War: Private Military and Security Companies under Public International Law* (Cambridge: Cambridge University Press, 2013); and for an overview of possibilities to regulate their activities Nigel D. White, "Regulatory Initiatives at the International Level" in Christine Bakker and Mirko Sossai (eds.), *Multilevel Regulation of Military and Security Contractors: The Interplay between International, European and Domestic Norms* (Oxford: Hart, 2012), pp. 1–30.

[95] See Montreux Document on Pertinent International Legal Obligations and Good Practices for States related to Operations of Private Military and Security Companies during Armed Conflict, UN Doc. A/63/467 and S/2008/636 (6 October 2008), Annex. The document is a joint initiative of like-minded states and the ICRC, with the inclusion of representatives from civil society and industry. On its drafting and content see James Cockayne, "Regulating Private Military Companies: The Content, Negotiation, Weaknesses and Promise of the Montreux Document""(2009) 13(3) *Journal of Conflict and Security Law* 401.

[96] Norms on the Responsibilities of Transnational Corporations and Other Business Enterprises with regard to Human Rights in Their Activities, UN Doc. E/CN.4/Sub.2/2003/12/Rev.2 (2003). On this proposal of the UN Sub-Commission on the Promotion and Protection of Human Rights, see UN Doc. E/CN.4/2006/11/Add.1 (3 March 2006), para. 28.

[97] See in greater detail Federico Lenzerini and Francesco Francioni, "The Role of Human Rights in the Regulation of Private Military and Security Companies" in Francesco Francioni and Natalino Ronzitti (ed.), *War by Contract: Human Rights, Humanitarian Law, and Private Contractors* (Oxford: Oxford University Press, 2011), pp. 55–79.

induced to comply with human rights in response to market pressures, i.e., where their clients demand respect for international human rights and humanitarian law in return for payment. Examples of such agreements between PMCs and states, which include respect for international humanitarian law and human rights, as well as concern for corporate social responsibility within PMCs, exist.[98]

[98] See Clapham, "Human Rights Obligations of Non-State Actors in Conflict Situations" (n. 32) 517.

15

Human rights in situations of occupation

15.1 Law of occupation: governing fragility in hostility

The law of occupation was inserted as Section III (Articles 42 to 56) in the 1899 Regulations respecting the Laws and Customs of War on Land annexed to Hague Convention II of 1899, and revised and attached under the same title to the Hague Regulations respecting the Laws and Customs of War on Land annexed to Hague Convention IV of 1907.[1] The delegates to the negotiations of the texts presumed that once the enemy was overpowered by force, this would lead to the enemy government being rendered dysfunctional and displaced by the victorious government's exercise of temporary authority with a view towards restoring peace again in a peace agreement.[2] As in other fields of international humanitarian law the drafters of these first rules on occupation could neither anticipate the rise of international human rights law nor could they imagine how occupations would become part of multi-faceted post-conflict scenarios.

Geneva Convention IV of 1949 followed the model provided in 1907. Section III of the Convention created, under the title "occupied territories," a set of protective rules for civilians under occupation to supplement the Hague Regulations[3] and envisaged also occupations which were not necessarily preceded by war.[4] Based on its nineteenth century foundations, the law of occupation soon began to evolve into a matrix of considerations which included, and needed to reconcile, the security needs of the occupier; the humanitarian concern for the fate of civilians; the idea of self-determination of peoples; the demands of nation (re)building; and the human rights of the occupied population. Additional Protocol I of 1977 also contains a number of rules on occupied

1 See Yoram Dinstein, *The International Law of Belligerent Occupation* (Cambridge: Cambridge University Press, 2009), pp. 4–5; and (on the historic evolution of the law of occupation) E. Benvenisti, *The International Law of Occupation* (Oxford: Oxford University Press, 2011), pp. 20–42. Article 42 of the Regulations respecting the Laws and Customs of War on Land, Annex to the Hague Convention IV of 1907, opens the section on occupation law: "[t]erritory is considered occupied when it is actually placed under the authority of the hostile army. The occupation extends only to the territory where such authority has been established and can be exercised."

2 See Benvenisti, *The International Law of Occupation* (n. 1) p. 20.

3 See Geneva Convention IV, Art. 154: "this . . . Convention shall be supplementary to Sections II and III of the Regulations annexed to the . . . Conventions of The Hague."

4 Geneva Convention IV, Art. 2 stipulates that the Convention applies to all cases of total or partial occupation "even if the said occupation meets with no armed resistance"; see also Dinstein, *The International Law of Belligerent Occupation* (n. 1) pp. 31–32, who cites the armed occupation of Denmark by Germany in 1940 as an example.

territories, most of them complementary to Geneva Convention IV, others more innovative and partly in response to such challenges.[5]

Systematically, the law of occupation is part of the law of international armed conflicts. Delimitating the two remains ambiguous, as is reflected in the continuing debate on the precise beginning and end of occupations.[6] The law of occupation is particular to international armed conflict and not applicable in internal conflict, not least because the tripartite relationship between occupier, occupied population and displaced sovereign on which the law of occupation is built can hardly be replicated in internal conflicts.[7] In reality, situations of occupations began to differentiate since 1949 along different lines not foreseen in the original legal texts. Short-term belligerent occupations, as envisaged in the Hague Regulations, were displaced by prolonged occupations, such as in the Occupied Palestinian Territories.[8] And transformative occupations with the explicit or implicit aim to bring about change in the political structure of the state and within society replaced the ultimately conservative approach of occupation, which was meant to preserve the law of the land as a kind of trusteeship.[9] The occupation of Iraq is an example of such a kind of transformative occupation.[10]

Finally, there are international territorial administrations such as in East Timor and Kosovo, where under a UN mandate and with the consent of the state concerned, territories were effectively governed in a mix of protectorate and trusteeship, which begs questions as to the applicability of occupation law in such situations.[11] Some consider the law of occupation clearly applicable, while others do not.[12] In addition, occupations are often carried out by multi-national coalitions, adding complexity to the attribution of responsibilities to the Occupying Powers. The linear sequence as envisaged in the Hague Regulations, whereby peace would give way to war to be followed by occupation to end in

[5] See Geneva Conventions, Common Art. 2: "The Convention shall also apply to all cases of partial or total occupation of the territory of a High Contracting Party, even if the said occupation meets with no armed resistance"; and Dinstein, *The International Law of Belligerent Occupation* (n. 1) p. 7.

[6] See Marten Zwanenburg, "The Law of Occupation Revisited: The Beginning of an Occupation" (2007) 10 *Yearbook of International Humanitarian Law* 99; and David Alonzo-Maizlish, "When Does It End? Problems in the Law of Occupation" in Roberta Arnold and Pierre-Robert Hildbrand (eds.), *International Humanitarian Law and the 21st Century's Conflicts: Changes and Challenges* (Lausanne: Edis, 2005), pp. 98–116.

[7] See Dinstein, *The International Law of Belligerent Occupation* (n. 1) pp. 33–34.

[8] See Orna Ben-Naftali, "PathoLAWgical Occupation: Normalizing the Exceptional Case of the Occupied Palestinian Territory and Other Legal Pathologies" in Orna Ben-Naftali (ed.), *International Humanitarian and International Human Rights Law* (Oxford: Oxford University Press, 2011), pp. 129–200.

[9] See Nehal Bhuta, "The Antinomies of Transformative Occupation" (2005) 16(4) *European Journal of International Law* 721; and Adam Roberts, "Transformative Military Occupation: Applying the Laws of War and Human Rights" in Michael N. Schmitt and Jelena Pejic (eds.), *International Law and Armed Conflict: Exploring the Faultlines* (Leiden: Nijhoff, 2007), pp. 439–95.

[10] See, e.g., Philip James Walker, "Iraq and Occupation" in David Wippman and Matthew Evangelista (eds.), *New Wars, New Laws?: Applying Laws of War in 21st Century Conflicts* (Ardsley: Transnational, 2005), pp. 259–88.

[11] Consensual occupations, e.g., the occupation of Iceland by the United States during the Second World War, are also referred to as *occupatio pacifica*, see Dinstein, *The International Law of Belligerent Occupation* (n. 1) p. 35. See also Steven Ratner, "Foreign Occupation and International Territorial Administration: The Challenges of Convergence" (2005) 16(4) *European Journal of International Law* 695.

[12] See Dinstein, *The International Law of Belligerent Occupation* (n. 1) p. 37, who argues against such a view, and Benvenisti, *The International Law of Occupation* (n. 1) p. 278, who argues for it.

peace again, is also no longer obvious. Rather, post-conflict situations are often characterized by prolonged instability and governed by a matrix of international norms which may be brought together under the rubric of an emerging *jus post bellum*.[13] In all these situations, international human rights law matters a great deal.

Given how far the reality of occupation has veered away from the law as it was initially conceived, it is today acknowledged that occupation law is under pressure and potentially also in need of reform. For many observers, the legal framework which governs situations of occupation and the way in which they are actually carried out are characterized by a "cognitive dissonance."[14] The ability of the law of occupation to effectively regulate post-conflict situations and provide adequate protection of those subjected to occupation is questionable to an extent that the law seems at a "turning point."[15]

In a way this is not surprising given the contradictory interests which need to be reconciled. The Occupying Power must take into account its own security interests, the rights and interests of the ousted government which it temporarily replaces, and the interests of the occupied population on behalf of whom it exercises a form of trusteeship.[16] It must be robust enough in its use of force to secure its power-base so as to fulfil its duties under the law of occupation, and sensitive enough to live up to the humanitarian demands which Geneva Convention IV contains with regard to the welfare of the occupied population. And a situation of occupation also means operating under temporal restrictions, as the Occupying Power assumes authority only for a given time during which it is meant to shoulder the responsibilities of the ousted government in a fragile and often hostile context.

15.2 Human rights and occupation law

This relationship between the Occupying Power as the temporary holder of authority and the population under its controls seems an invitation for human rights law, given that it is crafted for precisely such a relationship. Given these circumstances, the application of human rights in situations of occupation finds widespread support.[17] As in internal armed conflicts, a strong case can be made for the application of international human rights law as a matter of principle, but the precise interplay of human rights and humanitarian norms remains disputed and "extraordinarily complex."[18] Those critical of applying human rights in situations of occupation argue that state practice does not sufficiently support such a view; that applying international human rights law is impractical if compared to the specific obligations of international humanitarian law; that human rights

[13] See Carsten Stahn, "'*Jus Ad Bellum*,' '*Jus in Bello*' . . . '*Jus Post Bellum*'? Rethinking the Conception of the Law of Armed Force" (2006) 17(5) *European Journal of International Law* 921.

[14] Ratner, "Foreign Occupation and International Territorial Administration" (n. 11) 697, with reference both to situations of occupation and the territorial administration of territories under a UN mandate, such as in East Timor or Kosovo.

[15] Charles H.B. Garraway, "Occupation Responsibilities and Constraints" in Howard M. Hensel (ed.), *The Legitimate Use of Force: The Just War Tradition and the Customary Law of Armed Conflict* (Aldershot: Ashgate, 2008), p. 278.

[16] See Benvenisti, *The International Law of Occupation* (n. 1) p. 69.

[17] See, e.g., Noam Lubell, "Human Rights in Military Occupation" (2012) 94(885) *International Review of the Red Cross* 337; and Tristan Ferraro, "The Law of Occupation and Human Rights Law: Some Selected Issues" in Robert Kolb and Gloria Gaggioli (eds.), *Research Handbook on Human Rights and Humanitarian Law* (Cheltenham: Edward Elgar, 2013), p. 289.

[18] Roberts, "Transformative Military Occupation" (n. 9) p. 594.

law cannot cover acts of non-state armed groups; and that states would never accept the more constraining rules of international human rights law.[19]

But in reality, situations of occupation figure prominently in the practice and case law of human rights bodies, and the International Court of Justice (ICJ) (in its decision in *Democratic Republic of the Congo* v. *Uganda* concerning armed activities on the territory of the Congo) found that "both branches of international law, namely human rights law and international humanitarian law, would have to be taken into consideration in occupied territories."[20] The international community has also clearly agreed on such an application of human rights in occupation in the 1993 World Conference on Human Rights.[21] Eyal Benvenisti's seminal study of occupation law concludes by saying "that human rights law may complement the law of occupation in specific issues is by now an unchallenged proposition to which the US and Israel may be regarded as persistent objectors."[22] In state practice, human rights in occupation have also been an (often contentious) issue in various situations of occupation since 1945, most prominently in Northern Cyprus since 1974 and in the Occupied Palestinian Territory since 1967.[23]

Given the way in which an Occupying Power exercises authority, an overlap of international humanitarian law and international human rights law is to be expected, and their relationship may indeed be "symbiotic."[24] But views on the precise interplay of human rights and humanitarian law in situations of occupation differ. Some argue strongly that occupation law is *lex specialis* and excludes human rights.[25] But the International Committee of the Red Cross (ICRC) expert consultations on the law of occupation correctly considered that this argument is ultimately unconvincing, given that international human rights law can provide adequate or superior protection of civilians (or at least would not result in substantially different outcomes); would be flexible enough to accommodate the needs of law enforcement as well as the conduct of hostilities; could be interpreted according to the context of occupation; could be applied regardless of the status of those against which force is used; and would provide monitoring and remedial mechanisms.[26]

Indeed, human rights and humanitarian law can again both be considered "special," depending on the circumstances. One may see the many detailed rules of occupation law in the Hague Regulations, Geneva Conventions and Additional Protocol I as reflecting its specialty, or one may argue to the contrary that maintaining public order and security and enforcing laws is an area in which international human rights law and not international

[19] On these critical voices see International Committee of the Red Cross, *Expert Meeting on the Law of Occupation and Other Forms of Administration of Territory* (Geneva: ICRC, 2012), pp. 117–19.

[20] *Armed Activities on the Territory of the Congo (Democratic Republic of the Congo* v. *Uganda)*, International Court of Justice, Judgment of 19 December 2005 [2006] ICJ Reports, para. 216.

[21] Vienna Declaration and Programme of Action refers specifically to human rights in situations of occupation in its para. 3: "Effective international measures to guarantee and monitor the implementation of human rights standards should be taken in respect of people under foreign occupation, and effective legal protection against the violation of their human rights should be provided, in accordance with human rights norms and international law, particularly the Geneva Convention relative to the Protection of Civilian Persons in Time of War, of 14 August 1949, and other applicable norms of humanitarian law."

[22] Benvenisti, *The International Law of Occupation* (n. 1) pp. 14–15.

[23] See Roberts, "Transformative Military Occupation" (n. 9) pp. 595–99.

[24] Dinstein, *The International Law of Belligerent Occupation* (n. 1) p. 81. [25] Ibid. pp. 286–87.

[26] See ICRC, *Expert Meeting on the Law of Occupation and Other Forms of Administration of Territory* (n. 19) pp. 116–17.

humanitarian law is "special" with regard to its coverage, experience and expertise, including also in situations of crisis, emergency and international territorial administrations.[27] Human rights law in occupation can be useful for the way it helps define the means and ends of an occupation or fill gaps where humanitarian law is silent,[28] and more than that: "[t]he law of military occupation," it has been said, "arose with a 'human rights' purpose *ante litteram*."[29]

15.3 Identifying the duties of Occupying Powers

Some of the problems in applying human rights to situations of occupation mirror the legal obstacles discussed in previous chapters, while others are unique and reflect the specific context. Given that occupation means exercising authority beyond one's borders, the extra-territorial application of international human rights law is obviously again an issue, and the arguments with regard to the way in which the Occupying Power carries with it the human rights law by which it is bound to the occupied territory are all applicable. Alternatively (or cumulatively), the occupant may also be deemed to take over the ousted government's international human rights obligations without any necessity to consider the extra-territorial application of human rights law. Both scenarios are not without problems.

As has been argued above, the extra-territorial application of human rights norms in occupied territory necessitates the exercise of effective control over territory and/or persons. If one equates the "authority" required in Hague Regulations, Article 42 with such effective control, then every situation of occupation establishes a jurisdictional link strong enough to bring human rights treaty obligations to bear.[30] Both express the same idea that a state must, as a matter of fact, have a certain amount of control.[31] A situation without effective control is not conceivable, given that occupation is by definition a de facto situation of such control. The Hague Regulations and subsequent law are not interested in measuring the degree of control in order to establish specific duties. If control cannot be sustained, no occupation exists. Arguments that as Occupying Power one can exercise authority but not control (as seemingly put forward by the United Kingdom in the *Al-Skeini* case) are indeed contradictory.[32]

But it cannot be denied that the factual exercise of such authority or control is not always in analogy to the exercise of governmental authority, as envisaged under human rights law. There are differences: occupation is temporary (and sometimes also prolonged) but not permanent; the Occupying Power may comprise of a multi-national coalition of states with different human rights obligations; occupation is *bellica*, i.e., established and maintained by

[27] See Gloria Gaggioli and Robert Kolb, "A Right to Life in Armed Conflict? The Contribution of the European Court of Human Rights" (2007) 37 *Israel Yearbook on Human Rights* 163.

[28] Roberts, "Transformative Military Occupation" (n. 9) p. 580; and Dinstein, *The International Law of Belligerent Occupation* (n. 1) p. 84.

[29] Danio Campanelli, "The Law of Military Occupation Put to the Test" (2008) 90(871) *International Review of the Red Cross* 665.

[30] Hague Regulations 1907, Art. 42: "Territory is considered occupied when it is actually placed under the authority of the hostile army. The occupation extends only to the territory where such authority has been established and can be exercised."

[31] See Marco Sassòli, "Legislation and Maintenance of Public Order and Civil Life by Occupying Powers" (2005) 16(4) *European Journal of International Law* 661.

[32] See Campanelli, "The Law of Military Occupation Put to the Test of Human Rights Law" (n. 29) 665.

force against the will of the ousted government and (usually) against the will of the population or parts of it; it occurs in a fragile post-conflict context with high potential of relapse into conflict; it may be rolling and fluid (with pockets of resistance and hostilities in exchange for more peaceful periods); and obligations in situations of occupation need to be reconciled with the security demands, capabilities and realities of armed forces operating abroad under operational, logistical and resource constraints. The analogy to regular governmental function is thus often (but not always) limited.[33]

In particular, an occupation may comprise situations of stability and "peace" as well as hostilities and violence. The Occupying Power's capabilities (or lack thereof) thus come to bear in different scenarios where it exercises authority and control in varying degrees. It has consequently been suggested that in situations of hostilities, international humanitarian law may prevail, e.g., when targeting insurgents, while human rights law may play a greater role where it provides more detailed rules, for example, in situations of detention, and that particularly in prolonged occupations and with regard to socio-economic rights international human rights law is of importance.[34] One can see this once more as a collision of the two models of war-fighting and law enforcement under the premise that exercising quasi-governmental functions in a hostile environment may demand more robust enforcement of norms compared to regular situations. Furthermore, the (relatively) peaceful exercise of quasi-governmental functions can tilt any moment in situations of occupation, and give way to the open conduct of hostilities. The law of occupation is thus neither about peace nor war but falls in between.[35]

This seems to suggest that for combat operations international humanitarian law is the appropriate framework, while all other activities allow reliance on human rights law. But again the line between the two is blurred: responding to an attack by a rocket-propelled grenade in a given place may be an act of warfare governed by international humanitarian law, while firing upon a car which fails to stop at a checkpoint in the same place at the same time may be a law enforcement operation governed by international human rights law. In the first scenario, the attacker would be a lawful military target (as a civilian directly participating in hostilities) and may be killed, just as bystanders may be killed as long as such deaths are not excessive in relation to the anticipated result of the use of force. In the latter situation, both the driver and bystanders may only be killed as a last resort and when lesser means such as non-lethal weapons, physical force or arrest are futile and all possible measures of precautions to minimize damage have been taken.[36] This may require the individual soldiers to switch between the two legal paradigms in an instant, a difficult, impractical and perhaps impossible task.

There is thus considerable uncertainty as to which model – a "law enforcement" model or a "conduct of hostilities" model – ought to prevail when armed force is used in situations of occupation. The "law enforcement" model seems to be the default model in relation to the use of armed force in occupied territory, as the ICRC expert meeting on occupation law

[33] See Benvenisti, *The International Law of Occupation* (n. 1) p. 14; and Dinstein, *The International Law of Belligerent Occupation* (n. 1) pp. 67–69.

[34] See Oma Ben-Naftali and Yuval Shany, "Living in Denial: The Application of Human Rights in the Occupied Territories" (2004) 1(37) *Israel Law Review* 87–89.

[35] See Campanelli, "The Law of Military Occupation Put to the Test of Human Rights Law" (n. 29) 660.

[36] See Sassòli, "Legislation and Maintenance of Public Order and Civil Life by Occupying Powers" (n. 31) 666.

suggests.[37] In the experts' view it needs, however, (unspecified) criteria to allow a "conduct of hostilities model" to take over. There is no agreement on how to delimit the two. It could be done on the basis of a "sliding scale approach"[38] under which one model, and hence one legal regime, gradually blends into the other, depending on the occupant's assessment of the situation. Or it could be done on the basis of a "mixed model"[39] under which both international humanitarian law and international humanitarian law apply on a case-by-case analysis; or on the basis of a "jump theory"[40] under which objective criteria would trigger the application of one of the two models.

Given the potentially far-reaching duties of Occupying Powers to govern war-torn societies, a question also arises as to the scope of human rights obligations owed to the population. Obviously, in light of the broad range of existing humanitarian obligations which cover matters of labour rights;[41] the protection of workers;[42] the protection of judges and public officials;[43] the obligation to provide food and medical supplies;[44] obligations for hygiene, public health and hospitals;[45] spiritual assistance;[46] humanitarian assistance;[47] penal legislation; fair trial guarantees;[48] and detention conditions,[49] the complementary application of human rights law means that civil, political, economic, social and cultural rights are at stake.[50] But it is disputed whether Occupying Powers have negative and positive obligations or whether, at least, the latter should depend on the degree of control effectively exercised.[51] A capability approach, as suggested above for situations of armed conflict, may help in discerning which obligations are owed, but it would need to take into account that the exercise of authority leads already to the presumption of control and thus seems to advocate a far-reaching jurisdiction and broader subsequent obligations, compared to any other situation of armed conflict.

All of this is a particular problem in prolonged occupations which were not foreseen under humanitarian law. It has thus been suggested to distinguish between short-term and long-term (human rights) obligations of the Occupying Power, so that international humanitarian law governs short-term occupations while human rights law applies the longer the occupation lasts.[52] This is, however, not supported by the law. Rather, the specific circumstances of an occupation need to be taken into account.[53] There is no authoritative

[37] See ICRC, *Expert Meeting on the Law of Occupation and Other Forms of Administration of Territory* (n. 19) pp. 116 and 112–13 (on the differences between the two models).

[38] Ibid. p. 113. [39] Ibid. p. 115. [40] Ibid. p. 115. [41] See Geneva Convention IV, Art. 51.

[42] See ibid. Art. 52. [43] See ibid. Art. 54. [44] See ibid. Art. 55. [45] See ibid. Arts. 56 and 57.

[46] See ibid. Art. 58. [47] See ibid. Arts. 59–63. [48] See ibid. Arts. 64–75. [49] See ibid. Arts. 76–135.

[50] See Walter Kälin, *Human Rights in Times of Occupation: The Case of Kuwait* (Bern: Stämpfli, 1994), p. 17. For a detailed analysis of such rights see Yutaka Arai-Takahashi, "Fair Trial Guarantees in Occupied Territory: The Interplay between International Humanitarian Law and Human Rights Law" in Roberta Arnold and Noelle Quénivet (eds.), *International Humanitarian Law and Human Rights Law: Towards a Merger in International Law* (Leiden: Nijhoff, 2008), pp. 449–74; and Sylvain Vité, "The Interrelationship between the Law of Occupation and Economic, Social and Cultural Rights: The Examples of Food and Health", *Appendix to the Expert Meeting: Occupation and Other Forms of Administration of Foreign Territory* (Geneva: International Committee of the Red Cross, 2012), pp. 88–95.

[51] See the opinion of (unidentified) experts in ICRC, *Expert Meeting on the Law of Occupation and Other Forms of Administration of Territory* (n. 19) p. 63.

[52] See ibid. p. 63.

[53] See Vaios Koutroulis, "The Application of International Humanitarian Law and International Human Rights Law in Situation of Prolonged Occupation: Only a Matter of Time?" (2012) 94(885) *International Review of the Red Cross* 205.

assessment of the length of an occupation to decide whether a given situation is short-term or already long-term. Distinguishing between the two for the purposes of applying different laws might invite governments to deny any applicability of international human rights law to short occupations (measured at will) and would create different legal regimes for what may essentially be the same kind of situation with slightly varying lengths.

Similarly, it has been argued that in short-term occupation only civil-political rights should apply (because they allegedly can be realized immediately), while in long-term occupations socio-economic and cultural rights should apply additionally, given that the International Covenant on Economic, Social and Cultural Rights (ICESCR) requires the progressive implementation of the respective provisions.[54] But such a view not only misunderstands the nature of civil-political and socio-economic rights, as no such direct correlation exists, it also greatly complicates the applicable legal regime in merging the length of occupation with the coverage of norms, both of which are disputed.

In practice, human rights do find a place in situations of occupation.[55] In addition to some of the examples of the complementary application of human rights and humanitarian law discussed in previous chapters, the right to education may be highlighted as an additional case in point. The Occupying Power has different duties under occupation law with regard to education, including the duty to respect the right to education of persons in the occupied territory; facilitate the functioning of schools and educational institutions; protect them from attack, destruction and abuse; and fulfil the educational needs of the population, which includes making all necessary arrangements for the maintenance of education for all.[56] But humanitarian law says nothing, for example, on the content of education, which may be a particular problem in post-conflict settings with their often divided societies. Allowing education to sustain inter-ethnic discrimination and hatred is hardly the kind of thing which should be tolerated by Occupying Powers, but occupation law is seemingly uninterested in this matter. International human rights law, on the other hand, provides guidance on how education needs to be directed towards non-discrimination, participation of all in a democratic society and promoting understanding and tolerance, and can clarify the obligations of Occupying Powers in this respect.[57]

Finally, the attribution of responsibility for human rights violations in situations of occupation remains a matter of concern. International humanitarian law does not provide for obligations of non-state armed groups who control territory akin to the law of

[54] See the opinion of (unidentified) experts in ICRC, *Expert Meeting on the Law of Occupation and Other Forms of Administration of Territory* (n. 19) p. 63.

[55] See Dinstein, *The International Law of Belligerent Occupation* (n. 1) pp. 84–85. On selected problems see also Arai-Takahashi, "Fair Trial Guarantees in Occupied Territory" (n. 50) pp. 449–74; Michael S. Perry, "Worker and Trade Union Rights of Palestinian Arabs from the Occupied Palestinian Territories" (1993) 23 *Israel Yearbook on Human Rights* 27; and Sylvain Vité, "The Interrelation of the Law of Occupation and Economic, Social and Cultural Rights: The Examples of Food, Health and Property" (2008) 90(871) *International Review of the Red Cross* 629.

[56] See United Nations Office of the High Commissioner for Human Rights, *International Legal Protection of Human Rights in Armed Conflict* (New York and Geneva: United Nations, 2011), pp. 19–20.

[57] See Conor McCarthy, "Legal Reasoning and the Applicability of International Human Rights Standards during Military Occupation" in Roberta Arnold and Noelle Quénivet (eds.), *International Humanitarian Law and Human Rights Law: Towards a Merger in International Law* (Leiden: Nijhoff, 2008), pp. 127–28, with reference to this particular problem in post-conflict Croatia.

occupation even though many such situations exist.[58] The attribution of obligations in multi-national coalition warfare is likely to pose a problem, as is the involvement of international organizations. And the residual (human rights) obligations of the ousted government also need to be reconciled with the obligations under human rights and humanitarian law of the Occupying Power.[59] All of this adds to the complexity of occupation law which, in addition, can be seen as swerving between the two contradictory poles of preservation and transformation.

15.4 Occupation between preservation and transformation

The main thrust of the law of occupation can be derived from Article 43 of the Hague Regulations of 1907:

> The authority of the legitimate power having in fact passed into the hands of the occupant, the latter shall take all the measures in his power to restore, and ensure, as far as possible, public order and safety, while respecting, unless absolutely prevented, the laws in force in the country.[60]

As already discussed, this means that while there is no transfer of sovereignty, the occupant must exercise some form of effective control over territory ("authority") which replaces the one exercised by the former government, and that such a replacement of authority is not permanent but temporary. Thirdly, however, it also means that occupation is conservationist: the occupant is put in the position of a trustee which has to preserve, as far as possible, the *status quo ante* for the benefit of the population. In addition, it means that the duties of Occupying Powers cover the whole of societal life. It is noteworthy in this respect that the English translation of the (only authentic and binding) French text contains a grave error which has never been corrected. "[L]'ordre et la vie publique" in the French text is not equivalent to "public order and safety" in the English version. The former refers to the entire social and commercial life of the community, while the latter is more restricted and conveys the wrong expectation that only matters of public security should be the occupant's concern.[61] Finally, a balance also needs to be struck between such potentially far-reaching duties of the occupant and the capacity to fulfil the role of the ousted government in light of the specific circumstances of occupation which is, after all, perceived by international humanitarian law as an accessory part of a previous international armed conflict.

Together, these characteristics reflect a conservative as well as preservative attitude of occupation, which contradicts the idea and practice of occupations as transformative processes which not only lead from war to peace but create structures and societies capable of effectively enjoying and sustaining such a peace in the future. This paradox is built into humanitarian law and it has come to the forefront of the public debate in occupations such as in Iraq (from 2003 onwards). The way in which the United States as Occupying Power sought to change the country beyond what humanitarian law allowed challenged the idea of

[58] See Sandesh Sivakumaran, "Re-envisaging the International Law of Armed Conflict" (2001) 22(1) *European Journal of International Law* 244.

[59] Benvenisti, *The International Law of Occupation* (n. 1) pp. 103–6.

[60] Hague Regulations 1907, Art. 43 and (on the interpretation of this provision) Dinstein, *The International Law of Belligerent Occupation* (n. 1) p. 51.

[61] See ibid. p. 89.

occupation law. The US-led Coalition Provisional Authority (CPA), for example, issued altogether twelve regulations, 100 orders and seventeen explanatory memoranda which thoroughly reformed the Iraqi legal system, from criminal law to economic matters.[62]

If one adds to this the demands of human rights law with its inherent call for the dynamic development of a state's law, practice, structure and society, the problem magnifies. To reconcile the demands of humanitarian law to preserve the occupied territory for the benefit of the population with the need to ensure their human rights so as to empower individuals and develop societies along the coordinates of human rights seems to stretch the legal framework to breaking-point. What if, for example, a domestic norm (which needs to be preserved under humanitarian law) is incompatible with an international human rights norm? The often quoted case is that of a domestic penal law which stipulates that women who commit adultery can be stoned to death, a practice clearly prohibited as inhuman punishment under international human rights treaty law, which may nevertheless be the "law in force" under humanitarian law.[63]

This example seems to demonstrate the incompatibility of human rights and humanitarian law, but it fails to convince. First, the occupied state may be bound by an international human rights treaty which contains this very provision on inhuman punishment (if it is not already considered customary human rights law) and (at least where a norm is not derogated or otherwise affected by a reservation or declaration to a human rights treaty) makes the stoning illegal. The contradiction is thus not one between international humanitarian law and international human rights law but between the domestic penal law of the occupied state and the state's obligations under international law. All the Occupying Power needs to do is apply the applicable law, i.e., the domestic penal law in light of international human rights law. Furthermore, in 1907, when the occupation law was crafted, such laws have likely meant domestic laws only, but the Hague Regulations could not foresee the extent to which international human rights obligations would be seen as binding upon states a century later. Consequently, international legal obligations may well be considered also "laws in force" within the meaning of Hague Regulations, Article 43.[64] This is indeed the way in which, for example, the United States has considered various situations in occupied Iraq. The CPA relied on international (human rights) law when it redrafted the Iraqi Labour Code, based on Iraq's ratification of ILO Conventions Nos. 138 and 182. The CPA found Iraq to be under the legal obligation to take affirmative steps towards eliminating child labour, accepted such an obligation as the Occupying Power, argued that its duty to respect Iraq's laws in force would include the provisions of the ILO Conventions, and changed the Labour Code.[65]

[62] See, e.g., Kristen E. Boon, *The Future of the Law of Occupation* (2009), pp. 14 and 167, available at http://papers.ssrn.com/sol3/papers.cfm?abstract_id=1464443 (last accessed 15 April 2014).

[63] See Marko Milanovic, *Extraterritorial Application of Human Rights Treaties* (Oxford: Oxford University Press 2011), p. 257.

[64] See in support of this view Christopher Greenwood, "The Administration of Occupied Territory in International Law" in Emma Playfair (ed.), *International Law and the Administration of Occupied Territories: Two Decades of Israeli Occupation of the West Bank and Gaza Strip* (Oxford: Clarendon Press, 1992), p. 248; and McCarthy, "Legal Reasoning and the Applicability of International Human Rights Standards during Military Occupation" (n. 57) pp. 126–27.

[65] See International Committee of the Red Cross, Expert Meeting on the Law of Occupation and Other Forms of Administration of Territory, p. 65.

The argument that this would lead to limitless changes in violation of the very spirit of occupation law is unconvincing.[66] It is true that the way in which the law of occupation is informed by nineteenth century conceptions of international stability and order among (European) nation states prevents it from being used to remake states.[67] If a transformative occupation is defined as having the objective to overhaul the institutional, political and economic structure of the occupied territory in line with the occupant's own preferences, then such occupations indeed run counter to the very idea of occupation law.[68] But occupations which effectively seek "regime change" differ considerably from the immediate pressure faced by Occupying Powers to fix the destroyed infrastructure, secure the basic functioning of society, preserve the legal and political system of an industrialized country, rebuild a state whose very basic infrastructure and social fabric is in ruins, or ensure adherence to international human rights norms.[69] If one accepts that a purely statist and conservationist nature of occupation was not envisaged in 1899 and 1907, and that a degree of transformation is part of occupation law as it has been conceived, then international human rights law can inform the Occupying Power on the scope and limits of such a transformation. A combined reading of the Hague Regulations, Article 43, Geneva Convention IV, Article 64 and international human rights law would then require the abrogation of laws and practices which violate international human rights law obligations in occupied territories, whether they are derived from the extra-territorial application of international humanitarian law or as a continuation of the "laws in force" of the occupied country.[70]

Critics may say that this places an unreasonable burden on Occupying Powers way beyond what the law of occupation covers. International human rights law is essentially an agenda for social change, it may be argued, and differs from the conservative goals of humanitarian law, so that the two cannot be combined. Any such transformative acts would, however, only be acceptable within the boundaries of international human rights law.[71] The latter, and not self-proclaimed ideals (of free markets, religious beliefs or political ideologies) need to limit and guide such transformations. The argument that such changes amount to human rights imperialism for the way they export, in an intrusive manner, culturally alien and contextually inappropriate norms and force them on the local

66 See Jonathan Horowitz, "Human Rights, Positive Obligations, and Armed Conflict: Implementing the Right to Education in Occupied Territories" (2010) 1(2) *International Journal of Humanitarian Legal Studies* 326–27.

67 See Bhuta, "The Antinomies of Transformative Occupation" (n. 9) 740.

68 See International Committee of the Red Cross, Expert Meeting on the Law of Occupation and Other Forms of Administration of Territory, p. 67.

69 Ibid. pp. 69–70.

70 The Commentary on the Fourth Geneva Convention specifies particularly socio-economic rights such as child welfare, labour, food, hygiene and public health as susceptible to such transformations; see Jean Pictet (ed.), *Commentary to the Fourth Geneva Convention Relative to the Protection of Civilian Persons in Time of War* (Geneva: International Committee of the Red Cross, 1952), p. 337. Cases where international organization administer territory, such as in East Timor and Kosovo, remain special but invite even more human rights to be applied (without solving the resulting problems of accountability for human rights violations by international organizations), see Tobias H. Irmscher, "The Legal Framework for the Activities of the United Nations Administration Mission in Kosovo: The Charter, Human Rights, and the Law of Occupation" (2001) 44 *German Yearbook of International Law* 366.

71 See International Committee of the Red Cross, Expert Meeting on the Law of Occupation and Other Forms of Administration of Territory, p. 68.

population[72] seems exaggerated and (particularly where invasions and occupation are justified because they are meant to ensure human security and human rights of the population) hypocritical.

The conservationist approach expressed in the Hague Regulations and in Geneva Convention IV is thus not keen on putting preservation of local laws and practices above all other considerations. The law of occupation can, and must, be read in light of human rights standards so as to allow flexibility and make institutional and legal change possible on the basis of human rights law.[73] At the same time, international human rights law also sets the limits for such change. It seems thus unnecessary and perhaps even counter-productive to create exceptions and permit derogations from its strict conservative requirements only for certain types of occupations and not for others.[74]

In a more pragmatic manner, it needs to be noted that calls for a comprehensive document which would outline the rights and responsibilities of an Occupying Power under the various legal regimes have not led to, and seem not likely to lead to, any results.[75] The application of human rights in armed conflict will thus remain a complex matter to be debated on a case-by-case basis.[76] At the same time, international human rights law is also an important and intrinsic part in an emerging comprehensive *jus post bellum*.[77] If such a legal framework is meant to ensure fairness and justice in peace agreements, punishment of violations of the law, individual reparations and sanctions, justice and reconciliation, as well as governance centred on the people in a participatory manner within the framework of the rule of law, then international human rights needs to find a place, just as international humanitarian law remains important in post-conflict situations.

72 Ibid. pp. 68–69 (on the diverse views of experts).

73 See Kirsten Schmalenbach, "Das moderne Recht der Okkupation – ein Instrument des Regimewechsels?" in Hans-Joachim Heintze and Knut Ipsen (eds.), *Heutige bewaffnete Konflikte als Herausforderungen an das humanitäre Völkerrecht* (Berlin: Springer, 2011), p. 131.

74 See Garraway, "Occupation Responsibilities and Constraints" (n. 15) p. 278.

75 See the proposal of an "Occupation Document" in Brian Walsh and Ilan Peleg, "Human Rights under Military Occupation: The Need for Expansion" (1998) 2 *International Journal of Human Rights* 62.

76 See Roberts, "Transformative Military Occupation" (n. 9) p. 599.

77 See Ralphe Wilde, "Are Human Rights Norms Part of the Jus Post Bellum, and Should They Be?" in Carsten Stahn and Jann K. Kleffner (eds.), *Jus Post Bellum: Towards a Law of Transition from Conflict to Peace* (The Hague: T.M.C. Asser, 2008), pp. 163–86; and Matteo Tondini, "Putting an End to Human Rights Violations by Proxy: Accountability of International Organisations and Member States in the Framework of *Jus Post Bellum*" in Carsten Stahn and Jann K. Kleffner (eds.), *Jus Post Bellum: Towards a Law of Transition from Conflict to Peace* (The Hague: T.M.C. Asser, 2008), pp. 211–12.

16

Context: the humanization of international law

16.1 Humanity in international law

The debate on human rights in armed conflict reflects broader trends in international law and policy beyond concerns for the existing and future *jus in bello*. In particular, it represents and, at the same time, decisively fuels and contributes to three interlinked developments in international law which may be termed individualization, humanization and constitutionalization. Together, they describe the possible transformation of international law from a set of rudimentary inter-state agreements which regulate the coexistence and cooperation of sovereign nation states towards a normative framework which increasingly accommodates the human being as the ultimate beneficiary of any law. These intertwined processes are geared towards a legal order which protects and empowers individual human beings in a "humanitarian" way in the broadest sense, accommodates basic norms for inter- and intra-state behaviour in a constitutionalist sense, and provides for human rather than national security as a constituent concern of international law. While these trends are clearly discernible, they remain disputed as well as important for the debate on human rights in armed conflict.

The idea that international law is on such a trajectory of humanization means bringing community interests as well as the individual human being into the centre of law-making at the expense of the unquestioned and absolute sovereignty of states.[1] It invites a reflection on whether the development of international law is driven more by the will of states or occurs on the basis of shared values of the international community and human conscience, and how the two approaches go together.[2] In such a perspective and in light of the debate on the law of war, "humanity" transcends its meaning as merciful human kindness exchanged between individual persons and becomes a *Grundnorm* of an otherwise still state-based system.[3] While such a growing universalization of norms is obviously likely to be praised by cosmopolitans and fits into a constructivist worldview, it will create less enthusiasm in the realist quarter, particularly when it comes to matters of war and peace.[4]

But the humanization of international law is not only a theoretical construct or worldview. Elements of such a humanization can be detected at work in a variety of fields of

[1] See Theodor Meron, *The Humanization of International Law* (Leiden: Nijhoff, 2006).

[2] See Daniel Thürer, *International Humanitarian Law: Theory, Practice, Context* (The Hague: Hague Academy of International Law, 2011), p. 36.

[3] Anne Peters, "Humanity as the Alpha and Omega of Sovereignty" (2009) 20(3) *European Journal of International Law* 513.

[4] For a supportive cosmopolitan perspective see Mary Kaldor, *New and Old Wars: Organized Violence in a Global Era* (3rd edn., Cambridge: Polity, 2012), pp. 119–50.

international law.[5] The debate on human rights in armed conflict is a variation of this theme: "[b]oth humanitarian law and human rights law are involved in the transformation of the international legal order into something in which universal human values or goals take precedence over all other considerations."[6] Notwithstanding the intricacies of the interplay of human rights and humanitarian law, humanity is always the "*telos*"[7] of all regulatory activities in armed conflict. Whatever mechanical norms in a contractual legal system are being created and whatever humanitarian considerations need to be balanced, the idea and value of human dignity is at the core of them. "The essence of the whole corpus of international humanitarian law as well as human rights law," it has rightly been said, "lies in the protection of the human dignity of every person."[8]

But for humanitarian law as it stands, humanity is still more of an object and describes the product of its endeavours, whereas in human rights terms humanity is about individual entitlements and rights-holders around which the international legal order ultimately needs to be conceptualized. The humanization of international law, including *jus in bello*, is thus about conceiving humanity as both the object and subject of the law: "the human is a subject and a standard of treatment."[9] The ultimate benchmark for all law is human dignity as expressed in international human rights law and no other possible manifestation of humanity.

It has rightly been argued that the way in which international humanitarian law, international human rights law and international criminal law together gives rise to an altogether new type of international law which one may indeed call "humanity's law."[10] This describes not just the pragmatic confluence of three closely related fields but suggests that such a law has a transformative force which cuts across traditionally defined doctrinal borders, as well as the established dichotomy of peace-time and war-time.[11] Suggesting that human rights have a role to play in armed conflict (as well as arguing for the further development and reaffirmation of humanitarian law) is an openly humanistic project with the aim of advancing humanitarian considerations in matters of warfare (as which it has been presented in the introduction to this study), but it is also a reflection of such larger developments.[12]

Such a humanization of international law presupposes a human-centred perspective in which more and more rights are being reframed in order to reach beyond the interests of the state, and recognize instead the interests of persons and peoples.[13] This individualization of international law, too, is a paradigmatic change. International law is moving beyond its

[5] Wolfgang Benedek, "Challenges of a Humanization of International Relations by International Law" in MIha Pogacnik (ed.), *Challenges of Contemporary International Law and International Relations: Liber Amicorum in Honour of Ernest Petric* (Nova Gorica: European Faculty of Law, 2011), pp. 81–92.

[6] Thürer, *International Humanitarian Law* (n. 2) p. 138. [7] Ibid. p. 36.

[8] *Prosecutor* v. *Anto Furundžija*, IT-95_17/1.T, International Criminal Tribunal for the Former Yugoslavia, Judgment of 10 December 1998, para. 183.

[9] See Ruti G. Teitel, *Humanity's Law* (Oxford: Oxford University Press, 2011), p. 20. [10] Ibid. p. 13.

[11] Ibid. p. 21. For the author this new law is not merely the culmination of a state-based Westphalian law as most international lawyers would argue but is a process in law and politics towards transcending established approaches to international law altogether. For her this is a Grotian moment of reconceiving the international community, see pp. 31–32.

[12] See Orna Ben-Naftali, "Introduction: International Humanitarian and International Human Rights Law – *Pas de Deux*" in Orna Ben-Naftali (ed.), *International Humanitarian and International Human Rights Law* (Oxford: Oxford University Press, 2011), p. 4.

[13] See Teitel, *Humanity's Law* (n. 9) p. 17.

focus on inter-state relations towards acknowledging the individual human being, and again this can be observed in certain areas of the law with some clarity.[14] Human rights law is a particularly strong manifestation of this process and way ahead of other fields of international law where controversy over the role of individuals is the norm.[15] "The international human rights programme," it is said:

> is more than a piece-meal addition to the traditional corpus of international law, more than another chapter sandwiched into traditional textbooks of international law. By shifting the fulcrum of the system from the protection of sovereigns to the protection of people, it works qualitative changes in virtually every component.[16]

While humanization provides the direction in which international law is moving in its substance and individualization identifies the beneficiary of this development, then the idea of the constitutionalization of international law provides the framework in which this transformation takes place. In international legal scholarship, the idea of a constitutionalization of international law, which emanated primarily from German legal thought, has inspired a new thinking about the very form of international law in the twenty-first century. The essential argument of its proponents is that basic principles of international law resemble and echo developments in constitution-making on the national level. These principles represent a core of an emerging world constitution in its very broadest sense as an international community which feels bound together by some central values in an emerging legal framework which again emulates domestic constitutional developments.[17]

While this constitutionalization of international law is an "integrated, institutionalized, community-oriented and value-laden"[18] approach, it leaves space for sovereign nation states – but not at the cost of community interests. In such an imagined international legal order, human rights play a particularly important role, as they may accompany or replace state consent as the overriding principle for creating norms and binding the various elements together.[19] The way in which the humanitarian tradition of the law of armed conflict constitutes the first elements of such a constitutional idea has already been highlighted.[20] The application of human rights in armed conflicts necessarily supports such a view. When human rights are seen as a basic normative "bill of rights" of international law

[14] For an exhaustive analysis see Kate Parlett, "*The Individual in the International Legal System: Continuity and Change in International Law* (Cambridge: Cambridge University Press, 2011), in particular pp. 120–228 with regard to international humanitarian law.

[15] See Matthias C. Kettemann, *The Future of Individuals in International Law: Lessons from International Internet Law* (The Hague: Eleven, 2013), p. 81.

[16] W. Michael Reisman, "Sovereignty and Human Rights in Contemporary International Law" (1990) 84(4) *American Journal of International Law* 872.

[17] See, e.g., Erika de Wet, "The International Constitutional Order" (2006) 55(1) *International and Comparative Law Quarterly* 51 and Jan Klabbers, Anne Peters and Geir Ulfstein, *The Constitutionalization of International Law* (Oxford: Oxford University Press, 2009).

[18] Bruno Simma and Dirk Pulkowski, "Of Planets and the Universe: Self-Contained Regimes in International Law" (2003) 17(3) *European Journal of International Law* 498.

[19] See Joost Pauwelyn, *Conflict of Norms in Public International Law: How WTO Rules Relate to Other Rules of International Law* (Cambridge: Cambridge University Press, 2003), p. 95.

[20] See Daniel Thürer, "International Humanitarian Law as a Core of a 'Constitutional System' of Public International Law?" in Stefania Baldini and Guido Ravasi (eds.), *Humanitarian Action and State Sovereignty: International Congress on the Occasion of its 30th Anniversary, San Remo, 31 August–2 September 2000* (Sanremo: International Institute of Humanitarian Law, 2003), pp. 46–58.

then they necessarily penetrate all areas of law.[21] And when constitutionalism is about identifying "elementary principles above and within the law . . . and admit[ting] ethical and moral considerations to the resolution of issues of international law,"[22] then no field of law, including the law of war, can isolate itself from human rights as a cross-cutting issue. Some would even argue that in such a constitutional image of international law, human rights are not only universal but also potentially normatively higher than other law.[23]

It is also worth remembering that even humanitarian law, which may historically be perceived as a mere inter-state arrangement to regulate wars, was from its early days not only an inter-state law but expressed also interests other than that of states.[24] In this sense, its basic humanitarian principles are already part of such a constitutional core of international law where it invokes "unwritten basic principles and values of humanity and ideas like public conscience and global responsibility."[25] Such a tradition which is, for example, reflected in the Martens Clause (as discussed in the previous chapters) needs be revealed again and can be exploited because it connects with the current discourse on human rights in armed conflicts.

16.2 Human security and armed conflict

And finally, the idea of human security challenges any legal framework based on or geared towards putting national or military security above the security of the individual human being. This includes, in particular, the law of armed conflict. Since its first appearance in the 1994 United Nations Development Programme (UNDP) Human Development Report,[26] the concept of human security has advocated a shift from national and military security based on states' interests towards the security of individual human beings. Despite being criticized for its lack of analytical clarity, the concept has, in a vertical move, positioned the kind of security which people seek in their everyday lives rather than the security of borders or states as the ultimate goal.[27] In a horizontal move, the concept made clear that security is comprehensive because it means protection from armed conflicts, human rights violations, criminal activity and non-conventional and transnational threats and risks.

The concept of human security aptly reflects the threats and risks of today's variegated types of armed conflicts and connects easily with the ideas of humanization, individualization and constitutionalization of international law. And with its focus on managing threats,

[21] See Jochen Abr. Frowein, "Die Konstitutionalisierung des Völkerrechts" in Klaus Dicke, Waldemar Hummer, Daniel Girsberger, Katharina Boele-Woelki, Christoph Engel and Jochen Abr. Frowein (eds.), *Völkerrecht und internationales Privatrecht in einem sich globalisierenden System / Public and Private International Law in a Globalizing System. Berichte der deutschen Gesellschaft für Völkerrecht, Band 39* (Karlsruhe: C.F. Müller, 2000), p. 435.

[22] Klabbers, Peters and Ulfstein, *The Constitutionalization of International Law* (n. 17) p. 352.

[23] See Thürer, *International Humanitarian Law* (n. 2) p. 408.

[24] See Wolfram Karl, "Das humanitäre Völkerrecht auf dem Weg vom Zwischenstaats- zum Weltrecht" in Wolfgang Benedek, Renate Kicker and Hubert Isak (eds.), *Development and Developing International and European Law, Essays in Honour of Konrad Ginther on the Occasion of his 65th Birthday* (Frankfurt/Main: Peter Lang, 1999), p. 583.

[25] Thürer, *International Humanitarian Law* (n. 2) p. 415.

[26] United Nations Development Programme, *Human Development Report 1994: New Dimensions of Human Security* (1994), available at http://hdr.undp.org/reports/global/1994/en (last accessed 15 April 2014).

[27] See, e.g., Lloyd Axworthy, "Human Security and Global Governance: Putting People First" (2001) 7(1) *Global Governance* 19.

conflicts and violence in a human-centred perspective it also speaks the language of international humanitarian law. Given that it is widely acknowledged that human security needs to rely on international human rights law to give concrete meaning and normative substance to its propositions, the concept introduces the value and language of human dignity, as spelled out in international human rights law, into debates on security.[28] For human security, ensuring individual security as a goal of the international legal order necessitates the cumulative application of international humanitarian law and human rights to protect civilians from all forms of organized violence, including armed conflict.

The fate of civilians caught up in armed conflict is a prime concern of human security.[29] Some texts of humanitarian law, such as the Ottawa Convention in respect of anti-personnel mines, reflect human security concerns in the way they prioritize the long-term human impact of the use of these types of weapons over military considerations with a clear focus on the human impact of the use of these particular weapons.[30] The idea of human security has also found its way into the practice of international institutions and is invoked whenever human rights and humanitarian law are used in a complementary fashion to protect civilians in armed conflict. Whenever the UN Security Council adopts a resolution on this matter, for example in its Resolution 1325 on women, peace and security of 2000 (which links a gender perspective on human security with human rights, humanitarian law, international criminal law, refugee law, the spread of HIV/Aids and UN peace-keeping activities in a holistic framework)[31] or in Resolution 1894 on the protection of civilians in armed conflict of 2009,[32] it can be said to apply human security in all but name.[33]

Human security calls for "shap[ing] a security paradigm that captures the need to reach out in defence of people as well as states, and that can orchestrate and steer our endeavours in both directions."[34] The concept can thus be important as a benchmark when armed force is applied. But where humanitarian law regulates and restrains the use of force in relation to military necessity, human security measures the effects of the use of force within its overall concern of increasing individual security. In a human security perspective, measuring collateral damage recognizes other benchmarks than balancing civilian death with military advantage.[35] And given that human security relies on international human rights law to give clarity and substance to its conceptual ideas, a human security perspective on the

[28] See Gerd Oberleitner, "Human Security" in David P. Forsythe, *Encyclopedia of Human Rights* (Oxford: Oxford University Press, 2009), vol. II, pp. 486–93; and Wolfgang Benedek, "Human Rights and Human Security: Challenges and Prospects" in Alice Yotopolous-Marangopolous (ed.), *L'etat actuel des droits de l'homme dans le monde: Défis et perspectives* (Paris: Pedone, 2006), pp. 95–109.

[29] See, e.g., Commission on Human Security, *Human Security Now* (New York: Commission on Human Security, 2003), pp. 20–39.

[30] Convention on the Prohibition of the Use, Stockpiling, Production and Transfer of Anti-personnel Mines and on their Destruction (adopted 18 September 1997).

[31] Security Council Res. 1325, UN Doc. S/RES/1325 (31 October 2000).

[32] Security Council Res. 1894, UN Doc. S/RES/1894 (11 November 2009).

[33] On the way in which Canada sought to make the Security Council use human security more directly with regard to the protection of civilians and the trafficking in small arms and "blood diamonds" in the conflict in Angola, see Lloyd Axworthy, *Navigating a New World: Canada's Global Future* (Toronto: Alfred A. Knopf, 2003), p. 237.

[34] Sverre Lodgaard, *Human Security: Concept and Operationalization* (2007), available at www.cpdsindia.org/conceptandoperationalization.htm (last accessed 15 April 2014).

[35] See Teitel, *Humanity's Law* (n. 9) pp. 42–43.

law of armed conflict necessarily means the application of international human rights law in decisions on the use of force.

This is particularly so when military operations are conducted for the very purpose of enhancing human security. Where military force is being used for this goal, the idea of human security introduces more stringent benchmarks for the use of force and acceptable levels of damage to the civilian population.[36] Any use of force for human security purposes must then be measured against the impact it has on the security of those on whose behalf a military operation or "humanitarian intervention" is carried out, and not primarily along the lines of military advantage achieved. In such missions, the close link between human rights and human security entails a reassessment and upgrading of human rights in their design and conduct. This may, in turn, restrain the use of military means beyond what is expected by international humanitarian law. The latter accepts civilian deaths and destruction of civilian property as long as it is not excessive in relation to the military advantage achieved, an advantage measured in terms of military or national but not necessarily human security.[37] Examining international humanitarian law through a human security lens may thus force military operations to allow for more scrutiny on whether the means are adequate to the end. And because human rights are so important in the concept of human security, they will also have to be invoked more thoroughly in such calculations.

[36] See Mary Kaldor, *Human Security: Reflections on Globalization and Intervention* (Cambridge: Polity, 2007), p. 186.

[37] See Gerd Oberleitner, "Human Security: A Challenge to International Law?" (2005) 11(2) *Global Governance* 185.

Part V

Enforcement: practice and potential

Over the past decades a broad range of international institutions, mechanisms and procedures have been set up to promote human rights, assist states in implementing human rights norms, scrutinize states' adherence to these norms, prevent human rights violations and offer remedies for victims of such violations. The main human rights bodies created under international law – the UN Human Rights Council (and its predecessor, the Commission on Human Rights), the UN Office of the High Commissioner for Human Rights, the UN treaty bodies, the Inter-American Commission and Court of Human Rights, the European Court of Human Rights and the African Commission on Human and Peoples' Rights – have all repeatedly been confronted with situations of armed conflict. A certain practice of human rights bodies with regard to armed conflicts has emerged which necessarily reflects a human rights view of armed conflict. What these bodies have to say on the continued application of human rights law in such situations and on the interplay of humanitarian law and human rights law can inform the debate on human rights in armed conflict and carries with it the authority of institutions specifically designed to promote and protect human rights at all times, even though situations of armed conflict did not take centre-stage in the mind of their creators.

As will be shown, these bodies uniformly argue for the continued application of human rights in armed conflicts and, as a consequence, consider themselves authorized to deal with matters of human rights in such situations. While UN human rights bodies focus more on monitoring human rights in armed conflict, regional human rights systems have a stronger emphasis on "litigating" human rights through individual petitions, complaints and communication procedures before commissions and courts. The Inter-American Commission and Court of Human Rights, the European Court of Human Rights (and, prior to 1998, the European Commission on Human Rights) and the African Commission on Human and Peoples' Rights allow space for a victims' perspective in individual cases, different from the broader, policy-oriented monitoring of political human rights bodies such as the UN Human Rights Council.

As will also become clear, however, the concurrent application of international humanitarian law and human rights law remains troublesome in the practice of human rights bodies. The case law is uneven and inconclusive in this respect. Human rights bodies have not convincingly clarified the interplay of humanitarian law and human rights law, even though their preparedness to consider not only international human rights law but also international humanitarian law became evident already in the 1980s.[1]

[1] See Héctor Gros Espiell, "Humanitarian Law and Human Rights" in Janusz Symonides (ed.), *Human Rights: Concepts and Standards* (Aldershot and Paris: Ashgate and UNESCO, 2000), p. 354.

Their involvement in matters of human rights in armed conflict begs questions of law and policy, including the problem of whether they are legally entitled and competent to consider matters of humanitarian law; what complainants seek when they bring cases to treaty bodies and courts; and whether human rights bodies can and should stand in for the largely dysfunctional implementation mechanisms under international humanitarian law.

17

United Nations Human Rights Council: monitoring armed conflicts

17.1 A mandate for armed conflicts?

The UN Human Rights Council, created in 2006 as successor to the Commission on Human Rights, is at the centre of the UN's human rights system. The Council's many functions are laid down in General Assembly Resolution 60/251 of 2006 and include "promoting universal respect for the protection of all human rights and fundamental freedoms for all, without distinction of any kind and in a fair and equal manner,"[1] particularly in "situations of violations of human rights, including gross and systematic violations,"[2] upon which it can make recommendations. The Council is also meant to "respond promptly to human rights emergencies"[3] and "[s]erve as a forum for dialogue on thematic issues on all human rights."[4] In light of this mandate it comes as no surprise that the Council is regularly confronted with situations of armed conflicts where the kind of grave and serious human rights violations which the Council is meant to deal with are most likely to occur.

The Council has repeatedly held that it is mandated to consider the human rights situation in armed conflicts and that it sees human rights as applicable in such situations. To give one example: in Resolution 9/9 of 2008 on the protection of the human rights of civilians in armed conflict, the Council stated that the protection provided by human rights law continues in situations of armed conflict; that international human rights law and international humanitarian law are complementary and mutually reinforcing; that international humanitarian law has the status of *lex specialis*; and that certain rights of the ICCPR are non-derogable in times of armed conflict.[5] The resolution was adopted without a vote.[6] The Commission on Human Rights had used similar language in earlier thematic and country-specific resolutions, e.g., in Resolution 2005/34 on extra-judicial, summary or arbitrary executions, where it "[a]cknowledg[ed] ... that international human rights law and international humanitarian law are complementary and not mutually exclusive."[7]

With Resolution 9/9 of 2008 the Council also explicitly considered itself mandated to address systematic and gross violations of human rights of civilians in armed conflicts and

[1] General Assembly Res. 60/251, UN Doc. A/RES/60/251 (3 April 2006), para. 1. [2] Ibid. para. 3.
[3] Ibid. para. 5(f). [4] Ibid. para. 5(b).
[5] Human Rights Council Res. 9/9, UN Doc. A/HRC/RES/9/9 (24 September 2008), Preamble.
[6] See Report of the Human Rights Council on its Ninth Session, UN Doc. A/HRC/9/28 (2 December 2008), p. 25.
[7] Human Rights Commission Res. 2005/34, UN Doc. E/CN.4/RES/2005/34 (19 April 2005), Preamble. For more examples see Walter Kälin, *Report on the Situation of Human Rights in Kuwait under Iraqi Occupation*, UN Doc. E/CN.4/1992/26 (16 January 1992) (with reference to the involvement of the Council in Kuwait, Chile, Sri Lanka, El Salvador, Guatemala, Afghanistan and the former Yugoslavia).

to monitor human rights at all times, including in armed conflicts.[8] The Council also found other UN human rights bodies to be under the same obligation and requested that its own relevant special procedures as well as its subsidiary body, the Human Rights Council Advisory Committee and UN human rights treaty bodies address, within their respective mandates, "the relevant aspects of the protection of human rights of civilians in armed conflict."[9] The Commission's Sub-Commission on the Promotion and Protection of Human Rights (the precursor of the current Advisory Committee) also argued for the convergence of international human rights law and international humanitarian law in its Resolution 1989/24, entitled "Human rights in times of armed conflict."[10] The Council's mandate to act when the human rights situation in armed conflicts requests it is thus beyond question. The Council can monitor and discuss human rights in such situations in its regular and special sessions, through its country and thematic special procedures, in response to complaints of gross human rights violations, and in the Universal Periodic Review (UPR).[11] But the Council has no specific mandate to monitor norms other than human rights. Can it also resort to international humanitarian law when it deals with a situation of armed conflict?

The Council's and Commission's practice so far allows a positive answer. For roughly two decades, between the 1980s and 2006 (when it was replaced by the Council), the Commission on Human Rights has regularly treated international humanitarian law as within its remit and has always been supported by its parent body, the Economic and Social Council (ECOSOC), in this approach.[12] Given that General Assembly Resolution 60/251 (which set up the Human Rights Council) has mandated it to continue with all activities of the Commission, the Council saw no reason to change this approach. The matter was, however, seemingly not discussed when the Council was created in 2006.[13] As a consequence, international humanitarian law is not mentioned in General Assembly Resolution 60/251. A clear mandate of the Human Rights Council to invoke international humanitarian law also cannot be derived from the UN Charter. Neither Article 1(3) of the Charter (which mandates the UN to promote and encourage respect for human rights) nor Article 68 (which had set up the Commission on Human Rights as a subsidiary body of ECOSOC in 1945) mentions humanitarian law.[14]

[8] Human Rights Council Res. 9/9, UN Doc. A/HRC/RES/9/9 (24 September 2008), para. 6: "Resolves to address, in accordance with its mandate established by the General Assembly in its resolution 60/251, systematic and gross violations of the human rights of civilians in armed conflicts."

[9] Ibid. para. 7.

[10] See Alfred de Zayas, "Human Rights and Humanitarian Law" (1993) 61–62 *Nordic Journal of International Law* 259.

[11] For details on the Council's mandate and working methods, see Bertrand Ramcharan, *The Human Rights Council* (Abingdon: Routledge, 2011), pp. 15–105.

[12] See United Nations Office of the High Commissioner for Human Rights, *International Legal Protection of Human Rights in Armed Conflict* (New York and Geneva: United Nations, 2011), p. 103; and Philip Alston, Jason Morgan-Foster and William Abresch, "The Competence of the UN Human Rights Council and Its Special Procedures in Relation to Armed Conflicts: Extrajudicial Executions in the 'War on Terror'" (2008) 19 *European Journal of International Law* 198–99.

[13] See Alston, Morgan-Foster and Abresch, "The Competence of the UN Human Rights Council" (n. 12) 199.

[14] UN Charter, Art. 1(3): "The purposes of the United Nations are ... to achieve international co-operation ... in promoting and encouraging respect for human rights and for fundamental freedoms for all without distinction as to race, sex, language, or religion"; UN Charter, Art. 68: "The Economic and

But the fact that the Council has no specific mandate to determine violations of humanitarian law and denounce violations of the Geneva Conventions and Additional Protocols or other humanitarian law instruments does not mean that it necessarily acts outside its competence (*ultra vires*) and that consequently any matter involving international humanitarian law needs to be referred to other forums, such as the General Assembly (the competence of which extends to all matters of international law).[15] On the other hand, the Council is also not specifically barred from applying humanitarian law in its mandate. And indeed, the Council's practice (and that of its predecessor, the Commission) shows that it does use international humanitarian law without keeping it strictly separate from international human rights law.[16]

17.2 The Council's practice

Since the Commission became entitled to denounce human rights violations in specific countries under ECOSOC Resolution 1235 in 1967 (which brought an end to the Commission's "no power doctrine" on responding to complaints about human rights crises and emergencies), many countries it had to deal with were affected by armed conflict.[17] Situations examined by the Commission in pursuance of ECOSOC Resolution 1235 included El Salvador, Bolivia, Guatemala, Haiti, Cuba, Equatorial Guinea, Central African Republic, Uganda, Iran, Sri Lanka, Afghanistan, Iraq, Libya, Syria, and more.[18] Many of the Commission's country-specific resolutions contained references to international humanitarian law. The Commission denounced, for example, violations of international humanitarian law in Sri Lanka since the 1980s. In Resolution 1987/61 of 1987 it called upon all groups in Sri Lanka to respect universally accepted rules of humanitarian law, cooperate with the International Committee of the Red Cross (ICRC) and allow it to deliver humanitarian assistance.[19] In the conflict in the former Yugoslavia, the Commission also called upon the parties in 1992 to respect international humanitarian law and spoke out on violations of international humanitarian law, both in general terms as well as with reference to specific rules of humanitarian law. In Resolution 1992/S-1/1 on the situation of human rights in the territory of the former Yugoslavia, the Commission asked for full respect for humanitarian law and reminded the parties that they are:

Social Council shall set up commissions in economic and social fields and for the promotion of human rights."

15 See Theo van Boven, "Reliance on Norms of Humanitarian Law by United Nations' Organs" in Astrid J.M. Delissen and Gerard J. Tanja (eds.), *Humanitarian Law of Armed Conflict: Challenges Ahead, Essays in Honour of Frits Kalshoven* (Dordrecht: Nijhoff, 1991), p. 511.

16 See Louise Doswald-Beck and Sylvain Vité, "International Humanitarian Law and Human Rights Law" (1993) 33(293) *International Review of the Red Cross* 115.

17 The Commission's decision not to respond to complaints on human rights violations was taken in 1947, see *Report of the Commission on Human Rights*, Economic and Social Council Official Records, Supplement No. 3, UN Doc. E/259 (1947), para. 22, and was reversed with Economic and Social Council Res. 1235 (XLII), Economic and Social Council Official Records, Supplement No. 1, UN Doc. E/4393 (1967) which allowed the Commission to examine information relevant to gross violations of human rights and fundamental freedoms.

18 See van Boven, "Reliance on Norms of Humanitarian Law by United Nations' Organs" (n. 15) pp. 499–500.

19 See Commission on Human Rights, UN Doc. E/CN.4/1987/61 (12 March 1987), para. 1.

> bound to comply with their obligations under international humanitarian law, and in particular the third Geneva Convention relating to the treatment of prisoners of war and the fourth Geneva Convention relating to the protection of civilian persons in time of war, of 12 August 1949, and the Additional Protocols thereto of 1977.[20]

ECOSOC endorsed this resolution.[21] In Resolution 1994/72 the Human Rights Commission "[c]ondemn[ed] categorically all violations of human rights and international humanitarian law by all sides"[22] as well as "continued deliberate and unlawful attacks and uses of military force against civilians and other protected persons . . . non-combatants . . . and . . . relief operations."[23] Again ECOSOC approved this.[24] In Resolution S-3/1 on human rights in Rwanda in 1994, the Commission "[c]ondemn[ed] in the strongest terms all breaches of international humanitarian law . . . in Rwanda,"[25] and called upon all the parties to end these breaches and urged the government of Rwanda to put an end to all violations of international humanitarian law by all persons within its jurisdiction or under its control. Again, this was endorsed by ECOSOC.[26] In Resolution 1996/68, the Commission "call[ed] upon the Government of Israel, the occupying Power of territories in southern Lebanon and West Bekaa, to comply with the Geneva Conventions of 1949, in particular the Geneva Convention relative to the Protection of Civilian Persons in Time of War,"[27] and again ECOSOC approved this.[28]

Such practice is not beyond the limits of the Council's mandate for a number of reasons. First, it needs to be noted that the Council (as well is its predecessor, the Commission) is a "political" rather than a "legal" human rights body. Being composed of governmental representatives (as opposed to a legal human rights body, such as a treaty body composed of independent experts, or a human rights court), such political bodies are entrusted with a broad set of governance functions, different from the limited monitoring tasks of treaty bodies and courts. Political human rights bodies take decisions on human rights issues "on political lines, albeit in the light of appropriate international legal standards."[29] In contrast, legal bodies are expected to operate on the basis of human rights expertise and strict legal demands rather than political considerations. The boundaries between the two types of institutions are obviously blurred as both deal with legal and political issues, and given that independence and expertise are relative terms.[30] Still, in comparison to legal bodies, political bodies enjoy a larger degree of freedom to refer to international law as a standard of conduct rather than having to identify specific primary sources of the applicable law. This is particularly important where basic humanitarian obligations are invoked:

[20] Commission on Human Rights Res. S/1-1, UN Doc. E/CN.4/RES/1992/S-1/1 (14 August 1992), para. 1.

[21] See ECOSOC Decision 1992/305 (18 August 1992).

[22] Commission on Human Rights Res. 1994/72, UN Doc. E/CN.4/RES/1994/72 (9 March 1994), para. 4.

[23] Ibid. para. 7. [24] See ECOSOC Decision 1994/262 (22 July 1994).

[25] Commission on Human Rights Res. S-3/1, UN Doc. E/CN.4/RES/1994/S-3/1 (25 May 1994), para. 1.

[26] See ECOSOC Decision 1994/223 (6 June 1994).

[27] Commission on Human Rights Res. 1996/68, UN Doc. E/CN.4/RES/1996/68 (23 April 1996), para. 3.

[28] See ECOSOC Decision 1996/274 (23 July 1996).

[29] Philip Alston, "The Commission on Human Rights" in Philip Alston (ed.), *The United Nations and Human Rights: A Critical Appraisal* (Oxford: Clarendon Press, 1992), p. 193.

[30] See Gerd Oberleitner, *Global Human Rights Institutions: Between Remedy and Ritual* (Cambridge: Polity, 2007), pp. 63–66.

> [c]ourts of law may . . . establish legal rights and obligations. However, political organs of the United Nations, . . . in assessing the policies and actions of governments or of any other relevant entities . . . can base themselves on the premise that governments and other actors must comply with basic standards of humanitarian behaviour.[31]

Political bodies thus find it easier to avoid a precise legal assessment in favour of a broader prescription of politically desired outcomes by invoking general standards laid down in the law. If the Council's mandate is understood in such a way, i.e., as comprising concern for humanitarian principles found in human rights *and* humanitarian law, it is difficult to imagine a situation in which the Council would be barred from invoking such principles in light of its wide-ranging mandate. The Council's general references to core international humanitarian documents and the principles contained therein confirm this approach. Such a policy-oriented approach does not, however, remedy the legal limits of resorting to international humanitarian law. If a state has derogated a human rights provision under international human rights law in a situation of emergency, the Council is obviously barred from holding a state to account for a violation of such a norm, although the effects, limits and lawfulness of such derogations could again be scrutinized by the Council.

Alternatively, the Council's repeated references to humanitarian law can be justified by the argument that resorting to humanitarian law is never beyond the Council's mandate as long as it is related to human rights issues. The Council does, after all, look beyond international human rights law when it considers, for example, matters of state responsibility, and it can do the same with regard to other matters of international law. Reference to humanitarian law has also been justified by yet another argument: in Resolution 9/9 of 2008 (mentioned above) the Council held that violations of international humanitarian law, including grave breaches of the Geneva Conventions or Additional Protocol I, constitute at the same time gross human rights violations.[32] What the Council seemed to suggest is that in situations where two norms of both regimes substantially converge, the Council is entitled to consider this situation. The Council did not, however, qualify which "gross human rights violations" would be covered by this argument.

Whenever states have tried to reject the Council's view that it is mandated to invoke international humanitarian law and denounce violations of humanitarian law, they usually resorted to the *lex specialis* character of international humanitarian law rather than arguing that the Council is, in a literal reading of its mandate, legally barred from referring to humanitarian law. But their argument is built on weak ground: not only is the adequacy of the principle of *lex specialis* for explaining and regulating the relationship between human rights and humanitarian law questionable, as has been discussed above. It is also obvious that in determining the specialty of international humanitarian law, the Council needs to consider this legal regime rather than keep away from it.

Alternatively, states may question the Council's competence to refer to international humanitarian law by arguing that it is not legally but practically and operationally incompetent to do so. In other words, they may question the Council's suitability or capability to deliver the expected results. Matters of humanitarian law, this argument goes, should be

[31] van Boven, "Reliance on Norms of Humanitarian Law by United Nations' Organs" (n. 15) p. 503.

[32] See Human Rights Council Res. 9/9, UN Doc. A/HRC/RES/9/9 (24 September 2008), para. 1. The Council repeats the respective language of earlier resolutions of the Commission on Human Rights in this matter, see, e.g., Commission on Human Rights Res. 2005/63 on the protection of the human rights of civilians in armed conflicts, UN Doc. E/CN.4/RES/2005/63 (20 April 2005).

brought before a more suitable body the composition, expertise or aptitude of which exceeds that of the Human Rights Council. Such a decision on capability can, however, legally and reasonably be taken only by the concerned body itself. It is up to the member states of the respective body (or its parent body) to ascertain a majority decision to keep the matter on the agenda or relegate it to another institution. A related argument is that the Council's workload, time constraints and limited resources will not allow including any other matters than strictly human rights questions. This can be countered in a similar way: deciding whether such constraints allow the Council to deal with a particular question is the prerogative of the Council or the General Assembly. They would have to decide on how to remedy any shortcomings, for example, by allocating resources or setting up subsidiary bodies specifically entrusted with matters of international humanitarian law. No such decision has ever been sought.

17.3 Special procedures of the Human Rights Council and armed conflict

While the Council usually refers to humanitarian law in general terms when discussing situations of armed conflict, its special procedures – Special Rapporteurs, Independent Experts, Working Groups and Special Representatives of the UN Secretary General – are more important for dealing with situations of armed conflict. These procedures are the backbone of the Council's investigative, supervisory and protective activities and have, over time, covered a range of human rights issues and countries.[33] They serve functions which have been described by the mandate-holders of special procedures like this:

> Our task is clear: what we do is render the international norms that have been developed more operative. We do not merely deal with theoretical questions, but strive to enter into constructive dialogues with governments and to seek their cooperation as regards concrete situations, incidents and cases. The core of our work is to study and investigate in an objective manner with a view to understanding the situations and recommending to governments solutions to overcome the problem of securing respect for human rights.[34]

Special procedures considered situations of armed conflict on many occasions. Country procedures were frequently faced with armed conflicts and occupations since their emergence in the 1960s.[35] The Ad Hoc Working Group of Experts, for example, mandated in 1967 to "investigate and study the policies and practices which violate human rights in South Africa and Namibia,"[36] was asked to investigate cases of torture and ill-treatment of detainees and the deaths of detainees in South Africa. When the Working Group took up its work, it gave itself a list of applicable standards against which the measures taken by South

[33] See in greater detail Oberleitner, *Global Human Rights Institutions* (n. 30) pp. 54–62.

[34] Joint Declaration of the independent experts responsible for the special procedures for the protection of human rights, UN Doc. A/CONF.157/9 (18 June 1993).

[35] The first country procedure was established for Vietnam in 1963 although it did not materialize due to circumstances on the ground, see Lyal S. Sunga, "The Special Procedures of the UN Commission on Human Rights: Should They be Scrapped?" in Gudmundur Alfredsson, Jonas Grimheden, Bertrand Ramcharan and Alfred de Zayas (eds.), *International Human Rights Monitoring Mechanisms, Essays in Honour of Jakob Th. Möller* (The Hague: Nijhoff, 2001), pp. 236–41.

[36] Commission on Human Rights Res. 2 (XXIII) (6 March 1967), ECOSOC Official Records 42 (1967) Supplement 6, 76.

Africa could be assessed. This list included relevant provisions of the four Geneva Conventions of 1949.[37]

In the 1980s, conflict situations began to figure ever more prominently on the agenda of special procedures. Since this time, they have regularly invoked international humanitarian law alongside human rights. The Special Rapporteur on the Situation of Human Rights in Afghanistan (up to 1991), Felix Ermacora, considered all parties to the conflict bound by Common Article 3 of the Geneva Conventions and found violations of international humanitarian law through the use of antipersonnel mines (specifically the so-called toy-bombs); the indiscriminate killings of civilians; the use of heavy weapons with massively destructive effects; the systematic discrimination against persons not supporting the People's Democratic Party of Afghanistan; and the non-acceptance of members of Afghan opposition movements as prisoners of war. His findings were endorsed in a number of subsequent General Assembly Resolutions.[38]

In El Salvador (up to 1991) Special Representative Jose Antonio Pasto Ridruejo repeatedly emphasized the importance of Common Article 3 of the Geneva Conventions and criticized the military for the indiscriminate killing of civilians by air bombardments and the use of certain types of weapons (i.e., fragmentation and incendiary bombs as well as white phosphorus), and the guerilla forces for the use of antipersonnel mines against civilians and for attacking the economic infrastructure of El Salvador in violation of international humanitarian law. The General Assembly endorsed his findings and urged, in a detailed manner, the parties to the conflict to comply with international humanitarian law.[39] Similarly, the Rapporteurs mandated to deal with the conflicts in Rwanda, Burundi and the Democratic Republic of the Congo included references to international humanitarian law in their reports.[40]

Only occasionally did the special procedures express concern about using international humanitarian law. When the Council's Working Group on Arbitrary Detention was, in 1993, faced with the question of whether it should refer to international humanitarian law or not, it considered that international humanitarian law instruments were not within its remit but a prerogative of the ICRC. The Working Group decided that it:

> will not deal with situations of international armed conflict in so far as they are covered by the Geneva Conventions of 12 August 1949 and their Additional Protocols, particularly when the International Committee of the Red Cross (ICRC) has competence.[41]

By 2006, however, the Working Group had changed its opinion and argued that it is well within its mandate to deal with communications arising from a situation of international armed conflict, in particular when detained persons are denied the protection of Geneva

[37] See van Boven, "Reliance on Norms of Humanitarian Law by United Nations' Organs" (n. 15) p. 499.

[38] See the reports of Special Rapporteur Felix Ermacora on the situation of human rights in Afghanistan, UN Doc. A/40/843 (5 November 1985), para. 128; UN Doc. A/42/667 (23 October 1987), para. 123; UN Doc. A/44/669; and UN Doc. A/49/650 (8 November 1994); and van Boven, "Reliance on Norms of Humanitarian Law by United Nations' Organs" (n. 15) p. 504.

[39] Ibid. 505–6.

[40] See Michaela Ricca, "Human Rights and the UN Special Rapporteurs' System: Tendencies in Reporting on Conflict Areas" (2002) 15(3) *Journal of International Law of Peace and Armed Conflict* 169.

[41] *Report of the Working Group on Arbitrary Detention*, UN Doc. E/CN.4/1993/24 (12 January 1993), Annex IV, para. 16.

Convention III or IV.[42] When confronted with the situation of persons detained by the United States in Guantánamo Bay, it consequently applied both international humanitarian law and international human rights law. The joint report of the Working Group and several Special Rapporteurs on this matter repeated the position that human rights are applicable in times of armed conflict and that human rights and humanitarian law are complementary and not mutually exclusive.[43]

The Working Group on Enforced or Involuntary Disappearances seems to have been the only body which, for some time, explicitly avoided international humanitarian law as it was not prepared to deal with situations of international armed conflict for which it deemed the ICRC as solely competent.[44] But yet again, this position has changed, as the latest version of the document which outlines the Working Group's methods of work no longer mentions any such restriction.[45]

Apart from these instances, thematic procedures have repeatedly invoked international humanitarian law. The Representative of the Secretary-General on the human rights of internally displaced persons, for example, spoke out on violations of international humanitarian law and international human rights law in his report on Somalia and specifically mentioned indiscriminate attacks; the shelling of residential areas; the generalized use of force without the necessary precautions to minimize the impact on the civilian population; and referred to prohibited methods of warfare as possible war crimes and crimes against humanity.[46] The Special Rapporteurs on adequate housing as a component of the right to an adequate standard of living, on illicit movement and dumping of toxic and dangerous products and wastes, on the independence of judges and lawyers, and on the sale of children and child prostitution, have issued thematic reports in which they refer to the application of human rights standards in armed conflict and to international humanitarian law.[47]

[42] See Office of the United Nations High Commissioner for Human Rights, *Report on the Outcome of the Expert Consultation on the Issue of Protecting the Human Rights of Civilians in Armed Conflict*, UN Doc. A/HRC/11/31 (4 June 2009), para. 24.

[43] Chairperson-Rapporteur of the Working Group on Arbitrary Detention, Leila Zerrougui; Special Rapporteur on the independence of judges and lawyers, Leandro Despouy; Special Rapporteur on torture and other cruel, inhuman or degrading treatment or punishment, Manfred Nowak; Special Rapporteur on freedom of religion or belief, Asma Jahangir; and Special Rapporteur on the right of everyone to the enjoyment of the highest attainable standard of physical and mental health, Paul Hunt, *Report*, UN Doc. E/CN.4/2006/120 (27 February 2006), paras. 15–16. For references to international humanitarian law, see paras. 7, 9, 19, 21, 25, 28 and 83.

[44] See Office of the High Commissioner for Human Rights, *Enforced or Involuntary Disappearances*, Fact Sheet No. 6 (Rev.3) (Geneva: United Nations, 2009), p. 11.

[45] See *Report of the Working Group on Enforced or Involuntary Disappearances*, UN Doc. A/HRC/19/58/Rev.1, Annex II (Revised methods of work of the Working Group on Enforced or Involuntary Disappearances, adopted on 11 November 2011).

[46] See UN OHCHR, *Report on the Outcome of the Expert Consultation* (n. 42) para. 19.

[47] See, e.g., Special Rapporteur on adequate housing as a component of the right to an adequate standard of living, Miloon Kothari, *Report*, UN Doc. E/CN.4/2001/51 (25 January 2001), para. 73; Special Rapporteur on adequate housing as a component of the right to an adequate standard of living, Miloon Kothari, *Report*, UN Doc. E/CN.4/2004/48 (2 November 2004), paras. 18 and 92; Special Rapporteur on adverse effects of illicit movement and dumping of toxic and dangerous products and waste on the enjoyment of human rights, Okechukwu Ibeanu, *Report*, UN Doc. A/HRC/5/5 (11 June 2007), paras. 4 and 47–57; Special Rapporteur on the independence of judges and lawyers, Leandro Despouy, *Report*, UN Doc. E/CN.4/2006/52 (23 January 2006), paras. 14–15; and Special Rapporteur on the sale of children, child prostitution and child pornography, Juan Migueal Petit, *Report*, UN Doc. E/CN.4/2006/67 (12 January 2006), paras. 61–64.

The Special Rapporteur on the promotion and protection of human rights while countering terrorism has made the strongest arguments yet for international humanitarian law to be within the remit of special procedures. Given that the exercise of the Rapporteur's mandate depends on classifying when a situation amounts to an armed conflict (in which humanitarian law is applicable) and when to a law enforcement operation (in which human rights law is applicable), an in-depth analysis and application of international humanitarian law was seen as indispensible by the first mandate holder, Martin Scheinin.[48] He argued for the continued application of international human rights law in armed conflicts,[49] as well as for the complementary application of international human rights and humanitarian law. He did so, for example, in the report on Israel where he stated that the legal framework against which Israeli measures against terrorism are to be assessed is comprised of international humanitarian law and international human rights law.[50] His reports have considered targeted killings of civilians; the active participation of civilians in hostilities; the detention of persons charged with terrorism without access to judicial review; and security detention during an armed conflict; as well as non-recognition of prisoner of war status – all of these matters are (also) regulated by international humanitarian law.[51]

In a joint mission to Lebanon and Israel in September 2006, following the conflict between Israel and Lebanon, which was carried out by four other mandate holders (the Special Rapporteur on extra-judicial, summary or arbitrary executions, the Special Rapporteur on the right of everyone to the enjoyment of the highest attainable standard of physical and mental health, the Representative of the Secretary-General on human rights of internally displaced persons and the Special Rapporteur on adequate housing as a component of the right to an adequate standard of living), the complementary nature of international human rights law and humanitarian law was stressed again. Their report considered cases of land confiscation, forced evictions and displacement, dispossession of property and destruction of homes as a consequence of the armed conflict. They concluded that the demolition of homes in violation of international humanitarian law and the subsequent displacement amounted to forcible eviction and constituted also a violation of the right to adequate housing.[52] The report also suggested that internal armed conflicts involve the full applicability of relevant provisions of international humanitarian law and human rights law, except where states have derogated from human rights law.[53]

[48] See UN OHCHR, *Report on the Outcome of the Expert Consultation* (n. 42), para. 22. The Special Rapporteur's mandate covered the period August 2005 to July 2011.

[49] See Special Rapporteur on the promotion and protection of human rights and fundamental freedoms while countering terrorism, Martin Scheinin, *Report, Addendum: Mission to America*, UN Doc. A/HRC/6/17/Add.3 (22 November 2007), para. 7.

[50] See Special Rapporteur on the promotion and protection of human rights and fundamental freedoms while countering terrorism, Martin Scheinin, *Report, Addendum: Mission to Israel, including Visit to Occupied Palestinian territory*, UN Doc. A/HRC/6/17/Add.4 (16 November 2007), para. 6.

[51] See UN OHCHR, *Report on the Outcome of the Expert Consultation* (n. 42), para. 23.

[52] See Special Rapporteur on extra-judicial, summary or arbitrary executions, Philip Alston; Special Rapporteur on the right of everyone to the enjoyment of the highest attainable standard of physical and mental health, Paul Hunt; Representative of the Secretary-General on human rights of internally displaced persons, Walter Kälin; and Special Rapporteur on adequate housing as a component of the right to an adequate standard of living, Miloon Kothari, *Report: Mission to Lebanon and Israel*, UN Doc. A/HRC/2/7 (2 October 2006), in particular paras. 22–31 and 61.

[53] Ibid. paras. 15–17.

The concerned states have at times rejected such views. A particularly vivid debate ensued on whether the Special Rapporteur on extra-judicial, summary or arbitrary executions is allowed to consider international humanitarian law. When Special Rapporteur Asma Jahangir (who held the post from 1998–2004) reported on the killing of six men travelling in a car in Yemen by a missile launched from a US-controlled Predator drone aircraft on 3 November 2002, the US government responded that military operations conducted in the "War on Terror" would not fall within the mandate of the Rapporteur as they occurred in an armed conflict governed by international humanitarian law.[54] In this and in other cases the United States found the (then) Commission on Human Rights and its Rapporteurs to lack entirely the competence to consider matters pertaining to the law of armed conflict.[55] Cases included the alleged use of excessive force against civilians during demonstrations in Falluja, Iraq, in 2003;[56] the critique on the "shoot on sight" policy of US troops in the looting of property in Iraq;[57] and the killing of suspected terrorist Haitham al-Yemeni on the border between Pakistan and Afghanistan on 10 May 2005 by a US drone.[58] The United States also made clear that, in their view, similar references to international humanitarian law in resolutions of the General Assembly, such as in General Assembly Resolution 59/197 of 20 December 2004 which urged governments "to take all necessary and possible measures, in conformity with international human rights law and international humanitarian law, to prevent loss of life ... during ... armed conflicts,"[59] were legally and politically separate from the work of Special Rapporteurs.[60]

Asma Jahangir's successor as Special Rapporteur on extra-judicial, summary or arbitrary executions, Philip Alston (who held the mandate from 2004–2010) sought to reject these arguments. In his first report in 2005 (on the United States' responses to communications regarding the alleged extra-judicial killings in Yemen and Iraq) he pointed out that, in his opinion, humanitarian law "falls squarely within [the Rapporteur's] mandate."[61] He rested his view on three arguments: that (similar to the view held by UN treaty bodies) Special Rapporteurs may resort to any other source of law to decide on a human rights violation; that Special Rapporteurs need to interpret their mandate dynamically in light of new

[54] See Letter dated 14 April 2003 from the Chief of Section, Political and Specialized Agencies, of the Permanent Mission of the United States of America to the Secretariat of the Commission on Human Rights, UN Doc. E/CN.4/2003/G/80 (22 April 2004), pp. 2–3; see also Alston, Morgan-Foster and Abresch, "The Competence of the UN Human Rights Council" (n. 12) 186.

[55] See Letter dated 14 April 2003, UN Doc. E/CN.4/2003/G/80 (n. 54) p. 5.

[56] Communication of 12 May 2003, in Special Rapporteur, Asma Jahangir, *Report: Summary of Cases Transmitted to the Government and Replies Received*, UN Doc. E/CN.4/2004/7/Add.1 (2004), para. 579, see Alston, Morgan-Foster and Abresch, "The Competence of the UN Human Rights Council" (n. 12) 188.

[57] Communication of 12 May 2003, UN Doc. E/CN.4/2004/7/Add.1 (2004), para. 572; see Alston, Morgan-Foster and Abresch, "The Competence of the UN Human Rights Council" (n. 12) 188.

[58] Allegation letter sent on 26 August 2005, in UN Doc. E/CN.4/2006/53/Add.1 (27 March 2006), pp. 264–65; see Alston, Morgan-Foster and Abresch, "The Competence of the UN Human Rights Council" (n. 12) 188–89.

[59] General Assembly Res. 59/197, UN Doc. A/Res/59/197 (20 December 2004).

[60] Letter dated 4 May 2006 from the United States to the Special Rapporteur on extra-judicial, summary or arbitrary executions, p. 1, quoted in Alston, Morgan-Foster and Abresch, "The Competence of the UN Human Rights Council" (n. 12) 189.

[61] Special Rapporteur on extra-judicial, summary or arbitrary execution, Philip Alston, *Report*, UN Doc. E/CN.4/2005/7 (22 December 2004), para. 45.

developments; and that reliance on humanitarian law by Special Rapporteurs is acceptable as long as it is endorsed by the Human Rights Council.[62]

The first argument had already been developed by the UN Human Rights Committee when it pointed out (in its General Comment No. 29) that, despite its competence being limited to violations of the International Covenant on Civil and Political Rights (ICCPR), it has "the competence to take a State party's other international obligations into account when it considers whether the Covenant allows the State party to derogate from specific provisions of the Covenant."[63] The second of the Rapporteur's arguments is based on the consideration that the mandate of the Special Rapporteur on extra-judicial, summary or arbitrary executions was created in response to a phenomenon, i.e., to examine questions related to summary or arbitrary executions, and not to accommodate a specific legal regime.[64] Such a mandate, the Special Rapporteur argued, is evolutionary in nature: responding effectively to the phenomenon of summary or arbitrary executions entails considerations not envisaged in the original resolution which set up the post of the Special Rapporteur. The need to respond to new forms of violations and to increasing public demands for effective protection of victims would necessitate a more expansive analysis which includes, *inter alia*, considerations of international humanitarian law, he argued.[65] This would ensure that "mandates are not frozen in time and thus unable to respond to new and changing circumstances."[66]

And finally, the Special Rapporteur argued that any such dynamism needs ultimately to be accepted by the Human Rights Council and through it by the UN member states. Every annual report of the Special Rapporteur on extra-judicial, summary or arbitrary executions since 1992 had dealt with violations of the right to life in the context of international and non-international armed conflicts,[67] and indeed, the Council has always signalled its support for the approach of the Rapporteurs since the post was first established in 1982, usually through resolutions which endorsed their reports.[68]

The United States countered by pointing out that even if such practice had been established it could not heal the absence of any reference to international humanitarian law in the original mandate of the Special Rapporteur.[69] But there has been consistent state practice in support of the Rapporteur's position.[70] Already in the first ever report, Special

62 See Alston, Morgan-Foster and Abresch, "The Competence of the UN Human Rights Council" (n. 12) 199–200.

63 Human Rights Committee, *General Comment No. 29 on States of Emergency (Article 4)*, UN Doc. CCPR/C/21/Rev.1/Add.11 (31 August 2001), para. 10.

64 See Alston, Morgan-Foster and Abresch, "The Competence of the UN Human Rights Council" (n. 12) 202.

65 Special Rapporteur on extra-judicial, summary or arbitrary executions, *Report*, UN Doc. A/62/265 (16 August 2007), paras. 22–54.

66 Ibid. para. 53.

67 See Special Rapporteur on extra-judicial, summary or arbitrary executions, *Report*, UN Doc. E/CN.4/2005/7 (22 December 2004), para. 45.

68 Special Rapporteur on extra-judicial, summary or arbitrary executions, *Report*, UN Doc. A/62/265 (16 August 2007), para. 53.

69 Letter dated 4 May 2006 from the United States to the Special Rapporteur on extra-judicial, summary or arbitrary executions, p. 4, quoted in Alston, Morgan-Foster and Abresch, "The Competence of the UN Human Rights Council" (n. 12) 189.

70 See Alston, Morgan-Foster and Abresch, "The Competence of the UN Human Rights Council" (n. 12) 203–6.

Rapporteur S. Amos Wako (who held the position from 1982–1992) observed that summary and arbitrary executions frequently occur during armed conflicts and that consequently international humanitarian law is an important element of the Rapporteur's mandate. His report contained a section on "killings in war, armed conflict, and states of emergency."[71] He found the Geneva Conventions to be relevant given that they prohibit murder and other acts of violence against protected persons which are grave breaches of the Geneva Conventions.[72] The Commission endorsed his report.[73]

In 1992, his successor as mandate holder, Bacre Waly Ndiaye, Special Rapporteur from 1992–1998, included in his first report a section on "violations of the right to life during armed conflicts" under the heading "legal framework within which the mandate of the Special Rapporteur is implemented," where he noted that:

> [t]he Special Rapporteur receives many allegations concerning extrajudicial, summary or arbitrary executions during armed conflicts. In considering and acting on such cases, the Special Rapporteur takes into account the Geneva Conventions of 12 August 1949 and the Additional Protocols thereto of 1977. Of particular relevance are common article 3 of the 1949 Conventions, which protects the right to life of members of the civilian population as well as combatants who are injured or have laid down their arms, and article 51 of Additional Protocol I and article 13 of Additional Protocol II concerning the protection of the civilian population against the dangers arising from military operations.[74]

The Commission took note of this report "with appreciation."[75] In 1995, a joint report on Colombia, issued by two Special Rapporteurs (on extra-judicial, summary or arbitrary executions and on torture and inhuman and degrading treatment) referred to violations of international humanitarian law, including assassinations and hostage-taking.[76] In his report on Burundi, the Special Rapporteur on extra-judicial, summary or arbitrary executions qualified the conflict as a "low intensity civil war."[77] The Commission not only welcomed the report but commended the Rapporteur for his working methods.[78]

71 Special Rapporteur, Amos Wako, *Report*, UN Doc. E/CN.4/1983/16 (31 January 1983), paras. 29–39.

72 Ibid. paras. 33–34.

73 Commission on Human Rights Res. 1983/36, UN Doc. E/CN.4/RES/1998/36 (27 May 1983), para. 3.

74 Special Rapporteur on extra-judicial, summary or arbitrary executions, Bacre Waly Ndiaye, *Report*, UN Doc. E/CN.4/1993/46 (23 December 1992), para. 60. The Special Rapporteur has repeated his position in subsequent reports, see UN Doc. E/CN.4/1994/7 (7 December 1993), para. 10(l); UN Doc. E/CN.4/1995/61 (14 December 1994), para. 7(d) and paras. 394–96; UN Doc. E/CN.4/1996/4 (25 January 1996), para. 10(f) and paras. 587–89; UN Doc. E/CN.4/1997/60 (24 December 1996), paras. 38–41; UN Doc. E/CN.4/1998/68 (23 December 1997), paras. 42–43 and 126–27; see Alston, Morgan-Foster and Abresch, "The Competence of the UN Human Rights Council" (n. 12) 206, note 104.

75 Commission on Human Rights Res. 1993/71, UN Doc. E/CN.4/1993/71 (10 March 1993), para. 4.

76 Special Rapporteur on the question of torture, Nigel S. Rodley, and Special Rapporteur on extra-judicial, summary or arbitrary executions, Bacre Waly Ndiaye, *Joint Report: Mission to Colombia*, UN Doc. E/CN.4/1995/111 (16 January 1995), para. 57.

77 Special Rapporteur on extra-judicial, summary or arbitrary executions, Bacre Waly Ndiaye, *Report, Addendum: Mission to Burundi from 19 to 29 April 1995*, UN Doc. E/CN.4/1996/4/Add.1 (24 July 1995), para. 61.

78 Commission on Human Rights Res. 1996/74, UN Doc. E/CN.4/1996/74 (23 April 1996), Preamble.

17.4 Special sessions, fact-finding missions and commissions of inquiry

Before the Human Rights Council was created in 2006, the Commission on Human Rights found it difficult to respond adequately to situations of emergency as it was in session only once a year for six weeks, with limited possibilities to meet outside these dates. Rapid responses to the outbreak of situations of armed violence, such as installing a special procedure or establishing a commission of inquiry or fact-finding mission, were hampered by this fact. This changed when the Council was mandated in 2006 to hold special sessions as necessary.[79] Out of the Council's twenty special sessions held so far, fifteen were devoted to situations of armed conflict or violence around the threshold of such situations, and most of them involved questions of international humanitarian law: special sessions 1, 3, 6, 9 and 12 on the Occupied Palestinian Territory; session 2 on the Lebanon conflict; session 4 on Darfur; session 8 on the Democratic Republic of the Congo; session 11 on Sri Lanka; session 14 on Côte d'Ivoire; session 15 on Libya; sessions 16 to 19 on Syria; and session 20 on the Central African Republic.[80]

More than once, the outcome of such sessions was the establishment of fact-finding missions or commissions of inquiry tasked with, *inter alia*, monitoring adherence to international humanitarian law alongside human rights law. This was already the case in earlier missions, such as in Timor-Leste (1999)[81] and the occupied Palestinian territory (2000).[82] Since its establishment in 2006 the Human Rights Council has mandated thirteen such commissions and missions, including the Fact-Finding Mission headed by John Dugard, the Special Rapporteur on the situation of human rights in the Palestinian territories occupied since 1967;[83] the Commission of Inquiry on Lebanon in 2006;[84] the High-Level Fact-Finding Mission to Beit Hanoun in 2006;[85] the High-Level Mission on the situation of human rights in Darfur in 2006;[86] and the United Nations Fact-Finding Mission on the Gaza Conflict in

[79] Special sessions can be held any time on the request of one member of the Human Rights Council when supported by one-third of its members, see UN Doc. A/RES/60/251, para. 10.

[80] Special sessions unrelated to situations of violence were session 5 on Burma/Myanmar; session 7 on the world food crisis; session 10 on the global financial crisis; and session 13 on Haiti. See the constantly updated list of regular and special sessions at www.ohchr.org/EN/HRBodies/HRC/Pages/Sessions.aspx (last accessed 15 April 2014).

[81] Commission on Human Rights Res. S-4/1, UN Doc. E/CN.4/RES/S-4/1 (27 September 1999).

[82] Commission on Human Rights Res. S-5/1, UN Doc. E/CN.4/RES/S-5/1 (19 October 2000).

[83] Established by Human Rights Council Res. S-1/1, UN Doc. A/HRC/RES/S-1/1 (2 July 2006). The mission resulted in two reports, UN Doc. A/HRC/4/116 (20 December 2006) and UN Doc. A/HRC/5/11 (8 June 2007).

[84] Established by Human Rights Council Res. S-2/1, UN Doc. A/HRC/RES/S-2/1 (11 August 2006); the members were Stelios Perrakis, Mohamed Chande Othman and Joao Clemente Baena Soares. See the report of the Commission, UN Doc. A/HRC/3/2 (23 November 2006).

[85] Established by Human Rights Council Res. S-3/1, UN Doc. A/HRC/RES/2006/S-3/1 (15 November 2006). The mission was carried out by Desmond Tutu and Christine Chinkin; see the final report, UN Doc. A/HRC/9/26 (1 September 2008).

[86] Established by Human Rights Council Decision S-4/101 (13 December 2006). Members were Jody Williams, Bertrand Ramcharan, Martin Nutt, Makarim Wibisono, Patrice Tonda and the Special Rapporteur on the situation of human rights in Sudan, Sima Samar; see the report, UN Doc. A/HRC/4/80 (9 March 2007).

2009.[87] In 2008, a mission under the title "Technical assistance to the Government of the Democratic Republic of the Congo and urgent examination of the situation in the east of the country" was created, composed of the Special Rapporteurs on violence against women, on the independence of judges and lawyers, on the right to everyone to the enjoyment of the highest attainable standard of physical and mental health, on the situation of human rights defenders, and the Special Representatives of the Secretary-General on the human rights of internally displaced persons, on the issue of human rights and transnational corporations and other business, and for children and armed conflict.[88]

In 2010 the Human Rights Council mandated an International Fact-Finding Mission to "investigate violations of international law, including international humanitarian and human rights law, resulting from the Israeli attacks on the flotilla of ships carrying humanitarian assistance."[89] In the same year, the Committee of Independent Experts in International Humanitarian and Human Rights Law was created to monitor and assess the proceedings undertaken by Israel and the Palestinian side to carry out investigations in pursuance of General Assembly Resolution 64/254.[90] 2011 saw the creation of the UN Independent Commission of Inquiry on Libya[91] and the International Commission of Inquiry to investigate the facts and circumstances surrounding the allegations of serious abuses and violations of human rights committed in Côte d'Ivoire following the presidential election of 28 November 2010.[92] In the same year, commissions and missions were installed for the situation in Syria. The first was the Mission to the Syrian Arab Republic to investigate all alleged violations of international human rights law and to establish the facts and circumstances of such violations and of the crimes perpetrated.[93] In light of this mission, an Independent International Commission of Inquiry on the Syrian Arab Republic was created.[94] And in 2012 the Council established the International Fact-Finding Mission on Israeli Settlements in the Occupied Palestinian Territory to "investigate the implications of

[87] Established by Human Rights Council Res. S-9/1, UN Doc. A/HRC/RES/S-9/1 (12 January 2009) and composed of Richard Goldstone, Christine Chinkin, Hina Jilani and Desmond Travers; see the report, UN Doc. A/HRC/12/48 (23 September 2009).

[88] Established by Human Rights Council Res. UN Doc. A/HRC/RES/S-8/1 (1 December 2008); see the report, UN Doc. A/HRC/10/59 (5 March 2009).

[89] Human Rights Council Res. 14/1, UN Doc. A/HRC/RES/14/1 (23 June 2010), para. 8. The mission resulted in the report, UN Doc. A/HRC/15/21 (27 September 2010) and its members were Karl T. Hudson-Philipps, Desmond de Silva and Mary Shanthi Dairiam.

[90] General Assembly Res. 64/254, UN Doc. A/64/254 (25 March 2010) called on both sides to follow up on the report of the Fact-Finding Mission on the Gaza Conflict; see Human Rights Council Res. 13/9, UN Doc. A/HRC/RES/13/9 (14 April 2010). The committee members were Christian Tomuschat, Mary McGowan Davis and Param Cumaraswamy.

[91] Established by Human Rights Council Res. S-15/1, UN Doc. A/HRC/RES/S-15/1 (25 February 2011). The report is contained in UN Doc. A/HRC/19/68 (2 March 2012). The members were Philippe Kirsch, Cherif M. Bassiouni and Asma Khader.

[92] Established by Human Rights Council Res. 16/25, UN Doc. A/HRC/RES/16/25 (25 March 2011) and composed of Vitit Muntarbhorn, Reine Alapini Gansou and Suliman Baldo; see the report, UN Doc. A/HRC/17/48 (14 June 2011).

[93] See Human Rights Council Res. S-16/1, UN Doc. A/HRC/RES/S-16/1 (29 April 2011). The thirteen-member mission was headed by Deputy High Commissioner for Human Rights, Kyung-wha Kang.

[94] See Human Rights Council Res. S-17/1, UN Doc. A/HRC/RES/S-17/1 (22 August 2011). Commission members are Sergio Pinheiro, Yakin Erturk and Karin Abu Zeid; see the Commission's report, UN Doc. A/HRC/21/50 (16 August 2012).

the Israeli settlements on the civil, political, economic, social and cultural rights of the Palestinian people throughout the Occupied Palestinian Territory, including East Jerusalem."[95] In its report submitted to the 22nd session of the Human Rights Council in February/March 2013, the Mission explicitly concluded that Israel is in violation of Geneva Convention IV, Article 49, which forbids the transfer of civilian population in occupied territory.[96]

There is obviously no uniform format for such commissions of inquiry and fact-finding missions and their mandates vary, with some of them including humanitarian law and others not. In their reports, however, they all referred to international humanitarian law; some of them did more extensively so than others.[97] It seems that such commissions and missions are used with increasing frequency as a means (indeed as the prime means) to monitor situations of violence and armed conflict. At the same time, their establishment on an ad hoc basis entails considerable challenges as to their expertise, mandate, funding, functioning and follow-up to their findings. Issues such as lack of transparency, independence and impartiality, as well as practical matters such as limited access to information, security concerns and missing cooperation with states, non-state actors and other parts of the UN system and regional organizations have led to a vivid debates.[98]

17.5 Universal Periodic Review

When the Human Rights Council was created in 2006, it was given a new instrument to scrutinize states' implementation of human rights obligations. The Universal Periodic Review was introduced as a means to assess and discuss the human rights situation in every UN member state. In the words of General Assembly Resolution 60/251, the Council has now to:

> undertake a periodic review, based on objective and reliable information, of the fulfilment by each State of its human rights obligations and commitments in a manner which ensures universality of coverage and equal treatment with respect to all States; the review shall be a cooperative mechanism, based on an interactive dialogue, with the full involvement of the country concerned and with consideration given to its capacity-building needs; such a mechanism shall complement and not duplicate the work of the treaty bodies.[99]

After considerable debate on the scope of the human rights obligations and commitments mentioned in the resolution, the Council decided that the UPR should be based on the UN Charter, the Universal Declaration of Human Rights, human rights instruments to which a

[95] See Human Rights Council Res. 19/17, UN Doc. A/HRC/RES/19/17 (10 April 2012), para. 9.

[96] See *Report of the Independent International Fact-finding Mission to Investigate the Implications of the Israeli Settlements on the Civil, Political, Economic, Social and Cultural Rights of the Palestinian People Throughout the Occupied Palestinian Territory, including East Jerusalem*, UN Doc. A/HRC/22/63 (7 February 2013), para. 16. Geneva Convention IV, Art. 49 prohibits "[i]ndividual or mass forcible transfers, as well as deportations of protected persons from occupied territory to the territory of the Occupying Power or to that of any other country, occupied or not . . . regardless of their motive."

[97] See UN OHCHR, *International Legal Protection of Human Rights in Armed Conflict* (n. 12) p. 115.

[98] See Geneva Academy of International Humanitarian Law and Human Rights, *The UN Human Rights Council: Commissions of Inquiry Conference Brief* (December 2011), pp. 2–4, available at www.geneva-academy.ch/docs/news/HR-council-inquiry-conference-brief.pdf (last accessed 15 April 2014).

[99] General Assembly Res. 60/251, UN Doc. A/60/251 (3 April 2006), para. 5.

state is party and voluntary pledges and commitments made by states, including those they made when presenting their candidatures for election to the Human Rights Council. In addition to these four types of obligations a fifth was added: "given the complementary and mutually interrelated nature of international human rights law and international humanitarian law, the review shall take into account applicable international humanitarian law."[100]

The rationale for including humanitarian law was never publicly debated or explained. It may have been meant to prevent a state from escaping scrutiny of the UPR by declaring a state of emergency and derogating human rights provisions of treaties to which it is a party and to guarantee that the Council can monitor situations of conflict, tension and insecurity.[101] The qualification of international humanitarian law as "applicable" and the Council's mandate merely to "take into account" humanitarian law are vague and seem restrictive and could allow the Council only to use certain norms of humanitarian law and require it to refrain from speaking out on violations. But a closer look reveals that this is not the case. Given that the four Geneva Conventions are universally ratified and thus applicable to all states, together with the equally applicable customary international humanitarian law (as brought together in the ICRC study on customary humanitarian law), the overwhelming part of humanitarian law is covered; problems may arise with (non-customary) rules of the Additional Protocols to the Geneva Conventions. If, alternatively, the provision is meant to say that humanitarian law can be invoked only when an armed conflict exists, then it is a self-evident reference to the scope of application of humanitarian law regulated by the Geneva Conventions and Additional Protocols. Thus, the resolution does not create a specific subset of humanitarian rules applicable by the Council in the UPR. The provision must not be understood as allowing only for the application of those humanitarian norms which find an equivalent provision in international human rights law.

The Council's mandate to "take into account" humanitarian law in the UPR also allows a broad interpretation: neither does it specifically entitle the Council to denounce violations of international humanitarian law nor does it mean that humanitarian law is only a secondary interpretative device. If it is read (as it should be) in light of the Council's broad policy-oriented mandate to consider and discuss the general human rights situation in a given country in the framework of the cooperative mechanism of the UPR, then every form of "taking into account" humanitarian law, from sweeping references to general humanitarian principles as well as denouncing specific violations of the Geneva Conventions and Additional Protocols is possible.

But when the first cycle of reviews of all UN member states came to its end in 2011, there were no indications of any consistent practice of examining matters of international humanitarian law.[102] References to violations of international humanitarian law in the

[100] Human Rights Council Res. 5/1, Institution-building of the United Nations Human Rights Council, UN Doc. A/HRC/RES/5/1 (18 June 2006), Annex.

[101] See Miko Lempinen and Martin Scheinin, *The New Human Rights Council: The First Two Years*, Substantive Report of the Workshop organized by the European University Institute, Istituto Affari Internazionali, and the Institute for Human Rights at Abo Akademi University, European University Institute, 7–8 November 2007 (Abo: Abo Akademi Institute, 2007), p. 5, available at www.eui.eu/Documents/DepartmentsCentres/AcademyofEuropeanLaw/Projects/HRCReport.pdf (last accessed 15 April 2014).

[102] See Walter Kälin, "Universal Human Rights Bodies and International Humanitarian Law" in Robert Kolb and Gloria Gaggioli (eds.), *Research Handbook on Human Rights and Humanitarian Law* (Cheltenham: Edward Elgar, 2013), pp. 454–55.

final reports of the Working Group (which also contain the specific recommendations to the state under review) are scarce and general. Examples are the review of Somalia, where Denmark expressed "concern about violations of international humanitarian and human rights law in southern and central Somalia,"[103] or the review of the United States, where general remarks on the interplay between international human rights and international humanitarian law were made by the US delegation.[104] In the discussions of the UPR Working Group, references to international humanitarian law violations were also limited and superficial, as the examples of Afghanistan and the Central African Republic demonstrate.[105]

Only a few recommendations made by states in the UPR refer to international humanitarian law in a more detailed manner. In some cases states recommended, albeit still in general terms, to improve the training in international humanitarian law. This was the case with the Czech Republic with regard to Afghanistan,[106] Algeria with regard to Côte d'Ivoire[107] and Algeria, Belgium, Czech Republic and the United Kingdom with regard to the Central African Republic.[108] And only occasionally did states invoke specific questions of humanitarian law, for example, when France urged Israel to conform to its obligations under international humanitarian law to allow humanitarian access to the Gaza Strip,[109] and Iran accused Israel of violating international humanitarian law by using Palestinians as human shields.[110] Even in these cases, states refrained from mentioning the Geneva Conventions and Additional Protocols. Only Cuba, Mexico and Malaysia referred to them when commenting on the situation in Israel.[111] Otherwise, the preferred formulation was to ask a state to adhere to "its international humanitarian law obligations."[112]

[103] Human Rights Council, *Report of the Working Group of the Universal Periodic Review: Somalia*, UN Doc. A/HRC/18/6 (11 July 2011), para. 62.

[104] See Human Rights Council, *Report of the Working Group of the Universal Periodic Review: United States of America*, UN Doc. A/HRC/16/11 (4 January 2011), para. 53.

[105] See *Draft Report of the Human Rights Council on its Twelfth Session*, UN Doc. A/HRC/12/L.10 (2 October 2009), para. 386; and *Draft Report of the Human Rights Council on its Twelfth Session*, UN Doc. A/HRC/12/L.10 (2 October 2009), para. 220.

[106] See Human Rights Council, *Report of the Working Group of the Universal Periodic Review: Afghanistan*, UN Doc. A/HRC/12/9 (20 July 2009), Recommendation 66. This is the only reference to international humanitarian law in the entire report. Only a few comments relate to matters of armed conflict at all, such as Slovenia's concern about attacks against schools by Taliban insurgents, see para. 66.

[107] See Human Rights Council, *Report of the Working Group of the Universal Periodic Review: Côte d'Ivoire*, UN Doc. A/HRC/13/9 (5 January 2010), Recommendation 65.

[108] See *Report of the Working Group of the Universal Periodic Review: Central African Republic*, UN Doc. A/HRC/12/22 (4 June 2009), paras. 17, 40, 58 and 59.

[109] See Human Rights Council, *Report of the Working Group of the Universal Periodic Review: Israel*, UN Doc. A/HRC/10/76 (8 January 2010), para. 24.

[110] Ibid. para. 25.

[111] Cuba, Mexico and Malaysia, for example, invoked the Geneva Conventions and Additional Protocols when commenting on the situation in Israel, see Human Rights Council, *Report of the Working Group of the Universal Periodic Review: Israel*, UN Doc. A/HRC/10/76 (8 January 2010), paras. 57, 74 and 81.

[112] Switzerland used this language with regard to Israel, see Human Rights Council, *Report of the Working Group of the Universal Periodic Review: Israel*, UN Doc. A/HRC/10/76 (8 January 2010), para. 34. Similarly, Mexico recommended to Pakistan to "strictly adhere to international human rights and international humanitarian law and international refugee law in its fight against terrorism," Human Rights Council, *Report of the Working Group of the Universal Periodic Review: Pakistan*, UN Doc. A/HRC/8/42 (4 June 2008), Recommendation 25.

Even in states with massive and well-documented violations of international humanitarian law, the UPR failed to convincingly discuss the situation or provide the state under review with any meaningful recommendations in the first review cycle. The usual formula was to call for those responsible for violations of grave human rights and humanitarian law violations to be brought to justice.[113] In the review of the Democratic Republic of the Congo, for example, states merely resorted to general recommendations such as that by Niger to "[c]ontinue efforts to incorporate the standards of international humanitarian law into national legislation."[114] This is hardly the kind of response an effective human rights watchdog is expected to provide. This inconclusive practice reflects the general shortcomings of the UPR as a method of reviewing states' performance: the overall predominance of general and unspecific recommendations and inconsistencies among them; the negative impact of the UN group structure on scrutinizing states' performance in an unbiased way; and the uncertainty about adequate follow-up procedures.[115] As it stands, the UPR is thus a far cry from an effective supervisory mechanism for violations of humanitarian law in armed conflicts.

[113] As was the case, for example, in reviewing the Democratic Republic of the Congo, see Human Rights Council, *Report of the Working Group of the Universal Periodic Review: Democratic Republic of the Congo*, UN Doc. A/HRC/13/8 (4 January 2010), Recommendations 48, 77 and 87. Likewise, Greece urged Sri Lanka to "take all necessary measures to end impunity for perpetrators of violations of international human rights law and humanitarian law," Human Rights Council, *Report of the Working Group of the Universal Periodic Review: Sri Lanka*, UN Doc. A/HRC/8/46 (5 June 2008), para. 74.

[114] See Human Rights Council, *Report of the Working Group of the Universal Periodic Review: Democratic Republic of the Congo*, UN Doc. A/HRC/13/8 (4 January 2010), Recommendation 11.

[115] See in greater detail UPR Info, *Universal Periodic Review: On the Road to Implementation* (2012), available at www.upr-info.org/IMG/pdf/2012_on_the_road_to_implementation.pdf (last accessed 15 April 2014).

18

United Nations High Commissioner for Human Rights

Similar to the Human Rights Council, the mandate of the High Commissioner for Human Rights does not refer to armed conflict or international humanitarian law. It comprises the promotion and protection of all human rights, including the right to development, the provision of advisory services and technical assistance, the coordination and mainstreaming of human rights in the UN, being in dialogue with governments on human rights matters as well as carrying out any other task assigned by the competent UN bodies.[1] Similar to the Council, the High Commissioner is set up by the UN General Assembly and entrusted not with exercising legal scrutiny under international treaty law but to respond to political challenges which involve the application of international human rights law. The High Commissioner is neither mandated to monitor observance of international humanitarian law nor to speak out on violations of humanitarian law. But like the Human Rights Council, it may be faced with situations where an evaluation of the human rights situation may make it necessary to take into account other sources of international law, including international humanitarian law.

In situations of armed conflict the High Commissioner has regularly monitored human rights and humanitarian law and has used its mandate to engage in activities which are best described as humanitarian advocacy and humanitarian diplomacy, mediation and the provision of good offices.[2] In 2004, for example, Acting High Commissioner Bertrand Ramcharan dispatched an emergency mission to Chad and Darfur *ex officio*.[3] And in 2010, the Office of the High Commissioner was entrusted with carrying out fact-finding activities in Côte d'Ivoire following the 2010 presidential elections.[4] The report on the mission detailed violations of human rights and international humanitarian law "which

[1] See General Assembly Res. 48/141, UN Doc. A/RES/48/141 (20 December 1993), para. 4.

[2] See Loubna Freih, "The Role of the United Nations High Commissioner for Human Rights in Armed Conflict Situations" in International Institute of Humanitarian Law (ed.), *Strengthening Measures for the Respect and Implementation of International Humanitarian Law and Other Rules Protecting Human Dignity in Armed Conflict*, 28th Round Table on Current Problems of International Humanitarian Law, Sanremo, 2–4 September 2004 (Sanremo: International Institute of Humanitarian Law, 2004), pp. 62–69; and Chris Sidoti, "Role of the High Commissioner for Human Rights in Armed Conflict Situations" in International Institute of Humanitarian Law (ed.), *Strengthening Measures for the Respect and Implementation of International Humanitarian Law and Other Rules Protecting Human Dignity in Armed Conflict*, 28th Round Table on Current Problems of International Humanitarian Law, Sanremo, 2–4 September 2004 (Sanremo: International Institute of Humanitarian Law, 2004), pp. 139–40.

[3] The mission was led by Bacre Waly Ndiaye, Director of the UN Human Rights Office in New York; see Freih, "Role of the United Nations High Commissioner for Human Rights" (n. 2) p. 64.

[4] See Human Rights Council Res. S-14/1, UN Doc. A/HRC/RES/S-14/1 (4 January 2011), para. 12, which "[r]equests the United Nations High Commissioner for Human Rights to inform and present a report to

include summary executions, enforced disappearances, rape, torture, cruel, inhumane and degrading treatment, arbitrary arrests and detentions, pillaging and looting."[5] It did not, however, indicate any legal norms of humanitarian law which were violated by these acts and refrained entirely from mentioning the Geneva Conventions and Additional Protocols.

Field presences of the Office of the High Commissioner for Human Rights have also been entrusted with a dual mandate to monitor human rights and international humanitarian law. In 1996, the OHCHR office in Colombia was mandated to receive complaints on violations of human rights and international humanitarian law; in 2005, the office in Nepal was tasked with monitoring observance of human rights and international humanitarian law with a view to advising the authorities of Nepal; in 2006, the offices in Togo and Uganda were given a monitoring mandate for human rights and international humanitarian law; and in 2008, the agreement between the OHCHR and Mexico contained similar provisions.[6] The High Commissioner's reports also frequently referred to violations of both human rights and international humanitarian law, e.g., in the Occupied Palestinian Territory, Sudan, Nepal and Colombia.[7]

The High Commissioner's manifold diplomatic activities to solve humanitarian crises, negotiate solutions and provide good offices in situations where violations of humanitarian law may occur have also never been objected to by states.[8] Again, and similar to the Human Rights Council, it seems that the function originally entrusted to the International Humanitarian Fact-Finding Commission, set up under Additional Protocol I to the Geneva Convention in 1977, to "facilitate, through its good offices, the restoration of an attitude of respect for the Convention and this Protocol"[9] has been taken over to some extent by a human rights body. In addition, the Office of the High Commissioner also regularly calls upon states to ensure the dissemination of and education in international humanitarian law, and emphasizes the importance of integrating humanitarian law in human rights education and training.[10]

Critical observers of the High Commissioner's activities in relation to armed conflict have pointed out that its monitoring is inconsistent and depends heavily on factual circumstances and personal approaches of OHCHR staff on the ground.[11] Calls have been made for the clarification of a "core doctrine"[12] of human rights fieldwork which would include

the Council on the abuses and violations of human rights in Côte d'Ivoire in relation to the conclusion of the 2010 presidential elections."

5 See United Nations High Commissioner for Human Rights, *Report on the Situation of Human Rights in Côte d'Ivoire*, UN Doc. A/HRC/17/49 (14 June 2011), para. 22.

6 United Nations Office of the High Commissioner for Human Rights, *International Legal Protection of Human Rights in Armed Conflict* (New York and Geneva: United Nations, 2011), pp. 105–6.

7 Ibid. pp. 105–6.

8 William Schabas, "The United Nations High Commissioner for Human Rights and International Humanitarian Law" in International Institute of Humanitarian Law (ed.), *Strengthening Measures for the Respect and Implementation of International Humanitarian Law and Other Rules Protecting Human Dignity in Armed Conflict*, 28th Round Table on Current Problems of International Humanitarian Law, Sanremo, 2–4 September 2004 (Sanremo: International Institute of Humanitarian Law, 2004), p. 203.

9 Additional Protocol I, Art. 90(2)(a)(ii).

10 See Bertrand Ramcharan, *The United Nations High Commissioner for Human Rights and International Humanitarian Law*, Program on Humanitarian Policy and Conflict Research, Harvard University, Occasional Paper Series No. 3 (2005), pp. 41–42.

11 See Freih, "Role of the United Nations High Commissioner for Human Rights" (n. 2) p. 66.

12 See Michael O'Flaherty, "Human Rights Monitoring and Armed Conflict: Challenges for the UN" (2004) 3 *Disarmament Forum* 55.

reference to states' obligations under international humanitarian law, and strengthening expertise in humanitarian law in headquarters and in the field is seen as a matter of importance and concern, particularly by NGOs present in the respective region(s).[13]

Such informed, thorough and consistent monitoring and reporting on matters of humanitarian law in armed conflicts would, however, pose a challenge to the OHCHR as it adds yet another task to the already dauntingly impressive list of functions the Office is entrusted with. It would also require the establishment of ongoing policy dialogues with relevant parts of the UN system (first and foremost the Security Council and UN departments) and with relevant NGOs, interaction with the governments of countries in armed conflict and other parties to the conflict, and building professional expertise within the Office as well as ensuring that the Office has adequate operational capacities.[14] In theory, the High Commissioner would also be well placed to alert the Security Council to violations of human rights and humanitarian law in armed conflicts, but in reality this link is weak, even though already in the first ever appearance of the High Commissioner for Human Rights before the Security Council in 1999, then High Commissioner Mary Robinson referred extensively to the protection of civilians in armed conflict.[15]

[13] See Freih, "Role of the United Nations High Commissioner for Human Rights" (n. 2) p. 63.
[14] See O'Flaherty, "Human Rights Monitoring and Armed Conflict" (n. 12) 55.
[15] See Freih, "Role of the United Nations High Commissioner for Human Rights" (n. 2) p. 66.

19

United Nations human rights treaty bodies

19.1 Human Rights Committee

Different from the Human Rights Council and the High Commissioner for Human Rights, the UN treaty bodies are set up as monitoring bodies under a human rights treaty and are thus bound by specific treaty regulations which can include jurisdictional clauses *ratione temporis*, *personae* and *loci*. The mandate of UN treaty bodies in relation to situations of armed conflict and the use of international humanitarian law is thus more intricate than is the case for bodies set up under the UN Charter, such as the Human Rights Council and the High Commissioner for Human Rights.

Each of the nine core UN human rights treaties[1] provides for a treaty body the competences of which include the examination of state reports and (where so foreseen in the treaty or Optional Protocols) the decision on complaints submitted by states and individuals; some may also conduct on-site visits. The Committee on the Elimination of Racial Discrimination was the first to be established. It has monitored the implementation of the Convention on the Elimination of All Forms of Racial Discrimination (CERD) since 1969.[2] The Human Rights Committee took up its work under the International Covenant on Civil and Political Rights (ICCPR) in 1976, and since 1987 the Committee on Economic, Social and Cultural Rights has carried out a mandate under the International Covenant on Economic, Social and Cultural Rights (ICESCR) which before was entrusted to ECOSOC. The Committee on the Elimination of Discrimination Against Women has monitored the Convention on the Elimination of All Forms of Discrimination Against Women (CEDAW) since 1979,[3] and the Committee Against Torture has done the same since 1987 with regard to the Convention Against Torture and Other Cruel, Inhuman or Degrading Treatment (CAT).[4] Since 1990, the Committee on the Rights of the Child has monitored the Convention on the Rights of the Child (CRC), and since 2004 the Committee on Migrant Workers has supervised the Convention on the Protection of the Rights of All

1 Optional Protocol to the Convention Against Torture 2002, which establishes an inspection mechanism, and Optional Protocol to the Convention on the Rights of Persons with Disabilities 2007 on individual complaints, constitute what is commonly referred to as core UN human rights treaties. See in greater detail Julie Mertus, *The United Nations and Human Rights: A Guide for A New Era* (2nd edn., London: Routledge, 2009), pp. 64–97.

2 Convention on the Elimination of All Forms of Racial Discrimination, 7 March 1966, 660 UNTS 195.

3 Convention on the Elimination of All Forms of Discrimination Against Women, 18 December 1979, 1249 UNTS 13.

4 Convention Against Torture and Other Cruel, Inhuman or Degrading Treatment, 10 December 1984, 1465 UNTS 85.

Migrant Workers and Members of Their Families (CMW).[5] The Committee on the Rights of Persons with Disabilities took up its work under the Convention on the Rights of Persons with Disabilities (CRPD) in 2009, and the Committee on Enforced Disappearances has monitored the Convention on the Protection of All Persons from Enforced Disappearance (CED) since 2011. Individual complaint procedures are provided for in Optional Protocols to the ICCPR,[6] ICESCR,[7] CEDAW,[8] CRC[9] and CRPD,[10] while CAT is supplemented by an inspection system.[11]

The Human Rights Committee has repeatedly stated its view that international human rights law continues to apply in armed conflicts. In General Comment No. 31 of 2004, the Committee argued that "[w]hile, in respect of certain Covenant rights, more specific rules of international humanitarian law may be specially relevant for the purposes of the interpretation of Covenant rights, both spheres of law are complementary, not mutually exclusive."[12] Similarly, the Committee argued that international humanitarian law shares the goal of human rights law:

> [d]uring armed conflict, whether international or non-international, rules of international humanitarian law become applicable and help, in addition to the provisions in articles 4 and 5, paragraph 1, of the Covenant, to prevent abuse of a State's emergency powers.[13]

In General Comment No. 29 of 2001 on derogation, the Committee put forward a strict interpretation of states' ability to derogate from the ICCPR on the grounds of an emergency. It took the view that the Covenant requires that no measure derogating from the provisions of the Covenant may be inconsistent with the state party's other obligations under international law, in particular the rules of international humanitarian law, and that states parties may in no circumstance invoke the ICCPR's provisions on derogations as justification for acting in violation of humanitarian law or peremptory norms of international law, for instance, by taking hostages, imposing collective punishments, through arbitrary deprivations of liberty or by deviating from fundamental principles of fair trial, including the presumption of innocence.[14] In the same General Comment, the Committee also argued

[5] Convention on the Protection of the Rights of All Migrant Workers and Members of Their Families, 18 December 1990, 2220 UNTS 3.

[6] Optional Protocol to the International Covenant on Civil and Political Rights, 16 December 1966, 999 UNTS 171.

[7] Optional Protocol to the International Covenant on Economic, Social and Cultural Rights, 10 December 2008, UN Doc. A/63/435.

[8] Optional Protocol to the Convention on the Elimination of All Forms of Discrimination Against Women, 6 October 1999, 2131 UNTS 83.

[9] Optional Protocol to the Convention on the Rights of the Child on a communications procedure, 19 December 2011, UN Doc. A/RES/66/138.

[10] Optional Protocol to the Convention on the Rights of Persons with Disabilities, 13 December 2006, UN Doc. A/61/611.

[11] Optional Protocol to the Convention Against Torture and Other Cruel, Inhuman or Degrading Treatment or Punishment, 18 December 2002, 2375 UNTS 237.

[12] Human Rights Committee, *General Comment No. 31 on the Nature of the General Legal Obligation Imposed on States Parties to the Covenant (Article 2)*, UN Doc. CCPR/C/21/Rev.1/Add.13 (26 May 2004), para. 11.

[13] Human Rights Committee, *General Comment No. 29 on States of Emergency (Article 4)*, UN Doc. CCPR/C/21/Rev.1/Add.11 (31 August 2001), para. 3.

[14] *General Comment No. 29 on States of Emergency (Article 4)*, UN Doc. CCPR/C/21/Rev.1/Add.11 (31 August 2001), para. 11.

that it is mandated to consider treaties other than the ICCPR, which obviously includes international humanitarian law.[15] The Committee said that:

> [a]lthough it is not the function of the Human Rights Committee to review the conduct of a State party under other treaties, in exercising its functions under the Covenant the Committee has the competence to take a State party's other international obligations into account when it considers whether the Covenant allows the State party to derogate from specific provisions of the Covenant. Therefore, when invoking article 4, paragraph 1, or when reporting under article 40 on the legal framework related to emergencies, States parties should present information on their other international obligations relevant for the protection of the rights in question, in particular those obligations that are applicable in times of emergency. In this respect, States parties should duly take into account the developments within international law as to human rights standards applicable in emergency situations.[16]

In its concluding observations on state reports under the ICCPR, the Committee repeatedly considered the impact of armed conflicts on the observance of human rights[17] or spoke out on derogations in situations of emergency.[18] Direct references to humanitarian law are, however, not very frequent, and where they are made, they remain unspecific. On Israel's periodic report in 2003, for example, the Committee (while taking note of Israel's position that the Covenant does not apply beyond its own territory and not in the West Bank and in Gaza as long as there is a situation of armed conflict in these areas) commented that the application of international humanitarian law during armed conflict must not preclude the application of the Covenant.[19]

When it commented on Serbia's failure to investigate and prosecute violations of international humanitarian law in 2004, it referred to humanitarian law only in connection with the jurisdiction of the International Criminal Tribunal for the Former Yugoslavia (ICTY).[20] When it considered the report of the United States, it welcomed explicitly the US Supreme Court decision in *Hamdan* v. *Rumsfeld* of 2006 (which had established the applicability of Common Article 3 of the Geneva Conventions to the US-led "War on Terror") because it found that Common Article 3 of the Geneva Conventions "reflects fundamental rights guaranteed by the Covenant in any armed conflict."[21] With regard to the state report of the Central African Republic, the Committee noted in 2006 that the country had failed to investigate violations of international humanitarian law and international human rights

[15] See David Weissbrodt, "The Role of the Human Rights Committee in Interpreting and Developing Humanitarian Law" (2010) 31(4) *Pennsylvania Journal of International Law* 1212.

[16] *General Comment No. 29 on States of Emergency (Article 4)*, UN Doc. CCPR/C/21/Rev.1/Add.11 (31 August 2001), para. 10 (footnotes omitted).

[17] E.g. on Sudan in 1997, on Azerbaijan in 1994 and on Sri Lanka in 1995; see for the respective reports Weissbrodt, "The Role of the Human Rights Committee" (n. 15) 1222–23.

[18] E.g. on Guatemala and Croatia in 2001, on Serbia and Montenegro in 2004 and repeatedly on Israel; see Weissbrodt, "The Role of the Human Rights Committee" (n. 15) 1223–24.

[19] See Human Rights Committee, *Concluding Observations on Israel*, UN Doc. CCPR/CO/78/ISR (5 August 2003), para. 11.

[20] See Human Rights Committee, *Concluding Observations on Serbia and Montenegro*, UN Doc. CCPR/CO/81/SEMO (12 August 2004), para. 11.

[21] Human Rights Committee, *Concluding Observations on United States of America*, UN Doc. CCPR/CO/USA/CO/3/Rev.1 (18 December 2006), paras. 5 and 20.

law.[22] With regard to Belgium, the Committee expressed concern about domestic laws for prosecuting violations of humanitarian law (unrelated to any situation of armed conflict).[23] Colombia was asked by the Committee during the examination of the state report in 1980 rather bluntly whether its armed forces would apply the Geneva Conventions when combating insurgents (to which the state somewhat ambiguously responded that anyone who did not was regarded as an offender).[24]

The Committee had to decide only few individual communications under its Optional Protocol in which armed conflict played a role. Cases included Uruguay and Colombia, where the Committee saw the ICCPR as continually applicable and held that derogation is possible only within strict limits and that the ICCPR applies extra-territorially.[25] Nowhere did the Committee resort to international humanitarian law.[26] Altogether, the Committee neither seems to live up to its own rhetoric on the concurrent application of human rights and humanitarian law nor on its self-perception as being entitled to look beyond the ICCPR and resort to obligations under humanitarian law where appropriate. The importance of the Committee's statements on the application of human rights in armed conflicts is beyond question, but contrary to more optimistic assertions that the Committee considers violations of humanitarian law at least "framed through the Covenant,"[27] there is otherwise little substantive engagement with humanitarian law.

19.2 Committee on the Rights of the Child

The Committee on the Rights of the Child is in a special position, given that the CRC contains provisions borrowed from international humanitarian law with regard to the conscription or recruitment of child soldiers and their participation in conflict. As mentioned earlier, Article 38(1) of the CRC stipulates that "States Parties undertake to

[22] Human Rights Committee, *Concluding Observations on Central African Republic*, UN Doc. CCPR/C/CAF/CO/2 (27 July 2006), para. 8: "The Committee notes with concern that, to date, the authorities have not carried out any exhaustive and independent appraisal of serious violations of human rights and international humanitarian law in the Central African Republic and that the victims have received no reparations."

[23] See Human Rights Committee, *Concluding Observations on Belgium*, UN Doc. CCPR/CO/81/BEL (12 August 2004), para. 148; and *Fourth Periodic Report of Belgium*, UN Doc. CCPR/C/BEL/2004/4 (16 May 2003), p. 71 note 62.

[24] See Human Rights Committee, *Concluding Observations on Colombia*, UN Doc. CCPR/A/35/40 (1980), paras. 520 and 524.

[25] See Weissbrodt, "The Role of the Human Rights Committee" (n. 15) 1203, with reference to *Jorge Landinelli Silva and others* v. *Uruguay, Views*, Human Rights Committee, Communication No. 34/1978, UN Doc. CCPR/C/12/D/34/1978 (8 April 1981); *Lucia Sala da Touren* v. *Uruguay, Views*, Human Rights Committee, Communication No. 32/1978, UN Doc. CCPR/C/12/D/32/1978 (31 March 1981); *Luciano Weinberger Weisz* v. *Uruguay, Views*, Human Rights Committee, Communication No. 28/1978, UN Doc. CCPR/C/11/D/28/1978 (29 October 1980); *Ann Maria Garcia Lanza de Netto* v. *Uruguay, Views*, Human Rights Committee, Communication No. 8/1977, UN Doc. CCPR/C/9/D/8/1977 (3 April 1980); and *Husband of Maria Fanny Suarez de Guerrero* v. *Colombia, Admissibility*, Human Rights Committee, Communication No. R.11/45, UN Doc. Supp. No. 40, A/37/40 (1982), p. 137. See also Christine Byron, "A Blurring of the Boundaries: The Application of International Humanitarian Law by Human Rights Bodies" (2007) 47(4) *Virginia Journal of International Law* 849.

[26] See Weissbrodt, "The Role of the Human Rights Committee" (n. 15) 1203.

[27] Ibid. 1205.

respect and to ensure respect for rules of international humanitarian law applicable to them in armed conflicts which are relevant to the child."[28] The Optional Protocol on the involvement of children in armed conflict also refers to international humanitarian law[29] and, in its Preamble, requires all states to abide by the provisions of international humanitarian law.[30] While the Committee is the only UN treaty body with more substantial pronouncements on humanitarian law, it has so far not been able to receive individual complaints and has thus not examined the question of the interplay of human rights and humanitarian law in individual cases.[31]

In three of its General Comments, the Committee has dealt with international humanitarian law.[32] In General Comment No. 1 on the aims of education under CRC, Article 29(1) it emphasized the importance of education in humanitarian law.[33] In General Comment No. 6 on unaccompanied and separated children outside their country of origin, it stated that child soldiers should not normally be interned but where such internment is unavoidable on an exceptional basis (i.e., when they constitute a security threat), they must benefit from international human rights and humanitarian law.[34] This can be seen as an interpretation of a rule of international humanitarian law from a human rights perspective.[35] The same General Comment also interpreted CRC, Article 38 on child soldiers as obliging states not to return a child to a state in which it faces the risk of under-age recruitment or is likely to directly or indirectly participate in hostilities. The Committee found that:

> [a]s underage recruitment and participation in hostilities entails a high risk of irreparable harm involving fundamental human rights, including the right to life, State obligations deriving from article 38 of the Convention, in conjunction with articles 3 and 4 of the Optional Protocol to the Convention on the Rights of the Child on the involvement of children in armed conflict, entail extraterritorial effects and States shall refrain from returning a child in any manner whatsoever to the borders of a State where there is a real risk of underage recruitment, including recruitment not only as a combatant but also to provide sexual services for the military or where there is a real risk of direct or indirect

[28] CRC, Art. 38.

[29] Optional Protocol to the CRC on the involvement of children in armed conflict, Art. 5: "Nothing in the present Protocol shall be construed as precluding provisions in the law of a State Party or in international instruments and international humanitarian law that are more conducive to the realization of the rights of the child."

[30] Ibid. Preamble.

[31] The Optional Protocol to the CRC on a communications procedure has received the necessary number of ratifications for entry into force in January 2014.

[32] See David Weissbrodt, Joseph C. Hansen and Nathaniel H. Nesbitt, "The Role of the Committee on the Rights of the Child in Interpreting and Developing International Humanitarian Law" (2011) 24 *Harvard Human Rights Journal* 124.

[33] Committee on the Rights of the Child, *General Comment No. 1 on the Aims of Education*, UN Doc. CRC/GC/2001/1 (17 April 2001), para. 16: "Education about international humanitarian law also constitutes an important, but all too often neglected, dimension of efforts to give effect to article 29(1)."

[34] Committee on the Rights of the Child, *General Comment No. 6 on the Treatment of Unaccompanied and Separated Children Outside their Country of Origin*, UN Doc. CRC/GC/2005/6 (1 September 2005), paras. 56 and 57.

[35] See Weissbrodt, Hansen and Nesbitt, "The Role of the Committee on the Rights of the Child" (n. 32) 124–25.

participation in hostilities, either as a combatant or through carrying out other military duties.[36]

This can be seen as the contrary move, as it includes a norm of humanitarian law into human rights law.[37] In General Comment No. 11, the Committee interpreted CRC, Article 38 as obliging states to ensure respect for the rules of humanitarian law with regard to indigenous children affected by armed conflict.[38] In all three General Comments, the Committee not only reminded states of their obligations under humanitarian law but also linked those obligations to obligations under the CRC.

International humanitarian law also figures prominently in the Committee's general discussion days (an annual practice since 1992 with the participation of experts, geared towards different stakeholders and aimed at fostering better understanding of the Convention). In these events, the Committee consistently emphasized the continued relevance of human rights in armed conflict and of invoking norms of international humanitarian law as part of its mandate, albeit in general terms.[39]

In its Concluding Observations on state reports, the Committee repeatedly found states responsible for violations of humanitarian law in conjunction with violations of CRC, Article 38. A study of 2010 found references to international humanitarian law in fifteen such Concluding Observations, some more explicit than others.[40] With regard to Uganda, for example, the Committee was "deeply concerned that the rules of international humanitarian law applicable to children in armed conflict are being violated in the northern part of the country, in contradiction to the provisions of article 38 of the Convention."[41] In many of the other Concluding Observations, the Committee asked for compliance with international humanitarian law generally.[42] Nowhere, however, was the Committee more specific than with regard to Israel, where it referred to Geneva Convention IV and recommended that the country "fully comply with the rules of distinction (between civilians and combatants) and proportionality (of attacks that cause excessive harm to civilians)";[43] "refrain from the demolition of civilian infrastructure, including homes, water supplies and other utilities";[44] and "establish and strictly enforce rules of engagement for military

36 Committee on the Rights of the Child, *General Comment No. 6 on the Treatment of Unaccompanied and Separated Children Outside their Country of Origin*, UN Doc. CRC/GC/2005/6 (1 September 2005), para. 28.

37 See Weissbrodt, Hansen and Nesbitt, "The Role of the Committee on the Rights of the Child" (n. 32) 125.

38 Committee on the Rights of the Child, *General Comment No. 11 on Indigenous Children and their Rights under the Convention*, UN Doc. CRC/C/GC/11 (12 February 2009), para. 66.

39 See Weissbrodt, Hansen and Nesbitt, "The Role of the Committee on the Rights of the Child" (n. 32) 147–49.

40 On Bhutan, Burundi, Democratic Republic of the Congo, Ethiopia, India (twice), Indonesia, Iraq, Israel, Burma/Myanmar, Russian Federation, Sudan, Tajikistan, Uganda and Uzbekistan; see Weissbrodt, Hansen and Nesbitt, "The Role of the Committee on the Rights of the Child" (n. 32) 131.

41 Committee on the Rights of the Child, *Concluding Observations on Uganda*, UN Doc. CRC/C/15/Add.80 (21 October 1997), para. 34.

42 See Weissbrodt, Hansen and Nesbitt, "The Role of the Committee on the Rights of the Child" (n. 32) 132–33.

43 Committee on the Rights of the Child, *Concluding Observations on Israel*, UN Doc. CRC/C/15/Add.195 (9 October 2002), para. 51.

44 Ibid. para. 51.

and other personnel which fully respect the rights of children as contained in the Convention and protected under international humanitarian law."[45]

In its Concluding Observations under the Optional Protocol on children in armed conflict, the Committee likewise referred to international humanitarian law. It invoked, for example, the Geneva Conventions to ask Canada not to transfer detained persons under the age of eighteen years to states which are not willing and able to apply the Geneva Conventions.[46] But again, the Committee's approach is not entirely consistent as it refrained from making such explicit statements in other cases where international humanitarian law could have been applied.[47] The Committee also consequently refrained from identifying the nature of armed conflicts under international humanitarian law.[48]

While the Committee on the Rights of the Child spearheads the engagement of treaty bodies with international humanitarian law on the basis of CRC, Article 38 and regularly resorts to international humanitarian law, it has been criticized for not offering enough substantial analysis of specific norms, a critique which is mitigated by the fact that the lack of an individual complaints procedure did not allow the Committee to produce case law.[49] Given that, on the basis of CRC, Article 38, the Committee can be said to watch over two conventions with (near) universal ratification (the Geneva Conventions are universally ratified and only Somalia and the United States have not ratified the CRC) it has, in theory, enormous potential to explore the interplay of international humanitarian law and international human rights law within its mandate. Yet, the view that it is effectively "shaping and solidifying"[50] norms of international humanitarian law beyond what states are presently willing to agree on seems perhaps too optimistic in light of the Committee's practice.

19.3 Other human rights treaty bodies

The Committee on Economic, Social and Cultural Rights made it clear that socio-economic and cultural rights must be respected in armed conflicts and that they are part of international humanitarian law. In its Concluding Observations on Israel, for example, the Committee argued that:

> even in a situation of armed conflict, fundamental human rights must be respected and that basic economic, social and cultural rights as part of the minimum standards of human rights are guaranteed under customary international law and are also prescribed by international humanitarian law. Moreover, the applicability of rules of humanitarian law does not by itself impede the application of the Covenant or the accountability of the State under Article 2(1), for the actions of its authorities.[51]

The Committee on Racial Discrimination referred occasionally to international humanitarian law without further analyzing the interplay of human rights and humanitarian law, e.g., when it called upon states parties to disseminate international humanitarian law and respect the

[45] Ibid. para. 59.

[46] Committee on the Rights of the Child, *Concluding Observations on Canada*, UN Doc. CRC/C/OPAC/CAN/CO/1 (1 May 2007), para. 12.

[47] See Weissbrodt, Hansen and Nesbitt, "The Role of the Committee on the Rights of the Child" (n. 32) 146.

[48] Ibid. 137. [49] Ibid. 151–52. [50] Ibid. 140.

[51] Committee on Economic, Social and Cultural Rights, *Concluding Observations on Israel*, UN Doc. E/C.12/1/Add.90 (23 May 2004), para. 31.

principles of humanitarian law, or when it urged states to become parties to humanitarian instruments (as it did with regard to Sri Lanka in 1995).[52] In its Concluding Observations on Israel in 1998, it directly referred to international humanitarian law and voiced concern that changing the demographic composition of the Occupied Palestinian Territories would violate "contemporary international humanitarian law."[53] In its concluding observations on the United States, it asked the country to comply with international human rights law, international humanitarian law and refugee law when detaining and arresting non-US citizens in its fight against terrorism.[54] In its General Recommendation No. 30 (the only substantial mentioning of international humanitarian law apart from passing observations on international humanitarian law in two other General Recommendations),[55] the Committee noted that non-citizens are protected by international human rights law, international humanitarian law and refugee law.[56] In its urgent procedures, the Committee referred occasionally to international humanitarian law, e.g., with regard to the former Yugoslavia, Rwanda, the Democratic Republic of the Congo and Sudan, but like other treaty bodies, CERD's approach lacks overall coherence and predictability.[57]

The Committee on the Elimination of Discrimination Against Women would, in principle, also be well placed to consider humanitarian norms in examining the role of women in armed conflicts, a topic which has attracted much interest, not least since the Security Council adopted Resolution 1325 in 2000 which acknowledged gender perspectives in peace negotiations, humanitarian planning, peace-keeping operations and post-conflict peace-building.[58] And indeed, the Committee has dealt with the specific situation of women in armed conflicts, such as in its General Recommendation No. 19, where it examined gender-based and sexual violence in armed conflicts and noted that wars, armed conflicts and the occupation of territories often lead to increased prostitution, trafficking in women and sexual assault on women.[59] In General Recommendation No. 24, the Committee recommended that special attention be given to the health needs and rights of women belonging to vulnerable and disadvantaged groups, such as refugees and internally displaced women, and recommended further that states parties ensure adequate protection and health services, including trauma treatment and counselling for women in situations of armed conflict and women

[52] See in greater detail David Weissbrodt, "The Approach of the Committee on the Elimination of Racial Discrimination to Interpreting and Applying International Humanitarian Law" (2010) 19(2) *Minnesota Journal of International Law* 344 and 347.

[53] Committee on the Elimination of Racial Discrimination, *Concluding Observations on Israel*, UN Doc. CERD/C/304/Add.45 (30 March 1998), para. 10. See also Weissbrodt, "The Approach of the Committee on the Elimination of Racial Discrimination" (n. 52) 347.

[54] Committee on the Elimination of Racial Discrimination, *Concluding Observations on United States of America*, UN Doc. CERD/C/USA/CO/6 (8 May 2008), para. 24; see Weissbrodt, "The Approach of the Committee on the Elimination of Racial Discrimination" (n. 52) 348.

[55] See Weissbrodt, "The Approach of the Committee on the Elimination of Racial Discrimination" (n. 52) 350–51.

[56] Committee on the Elimination of Racial Discrimination, *General Recommendation No. 30 on Discrimination against Non-citizens*, UN Doc. CERD/C/64/Misc.11/rev.3 (1 October 2004), para. 20.

[57] See Weissbrodt, "The Approach of the Committee on the Elimination of Racial Discrimination" (n. 52) 352–55.

[58] Security Council Res. 1325, UN Doc. S/RES/1325 (31 October 2000).

[59] Committee on the Elimination of Discrimination Against Women, *General Recommendation No. 19 on Violence Against Women* (1992), para. 16, available at www.un.org/womenwatch/daw/cedaw/recommendations/recomm.htm#recom20 (last accessed 15 April 2014).

refugees.[60] Regarding some state reports, e.g., on Indonesia, the Committee deplored the lack of information on the participation of women in the armed forces and the vulnerability of women to sexual exploitation in conflict situations.[61] The Committee also suggested to Uganda to include in peace negotiations measures of accountability, redress and rehabilitation for women and girls who have been victims of violence, including enslavement, in those conflicts.[62] There is, however, no direct reference to humanitarian law in any of these texts.

It seems thus correct to conclude, as an expert consultation convened by the UN High Commissioner for Human Rights in 2002 did, that despite a modest surge in the use of humanitarian law by UN treaty bodies in recent years, there is no common approach on how to deal with violations of humanitarian law.[63] Where humanitarian law is invoked it is done (with a few exceptions) in the most general terms. One can see this simply as a relaxed attitude by treaty bodies which see no need for a technical analysis of the specificities of international humanitarian law, or as reflecting the lack of humanitarian expertise in treaty bodies, or as a deliberate attempt to gloss over the categorization of forms of conflicts and apply a common standard of protection in all situations.[64] In any case, it remains uncertain to what extent they perceive themselves as guardians of humanitarian law.

Suggestions for reforming the treaty body system with a view towards allowing the inclusion of humanitarian law have occasionally been made but have led nowhere. They included on-site visits and observation of violations of humanitarian law in the field; establishing a committee on the protection of civilians in armed conflict; developing a reporting and monitoring system for children in armed conflict (which is now partly realized in the Security Council); and establishing a mandate in (some) treaty bodies with quasi-prosecutorial functions to ensure respect of international humanitarian law and international human rights law in armed conflicts.[65] There is also no evidence that treaty bodies would use humanitarian law where it overlaps with human rights norms, or argue that the *lex specialis* nature of humanitarian law necessitates an analysis of provisions of the Geneva Conventions or the Additional Protocols so as to adequately apply human rights treaties as *lex generalis*, or search for the norm which provides the greatest protection to the individual in a concrete situation, whether it stems from human rights or humanitarian law. This is, however, exactly what the Inter-American Commission on Human Rights has done for the past twenty-five years and which provides an altogether different example of a human rights body's approach to armed conflict and the application of humanitarian law.

[60] Committee on the Elimination of Discrimination Against Women, General Recommendation No. 24 on Women and Health (1999), para. 16, available at www.un.org/womenwatch/daw/cedaw/recommendations/recomm.htm#recom24 (last accessed 15 April 2014).

[61] See *Report of the Committee on the Elimination of Discrimination against Women*, UN Doc. A/53/38/Rev.1 (14 May 1998), para. 295.

[62] See *Report of the Committee on the Elimination of Discrimination against Women*, UN Doc. A/57/38 (2 May 2002), para. 156.

[63] Office of the High Commissioner for Human Rights, *Report on the Outcome of the Expert Consultation on the Issue of Protecting the Human Rights of Civilians in Armed Conflict*, UN Doc. A/HRC/14/40 (2 June 2010), para. 38. The expert consultation was convened on request of the Human Rights Council; see Human Rights Council Res. 9/9, UN Doc. A/HRC/RES/9/9 (24 September 2008).

[64] See Weissbrodt, Hansen and Nesbitt, "The Role of the Committee on the Rights of the Child" (n. 32) 138–39, with regard to the Committee on the Rights of the Child.

[65] See Bertrand Ramcharan, *The United Nations High Commissioner for Human Rights and International Humanitarian Law*, Program on Humanitarian Policy and Conflict Research, Harvard University, Occasional Paper Series No. 3 (2005), p. 11.

20

The Inter-American human rights system

20.1 Inter-American Commission on Human Rights

(a) Applying humanitarian law

The Inter-American Commission was faced with situations of armed conflict in the southern hemisphere of the Inter-American human rights system soon after it had become operational in 1960.[1] To date, no other human rights monitoring body has gone further than the Commission in speaking out on violations of human rights *and* humanitarian law in situations of armed conflict. Unlike other human rights bodies, it has deliberately sought to accommodate international humanitarian law alongside human rights law when considering such situations.[2]

In the first decade of its existence, from 1959 to 1973, however, the Commission made no reference to international humanitarian law in its jurisprudence, despite the occurrence of armed conflicts in the region, e.g., in Cuba, the Dominican Republic and Chile. Only with the armed conflict in Nicaragua and its on-site visit to the country in 1978 did the Commission take an interest in this matter.[3] The Commission considered this situation as an internal armed conflict under Common Article 3 of the Geneva Conventions and held that the use of heavy artillery and bombardments by the Nicaraguan National Guard against the Sandinista Front for National Liberation amounted to violations of "a basic humanitarian norm."[4] The precise meaning of this term was not clarified and in the report on Argentina two years later, in 1980, the Commission held that it had no other competence than to investigate human rights

[1] The Inter-American Commission on Human Rights was created in 1959 and held its first session in 1960. It has carried out country visits since 1961 and, since 1965, has examined individual complaints on human rights violations. It operates under both the American Declaration of the Rights and Duties of Man of 1948 and the 1969 American Convention of Human Rights.

[2] See Noam Lubell, "Parallel Application of International Humanitarian Law and International Human Rights Law: An Examination of the Debate" (2007) 40(2) *Israel Yearbook of Human Rights* 650.

[3] See Christina Cerna, "The History of the Inter-American System's Jurisprudence as Regards Situations of Armed Conflict" (2011) 2(1) *Journal of International Humanitarian Legal Studies* 10–11.

[4] The visit was carried out from 3–12 October 1978 and concluded, *inter alia*, that "[t]he Commission is totally convinced that the Nicaraguan National Guard not only used its firepower indiscriminately causing a great number of casualties and tremendous suffering to the civilian population, but that it also ordered the people to remain inside their homes before the bombing, without even allowing them to evacuate, thus violating a basic humanitarian norm," Inter-American Commission on Human Rights, *Report on the Situation of Human Rights in Nicaragua*, OAS Doc. OEA/SEr.L/V/II/45 Doc. 18 rev. 1 (17 November 1978), ch. II. See also Cerna, "The History of the Inter-American System's Jurisprudence" (n. 3) 11–12.

violations and would not examine violations of international humanitarian law in armed conflicts. The reason for this restraint may be found in the repeated requests by the General Assembly of the Organization of American States (OAS) to the Commission to investigate not only human rights abuses by governmental authorities but also by non-state armed groups and terrorist organizations. The Commission seemingly did not want to be drawn into examining their conduct even though it began to do so later when it considered the human rights situation in Peru in 1993.[5]

The case of *Disabled Peoples' International* v. *United States* in 1987 was the first time the Commission was confronted with allegations of international humanitarian law in a situation of armed conflict under the individual complaints procedure of the American Convention on Human Rights (ACHR).[6] The Commission had to consider an aerial bombing attack carried out by the United States on 24 October 1983 (during the US invasion of Grenada) against the Peoples' Revolutionary Army, which left sixteen inmates of a psychiatric hospital dead and caused injuries to several others. The NGO *Disabled Peoples' International* brought the case before the Inter-American Commission under Article 1 (right to life) of the American Declaration of the Rights and Duties of Man. The US government took the view that the Commission was not competent to decide on the allegations because its mandate was limited to the American Declaration, whereas this particular situation was governed by international humanitarian law. In the United States' view, the Commission was not an "appropriate organ to apply the Fourth Geneva Convention to the United States."[7] In order to be able to find a violation, the United States argued, the Commission would have to apply international humanitarian law, an activity for which it had never been mandated by the OAS member states.[8] The Commission nevertheless declared the petition admissible but did not decide on the merits as the petitioners requested the case to be closed in 1995, following fruitless attempts by the Commission to receive further information on the case.[9]

In 1998, a triad of cases allowed the Commission to formulate a new position towards international humanitarian law and present itself as a guardian of both human rights and humanitarian law. In *Arturo Ribón Avilán* v. *Colombia*,[10] *Hugo Bustios Saavedra* v. *Peru*[11]

[5] Cerna, "The History of the Inter-American System's Jurisprudence" (n. 3) 14–25.

[6] *Disabled Peoples' International* v. *United States*, Inter-American Commission on Human Rights, Case No. 9213, Decision as to the Admissibility of 22 September 1997, OAS Doc. OEA/Ser.L/V/II.71 Doc. 9 rev. 1.

[7] Ibid. ch. IV.B para. 3.

[8] See also David Weissbrodt, "The Right to Life in Armed Conflict: Disabled Peoples' International v. United States" (1988) 29(1) *Harvard International Law Journal* 65.

[9] The petitioners were satisfied with having received financial aid from the United States Agency for International Development (USAID) to rebuild the hospital and compensate victims, while the United States put on record that their actions had been lawful under the law of armed conflict and such aid should not to be seen as any form of compensation for damages; see Inter-American Commission on Human Rights, Case No. 9213, Report No. 3/96 of 22 September 1987, Annual Report 1986–1987, OAS Doc. OEA/Ser.L/V/II.91 Doc. 7at 201.

[10] *Arturo Ribón Avilán and ten others ("The Milk")* v. *Colombia*, Inter-American Commission on Human Rights, Case No. 11.142 of 30 September 1997, Report No. 26/97 of 13 April 1998, OAS Doc. OEA/Ser.L/V/II.98, Doc. 6 rev.

[11] *Hugo Bustios Saavedra* v. *Peru*, Inter-American Commission on Human Rights, Case No. 10.548 of 16 October 1997, Report No. 38/97 of 13 April 1998, OAS Doc. OEA/Ser.L/V/II.98 Doc. 6 rev.

and *Juan Carlos Abella* v. *Argentina* (also known as the "*La Tablada*" case)[12] the Commission formulated what remains the most far-reaching interpretation of the mandate of a human rights body to consider violations of international humanitarian law. The Commission may have been influenced by the International Court of Justice (ICJ)'s Advisory Opinion in the *Nuclear Weapons* case of 1996 which had come out shortly before the cases were decided. On the basis of the ICJ's view that international human rights law continues to apply in armed conflicts and international humanitarian law constitutes the *lex specialis*, the Commission began to argue that it is not only allowed but obliged to resort to international humanitarian law.

In addition to the ICJ's Advisory Opinion, the Commission also relied on the Advisory Opinion of the Inter-American Court of Human Rights in the "*Other Treaties*" case of 1982. In this case, Peru had asked the Court (under ACHR, Article 64) which treaties other than the ACHR would fall within the Court's jurisdiction.[13] The Inter-American Court had found that:

> [t]he need of the regional system to be complemented by the universal finds expression in the practice of the Inter-American Commission on Human Rights and is entirely consistent with the object and purpose of the Commission. The Commission has properly invoked in some of its reports and resolutions "other treaties concerning the protection of human rights in the American States", regardless of their bilateral or multilateral character, or whether they have been adopted within the framework or under the auspices of the inter-American system.[14]

The Commission used and further developed the arguments made in both Advisory Opinions in its jurisprudence. In the first case, *Arturo Ribón Avilán* v. *Colombia*, it had to decide on the death of members of the M-19 guerilla movement killed by the Colombian army. The *guerilleros* had distributed milk from a stolen milk truck in Bogotá when they were approached by a massive contingent of army, police and state security agents. The subsequent pursuit resulted in eleven persons being killed (including one bystander) all of which the police forces claimed were "killed in combat."[15] The Commission found Colombia to have violated several provisions of the ACHR as well as Common Article 3 of the Geneva Conventions. It did not dispute Colombia's right to use military force against what it called "armed combatants" and "legitimate military objects"[16] but considered that once such persons were in the custody of the Colombian authorities, they were entitled to protection under the ACHR as well as under Common Article 3 of the Geneva Conventions.[17] It went on to interpret the content of Common Article 3 of the Geneva Conventions and said that, with regard to the wounded persons and those in the custody of the authorities:

[12] *Juan Carlos Abella* v. *Argentina*, Inter-American Commission on Human Rights, Case No. 11.137 of 18 November 1997, Report No. 55/97 of 14 April 1998, OAS Doc. OEA/Ser.L/V/II.98 Doc. 6 rev. at 161.

[13] *Other Treaties Subject to the Consultative Jurisdiction of the Court (Art. 64 American Convention on Human Rights)*, Inter-American Court of Human Rights, Advisory Opinion of 24 September 1982, OC-1/82, Ser. A, No. 1, para. 8. ACHR, Art. 64 provides that "[t]he member states of the Organization may consult the Court regarding the interpretation of this Convention or of other treaties concerning the protection of human rights in the American states."

[14] *Other Treaties* Advisory Opinion (n. 13) para. 43.

[15] *Arturo Ribón Avilán* v. *Colombia* (n. 10) para. 22. [16] Ibid. para. 133. [17] Ibid. para. 134.

> [m]ilitary operations must always be conducted within the regulations and prohibitions imposed by the application of the rules of international humanitarian law. The first of these rules is that a wounded person and/or a combatant who is captured or *hors de combat* must be afforded humane treatment. This rule recognizes that when some combatants have ceased participating in the hostilities and no longer pose a threat or the possibility of immediate harm to the adversary, they do not qualify as legitimate military targets. Mistreatment, and even more so extrajudicial executions, of wounded or captured combatants are grave violations of Common Article 3.[18]

Those persons who had surrendered in unclear circumstances, the Commission argued, were also under the protection of Common Article 3 of the Geneva Conventions[19] so that all deaths constituted:

> a flagrant violation of common Article 3 of the Geneva Conventions in that state agents were absolutely required to treat humanely all the persons within their power due to injury, surrender or detention, whether or not they had previously participated in hostilities.[20]

It needs to be noted that the Inter-American Commission had raised the issue of violation of international humanitarian law on its own without the petitioners having claimed violations of international humanitarian law. Colombia rejected the Commission's view that the simultaneous application of international humanitarian law and human rights law is within its powers and is its duty and argued that the Commission was not competent to apply international humanitarian law.[21] In response, the Commission rejected this argument on two grounds: first it pointed out that the state had indicated that an armed confrontation exists and had thus "opened the door"[22] to the Commission's use of international humanitarian law. Secondly, it said that whether or not the state had (implicitly) agreed on the application of humanitarian law, the Commission considered itself "competent to apply directly provisions of international humanitarian law or to refer to these norms to inform its interpretations of relevant provisions of the American Convention."[23] It argued that:

> in cases such as this one, which involve situations of armed conflict, and particularly where the State makes special reference to the armed conflict, the Commission should apply humanitarian law to analyze the actions of State agents in order to determine whether they have exceeded the limits of legitimate action.[24]

More specifically, the Commission defended the application of international humanitarian rights law with several inter-linked arguments: first, and with reference to the decision of the Inter-American Court of Human Rights in the "*Other Treaties*" case mentioned above, the Commission invoked ACHR, Article 29(2) which stipulates that no provision of the Convention may be interpreted so as to exclude or limit the effect of other treaties (the so-called "savings clause" or "most-favourable clause").[25] The Commission said that:

> Article 29 of the American Convention establishes that no provision of the Convention may be interpreted as "excluding or limiting the effect" of other international acts of the

[18] Ibid. para. 140. [19] Ibid. para. 141. [20] Ibid. para. 202. [21] Ibid. para. 170. [22] Ibid. para. 169.
[23] Ibid. para. 170. [24] Ibid. para. 168.
[25] ACHR, Art. 29(2): "No provision of this Convention shall be interpreted as . . . restricting the enjoyment or exercise of any right or freedom recognized by virtue of the laws of any State Party or by virtue of another convention to which one of the said states is a party."

> same nature, or of another convention, to which a State is party. Consequently, the Commission is competent to directly apply norms of international humanitarian law, i.e. the law of war, or to inform its interpretation of the Convention provisions by reference to these norms.[26]

Secondly, it pointed to the non-derogable nature of the right to life under ACHR, Article 27 which, in its opinion, "applies along with and is informed by the provisions of international humanitarian law for internal hostilities."[27] Colombia, however, had not derogated the ACHR and the Commission raised this point on its own. Thirdly, the Commission considered it necessary to use humanitarian law as it "generally provide[s] for more specific protection for the victims of armed conflicts than the guarantees set forth in more general terms in the American Convention."[28] The Commission therefore "must necessarily refer to and apply definitional provisions and relevant rules from humanitarian law as authoritative sources which provide orientation in the resolution of these cases."[29] While the Commission did not explicitly refer to humanitarian law as *lex specialis* in its decision, this seems to express a similar idea, namely, that humanitarian law is the more appropriate (although not the only) legal framework for armed conflicts. It stated that:

> [e]ven though technically the American Convention and the other human rights treaties are applicable in times of peace and situations of armed conflict, none of these human rights instruments has been designed to regulate situations of armed conflict, and therefore they do not include norms that govern the means and methods of such conflicts.[30]

Fourthly, the Commission argued in more general terms that human rights and humanitarian law "converge and reinforce one another"[31] and it thus saw the need to apply both bodies of law simultaneously. Fifthly, and related to this argument, the Commission found the provisions of Common Article 3 of the Geneva Conventions and ACHR, Article 5 identical to the extent that their simultaneous application would "not impose additional burdens"[32] on the state. And sixthly, the Commission pointed out that the Colombian Constitution contained a provision according to which the rules of international humanitarian law must be respected in all cases. It found that with this provision Colombia had recognized the right to an effective remedy against violations of international humanitarian law. It linked this fact with ACHR, Article 25 (which obliges states parties to provide judicial remedies for violations of rights recognized by the constitution or laws of the state) and argued that the Commission is authorized to directly apply international humanitarian law where a violation of Article 25 (i.e., on insufficient domestic investigations for violations of Common Article 3 of the Geneva Conventions) is alleged.[33]

[26] *Arturo Ribón Avilán* v. *Colombia* (n. 10) para. 132.

[27] Ibid. para. 134. ACHR, Art. 27: "1. In time of war, public danger, or other emergency that threatens the independence or security of a State Party, it may take measures derogating from its obligations under the present Convention to the extent and for the period of time strictly required by the exigencies of the situation, provided that such measures are not inconsistent with its other obligations under international law and do not involve discrimination on the ground of race, color, sex, language, religion, or social origin."

[28] *Arturo Ribón Avilán* v. *Colombia* (n. 10) para. 171. [29] Ibid. para. 173. [30] Ibid. para. 171.

[31] Ibid. para. 174. [32] Ibid. para. 172.

[33] Ibid. paras. 176–78. ACHR, Art. 25 reads: "Right to judicial protection: 1. Everyone has the right to simple and prompt recourse, or any other effective recourse, to a competent court or tribunal for protection

The Commission confirmed its views in the decision in *Hugo Bustíos Saavedra* v. *Peru*. The case was about the death of journalist Hugo Bustíos and injuries sustained by a colleague of his in an incident which involved the Peruvian security forces and military. The journalists had been attacked by unidentified men when they were trying to interview members of the police and military during the investigation of a murder case.[34] Again, the Commission argued that Common Article 3 of the Geneva Conventions is applicable in this situation which forms part of the internal armed conflict occurring in Peru,[35] and that Common Article 3 of the Geneva Conventions and ACHR, Article 4 on the right to life apply "simultaneously."[36] It found Peru in violation of ACHR, Article 4 and Common Article 3 of the Geneva Conventions.[37] In this decision it also referred to customary international humanitarian law although it did not consider any such rules.[38]

It repeated and further developed its arguments in the *La Tablada* case against Argentina of 1998, which remains the most widely cited example of the Commission's approach to international humanitarian law. Following an attack of forty-two armed individuals – members of the armed group *Moviemento Todos por la Patria* – on military barracks in La Tablada in the province of Buenos Aires in 1989, the national armed forces (fearing a coup d'état) retook the barracks in a thirty-hour exchange of fire which resulted in twenty-nine attackers and several state agents being killed (out of a total of approximately 3,500 persons involved in the incident).[39] Both the petitioners and the state agreed that the situation constituted an "armed confrontation"[40] and Argentina qualified its conduct specifically as a "military operation"[41] but rejected the applicability of international humanitarian law to this situation. In contrast, the petitioners claimed that Argentina had not only violated several obligations under the ACHR but that the armed forces had also violated international humanitarian law.[42] The petitioners specifically pointed out that the Argentine military had rejected an offer to surrender and had used weapons that caused unnecessary suffering.[43]

The Commission found that qualifying the nature of the armed confrontation constitutes a prerequisite for evaluating the merits of the case. It said that:

> before it can properly evaluate the merits of the petitioner's claims concerning the recapture of the La Tablada base by the Argentine military, it must first determine whether the armed confrontation at the base was merely an example of an "internal disturbance or tensions" or whether it constituted a non-international or internal armed conflict within the meaning of Article 3 common to the four 1949 Geneva conventions ("Common Article 3"). Because the legal rules governing an internal armed conflict vary significantly from those governing situations of internal disturbances or tensions, a proper characterization of the events at the La Tablada military base on January 23 and 24, 1989 is necessary to determine the sources of applicable law. This, in turn,

against acts that violate his fundamental rights recognized by the constitution or laws of the state concerned or by this Convention, even though such violation may have been committed by persons acting in the course of their official duties. 2. The States Parties undertake: (a) to ensure that any person claiming such remedy shall have his rights determined by the competent authority provided for by the legal system of the state; (b) to develop the possibilities of judicial remedy; and (c) to ensure that the competent authorities shall enforce such remedies when granted."

[34] See *Hugo Bustíos Saavedra* v. *Peru*, Inter-American Commission on Human Rights, Case 10.548 of 13 April 1998, OAS Doc. OEA/Ser.L/V/II.98 Doc. 6, paras. 4–13.

[35] Ibid. para. 58. [36] Ibid. para. 59. [37] Ibid. para. 63. [38] Ibid. para 61.

[39] *Juan Carlos Abella* v. *Argentina* (n. 12) paras. 7–37. [40] Ibid. para. 147. [41] Ibid. para. 147.

[42] Ibid. para. 147. [43] Ibid. para. 158.

> requires the Commission to examine the characteristics that differentiate such situations from Common Article 3 armed conflicts in light of the particular circumstances surrounding the incident at the La Tablada base.[44]

It did so at length and concluded that the concerted nature of the attacks, the involvement of armed forces, the military planning and coordination as well as the nature and level of violence demonstrated the existence of an internal armed conflict governed by Common Article 3 of the Geneva Conventions, despite the short duration of the armed confrontation.[45]

The Commission then restated its position that "human rights treaties apply both in peace-time, and during situations of armed conflict"[46] and said that "the general rules contained in international instruments relating to human rights apply to non-international armed conflicts as well as the more specific rules of humanitarian law."[47] As before, the Commission argued that international human rights law and international humanitarian law share a common nucleus of non-derogable rights and a common purpose of protecting human life and dignity, but that despite the continued applicability of human rights in armed conflict human rights instruments were not meant to regulate warfare and that international humanitarian law provides more protection for victims of armed conflicts.[48] Again, however, it did not explicitly refer to humanitarian law as *lex specialis*. The Commission also repeated its view that Common Article 3 of the Geneva Conventions and ACHR, Article 4 converge and reinforce each other:

> both Common Article 3 and Article 4 of the American Convention protect the right to life and, thus, prohibit, *inter alia*, summary executions in all circumstances. Claims alleging arbitrary deprivations of the right to life attributable to State agents are clearly within the Commission's jurisdiction. But the Commission's ability to resolve claimed violations of this non-derogable right arising out of an armed conflict may not be possible in many cases by reference to Article 4 of the American Convention alone. This is because the American Convention contains no rules that either define or distinguish civilians from combatants and other military targets, much less specify when a civilian can be lawfully attacked or when civilian casualties are a lawful consequence of military operations.[49]

It maintained that it must necessarily look to and apply definitional standards and relevant rules of humanitarian law as sources of authoritative guidance in its resolution of this and other kinds of claims alleging violations of the American Convention in combat situations,[50] as otherwise it would have to decline its jurisdiction in many cases which would be "manifestly absurd in light of the underlying object and purposes of both the American Convention and humanitarian law treaties."[51] After it made a general comment that states parties to the Geneva Conventions are required to respect and ensure respect for the provisions of the Convention, it repeated that its competence to refer to humanitarian law is derived from ACHR, Articles 25, 27, 29 and 64. With regard to the latter provision it restated its views expressed in the *Avilán* case.[52] Concerning ACHR, Article 25 it held that when a claimed violation by state agents of fundamental rights:

[44] Ibid. para. 148. [45] Ibid. paras. 149–56. [46] Ibid. para. 158. [47] Ibid. para. 160.

[48] Ibid. paras. 158–59.

[49] Ibid. para. 161. See also para. 160 where the Commission repeats its views on the convergence of the two fields expressed earlier in the *Avilán* case.

[50] Ibid. para. 161. [51] Ibid. para. 161 [52] Ibid. para. 171.

> is not redressed on the domestic level and the source of the right is a guarantee set forth in the Geneva Conventions, which the State Party concerned has made operative as domestic law, a complaint asserting such a violation can be lodged with and decided by the Commission under Article 44 of the American Convention.[53]

It elaborated on its duty to take into account the norm most favourable to the individual under ACHR, Article 29(2) and argued that in case of the same or comparable rights under the ACHR and humanitarian law, the Commission is duty bound to give effect to the treaty with the higher standard(s) applicable to the right(s) or freedom(s) in question and found that "[i]f that higher standard is a rule of humanitarian law, the Commission should apply it."[54] It also repeated its view that although the derogation clause of ACHR, Article 27(1):

> cannot be interpreted as incorporating by reference into the American Convention all of a State's other international legal obligations, [it] does prevent a State from adopting derogation measures that would violate its other obligations under conventional or customary international law.[55]

As in the *Avilán* case, however, the state had not derogated from the Convention. As it had done in *Hugo Bustios Saavedra*, the Commission also made a passing reference to customary international humanitarian law as applicable.[56] It did not, however, repeat its earlier position that Common Article 3 of the Geneva Conventions requires states to do no more than they are already legally obliged to do under the American Convention and would thus impose no additional burden upon them.

It seems that in *Avilán* and in *La Tablada*, the Commission wanted to argue for a twofold competence: to directly apply humanitarian law and to use humanitarian law as an interpretative yardstick for the application of the ACHR.[57] In *Avilán* v. *Colombia*, the Commission said that it "is competent to directly apply norms of international humanitarian law, i.e. the law of war, or to inform its interpretation of the Convention provisions by reference to these norms."[58] In *La Tablada* it said:

> [b]efore addressing petitioner's specific claims, the Commission thinks it useful to clarify the reasons why it has deemed it necessary at times to apply directly rules of international humanitarian law or to inform its interpretations of relevant provisions of the American Convention by reference to these rules.[59]

But in *Avilán* the statement on interpretation was followed by the straightforward comment that the Commission "should apply both bodies of law."[60] This was omitted in the *La Tablada*. And indeed, the Commission found Peru in violation of Common Article 3 of the Geneva Conventions, in addition to the ACHR in the *Avilán* case, while it held Argentina responsible for violations of ACHR Articles 4, 5 and 25 in *La Tablada*.[61] Even so, the Commission analyzed the facts in *La Tablada* more thoroughly from a humanitarian law perspective than any other human rights body has ever done before or after. It qualified the attackers as "subject to direct individualized attack to the same extent as combatants"[62] who had temporarily lost the protection granted to civilians; spoke about the choice of means

[53] Ibid. para. 163. [54] Ibid. para. 165. [55] Ibid. para. 168. [56] Ibid. para. 177.
[57] *Arturo Ribón Avilán* v. *Colombia* (n. 10) para 132. [58] Ibid. para. 157.
[59] *Juan Carlos Abella* v. *Argentina* (n. 12) para. 157.
[60] *Arturo Ribón Avilán* v. *Colombia* (n. 10) para. 174.
[61] *Juan Carlos Abella* v. *Argentina* (n. 12) paras. 245–47. [62] Ibid. para. 178.

and methods of the military;[63] referred to the circumstances of surrender and denial of quarter and the use of weapons of a nature to cause superfluous injury or unnecessary suffering (all terms common to international humanitarian law instruments); and invoked the Protocol on Prohibitions or Restrictions on the Use of Incendiary Weapons and commented on the fact that Argentina had not ratified it.[64]

But it found the applicants had misconceived their role in the events: the application of international humanitarian law, the Commission argued, means that only persons *hors de combat* and civilians are protected from the direct use of force against them but not civilians directly taking part in hostilities (such as the applicants) who temporarily lose their protection under international humanitarian law when and as long they participated in hostilities. Consequently, the actions of the state agents in retaking the barracks had not violated international humanitarian law.[65] The Commission concluded that because of the lack of sufficient evidence to establish the use of "illegal methods and means of combat"[66] by the state agents:

> the deaths of and wounds inflicted on the attackers, while they were active participants in the conflict, were legitimately related to the combat, and do not constitute violations of the American Convention or of the applicable provisions of humanitarian law.[67]

In contrast, the Commission said, any inhumane treatment of persons following their surrender, such as executions and disappearances, did amount to a violation of Common Article 3 of the Geneva Conventions and the ACHR. Those who had surrendered, were captured or had been wounded and ceased their hostile acts were fully protected by Common Article 3 of the Geneva Conventions and ACHR, Article 5: "[t]he intentional mistreatment, much less summary execution, of such wounded or captured persons would be a particularly serious violation of both instruments."[68] It did not, however, repeat this conclusion in the part of the decision which established which Articles of the ACHR had been violated.

The Commission's arguments on its competence to apply humanitarian law have met with scepticism, and its reliance on ACHR, Article 25 seems particularly troublesome. As mentioned, Article 25 provides that individuals have a right to a domestic judicial remedy in case of violations of fundamental rights recognized by the constitution or laws of the state concerned.[69] The Commission seemed to interpret the inclusion of remedies against violations of the Geneva Conventions in domestic legislation as covered by the notion of "fundamental rights" when it said that:

> when the claimed violation is not redressed on the domestic level and the source of the right is a guarantee set forth in the Geneva Conventions, which the State Party concerned has made operative as domestic law, a complaint asserting such a violation can be lodged with and decided by the Commission.[70]

This seems acceptable in the cases at hand where the fundamental rights under Common Article 3 of the Geneva Conventions are at stake, but the blanket reference to the Geneva Conventions remains questionable.[71] The Commission's argument that humanitarian law

[63] Ibid. para. 179. [64] Ibid. paras. 176–89. [65] Ibid. paras. 172–79 and 182. [66] Ibid. para. 188.
[67] Ibid. para. 328. [68] Ibid. para. 189. [69] ACHR, Art. 25.
[70] *Juan Carlos Abella* v. *Argentina* (n. 12) para. 163.
[71] See for a similar critique also Liesbeth Zegveld, "The Inter-American Commission on Human Rights and International Humanitarian Law: A Comment on the Tablada Case" (1998) 38(324) *International Review*

can be directly applied as long as it is identical with human rights law (e.g., when the Commission found Common Article 3 of the Geneva Conventions to be "pure human rights law")[72] is more to the point but also problematic. It can be understood as arguing for the complementarity of human rights and humanitarian law but also seems to equate the existence of the same substantive norms in two different treaties with the procedural competence to apply both.[73] Furthermore, if two norms of humanitarian and human rights law were indeed identical and entirely interchangeable, the only reason to apply both seems to be to emphasize the gravity of the violation. And the argument also does not seem to reach far beyond norms such as Common Article 3 of the Geneva Conventions, i.e., to rules on the lawful means and methods of warfare in humanitarian law which have no equivalent in human rights law.

The Commission's reliance on the Inter-American Court's Advisory Opinion in *Other Treaties* (where it had accepted the Commission's reference to other treaties than the ACHR) is also less straightforward than it seems. The Inter-American Court had said that:

> [t]he Commission has properly invoked in some of its reports and resolutions "other treaties concerning the protection of human rights in the American states," regardless of their bilateral or multilateral character, or whether they have been adopted within the framework or under the auspices of the Inter-American system.[74]

A literal reading of the phrase "other treaties concerning the protection of human rights" seems to exclude international humanitarian treaties. Commentators remain divided over this matter. Some argue that humanitarian treaties should be considered as included[75] while others argue against.[76] The blanket equation of the Geneva Conventions with "other treaties concerning the protection of human rights" seems not tenable. The Court itself had argued in its Advisory Opinion that "the broadest interpretation would include within the Court's advisory jurisdiction any treaty concerning the protection of human rights in which one or more American States are Parties."[77]

The Commission's strongest argument seems to be the use of ACHR, Article 29 to allow the application of the norm of human rights or humanitarian law which is most favourable to the individual.[78] As mentioned, the Commission argued that in light of ACHR, Article 29 it feels obliged to apply the provision which offers the highest level of protection as otherwise it fail in its duties. It said that:

of the Red Cross 509; and Lindsay Moir, "Decommissioned? International Humanitarian Law and the Inter-American Human Rights System" (2003) 25(1) *Human Rights Quarterly* 196. Both seem to understand the Commission's statement as to allow it to directly consider violations of humanitarian law rather than legal remedies and reject it as not covered by the text of the ACHR.

72 *Juan Carlos Abella* v. *Argentina* (n. 12) para. 158.

73 See Zegveld, "The Inter-American Commission on Human Rights" (n. 71) 508; and Moir, "Decommissioned?" (n. 71) 194.

74 *Other Treaties* Advisory Opinion (n. 13) para. 43.

75 See Thomas Buergenthal, "The Advisory Practice of the Inter-American Human Rights Court" (1985) 79(1) *American Journal of International Law* 6.

76 See Moir, "Decommissioned?" (n. 71) 199, who also points out that the Court meant to establish its own competence in the Advisory Opinion and not that of the Commission.

77 *Other Treaties* Advisory Opinion (n. 13) para. 32.

78 ACHR, Art. 29(2): "No provision of this Convention shall be interpreted as . . . restricting the enjoyment or exercise of any right or freedom recognized by virtue of the laws of any State Party or by virtue of another convention to which one of the said states is a party."

> in those situations where the American Convention and humanitarian law instruments apply concurrently, Article 29(b) of the American Convention necessarily require[s] the Commission to take due notice of and, where appropriate, give legal effect to applicable humanitarian law rules.[79]

From this it concluded that:

> where there are differences between legal standards governing the same or comparable rights in the American Convention and a humanitarian law instrument, the Commission is duty bound to give legal effect to the provision(s) of that treaty with the higher standard(s) applicable to the right(s) or freedom(s) in question. If that higher standard is a rule of humanitarian law, the Commission should apply it.[80]

The way in which the Commission used the savings clause as a blanket permission to decide on matters of humanitarian law has been viewed critically, given that such clauses are formulated negatively: no provision of the ACHR may be interpreted as restricting the enjoyment or exercise of rights recognized elsewhere. In contrast, the Commission saw it as a positive obligation to compare the content of human rights and humanitarian treaties and choose the more appropriate one.[81] The rationale and *travaux préparatoires* of savings clauses in the ACHR and elsewhere, e.g., in International Covenant on Civil and Political Rights (ICCPR), Article 5(2)[82] and European Convention on Human Rights, Article 53[83] are not fully clear with regard to such an approach, as it is not obvious whether the "other international obligations" mentioned in such clauses extend solely to other human rights conventions or all international treaties; the wording of some of the clauses seems to allow for both interpretations.[84]

It also seems that savings clauses were meant to prevent the deliberately abusive application of the respective human rights treaty to the detriment of the victim (as becomes clear from the insertion of the words "on the pretext" in ICCPR, Article 5),[85] and not to allow choosing between international treaty law. One would thus need to understand such savings clauses as allowing for positive obligations which also apply to situations where (different) levels of protection exist and argue – with a view towards the systemic coherence of the law and the shared humanitarian goal of human rights and humanitarian law to provide the highest level of protection – for their complementarity. Even though this argument seems possible, the case law of the Inter-American Commission is not conclusive in this regard as

[79] *Juan Carlos Abella* v. *Argentina* (n. 12) para. 164. [80] Ibid. para. 165.

[81] Conor McCarthy, "Human Rights and the Laws of War under the American Convention on Human Rights" (2008) 6 *European Human Rights Law Review* 772. For a critical view see Zegveld, "The Inter-American Commission on Human Rights" (n. 71) 509.

[82] ICCPR, Art. 5(2): "There shall be no restriction upon or derogation from any of the fundamental human rights recognized or existing in any State Party to the present Covenant pursuant to law, conventions, regulations or custom on the pretext that the present Covenant does not recognize such rights or that it recognizes them to a lesser extent."

[83] ECHR, Art. 53: "Nothing in this Convention shall be construed as limiting or derogating from any of the human rights and fundamental freedoms which may be ensured under the laws of any High Contracting Party or under any other agreement to which it is a Party."

[84] See Manfred Nowak, *UN Covenant on Civil and Political Rights: CCPR Commentary* (2nd edn., Kehl: Engel, 2005), p. 118.

[85] ICCPR, Art. 5(2): "There shall be no restriction upon or derogation from any of the fundamental human rights . . . on the pretext that the present Covenant does not recognize such rights or that it recognizes them to a lesser extent."

it is about Common Article 3 of the Geneva Conventions, the application of which (as the Commission itself had argued) is identical to the provisions of the ACHR which were alleged to have been violated.[86]

In *Lucio Parada Cea and others* v. *El Salvador*, decided in 1999, the Commission again found the state to have violated Common Article 3 of the Geneva Conventions and Article 4 of Protocol II, very much in line with its findings in *Avilán*.[87] The case was situated in the armed conflict of El Salvador (1980 to 1991) and involved the detention, torture and death of farm workers by the Salvadoran army. The Commission based its decision on its competence to "directly enforce rules of international humanitarian law or interpret provisions of the American Convention, using those rules as reference."[88] Unlike in the previous cases, the Commission also applied Additional Protocol II.[89]

(b) Interpreting human rights law

The Commission's argument to use humanitarian law as an interpretative yardstick is less controversial.[90] Its view that it must:

> necessarily look to and apply definitional standards and relevant rules of humanitarian law as sources of authoritative guidance in its resolution of . . . claims alleging violations of the American Convention in combat situations[91]

is supported by other sources. The International Law Commission (ILC) study on the fragmentation of international law, for example, also argued that treaty bodies are not only allowed but may be required to interpret provisions of their respective treaties against the background of "other" international law as a reflection of the principle enshrined in Vienna Convention on the Law of Treaties (VCLT), Article 31(3)(c) on the general interpretation of treaties.[92] The phrase "any relevant rules of international law" in VCLT, Article 31(3)(c) can be understood as an expression of the systemic approach of interpretation which mitigates

86 Heike Krieger, "Die Verantwortlichkeit Deutschlands nach der EMRK für seine Streitkräfte im Auslandseinsatz" (2002) 62 *Zeitschrift für ausländisches öffentliches Recht und Völkerrecht* 695.

87 *Lucio Parada Cea, Héctor Jaoquín Miranda Marroquín, Fausto García Funes, Andrés Hernández Carpio, Jose Catalino Meléndez and Carlos Antonio Martiínez* v. *El Salvador*, Inter-American Commission on Human Rights, Case 10.480, Report No. 1/99 of 27 January 1999, OAS Doc. OEA Ser.L/V/II.102 Doc. 6 rev., para. 160.

88 *Lucio Parada Cea and others* v. *El Salvador* (n. 87) paras. 66 and 99.

89 It found a violation of Additional Protocol II, Art. 4 (Fundamental Guarantees) which prohibits violence to the life, health and physical or mental well-being of persons, in particular murder and torture.

90 See Moir, "Decommissioned?" (n. 71) 191–93. 91 *Juan Carlos Abella* v. *Argentina* (n. 12) para. 161.

92 VCLT, Art. 31(3)(c): "There shall be taken into account, together with the context: . . . any relevant rules of international law applicable in the relations between the parties." See Report of the Study Group of the International Law Commission, finalized by Martii Koskenniemi, *Fragmentation of International Law: Difficulties Arising from the Diversification and Expansion of International Law*, UN Doc. A/CN.4/L.682 (13 April 2006) ("ILC Study on Fragmentation"), para. 423; and Oliver Dörr, "General Rule of Interpretation" in Oliver Dörr and Kirsten Schmalenbach (eds.), *The Vienna Convention on the Law of Treaties: A Commentary* (Heidelberg: Springer, 2012), p. 562, on the basis of the ICJ's decision in the *Namibia* case that "[a]n international instrument has to be interpreted and applied within the framework of the entire legal system prevailing at the time of the interpretation", *Legal Consequences for States of the Continued Presence of South Africa in Namibia (South West Africa) notwithstanding Security Council Resolution 276*, International Court of Justice [1970] ECJ Reports 16, para 53.

the fragmentation of international law.[93] But yet again, the case law produced by the Inter-American Commission is largely restricted to situations where the fundamental guarantees of Common Article 3 of the Geneva Conventions overlap with provisions of the AHCR.

In its later cases, the Inter-American Commission departed from its view that it can denounce violations of specific norms of international humanitarian law and seemingly moved towards using international humanitarian law so as to interpret provisions of the ACHR.[94] First, however, it lost its confidence in denouncing violations of Common Article 3 of the Geneva Conventions. In *Jose Alexis Fuentes Guerrero and others* v. *Colombia*, the Commission had found violations only of "standards of common Article 3 of the Geneva Conventions"[95] even though the petitioners had not claimed any such violations. In this case about the killing of eight unarmed civilians by the armed forces in the hamlet of Puerto Lleras, the Commission also analysed in considerable detail Additional Protocol II, Article 13 on civilian immunity and applied it to the situation at hand.[96] It also qualified the direct participation in hostilities as contained in Additional Protocol II, Article 13, i.e., the loss of civilian immunity unless and for such times as civilians take a direct part in hostilities, a legal concept not found in international human rights law (even though it refrained from indicating whether Article 13 had actually been violated):

> In the case of the residents of Puerto Lleras, the alleged expression of sympathy for the cause of one of the parties to the conflict is not equivalent to carrying out acts of violence that constitute a real and immediate threat to the adversary. Therefore, even if the expressions of Lt. Otálora Amaya in terms of the alleged sympathies of the civilian population for the armed dissidents were authentic, the members of the Army involved were not authorized to treat the victims in this case as legitimate targets of attack.[97]

In *Ellacuria and others* v. *El Salvador*, which concerned the extra-judicial execution of six Jesuit priests and a woman in San Salvador by the armed forces, the Commission held that the state had violated the right to life enshrined in Article 4 of the American Convention without any reference to international humanitarian law, even though the petitioners had claimed that the state "has violated the precepts of humanitarian law."[98] In *Romero y Galdámez* v. *El Salvador* in 2000 (on the killing of the Archbishop of San Salvador by a death squad on 24 March 1980), the Commission used ambiguous language again when it

93 Dörr, "General Rule of Interpretation" (n. 2) pp. 560–61.

94 See Emiliano J. Buis, "The Implementation of International Humanitarian Law by Human Rights Courts: The Example of the Inter-American Human Rights System" in Roberta Arnold and Noelle Quénivet (eds.), *International Humanitarian Law and Human Rights Law: Towards a Merger in International Law* (Leiden: Nijhoff, 2008), pp. 282–83 and 290.

95 *Jose Alexis Fuentes Guerrero and others* v. *Colombia*, Inter-American Commission on Human Rights, Case No. 11.519, Report No. 61/99 of 13 April 1999, OAS Doc. OEA Ser.L/V/II.106 Doc. 7 rev., para. 43.

96 Additional Protocol II, Art. 13 reads: "1. The civilian population and individual civilians shall enjoy general protection against the dangers arising from military operations. To give effect to this protection, the following rules shall be observed in all circumstances. 2. The civilian population as such, as well as individual citizens, shall not be the object of attack. Acts or threats of violence the primary purpose of which is to spread terror among the civilian population are prohibited. 3. Civilians shall enjoy the protection afforded by this Part, unless and for such time as they take a direct part in hostilities."

97 *Jose Alexis Fuentes Guerrero and others* v. *Colombia* (n. 95) para. 41.

98 *Ignacio Ellacuria, SJ, Segundo Montes, SJ, Armando López, SJ, Ignacio Martin-Baró, SJ, Joaquin López y López, SJ, Juan Ramón Moreno, SJ, Julia Elba Ramos and Celina Mariceth Ramos* v. *El Salvador*, Inter-American Commission on Human Rights, Case No. 10.488, Report No. 136/99 of 22 December 1999, OAS Doc. OEA Ser.L/V/II.106 Doc. 3 rev., para. 37.

found that the state had "violated . . . Article 4 of the American Convention, in conjunction with the principles codified in common Article 3."[99]

Whether such reference to "standards" and "principles" of Common Article 3 of the Geneva Conventions means that the Commission directly applied both provisions or interpreted them in light of the other must be left unanswered. In a decision taken a year later, in 2001, in the *Riofrio Massacre* case against Colombia (the murder of thirteen persons in the village of El Bosque in the municipality of Riofrió by members of the armed forces and killers in plain clothes), the Commission referred to Common Article 3 of the Geneva Conventions in passing (as did the complainants who also alleged violations of Additional Protocol II, Article 2 without giving further reasons why this provision was referred to); but the Commission found only violations of ACHR, Article 4.[100]

In *Prada Gonzalez and others* v. *Colombia* in 2001 (on extra-judicial executions by members of the army in 1993) the Commission invoked Common Article 3 of the Geneva Conventions but found only a violation of ACHR, Article 4.[101] *Marino Lopez and others* v. *Colombia* of 2004 concerned the murder and forced displacement of members of communities of African descent who fled from aerial and land-based bombardments and attacks in the counter-guerilla "Operation Genesis" carried out by the armed forces.[102] The Commission upheld its competence to interpret the ACHR under ACHR, Article 29 "based on other international instruments relevant to the case."[103] It found the killing of Marino Lopez in violation of the ACHR without referring to Common Article 3 of the Geneva Conventions[104] but invoked international humanitarian law with regard to the forced displacement when it held that "the bombings in the said operation were carried out indiscriminately, with no respect for the principle of distinction set out in Additional Protocol II to the Geneva Conventions."[105] It said no more than that, however, on Additional Protocol II.

All of these cases concerned internal armed conflicts. Only *Coard and others* v. *United States* in 1999 allowed the Commission to consider an international armed conflict.[106] The case was about seventeen individuals detained and allegedly mistreated by US armed forces during the 1983 invasion of Grenada. While the petitioners only claimed violations of the ACHR, the United States stated that it had fully complied with the "applicable international rules concerning the law of armed conflict, including the rules governing the treatment of civilian detainees and military prisoners."[107] The Commission and the state then had a lengthy exchange of views on the status of these persons under international humanitarian

[99] *Monsignor Oscar Amulfo Romero y Galdámez* v. *El Salvador*, Inter-American Commission on Human Rights, Case No. 10.481, Report No. 37/00 of 13 April 2000, OAS Doc. OEA Ser.L/V/II.106 Doc. 3 rev., para. 72.

[100] See *Riofrió Massacre – Colombia*, Inter-American Commission on Human Rights, Case No. 11.654, Report No. 62/01 of 6 April 2001, OAS Doc. OEA/Ser.L/V/II.111 Doc. 20 rev. at 758, paras. 14 and 54. Additional Protocol II, Art. 2 is on the personal field of application of the Protocol.

[101] See *Carlos Manuel Prada Gonzalez and Evelio Antonio Bolaño Castro* v. *Colombia*, Inter-American Commission on Human Rights, Case No. 11.710, Report 63/01 of 6 April 2001, OAS Doc. OEA/Ser.L/V/II.111 Doc. 20 rev. at 781, para. 32.

[102] See *Marino Lopez and others* v. *Colombia*, Inter-American Commission on Human Rights, Case No. 12.573, Report 64/11 of 31 March 2011, OAS Doc. OEA/Ser.L/V/II.127 Doc. 4 rev. 1.

[103] Ibid. para. 214. [104] Ibid. paras. 5 and 244–65. [105] Ibid. para. 240.

[106] *Bernard Coard and others* v. *United States*, Inter-American Commission on Human Rights, Case No. 10.951, Report No. 109/99 of 29 September 1999, OAS Doc. OEA/Ser.L/V/II.106 Doc. 3 rev.

[107] Ibid. para. 21.

law, i.e., whether they were civilian detainees under Geneva Convention IV or prisoners of war under Geneva Convention III.[108] Finally, the United States denied the Commission's competence altogether as in the view of the US government the situation was completely and exclusively regulated by international humanitarian law.[109] The Commission again defended its competence with reference to the arguments made in its earlier cases.[110] It repeated its opinion that:

> international humanitarian law pertains primarily in times of war and the international law of human rights applies most fully in times of peace, the potential application of one does not necessarily exclude or displace the other. There is an integral linkage between the law of human rights and humanitarian law because they share a "common nucleus of non-derogable rights and a common purpose of protecting human life and dignity," and there may be a substantial overlap in the application of these bodies of law. Certain core guarantees apply in all circumstance, including situations of conflict.[111]

It then proceeded to analyze the provisions of international humanitarian law on detention contained in Geneva Conventions III and IV, including the right to appeal in Geneva Convention IV, Article 78, which provides that the procedure for decisions on assigned residence or internment of civilians shall include the right to appeal "with the least possible delay."[112] The Commission concluded that the time of internment (up to nine days after the cessation of hostilities) was "incompatible with the terms of the American Declaration of the Rights and Duties of Man as understood with reference to Article 78 of the Fourth Geneva Convention."[113] It concluded, without further reference to Geneva Convention IV, that a violation of the American Declaration of the Rights and Duties of Man had occurred.[114]

More recently, in the inter-state complaint *Ecuador* v. *Colombia* concerning Franklin Guillermo Aisalle Molina, which was declared admissible in 2010, Ecuador alleged the extra-judicial executions of twenty-five individuals (civilians and *guerilleros*) by Colombian armed forces in an attack on a camp of the Colombian Revolutionary Armed Forces in Ecuador (FARC) in the immediate proximity of the Colombian border.[115] The individuals had been shot at short range or had died after having been beaten. Ecuador alleged violations of the right to life under the ACHR while Colombia maintained that the ACHR was inapplicable as "Operation Phoenix" (the military operation against FARC in which the deaths occurred) was solely governed by international humanitarian law. In particular, Colombia argued that only under humanitarian law may it be "established whether or not the deprivation of the right to life of an individual resulting from hostilities associated with a military operation which in turn unfolded in the context of an armed

[108] Ibid. paras. 21–27 and 30–33. Eventually the United States confirmed their status as civilian detainees "treated de facto to the highest legally available standard of protection," para. 32.

[109] Ibid. para. 35. [110] Ibid. paras. 38–43. [111] Ibid. para. 39.

[112] Geneva Convention IV, Art. 78; see *Bernard Coard and others* v. *United States* (n. 106) para. 55.

[113] Ibid. para. 57. The American Declaration on the Rights and Duties of Man contains in its Art. XXV a provision similar to Geneva Convention IV, Art. 78 which requires supervisory control of detentions to be made available "without delay."

[114] *Bernard Coard and others* v. *United States* (n. 106) para. 61.

[115] See *Franklin Guillermo Aisalle Molina (Ecuador* v. *Colombia)*, Inter-American Commission on Human Rights, Report No. 112/10 of 21 October 2010 on Admissibility, Inter-State Petition IP-02, OAS Doc. OEA/Ser.L/V/II.140 Doc. 10.

conflict, was arbitrary."[116] The Commission responded that the American Convention and the Geneva Conventions share a common core of non-derogable rights, specifically Article 4 and Common Article 3 of the Geneva Conventions which protect the right to life.[117] It said that as a consequence, any act of killing is within the remit of the Commission in exercising its jurisdiction under the ACHR and that in circumstances such as these it needs to consider international humanitarian law.[118]

Finally, the Commission also invoked humanitarian law when it ordered interim measures with regard to the situation of the detainees held by the United States in Guantánamo Bay, Cuba, in 2002, and asked the United States to have the status of the detainees clarified.[119] It repeated its position on the role of human rights in armed conflict, the interplay of human rights and humanitarian law and its competence to apply international humanitarian law as *lex specialis*:

> In addition, while its specific mandate is to secure the observance of international human rights protections in the Hemisphere, this Commission has in the past looked to and applied definitional standards and relevant rules of international humanitarian law in interpreting the American Declaration and other Inter-American human rights instruments in situations of armed conflict. In taking this approach, the Commission has drawn upon certain basic principles that inform the interrelationship between international human rights and humanitarian law ... In certain circumstances, however, the test for evaluating the observance of a particular right, such as the right to liberty, in a situation of armed conflict may be distinct from that applicable in time of peace. In such situations, international law, including the jurisprudence of this Commission, dictates that it may be necessary to deduce the applicable standard by reference to international humanitarian law as the applicable *lex specialis*.[120]

In this document the Commission also invoked the Martens Clause as proof for its position that no one is outside the law and linked Geneva Convention III, Article 5 to Article XVIII of the American Declaration on the Rights and Duties of Man to remind the United States of its duty to have the legal status of the detainees decided by a competent court of tribunal.[121] In its subsequent Resolution No. 2/06, it urged the United States to close Guantánamo Bay and remove the detainees in accordance with international humanitarian law and international human rights law.[122] And in Resolution No. 2/11 on the same matter in 2011, the Commission again reminded the United States that human rights law and

[116] Ibid. para. 115. [117] Ibid. paras. 117–18. [118] Ibid. para. 118.

[119] *Detainees at Guantanamo Bay, Cuba*, Inter-American Commission on Human Rights, Precautionary Measure of 12 March 2002 (footnotes omitted).

[120] Ibid.

[121] See *Detainees at Guantanamo Bay, Cuba*, Precautionary Measure (n. 119). Geneva Convention III, Art. 5 reads: "should any doubt arise as to whether persons, having committed a belligerent act and having fallen into the hands of the enemy, belong to any of the categories enumerated in Article 4, such persons shall enjoy the protection of the present Convention until such time as their status has been determined by a competent tribunal"; and American Declaration of the Rights and Duties of Man, Art. XVIII, OAS Res. XXX (1948), reprinted in OEA/Ser.L.V/II.82 Doc. 6 rev. 1 at 17 (1992), reads "Every person may resort to the courts to ensure respect for his legal rights. There should likewise be available to him a simple, brief procedure whereby the courts will protect him from acts of authority that, to his prejudice, violate any fundamental constitutional rights."

[122] Inter-American Commission on Human Rights, Resolution No. 2/06 on Guantánamo Bay Precautionary Measures, United States (28 July 2006).

international humanitarian law apply to the situation in Guantánamo.[123] In its 2002 Report on Terrorism and Human Rights, the Commission also repeated its position on the interplay of humanitarian law and human rights.[124] With regard to its competence in matters of humanitarian law it said (very much in line with the position of the Inter-American Court) that "[i]t is therefore appropriate, and indeed imperative, for the Commission to consider all relevant international norms, including those of international humanitarian law, while interpreting the international human rights law instruments for which it is responsible."[125]

The Commission dealt with violations of international humanitarian law not only in individual complaints but also in some country reports where it used humanitarian law as an interpretative yardstick to understand the human rights obligations of states parties but also spoke out on obligations under humanitarian law, including those of non-state armed groups.[126] In its third report on Colombia in 1999, the Commission mentioned international humanitarian law for the first time explicitly and in order to analyze the "violence which occurs constantly and with extreme intensity in Colombia."[127] The report stands out for the Commission's detailed analysis of humanitarian law. Prior to this, the Commission had only noted the state's position towards the existence of an emergency situation, e.g., when Chile declared a state of siege in 1983 to which the Commission did not react.[128] In its report on El Salvador of 1978 it had merely noted the international humanitarian treaties to which the country was party.[129] When discussing military operations in rural areas in Colombia in its report of 1981, it had also refrained from referring to international humanitarian law.[130] The same can be said about the Commission's comments on the armed conflict in El Salvador.[131]

In the third report on Colombia, however, the Commission devoted a whole section to the Commission's use of international humanitarian law.[132] It repeated its position that the Inter-American Convention continues to apply during armed conflicts.[133] Then it recalled that it had already made clear its intention to invoke "the norms provided by both human rights law and international humanitarian law in analyzing specific petitions involving alleged abuses by state agents and their proxies which arise in the context of internal armed

[123] Inter-American Commission on Human Rights, Resolution No. 2/11 regarding the situation of the detainees at Guantánamo Bay (22 July 2011).

[124] Inter-American Commission on Human Rights, *Report on Terrorism and Human Rights*, OAS Doc. EA/Ser.L/V/II.116 Doc. 5 rev. 1 corr. (22 October 2002), para. 61.

[125] Ibid. para. 62.

[126] See Cerna, "The History of the Inter-American System's Jurisprudence" (n. 3) 41–45.

[127] Inter-American Commission on Human Rights, *Report on the Situation of Human Rights in Colombia*, OAS Doc. OEA/Ser.L/V/II.102 Doc. 9 rev. 1 (26 February 1999), ch. IV, para. 1.

[128] See Inter-American Commission on Human Rights, *Report on the Status of Human Rights in Chile*, OAS Doc. OEA/Ser.L/V/II.34 Doc. 21 corr. 1 (25 October 1974), ch. IV, paras. 2–3.

[129] See Inter-American Commission on Human Rights, *Report on the Situation of Human Rights in El Salvador*, OAS Doc. OEA/Ser.L/V/II.46 Doc. 23 rev. 1 (17 November 1978), ch. I.G.

[130] See Inter-American Commission on Human Rights, *Report on the Situation of Human Rights in the Republic of Colombia*, OAS Doc. OEA/Ser.L/V/II.53 Doc. 22 (30 June 1981), ch. VII.

[131] See Inter-American Commission on Human Rights, *Report on the Situation of Human Rights in El Salvador*, OAS Doc. OEA/Ser.L/II.85 Doc. 28 rev. (11 February 1994), ch. I.1 (entitled "El Salvador: from conflict to the quest for peace. The position of the Inter-American Commission on Human Rights during the armed conflict").

[132] Inter-American Commission on Human Rights, *Report on the Situation of Human Rights in Colombia* (1999), ch. IV.2.

[133] Ibid. ch. IV, para. 9.

conflicts"[134] and that it would do the same in considering state reports.[135] It acknowledged the *lex specialis* nature of international humanitarian law from which it concluded that it "must necessarily look to and apply definition standards and relevant rules of international humanitarian law as sources of authoritative guidance . . . ,"[136] the phrase it had also used repeatedly in its case law.

The Commission also highlighted that invoking international humanitarian law would allow it to scrutinize the behaviour of non-state armed actors and thus provide greater protection of those affected by armed conflicts. And more than that: not looking at international humanitarian law, the Commission argued, would place it "in the extremely difficult situation of being asked to analyze the conduct of dissident groups without reference to any previously-established standards."[137] Given that it had been asked by OAS organs to examine the conduct of non-state armed groups, reference to international humanitarian law was now seen as a necessity for the Commission "in order to fairly and adequately address the activities of those groups in its reporting."[138] The Commission also rejected Colombia's assertion that in doing so these groups would be elevated to the same level as the state.[139]

These preliminary remarks are followed by more than 300 paragraphs which apply the fundamental principles of humanitarian law to the situation in Colombia,[140] lay down the humanitarian obligations of non-state actors[141] and discuss in detail acts of torture, perfidy, attacks on civilian objects and health services, forced displacement and disappearances, massacres of civilians, extra-judicial executions, and the use of child soldiers in light of human rights and humanitarian law.[142] Nowhere has a human rights body gone further in scrutinizing the situation of an internal armed conflict in such a legally comprehensive manner.

20.2 Inter-American Court of Human Rights

(a) Las Palmeras: *delimiting interpretation*

The Inter-American Court of Human Rights adopted a more restrictive approach with regard to international humanitarian law in *Las Palmeras* v. *Colombia* in 2000.[143] This is all the more important as the Court's decisions are binding whereas the Commission may only make recommendations and proposals.[144] The case concerned the death of seven persons in the hands of the national police force and armed forces in Las Palmeras in the department of Putumayo in Colombia. When the case had been before the Inter-American Commission on Human Rights it had established the existence of an international armed conflict under Common Article 3 of the Geneva Conventions and found a violation of this provision together with ACHR, Article 4, and had consequently asked the Court to decide on Colombia's responsibility for violations of "the right to life, embodied in Article 4 of the Convention and Article 3 common to all the 1949 Geneva Conventions."[145]

[134] Ibid. ch. IV.2, para. 11. [135] Ibid. ch. IV.2, para. 13. [136] Ibid. ch. IV.2, para. 12.
[137] Ibid. ch. IV.2, para. 14. [138] Ibid. ch. IV.2, para. 14. [139] Ibid. ch. IV.2, para. 18.
[140] Ibid. ch. IV.2, paras. 36–80. [141] Ibid. ch. IV.2, paras. 37–132. [142] Ibid. ch. IV.2, paras. 133–347.
[143] *Las Palmeras* v. *Colombia*, Inter-American Court of Human Rights, Judgment (Preliminary Objections) of 4 February 2000, Ser. C, No. 67.
[144] See ACHR, Art. 63(1) and ACHR, Art. 50(3). [145] Ibid. para. 12.

Colombia responded by filing several preliminary objections to the Court, claiming, *inter alia*, that neither the Inter-American Commission nor the Court were competent to apply international humanitarian law and other international treaties.[146] The government did not object to the argument that the incident was part of an internal armed conflict and thus covered by Common Article 3 of the Geneva Conventions. It also did not object to the application of the ACHR in an armed conflict and contended that the Court may interpret the Geneva Conventions and other international treaties. But it stated that the Commission may only apply the American Convention and concluded that under ACHR, Article 62 in conjunction with ACHR, Article 33 the jurisdiction of the Court is limited to the application of the American Convention.[147]

The Commission requested the Inter-American Court to dismiss the objections of Colombia and confirm its view that it can directly apply international humanitarian law.[148] The Court, however, followed Colombia's arguments and concluded that the Commission is restricted to the ACHR when it submits a case to the Court. "Although the Inter-American Commission has broad faculties as an organ for the promotion and protection of human rights," the Court argued:

> it can clearly be inferred from the American Convention that the procedure initiated in contentious cases before the Commission, which culminates in an application before the Court, should refer specifically to rights protected by that Convention . . . Cases in which another Convention, ratified by the State, confers competence on the Inter-American Court or Commission to hear violations of the rights protected by that Convention are excepted from this rule; these include, for example, the Inter-American Convention on Forced Disappearance of Person.[149]

With regard to its own mandate, the Court held that the Convention has given it only the competence to determine whether the acts and norms of states are compatible with the Convention itself and not with the Geneva Conventions. It held that it is competent to determine whether any norm of domestic or international law applied by a state, in times of peace or armed conflict, is compatible with the American Convention. In this activity, the Court said, it is unlimited: "any legal norm may be submitted to this examination of compatibility."[150] But specifically with regard to international humanitarian law it said that:

> [i]n order to carry out this examination, the Court interprets the norm in question and analyzes it in the light of the provisions of the Convention. The result of this operation will always be an opinion in which the Court will say whether or not that norm or that fact is compatible with the American Convention. The latter has only given the Court competence to determine whether the acts or the norms of the States are compatible with the Convention itself, and not with the 1949 Geneva Conventions.[151]

This decision was largely understood as preventing the Commission and the Court from applying international humanitarian law.[152] But critics have accused the Court of ignoring its mandate (and that of the Commission) to consider other obligations under international law when a derogation is made under ACHR, Article 27, sidelining the savings clause of

[146] Ibid. para. 16. [147] Ibid. para. 28. [148] Ibid. para. 31. [149] Ibid. para. 34. [150] Ibid. para. 32.
[151] Ibid. para. 33.
[152] See Liesbeth Zegveld, "Remedies for Victims of Violations of International Humanitarian Law" (2003) 85(851) *International Review of the Red Cross* 516; and Buis, "The Implementation of International Humanitarian Law by Human Rights Courts" (n. 94) p. 286.

ACHR, Article 29 and disregarding the ICJ's Advisory Opinion on Nuclear Weapons.[153] It must be noted, however, that the Court's decision was not a wholesale rejection of the Commission's approach. It had restricted the Commission's competence to using humanitarian law for the purpose of interpretation, as the Commission itself had argued in its cases.[154]

The Court had argued similarly with regard to other human rights treaties in *Villagrán-Morales* v. *Guatemala* (also known as the "Street Children" case) which was decided shortly before *Las Palmeras*. In this case the Court found the Inter-American Convention to Prevent and Punish Torture[155] as well as the UN Convention on the Rights of the Child (CRC) to form part of a comprehensive international *corpus iuris* which helps it to decide on an alleged violation of the ACHR by way of an evolutionary interpretation of the Convention as a living instrument.[156] The Court did the same in *Las Palmeras* with regard to humanitarian law treaties which, in its view, help in defining the substance of human rights law in armed conflicts.[157] In light of the Commission's own ambiguity with regard to denouncing violations of Common Article 3 of the Geneva Conventions, this position is not as remote from the Commission's own approach as it may seem.

(b) *Beyond* Las Palmeras

In *Bámaca Velàsquez* v. *Guatemala*, decided in the same year as *Las Palmeras*, the Court took a different view, based on Guatemala's specific consent to apply humanitarian law.[158] In this case, the Court was asked to decide on the responsibility of Guatemala for violations of the ACHR as well the Inter-American Convention to Prevent and Punish Torture and Common Article 3 of the Geneva Conventions.[159] A guerrilla fighter had been captured, tortured and executed by the military forces of Guatemala, and the Inter-American Commission had once more argued that Common Article 3 of the Geneva Conventions is not only important for the interpretation of the ACHR's provisions but that the provisions of the ACHR must not be interpreted as restricting Common Article 3 of the Geneva Conventions. "Article 3, common to the Geneva Conventions," it had said, "constitutes a valuable parameter for interpreting the provisions of the American Convention".[160]

When the case came to the Court the state argued that

[153] See Cerna, "The History of the Inter-American System's Jurisprudence" (n. 3) 49–50. See also Fanny Martin, "Application du droit international humanitaire par la Cour interaméricaine des droits de l'hommes" (2001) 83(844) *Revue international de la Croix-Rouge* 1064, who points out that somewhat ironically the Court's decision was to some extent thwarted by the fact that a few days after it had delivered its judgment the government of Colombia installed a commission (Comisión intersectorial permanente para los derechos humanos y el derecho humanitario) to ensure respect for both international humanitarian law and international human rights law in the country.

[154] See Buis, "The Implementation of International Humanitarian Law" (n. 94) pp. 281–84.

[155] Inter-American Convention to Prevent and Punish Torture, 12 September 1985, OAS Treaty Series No. 67.

[156] *Villagrán-Morales and others* v. *Guatemala (Case of the Street Children)*, Inter-American Court of Human Rights, Judgment (Merits) of 19 November 1999, Series C, No. 63, paras. 193–94.

[157] Buis, The Implementation of International Humanitarian Law" (n. 94) p. 288.

[158] *Bámaca Velásquez* v. *Guatemala*, Inter-American Court of Human Rights, Judgment (Merits) of 25 November 2000, Series C, No. 70.

[159] Ibid. para. 2. [160] Ibid. para. 203.

> although the case was instituted under the terms of the American Convention, since the Court had "extensive faculties of interpretation of international law, it could [apply] any other provision that it deemed appropriate."[161]

On this basis the Court confirmed the existence of an internal armed conflict and applied international humanitarian law.[162] It found that:

> as established in Article 3 common to the Geneva Conventions of August 12, 1949, confronted with an internal armed conflict, the State should grant those persons who are not participating directly in the hostilities or who have been placed *hors de combat* for whatever reason, humane treatment, without any unfavorable distinctions. In particular, international humanitarian law prohibits attempts against the life and personal integrity of those mentioned above, at any place and time. Although the Court lacks competence to declare that a State is internationally responsible for the violation of international treaties that do not grant it such competence, it can observe that certain acts or omissions that violate human rights, pursuant to the treaties that they do have competence to apply, also violate other international instruments for the protection of the individual, such as the 1949 Geneva Conventions and, in particular, common Article 3.[163]

The precise meaning of this remains unclear, given that the Court declares that it is incompetent to find violations of humanitarian law while at the same observing that such violations have occurred. To some commentators, the case seems to indicate that international humanitarian law can be directly applied by the Inter-American Court, contrary to what was said in *Las Palmeras*.[164] But in the paragraph which follows this ambiguous statement, the Court said that Common Article 3 of the Geneva Conventions and provisions of the ACHR bear a "similarity,"[165] and that other treaties may be taken into consideration "as elements for the interpretation of the American Convention."[166] This may mean that the Court suggests that insofar as human rights and humanitarian law overlap, it can hold a state responsible for violations of the ACHR and the Geneva Conventions.

Whatever the Court wanted to say – whether state consent or the similarity of norms is a prerequisite for observing violations of humanitarian law – it seems to contradict its earlier views that a direct application of humanitarian law (i.e., a decision on violations of specific norms of the Geneva Conventions and Additional Protocols) is absolutely ruled out. In the end, the Court found Guatemala responsible for violations of human rights provision but not for violations of international humanitarian law.[167]

Serrano-Cruz Sisters v. *El Salvador* (on the abduction of two children in 1982 by the Salvadoran army during a military operation), decided in 2004, is equally ambiguous. While the Commission and the Court used humanitarian law in this case in a very specific way they still stopped short of denouncing a violation of humanitarian law. The Commission had invoked the very general provision on family life of ACHR, Article 17 with regard to the state's obligations to investigate and determine the whereabouts of the disappeared sisters and had explicitly found the state to be in violation of this provision.[168] To this it had added,

[161] Ibid. para. 204. [162] Ibid. paras. 121 and 207. [163] Ibid. para. 208.

[164] See Hans-Joachim Heintze, "On the Relationship between Human Rights Law Protection and International Humanitarian Law" (2004) 86(856) *International Review of the Red Cross* 805.

[165] *Bámaca Velàsquez* v. *Guatemala* (n. 158) para. 209. [166] Ibid. para. 209. [167] Ibid. paras. 213–14.

[168] *Serrano-Cruz Sisters* v. *El Salvador*, Inter-American Court of Human Rights, Judgment (Merits, Reparations and Costs) of 1 March 2005, Ser. C, No. 118, para. 116. ACHR, Art. 17 stipulates that "[t]he family . . . is entitled to protection by society and the state."

in a more ambiguous way, that under Additional Protocol II the state has the obligation to provide the family with timely measures such as the identification and registration of children to ensure reunification, and had found that the "[t]he state did not adopt any measure to comply with the obligations established for the protection of the Serrano Cruz sisters."[169] This can be understood as a decision that El Salvador had violated a specific norm of humanitarian law (as the measures referred to are not contained in the ACHR) or as interpreting ACHR, Article 17 in light of humanitarian law.

When the case came to the Court, the state declined the Court's competence to deal with the case as the military operation in question was, in its opinion, solely covered by international humanitarian law for the supervision of which the Commission and Court has no mandate.[170] In its decision on the preliminary objections the Court repeated its view that human rights and humanitarian law are complementary and that:

> all persons, during internal or international armed conflict, are protected by the provisions of international human rights law, such as the American Convention, and by the specific provisions of international humanitarian law.[171]

It stressed the complementarity and convergence of human rights and humanitarian law, particularly with regard to Common Article 3 of the Geneva Conventions and the Fundamental Guarantees of Article 75 of Additional Protocol I.[172] The Court repeated its view that it may "use the provisions of international humanitarian law, ratified by the defendant State, to give content and scope to the provisions of the American Convention."[173]

When the Court later decided on the merits, it even specified the Commission's general reference to the Additional Protocol by explicitly quoting Additional Protocol II, Article 4(3)(b) as applicable source for its decision.[174] This was clearly meant to provide additional protection in a matter not regulated at all in the ACHR, very much in line with what the Commission had consistently argued: that human rights and humanitarian law converge and reinforce each other; that humanitarian law can provide more specific rules in certain situations; and that the (humanitarian law) provision which is most favourable to the individual must be chosen when the ACHR provides less protection. The Court obviously used this provision of humanitarian law to interpret the scope of ACHR, Article 17, but again stopped short of finding a violation of a norm of humanitarian law, seemingly different from the Commission, provided one accepts the cautious words on "non-compliance with Additional Protocol II" in its decision as denouncing a breach of a provision of a humanitarian treaty. Judge Cançado Trindade used his dissenting opinion in this case not only to disagree with this approach but to open up another avenue for the application of humanitarian law in this and other cases. He argued that the peremptory nature of Common Article 3 of the Geneva Conventions together with the Fundamental Guarantees of Additional Protocol I, Article 75 and Additional Protocol II, Articles 4 to 6, all

169 *Serrano-Cruz Sisters* v. *El Salvador*, Judgment (Merits, Reparations and Costs) (n. 168) para. 116.

170 Ibid. para. 108. 171 Ibid. para. 112. 172 Ibid. paras. 111–16. 173 Ibid. para. 119.

174 *Serrano-Cruz Sisters* v. *El Salvador*, Judgment (Merits, Reparations and Costs), para. 145. Additional Protocol II, Art. 4(3)(b) provides that "all appropriate steps shall be taken to facilitate the reunion of families temporarily separated."

of which are *jus cogens*, would suffice to reject, in all cases, the objection of lack of jurisdiction of the Commission and Court *ratione materiae*.[175]

The Court repeated its view that humanitarian law is helpful for interpreting human rights obligations in the case of the *Mapiripán Massacre* in Colombia which was decided in the same year. Upon consideration of the mass killings carried out by paramilitary groups in Colombia in 1997, the Court remarked that "while it cannot attribute international responsibility under International Humanitarian Law [*sic*!], as such, said provisions are useful to interpret other aspects of the violations alleged in the instant case."[176] The Court did not find a violation of humanitarian law but ordered the state to train members of its military and security forces in human rights and international humanitarian law so as to comply with the "obligations derived from Protocol II to disseminate international humanitarian law."[177] Interestingly, the Court seemed at ease finding such a positive obligation contained in a humanitarian law treaty on the compliance with which it allegedly had nothing to say.

In a similar case on the forced disappearance and extra-judicial execution of peasants in the village of Pueblo Bello in Colombia in 1990 – the *Pueblo Bello Massacre* – the Court refrained from mentioning international humanitarian law entirely.[178] In his dissenting opinion in this case, Judge Cançado Trindade again strongly disagreed with this approach and argued, as he had done in *Serrano Cruz Sisters* v. *El Salvador*, that in as far as fundamental guarantees common to human rights and humanitarian law constitute *jus cogens* the Court should in all cases apply them directly.[179] In the *Plan de Sánchez* case, the Court also refrained from using international humanitarian law. The events occurred on 18 July 1982 in Guatemala in the context of the internal armed conflict in the country and included the firing of mortar grenades, followed by the abuse, rape and murder of women and girls and the killings of altogether more than 260 persons in the village of Plan de Sánchez (inhabited mostly by members of the Mayan indigenous people) by members of the military, paramilitary forces and civilian state agents.[180]

Finally, it should be noted that the Court also accepted violations of international humanitarian law as triggering the adoption of provisional measures to protect persons affected by armed conflicts. One example is the *Matter of the Indigenous Community of Kankuamo*, where violations of international humanitarian law (together with threats against the life and personal integrity of some leaders, violations of the rights of women

[175] *Serrano-Cruz Sisters* v. *El Salvador*, Judgment (Merits, Reparations and Costs) (n. 168), Dissenting Opinion of Judge Antônio Augusto Cançado Trindade, para. 40.

[176] *Mapiripán Massacre* v. *Colombia*, Inter-American Court of Human Rights, Judgment (Merits, Reparations and Costs) of 15 September 2005, Ser. C, No. 134, para. 115.

[177] Ibid. para. 317.

[178] *Pueblo Bello Massacre* v. *Colombia*, Inter-American Court of Human Rights, Judgment (Merits, Reparations and Costs) 31 January 2006, Ser. C, No. 140.

[179] Ibid. Dissenting Opinion of Judge Antônio Augusto Cançado Trindade, para. 64.

[180] See *Plan de Sánchez Massacre* v. *Guatemala*, Inter-American Court of Human Rights, Judgment (Merits) of 29 April 2004, Ser. C, No. 105, para. 42. Again Judge Cançado Trindade used a separate opinion to dwell on the relationship between human rights and humanitarian law in general terms, this time referring to the fundamental norms of humanitarian law as general principles of international law, see *Plan de Sánchez Massacre* v. *Guatemala*, Separate Opinion of Judge Antônio Augusto Cançado Trindade, paras. 18–23.

and the presence of non-state armed groups) led the Court to request Colombia to adopt adequate measures of protection.[181]

In light of the practice of the Inter-American Commission and Court it seems too optimistic to argue that they have shown the way in reconciling international humanitarian law and international human rights law.[182] They moreover never considered a situation of normative conflict between humanitarian law and human rights law, so that the lessons to be learned on the interplay of human rights and humanitarian law in such situations remain limited.[183] But it is also not fully correct to argue that both have finally settled on the view that humanitarian law can be used only as an "interpretative reference or a contextualizing guideline"[184] for discerning obligations under human rights law in light of similar obligations of humanitarian law given that a sizeable number of cases were decided on the basis of humanitarian law, and in others ambiguous language on violations of humanitarian law was used.

[181] See the most recent of four orders: Order of the Inter-American Court of Human Rights, Provisional Measures regarding the Republic of Colombia, Matter of the Indigenous Community of Kankuamo (21 November 2011), para. 11.

[182] Françoise Hampson, "The Relationship between International Humanitarian Law and Human Rights Law from the Perspective of a Human Rights Treaty Body" (2008) 90(871) *International Review of the Red Cross* 572.

[183] See McCarthy, "Human Rights and the Laws of War" (n. 81) 775–76 and 779.

[184] Buis, "The Implementation of International Humanitarian Law" (n. 94) p. 293.

21

The European Court of Human Rights

21.1 From *Cyprus* v. *Turkey* to *Al-Skeini*: international conflicts and occupation

Like the Inter-American Commission and Court on Human Rights, the European Court of Human Rights (and, prior to 1998, the European Commission on Human Rights which functioned as the Court's filtering mechanism until the establishment of the Court as a single and permanent monitoring mechanism) has produced case law on human rights in armed conflict and was confronted with claims of violations of international humanitarian law. Like other human rights bodies, the European Court of Human Rights sees human rights as continuously applicable in armed conflicts, even though it has never been as explicit about this. The way in which the Court has frequently invoked the right to life and the duty to investigate killings and disappearances, and has adjudicated on detention, the right to property and private and family life in internal armed conflicts confirms this view.[1] But the Court has not developed a consistent approach towards international humanitarian law, quite to the contrary: its case law is ambiguous in this respect and seemingly characterized by the attempt to keep away from humanitarian law as much as possible.[2]

Under the European Convention on Human Rights (ECHR), the Court is mandated to "ensure the observance of the engagements undertaken by the High Contracting Parties in the Convention and in the Protocols thereto."[3] No reference is made in this mandate to international humanitarian law.[4] The importance of cases decided by the European

[1] See Andrea Gioia, "The Role of the European Court of Human Rights in Monitoring Compliance with Humanitarian Law in Armed Conflict" in Orna Ben-Naftali (ed.), *International Humanitarian Law and International Human Rights Law* (Oxford: Oxford University Press, 2011), p. 205.

[2] Ibid. p. 203; and Vera Gowlland-Debbas and Gloria Gaggioli, "The Relationship between International Human Rights Law and Humanitarian Law: An Overview" in Robert Kolb and Gloria Gaggioli (eds.), *Research Handbook on Human Rights and Humanitarian Law* (Cheltenham: Edward Elgar, 2013), p. 93.

[3] ECHR, Art. 19.

[4] "War" is mentioned, however, in the derogation provision of Art. 15: "1. In time of war or other public emergency threatening the life of the nation any High Contracting Party may take measures derogating from its obligations under this Convention to the extent strictly required by the exigencies of the situation, provided that such measures are not inconsistent with its other obligations under international law. 2. No derogation from Article 2, except in respect of deaths resulting from lawful acts of war, or from Articles 3, 4 (paragraph 1) and 7 shall be made under this provision." If one takes into account the time of drafting of the Convention (shortly after the Geneva Conventions and the general shift in terminology from "war" to "armed conflict") the term "war" can be seen as a reference to international armed conflicts whereas the term "other public emergency" applies to non-international armed conflicts and events beyond the threshold of an armed conflict, see Gioia, "The Role of the European Court of Human Rights" (n. 1) pp. 216–17.

Commission and Court of Human Rights with regard to the extra-territorial application of the Convention (and beyond) has already been discussed above. But these cases, and others, can also be seen in light of how they consider international humanitarian law as jointly applicable with the European Convention as a matter of substance. The European Commission on Human Rights was first faced with the application of the Convention in a situation of occupation when it had to consider cases on Northern Cyprus. After Turkey had invaded the island in 1974, the Commission had to decide on alleged violations of the ECHR by Turkish armed forces in the inter-state complaint of *Cyprus* v. *Turkey* in 1974. Cyprus alleged that Turkish military operations had resulted in indiscriminate killings of civilians and in torture, forced labour, the deprivation of life and the displacement of more than 1,000 persons.[5] The Commission avoided characterizing the situation as an occupation governed by humanitarian law even though the UN Security Council spoke of the "occupied parts of Cyprus" in its resolutions on the situation.[6] It considered Turkey to be bound by the Convention because it exercised jurisdiction either through Turkish armed forces or through the local government which depended heavily on Turkey.

With regard to Cypriot Greeks detained by Turkey, some of whom were considered prisoners of war, the Commission took note of the fact that both states were party to Geneva Convention III on prisoners of war and that Turkey had indicated that it would respect the Convention and allow visits by the International Red Cross (ICRC). In light of these facts the Commission concluded that it need not examine ECHR, Article 5 (on the right to liberty and security) with regard to these persons.[7] Important as this case is for the extra-territorial application of the Convention to situations of occupation, humanitarian law was not further mentioned other than in the dissenting opinion of Judge Sperduti who pointed out that Article 49 of Geneva Convention IV would be applicable as it prohibits deportations of protected persons.[8]

The Court stuck to this approach in its subsequent cases on Northern Cyprus, for example when it decided *Loizidou* v. *Turkey* in 1996.[9] The claimant had been denied permission by the Turkish authorities to repossess property in Northern Cyprus, her previous place of residence, and the Court considered this a denial of the enjoyment of her property under Article 1 of the first Additional Protocol to the ECHR.[10] In line with the Commission's earlier reasoning, the Court refrained from calling the situation a belligerent occupation to which humanitarian law would apply and argued for the extra-territorial application of the Convention by virtue of the effective control exercised by Turkey in Northern Cyprus: "the responsibility of a Contracting Party could also arise when as a

[5] *Cyprus* v. *Turkey*, European Commission on Human Rights, Appl. Nos. 6780/74 and 6950/75, Decision of 10 July 1976. A third inter-state complaint was brought to the Commission soon after, *Cyprus* v. *Turkey*, Appl. No. 8007/77, Decision of 10 July 1978; see on the following also Van Coufoudakis, "Cyprus and the European Convention on Human Rights: The Law and Politics of *Cyprus* v. *Turkey*, Applications 6780/74 and 6950/75" (1982) 4(4) *Human Rights Quarterly* 450.

[6] Security Council Res. 550, UN Doc. S/550/1984 (11 May 1984), Preamble.

[7] *Cyprus* v. *Turkey* (n. 5) para. 313; see also Gioia, "The Role of the European Court" (n. 1) pp. 216–17.

[8] See *Cyprus* v. *Turkey* (n. 5) Dissenting Opinion of G. Sperduti, joined by S. Trechsel, on Art. 15 of the Convention, para. 6. See also Heike Krieger, "A Conflict of Norms: The Relationship between Humanitarian Law and Human Rights Law in the ICRC Customary Law Study" (2006) 11(2) *Journal of Conflict and Security Law* 278.

[9] *Loizidou* v. *Turkey*, European Court of Human Rights, Appl. No. 15318/89, Judgment of 18 December 1996.

[10] Ibid. para. 6.

consequence of military action – whether lawful or unlawful – it exercises effective control of an area outside its territory."[11] Humanitarian law was not mentioned even though it might have supported the Court's findings.[12] This was particularly criticized by Judge Pettiti in his dissenting opinion where he remarked that the Court should have clarified the situation in Northern Cyprus by, *inter alia*, referring to the concept of occupation under humanitarian law.[13]

When the Court was confronted with an international armed conflict in the *Banković* case (discussed with regard to the extra-territorial application of the Convention previously), it refrained from any reference to international humanitarian law in its decision on admissibility.[14] In another case where the armed conflict could have been viewed (at least potentially and partly) of an international character, *Issa* v. *Turkey* (also mentioned previously), the Court refrained from a decision on the merits, too. The six applicants, shepherds who lived in Northern Iraq close to the Turkish border, were killed and mutilated by Turkish soldiers operating outside Turkish territory.[15] As the Court could not find sufficient evidence for the presence of Turkish troops in the area it concluded that no jurisdictional link to Turkey existed and did not consider humanitarian law any further.[16]

When the obligations of the United Kingdom as Occupying Power in Iraq from 2003 onwards became a matter for the Court, the question of the interplay of human rights and humanitarian law in such situations arose again. In its judgment in *Al-Jedda*, a case lodged against the United Kingdom on grounds of the security detention of Mr Al-Jedda in Basrah by UK forces between 2004 and 2007, the Court found the United Kingdom to be in breach of ECHR, Article 5(1) on the right to liberty and security of the person. The applicant had been detained on security grounds in a British detention facility, but the United Kingdom had argued that on the basis of UN Security Council Resolution 1546 (which mandated the multi-national coalition of states to take all necessary measures to contribute to the maintenance of security in Iraq), the internment was attributable to the United Nations.[17] While the case is most important for the way it departs from the much criticized decisions of the Court in the *Behrami* and *Saramati* cases (where the Court had argued to the contrary)[18] and the role of Security Council Resolutions with regard to detentions in multi-national operations, it also contains references to international humanitarian law.

[11] Ibid. para. 52.

[12] See Hans-Joachim Heintze, "On the Relationship between Human Rights Law Protection and International Humanitarian Law" (2004) 86(856) *International Review of the Red Cross* 807–8.

[13] *Loizidou* v. *Turkey* (n. 9), Dissenting Opinion of Judge Pettiti.

[14] Heintze, "On the Relationship" (n. 12) 809. Whether or not the Court would have invoked international humanitarian law if the case had been declared admissible remains speculation. Most likely it would not have done so, see Peter Rowe, "Non-international Armed Conflict and the European Court of Human Rights: Chechnya from 1999" (2007) 4 *New Zealand Yearbook of International Law* 207.

[15] See *Issa and others* v. *Turkey*, European Court of Human Rights, Appl. No. 31821/96, Judgment of 11 November 2004, paras. 12–25. The government disputed the events, relied on the Court's decision in *Banković* and denied that the area was covered by the jurisdiction of the European Convention, see para. 52.

[16] Ibid. paras. 72–82. See also Gioia, "The Role of the European Court of Human Rights" (n. 1) pp. 209–10.

[17] See *Al-Jedda* v. *United Kingdom*, European Court of Human Rights, Appl. No. 27021/08, Judgment of 7 July 2011, para. 60.

[18] See Frederik Naert, "The European Court of Human Rights' *Al-Jedda* and *Al-Skeini* Judgments: An Introduction and Some Reflections" (2011) 50(3–4) *Military Law and the Law of War Review* 317.

One particular issue in this case was that security detention in the context of armed conflicts or occupation is not mentioned as an exception to the right to liberty and security in ECHR, Article 5(1). The Court felt it thus necessary to refer to humanitarian law, specifically to Article 43 of the Hague Regulations 1907 which obliges Occupying Powers to take all the measures in their power to restore, and ensure, as far as possible, public order and safety and which arguably includes detaining persons for security reasons.[19] It did so to establish if any other legal basis apart from Security Council Resolution 1546 would render Article 5(1) inapplicable and concluded that it did not find it established that international humanitarian law placed an obligation on an Occupying Power to use indefinite internment without trial. It interpreted Article 43 of the Hague Regulations not as an obligation of the Occupying Power to use internment but as a measure of last resort.[20] The Court declared that it:

> does not find it established that international humanitarian law places an obligation on an Occupying Power to use indefinite internment without trial. Article 43 of the Hague Regulations requires on Occupying Power to take "all the measures in his power to restore, and ensure, as far as possible, public order and safety, while respecting, unless absolutely prevented, the laws in force in the country . . . In the Court's view it would appear from the provisions of the Fourth Geneva Convention that under international humanitarian law internment is to be viewed not as an obligation on the Occupying Power but as a measure of last resort.[21]

The decision has attracted criticism as a misreading of international humanitarian law (in particular Geneva Convention IV)[22] and as "a potential and serious revision of a legal regime [international humanitarian law] agreed to by all states in the world and one generally considered to constitute the applicable *lex specialis* in international armed conflicts."[23] Different from *Al-Jedda*, the Court saw no need to analyze the United Kingdom's obligations under international humanitarian law in *Al-Skeini* v. *United Kingdom*, discussed previously.[24]

21.2 Internal violence: the Kurdish cases

The European Court has always seen it as within its remit to deal with the activities of military and security forces in response to internal violence. To start with, it had to decide a sequence of cases on measures taken by the United Kingdom against the activities of the Irish Republican Army (IRA) in Northern Ireland. The situation had not been characterized by the United Kingdom as an internal armed conflict under Common Article 3 of the Geneva Conventions or Additional Protocol II but as a terrorist threat to which domestic

[19] See *Al-Jedda* v. *United Kingdom* (n. 17) paras. 42–43. Hague Regulations, Art. 43 reads: "The authority of the legitimate power having in fact passed into the hands of the occupant, the latter shall take all the measures in his power to restore, and ensure, as far as possible, public order and safety, while respecting, unless absolutely prevented, the laws in force in the country."

[20] Ibid. para. 107 [21] Ibid. para. 107.

[22] See Jelena Pejic, "The European Court of Human Rights' *Al-Jedda* Judgment: The Oversight of International Humanitarian Law" (2012) 93(838) *International Review of the Red Cross* 845.

[23] Ibid. 851.

[24] See Max Schaefer, "Al Skeini and the Elusive Parameters of Extraterritorial Jurisdiction" (2011) 16 *European Human Rights Law Review* 580.

anti-terrorism measures and laws had to be applied.[25] The leading case remains *McCann and others* v. *United Kingdom*, which continues to inform the Court's approach to situations involving the right to life under ECHR, Article 2 in situations of large-scale internal violence.[26]

In *McCann*, the United Kingdom authorities had become aware of a planned terrorist attack and confronted three IRA members in Gibraltar who were thought to be planting a car bomb. Minimum force was to be used in order to arrest the suspects but when the UK soldiers felt threatened they opened fire, eventually killing the three men, even though, as it turned out, neither of them carried a weapon or a detonator nor was there actually a car-bomb at the site (such a bomb was found later in another car).[27] The UK government considered the use of force in this situation "no more than absolutely necessary in defence of the people of Gibraltar from unlawful violence"[28] and thus in accordance with ECHR, Article 2(2)(a). The Court went along with this position but found a violation of ECHR, Article 2 given that the conduct and planning of the operation was not organized in such a way so as to "minimize, to the greatest extent possible, recourse to lethal force."[29] The Court also lamented the absence of an "effective official investigation" into the incident.[30] The reasoning in this case was later quoted extensively also in situations which (potentially) amounted to internal armed conflicts under humanitarian law, such as in Eastern Turkey and Chechnya.

The former of these two situations – the conduct of military and security operations by Turkey against the PKK – led to a range of cases decided by the European Court of Human Rights. The views on the situation differed from the start: while Turkey found it was engaged in anti-terrorism operations and never accepted the application of Common Article 3 of the Geneva Conventions to the situation (nor has it ratified Additional Protocol II), others consider the situation as an internal armed conflict (and, where Turkish forces intruded into the territory of Iraq, an international armed conflict).[31] The European Court of Human Rights never expressed an opinion as to whether the events passed the threshold of Common Article 3 of the Geneva Conventions and constituted an armed conflict under international humanitarian law. Many of the cases before the Court could therefore have potentially led to considerations of international humanitarian law.[32]

In one of the first cases of interest here, *Ergi* v. *Turkey*, decided in 1998, Turkish security forces had resorted to the indiscriminate bombardment of civilian houses in their pursuit of members of the PKK in 1993, which had resulted in the death of the applicant.[33] Turkey was held responsible for violations of the right to life under the ECHR as it had not properly

[25] See Roberta Arnold, "Human Rights in Times of Terrorism" (2006) 66(2) *Zeitschrift für ausländisches öffentliches Recht und Völkerrecht* 299; and Heintze, "On the Relationship" (n. 12) 806.

[26] Federico Sperotto, *Violations of Human Rights during Military Operations in Chechnya* (2008), p. 2, available at http://papers.ssrn.com/sol3/papers.cfm?abstract_id=1081199 (last accessed 15 April 2014).

[27] *McCann and others* v. *United Kingdom*, European Court of Human Rights, Appl. No. 18984/91, Judgment of 27 September 1995, paras. 1–18, 100 and 141.

[28] Ibid. para. 143. [29] Ibid. para. 194; see also paras. 202–14. [30] Ibid. para. 161.

[31] On the situation see in greater detail Kerim Yildiz and Susan Breau, *The Kurdish Conflict: International Humanitarian Law and Post-Conflict Mechanisms* (London: Routledge, 2010).

[32] Aisling Reidy, Françoise Hampson and Kevin Boyle, "Gross Violations of Human Rights: Invoking the European Convention on Human Rights in the Case of Turkey" (1997) 15(2) *Netherlands Quarterly of Human Rights* 162.

[33] *Ergi* v. *Turkey*, European Court of Human Rights, Appl. No. 23818/94, Judgment of 28 July 1998, para. 7.

organized the military operation and had put the inhabitants at risk of being caught in the crossfire between its security forces and members of the PKK.[34] The Court held that the responsibility of the state was not limited to misdirected fire but includes situations where the state fails to take all feasible precautionary measures "in the choice of means and methods of a security operation mounted against an opposing group with a view to avoiding and, in any event, to minimizing, incidental loss of civilian life."[35] In line with its reasoning in *McCann*, the Court argued that under ECHR, Article 2(2) "force used must be strictly proportionate to the achievement of the aims."[36]

The decision was taken in the absence of any reference to international humanitarian law but it has often been remarked how strikingly the Court's language resembled that of international humanitarian law.[37] The Court referred to the means and methods of military operations and used notions such as "civilian life,"[38] "indiscriminate bombardment of civilian houses,"[39] "civilian areas"[40] and "incidental loss,"[41] all of which seem borrowed from international humanitarian law.[42] Nowhere has the Court gone further in resorting to the terminology of international humanitarian law on lawful targets, proportionality and military advantage, even though it did not refer to a particular norm of humanitarian law. The Court also did not consider the situation as an armed conflict but referred to "armed clashes"[43] instead (when it concluded that even in such a situation the state has the duty to investigate the circumstances surrounding the applicant's death).

But *Ergi* v. *Turkey* remains exceptional. In *Güleç* v. *Turkey*, decided around the same time, the Court did not resort to such language.[44] In this case, Turkish security forces had used a machine gun to confront a demonstration in which (as they claimed) terrorists had

[34] Ibid. para. 80; see William Abresch, "A Human Rights Law of Internal Armed Conflict: The European Court of Human Rights in Chechnya" (2005) 16(4) *European Journal of International Law* 763.

[35] *Ergi* v. *Turkey* (n. 33) para. 79; see Heintze, "On the Relationship" (n. 12) 810.

[36] *Ergi* v. *Turkey* (n. 33) para. 79. ECHR, Art. 2(2) stipulates that "[d]eprivation of life shall not be regarded as inflicted in contravention of this article when it results from the use of force which is no more than absolutely necessary."

[37] See Heike Krieger, "Die Verantwortlichkeit Deutschlands nach der EMRK für seine Streitkräfte im Auslandseinsatz" (2002) 62 *Zeitschrift für ausländisches öffentliches Recht und Völkerrecht* 692; and Heintze, "On the Relationship" (n. 12) 810.

[38] *Ergi* v. *Turkey* (n. 33) para. 79. [39] Ibid. para. 10. [40] Ibid. paras. 45 and 84. [41] Ibid. para. 79.

[42] The terminology could indeed have been taken from Additional Protocol I, Art. 57 on precautionary measures: "1. In the conduct of military operations, constant care shall be taken to spare the civilian population, civilians and civilian objects. 2. With respect to attacks, the following precautions shall be taken: (a) those who plan or decide upon an attack shall: (i) do everything feasible to verify that the objectives to be attacked are neither civilians nor civilian objects . . .; (ii) take all feasible precautions in the choice of means and methods of attack with a view to avoiding, and in any event to minimizing, incidental loss of civilian life, injury to civilians and damage to civilian objects; (iii) refrain from deciding to launch any attack which may be expected to cause incidental loss of civilian life, injury to civilians, damage to civilian objects, or a combination thereof, which would be excessive in relation to the concrete and direct military advantage anticipated; (b) an attack shall be cancelled or suspended if it becomes apparent that the objective is not a military one or is subject to special protection or that the attack may be expected to cause incidental loss of civilian life, injury to civilians, damage to civilian objects, or a combination thereof, which would be excessive in relation to the concrete and direct military advantage anticipated; (c) effective advance warning shall be given of attacks which may affect the civilian population, unless circumstances do not permit."

[43] *Ergi* v. *Turkey* (n. 33) para. 85.

[44] *Güleç* v. *Turkey*, European Court of Human Rights, Appl. No. 21593/93, Judgment (Merits and Just Satisfaction) of 27 July 1998.

participated and had opened fire at the security forces. A young boy was killed by shots fired into the crowd and the applicants alleged a violation of ECHR, Article 2(2)(c).[45] The Court dismissed, for lack of evidence, the Turkish government's argument that the demonstration had suddenly changed into an insurrection because PKK members had began to open fire on the security forces.[46] It considered the use of force justified as a matter of principle but not to the extent applied, and reminded Turkey of the proportionality "between the aim pursued and the means employed to achieve it."[47] Because the security forces were insufficiently equipped to control the situation they had to use battlefield weapons against the demonstrators. The Court found this particularly difficult to understand given that a state of emergency had been declared in the region and public disturbances had to be anticipated:

> The gendarmes used a very powerful weapon because they apparently did not have truncheons, riot shields, water cannon, rubber bullets or tear gas. The lack of such equipment is all the more incomprehensible and unacceptable because the province of Þýrnak, as the Government pointed out, is in a region in which a state of emergency has been declared, where at the material time disorder could have been expected.[48]

It thus considered the use of combat weapons as not absolutely necessary, disproportionate and in violation of ECHR, Article 2.[49] But in light of the Court's view that a law enforcement operation was conducted with inappropriate means it seems doubtful to construct its views as borrowing the proportionality principle of humanitarian law, as some seem to suggest.[50]

In *Akdivar and others* v. *Turkey*, Turkish soldiers destroyed several houses in a village in their fight against the PKK and the Court concluded that these actions constituted a violation of Article 8 (on respect for private and family life) and Article 1 of the First Optional Protocol to the Convention (on the right to property).[51] In *Selçuk and Asker* v. *Turkey*, the Court similarly found the deliberate burning of houses (with the residents escaping just in time) on the grounds that they had been used by members of the PKK as a violation of the Convention.[52] Nowhere did the Court consider the events as also governed by humanitarian law.

But in *Ahmet Özkan and others* v. *Turkey*, the Court was more forthcoming and explicitly established the existence of "serious disturbances in south-east Turkey involving an armed conflict between the security forces and members of the PKK."[53] In a search operation for PKK members, Turkish security forces had responded to shots from a village by opening fire and the Court accepted this as compatible with ECHR, Article 2 in light of the gravity of threat which the security forces were facing.[54] Despite the intensity of the exchange of fire

[45] ECHR, Art. 2(2)(c): "Deprivation of life shall not be regarded as inflicted in contravention of this article when it results from the use of force which is no more than absolutely necessary: . . . (c) in action lawfully taken for the purpose of quelling a riot or insurrection."

[46] *Güleç* v. *Turkey* (n. 44) paras. 72 and 76. [47] Ibid. para. 71. [48] Ibid. para. 71. [49] Ibid. para. 83.

[50] See, e.g., Louise Doswald-Beck, "The Right to Life in Armed Conflict: Does International Humanitarian Law Provide All the Answers?" (2007) 88(864) *International Review of the Red Cross* 886; and Krieger, "Die Verantwortlichkeit Deutschlands" (n. 37) 692.

[51] *Akdivar and others* v. *Turkey*, European Court of Human Rights, Appl. No. 21893/93, Judgment of 16 September 1996, paras. 15–18 and 88.

[52] *Selcuk and Asker* v. *Turkey*, European Court of Human Rights, Appl. Nos. 23184/94 and 23185/94, Judgment of 24 April 1998, paras. 11–16, 75 and 79.

[53] *Ahmet Özkan and others* v. *Turkey*, European Court of Human Rights, Appl. No. 21689/93, Judgment of 6 April 2004, para. 85.

[54] Ibid. para. 306.

with rocket-propelled grenades and even though the Court had already hinted at the existence of an armed conflict, no mention was made of humanitarian law in the case.

21.3 Internal violence: Chechnya

The situation in Chechnya since 1994 brought another set of cases before the Court.[55] Chechnya had sought independence from Russia which in turn had led to conflicts colloquially referred to as the two Chechen "wars" from 1994 to 1996 and from 1999 onwards. Russia had never qualified the situation as an internal armed conflict but understood the situation as a counter-terrorism operation.[56] Russia had also not declared a state of emergency or derogated from the ECHR.[57] The resulting cases before the European Court of Human Rights were welcomed by human rights NGOs as breaking the silence on human rights violations in Chechnya and putting an end to the impunity of Russian law enforcement agencies and security services, but they would also have given the Court the chance to revisit its approach to international humanitarian law and the way in which it invokes the Convention in an armed conflict. The Court, however, chose not to opt for a new approach and rather created more ambiguous case law.

In the first case, *Isayeva, Yusupova and Bazayeva* v. *Russia*, decided in 2005, the applicants claimed to be victims of indiscriminate bombing.[58] On 29 October 1999, Russian military planes had attacked a civilian convoy near Chechnya's capital Grozny. The convoy had formed after the inhabitants of the town had been informed through the media that a humanitarian corridor would be opened to allow civilians to leave for neighbouring Ingushetia. Soon several hundred vehicles queued up for more than 12 kilometres. The convoy, which included Red Cross vehicles, was attacked by two Russian military planes which repeatedly fired missiles and rockets, resulting in a great number of casualties. Russia offered different explanations for the attack, some in contrast to eye-witness accounts (such as claims that the planes had been attacked from trucks with automatic weapons), some putting the blame on the circumstances (such as lack of information and allegations that the Red Cross vehicles were not clearly visible), and some hard to comprehend (that in the time it took the missiles to reach the target after they had been fired the queue of vehicles had materialized from out of nowhere, making it impossible for the pilots to cancel the attack).[59]

The applicants alleged, *inter alia*, that the planning and control of the operation had violated the principle of ECHR, Article 2 and that the choice of means used by the Russian military was disproportionate to the military aim. They pointed to the Court's judgment in *Güleç* v. *Turkey* where the Court had found the use of combat weapons against demonstrators to constitute a violation of the Convention.[60] They also specifically claimed

[55] See on the Court's role with regard to Chechnya in general Philip Leach, "The Chechen Conflict: Analysing the Oversight of the European Court of Human Rights" (2008) 6 *European Human Rights Law Review* 732.

[56] On the respective and partly inconsistent views of the Russian Federation on the situation see Federico Sperotto, "Law in Times of War: The Case of Chechnya" (2008) 8 *Global Jurist* 2, 3–4.

[57] See Hans-Joachim Heintze, "The European Court of Human Rights and the Implementation of Human Rights Standards during Armed Conflict" (2002) 45 *German Yearbook of International Law* 63.

[58] *Isayeva, Yusupova and Bazayeva* v. *Russia*, European Court of Human Rights, Appl. Nos. 57947/00, 57948/00 and 57949/00, Judgment of 24 February 2005, para. 3.

[59] Ibid. paras. 10–34. [60] Ibid. para. 166.

a violation of Common Article 3 of the Geneva Conventions.[61] The Russian government responded that the use of force had been justified and necessary under ECHR, Article 2(2)(a) in response to unlawful violence against its state agents.[62]

The Court again drew on its decision in *McCann* and argued that under ECHR, Article 2 the use of force must be no more than absolutely necessary for the achievement of one or more of the purposes set out in this provision and must be strictly proportionate to the achievement of the permitted aims, and that any operation must be planned and controlled by the authorities so as to minimize, to the greatest extent possible, recourse to lethal force.[63] At the same time, the Court accepted that Russia had to take exceptional measures to regain control over parts of its territory and to "suppress the illegal armed insurgency."[64] It did not define this term any further but saw the use of military planes equipped with heavy combat weapons as acceptable and found the use of lethal force against attacks by illegal armed groups as conforming to the ECHR.[65] The Court's reference to "insurgency" may be seen as an implicit judgement on the nature of the events as an internal armed conflict but the Court did not specify this any further.[66] It ignored the reference made to Common Article 3 of the Geneva Conventions by the applicants (who had cited a report by Human Rights Watch in support)[67] and found Russia to be in violation of ECHR, Article 2 because the government had insufficiently planned and executed the operation and not taken adequate care for the lives of the civilian population:

> To sum up, even assuming that the military were pursuing a legitimate aim in launching 12 S-24 non-guided air-to-ground missiles on 29 October 1999, the Court does not accept that the operation ... was planned and executed with the requisite care for the lives of the civilian population.[68]

In the second case, *Isayeva* v. *Russia*, the applicant also alleged indiscriminate bombing by the Russian military.[69] The Russian military had tried to lure Chechen fighters out of Grozny and, as a result, they ended up hiding in the village of Katyr-Yurt which had previously been declared a safe zone. The Chechen fighters seemingly used the population of the village as human shields and the Russian military responded with an aerial bombardment of the village which included the use of free-falling high explosive weapons with an impact radius of 1,000 metres in a densely populated area.[70] The applicant's son and others

[61] Ibid. para. 157. The use of this argument was obviously disputed among the legal representatives of the claimants, in particular with regard to the jurisprudence of the International Criminal Tribunal for the Former Yugoslavia (ICTY) as supporting the applicants' claim, see Bill Bowring, "Fragmentation, *Lex Specialis* and the Tensions in the Jurisprudence of the European Court of Human Rights" (2010) 14(3) *Journal of Conflict and Security Law* 488.

[62] *Isayeva, Yusupova and Bazayeva* v. *Russia* (n. 58) para. 181. ECHR, Art. 2(2)(a) stipulates that "[d]eprivation of life shall not be regarded as inflicted in contravention of this article when it results from the use of force which is no more than absolutely necessary in defence of any person from unlawful violence."

[63] See *Isayeva, Yusupova and Bazayeva* v. *Russia* (n. 58) paras. 169 and 171. [64] Ibid. para. 178.

[65] Ibid. para. 178

[66] Noelle Quénivet, "*Isayeva* v. *Russian Federation* and *Isayeva, Yusupova and Bazayeva* v. *Russian Federation*: Targeting Rules according to Article 2 of the European Convention on Human Rights" (2005) 3 *Journal of International Law of Peace and Armed Conflict* 222.

[67] See *Isayeva, Yusupova and Bazayeva* v. *Russia* (n. 58) para. 102. [68] Ibid. 199.

[69] See *Isayeva* v. *Russia*, European Court of Human Rights, Appl. No. 57950/00, Judgment (Merits and Just Satisfaction) of 24 February 2005, para. 3.

[70] Ibid. paras. 10–28.

were killed, which the applicant claimed to be a violation of ECHR, Article 2. Common Article 3 of the Geneva Conventions was invoked by the applicants only incidentally, together with Additional Protocol II, Article 13(2), by citing a report of Human Rights Watch.[71] Again, the Russian government claimed that the use of force was necessary and proportionate "to suppress the active resistance of the illegal armed groups, whose actions were a real threat to the life and health of the servicemen and civilians, as well as to the general interests of society and the state."[72]

In its decision, the Court took recourse to the cases of *McCann*[73] and *Ergi*[74] and once more accepted that exceptional measures had to be taken by Russia and that the presence and resistance of a large group of Chechen fighters in the village justified the use of lethal force.[75] It went on to examine if the weapons employed were proportionate to the aim pursued.[76] Since the military had known in advance and perhaps even planned that Chechen fighters would end up in Katyr-Yurt, there should have been, in the Court's view, sufficient time to give at least some advance warning to the population.[77] The Court concluded that the military had not paid sufficient attention to the dangers arising out of the use of heavy combat weapons in densely populated areas and that there had not been a "comprehensive evaluation of the limits of and constraints on the use of indiscriminate weapons within a populated area."[78] It found that the "massive use of indiscriminate weapons was incompatible with the standard of care prerequisite to an operation of this kind involving the use of lethal force by State agents"[79] and that, since the operation was not "planned and executed with the requisite care for the lives of the civilian population,"[80] ECHR, Article 2 had been violated.[81]

Since no martial law had been enacted, no state of emergency declared and no derogation been made, the Court analyzed these cases against what it called "a normal legal background."[82] It effectively saw them as law enforcement measures and not as a military operation in a non-international armed conflict.[83] It seems that Russia's non-derogation from the ECHR sufficed for the Court to conclude that no such conflict existed. This seemingly allowed the Court to avoid any reference to international humanitarian law and keep the case strictly within the boundaries of the European Convention.[84] While the majority of commentators see no particular problem in this approach, it has rightly been argued that the Court's assessment that the operation by the Russian military was a law

[71] Ibid. para. 114. Additional Protocol, Art. 13(2) protects the civilian population and reads "The civilian population as such, as well as individual civilians, shall not be the object of attack. Acts or threats of violence the primary purpose of which is to spread terror among the civilian population are prohibited."

[72] *Isayeva* v. *Russia* (n. 69) para. 170.

[73] Ibid. para. 175, where the Court analyzed whether the operation was planned and controlled by the authorities so as to minimize, to the greatest extent possible, recourse to lethal force.

[74] Ibid. para. 176, where the Court pointed out that security forces have to take all feasible precautions in the choice of means and methods of a security operation mounted against an opposing group with a view to avoiding and, in any event, minimizing, incidental loss of civilian life.

[75] Ibid. para. 180. [76] Ibid. para. 180. [77] Ibid. para. 187. [78] Ibid. para. 189. [79] Ibid. para. 191.

[80] Ibid. para. 200. [81] Ibid. para. 201. [82] Ibid. para. 191.

[83] See *Isayeva, Yusupova and Bazayeva* v. *Russia* (n. 58) para. 191; and David Kaye, "International Decision (Comment on *Khasyivev and Akayeva* v. *Russia*; *Isayeva, Yusupova and Bazayeva* v. *Russia*; *Isayeva* v. *Russia*)" (2005) 99(4) *American Journal of International Law* 878.

[84] Commentators have called this a "business as usual approach," see Sperotto, "Law in Times of War" (n. 56) 12.

enforcement operation and not an operation within an internal armed conflict was factually and legally wrong.[85]

At the very least, the Court's law enforcement approach was contradictory, given that it had already assessed the circumstances as "illegal armed insurgency,"[86] which would allow Russia to respond with massive air strikes. To complicate matters, the Court also referred to principles of humanitarian law such as lawful targeting, the prohibition of indiscriminate weapons, and the distinction between civilians and "fighters."[87] The Court's repeated use of this terminology has rightly led commentators to wonder how it can do so without at least *sub silentio* referring to the respective categorization undertaken by international humanitarian law.[88] The Court also assessed the proportionality of the use of force against the standards in the Russian Army Field Manual and claimed that this document was insufficient for such operations without further domestic legislation to authorize the use of force.[89] And it seemed to rely on the precautionary principles of international humanitarian law when it said that "it was at least open to [the authorities] to warn the residents in advance."[90]

Similarly, the Court criticized the government for not "assessing and preventing possible harm to the civilians who might have been present on the road or elsewhere in the vicinity of what the military could have perceived as legitimate targets,"[91] a remark which relies heavily on the language of humanitarian law without saying so.[92] The Court also referred to "incidental loss of civilian life"[93] which must be avoided and minimized in a military operation. Likewise, the Court's judgment that "the military reasonably considered that there was an attack or a risk of attack from illegal insurgents, and that the air strike was a legitimate response to that attack"[94] seems to strike a balance between military requirements and humanitarian concerns just as is required under international humanitarian law. Nowhere, however, is a reasoning to be found why the Court chose to refrain from any reference to international humanitarian law despite repeatedly invoking its language.[95] Even so, it seems that the Court was clearly aware of international humanitarian law and borrowed from its language so as to do justice to the situation without explicitly referring to international humanitarian law norms.[96]

[85] See Guglielmo Verdirame, "Human Rights in Wartime: A Framework for Analysis" (2008) 6 *European Human Rights Law Review* 701.

[86] *Isayeva, Yusupova and Bazayeva* v. *Russia* (n. 58) para. 178.

[87] See Cordula Droege, "The Interplay between International Humanitarian Law and International Human Rights Law in Situations of Armed Conflict" (2007) 40(2) *Israel Law Review* 315, 347.

[88] See *Isayeva, Yusupova and Bazayeva* v. *Russia* (n. 5) paras. 175, 177, 185 and 199; and *Isayeva* v. *Russia* (n. 69) paras. 176, 182, 183, 190 and 198.

[89] *Isayeva* v. *Russia* (n. 69) para. 199.

[90] Ibid. para. 187. Additional Protocol I, Art. 57(2)(c) reads: "With respect to attacks, the following precautions shall be taken: . . . effective advance warning shall be given of attacks which may affect the civilian population, unless circumstances do not permit"; see also Doswald-Beck, "The Right to Life in Armed Conflict" (n. 49) 884.

[91] *Isayeva, Yusupova and Bazayeva* v. *Russia* (n. 58) para. 175.

[92] Quénivet, "*Isayeva* v. *Russian Federation*" (n. 66) 225.

[93] *Isayeva* v. *Russia* (n. 69) para. 176 with reference to *Ergi* v. *Turkey* (n. 33) para. 79.

[94] *Isayeva, Yusupova and Bazayeva* v. *Russia* (n. 58) para. 181.

[95] See Kaye, "International Decision" (n. 83) 879.

[96] See Quénivet, "*Isayeva* v. *Russian Federation*" (n. 66) 224.

The Court also found Russia to be in violation of the ECHR in *Khashiyev and Akayeva* v. *Russia* in 2005.[97] In this case, the applicants had fled Grozny in 2000 when Russian forces approached and, upon return, found their relatives dead and mutilated. They claimed a violation of ECHR, Articles 2 and 3 (right to life and prohibition of torture and inhuman or degrading treatment or punishment).[98] Given that the Russian armed forces had had exclusive control over the events at the time in question, the Court concluded that the victims' deaths were attributable to Russia and that ECHR, Article 2 had been violated. It also found that the authorities had failed to carry out an effective criminal investigation into the circumstances surrounding the deaths as required by Article 2. While the Court was unable to clearly establish cases of torture and ill-treatment, it also considered Article 3 violated by the inadequate and ineffective domestic investigation.[99] No reference to international humanitarian law was made. The same can be said for the similar case of *Estamirov and others* v. *Russia*.[100]

In *Umayeva* v. *Russia*,[101] another case on injured civilians who had tried leaving Grozny through a humanitarian corridor, the Court repeated its findings made in the earlier cases. In *Trapeznikova* v. *Russia*, the Court had to decide, *inter alia*, on the destruction of the applicant's property during a military operation.[102] The applicant's apartment had been hit by what the applicant claimed was a Russian missile.[103] The applicant based her claims on "generally known facts concerning the use of heavy force and indiscriminate shelling by the federal armed forces in Chechnya."[104] The Court refrained from any assessment of the "indiscriminate" nature of the bombings and ignored the applicant's reference to international humanitarian law. For the events itself it used the word "violent confrontations"[105] and found Russia not to have violated the ECHR.[106]

In a series of cases the Court dealt with the disappearance of persons in Chechnya and all of them were decided without reference to humanitarian law. In *Imakayeva* v. *Russia*, for example, the Court considered the lack of an effective, prompt and thorough investigation into the disappearance of the applicant's son and husband as a violation of ECHR, Article 2.[107] In *Bitiyeva and X* v. *Russia*, the Court had to deal with the ill-treatment and illegal detention of the applicants and the subsequent killing of one of them. The victims were detained after a passport control in their house and repeatedly ill-treated and tortured

[97] *Khashiyev and Akayeva* v. *Russia*, European Court of Human Rights, Appl. Nos. 57942/00 and 57945/00, Judgment of 24 February 2005.

[98] Ibid. paras. 3 and 11–27. [99] Ibid. paras. 166 and 174–80.

[100] *Estamirov and others* v. *Russia*, European Court of Human Rights, Appl. No. 60272/00, Judgment of 12 October 2006.

[101] *Umayeva* v. *Russia*, European Court of Human Rights, Appl. No. 1200/03, Judgment of 4 December 2008.

[102] *Trapeznikova* v. *Russia*, European Court of Human Rights, Appl. No. 21539/02, Judgment of 11 December 2008.

[103] Ibid. para. 8. [104] Ibid. para. 98. [105] Ibid. para. 109. [106] Ibid. para. 110.

[107] See *Imakayeva* v. *Russia*, European Court of Human Rights, Appl. No. 7615/02, Judgment of 9 November 2006, para. 160. Other cases with similar conclusions are *Bazorkina* v. *Russia*, European Court of Human Rights, Appl. No. 69481/01, Judgment of 27 July 2006; *Baysayeva* v. *Russia*, European Court of Human Rights, Appl. No. 74237/01, Judgment of 5 April 2007; *Akhmadova and Sadulayeva* v. *Russia*, European Court of Human Rights, Appl. No. 40464/02, Judgment of 10 May 2007; *Alikhadzhiyeva* v. *Russia*, European Court of Human Rights, Appl. No. 68007/01, Judgment of 5 July 2007.

by Russian soldiers. The Court found a violation of ECHR, Article 3 on the grounds of inhuman and degrading treatment.[108]

But the Court seemingly changed its approach in *Akhmadov and others* v. *Russia*, where it was asked to adjudicate, *inter alia*, on the killing of the applicants' relatives by a Russian helicopter while harvesting a field and transporting the crop, despite having received prior authorization to do so.[109] The applicants considered the lethal use of force as disproportionate and complained that the authorities had never given "any explanations as to how civilians were expected to behave within the area of the counter-terrorist operation."[110] The Court assessed the general situation in Chechnya and, with reference to *Isayeva, Yusupova and Bazayeva* v. *Russia*, recognized "the difficult situation in the Chechen Republic at the material time, which called for exceptional measures on the part of the State to suppress the illegal armed insurgency."[111] But despite both the applicants' and the Russian government's reference to the events as part of a "counter-terrorist operation,"[112] the Court, quite remarkably, explicitly characterized the events as an armed conflict: "an armed conflict such as that in Chechnya," the Court said, "may entail developments to which State agents are called upon to react without prior preparation."[113] The Court found a violation of ECHR, Article 2 based on the lack of information provided by the Russian state.[114] The Court repeated this in the similar case of *Khatsiyeva and others* v. *Russia* concerning a helicopter attack on civilians in neighbouring Ingushetia.[115]

In *Dzhabrailova* v. *Russia*,[116] the Court found Russia responsible, under ECHR, Article 2, for the disappearance of the applicant's relative who had been detained by the Russian military.[117] In yet another turn of arguments it was now the Russian government which used the term "armed conflict" when it stated that "groups of Ukrainian or ethnic Russian mercenaries had participated in the armed conflict together with Chechen rebel fighters and committed crimes in the territory of the Chechen Republic."[118] But now the Court departed from its earlier qualification of the situation and chose to ignore Russia's comment on the existence of an armed conflict. The Chechen cases are thus not characterized by a consistent approach to these questions.

21.4 Exceptional references to humanitarian law

The European Court did apply international humanitarian law more straightforwardly only in very few cases. In *Varnava and others* v. *Turkey*, it had to decide on applications against Turkey with regard to eighteen persons who had disappeared in Northern Cyprus in

[108] See *Bitiyeva and X* v. *Russia*, European Court of Human Rights, Appl. Nos. 57953/00 and 37392/03, Judgment of 21 June 2007, para. 107.

[109] See *Akhmadov and others* v. *Russia*, European Court of Human Rights, Appl. No. 21586/02, Judgment of 14 November 2008, paras. 9–16.

[110] Ibid. para. 86. [111] Ibid. para. 97. [112] Ibid. paras. 86–88 and 91. [113] Ibid. para. 97.

[114] Ibid. para. 102.

[115] See *Khatsiyeva and others* v. *Russia*, European Court of Human Rights, Appl. No. 5108/02, Judgment of 17 January 2008, paras. 134–47, with specific reference to an "armed conflict" in para. 139.

[116] *Dzhabrailova* v. *Russia*, European Court of Human Rights, Appl. No. 1586/05, Judgment of 9 April 2009.

[117] Ibid. paras. 57–66. [118] Ibid. para. 56.

1974.[119] The Court found Turkey in violation of ECHR, Article 2 on account of the authorities' failure to effectively investigate the disappearances. But unlike other cases on Northern Cyprus it stated that:

> Article 2 must be interpreted in so far as possible in light of the general principles of international law, including the rules of international humanitarian law which play an indispensable and universally-accepted role in mitigating the savagery and inhumanity of armed conflict. The Court therefore concurs with the reasoning of the Chamber in holding that in a zone of international conflict Contracting States are under obligation to protect the lives of those not, or no longer, engaged in hostilities. This would also extend to the provision of medical assistance to the wounded; where combatants have died, or succumbed to wounds, the need for accountability would necessitate proper disposal of remains and require the authorities to collect and provide information about the identity and fate of those concerned, or permit bodies such as the ICRC to do so.[120]

In *Kononov* v. *Latvia* in 2008, the Court had to decide on an alleged violation of the principle of legality with regard to the applicants' conviction of war crimes for acts committed in occupied Latvia in 1944.[121] The dispute around the lawfulness of the applicant's conviction for war crimes by Latvian courts in 2004 centred on the question whether the persons killed by the applicant in 1944 were protected civilians (as the Latvian courts had said) or combatants under international humanitarian law (as the applicant had claimed). The European Court concluded that some of the persons killed indeed had combatant status while others had not, and found Latvia to have violated ECHR, Article 7.[122] In its reasoning, the Court referred to the 1907 Hague Convention, customary humanitarian law and Additional Protocol I (which it found to have been applied retroactively and incorrectly).[123] While the Court's interpretation of the norms of humanitarian law has been criticized,[124] the case seems to demonstrate the Court's preparedness to apply specific provisions of international humanitarian norms in deciding on a violation of the ECHR.

In *Engel and others* v. *The Netherlands*, the Court also applied international humanitarian law.[125] The case was about the unequal treatment of different military ranks in the disciplinary punishments of five Dutch conscript soldiers unrelated to any armed conflict. The nature of their penalties depended on the different ranks of the offenders. The applicants claimed, *inter alia*, a deprivation of liberty, and the Court referred explicitly to the Geneva Conventions even though the applicants themselves had not claimed a violation of international humanitarian law.[126] The Court took the view that the different ranks and

[119] *Varnava and others* v. *Turkey*, European Court of Human Rights, Appl. Nos. 16064/90, 16065/90, 16066/90, 160668/90, 160669/90, 16070/90, 16071/90, 16072/90 and 16073/90, Judgment of 18 September 2009.

[120] Ibid. para. 185; the footnote (omitted) quotes the Geneva Conventions and Additional Protocols.

[121] *Kononov* v. *Latvia*, European Court of Human Rights, Appl. No. 35376/04, Judgment of 24 July 2008.

[122] Ibid paras. 188–246.

[123] Ibid. para. 174. See in greater detail Giulia Pinzauti, "The European Court of Human Rights' Incidental Application of International Criminal and Humanitarian Law: A Critical Discussion of *Kononov* v. *Latvia*" (2008) 6(5) *Journal of International Criminal Justice* 1052.

[124] See Pinzauti, "The European Court of Human Rights' Incidental Application" (n. 123) 1058–59.

[125] *Engel and others* v. *The Netherlands*, European Court of Human Rights, Appl. Nos. 5100/71, 5101/71, 5102/71, 5354/72, and 5370/72, Judgment of 23 November 1976.

[126] Ibid. paras. 33–51.

their correspondingly different responsibilities would justify different treatment in disciplinary punishments and stated that such inequalities "are tolerated by international humanitarian law."[127] The decision explicitly mentions Article 88 of Geneva Convention III.[128] This remains a singular incident but it demonstrates that, while in cases which involve large-scale military occurrences, such as in Northern Cyprus, Eastern Turkey or Chechnya, the Court seems to be held back by considerations of the politically sensitive environment and does not wish to be drawn into any debate on the nature of the occurrences, it readily drops this sensitivity in politically less significant cases.[129]

21.5 A European human rights law of armed conflict?

Altogether, the European Court's approach to international humanitarian law is inconsistent. While the Court shares the view of all other human rights bodies that international human rights law continues to apply in armed conflict, it is unwilling to take any traceable position on whether or not the Court can and should use international humanitarian law to interpret the Convention or directly find violations of international humanitarian law.[130] Only in cases which involved matters of humanitarian law in a historic perspective (such as *Kononov* on alleged violations in the Second World War) and outside armed conflict (such as *Engel*) was the European Commission seemingly at ease with direct reference to specific humanitarian norms.

In all other cases, the European Court limited itself to finding violations of the ECHR and ignored claims by the applicants on violations of international humanitarian law.[131] It seems thus too optimistic to say that the Court is inspired by international humanitarian law,[132] so little does the Court reveal of its motivation. The Court also does not use international humanitarian law as guidance, as some claim,[133] and it does not see international humanitarian law and international human rights law as interchangeable.[134] Instead, it constructs the situation before it as a law enforcement operation regardless of the context and the views of the parties even when this means feigning a "normal legal background" in the midst of the heaviest fighting – with the exceptional slip of the tongue when the

[127] Ibid. para. 72. [128] Ibid. para. 72. [129] Heintze, "On the Relationship" (n. 12) 812.

[130] Noam Lubell, "Challenges in Applying Human Rights Law to Armed Conflict" (2005) 87(860) *International Review of the Red Cross* 746.

[131] See Heintze, "The European Court of Human Rights" (n. 57) 75. This is even reflected in scholarly literature on the subject, e.g., when a thorough legal assessment of the Court's jurisprudence in the Chechen cases meticulously traces the Court's application of the ECHR but, despite explicitly acknowledging that the situation in the two Chechen "wars" of 1994–1996 and 1999 amounted to an internal armed conflict governed by international humanitarian law, omits any reference to international humanitarian law (other than by way of comparison with the ACHR), see Kiril Koroteev, "Legal Remedies for Human Rights Violations in the Armed Conflict in Chechnya: The Approach of the European Court of Human Rights in Context" (2010) 2(1) *Journal of International Humanitarian Legal Studies* 275.

[132] Quénivet, "*Isayeva* v. *Russian Federation*" (n. 66) 220–26.

[133] Liesbeth Zegveld, "Remedies for Victims of Violations of International Humanitarian Law" (2003) 85(851) *International Review of the Red Cross* 516, 519.

[134] Alexander Orakhelashvili, "The Interaction between Human Rights and Humanitarian Law: Fragmentation, Conflict, Parallelism, or Convergence?" (2008) 19(1) *European Journal of International Law* 169.

existence of an "armed conflict" is established *en passant*.[135] Despite its (inconsistent reference) to the situation in Chechnya as an armed conflict, an insurgency and an anti-terrorist operation, the Court ultimately saw only law enforcement operations, up to and including battles with thousands of insurgents, aerial bombardments and artillery attacks with some of the heaviest weaponry in the Russian arsenal.

At the same time, it repeatedly used the language, conceptual framework and terminology of international humanitarian law when addressing situations of armed conflict without resorting to the rules of international humanitarian law or mentioning the Geneva Conventions and Additional Protocols.[136] It sometimes relied on principles of, or at least close to, humanitarian law but only directly applied the European Convention even though *sub silentio* humanitarian law seems to be present.[137] The reasons for the Court's reluctance to refer to humanitarian law are not obvious. It has been speculated that the Court exercises judicial self-restraint[138] or that it sees human rights law as a self-contained regime into which international humanitarian law should not intrude.[139] But the Court's complete ignorance of humanitarian law, in stark contrast to the Inter-American Commission and Court of Human Rights, is obvious. Commentators on earlier cases of the Court (prior to the first Chechen case) could not imagine that the Court would indeed simply ignore international humanitarian law in a situation such as Chechnya.[140]

Most observers seem to agree that the Court has not clarified its position on the interplay of international human rights and humanitarian law.[141] Instead, it seems to advocate a single body of law which it derives from the provisions of the ECHR and which is capable of covering every violent encounter imaginable in internal conflicts such as in Chechnya. It has been argued that this amounts to the creation of a "human rights law of internal armed conflict"[142] which replaces the need to apply fundamental norms and principles of international humanitarian law, such as the distinction between civilians and combatants, the rules on targeting and the precautionary principles, in favour of the Court's interpretation of the lawful use of lethal force under ECHR, Article 2.

In the absence of clear statements by the Court, it remains uncertain if this is indeed how the Court sees it but such an approach is clearly in contrast to that taken by the Inter-American Commission in Human Rights. The Inter-American Commission seems

135 Abresch, "A Human Rights Law of Internal Armed Conflict" (n. 34) 753. 136 Ibid. 746.

137 See Droege, "The Interplay" (n. 87) 345–46 and Abresch, "A Human Rights Law of Internal Armed Conflict" (n. 34) 746. At the very least, the Court has never contradicted international humanitarian law, see Gioia, "The Role of the European Court of Human Rights" (n. 1) p. 248.

138 See Michael Bothe, "Die Anwendung der Europäischen Menschenrechtskonvention in bewaffneten Konflikten – eine Überforderung?" (2005) 65 *Zeitschrift für ausländisches öffentliches Recht und Völkerrecht* 633.

139 See Sperotto, "Law in Times of War" (n. 56) 11.

140 See Heintze, "The European Court of Human Rights" (n. 57) 70, who argues that in future cases the Court will not be in a position to avoid taking international humanitarian law into consideration.

141 Few seem to be willing to credit the Court with an overall commendable and only occasionally unsatisfactory approach with regard to humanitarian law, such as, for example, Lindsay Moir, "The European Court of Human Rights and International Humanitarian Law" in Robert Kolb and Gloria Gaggioli (eds.), *Research Handbook on Human Rights and Humanitarian Law* (Cheltenham: Edward Elgar, 2013), 495–96.

142 See Abresch, "A Human Rights Law of Internal Armed Conflict" (n. 34) 743 and 748, and similarly Krieger, "A Conflict of Norms" (n. 8) 13, who argues that the Court is able to define human rights applicable in situations of armed conflict.

to see international human rights law as insufficient to regulate events in internal armed conflicts so that it turns to international humanitarian law and tries to apply it directly, while the European Court seems to view international humanitarian law as inappropriate and sticks to international human rights law. Compared to the ICRC's approach, which seeks to apply international humanitarian norms developed for international armed conflicts to internal armed conflicts, as discussed earlier, the European Court of Human Rights' approach seems to be a competing project.[143] It is not clear if the Court wishes to argue that there is no more space for international humanitarian law in internal armed conflict and that human rights law should apply exclusively. The case law of the Court does not really provide an answer in this regard.[144]

Mostly, this ignorance which the Court displays towards humanitarian law is viewed critically. The Court's silence on international humanitarian law, its reference to international humanitarian law principles only *sub silentio*, and the way in which the Court seems to gloss over objective criteria as well as disregard the views of the parties to a conflict are seen as a mistake.[145] It seems indeed that open reference to humanitarian law would at least allow greater coherence in the Court's jurisprudence. But the Court's approach could also represent a new approach to reconsidering the law applicable in internal armed conflicts. The way the Court seems to replace the precautionary principles of international humanitarian law by international human rights law standards may well have "the potential to drive military reform and improvement at the institutional level."[146] If this is the Court's intention, then all acts in internal armed conflicts are ultimately law enforcement measures and should not be modelled along the image of international armed conflicts. The only goal of the state in such situations of internal violence may then be the restoration of law and order as a means to defend society and its laws.[147] The Court's insistence on human rights can indeed be seen as "part of a law enforcement package rather than a power given to the State to use armed force to kill those who would use violence or otherwise break the laws."[148]

It has rightly been remarked that such views of the European Court of Human Rights are "likely to be received by specialists in humanitarian law with some disquiet."[149] If the Court's approach is alternatively seen only as a complementary application of human rights and (*sub silentio*) humanitarian law it could be argued that the Court's insistence on the adequate planning of military operations in an internal armed conflict (whether or not the state has agreed to its existence) fills a gap, given that the precautionary principles of Additional Protocol I were drafted for international armed conflicts.[150] But as it stands, the Court's case law is insufficient to allow conclusions along any of these lines.[151]

[143] See Abresch, "A Human Rights Law of Internal Armed Conflict" (n. 34) 749. [144] Ibid. 756–60.
[145] See Gioia, "The Role of the European Court of Human Rights" (n. 1) pp. 217–18.
[146] Abresch, "A Human Rights Law of Internal Armed Conflict" (n. 34) 764. [147] Ibid. 764–65.
[148] Rowe, "Non-international Armed Conflict and the European Court of Human Rights" (n. 14) 225.
[149] Abresch, "A Human Rights Law of Internal Armed Conflict" (n. 34) 767.
[150] See Gioia, "The Role of the European Court of Human Rights" (n. 1) p. 233.
[151] Droege, "The Interplay" (n. 87) 347.

22

The African Commission on Human and Peoples' Rights

The African Commission on Human and Peoples' Rights has even less to contribute to the role of human rights in armed conflicts and the interplay of humanitarian law and human rights law. Even though the number of potential situations of armed conflicts which one would expect to end up before the African Commission is higher than in the European and Inter-American system, given the persistence of internal and cross-border violence in Africa, the Commission's case law on this matter is scarce. As far as the role of human rights in armed conflict is concerned, it has consistently seen the African Charter on Human and Peoples' Rights (ACHPR) as applying in situations of armed conflict and has argued for a convergence of human rights and humanitarian law, in line with all other human rights bodies.[1] In 1995, the Commission applied the African Charter to human rights violations in the internal armed conflict in Chad but merely argued that "even a civil war in Chad cannot be used as an excuse by the State violating or permitting violations of rights in the African Charter."[2] It used similar language with regard to Sudan in 1999.[3] Otherwise, there is no evidence that the Commission invoked humanitarian law in dealing with individual communications under the Charter, even in situations where an armed conflict occurred.[4]

The Commission also repeatedly called upon parties to an armed conflict, in general terms, to respect human rights and humanitarian law, for example, with regard to the

[1] This is also due to the inclusion of the right to peace in the African Charter. ACHPR, Art. 23 stipulates that "[a[ll peoples have the right to national and international peace and security." This has arguably led the Commission to repeatedly stress the link between human rights and peace and see human rights violations as root causes of war; see Rachel Murray, *The African Commission on Human and Peoples' Rights and International Law* (Oxford: Hart, 2000), p. 133. See also Clive Baldwin and Cynthia Morel, "Group Rights" in Malcolm Evans and Rachel Murray (eds.), *The African Charter of Human and Peoples' Rights: The System in Practice, 1986–2006* (2nd edn., Cambridge: Cambridge University Press, 2008), pp. 279–83.

[2] *Commission nationale des droits de l'homme et des libertés* v. *Chad*, African Commission on Human and Peoples' Rights, Case No. 74/92, Decision of 11 October 1995, Ninth Activity Report 1995–1996, para. 21.

[3] *Amnesty International, Comité Loosli Bachelard, Lawyers' Committee for Human Rights and Association of Members of the Episcopal Conference of East Africa* v. *Sudan African Commission on Human and Peoples' Rights*, Case No. 48/90-50/91-52/91-89/93, Decision of 15 November 1999, Thirteenth Activity Report 1999–2000, para. 50: "[e]ven if Sudan is going through a civil war, civilians in areas of strife are especially vulnerable and the State must take all possible measures to ensure that they are treated in accordance with international humanitarian law."

[4] See Bronwen Manby, "Civil and Political Rights in the African Charter on Human and Peoples' Rights: Articles 1-7" in Malcolm Evans and Rachel Murray (eds.), *The African Charter of Human and Peoples' Rights: The System in Practice, 1986–2006* (2nd edn., Cambridge: Cambridge University Press, 2008), pp. 171–212.

situation in Mali in 2013 where it said that "human rights must be respected at all times" and called upon all parties to the conflict "to fully respect international humanitarian law and protect civilian populations and their property."[5] It had already done so earlier with regard to Rwanda and Sudan.[6] In its fact-finding missions and commissions of inquiry, the Commission seems to have largely avoided the issue of states' obligations under humanitarian law.[7] At its Fourteenth Ordinary Session in 1993, the African Commission adopted a resolution on the promotion and respect of international humanitarian law and human and peoples' rights in which it noted that the two aim at protecting human beings and their fundamental rights, and invited all states parties to the African Charter to ensure the promotion of the provisions of international humanitarian law and human and peoples' rights and provide instruction and education in both fields.[8]

Democratic Republic of Congo v. *Republics of Burundi, Rwanda and Uganda*, decided in 2003, is seemingly the only time the Commission referred to humanitarian law more specifically.[9] It had to consider a complaint brought before it by the Democratic Republic of Congo on systematic rape and sexual violence perpetrated by Rwandan and Ugandan soldiers. The Democratic Republic of the Congo specifically alleged violations of the Geneva Conventions and Additional Protocol I in addition to violations of the ACHPR.[10] In response to the arguments by the respondent states (which had not denied the occurrence of mass rape and subsequent infection with HIV/Aids but argued that there was no group responsibility for such acts) the Commission noted that systematic rape is a violation of Additional Protocol I, Article 76.[11] It also stated that under Articles 60 and 61 of the African Charter it was entitled to take into account international humanitarian law, even though these Articles do not mention humanitarian instruments specifically.[12]

5 Statement by the African Commission on the situation in Mali, 18 January 2013, available at www.achpr.org/press/2013/01/d140 (last accessed 15 April 2014).

6 See African Commission on Human and Peoples' Rights, Resolution on Rwanda, Seventh Annual Activity Report 1993–1994: "The Commission . . . calls on all parties to respect the African Charter on Human and Peoples' Rights, the principles of international humanitarian law as well as the activities of the humanitarian organizations operating in the field"; see Murray, *The African Commission on Human and Peoples' Rights*, p. 139.

7 See Rachel Murray, "Evidence and Fact-Finding by the African Commission" in Malcolm Evans and Rachel Murray (eds.), *The African Charter of Human and Peoples' Rights: The System in Practice, 1986–2006* (2nd edn., Cambridge: Cambridge University Press, 2008), pp. 139–70.

8 See African Commission on Human and Peoples' Rights, Resolution on the promotion and respect of international humanitarian law and human and peoples' rights, Fourteenth Ordinary Session, 1–10 December 1993, available at www.achpr.org/sessions/14th/resolutions/7 (last accessed 15 April 2014). For more details on the Commission's views on the dissemination of humanitarian law see Murray, *The African Commission on Human and Peoples' Rights* (n. 1) p. 145.

9 *Democratic Republic of Congo* v. *Republics of Burundi, Rwanda and Uganda*, African Commission on Human and Peoples' Rights, Case No. 227/99, Decision of 29 May 2003, Twentieth Activity Report January–June 2006.

10 Ibid. para. 9.

11 Additional Protocol I, Art. 75 provides that "[w]omen shall be the object of special respect and shall be protected in particular against rape, forced prostitution and any other forms of indecent assault."

12 *Democratic Republic of Congo* v. *Republics of Burundi, Rwanda and Uganda* (n. 9) para. 70. ACHPR, Art. 60 allows the Commission to draw inspiration from the provisions of African instruments on Human and Peoples' Rights, the Charter of the United Nations, the Charter of the Organisation of African Unity, the Universal Declaration of Human Rights, other instruments adopted by the United Nations and by African countries in the field of Human and Peoples' Rights, as well as from instruments adopted by the

The Commission argued that "the Four Geneva Conventions and the two Additional Protocols covering armed conflicts constitute part of the general principles of law recognised by African States"[13] and that it can consider them in deciding the case. In addition to violations of the ACHPR, the Commission also found:

> the killings, massacres, rapes, mutilations and other grave human rights abuses committed while the Respondent States' armed forces were still in effective occupation of the eastern provinces of the Complainant State are reprehensible and also inconsistent with their obligations under Part III of the Geneva Convention Relative to the Protection of Civilian Persons in Time of War of 1949 and Protocol 1 of the Geneva Convention.[14]

The African Commission thus condemned the countries for violations of humanitarian law in strong terms.[15] However, its reference to humanitarian law as general principles of international law is not persuasive, and the Commission provides no further arguments to sustain it. General principles of international law are usually understood as a very limited set of principles derived from municipal law, separate from treaty law and customary law, which fill gaps where no norms exists at all.[16] Humanitarian law *in toto* is thus not a general principle of international law. Even if the reference to general principles was meant to suggest customary law, the argument would fail as the customary nature of humanitarian law would not include a customary authorization of human rights bodies to apply humanitarian law. It is also unclear whether the Commission's conclusion that the alleged acts are "inconsistent" with obligations under the Geneva Conventions and the Additional Protocol are meant to denounce a violation of these treaties. This leaves it open how the Commission views the interplay of human rights and humanitarian law in such situations, particularly whether it considers violations of these norms only when they overlap with violations of the ACHPR.

In examining state reports, the Commission has largely refrained from referring to humanitarian law, including when it examined the reports of states affected by internal violence and armed conflict. The state reports of the Democratic Republic of the Congo, for example, do not contain reference to humanitarian law other than mentioning the Geneva Conventions and Additional Protocols, and the

UN Specialised Agencies. ACHPR, Art. 61 provides that the Commission shall also take into consideration other general or special international conventions as subsidiary measures to determine the principles of law, African practices consistent with international norms on Human and Peoples' Rights, customs and general principles of law recognized by African states.

13 *Democratic Republic of Congo* v. *Republics of Burundi, Rwanda and Uganda* (n. 9) para. 70. The same argument is also made in para. 64; and the Commission also bolstered it with reference to ACHPR, Art. 23 which it found applicable for this purpose, although it did not indicate the rationale for invoking this provision which provides (under the heading "right to national and international security and peace") that all peoples shall have the right to national and international peace and security.

14 *Democratic Republic of Congo* v. *Republics of Burundi, Rwanda and Uganda* (n. 9) para. 79.

15 See in greater detail Djacoba Liva Tehindrazanarivelo, "The African Union and International Humanitarian Law" in Robert Kolb and Gloria Gaggioli (eds.), *Research Handbook on Human Rights and Humanitarian Law* (Cheltenham: Edward Elgar, 2013), pp. 510–11.

16 See, e.g., Malcolm Shaw, *International Law* (6th edn., Cambridge: Cambridge University Press, 2008), pp. 98–109.

Commission has not invoked humanitarian law in examining these reports, either.[17] A similar approach can be identified with regard to Sudan.[18] Apart from the deliberations on one single communication to the Commission there is thus no discernible position of the Commission towards the application of international humanitarian law.

[17] As the Democratic Republic of the Congo had failed to submit any report since its ratification of the ACHPR, it provided the Commission with a single report combining its overdue initial report and six period reports in 2003, and submitted the seventh report in 2002 and the eighth to tenth reports in 2010. The Concluding Observations to the first combined report, adopted in the Thirty-first Ordinary Session of the Commission (6–20 November 2003) mention violations of humanitarian law briefly as a general area of concern (see para. 17); for all documents see www.achpr.org/states/democratic-republic-of-congo/reports/1st-1997-2001-old (last accessed 15 April 2014).

[18] See the combined fourth and fifth reports submitted in 2012; no Concluding Observations are publicly available, see www.achpr.org/states/sudan/reports/4thand5th-2008-2012 (last accessed 15 April 2014).

23

Monitoring and litigating humanitarian rights: prospects

23.1 Lack of humanitarian law enforcement

The notorious weakness of international humanitarian law to enforce respect for its provisions and providing effective remedies for violations is well acknowledged.[1] Calls for an effective monitoring mechanism for violations of humanitarian obligations in armed conflicts have resounded for decades in humanitarian circles and academia.[2] The importance of ensuring respect for international norms is obvious:

> [w]hat is important in regard to human rights whether in peace or war is not so much what the law proclaims as a right as what it provides for the protection and enforcement of those rights when breached.[3]

At the same time, the application of human rights in armed conflict introduces not only the substantial norms of human rights law into these situations but also the human rights procedural "infrastructure" at the core of which are the bodies, institutions and procedures just described. They have proliferated in the field of human rights law but – as has been demonstrated – they have also been confronted with and have responded to situations of armed conflict. Should they stand in for the lack of humanitarian law enforcement, and if so, under which conditions, and which consequences would this entail?

The means and institutions which international humanitarian law has to offer to enforce the law are limited. Belligerent reprisals, the oldest method of ensuring respect for humanitarian law by reciprocal violations of the law in response to the opponent's earlier violations, are largely outlawed because of their counter-productive effect of creating a spiral

[1] See, e.g., Timothy McCormack, "The Importance of Effective Multilateral Enforcement of International Humanitarian Law" in Liesbeth Lijnzaad, Johanna van Sambeek and Bahia Tahzib-Lie (eds.), *Making the Voice of Humanity Heard, Essays on Humanitarian Assistance and International Humanitarian Law in Honour of HRH Princess Margriet of the Netherlands* (Leiden: Nijhoff, 2004), pp. 319–38; Michel Veuthey, "Implementing International Humanitarian Law: Old and New Ways" in Bertrand Ramcharan (ed.), *Human Rights Protection in the Field* (Leiden: Nijhoff, 2006), pp. 87–117; and Marco Sassòli, "The Implementation of International Humanitarian Law: Current and Inherent Challenges" (2007) 10 *Yearbook of International Humanitarian Law* 45.

[2] See, e.g., Dietrich Schindler, "International Humanitarian Law: Its Remarkable Development and Its Persistent Violation" (2003) 5(2) *Journal of the History of International Law* 187: "[a] continued and professional control by a special organ or institution could greatly enhance respect for humanitarian law."

[3] Leslie C. Green, "Human Rights Law and International Humanitarian Law: A Historical Overview" in Susan C. Breau and Agnieszka Jachec Neale (eds.), *Testing the Boundaries of International Humanitarian Law* (London: British Institute of International and Comparative Law, 2006), p. 83.

of violence.[4] The institution of the Protecting Power, introduced by the Geneva Conventions in 1949 to allow third states to uphold the interests of the belligerents, has never been effective because of its reliance on state consent which hardly ever materialized.[5] The dual mandate of Protecting Powers (a "political" function as a sort of arbiter between belligerents, the so-called "Vienna mandate" and a "humanitarian" function which allows providing relief, the so-called "Geneva" mandate) remain unused, and the latter has been taken over entirely by the International Committee of the Red Cross (ICRC) when it acts as Protecting Power. Calls to replace Protecting Powers by an independent agency have already been made (unsuccessfully) in the early 1960s, for example, by the International Commission of Jurists.[6] The International Humanitarian Fact-Finding Commission, set up under Additional Protocol I, Article 90 to inquire into allegations of serious violations of the Geneva Conventions and to "facilitate, through its good offices, the restoration of an attitude of respect for the Conventions and the Protocols,"[7] shares the same fate. So far, it has never been called upon and its attempts to offer good offices and engage in other forms of assistance have gone nowhere.[8]

Apart from national implementation measures, the humanitarian and protective work of the ICRC is of great importance for ensuring respect for humanitarian law on the international level. Its Statute enables the organization to protect those affected by armed conflict and to "work for the faithful application of international humanitarian law applicable in armed conflicts and to take cognizance of any complaints based on alleged breaches of that law."[9] While the ICRC is often referred to as the guardian of humanitarian law, it has rightly been pointed out that it is "not the guarantor of humanitarian law."[10] Active as the organization is in promoting respect for humanitarian law, assisting with its dissemination and national implementation, engaging with governments, the armed forces and non-state armed actors and carrying out operational relief activities in armed conflicts, it is not an enforcement agency.[11]

The obligation to repress grave breaches of humanitarian law by means of criminal justice in the Geneva Conventions has paved the way for international criminal jurisdiction on war crimes and crimes against humanity.[12] While the emergence of international criminal law and, more specifically, the jurisprudence of the International Criminal Tribunal for the

4 See Shane Darcy, "The Evolution of the Law of Belligerent Reprisals" (2003) 175(184) *Military Law Review* 244.

5 See Toni Pfanner, "Various Mechanisms and Approaches for Implementing International Humanitarian Law and Protecting and assisting War Victims" (2009) 91(874) *International Review of the Red Cross* 287.

6 Christina Cerna, "Human Rights in Armed Conflict: Implementation of International Humanitarian Law Norms by Regional Intergovernmental Human Rights Bodies" in Frits Kalshoven and Yves Sandoz (eds.), *Implementation of International Humanitarian Law* (Dordrecht: Nijhoff, 1989), pp. 36–39.

7 Additional Protocol I, Art. 90.

8 See in greater detail Aly Mokhtar, "Will This Mummification Saga Come to an End? The International Fact-Finding Commission: Article 90 of Protocol 1" (2003) 22(2) *Penn State International Law Review* 243; and Charles H.B. Garraway, "The International Humanitarian Fact-Finding Commission" in Aldo Zammit Borda (ed.), *International Humanitarian Law and the International Red Cross and Red Crescent Movement* (London: Routledge, 2010), p. 75.

9 Statutes of the International Committee of the Red Cross, Art. 4(1)(c).

10 Pfanner, "Various Mechanisms and Approaches" (n. 5) 291.

11 Ibid. 291–304.

12 Grave breaches are found in Geneva Convention I, Arts. 49–54; Geneva Convention II, Arts. 50–53; Geneva Convention III, Arts. 129–32; Geneva Convention IV, Arts. 146–49; and Additional Protocol I, Arts. 85–89, and entail the duty of states parties to prosecute and punish such acts as war crimes.

Former Yugoslavia (ICTY) and the adoption of the Rome Statute of the International Criminal Court in 1998 have increased awareness of humanitarian law and led to the prosecution and adjudication of a number of war crimes and crimes against humanity, international criminal law, too, has limits. It allows responses only *ex post*; extends only to the most serious international crimes and breaches of international humanitarian law; is not directly accessible by victims; is applied inconsistently and not universally to all conflicts, parties and perpetrators in practice; cannot prevent or halt ongoing violations of the law; and cannot award individual damages or reparations.[13]

International humanitarian law thus still lacks appropriate enforcement mechanisms which regularly, consistently and independently monitor situations of armed violence, compel parties to the conflict to end violations, and provide appropriate remedies to victims. It may well be true that "[w]e should perhaps not so much complain that the law of war does not work well, as marvel that it works at all."[14] But the creation of mechanisms to monitor compliance with the provisions of international humanitarian law has recently once more been identified by the ICRC as a particular challenge and priority.[15] In order to improve the enforcement of humanitarian law one could, of course, strengthen existing procedures under humanitarian law, such as the International Humanitarian Fact-Finding Commission, or create new mechanisms under the umbrella of the Geneva Conventions and Additional Protocols. One could add additional supervisory and monitoring mechanisms or create a framework which gives victims procedural rights under humanitarian law, such as the right to an effective remedy, the right to reparations and the right to an effective investigation, in analogy to international human rights law.[16]

So far, however, suggestions for creating new procedures under international humanitarian law have failed to progress.[17] As early as 1949, the establishment of a High International Committee to monitor the Geneva Conventions was proposed.[18] In 1970, the UN Secretary-General suggested setting up an Observer-General or Commissioner-General to supervise asylum for displaced civilians.[19] In 1971, the ICRC recommended using existing international or regional organizations to monitor observance of the Additional Protocol which were being drafted or to create an ad hoc commission for this purpose.[20] The UN Millennium Summit report also suggested a monitoring mechanism for violations

[13] See International Committee of the Red Cross, *Strengthening Legal Protection for Victims of Armed Conflict, International Conference of the Red Cross and Red Crescent Societies (28 November–1 December 2011)*, ICRC Doc. 31IC/11/5.1.1 (October 2011), pp. 12–13; and Pfanner, "Various Mechanisms and Approaches" (n. 5) 283–85.

[14] Geoffrey Best, *Humanity in Warfare: The Modern History of the International Law of Armed Conflict* (New York: Columbia University Press, 1980), p. 11.

[15] See ICRC, *Strengthening Legal Protection for Victims of Armed Conflict* (n. 13) pp. 12–13.

[16] See Daniel Thürer, *International Humanitarian Law: Theory, Practice, Context* (The Hague: Hague Academy of International Law, 2011), p. 424.

[17] See ICRC, *Strengthening Legal Protection for Victims of Armed Conflict* (n. 13) pp. 14–15.

[18] See Final Record of the Diplomatic Conference of Geneva of 1949 (1963), vol. 3, annex 21, and vol. 2, sec. (b)B p. 61.

[19] See *Report of the Secretary-General on Respect for Human Rights in Armed Conflicts*, UN Doc. A/8052 (1970).

[20] See International Committee of the Red Cross, *Protection of Victims of Non-International Armed Conflicts, Submitted to the Conference of Government Experts on the Reaffirmation and Development of International Humanitarian Law Applicable in Armed Conflicts* (Geneva: ICRC, 1971), pp. 77–78.

of international humanitarian law.[21] In 2003, the ICRC proposed to look into the establishment of various mechanisms, including a reporting system, individual complaints mechanisms, fact-finding missions and the quasi-individual investigation of violations.[22] The creation of a commission dedicated to monitoring violations of humanitarian law seemed to have been the preferred suggestion, even though uncertainties and different opinions as to its composition and function were obvious.[23]

More recently, an initiative to strengthen compliance with international humanitarian law, facilitated by Switzerland and the ICRC and involving a group of interested states, is a more promising attempt to establish monitoring mechanisms for humanitarian law. Pursuant to Resolution 1 of the Thirty-first International Conference of the Red Cross and Red Crescent in 2011 on strengthening the legal protection of victims of armed conflicts, interested states are now negotiating a reporting mechanism for humanitarian obligations to be undertaken in dedicated meetings of states parties to the Geneva Conventions. The outcome of this process is at present uncertain; its aim seems to be the creation of a state reporting mechanism on obligations under international humanitarian law in a regular peer-review monitoring process.[24]

The UN Security Council also takes an interest in the protection of civilians since its first report on this topic in 1999 in which the Council identified several legal and policy gaps which hinder such effective protection, *inter alia*, in the fields of internal displacement; child soldiers; humanitarian access; protection of children and women; small arms; anti-personnel landmines; safe zones; disarmament and demobilization; effective intervention; and peace-keeping.[25] In doing so, it has developed into what some consider a "supreme guardian of international humanitarian law,"[26] even though its impact was largely restricted to adopting repetitive resolutions. Two things seem important, though.

First, the Council has succeeded in establishing mechanisms to enhance compliance with and monitor the application of protective norms. In Resolution 1539 of 2004, the Council dealt with the multitude of violations of humanitarian and human rights law of children in armed conflict and considered the recruitment and use of child soldiers to constitute a threat to international peace and security.[27] In Resolution 1612 of 2005 it set up a monitoring and reporting mechanism to enforce compliance among non-state armed groups which use child soldiers.[28]

[21] UN Secretary-General, *We, the Peoples: The Role of the United Nations in the Twenty-First Century*, UN Doc. A/54/2000 (27 March 2000), para. 212.

[22] See International Committee of the Red Cross, *Improving Compliance with International Humanitarian Law, ICRC Expert Seminar* (Geneva: ICRC, October 2003), pp. 16–19.

[23] See Paolo Benvenuti and Guilio Bartolini, "Is There a Need for New International Humanitarian Law Implementation Mechanisms?" in Robert Kolb and Gloria Gaggioli (eds.), *Research Handbook on Human Rights and Humanitarian Law* (Cheltenham: Edward Elgar, 2013), pp. 615–16.

[24] Thirty-first International Conference of the Red Cross and Red Crescent (2011), Resolution 1, Strengthening legal protection of victims of armed conflicts, see www.icrc.org/eng/what-we-do/other-activities/development-ihl/strengthening-legal-protection-compliance.htm (last accessed 15 April 2014).

[25] *Report of the Secretary-General to the Security Council on the Protection of Civilians in Armed Conflict*, UN Doc. S/1999/957 (8 December 1999).

[26] See Schindler, "International Humanitarian Law" (n. 2) 174.

[27] Security Council Res. 1539, UN Doc. S/RES/1539 (22 April 2004).

[28] Security Council Res. 1612, UN Doc. S/RES/1612 (26 July 2005).

And secondly, the Council routinely combines obligations arising from human rights and humanitarian law when it reminds states of their duties under international law. The Council obviously sees human rights as an indispensible legal framework to be used in times of armed conflict, in conjunction with humanitarian law. This is the case in a range of text adopted since 1999, particularly in the field of children in armed conflict and on the role of women in armed conflict, such as in Resolution 1325, with which the Security Council specifically called upon states to respect the rights of women and girls in armed conflicts and implement the respective obligations under humanitarian and human rights law to protect women and girls from all forms of sexual and gender-based violence.[29]

23.2 Human rights bodies in armed conflict: lessons learned

Notwithstanding the present negotiations on a reporting mechanism for humanitarian law, the current absence of a functioning monitoring procedure under international humanitarian law seems to speak for using human rights bodies as the second-best yet more realistic option to ensure respect for humanitarian law.[30] This could be done within the existing legal, political and operational limits of these bodies or by introducing reforms which specifically allow them to supervise states' obligations under human rights and humanitarian law in situations of armed conflict. Such supervisory activities could include the monitoring of states' adherence to their obligations under humanitarian law in situations of emergency and armed conflict, including through on-site visits; it could comprise the regular examination of states' adherence to specific norms of humanitarian law; and it could allow treaty bodies and human rights courts to accept complaints alleging violations of humanitarian law.

As has been demonstrated, human rights bodies have already entered into this field. Does this mean that human rights bodies are suited to such tasks? In light of their ambiguous practice the answer is not going to be a resounding "yes." And indeed the views on their suitability to supervise compliance with human rights and international humanitarian law remain divided. Calls for using international human rights bodies to scrutinize violations of international humanitarian law have repeatedly been made but have found limited resonance in academia, as well as in policy, military and humanitarian circles.[31] The lessons learned in the past twenty-five years on the aptitude of human rights bodies to act as guardians of humanitarian law are not promising. It is beyond doubt that they all consider

[29] See Security Council Res. 1325, UN Doc. S/RES/1325 (31 October 2000), paras. 9–12 and 16. On the content and impact of the resolution see, e.g., Torunn L. Tryggestad, "Trick or Treat? The UN and Implementation of Security Council Resolution 1325 on Women, Peace, and Security" (2009) 15(4) *Global Governance* 539. For more examples, see *Report of the Secretary-General to the Security Council on the Protection of Civilians in Armed Conflict*, UN Doc. S/2009/277 (29 May 2009), paras. 26–73, issued on the tenth anniversary of the Council's first resolution on the protection of civilians.

[30] Hans-Joachim Heintze, "Konsequenzen der Konvergenz von Menschenrechtsschutz und humanitärem Völkerrecht" in Horst Fischer, Ulrike Froissart, Wolff Heinegg von Heintschel and Christian Raap (eds.), *Krisensicherung und humanitärer Schutz / Crisis Management and Humanitarian Protection. Festschrift für Dieter Fleck* (Berlin: Berliner Wissenschaftsverlag, 2004), p. 252.

[31] Beginning with Cerna, "Human Rights in Armed Conflict" (n. 6) pp. 32–33; followed by, e.g., Judith Gardam, "The Contribution of the International Court of Justice to International Humanitarian Law" (2001) 14(2) *Leiden Journal of International Law* 353; Heintze, "Konsequenzen der Konvergenz" (n. 30) pp. 251 52; and Cordula Droege, "The Interplay between International Humanitarian Law and International Human Rights Law in Situations of Armed Conflict" (2007) 40(2) *Israel Law Review* 350.

human rights fully applicable in situations of armed conflict alongside international humanitarian law. For all of them the continued application of international human rights law in all types of armed conflicts – international and non-international conflicts as well as situations of occupation and all forms of internal and trans-border violence – is now a matter of fact which deserves hardly any further justification or explanation, and passing references to earlier jurisprudence suffice when they are confronted with such situations.

Beyond that, their contribution to ensuring respect for humanitarian law is less convincing, even though they have all been faced with alleged violations of the law. What their practice demonstrates is that applying international humanitarian law, while disputed, is not entirely out of the question, but they have not solved the complex interplay of human rights and humanitarian law. The impact of their decisions has also been uneven and limited. Treaty bodies and courts have occasionally condemned violations of humanitarian law alongside human rights, urged investigations into states' conduct in armed conflict, granted compensation and damages for the victims, and contributed to clarifying the human rights responsibilities of states during armed conflicts. The missions of inquiry and fact-finding missions of the Human Rights Council have established facts and recommended action and have attracted considerable attention, scholarly interest and media coverage even though (or because) they have not always found the support of concerned states. But overall, their impact on the ground remains limited. What has mattered most so far is not substance but form: human rights law has been able to increasingly position itself as the prime international framework for publicly alleging violations of humanitarian law, debating the humanitarian responsibility of states and exerting pressure on states. That in itself was an important move.

The readiness of treaty bodies to apply humanitarian law varies and may stem from humanitarian law expertise among their members or may depend on the applicant's counsel being an expert in the field of international humanitarian law.[32] It may also be that a human rights NGO deems it useful to boost its arguments with a shot of international humanitarian law. And with all their shortcomings, the proceedings before international human rights bodies provide welcome publicity sought by victims and their representatives to put pressure on states.[33]

Where humanitarian law was used it regularly complemented human rights law; only in a few cases has reference to humanitarian law added value and increased the protection of individuals. For monitoring bodies such as the Human Rights Council, reference to the tandem "human rights/humanitarian law" has become a rhetorical tool to describe fundamental humanitarian principles applicable in armed conflicts without adding much clarity to the relationship of the two fields. In individual cases decided so far by human rights treaty bodies and courts, the norms of human rights and humanitarian law at stake were largely congruent: in internal armed conflicts, deliberate attacks on civilians, murder, mutilation, inhuman and degrading treatment, and torture were covered by the respective human rights treaty and Common Article 3 of the Geneva Conventions.

[32] It has been argued that this was the case in *Ergi* v. *Turkey* before the European Court of Human Rights, which strongly invoked the language of humanitarian law, see Noam Lubell, "Challenges in Applying Human Rights Law to Armed Conflict" (2005) 87(860) *International Review of the Red Cross* 743.

[33] See Dietrich Schindler, "The International Committee of the Red Cross and Human Rights" (1979) 19 *International Review of the Red Cross* 13.

Humanitarian law was thus largely used to emphasize the gravity of a violation and reinforce the protection offered by human rights.[34] In addition, the human rights bodies have taken different approaches towards humanitarian law, with the Inter-American Commission occasionally alleging violations of humanitarian law; the Inter-American Court arguing for its use only as an interpretative yardstick; the European Court ignoring humanitarian law altogether (albeit in an ambiguous way); and the UN human rights treaty bodies using strong rhetoric but producing less substantial output (with the exception of the Committee on the Rights of the Child and its specific role under the Convention on the Rights of the Child (CRC)). No cases of contradictory or incompatible standards under human rights and humanitarian norms had yet to be decided by them; should such a case arise their approach is unpredictable.[35]

These are not very strong grounds for positioning human rights bodies as guardians of humanitarian law. But even so, human rights bodies have been and will be confronted with situations of armed conflict and thus with the application of humanitarian law. Whether or not one wishes to see them further engaging with armed conflicts, they will in all likelihood find themselves repeatedly confronted with such situations.[36] The examination of human rights issues in armed conflict is always likely to involve questions on the conduct of hostilities, the means and methods used by the parties to the conflict, their impact on the civilian population, and the humanitarian situation of the civilian population. These are matters of human rights as much as considerations of humanitarian law, and so far human rights bodies have neither been able nor willing to neatly separate the two.[37] As a consequence, human rights bodies will be requested to monitor the adherence to human rights and humanitarian law in armed conflicts, will have to decide on individual complaints, and will be asked to provide appropriate remedies for war victims. Which potential do they offer in each of these fields?

23.3 Monitoring human rights and humanitarian law

As mentioned earlier, the special procedures, fact-finding missions and commissions of inquiry of the Human Rights Council are now the standard tool for establishing facts and come forward with recommendations in situations of alleged violations of human rights and humanitarian law in conflict scenarios.[38] The Council regularly refers to humanitarian law and denounces violations of humanitarian law on the basis of its "Charter-based *droit de*

[34] Hans-Joachim Heintze, "*Las Palmeras* v. *Bámaca-Velásquez* und *Banković* v. *Loizidou*? Widersprüchliche Entscheidungen zum Menschenrechtsschutz in bewaffneten Konflikten" (2004) 3 *Journal of International Law of Peace and Armed Conflict* 177.

[35] See Heintze, "Konsequenzen der Konvergenz" (n. 30) p. 263.

[36] See Liesbeth Zegveld, "Remedies for Victims of Violations of International Humanitarian Law" (2003) 85(851) *International Review of the Red Cross* 515.

[37] See Theo van Boven, "Reliance on Norms of Humanitarian Law by United Nations' Organs" in Astrid J.M. Delissen and Gerard J. Tanja (eds.), *Humanitarian Law of Armed Conflict: Challenges Ahead, Essays in Honour of Frits Kalshoven* (Dordrecht: Nijhoff, 1991), p. 495.

[38] See also Ulrika Sundberg, "The Role of the United Nations Commission on Human Rights in Armed Conflict Situations" in International Institute of Humanitarian Law (ed.), *Strengthening Measures for the Respect and Implementation of International Humanitarian Law and Other Rules Protecting Human Dignity in Armed Conflict, 28th Round Table on Current Problems of International Humanitarian Law, Sanremo, 2–4 September 2004* (Sanremo: International Institute of Humanitarian Law, 2004), p. 34.

regard."[39] It does so in general terms, i.e., by invoking the spirit and principles of humanitarian law rather than specific norms and regardless whether specific violations of treaty law are at stake or not. States have, with notable exceptions, largely consented to this, and the consistency with which the Human Rights Council now refers to international humanitarian law suggests that the Council has effectively assumed (some) functions of the Humanitarian Fact-Finding Commission.

But the shortcomings of the Council with regard to its role of monitoring situations of armed conflict are obvious. As a political body it remains plagued by an inconsistency towards the situations it considers, which in turn leads to accusations of double-standards in scrutinizing states' adherence to the law. The (much criticized) announcement of Israel in January 2013 not to participate in the second round of the Universal Periodic Review (UPR) (which eventually it did) serves as a reminder that not all is well.[40] The mostly general and sweeping references to humanitarian law also question the Council's competence in this field. Where the Council denounces humanitarian law violations in country resolutions it often does so haphazardly and largely unsupported by legal reasoning. Such references are more policy statements rather than specific recommendations derived from legal obligations. The Council is also not sufficiently synchronized with other human rights bodies, particularly UN treaty bodies, when considering situations of armed conflicts. And there is little to learn from the Council's practice on the relationship between international humanitarian law and international human rights other than that they apply concurrently.

But the Council remains important as it keeps the doors open for NGOs wishing to denounce not only violations of human rights law but also of humanitarian law. The holding of public hearings which include NGOs, such as by the United Nations Fact-Finding Mission on the Gaza Conflict (the Goldstone Commission) are an example for the Council's potential to include civil society actors and stakeholders in matters of human rights in armed conflicts (the Commission held two public hearings in Gaza City and in Geneva during which forty witnesses, victims and experts gave their testimony).[41] As a way forward and to improve the Council's approach, an expert consultation suggested in 2009 that a permanent UN Commission of Inquiry for international humanitarian law violations should be established.[42]

[39] Philip Alston, Jason Morgan-Foster and William Abresch, "The Competence of the UN Human Rights Council and Its Special Procedures in Relation to Armed Conflicts: Extrajudicial Executions in the 'War on Terror'" (2008) 19 *European Journal of International Law* 201.

[40] See Universal Periodic Review Media Brief (29 October 2013), available at www.ohchr.org/EN/HRBodies/UPR/Pages/Highlights29October2013pm.aspx (last accessed 15 April 2014).

[41] See www.ohchr.org/EN/HRBodies/HRC/SpecialSessions/Session9/Pages/FactFindingMission.aspx (last accessed 15 April 2014). In a similar way, Human Rights Council Res. 9/9, UN Doc. A/HRC/RES/9/9 (24 September 2008) also called for an expert consultation on the protection of human rights of civilians in armed conflict open to governments, regional organizations, relevant United Nations bodies and civil society organizations and the International Committee of the Red Cross. The report of the first consultation is contained in United Nations High Commissioner for Human Rights, *Report on the Outcome of the Expert Consultation on the Issue of Protecting the Human Rights of Civilians in Armed Conflict*, UN Doc. A/HRC/11/31 (4 June 2009); and the report of the second consultation, convened by Human Rights Council Res. 12/5, UN Doc. A/HRC/RES/12/5 (12 October 2009) in United Nations High Commissioner for Human Rights, *Report on the Outcome of the Expert Consultation on the Issue of Protecting the Human Rights of Civilians in Armed Conflict*, UN Doc. A/HRC/14/40 (2 June 2010).

[42] See UNHCHR, *Report on the Outcome of the Expert Consultation*, UN Doc. A/HRC/11/31 (n. 41) para. 42.

The same expert consultation suggested also allowing human rights treaty bodies to regularly monitor violations of human rights and humanitarian law.[43] Such ideas, including setting up a specific reporting procedure under humanitarian law to bodies within or outside humanitarian law, had been floated earlier.[44] Given that treaty bodies see less of a problem in applying humanitarian law in examining state reports than in individual complaints, this seems a viable way. The example of the Inter-American Commission's detailed scrutiny of Colombia in the examination of its third state report, mentioned above, proves that such an approach is possible.

Such a reporting obligation on humanitarian law to bodies outside the sphere of international humanitarian law is also not per se problematic, as the example of the 1954 Hague Convention for the Protection of Cultural Property in the Event of Armed Conflict demonstrates. The Convention obliges states to report to the Director-General of UNESCO on the implementation of the Convention every four years.[45] The system also demonstrates, however, the shortcomings of reporting on violations of humanitarian law as it is hampered by a low rate of replies to UNESCO's requests for such reports. Its value for the protection of cultural property in armed conflicts seems limited.[46] It must also be feared that in discussing matters of humanitarian law in state reports, the approach of the Human Rights Council to denounce violations of the spirit and principles of humanitarian law in the most general terms rather than examine specific challenges and shortcomings will be replicated. The obligation of states to report on matters of humanitarian law in the UPR of the Human Rights Council and its shortcomings has already been mentioned above and it does not constitute an example of best practice.

The creation of specific bodies or procedures for such reporting seems thus a less realistic and promising option than building upon existing procedures and including an obligation to report to human rights bodies on humanitarian obligations where appropriate.[47] With regard to declared situations of emergency and derogations, for example, there is already the duty to report under various treaties, e.g., in International Covenant on Civil and Political

[43] See ibid. para. 42.

[44] See, e.g., Krzysztof Drzewicki, "The Possible Shape of a Reporting System for International Humanitarian Law: Topics to be Addressed" in Michael Bothe (ed.), *Towards a Better Implementation of International Humanitarian Law, Proceedings of an Expert Meeting Organised by the Advisory Committee on International Humanitarian Law of the German Red Cross, Frankfurt/Main, 28–30 May 1999* (Berlin: Berlin Verlag Arno Spitz, 2001), pp. 73–81; Heike Spieker, "The Possible Shape of a Reporting System for International Humanitarian Law: Composition and Status of an Evaluating Body" in Michael Bothe (ed.), *Towards a Better Implementation of International Humanitarian Law, Proceedings of an Expert Meeting Organised by the Advisory Committee on International Humanitarian Law of the German Red Cross, Frankfurt/Main, 28–30 May 1999* (Berlin: Berlin Verlag Arno Spitz, 2001), pp. 83–103; and Rainer Hofmann, "Can Victims of Human Rights Violations Claim Damages?" in Thomas Giegerich (ed.), *A Wiser Century? Judicial Dispute Settlement, Disarmament and the Laws of War 100 Years after the Second Hague Peace Conference* (Berlin: Duncker & Humblot, 2009), pp. 322–32.

[45] Hague Convention for the Protection of Cultural Property in the Event of Armed Conflict, Art. 26(2): "Furthermore, at least once every four years, [states parties] shall forward to the Director-General a report giving whatever information they think suitable concerning any measures being taken, prepared or contemplated by their respective administrations in fulfilment of the present Convention and of the Regulations for its execution."

[46] See Jan Hladik, "Reporting System under the 1954 Convention for the Protection of Cultural Property in the Event of Armed Conflict" (2000) 82(840) *International Review of the Red Cross* 1005.

[47] Hans-Joachim Heintze, "On the Relationship between Human Rights Law Protection and International Humanitarian Law" (2004) 86(856) *International Review of the Red Cross* 798–99.

Rights (ICCPR), Article 4(3),[48] European Convention on Human Rights (ECHR), Article 15(3)[49] and American Convention on Human Rights (ACHR), Article 27(3).[50] It has been suggested that these reports could include specific information on humanitarian law,[51] but given the reluctance of states to formally derogate (and more than that, discussing such situations publicly) the impact will be limited. The experiences with the state reporting procedure under human rights treaties cautions that any further expansion of reporting duties is likely to lead to more overdue and inadequate reports rather than to strengthening states' adherence to humanitarian norms.[52] In any case, such reporting needs to fit into the already overstretched capacities of treaty bodies to effectively and efficiently deal with submitted reports.

23.4 Duty to investigate and the "right to truth"

International humanitarian law obliges states to investigate violations of the law in several ways. First, as Rule 158 of the ICRC study on customary law explains, states must investigate war crimes allegedly committed by their nationals or armed forces, or on their territory, and prosecute the suspects if appropriate, and investigate other war crimes over which they have jurisdiction.[53] This obligation extends to international and non-international armed conflicts and is supported by state practice and expressed in resolutions by the UN General Assembly and the Human Rights Council and its predecessor, the UN Commission on Human Rights.[54] A duty to investigate exists also with regard to the death of a prisoner of war.[55] Such investigations are, however, restricted either to the most serious acts, such as war crimes, or particular situations. Again, human rights law and the jurisprudence of human rights bodies, with its emphasis on the importance of prompt, thorough, effective, independent and impartial investigations, can support this comparable limited and often unspecified obligation under humanitarian law.[56] The duty to

[48] ICCPR, Art. 4(3): "Any State Party to the present Covenant availing itself of the right of derogation shall immediately inform the other States Parties to the present Covenant, through the intermediary of the Secretary-General of the United Nations, of the provisions from which it has derogated and of the reasons by which it was actuated. A further communication shall be made, through the same intermediary, on the date on which it terminates such derogation."

[49] ECHR, Art. 15(3): "Any High Contracting Party availing itself of this right of derogation shall keep the Secretary General of the Council of Europe fully informed of the measures which it has taken and the reasons therefor. It shall also inform the Secretary General of the Council of Europe when such measures have ceased to operate and the provisions of the Convention are again being fully executed."

[50] ACHR, Art. 27(3): "Any State Party availing itself of the right of suspension shall immediately inform the other States Parties, through the Secretary General of the Organization of American States, of the provisions the application of which it has suspended, the reasons that gave rise to the suspension, and the date set for the termination of such suspension."

[51] See Heintze, "Konsequenzen der Konvergenz" (n. 30) 253.

[52] See Gerd Oberleitner, *Global Human Rights Institutions: Between Remedy and Ritual* (Cambridge: Polity, 2007), pp. 94–97; and Heintze, "On the Relationship" (n. 47) 799–800.

[53] See Jean-Marie Henckaerts and Louise Doswald-Beck, *Customary International Humanitarian Law* (Cambridge: Cambridge University Press, 2005), vol. I, Rule 158, p. 607.

[54] Ibid. pp. 608–10. [55] Geneva Convention III, Art. 121.

[56] See Sandesh Sivakumaran, "International Humanitarian Law" in Daniel Moeckli, Sangeeta Shah and Sandesh Sivakumaran (eds.), *International Human Rights Law* (Oxford: Oxford University Press, 2010), p. 528.

account for persons in detention or for disappeared persons is firmly embedded in human rights law and reflected in human rights jurisprudence.[57] The criteria for effective investigations under human rights law are, in principle, also applicable in situations of armed conflict, as the European Court of Human Rights has repeatedly made clear.[58] In *Kaya* v. *Turkey*, for example (a case on the alleged inadequate investigation into the killing of the applicant during an anti-terrorist military operation in his village), the Court concluded that "neither the prevalence of armed clashes nor the high incidence of fatalities can displace the obligation [to investigate]."[59] The Court repeated this in *Akpar and Altun* v. *Turkey* when it adjudicated on killings by security forces.[60]

In addition to this emphasis on investigation, human rights bodies increasingly ask for the criminal prosecution and punishment of perpetrators of serious breaches of human rights *and* humanitarian law.[61] The Human Rights Committee has done so in the cases of Croatia (where it asked for the perpetrators to be brought to court),[62] Colombia (where it called for the investigation and prosecution of perpetrators and compensation of the victims)[63] and Democratic Republic of the Congo and Suriname (where it called for bringing those responsible for human rights violations to justice).[64] Such recommendations to institute domestic criminal proceedings for perpetrators of grave human rights violations tend to blur the lines between human rights and humanitarian law violations in the way in which they cover serious violations of humanitarian norms and principles.[65]

While a "right to truth"[66] for victims of armed conflicts does not exist as such, the right to an effective investigation, the duty to provide an effective remedy and reparations, as well as the obligation of states to combat impunity for violations of human rights in armed conflicts, are well established. Where human rights bodies refer to concurrent violations of human rights and humanitarian law, such an obligation necessarily extends also to the latter.

[57] See Sandra Krähenmann, "Positive Obligations in Human Rights Law During Armed Conflicts" in Robert Kolb and Gloria Gaggioli (eds.), *Research Handbook on Human Rights and Humanitarian Law* (Cheltenham: Edward Elgar, 2013), p. 173.

[58] Droege, "The Interplay" (n. 31) 351.

[59] *Kaya* v. *Turkey*, European Court of Human Rights, Application No. 22729/93, Judgment of 28 March 2000, para. 91.

[60] See *Akpar and Altun* v. *Turkey*, European Court of Human Rights, Appl. No. 56760/00, Judgment of 27 May 2007, para. 59.

[61] See Christine Byron, "A Blurring of the Boundaries: the Application of International Humanitarian Law by Human Rights Bodies" (2007) 47(4) *Virginia Journal of International Law* 887.

[62] See Human Rights Committee, *Concluding Observations on Croatia*, UN Doc. CCPR/C/79/Add.15 (28 December 1992), para. 9.

[63] See Human Rights Committee, *Concluding Observations on Colombia*, UN Doc. CCPR/C/79/Add.76 (5 May 1997), paras. 32 and 34.

[64] See, e.g., *Mulezi* v. *Democratic Republic of the Congo*, Human Rights Committee, Communication No. 962/2001, UN Doc. CCPR/C/81/D/962/2001 (23 July 2004), para. 7; *Baboeram* v. *Suriname*, Human Rights Committee, Communication No. 146/1983, UN Doc. CCPR/C/24/D/146/1983 (4 April 1985), para. 16.

[65] Christina Cerna, "The History of the Inter-American System's Jurisprudence as Regards Situations of Armed Conflict" (2011) 2(1) *Journal of International Humanitarian Legal Studies* 8.

[66] Ana Salado-Osuna, "The Victims of Human Rights Violations in Armed Conflicts: The Right to Justice, Truth and Compensation" in Pablo Antonio Fernández-Sánchez (ed.), *The New Challenges of Humanitarian Law in Armed Conflicts* (Leiden: Brill, 2005), p. 315.

23.5 Individual complaints and litigation

(a) Importance of legal proceedings

Individual petitions on alleged violations of legal obligations are not entirely unknown to international humanitarian law:[67] prisoners of war, for example, have the right to make requests to the detaining military authorities with regard to their conditions of detention and can apply to the representatives of the Protecting Powers.[68] They may specifically complain about being forced to do prohibited work,[69] being confined as a disciplinary punishment[70] and sentenced to a penalty which deprives them of their liberty.[71] Geneva Convention IV mirrors Geneva Convention III. It allows internees to present petitions to the detaining authority or the Protecting Power[72] and grants the right of petition to the Protecting Power when working rights of protected persons are infringed.[73] More generally, all protected persons under the Geneva Conventions may make petitions to the Protecting Powers, the ICRC or the national Red Cross societies and "any organization that may assist them."[74] These are not accidental formulations, quite to the contrary. The drafters of the Conventions argued that it is not enough to grant rights to protected persons but they must rather be given the support which they require to obtain their rights.[75] Such complaints have so far only been made to the ICRC.[76]

But no general individual right of petition under international humanitarian law can be derived from these provisions, even though they serve as a reminder that international humanitarian law is neither blind to the need of allowing for individual complaints on violations nor, as a matter of principle, incapable of accommodating such complaints. An Additional Protocol to the Geneva Conventions has thus been suggested which would set up

[67] See Roman Wieruszewski, "Application of International Humanitarian Law and Human Rights: Individual Complaints" in Frits Kalshoven and Yves Sandoz (eds.), *Implementation of International Humanitarian Law* (Dordrecht: Nijhoff, 1989), pp. 447–48.

[68] Geneva Convention III, Art. 78: "Prisoners of war shall have the right to make known to the military authorities in whose power they are, their requests regarding the conditions of captivity to which they are subjected. They shall also have the unrestricted right to apply to the representatives of the Protecting Powers either through their prisoners' representative or, if they consider it necessary, direct, in order to draw their attention to any points on which they may have complaints to make regarding their conditions of captivity."

[69] Geneva Convention III, Art. 50: "should the above provisions be infringed, prisoners of war shall be allowed to exercise their right of complaint, in conformity with Article 78."

[70] Ibid. Art. 98. [71] Ibid. Art. 108.

[72] Geneva Convention IV, Art. 101: "Internees shall have the right to present to the authorities in whose power they are, any petition with regard to the conditions of internment to which they are subjected. They shall also have the right to apply without restriction through the Internee Committee or, if they consider it necessary, direct to the representatives of the Protecting Power, in order to indicate to them any points on which they may have complaints to make with regard to the conditions of internment."

[73] Geneva Convention III, Art. 52.

[74] Geneva Convention IV, Art. 30. The state may, however, suspend any rights of communication under ibid. Art. 5 for security reasons: "Where in occupied territory an individual protected person is detained as a spy or saboteur, or as a person under definite suspicion of activity hostile to the security of the Occupying Power, such person shall, in those cases where absolute military security so requires, be regarded as having forfeited rights of communication under the present Convention."

[75] See Wieruszewski, "Application of International Humanitarian Law and Human Rights" (n. 67) pp. 448–50, who refers to the Final Record of the Diplomatic Conference of Geneva of 1949.

[76] See Wieruszewski, "Application of International Humanitarian Law and Human Rights" (n. 67) p. 448.

a Humanitarian Law Committee mandated to consider individual complaints.[77] The problems in creating such an institution are manifold but not insurmountable. One would need to identify which violations of international humanitarian law would come before such a body, i.e., only grave breaches of the Geneva Conventions and Additional Protocols or all types of violations. In order not to duplicate international criminal procedures, the latter seems preferable. To be meaningful, the mandate would also need to include non-international armed conflicts and situations of occupation. One would also need to establish whether all provisions of international humanitarian law or only those which explicitly grant individual rights should be covered. And the question would arise whether complaints can also be brought against non-state actors – this would be particularly difficult to solve in practice. And finally, one would need to clarify if such a body can decide on reparations for individual violations.[78] So far, states have shown no interest in pursuing this idea.[79]

In contrast, international human rights law allows individuals to submit complaints to treaty bodies and litigate their cases before courts. As has been shown, victims of violations of humanitarian law have long discovered the potential of human rights bodies to deal with their claims. The use of such legal remedies for humanitarian law violations has been rejected by humanitarian law experts for decades. But the arguments which have continuously been advanced against individual remedies for violations of humanitarian law, namely, that "legal proceedings are not appropriate to remedy breaches committed by soldiers"; that international humanitarian law "protects primarily persons who, helpless and defenseless, normally would be in no position to resort to any legal process, whether national or international"; and that "[t]he implementation of the humanitarian conventions is therefore better secured by the intervention of a neutral body, acting independently, and by complementary penal sanctions"[80] are no longer tenable in light of recent developments.

It has also been claimed that human rights complaints procedures cannot accommodate situations of armed conflicts because of the requirement of exhaustion of domestic remedies and applicable time limits for filing complaints, demands which are difficult to achieve in situations of armed conflicts.[81] This argument, too, is not persuasive as the case law of human rights bodies shows that the requirement of domestic remedies can be interpreted flexibly in light of the situation on the ground. In addition, humanitarian law provides even less avenues to seek redress, and at least some human rights bodies may act *ex officio* and inquire information or set in motion urgent procedures.[82]

[77] See Jann Kleffner and Liesbeth Zegveld, "Establishing an Individual Complaints Procedure for Violations of International Humanitarian Law" (2000) 3 *Yearbook of International Humanitarian Law* 386. The idea was also part of the so-called Hague Agenda for Peace and Justice for the Twenty-first Century, adopted by the non-governmental initiative Hague Appeal for Peace in 1999, para. 20, available at www.haguepeace.org/resources/HagueAgendaPeace+Justice4The21stCentury.pdf (last accessed 15 April 2014).

[78] See Kleffner and Zegveld, "Establishing an Individual Complaints Procedure" (n. 77) 392–400.

[79] See Giulia Pinzauti, "Good Time for a Change: Recognizing Individuals' Rights under the Rules of International Humanitarian Law on the Conduct of Hostilities" in Antonio Cassesse (ed.), *Realizing Utopia: The Future of International Law* (Oxford: Oxford University Press, 2012), p. 578.

[80] All quotes from Schindler, "The International Committee of the Red Cross and Human Rights" (n. 33) 12.

[81] See Dietrich Schindler, "Human Rights and Humanitarian Law: Interrelationship of the Laws" (1982) 31(4) *American University Law Review* 941.

[82] See Byron, "A Blurring of the Boundaries" (n. 61) 884–85.

It has also been argued that international human rights law instruments are adequate for individual claims but cannot cope with the kind of gross and systematic violations of human rights in armed conflict.[83] This argument, too, can be rejected as a matter of principle, although its operational and financial consequences need to be considered carefully. Human rights bodies have always dealt with situations of prolonged and massive human rights violations, as the repeated involvement of the Inter-American Commission in Colombia or Ecuador and the range of cases against Turkey and Chechnya before the European Court of Human Rights demonstrate.[84] Indeed, it would be absurd to ask human rights bodies to refrain from considering the most serious violations of human rights and restrict themselves to "minor" cases.

What is true, though, is that individual complaints are not an adequate, or the only, response to situations of deep political divisions characterized by internal violence.[85] The willingness and capacity of individual judges to assess such conflict situations in their context may also differ, as two dissenting opinions in the *Louzidou* case before the European Court of Human Rights seem to demonstrate: while one judge feared that analyzing the whole context of an occupation under humanitarian law is beyond the Court's remit to examine individual cases,[86] another judge argued that humanitarian law is indispensable to arrive at reasonable conclusions in this specific case.[87]

While there are strong arguments in favour of using individual complaints procedures for cases arising out of armed conflicts, the existing case law is less convincing. Twenty-five years on, the conclusion reached by one commentator in 1989 that neither the Inter-American Commission and Court of Human Rights nor the European Court of Human Rights has systematically and consistently applied the provisions of the Geneva Conventions or Additional Protocols is still valid.[88] The cases of *Arturo Ribón Avilán* v. *Colombia*, *Hugo Bustios Saavedra* v. *Peru* and *Juan Carlos Abella* v. *Argentina* before the Inter-American Commission in 1998 still mark the limits to which a human rights body would go in speaking out on violations of international humanitarian law, and even in these cases the Commission's position on the direct applicability of humanitarian law remains ambiguous.

And yet, there is potential in adjudicating individual complaints of concrete violations of humanitarian law, as it would allow and force treaty bodies and courts to clarify the interplay of human rights and humanitarian law in concrete situations rather than prolonging theoretical debates on their relationship. Indeed, the debate on human rights in armed conflict is no longer merely a theoretical discussion but also a "litigation-driven phenomenon."[89] Such proceedings could provide specific guidance to states (and allow

[83] Heike Krieger, "Die Verantwortlichkeit Deutschlands nach der EMRK für seine Streitkräfte im Auslandseinsatz" (2002) 62 *Zeitschrift für ausländisches öffentliches Recht und Völkerrecht* 692.

[84] See Aisling Reidy, Françoise Hampson and Kevin Boyle, "Gross Violations of Human Rights: Invoking the European Convention on Human Rights in the Case of Turkey" (1997) 15(2) *Netherlands Quarterly of Human Rights* 161; and Hans-Joachim Heintze, "The European Court of Human Rights and the Implementation of Human Rights Standards during Armed Conflict" (2002) 45 *German Yearbook of International Law* 71.

[85] Heintze, "On the Relationship" (n. 47) 809.

[86] See *Loizidou* v. *Turkey*, European Court of Human Rights, Appl. No. 15318/89, Judgment of 18 December 1996, Dissenting Opinion of Judge Bernhard, joined by Judge Lopes Rocha.

[87] Ibid. Dissenting Opinion of Judge Pettiti.

[88] Cerna, "Human Rights in Armed Conflict" (n. 6) p. 32.

[89] Guglielmo Verdirame, "Human Rights in Wartime: A Framework for Analysis" (2008) 6 *European Human Rights Law Review* 691.

them to disagree with the findings of human rights bodies in specific rather than general terms), enable greater pressure to be put on violators of international humanitarian law, and make humanitarian law better known to a broader public.[90] They would complement criminal trials due to their greater flexibility, their competence to establish state responsibility, and the provision of remedies and damages, different from criminal law with its focus on individual punishment and deterrence.

(b) Humanitarian norms before human rights bodies

It seems that in the absence of legal reforms which allow human rights bodies and courts to specifically accept complaints on violations of humanitarian law, four approaches can be discerned for human rights bodies to decide on violations of humanitarian law: using humanitarian law through the practice of *renvoi*; applying humanitarian law where it is congruent with human rights law; interpreting savings clauses so as to oblige them to apply the highest available standard of protection; and applying human rights law instead of humanitarian law. None of these options is without problems.

The practice of using norms outside the respective human rights treaty reflects established legal doctrine that an organ of an international organization may refer to, invoke and adopt a position on other sources of law than the document under which it has been founded.[91] This is regularly the case where the domestic law of states parties needs to be analyzed with a view towards assessing its compliance with human rights.[92] References to norms of international law are more problematic but equally common. Human rights treaties allow human rights bodies to take into account "general principles of international law"[93] as well as "other obligations under international law."[94] The former is one of the sources of international law mentioned in Article 38 of the ICJ Statute, but with the exception of the unconvincing argument made by the African Commission on Human and Peoples' Rights in one of its cases, no treaty body has invoked general principles of international law to defend a reference to humanitarian law. "Other obligations under international law" undoubtedly comprise international humanitarian law, as human rights bodies have repeatedly pointed out (first and foremost the Inter-American Commission on Human Rights), even though explicit references to "international criminal law" or "international humanitarian law" are not common in human rights treaties.[95] But such references do not incorporate external norms in a given treaty or make such norms directly applicable

90 Louise Doswald-Beck and Sylvain Vité, "International Humanitarian Law and Human Rights Law" (1993) 33(293) *International Review of the Red Cross* 117.

91 See Héctor Gros Espiell, "Humanitarian Law and Human Rights" in Janusz Symonides (ed.), *Human Rights: Concepts and Standards* (Aldershot and Paris: Ashgate and UNESCO, 2000), p. 356.

92 See, e.g. ECHR, Arts. 5, 6, 8–11; ACHR, Arts. 4, 7, 11–16, 21 and 22; and ICCPR, Arts. 5, 6, 8, 9, 12–14, 17–19 and 22; see Giulia Pinzauti, "The European Court of Human Rights' Incidental Application of International Criminal and Humanitarian Law: A Critical Discussion of *Kononov* v. *Latvia*" (2008) 6(5) *Journal of International Criminal Justice* 1045 note 3.

93 See, e.g., ECHR Optional Protocol 1, Art. 1: "No one shall be deprived of his possessions except in the public interest and subject to the conditions provided for by law and by the general principles of international law."

94 Derogation clauses regularly employ these words, e.g. ECHR, Art. 15; ACHR, Art. 27; and ICCPR, Art. 4.

95 Noelle Quénivet, "*Isayeva* v. *Russian Federation* and *Isayeva, Yusupova and Bazayeva* v. *Russian Federation*. Targeting Rules according to Article 2 of the European Convention on Human Rights" (2005) 3 *Journal of International Law of Peace and Armed Conflict* 220.

by a treaty body. Rather, they serve a twofold purpose: they ensure the unity of the international legal order and, more specifically, allow a monitoring body to decide on a violation of the human rights treaty when such a decision hinges on the external norm and a treaty violation cannot be established without analysis of that norm.[96]

The Inter-American Commission on Human Rights has insisted that such an inherent power to examine external norms is a necessity; if it were to refrain from doing so it would fail in its duties.[97] Similarly, the European Court of Human Rights has repeatedly stated that the Convention cannot be applied in a vacuum but needs to be read in the totality of international law.[98] This power may be described as incidental or instrumental jurisdiction (as opposed to the monitoring body's principal or direct jurisdiction under the respective human rights instrument). Even though it is a secondary form of jurisdiction it is not restricted to merely taking cognizance of the existence of an external rule but may rather require analyzing, scrutinizing or interpreting the external rule through "a certain degree of hermeneutic activity."[99]

Even then, however, such references to other norms only allow the monitoring body to decide on a violation of the respective human rights treaty and not to review the conduct of a state party under humanitarian instruments as such.[100] One can thus expect human rights treaty bodies and courts to find violations of humanitarian law so as to emphasize and support their condemnation of a violation of the respective human rights treaty. In practice it does seem, however, that such an approach leads merely to the use of ambiguous phraseology which indicates a violation of humanitarian law without clearly saying so, as the case law mentioned earlier demonstrates. In contrast, using international humanitarian law to interpret and give meaning to human rights law in specific situations not adequately regulated by the latter is largely seen as unproblematic.[101] But where human rights bodies wish to decide that a violation of the Geneva Conventions or the Additional Protocols has occurred they need to resort to further arguments.

One possibility could be to argue for the identity, similarity or substantial overlap between a norm of human rights and humanitarian law, as the Inter-American Commission has suggested in its early case law, i.e., by considering Common Article 3 of the Geneva Conventions as "pure human rights law."[102] This argument is obviously strongest where the respective norm constitutes also *jus cogens*, e.g., with regard to

[96] ICJ Statute, Art. 38; see Pinzauti, "The European Court of Human Rights' Incidental Application" (n. 92) 1047–48.

[97] Ibid. 1049.

[98] See Andrea Gioia, "The Role of the European Court of Human Rights in Monitoring Compliance with Humanitarian Law in Armed Conflict" in Orna Ben-Naftali (ed.), *International Humanitarian Law and International Human Rights Law* (Oxford: Oxford University Press, 2011), p. 217.

[99] Pinzauti, "The European Court of Human Rights' Incidental Application" (n. 92) 1049.

[100] See Human Rights Committee, *General Comment No. 29 on States of Emergency (Article 4)*, UN Doc. CCPR/C/21/Rev.1/Add.11 (31 August 2001), para. 10: "Although it is not the function of the Human Rights Committee to review the conduct of a State party under other treaties, in exercising its functions under the Covenant the Committee has the competence to take a State party's other international obligations into account when it considers whether the Covenant allows the State party to derogate from specific provisions of the Covenant."

[101] See Pinzauti, "Good Time for a Change" (n. 79) p. 580.

[102] *Juan Carlos Abella* v. *Argentina*, Inter-American Commission on Human Rights, Case No. 11.137 of 18 November 1997, Report No. 55/97 of 14 April 1998,OAS Doc. OEA/Ser.L/V/II.98 Doc. 6 rev., para. 158.

(at least certain of) the elements of Common Article 3 of the Geneva Conventions, as Judge Cançado Trindade argued in various dissenting opinions mentioned above.[103] In light of the increasing acknowledgment of the convergence of human rights and humanitarian law, these seem potentially strong arguments which could be further exploited. They do not extend, however, beyond those norms which can reasonably be deemed identical or similar and certainly not to the whole of humanitarian law. They also cannot be used where derogations of human rights or non-ratification of humanitarian treaties are at stake.

As a third option it could be argued that there is a duty of human rights bodies to ensure the highest level of protection for individuals. This is what the Inter-American Commission on Human Rights did when it invoked the savings clause of the ACHR in situations where it found the ACHR to provide less protection than international humanitarian law instruments. The Commission justified this by interpreting the savings clause so as to allow the application of that legal instrument which provides the highest protection to the individual, regardless of whether it is a human rights instrument in the Inter-American human rights system, a human rights instrument outside this system, or a humanitarian law instrument. The example of the European Court of Human Rights, however, points towards an altogether different approach, namely, to ignore humanitarian law in situations which are arguably, in fact and law, situations of armed conflict while at the same time *sub silentio* invoking the fundamental concepts and the language of humanitarian law to do justice to the situation. As mentioned, one can see this approach as an emerging human rights law of armed conflict and highlight its benefits. Given that states often resist applying international humanitarian law to internal armed conflicts by denying that a situation amounts to an armed conflict at all, the Court's adaptation of international human rights law in light of international humanitarian law is seen by some as a promising base for supervising violent interactions between the state and its citizens and ensuring protection.[104]

Yet, it also means ignoring the claims of the applicants and the views of the involved state and may require feigning situations as peace-time scenarios in the midst of war. One would also have to accept that a human rights body consciously disregards (even only for interpretative purposes) the hundreds of specific provisions of the universally ratified Geneva Conventions which have been created and accepted by states to regulate precisely the kind of conduct in combat in question. This seems neither a politically sound position nor a convincing act of legal reasoning. Consequently, some commentators see human rights bodies which do not resort to international humanitarian law as simply expressing an extremist version of the separatist view turned up-side-down; a version in which one, and only one, legal regime (namely, international human rights law) governs armed conflicts.[105]

[103] See *Serrano-Cruz Sisters* v. *El Salvador*, Inter-American Court of Human Rights, Judgment (Merits, Reparations and Costs) of 1 March 2005, Ser. C, No. 118, Dissenting Opinion of Judge Antônio Augusto Cançado Trindade, para. 40.

[104] See William Abresch, "A Human Rights Law of Internal Armed Conflict: The European Court of Human Rights in Chechnya" (2005) 16(4) *European Journal of International Law* 743.

[105] See Christopher Greenwood, "Rights at the Frontier: Protection of the Individual in Time of War" in Barry A.K. Rider (ed.), *Law at the Centre: The Institute of Advanced Legal Studies at Fifty* (Dordrecht: Kluwer, 1999), p. 79.

Ignoring humanitarian law in situations where it is obviously applicable is thus no way forward.[106]

(c) *Reforming individual complaints procedures?*

In light of this diagnosis one may be inclined to suggest reforms to allow human rights bodies to put an end to this ambiguity and consider violations of international humanitarian law alongside human rights violations, akin to the approach which the Inter-American Commission seemed to suggest in its very early cases.[107] One way forward would be to establish special individual complaints procedures for human rights bodies to deal specifically with violations of humanitarian law.[108] The main obstacles to such an approach lie not in the legal technicalities: one could, for example, adopt an Optional Protocol which allows them to consider violations of humanitarian law with respect to the states parties to such a Protocol.

But such complaints procedures would artificially separate the two fields, which goes against the convergence of the two. It is also likely to create even more heterogeneous groups of states: some states would accept such complaints against them while others would not, and states affected by armed conflicts would most likely be in the second category. In addition, cases involving armed conflicts would still end up before treaty bodies provided they are not specifically barred from dealing with armed conflicts, which in turn would question the continued application of human rights in armed conflicts and infringe their competence to consider other obligations of international law, including humanitarian law, and thus seems no option.[109] It has also been pointed out that it seems unlikely to secure the support of states for such a project.[110]

As a more pragmatic and viable alternative it has been suggested to allow treaty bodies – first and foremost the UN Human Rights Committee – to cover international humanitarian law violations within their existing mandate. This would reflect their current practice, ensure coherent jurisprudence, and would seem operationally and financially reasonable.[111] Given that the Geneva Conventions are universally ratified there should be no problem regarding the states parties' obligations (the situation is, however, different with regard to the Additional Protocols). The lack of expertise should be no argument against it, as such an approach would precisely allow the treaty bodies to acquire such expertise over time, and the treaty bodies could give clarity to the interplay of human

[106] See Françoise Hampson and Ibrahim Salama, *Working Paper of the UN Sub-commission on the Promotion and Protection of Human Rights on the Relationship between Human Rights Law and International Humanitarian Law*, UN Doc. E/CN.4/2005/14 (21 June 2005), p. 18; and Aisling Reidy, "The Approach of the European Commission and Court of Human Rights to International Humanitarian Law" (1998) 80(324) *International Review of the Red Cross* 521.

[107] Heintze, "On the Relationship" (n. 47) 804.

[108] See Kleffner and Zegveld, "Establishing an Individual Complaints Procedure" (n. 77) pp. 384–401.

[109] See Byron, "A Blurring of the Boundaries" (n. 61) 895.

[110] Emiliano J. Buis, "The Implementation of International Humanitarian Law by Human Rights Courts: The Example of the Inter-American Human Rights System" in Roberta Arnold and Noelle Quénivet (eds.), *International Humanitarian Law and Human Rights Law: Towards a Merger in International Law* (Leiden: Nijhoff, 2008), p. 293.

[111] See David Weissbrodt, "The Role of the Human Rights Committee in Interpreting and Developing Humanitarian Law" (2010) 31(4) *Pennsylvania Journal of International Law* 1234–35.

rights and humanitarian law in concrete cases to take the respective academic discussion an important step further.[112]

In light of the practice of human rights bodies in dealing with humanitarian law, the broad agreement of states to this and their willingness to report on matters of humanitarian law, human rights bodies could build on the increasing convergence of human rights and humanitarian law and further expand their supervision of at least the core norms of humanitarian law in their various activities. In addition, interested and competent NGOs could be invited to contribute and provide information on humanitarian law in their "shadow reports" in the state reporting system and submit *amicus curiae* briefs on matters of humanitarian law to human rights treaty bodies and courts.[113]

23.6 Remedy and compensation

The form in and extent to which war victims are entitled to claim remedies and compensation remains disputed. The Statute of the International Criminal Court contains a provision on reparations to victims which enables the Court to "make an order directly against a convicted person specifying appropriate reparations to, or in respect of, victims, including restitution, compensation and rehabilitation."[114] Still, the general lack of remedies and reparations for victims of armed conflicts has been repeatedly deplored and criticized by many commentators as out of step with developments in other fields of law.[115] The ICJ as well as arbitral tribunals and claims commissions (where they exist) are accessible only to states,[116] and Article 91 of Additional Protocol 1, as well as Article 3 of the Hague Regulations, provide remedies only in a very unspecific way.[117] Such provisions do not reflect the idea of effective remedies for victims of violations of the law but rest on the public order character of international humanitarian law norms.[118]

[112] Ibid. 1237.

[113] ECHR, Art. 36(2) would, for example, open such a possibility for a third party intervention when it states that "[t]he President of the Court may, in the interest of the proper administration of justice, invite any High Contracting Party which is not a party to the proceedings or any person concerned who is not the applicant to submit written comments or take part in the hearing."

[114] Statute of the International Criminal Court, Art. 75.

[115] See Emanuela-Chiara Gillard, "Reparation for Violations of International Humanitarian Law" (2003) 85 (851) *International Review of the Red Cross* 529; and Rainer Hofmann, "Victims of Violations of International Humanitarian Law: Do They Have an Individual Right to Reparations against States under International Law?" in Pierre-Marie Dupuy, Bardo Fassbender, Malcolm N. Shaw and Karl-Peter Sommermann (eds.), *Common Values in International Law, Essays in Honour of Christian Tomuschat* (Kehl: Engel, 2006), pp. 341–59. On the underlying difficulties in reaching consensus on reparations see Abdullah Ahmed An-Na'im, "Toward a Universal Doctrine of Reparation for Violations of International Human Rights and Humanitarian Law" (2003) 5(1) *International Law Forum* 27.

[116] See Pinzauti, "Good Time for a Change" (n. 79) pp. 573–74.

[117] Hague Regulations, Art. 3 demands that "[a] belligerent party which violates the provisions of the said Regulations shall, if the case demands, be liable to pay compensation. It shall be responsible for all acts committed by persons forming part of its armed forces"; and Additional Protocol I, Art. 91 largely repeats this formula: "[a] Party to the conflict which violates the provisions of the Conventions or of this Protocol shall, if the case demands, be liable to pay compensation. It shall be responsible for all acts committed by persons forming part of its armed forces."

[118] See René Provost, *International Human Rights and Humanitarian Law* (Cambridge: Cambridge University Press, 2002), p. 54.

War victims also regularly fail to bring their cases successfully before domestic courts because states reject the admissibility of such claims on different grounds: they point out that they are not liable under international law for particular kinds of state conduct such as warfare; that warfare is a non-justiciable "political issue"; and that state immunity shields them from the jurisdiction of foreign courts. In the *Vavarin* case, for example, the German regional court (Landgericht) Bonn in 2003 dismissed claims brought before it by relatives of victims of a NATO air attack on a bridge near the Serbian town of Vavarin in 1999. Their demand for compensation was rejected on the grounds that neither public international law nor German law sustains their arguments and that violations of international humanitarian law can only be obtained through means of diplomatic protection exercised by the claimants.[119] And even if war victims succeed in obtaining a court judgment, it is unlikely to be enforced by the executive organs of the respective state or such enforcement will be delayed unduly.[120]

While the punishment of war criminals before international criminal courts and tribunals is now an established element of international law, the rights and interests of victims of war remain largely ignored. Arguments for respecting the victims' claims of access to justice, information, investigation, reparations, compensation, rehabilitation and guarantees of non-repetition have not been received favourably by the international community, despite the endorsement of documents such as the Basic Principles and Guidelines on the Right to a Remedy and Reparations for Victims of Violations of International Human Rights and Humanitarian Law.[121] The matter of reparations for war victims remains highly contentious among states. When the ICRC put the recommendations it had made in this respect in its report on strengthening the protection of war victims in 2011 up for discussion, the majority of states remained uninterested in the matter and many rejected any proposal to consider such reparations outright.[122] The idea that victims of armed conflicts are entitled to remedies against the use of force is still anathema to many, particularly when it comes to individual compensations for war-related damages.[123]

[119] See Landgericht Bonn (Regional Court of Bonn), Az. 1 O 361/02, Judgment of 10 December 2003, para. 122 ("*Varvarin* case"). See in greater detail Noelle Quénivet, "The *Vavarin* Case: The Legal Standing of Individuals as Subjects of International Law" (2004) 3 *Journal of Military Ethics* 2; and Giovanni Carlo Bruno, "'Collateral Damages' of Military Operations: Is Implementation of International Humanitarian Law Possible Using International Human Rights Law Tools?" in Roberta Arnold and Noelle Quénivet (eds.), *International Humanitarian Law and Human Rights Law: Towards a Merger in International Law* (Leiden: Nijhoff, 2008), pp. 298–300.

[120] See Pinzauti, "Good Time for a Change" (n. 79) p. 573; and in greater detail Natalino Ronzitti, "Access to Justice and Compensation for Violations of the Law of War" in Francesco Francioni (ed.), *Access to Justice as a Human Right* (Oxford: Oxford University Press, 2002), pp. 95–119.

[121] The Guidelines were adopted by the UN Commission on Human Rights at its Fifty-Sixth Session in 2000 as UN Doc. E/CN.4/2000/62 (18 January 2000) and by the UN General Assembly in 2006 as Basic Principles and Guidelines on the Right to a Remedy and Reparations for Victims of Violations of International Human Rights and Humanitarian Law, UN Doc. A/RES/60/147 (16 December 2005). On the content of the Principles see in greater detail Christian Tomuschat, "Reparation in Favour of Individual Victims of Gross Violations of Human Rights and International Humanitarian Law" in Marcelo G. Kohen (ed.), *Promoting Justice, Human Rights and Conflict Resolution Through International Law, Liber Amicorum Lucius Caflisch* (Leiden: Nijhoff, 2007), pp. 569–90.

[122] See ICRC, *Strengthening Legal Protection for Victims of Armed Conflict* (n. 13) p. 27.

[123] See Kenneth Watkin, "Controlling the Use of Force: A Role for Human Rights Norms in Contemporary Conflicts" (2004) 98(1) *American Journal of International Law* 34.

At the same time, there is evolving practice of remedies in international humanitarian law and the right to reparations is increasingly recognized.[124] In its Advisory Opinion in the *Wall* case, the ICJ, for example, saw individuals as entitled to reparations from Israel "for the damage caused by the construction of the wall in the Occupied Palestinian Territory, including in and around East Jerusalem."[125] Texts of the international legal community, such as the Chicago Principles on Post-Conflict Justice[126] or the Declaration on International Law Principles on Reparations for Victims of Armed Conflict, drafted by the International Law Association,[127] call for the victims' rights to remedy and reparations. National judicial practice, though scarce, cautiously supports this trend, such as when the Hague Court of Appeals ordered the Netherlands to pay compensation for the deaths of Muslims murdered in Srebrenica in 1995.[128] It has been argued that *de lege ferenda* such developments are likely to cumulate and lead towards individuals being entitled to remedies and reparations for violations of humanitarian law.[129] But the legal and practical obstacles are manifold and range from delineating state responsibility for individual violations of humanitarian norms to deciding on adequate forms of reparation.[130]

International human rights law may thus be able to make an important contribution with regard to remedies for war victims and human rights treaty bodies and courts can have a role to play in this respect.[131] The European Court of Human Rights, in particular, has developed extensive case law on compensation of victims of human rights violations, including in situations of internal violence. But the shortcomings of such compensation are also obvious: even when one considers the respective treaties fully applicable in armed conflicts, treaty bodies and courts can only decide within the limits of the alleged violations and not award more comprehensive compensation. And as far as the European Court of Human Rights is concerned, the financial compensation is rather symbolic, different from the Inter-American Court of Human Rights.

23.7 Human rights bodies in armed conflict: challenges and potential

As has been argued above, the way in which humanitarian law gradually acquires more of a subjective dimension and is increasingly capable of understanding its provisions as

124 See Droege, "The Interplay" (n. 31) 354; and Elke Schwager, "Reparation for Individual Victims of Armed Conflict" in Robert Kolb and Gloria Gaggioli (eds.), *Research Handbook on Human Rights and Humanitarian Law* (Cheltenham: Edward Elgar, 2013), p. 628.

125 *Legal Consequences of the Construction of a Wall in the Occupied Palestinian Territory*, International Court of Justice, Advisory Opinion of 9 July 2004 [2004] ICJ Reports, para. 163(3)(C).

126 See International Human Rights Law Institute, Chicago Principles on Post-Conflict Justice (2007).

127 See International Law Association, Declaration on International Law Principles on Reparations for Victims of Armed Conflict, Res. No.2/2010 (August 2010).

128 *Mustafic* v. *The Netherlands*, The Hague Court of Appeal, Case No. 200.020.173/01, Judgment of 5 July 2011; and *Nehanovic* v. *The Netherlands*, The Hague Court of Appeal, Case No. 200.020.174/01, Judgment of 5 July 2011; on both cases see Pinzauti, "Good Time for a Change" (n. 79) p. 577.

129 Ibid. p. 578. 130 Ibid. pp. 578–80.

131 See Ruona Iguyovwe, "The Interplay between International Humanitarian Law and International Human Rights Law" in Aldo Zammit Borda (ed.), *International Humanitarian Law and the International Red Cross and Red Crescent Movement* (London: Routledge, 2010), pp. 16–17; and Rob McLaughlin, "The Law of Armed Conflict and International Human Rights Law: Some Paradigmatic Differences and Operational Implications" (2010) 13 *Yearbook of International Humanitarian Law* 219.

individual rights speaks in favour of supervising adherence to humanitarian norms in the framework of human rights institutions.[132] But at the same time it has been argued that "a rights-based approach will not likely be the most effective in bringing needed protection to individuals during periods of armed conflict."[133] The ICRC, in particular, seems unconvinced that international human rights law mechanisms are suitable for monitoring violations of the law in armed conflict. Whenever the ICRC argues for the better enforcement of humanitarian law, it always emphasizes that any new mechanisms need to be independent, impartial and preferably capable of delivering legally binding decisions rather than recommendations. The main fear of the ICRC – that everything the United Nations touches becomes politically tainted – seems to include not only the Human Rights Council but also UN treaty bodies.[134]

The approach of human rights bodies to situations of armed conflicts has also rightly been criticized as lacking specificity.[135] Military lawyers, in particular, are likely to find the results of their deliberations too vague to provide specific guidance on the conduct of hostilities. This, in turn, invites those critical of the application of human rights in armed conflicts to dismiss human rights altogether as vague aspirations with limited value for battlefield operations and confirms their preference for relying exclusively on international humanitarian law.

Human rights bodies are also frequently accused of lacking expertise in humanitarian law which leads them to reach conclusions that humanitarian law experts find problematic.[136] A rough survey of the humanitarian law expertise has led one commentator to conclude that between 14 and 50 per cent of the members of the European Court of Human Rights, the Inter-American Commission on Human Rights and the UN Committee on Human Rights have a humanitarian law expertise while the others do not.[137] However, measuring "humanitarian law expertise" is tricky, as the author herself admits. Asking for "expertise" as a prerequisite for forming and expressing an opinion on international humanitarian law (beyond general qualifications in the field of law) is an understandable but vague demand. Where it leads to downgrading the (legal) opinions of non-members of a circle of established publicists and practitioners in humanitarian law and, more particularly, excluding renowned publicists and practitioners in human rights law because their opinions do not conform to mainstream legal doctrines, this would be an unacceptable restriction. Lack of expertise can be solved through training, external expertise, exchange with humanitarian experts and other means, and it can be expected that human rights bodies would grow in the face of the challenge as other institutions have done.[138]

132 See Michael Bothe, "Die Anwendung der Europäischen Menschenrechtskonvention in bewaffneten Konflikten – eine Überforderung?" (2005) 65 *Zeitschrift für ausländisches öffentliches Recht und Völkerrecht* 621.

133 Provost, *International Human Rights and Humanitarian Law* (n. 118) p. 349.

134 See ICRC, *Strengthening Legal Protection for Victims of Armed Conflict* (n. 13) pp. 14–15.

135 See John Tobin, "Seeking Clarity in relation to the Principle of Complementarity: Reflections on the Recent Contributions of Some International Bodies" (2007) 8(2) *Melbourne Journal of International Law* 359, 367; with reference to the UN human rights bodies and the Special Rapporteurs of the Human Rights Council.

136 See Hampson and Salama, *Working Paper on the Relationship between Human Rights Law and International Humanitarian Law* (n. 106) paras. 9–37.

137 See Byron, "A Blurring of the Boundaries" (n. 61) 882.

138 See Bothe, "Die Anwendung der Europäischen Menschenrechtskonvention" (n. 132) 622.

Some also fear that allowing a multitude of human rights bodies to deal with humanitarian law, and particularly those entrusted with securing respect for human rights in a specific region, will dilute the universal character of humanitarian law. This might, it is feared, lead to a "regionalization" of humanitarian norms in the Inter-American, African and European human rights systems, allow "forum-shopping" by claimants and produce contradictory decisions, inconsistent case law and double standards.[139] Such arguments should not be dismissed, but in light of the scarce means available to victims of violations of humanitarian law to complain about such violations, these concerns seem exaggerated. The room for different interpretations of humanitarian norms is narrow compared to international human rights standards, and while diverging jurisprudence cannot be ruled out there is no reason to expect fundamental deviations in jurisprudence with regard to core norms of humanitarian law. The overlap with international criminal proceedings is also no argument, given the very different kind of jurisprudence they exercise and the scarcity of international criminal proceedings after the criminal tribunals for the former Yugoslavia and Rwanda will have ended their work.

The organizational capacity of human rights bodies to deal with the number of cases is another serious issue, at least for some human rights institutions. The more victims and their legal representatives assume that the European Court is an appropriate forum to consider allegations of humanitarian law in support of their claims to decide on violations of the ECHR and to award damages, the more the caseload may increase. But even if the further engagement of human rights bodies in armed conflicts (including by taking into account international humanitarian law) is a challenge, it is not a valid reason to shy away from it in judicial self-restraint or in anticipation of an increased workload.[140]

The human rights obligations of non-state actors (or the lack thereof) will again pose a considerable problem in need of further scrutiny: How can they be held accountable by human rights bodies for violations of the law? The practice of treaty bodies in monitoring human rights (through special procedures, commissions of inquiry and fact-finding missions of the Human Rights Council and in examining state reports by treaty bodies) demonstrates the willingness and ability to denounce violations of human rights and humanitarian law by non-state actors, even though the situation is obviously different with regard to individual complaints brought to human rights courts.

In conclusion, the benefits of allowing human rights bodies to speak out on violations of humanitarian law in addition to human rights law violations seem to outweigh the challenges and obstacles. Their main contribution may be in establishing an unquestioned right of investigation and reparations for victims of armed conflicts and to allow for transparency and victims' participation as important elements in further developing international humanitarian law, as has been pointed out.[141] Human rights courts, in particular, have the autonomy and independence to deal with matters of humanitarian law and integrate human rights and international humanitarian law into a more coherent protective system.[142]

This does not mean that international humanitarian law procedures should not be strengthened. One could envisage, for example, an annual report on respect for international humanitarian law published by the ICRC which also highlights specific

[139] See ICRC, *Strengthening Legal Protection for Victims of Armed Conflict* (n. 13) p. 14.
[140] See Bothe, "Die Anwendung der Europäischen Menschenrechtskonvention" (n. 132) 622–33.
[141] Droege, "The Interplay" (n. 31) 354–55. [142] Cerna, "Human Rights in Armed Conflict" (n. 6) p. 60.

violations, or an annual report by the UN on human rights and humanitarian law violations.[143] But since the creation of new international humanitarian law supervisory bodies seems unlikely at present, recourse to human rights bodies to enforce international humanitarian law may be the only reasonable possibility regardless of the flaws.[144]

Whatever solution one envisages, human rights bodies are likely to be confronted with situations of armed conflicts in the future, and perhaps increasingly so. The regional human rights supervisory mechanisms exercise a particularly inescapable pull in light of the dysfunctional means of enforcement available under humanitarian law. In light of the persistent failures to secure respect for humanitarian law, their engagement in this area can rightly be seen as a necessity.[145] If states do not wish human rights bodies to be used to monitor their conduct in armed conflicts and provide remedies for victims of violence, then they will have to create effective mechanisms under international humanitarian law. As long as they do not, victims of state and non-state violence will increasingly and understandably refer themselves to human rights treaty bodies and courts.

143 See Bertrand Ramcharan, *The United Nations High Commissioner for Human Rights and International Humanitarian Law*, Program on Humanitarian Policy and Conflict Research, Harvard University, Occasional Paper Series No. 3 (2005), p. 37.

144 Heintze, "*Las Palmeras* v. *Bámaca-Velásquez* und *Bankovic* v. *Loizidou*?" (n. 34) 181.

145 See Francesco Bruscoli, "The Rights of Individuals in Times of Armed Conflict" (2002) 6(1) *International Journal of Human Rights* 58.

CONCLUSION

The laws which regulate warfare are a reflection of their time and the structure of society, its political and social order, the prevailing economic system and the dominant moral and political discourses on war and law.[1] Transformation and adaptation, not only to new circumstances and factual demands of war and warfare but also to the perceptions and expectations of society at large, are characteristic of the law. Historically, the law of armed conflict has gone through a series of transformations from medieval customary rules to the rational balancing of military advantage and human suffering in the Hague law, and the humanitarian advocacy tradition in the Geneva law, which finally allowed the creation of international humanitarian law in 1949. The debate on human rights in armed conflict is the response of our times to the dynamics of war and law.

With its mix of charity as an expression of faith and chivalry as a reflection of class and professionalism, and the rational and calculating positivism and philanthropic activism of the nineteenth century, the law of armed conflict is informed by a strong and vibrant humanitarian legacy; yet it does not adequately reflect the cosmopolitan views of the twenty-first century. This does not question its importance as an indispensible legal framework which mitigates the consequences of armed conflicts in all their forms. The debate on human rights in armed conflict is, or should be, a debate on the interplay of human rights *and* humanitarian law, and not an attempt to relegate international humanitarian law from the battlefield as the result of a competition in which one legal regime trumps the other. Today, the notion of "humanitarian" in humanitarian law can be understood properly only with reference to the idea, language, law and policy of human rights as the dominant moral and legal discourse of our times. Since the adoption of the Universal Declaration of Human Rights in 1948, humanity is no longer a grace but a right.

The influence of international human rights law began, cautiously at first, after 1948/49, when the Universal Declaration and the Geneva Conventions were drafted in parallel processes, and has since become ever more obvious. The convergence of human rights and humanitarian law is not an invention of current human rights scholarship and advocacy. It has its roots in the interaction of the images of war and the role assigned to the law in such situations; an interaction which stretches back for centuries. It can also build on a tradition of respect for human dignity as individual entitlement under international humanitarian law beyond the emotive compassion for human suffering and the coolly

[1] See Paul Kennedy and George J. Andreopoulos, "The Laws of War: Some Concluding Reflections" in Michael Howard, George J. Andreopoulos and Mark R. Shulman (eds.), *The Laws of War: Constraints on Warfare in the Western World* (New Haven, CT: Yale University Press, 1994), p. 214.

calculated balancing of military necessity and humanitarian concern. This tradition of humanitarian law, which invokes the "dictates of public conscience" and the "laws of humanity" (as found in the Martens Clause), can be unravelled again because it connects with the humanitarian discourse of our times.[2]

But even with this legacy, international humanitarian law is not a cosmopolitan legal framework. There is a growing awareness that what is right and wrong in times of armed conflict can today only be identified by reference to international humanitarian law *and* international human rights law.[3] Developments in law, policy, state practice and jurisprudence confirm that considerations of human rights have a place in regulating matters of armed conflict, in restraining the use of force and in protecting civilians. Self-proclaimed ideals of military professionalism and attempts to court the "hearts and minds" of those who have to bear the brunt of warfare can only sound hollow in comparison: those who have a (human) right to claim are not in need of mercy. Applying human rights in armed conflict is thus a threefold shift: a shift of ethos from a benevolent humanitarianism towards individual human rights; a shift of policy which allows human rights with their universal appeal and focus on individual rights to reflect the concerns and demands of stakeholders other than governments and the military; and a shift of law which critically questions the regulatory framework for armed conflicts from the perspective of international human rights law.

Retrospectively, the complementarity of international humanitarian law and international human rights law is obvious since 1948/49. All legal texts on war adopted since then have had an eye on human rights, and some have explicitly sought to connect the two worlds. Since the 1970s, the convergence of human rights and humanitarian law is no longer a construct of legal theory or an academic exercise but has become a substantial intersection, as demonstrated by the pronouncements of the International Court of Justice (ICJ) on the continued application of human rights; the inclusion of human rights law in humanitarian documents and of humanitarian norms in human rights documents; the litigation of human rights in armed conflict before international human rights commissions and courts; the monitoring of human rights and humanitarian law by UN human rights bodies and the Security Council; the confluence of human rights and humanitarian law in international criminal law; the identification of the interplay of human rights and humanitarian law in the International Committee of the Red Cross (ICRC)'s study on customary humanitarian law; the use of human rights and humanitarian law in civil society advocacy; and the emergence of broad, albeit not uniform, state practice which allows the application of human rights in armed conflict. Human rights have found a place in armed conflict alongside humanitarian law and there is indeed "no going back to a complete separation of the two realms"[4] as a matter of law and policy.

At the same time, the interplay of human rights and humanitarian law is still not sufficiently well understood in theory and practice and in need of further clarification.

[2] See Yves Sandoz, "Le demi-siècle des Conventions de Genève" (1999) 81 (834) *International Review of the Red Cross* 260.

[3] See Hans-Joachim Heintze, "Fortentwicklung des humanitären Völkerrechts durch den Menschenrechtsschutz" in Hans-Joachim Heintze and Knut Ipsen (eds.), *Heutige bewaffnete Konflikte als Herausforderungen an das humanitäre Völkerrecht* (Berlin: Springer, 2011), p. 165.

[4] Cordula Droege, "Elective Affinities? Human Rights and Humanitarian Law" (2008) 90(871) *International Review of the Red Cross* 548.

The dominant idea of *lex specialis*, however, is not an adequate device for explaining this relationship. Despite its seductive appeal as a purported means of legal logic it has, in the decades in which it has been invoked (on the basis of the ICJ's Advisory Opinions in the *Nuclear Weapons* and *Wall* cases), not allowed the meaningful, consistent and predictable clarification of the complementary application of human rights and humanitarian law. Ultimately, the very idea of complementarity is not compatible with the principle of *lex specialis derogat legi generali*, because the latter is about prevalence and not coherence. There is no relationship of "general" versus "special" which allows the meaningful application of the principle: both human rights and humanitarian law are special fields of law which can complement each other, and each of them can be "special," given the circumstances. The principle of *lex specialis* is an artificial solution for a real problem and has effectively only served to argue for the exclusivity of humanitarian law and to keep human rights at bay, where the search should instead have been for their complementary application to achieve the highest possible level of protection of individuals.

Instead, the overall goal must be to allow the mutual interpretation of human rights and humanitarian law with a view towards ensuring such a maximum protection as the guiding principle. This will preserve the systemic coherence of international law while at the same time guaranteeing operational clarity. There is no quick fix for this difficult task and no overall convincing theory which ensures the consistency of human rights and humanitarian law as expressed in their respective goals, values and objectives while still respecting existing differences between the two legal frameworks. The interpretative aim, however, must not be to search for prevalence but to ensure systemic coherence.

Such an interpretative framework needs to be guided by the idea of maximum protection through the norm(s) which are most favourable to the concerned individual(s). It presumes that it is the intent of states parties to instruments of humanitarian law and human rights law alike to be bound by the highest possible standard with regard to the protection of individuals in times of armed conflicts and to use international humanitarian law and human rights law to this end. The complementarity of human rights and humanitarian law must be understood not as a static parallelism of norms but as their active interplay and mutual influence and as a process geared towards this policy goal.

Whether a graduated interpretative approach which accepts, as a matter of principle, the application of human rights in armed conflicts and adjusts the application of norms, depending on their association with situations of "war-fighting" and "law enforcement," is a way forward remains to be seen. Such an approach reflects the (understandable) concern for preserving the integrity and operability of humanitarian law. It is argued that where situations of armed conflict conform to "war-fighting," such as "in combat" or on the "battlefield," (more) humanitarian law should apply, while in situations which resemble law enforcement operations, i.e., in situations of occupation and peace operations but also when individuals are detained in armed conflict or find themselves otherwise "in the hands of the enemy," (more) human rights law should be relevant. Ultimately, it must be feared that such an approach allows defining situations at will, depending on the distance to the "battlefield," and similar rickety constructions which are likely to collapse under closer scrutiny. It seems more appropriate to understand human rights as applicable in all situations of armed conflict rather than to create a *cordon sanitaire* to shield those parts of humanitarian law which deal with the use of force from the influence of human rights.

This, in turn, means arguing for a human rights-based approach to *jus in bello* as the more suitable way forward. Such an approach rests on three pillars: first, it understands the law of armed conflict as a regulatory framework which comprises international humanitarian law and international human rights law in a complementary manner under the prerogative of solving their relationship through the idea of maximum protection to achieve systemic coherence of the law. Secondly, it means that human rights (in the form of international human rights law) become integrated into this emerging new *jus in bello* (and thus also in the established law of armed conflict/humanitarian law) not as a concurrent or competing set of rules, but as a foundational normative value. And thirdly, it means that as such a foundational value international human rights law defines the operational direction and future development of the law in a human rights-based *jus in bello*. The debate on human rights in armed conflict is a challenging long-term transformational process in search of "the proper balance between security/military needs and individual liberty in light of modern standards."[5]

The contours of such a transformative interpretation of the term "humanity" are uncertain, and not all its consequences are foreseeable.[6] There remains considerable scepticism in many quarters as to whether such a transformation is at all feasible, together with concern about the repercussions it might have on the very idea of human rights.[7] One expectation is that the reliance on human rights will allow for a more graduated use of force which, in turn, will have a considerable impact on foundational elements of the law of armed conflict.[8] Another consequence feared by some is that human rights may have to leave behind their legacy as the pacifist peace project of the post-Second World War era and instead provide guidance for the humane use of force in war, which is obviously a contradictory term.[9] For some, this might ultimately lead to the "philosophical aberration of war with a human face."[10] Such arguments need to be taken seriously, but they could also be used against international humanitarian law, and indeed against any attempt to employ law to mitigate the consequences of war. They fail to convince for reasons of principle as well as on pragmatic grounds.

[5] Louise Doswald-Beck, "Background Paper" in University Centre for International Humanitarian Law, *Expert Meeting on the Supervision of the Lawfulness of Detention During Armed Conflict* (2004), p. 9, available at www.geneva-academy.ch/docs/expert-meetings/2004/4rapport_detention.pdf (last accessed 15 April 2014).

[6] It has rightly been said that "systemic coherence is not the hallmark of this emerging human rights law of armed conflict," Guglielmo Verdirame, "Human Rights in Wartime: A Framework for Analysis" (2008) 6 *European Human Rights Law Review* 690.

[7] See Christopher Greenwood, "Rights at the Frontier: Protection of the Individual in Time of War" in Barry A.K. Rider (ed.), *Law at the Centre: The Institute of Advanced Legal Studies at Fifty* (Dordrecht: Kluwer, 1999), p. 293, who argues that human rights lawyers should rather "abandon . . . any notion that the broad principles of human rights law can be used to set aside the mass of painstakingly negotiated compromises of the laws of war and transform the nature of warfare."

[8] See Daniel Thürer, *International Humanitarian Law: Theory, Practice, Context* (The Hague: Hague Academy of International Law, 2011), p. 71.

[9] See William Schabas, "*Lex specialis*? Belts and Suspenders? The Parallel Operation of Human Rights Law and the Law of Armed Conflict, and the Conundrum of Jus ad Bellum" (2007) 40(2) *Israel Law Review* 608.

[10] Verdirame, "Human Rights in Wartime" (n. 6) 692.

Quite to the contrary, the call for applying human rights in armed conflicts is in tune with, reflects and impacts upon larger transformation processes in international law. The idea that international law is on a trajectory towards a "humanization," "individualization" and "constitutionalization" describes the transformation of the law from a set of inter-state agreements towards a normative framework which accommodates the human being as the ultimate beneficiary of any law. In such a view, international law is ultimately geared towards a legal order which protects and empowers individual human beings in a "humanitarian" way in the broadest sense, accommodates basic norms for inter- and intra-state behaviour in a constitutionalist sense, and provides for human security rather than (inter-)state security. All of this corresponds to and reflects the need to apply international human rights law in armed conflict. In a constitutionalized and people-centred view of the international legal order, the law of war cannot isolate itself from human rights as a cross-cutting issue, and the interests of the (potential) victims of acts of war need to dictate the applicable rules, akin to how the interest of the state, and particularly the interests of large military powers, have informed the law of armed conflict. A human security perspective of the law of armed conflict, in particular, accommodates human rights, leads to measuring military advantage differently than under current humanitarian rules, and guides the use of force for community-oriented purposes along stricter lines than does the present law of armed conflict.

More pragmatically, the rationale for applying human rights in armed conflict can be found in considerations of necessity and utility because the complementary application of human rights and humanitarian law fills gaps in the protection and allows humanitarian norms to be interpreted in light of human rights standards without giving up the tested operational framework of humanitarian law in situations of armed conflict and occupation. Examples of this have been discussed throughout this study. Even the paradigmatic differences between the right to life under human rights law and the permissive approach of humanitarian law towards the use of deadly force are gradual rather than absolute. Obviously, the principles of proportionality and necessity which are used to avoid arbitrary killing and collateral damage under the respective legal frameworks differ. The necessity test under human rights law is absolute and allows the use of deadly force only as a last resort, while the killing of enemy combatants is lawful *qua* their status, and injury and death inflicted upon civilians as a result of acts of war fall under a contingent necessity which factors in military necessity.

But the idea of proportionality in humanitarian law is not incapable of absorbing, within limits, a human rights proportionality which may introduce additional stricter requirements for the use of deadly force, particularly in situations of internal conflicts, with a view towards a heightened protection for civilians. Under a human rights-based approach, such restraint in the use of force does not solely flow from utilitarian and tactical considerations of winning the "hearts and minds" of locals but reflects individual entitlements and corresponding duties. Even the permissiveness of humanitarian law with regard to killing enemy soldiers can be questioned within a human rights-based framework, as it corresponds with larger trends of modern warfare and the changing perception of the rights and duties of combatants, which cast doubt over the strictly status-based approach of humanitarian law.

The extra-territorial application of international human rights treaty law in situations of armed conflict – a prerequisite for any further debate on human rights in armed conflict whenever military operations take place outside a state's borders – can be accommodated within international human rights treaty law. It is accepted in jurisprudence and seems to be increasingly accepted in state practice (save the continuing objections of the United States and Israel, in particular). As a matter of principle, armed forces thus carry their state's human rights obligations with them when acting abroad. Beyond this statement of principle, however, the contours and consequences of the extra-territorial application of international human rights treaty law have yet to be delineated. Even though jurisprudence and case law are not overly helpful in this regard due to their ambiguity, the respective questions will ultimately have to be resolved on a case-by-case basis.

While the perception of jurisdiction as the exercise of control over persons remains the preferred view to understand the limits of the extra-territorial application of human rights, a capability approach seems to emerge which prevents states from deliberately lowering their human rights standard when acting abroad and at the same time taking into account the realities of armed conflict and occupation. Such an approach needs to reconcile the universal reach of human rights, the moral and legal demand to avoid double standards and the indivisibility of human rights as positive and negative obligations, with the capacity of a state to adhere to such obligations in the variegated contexts of armed conflict and occupation in a complementary fashion with international humanitarian law and in an operationally feasible manner. The presently prevailing view that human rights law applies whenever physical control is exercised over persons (for example, in detention), while the same is not the case if such control is exercised outside military facilities or in military operations or when force is projected over greater distances, is unsatisfactory. It can only be the beginning and not the end of the exploration of the boundaries of the extra-territorial application of human rights in armed conflicts.

In contrast to the importance of this question, the derogation provisions in international human rights treaties only pretend to be an obstacle to the full application of human rights in armed conflict. The idea and law of derogation (i.e., the suspension of certain rights when the life of the nation is in danger) remain under-theorized, over-rated and of limited practical importance. While derogation provides a firm legal argument that all human rights (other than those derogated) continue to apply in armed conflict, the unclear nature of an emergency under international human rights treaties, the strict substantial and procedural requirements of derogation, the existence of human rights conventions without such clauses, and the abandonment of such clauses in recent human rights treaties mean that derogation is in practice less significant an obstacle to the application of human rights in armed conflicts than is usually thought.

The view that humanitarian law and human rights law are incompatible in their legal structure because the former is about state obligations and the latter about individual rights also does not withstand closer scrutiny. Notwithstanding the existing differences as a matter of secondary procedural rights, both legal regimes recognize rights and corresponding duties, and humanitarian law contains individual entitlements which can be clustered as obligations to protect, respect and fulfil humanitarian norms. *De lege lata* as well as in light of larger developments of a re-orientation of the matrix of individual rights, obligations and responsibilities *de lege ferenda*, the differences between humanitarian "obligations" and human "rights" seem exaggerated.

At the same time, it is true that the individualistic framework of human rights with its emphasis on the human person introduces a different language and law into humanitarian law's concern with status and group association. This, too, may be a force of change and not merely a concurrence of different legal frameworks. It may mean revisiting the value of individual lives as a matter of morality and law under the law of armed conflict. This is not meant to, and will not, challenge the prerogative of humanitarian law to protect civilians through the important principle of distinction. But a human rights-based understanding of humanitarian rules cannot gloss over the way in which different values are assigned to lives in armed conflict. The strictly status-based approach of humanitarian law is certainly challenged by human rights, which see the individual less as an object but rather as a rights-holder under international law.

The operational consequences of the application of human rights in armed conflicts need yet to be discerned. So far, the debate on practical matters seems grounded more in fears of unforeseen and burdensome changes than in a sound rational analysis of operational and practical consequences. The concerns that human rights law in armed conflict will confuse operations and strain resources and put burdens on armed forces; that such a development leaves them unprepared through legal and operational training in these matters; that a human rights-based approach will not be accepted because it is incompatible with the self-perception of soldiers; and that it will restrict military operations and expose troops to greater risks need all to be taken very seriously. At the same time, most of them are operational concerns to be tackled with operational responses, rather than a rejection of human rights in armed conflict as a matter of principle.

The changing character of what once was termed "war" and the resulting dynamics of war and law are the other major driving force of the debate on human rights in armed conflict, next to the shift of the humanitarian discourse along the lines of human rights. The emergence of so-called "new wars," the continued blurring of the boundaries between war and peace, and the intricate interplay of the ideas of war-fighting and law enforcement are at the heart of the suggestion that human rights need to have a place in armed conflict. It is somewhat paradoxical that while we acknowledge the emergence of post-modern wars to which established categories of nationality, territory and politics can hardly be applied, and speak of hybrid wars which cut through the conventional criteria of public and private space, state and non-state regulation and formal and informal responses to violence, we cling on to a nineteenth century conceptualization of war and law. There are, of course, good reasons for this; after all, international humanitarian law – built on these foundations – is the only law there is.

But war and law are both dynamic, and the changing character of war necessitates the application of international human rights law as much as the application of human rights law changes the image of war. Today's wars are fought between, within and across nation states. They are not about conquest but about risk management, law enforcement and international policing. Such peace and human security missions are cosmopolitan responses to crisis and violence in a globalized environment in which human rights must have their place. Or, alternatively, they are asymmetric forms of violence which mesh crime with economic opportunities, "privatized" and "civilianized" wars in which warlords, criminal organizations and terrorist networks, as well as private military and security contractors, replace the state's monopoly of warfare and which affect civilians disproportionately. These conflicts, too, cannot be understood along the lines of humanitarian law alone.

In such situations, the concepts of war and peace, together with the images and laws of war-fighting and law enforcement become blurred. As a consequence, disagreements and misunderstandings between advocates of a human rights-oriented law enforcement paradigm and a security-oriented armed conflict paradigm stand often at the centre of the debate on human rights in armed conflict. But it is obvious that all such forms of armed conflicts cannot (solely) be regulated by international humanitarian law with its conventional typology of conflicts and imagery of warfare. This is not to deny the law its place as a protective force, and even less allow it to be replaced by self-designed new rules or allow legal black holes, as the United States did in their "War against Terrorism." Rather, it means that such conflicts are not only susceptible to the complementary application of international human rights law, but that there is a necessity to rely on human rights law in all of them.

The associated question of how to oblige non-state armed groups to adhere to international human rights law (as opposed to humanitarian law, which captures them as a party to the conflict) remains an important matter. For the critics of human rights in armed conflicts, as well as for those concerned about the practical adherence to humanitarian norms, such as the ICRC, this is a serious concern, and rightly so. At the same time, the ability of humanitarian law to effectively ensure adherence of non-state armed groups to the law seems exaggerated, just as the ability of human rights law to do the same is under-estimated. Non-state armed groups are often, in the practice of the Security Council and the Human Rights Council even routinely, called upon to adhere to humanitarian law *and* human rights law. The legal grounds for such calls are gradually better understood and making such groups comply with humanitarian obligations is a problem which humanitarian law and human rights law share. While humanitarian law is, as a matter of law and through the involvement of the ICRC, better suited to reach out to such groups, there is a growing awareness that both humanitarian law and human rights law impose obligations on non-state actors, even though the resulting challenges and pitfalls need to be considered very carefully.

The importance of human rights in situations of occupation is particularly obvious. The shift in the practice of occupation from the short-term "trusteeship" model, which ends with a formal peace agreement, towards occupations of various sorts not foreseen under the law (particularly long-term occupations and transformative occupations with the explicit or implicit aim to bring about change in the political structure and society of the occupied territory) is a challenge in law and practice. Human rights law matters in such situations, because it reflects the relationship between the Occupying Power as a temporary holder of authority over the population, and because it informs the Occupying Power in greater detail on the scope of its obligations. But even though the application of human rights can nowhere be argued more easily than in situations of occupation, it is also nowhere more complex in practice, given the matrix of applicable laws and the contradictory demands of reconciling a law enforcement approach in "peaceful" times and spaces of occupation with a "war-fighting" approach where hostilities persist. Even so, in the grander project of reconciling these norms into a consolidated *jus post bellum* which reflects considerations of fairness and justice, punishment of violations of the law, individual reparations and sanctions, justice and reconciliation, re-establishing sustainable peace, and people-centred governance under the rule of law within a fragile and violent environment, international human rights law obviously has to have a prominent place.

The application of international human rights law in armed conflicts also brings with it the institutional framework of international human rights law. The UN Human Rights

Council, the UN treaty bodies and the UN High Commissioner for Human Rights, as well as the Inter-American Commission and Court of Human Rights, the European Court of Human Rights and the African Commission on Human and Peoples' Rights have been confronted with situations of armed conflict and have responded to them in different ways. UN human rights bodies, first and foremost the UN Human Rights Council, now regularly monitor the law in armed conflict, i.e., human rights law and humanitarian law in a complementary fashion, albeit in a broad policy-oriented manner. The Human Rights Council's special procedures are of particular importance in this regard. The increasing use of fact-finding missions and commissions of inquiry by the Council makes such missions the current standard format of investigation and monitoring, and they have effectively displaced the dysfunctional Humanitarian Fact Finding Commission under humanitarian law. The UN High Commissioner for Human Rights, too, has partly taken over the function of good offices which the Humanitarian Fact-Finding Commission does not exercise, even though it remains affected by problems of inconsistency, funding and expertise. But even though the missions of inquiry and fact-finding missions of the Human Rights Council have established facts and recommended action and have attracted considerable attention and media coverage, they are plagued by shortcomings inherent in the work of the Council. The establishment of a permanent UN Commission of Inquiry or similar measures might be a way out and strengthen the interplay of human rights and humanitarian law.

In contrast, the Universal Periodic Review (UPR) of the Human Rights Council, which contains a reporting obligation on international humanitarian law, has proven to be next to useless in practice when it comes to scrutinizing humanitarian obligations. The next cycle of reporting obligations under this procedure could well be used to reflect on this problem and discuss whether a consistent and permanent reporting obligation for humanitarian obligations should be envisaged under the UPR or not. UN treaty bodies are only partly performing such a task in their examination of state reports, and only the Human Rights Committee and the Committee on the Rights of the Child have developed a sufficiently sound basis in this regard. Individual complaints on violations to treaty bodies on war-related issues also play a comparatively minor role before UN treaty bodies. One could think of ways to strengthen the treaty bodies with regard to monitoring situations of armed conflict, for example, by instituting on-site visits or establishing special monitoring, reporting, communication or complaints procedures for matters of humanitarian and human rights law. Such proposals are easily made, but they need also to be seen in light of resource constraints, workload and other feasibility considerations, and need to fit into ongoing reform processes so as not to lead to a normative overstretch.

In contrast to the way in which UN human rights bodies monitor adherence to the law, regional human rights courts and commissions allow consideration of human rights in armed conflicts from a victim's perspective. The involvement of the European Court of Human Rights, in particular, in such situations has made human rights in armed conflict also a litigation-driven phenomenon. From such a perspective, the law in armed conflict is no longer an inter-state affair but a profoundly individual matter. The emphasis of courts on procedural rights of investigation, transparency and accountability in military operations and their ability to provide a remedy for war-related damages could introduce important aspects into armed conflicts which the law so far has largely failed to cover.

At present, however, no clear guidance can be inferred from the jurisprudence on the interplay of human rights and humanitarian law. Overall, the impact of their deliberations and decisions has been limited. The Inter-American Commission's decisions in cases such as *La Tablada* and others still mark the outer limits to which human rights bodies are willing to go. In contrast, the European Court ignores humanitarian law altogether and seems to construct a human rights law of (internal) armed conflict which, at least at present, cannot convince.

Given the lack of enforcement procedures under humanitarian law (notwithstanding recent attempts to create a sort of reporting obligation for states parties to the Geneva Conventions), it seems advisable to allow human rights bodies to stand in for this lack of enforcement as the second best alternative. This could provide guidance to states, allow a more informed debate on human rights in armed conflict in concrete situations, put pressure on violators of the law, make humanitarian obligations better known and help to ensure the systemic coherence of the law. In any case, war victims are likely to continue knocking on the doors of human rights courts, which is more than understandable in light of the persistent failure of humanitarian law to provide individual remedies.

This unwillingness of states to effectively reaffirm and develop international humanitarian law is another explanation for the increased reliance on international human rights. For most advocates of human rights in armed conflict, the debate is about the role of human rights law as much as about the development of humanitarian law. Their concern is that the law needs to keep up with changing circumstances and larger societal and global developments and must be prevented from becoming marginalized or meaningless. And finally, the debate on human rights in armed conflict is also about legitimacy. States, and particularly democratic states, find it increasingly difficult to argue for higher standards of behaviour for those under their jurisdiction at home and lower standards for those abroad by invoking the rhetoric and law of war. Such a differentiation seems ever less tenable, even when it is compatible with the law and spirit of humanitarian law. The importance which democratic societies attach to the rule of law and human rights cannot leave the law of armed conflict completely untouched.

Overall, the history of the law of war is driven by a move from *raison d'État* to *raison d'humanité*.[11] Humanitarian considerations have supplanted much of the regulatory framework within which states were free to wage wars against each other as a means of politics in disregard of individual human dignity. What we witness at present is the next move from *raison d'humanité* to *raison de droit de l'homme* in situations of armed conflict: the inclusion of the individual, inalienable and inherent legal entitlement to human dignity of everyone in situations where armed force is being used. This seems only appropriate; after all, we live in the age of rights.[12] This, in itself, is unlikely to change the realities of warfare. But the combined moral pull of the global human rights discourse and the pragmatic push of human rights supervisory mechanisms, together with the increased influence of civil society actors may, at least in situations of armed conflicts which are no longer wars in the traditional sense, provide a direction for the development of tomorrow's *jus in bello*.

Perhaps such a perspective can give new meaning to Hersch Lauterpacht's famous dictum that "[i]f international law is in some ways at the vanishing point of law, the law

[11] Antônio Augusto, *Cançado Trindade, International Law of Humankind: Towards a New Jus Gentium* (Leiden: Nijhoff, 2010), p. 528.

[12] See Louis Henkin, *The Age of Rights* (New York: Columbia University Press, 1990).

of war is perhaps even more conspicuously at the vanishing point of international law."[13] He referred to the elusive character of the law. In geometry, however, the vanishing point is the point in the distance where two seemingly parallel lines converge so as to confirm that they have, in fact, never really been parallel but were always meant to meet, even if only in the distance. And the vanishing point also functions as a point of reference which allows the viewer to judge the radius of two verges (of a road, for example) and thus set the optimum speed and track to ensure a safe ride. Such a more positive reading of Lauterpacht's statement, it is hoped, may emerge from the preceding analysis of the role of human rights in armed conflicts and their interplay with international humanitarian law.

[13] Hersch Lauterpacht, "The Problem of the Revision of the Law of War" (1952) 29 *British Yearbook of International Law* 382.

BIBLIOGRAPHY

Books

Alston, Philip, "The Commission on Human Rights" in Philip Alston (ed.), *The United Nations and Human Rights: A Critical Appraisal* (Oxford: Clarendon, 1992)

Axworthy, Lloyd, *Navigating a New World: Canada's Global Future* (Toronto: Alfred A. Knopf, 2003)

Babiker, M.A., *Application of International Humanitarian and Human Rights Law to the Armed Conflict of the Sudan: Complementary or Mutually Exclusive Regimes?* (Antwerp: Intersentia, 2007)

Benvenisti, Eyal, *The International Law of Occupation* (Oxford: Oxford University Press, 2011)

Best, Geoffrey, *Humanity in Warfare: The Modern History of the International Law of Armed Conflict* (New York: Columbia University Press, 1980)

War and Law since 1945 (Oxford: Clarendon, 1994)

Blum, Gabriella and Heymann, Philip B., *Laws, Outlaws, and Terrorists: Lessons from the War on Terrorism* (Cambridge MA: MIT Press, 2010)

Bluntschli, Johann Caspar, *Das moderne Kriegsrecht der civilisirten Staaten als Rechtsbuch dargestellt* (Nördlingen: Beck, 1866)

Das moderne Völkerrecht der civilisierten Staaten als Rechtsbuch dargestellt (Nördlingen: Beck, 1868)

Bothe, Michael, Partsch, Karl-Josef and Solf, Waldemar A., *New Rules for Victims of Armed Conflicts: Commentary on the Two 1977 Protocols Additional to the Geneva Conventions of 1949* (The Hague: Nijhoff, 1982)

Byers, Michael, *War Law* (New York: Grove Press, 2005)

Cameron, Lindsey and Chetail, Vincent, *Privatizing War: Private Military and Security Companies under Public International Law* (Cambridge: Cambridge University Press, 2013)

Cançado Trindade, Antonio Augusto, *International Law of Humankind: Towards a New Jus Gentium* (Leiden: Nijhoff, 2010)

Cassesse, Antonio, *International Criminal Law* (2nd edn., Oxford: Oxford University Press, 2008)

Coker, Christopher, *War in an Age of Risk* (Cambridge: Polity, 2009)

Commission on Human Security, *Human Security Now* (New York: Commission on Human Security, 2003)

Detrick, Sharon, *A Commentary on the United Nations Convention on the Rights of the Child* (The Hague: Nijhoff, 1999)

Detter, Ingrid, *The Law of War* (Cambridge: Cambridge University Press, 2000)

Dinstein, Yoram, *The International Law of Belligerent Occupation* (Cambridge: Cambridge University Press, 2009)

The Conduct of Hostilities under the Law of International Armed Conflict (2nd edn., Cambridge: Cambridge University Press, 2010)

Donnelly, Jack, *International Human Rights: Dilemmas in World Politics* (Boulder: Westview, 2007)

Doswald-Beck, Louise, *Human Rights in Times of Conflict and Terrorism* (Oxford: Oxford University Press, 2011)

Forsythe, David, *The Humanitarians: The International Committee of the Red Cross* (Cambridge: Cambridge University Press, 2005)

Gasser, Hans-Peter, *Humanitäres Völkerrecht: eine Einführung* (Baden-Baden: Nomos, 2007)

Gat, Azar, *The Origins of Military Thought from the Enlightenment to Clausewitz* (Oxford: Clarendon, 1989)

Glendon, Mary Ann, *A World Made New: Eleanor Roosevelt and the Universal Declaration of Human Rights* (New York: Random House, 2002)

Green, Leslie C., *The Contemporary Law of Armed Conflict* (Manchester: Manchester University Press, 2008)

Griffin, James, *On Human Rights* (Oxford: Oxford University Press, 2008)

Gross, Oren and Ní Aoláin, Fionnuala, *Law in Times of Crisis: Emergency Powers in Theory and Practice* (Cambridge: Cambridge University Press, 2006)

Grotius, Hugo, *On the Law of War and Peace* (1625, edited and annotated by Stephen C. Neff, Cambridge: Cambridge University Press, 2012)

Henckaerts, Jean-Marie and Doswald-Beck, Louise, *Customary International Humanitarian Law*, vol. I, *Rules* and vol. II, *Practice* (Cambridge: Cambridge University Press, 2005)

Henkin, Louis, *The Age of Rights* (New York: Columbia University Press, 1990)

Ignatieff, Michael, *The Warrior's Honor: Ethnic War and the Modern Conscience* (New York: Henry Hold, 1998)

International Commission of Jurists, *States of Emergency: Their Impact on Human Rights* (Geneva: International Commission of Jurists, 1983)

International Institute of Humanitarian Law, *The Manual on the Law of Non-International Armed Conflict* (Sanremo: International Institute of Humanitarian Law, 2006)

Isenberg, David, *Shadow Force: Private Security Contractors in Iraq* (Westport, CT: Praeger, 2009)

Johann, Christian, *Menschenrechte im bewaffneten Konflikt. Zur Anwendbarkeit der Europäischen Menschenrechtskonvention und des Internationalen Pakts über bürgerliche und politische Rechte auf Kriegshandlungen* (Berlin: Berliner Wissenschaftsverlag, 2012)

Kaldor, Mary, *Human Security: Reflections on Globalization and Intervention* (Cambridge: Polity, 2007)
New and Old Wars: Organized Violence in a Global Era (3rd edn., Cambridge: Polity, 2012)

Kälin, Walter, *Human Rights in Times of Occupation: The Case of Kuwait* (Bern: Stämpfli, 1994)

Kälin, Walter and Künzli, Jörg, *The Law of International Human Rights Protection* (Oxford: Oxford University Press, 2009)

Kalshoven, Frits and Zegveld, Liesbeth, *Constraints on the Waging of War: An Introduction to International Humanitarian Law* (4th edn., Cambridge: Cambridge University Press, 2011)

Katanayagi, Mary, *Human Rights Functions of United Nations Peacekeeping Operations* (The Hague: Nijhoff, 2002)

Keen, Maurice Hugh, *The Laws of War in the Late Middle Ages* (London: Routledge and Kegan Paul, 1965)

Kennedy, David, *Of War and Law* (Princeton, NJ: Princeton University Press, 2006)

Kettemann, Matthias C., *The Future of Individuals in International Law: Lessons from International Internet Law* (The Hague: Eleven, 2013)

Klabbers, Jan, Peters, Anne and Ulfstein, Geir, *The Constitutionalization of International Law* (Oxford: Oxford University Press, 2009)

Kolb, Robert and Hyde, Richard, *An Introduction to the International Law of Armed Conflict* (Oxford: Hart, 2008)

Kuper, Jenny, *International Law Concerning Child Civilians in Armed Conflict* (Oxford: Clarendon, 1997)

Lemarchand, René, *The Dynamics of Violence in Central Africa* (Philadelphia, PA: University of Pennsylvania Press, 2009)

Locke, John, *The Second Treatise of Civil Government* (1690, reprinted with an introduction by Joseph Carrig, New York: Barns and Nobles, 2008)

Lubell, Noam, *Extraterritorial Use of Force against Non-State Actors* (Oxford: Oxford University Press, 2010)

McCoubrey, Hilaire, *International Humanitarian Law: Modern Developments in the Limitation of Warfare* (Aldershot: Ashgate, 1998)

McCoubrey, Hilaire and White, Nigel D., *International Law and Armed Conflict* (Aldershot: Ashgate, 1992)

Meron, Theodor, *Human Rights in Internal Strife: Their International Protection* (Cambridge: Grotius, 1987)

Human Rights and Humanitarian Norms as Customary Law (Oxford: Oxford University Press, 1989)

Henry's Wars and Shakespeare's Laws: Perspectives on the Law of War in the Later Middle Ages (Oxford: Clarendon, 1993)

Bloody Constraint: War and Chivalry in Shakespeare (New York: Oxford University Press, 1998)

The Humanization of International Law (Leiden: Nijhoff, 2006)

Mertus, Julie, *The United Nations and Human Rights: A Guide for A New Era* (2nd edn., London: Routledge, 2009)

Milanovic, Marko, *Extraterritorial Application of Human Rights Treaties: Law, Principles, and Policy* (Oxford: Oxford University Press, 2011)

Moir, Lindsay, *The Law of Internal Armed Conflict* (Cambridge: Cambridge University Press, 2002)

Murray, Rachel, *The African Commission on Human and Peoples' Rights and International Law* (Oxford: Hart, 2000)

Neff, Stephen C., *War and the Law of Nations: A General History* (Cambridge: Cambridge University Press, 2005)

Normand, Roger and Zaidi, Sarah, *Human Rights at the UN: The Political History of Universal Justice* (Bloomington, IN: Indiana University Press, 2008)

Nowak, Manfred, *UN Covenant on Civil and Political Rights: CCPR Commentary* (2nd edn., Kehl: Engel, 2005)

O'Keefe, Roger, *The Protection of Cultural Property in Armed Conflict* (Cambridge: Cambridge University Press, 2006)

Oberleitner, Gerd, *Global Human Rights Institutions: Between Remedy and Ritual* (Cambridge: Polity, 2007)

Oraá, Jaime, *Human Rights in States of Emergency in International Law* (Oxford: Clarendon, 1992)

Parlett, Kate, *The Individual in the International Legal System: Continuity and Change in International Law* (Cambridge: Cambridge University Press, 2011)

Pauwelyn, Joost, *Conflict of Norms in Public International Law: How WTO Rules Relate to Other Rules of International Law* (Cambridge: Cambridge University Press, 2003)

Pictet, Jean (ed.), *Commentary on the First Geneva Convention for the Amelioration of the Condition of the Wounded and Sick in Armed Forces in the Field* (Geneva: International Committee on the Red Cross, 1952)

Commentary on the Fourth Geneva Convention Relative to the Protection of Civilian Persons in Time of War (Geneva: International Committee of the Red Cross, 1952)

Pictet, Jean, *The Principles of International Humanitarian Law* (Geneva: International Committee of the Red Cross, 1967)

Development and Principles of International Humanitarian Law (Dordrecht: Nijhoff, 1985)

Provost, René, *International Human Rights and Humanitarian Law* (Cambridge: Cambridge University Press, 2002)

Ramcharan, Bertrand, *Contemporary Human Rights Ideas* (New York: Routledge, 2008)

The Human Rights Council (Abingdon: Routledge, 2011)

Rehman, Javaid, *International Human Rights Law* (Edinburgh: Pearson, 2010)

Reyntjens, Filip, *The Great African War: Congo and Regional Geopolitics, 1996–2006* (Cambridge: Cambridge University Press, 2011)

Roberts, Adam and Guelff, Richard, *Documents on the Law of War* (3rd edn., Oxford: Oxford University Press, 2000)

Rogers, A.P.V., *Law on the Battlefield* (3rd edn., Manchester: Manchester University Press, 2012)

Rousseau, Jean-Jacques, *The Social Contract*, Book I (1762, translated and introduced by Maurice Cranston, London: Penguin, 1968)

Rowe, Peter, *The Impact of Human Rights Law on Armed Forces* (Cambridge: Cambridge University Press, 2006)

Sandoz, Yves, Swinarski, Christophe and Zimmermann, Bruno (eds.), *Commentary on the Additional Protocols of 8 June 1977 to the Geneva Conventions of 12 August 1949* (Geneva: Nijhoff, 1987)

Schäfer, Bernhard, *Zum Verhältnis Menschenrechte und humanitäres Völkerrecht. Zugleich ein Beitrag zur extraterritorialen Geltung von Menschenrechtsverträgen* (Potsdam: Universitätsverlag Potsdam, 2006)

Seiderman, Ian D., *Hierarchy in International Law: The Human Rights Dimension* (Antwerpen: Intersentia, 2001)

Shaw, Malcolm, *International Law* (6th edn., Cambridge: Cambridge University Press, 2008)

Sigg, Alain, *International Human Rights Law, International Humanitarian Law, Refugee Law: Geneva from Early Origins to the 21st Century* (Berne: Swiss Federal Department of Foreign Affairs, 2003)

Singh, Nagendra, *Enforcement of Human Rights in Peace and War and the Future of Humanity* (Dordrecht: Nijhoff, 1986)

Sivakumaran, Sandesh, *The Law of Non-International Armed Conflict* (Oxford: Oxford University Press, 2012)

Smith, Rhona K., *Textbook on International Human Rights* (4th edn., Oxford: Oxford University Press, 2010)

Solis, Gary D., *The Law of Armed Conflict* (Cambridge: Cambridge University Press, 2010)

Teitel, Ruti G., *Humanity's Law* (Oxford: Oxford University Press, 2011)

Thürer, Daniel, *International Humanitarian Law: Theory, Practice, Context* (The Hague: Hague Academy of International Law, 2011)

Tomuschat, Christian, *Human Rights between Idealism and Realism* (2nd edn., Oxford: Oxford University Press, 2008)

UK Ministry of Defence, *The Manual of the Law of Armed Conflict* (Oxford: Oxford University Press, 2004)

US Army Marine Corps, *Counterinsurgency Field Manual* (Chicago, IL: University of Chicago Press, 2007)

von Clausewitz, Carl, *On War* (1832, edited and translated by Michael Eliot Howard and Peter Paret, Princeton, NJ: Princeton University Press, 1976)

Weiss, Thomas G., *Humanitarian Intervention* (Cambridge: Polity, 2013)

Yildiz, Kerim and Breau, Susan, *The Kurdish Conflict: International Humanitarian Law and Post-Conflict Mechanisms* (London: Routledge, 2010)

Zegveld, Liesbeth, *Accountability of Armed Opposition Groups in International Law* (Cambridge: Cambridge University Press, 2002)

Zwanenburg, Marten, *Accountability of Peace Support Operations* (Leiden: Nijhoff, 2005)

Articles and book chapters

Abdel-Monem, Tarik, "How Far do the Lawless Areas of Europe Extend? Extraterritorial Application of the European Convention on Human Rights" (2005) 2 *Journal of Transnational Law and Policy* 159–215

Abi-Saab, Georges, "The Specificities of Humanitarian Law" in Christophe Swinarski (ed.), *Studies and Essays on International Humanitarian Law and Red Cross Principles in Honour of Jean Pictet* (The Hague: Nijhoff, 1984), pp. 265–80

Abi-Saab, Rosemary, "Humanitarian Law and Internal Conflicts: The Evolution of Legal Concern" in Astrid J.M. Delissen and Gerard J. Tanja (eds.), *Humanitarian Law of Armed Conflict: Challenges Ahead, Essays in Honour of Frits Kalshoven* (Dordrecht: Nijhoff, 1991), pp. 209–23

Abresch, William, "A Human Rights Law of Internal Armed Conflict: The European Court of Human Rights in Chechnya" (2005) 16 *European Journal of International Law* 741–67

af Jocknick, Chris and Normand, Roger, "The Legitimation of Violence: A Critical History of the Laws of War" (1994) 35(1) *Harvard International Law Journal* 49–95

Alam, Aftab, "The Islamic Concept of Humanitarian Law" in V.S. Mani (ed.), *Handbook of International Humanitarian Law* (New Delhi: Oxford University Press, 2007), pp. 36–45

Aldrich, George H., "Human Rights and Armed Conflict: Conflicting Views" (1973) 67 *American Journal of International Law Proceedings* 141–2

"Human Rights in Armed Conflict: Development of the Law" (1973) 68 *Department of State Bulletin* 876–82

"Some Reflections on the Origins of the 1977 Geneva Protocols" in Christophe Swinarski (ed.), *Studies and Essays on International Humanitarian Law and Red Cross Principles in Honour of Jean Pictet* (The Hague: Nijhoff, 1984), pp. 129–37

"The Laws of War on Land" (2000) 94(1) *American Journal of International Law* 31–41

al-Fallouji, Iqbal, "Pour une thèse plus humaniste de 'tous les droits de l'homme'" in Christophe Swinarski (ed.), *Studies and Essays on International Humanitarian Law and Red Cross Principles in Honour of Jean Pictet* (The Hague: Nijhoff, 1984), pp. 625–33

Alonzo-Maizlish, David, "When Does It End? Problems in the Law of Occupation" in Roberta Arnold and Pierre-Robert Hildbrand (eds.), *International Humanitarian Law and the 21st Century's Conflicts: Changes and Challenges* (Lausanne: Edis, 2005), pp. 98–116

Alston, Philip, Morgan-Foster, Jason and Abresch, William, "The Competence of the UN Human Rights Council and Its Special Procedures in Relation to Armed Conflicts: Extrajudicial Executions in the 'War on Terror'" (2008) 19 *European Journal of International Law* 183–209

Altiparmak, Kerem, "Banković: An Obstacle to the Application of the European Convention on Human Rights in Iraq?" (2004) 9(2) *Journal of Conflict and Security Law* 213–51

An-Na'im, Abdullah Ahmed, "Toward a Universal Doctrine of Reparation for Violations of International Human Rights and Humanitarian Law" (2003) 5(1) *International Law Forum* 27–35

Arai-Takahashi, Yutaka, "Fair Trial Guarantees in Occupied Territory: The Interplay between International Humanitarian Law and Human Rights Law" in Roberta Arnold and Noelle Quénivet (eds.), *International Humanitarian Law and Human Rights Law: Towards a Merger in International Law* (Leiden: Nijhoff, 2008), pp. 449–74

Arnold, Roberta, "Human Rights in Times of Terrorism" (2006) 66(2) *Zeitschrift für ausländisches öffentliches Recht und Völkerrecht* 297–319

"The New War on Terror: Legal Implications under International Humanitarian Law" in Susan C. Breau and Agnieszka Jachec-Neale (eds.), *Testing the Boundaries of International Humanitarian Law* (London: British Institute of International and Comparative Law, 2006), pp. 85–112

"Terrorism in International Humanitarian Law and Human Rights Law" in Roberta Arnold and Noelle Quénivet (eds.), *International Humanitarian Law and Human Rights Law: Towards a Merger in International Law* (Leiden: Nijhoff, 2008), pp. 475–97

Axworthy, Lloyd, "Human Security and Global Governance: Putting People First" (2001) 7(1) *Global Governance* 19–23

Baldwin, Clive and Morel, Cynthia, "Group Rights" in Malcolm Evans and Rachel Murray (eds.), *The African Charter of Human and Peoples' Rights the System in Practice, 1986–2006* (2nd edn., Cambridge: Cambridge University Press, 2008), pp. 244–88

Balendra, Natasha, "Defining Armed Conflict" (2008) 29(6) *Cardozo Law Review* 2461–516

"International Human Rights Law and International Humanitarian Law: Alternative Frameworks for Interaction" in Christoffer C. Eriksen and Marius Emberland (eds.), *The New International Law* (The Hague: Nijhoff, 2010), pp. 117–37

Bangerter, Olivier, "Reasons Why Armed Groups Choose to Respect International Humanitarian Law or Not" (2011) 93(882) *International Review of the Red Cross* 353–84

Baxter, R.R., "Human Rights in War" (1977) 31(4) *Bulletin of the American Academy of Arts and Sciences* 4–13

Bederman, David J., "International Law in the Ancient World" in David Armstrong (ed.), *Routledge Handbook of International Law* (London: Routledge, 2009), pp. 115–25

Bellinger, John B. II, "Legal Issues in the War on Terrorism: A Reply to Silja N. Vöneky" (2007) 8(9) *German Yearbook of International Law* 871–78

Benedek, Wolfgang, "Human Rights and Human Security: Challenges and Prospects" in Alice Yotopolous-Marangopolous (ed.), *L'etat actuel des droits de l'homme dans le monde. Défis et perspectives* (Paris: Pedone, 2006), pp. 95–109

"Mainstreaming Human Security in United Nations and European Union Peace and Crisis Management Operations: Policies and Practice" in Wolfgang Benedek, Matthias C. Kettemann and Markus Möstl (eds.), *Mainstreaming Human Security in Peace Operations and Crisis Management: Policies, Problems, Potential* (London: Routledge, 2010), pp. 13–31

"Challenges of a Humanization of International Relations by International Law" in MIha Pogacnik (ed.), *Challenges of Contemporary International Law and International Relations, Liber Amicorum in Honour of Ernest Petric* (Nova Gorica: European Faculty of Law, 2011), pp. 81–92

Ben-Naftali, Orna, "Introduction: International Humanitarian and International Human Rights Law: *Pas de Deux*" in Orna Ben-Naftali (ed.), *International Humanitarian and International Human Rights Law* (Oxford: Oxford University Press, 2011), pp. 3–10

"PathoLAWgical Occupation: Normalizing the Exceptional Case of the Occupied Palestinian Territory and Other Legal Pathologies" in Orna Ben-Naftali (ed.), *International Humanitarian and International Human Rights Law* (Oxford: Oxford University Press, 2011), pp. 129–200

Ben-Naftali, Orna and Shany, Yuval, "Living in Denial: The Application of Human Rights in the Occupied Territories" (2004) 37(1) *Israel Law Review* 17–118

Bennoune, Karima, "Toward a Human Rights Approach to Armed Conflict: Iraq 2003" (2004) 11(1) *University of California Davis Journal of International Law and Policy* 171–228

Benvenuti, Paolo and Guilio Bartolini, "Is There a Need for New International Humanitarian Law Implementation Mechanisms?" in Robert Kolb and Gloria Gaggioli (eds.), *Research Handbook on Human Rights and Humanitarian Law* (Cheltenham: Edward Elgar, 2013), pp. 590–627

Bergal, Carina, "The Mexican Drug War: The Case for a Non-International Armed Conflict Classification" (2011) 34(4) *Fordham International Law Journal* 1042–88

Bernard, Vincent, "Editorial: Engaging Armed Groups" (2011) 93(883) *International Review of the Red Cross* 581–86

Bhuta, Nehal, "The Antinomies of Transformative Occupation" (2005) 16(4) *European Journal of International Law* 721–40

Bianchi, Andrea, "Dismantling the Wall: The ICJ's Advisory Opinion and Its Likely Impact on International Law" (2004) 47 *German Yearbook of International Law* 343–91

Blischchenko, Igor P., "Armed Conflict and Protection of Human Rights" (1971) 18 *Review of Contemporary Law* 23–38

Blum, Gabriella, "The Dispensable Lives of Soldiers" (2012) 2(1) *Journal of Legal Analysis* 69–124

Bothe, Michael, "Durchsetzung der Menschenrechte und des humanitären Völkerrechts – ein Paradigmenwechsel?" in Thilo Marauhn (ed.), *Die Rechtsstellung des Menschen Im Völkerrecht* (Tübingen: Mohr, 2003), pp. 115–30

"The Historical Evolution of International Humanitarian Law, International Human Rights Law, Refugee Law and International Criminal Law" in Horst Fischer, Ulrike Froissart, Wolff Heinegg von Heintschel and Christian Raap (eds.), *Krisensicherung und humanitärer Schutz / Crisis Management and Humanitarian Protection, Festschrift für Dieter Fleck* (Berlin: Berliner Wissenschaftsverlag, 2004), pp. 37–45

"Die Anwendung der Europäischen Menschenrechtskonvention in bewaffneten Konflikten – eine Überforderung?" (2005) 65 *Zeitschrift für ausländisches öffentliches Recht und Völkerrecht* 615

"Humanitäres Völkerrecht und Schutz der Menschenrechte: Auf der Suche nach Synergien und Schutzlücken" in Pierre-Marie Dupuy, Bardo Fassbender, Malcolm N. Shaw and Karl-Peter Sommermann (eds.), *Common Values in International Law, Essays in Honour of Christian Tomuschat* (Kehl: Engel, 2006), pp. 63–90

Boutruche, Théo, "Le statut de l'eau en droit international humanitaire" (2000) 82(840) *International Review of the Red Cross* 887–915

Bowring, Bill, "Fragmentation, *Lex Specialis* and the Tensions in the Jurisprudence of the European Court of Human Rights" (2010) 14(3) *Journal of Conflict and Security Law* 485–98

Brannagan, Craig A., "The Copenhagen Process on the Handling of Detainees in International Military Operations: A Canadian Perspective on the Challenges and Goals of Warfare" (2010) 15(3) *Journal of Conflict and Security Law* 501–32

Brett, Rachel, "The Role of NGOs" in International Institute of Humanitarian Law (ed.), *Strengthening Measures for the Respect and Implementation of International Humanitarian Law and Other Rules Protecting Human Dignity in Armed Conflict, 28th Round Table on Current Problems of International Humanitarian Law, Sanremo, 2–4 September 2004* (Sanremo: International Institute of Humanitarian Law, 2004), pp. 40–46

Bring, Ove, "Hugo Grotius and the Roots of Human Rights Law" in Jonas Grimheden and Rolf Ring (eds.), *Human Rights Law: From Dissemination to Application, Essays in Honour of Göran Melander* (Leiden: Nijhoff, 2006), pp. 131–47

Bruno, Giovanni Carlo, "'Collateral Damages' of Military Operations: Is Implementation of International Humanitarian Law Possible Using International Human Rights Law Tools?" in Roberta Arnold and Noelle Quénivet (eds.), *International Humanitarian Law and Human Rights Law. Towards a Merger in International Law* (Leiden: Nijhoff, 2008), pp. 295–307

Bruscoli, Francesco, "The Rights of Individuals in Times of Armed Conflict" (2002) 6(1) *International Journal of Human Rights* 45–60

Buergenthal, Thomas, "The Advisory Practice of the Inter-American Human Rights Court" (1985) 79(1) *American Journal of International Law* 1–27

Bugnion, François, "International Red Cross and Red Crescent Movement" in David P. Forsythe (ed.), *Encyclopedia of Human Rights* (Oxford: Oxford University Press, 2009), pp. 170–77

Buis, Emiliano J., "The Implementation of International Humanitarian Law by Human Rights Courts: The Example of the Inter-American Human Rights System" in Roberta Arnold and Noelle Quénivet (eds.), *International Humanitarian Law and Human Rights Law: Towards a Merger in International Law* (Leiden: Nijhoff, 2008), pp. 269–93

Byron, Christine, "A Blurring of the Boundaries: The Application of International Humanitarian Law by Human Rights Bodies" (2007) 47(4) *Virginia Journal of International Law* 839–96

Calogeropoulos-Stratis, Aristides, "Droit humanitaire, droits de l'homme et victimes des conflits armés" in Christophe Swinarski (ed.), *Studies and Essays on International Humanitarian Law and Red Cross Principles in Honour of Jean Pictet* (The Hague: Nijhoff, 1984), pp. 655–62

Campanelli, Danio, "The Law of Military Occupation Put to the Test" (2008) 90(871) *International Review of the Red Cross* 653–68

Cannizzaro, Enzo and de Vittor, Francesco, "Proportionality in the European Convention on Human Rights" in Robert Kolb and Gloria Gaggioli (eds.), *Research Handbook on Human Rights and Humanitarian Law* (Cheltenham: Edward Elgar, 2013), pp. 125–45

Cassel, Douglas, "Extraterritorial Application of Inter-American Convention Human Rights Instruments" in Fons Coomans and Menno T. Kamminga (eds.), *Extraterritorial Application of Human Rights Treaties* (Antwerp: Intersentia, 2004), pp. 175–81

Cassese, Antonio, "The Martens Clause: Half a Loaf or Simply Pie in the Sky?" (2000) 11(1) *European Journal of International Law* 187–216

Cerna, Christina, "Human Rights in Armed Conflict: Implementation of International Humanitarian Law Norms by Regional Intergovernmental Human Rights Bodies" in Frits Kalshoven and

Yves Sandoz (eds.), *Implementation of International Humanitarian Law* (Dordrecht: Nijhoff, 1989), pp. 31–67

"Extraterritorial Application of the Human Rights Instruments of the Inter-American System" in Fons Coomans and Menno T. Kamminga (eds.), *Extraterritorial Application of Human Rights Treaties* (Antwerp: Intersentia, 2004), pp. 141–74

"The History of the Inter-American System's Jurisprudence as regards Situations of Armed Conflict" (2011) 2(1) *Journal of International Humanitarian Legal Studies* 3–52

Cerone, John, "Human Rights on the Battlefield" in Stéphanie Lagoutte, Hans-Otto Sano and Peter Scharff Smit (eds.), *Human Rights in Turmoil: Facing Threats, Consolidating Achievements* (Leiden: Nijhoff, 2007), pp. 97–113

Chinkin, Christine, "International Humanitarian Law, Human Rights and the UK Courts" in Laurence Boisson de Chazournes and Marcelo G. Kohen, *International Law and the Quest for its Implementation* (Leiden: Nijhoff, 2010), pp. 239–60

Clapham, Andrew, "Human Rights Obligations of Non-State Actors in Conflict Situations" (2006) 88(863) *International Review of the Red Cross* 491–523

Cockayne, James, "Regulating Private Military Companies: The Content, Negotiation, Weaknesses and Promise of the Montreux Document" (2009) 13(3) *Journal of Conflict and Security Law* 401

Coker, Christopher, "The Collision of Modern and Post-Modern War" in Julian Lindley-French and Yves Boyer (eds.), *The Oxford Handbook of War* (Oxford: Oxford University Press, 2012), pp. 57–68

Condorelli, Luigi, "La protection des droits de l'homme lors d'actions militaires menées à l'étranger" in College d'Europe (ed.), *The Need for Justice and Requirements for Peace and Security: Proceedings of the Bruges Colloquium, 9–10 September 2004* (Bruges: College d'Europe, 2005), pp. 89–104

Corn, Geoffrey, "Mixing Apples and Hand Grenades: The Logical Limit of Applying Human Rights Norms to Armed Conflicts" (2010) 1(1) *International Humanitarian Legal Studies* 52–94

Corn, Geoffrey S. and Jensen, Eric Talbot, "Transnational Armed Conflict: A 'Principled' Approach to the Regulation of Counter-Terror Combat Operations" (2009) 42(1) *Israel Law Review* 46–79

Coomans, Fons, "Some Remarks on the Extraterritorial Application of the International Covenant on Economic, Social and Cultural Rights" in Fons Coomans and Menno T. Kamminga (eds.), *Extraterritorial Application of Human Rights Treaties* (Antwerp: Intersentia, 2004), pp. 183–99

Coufoudakis, Van, "Cyprus and the European Convention on Human Rights: The Law and Politics of *Cyprus* v. *Turkey*, Applications 6780/74 and 6950/75" (1982) 4(4) *Human Rights Quarterly* 450

Cowan, Anna, "A New Watershed: Re-evaluating *Banković* in Light of *Al-Skeini*" (2012) 1(1) *Cambridge Journal of International and Comparative Law* 213–27

Cryer, Robert, "The Interplay of Human Rights and Humanitarian Law: The Approach of the ICTY" (2009) 14(3) *Journal of Conflict and Security Law* 511–27

Cullen, Peter M., "The Role of Targeted Killings in the Campaign Against Terror" (2008) 48(1) *Joint Force Quarterly* 22–29

Dahl, Arne Willy, "The Role of Non-Governmental Organizations in Strengthening the Respect of International Humanitarian Law" in International Institute of Humanitarian Law (ed.), *Strengthening Measures for the Respect and Implementation of International Humanitarian Law and Other Rules Protecting Human Dignity in Armed Conflict, 28th Round Table on Current Problems of International Humanitarian Law, Sanremo, 2–4 September 2004* (Sanremo: International Institute of Humanitarian Law, 2004), pp. 54–56

Danchin, Peter G., "Human Rights, Humanitarian Law and the 'War on Terrorism' in Afghanistan" in Dennis Dijkzeul (ed.), *Between Force and Mercy: Military Action and Humanitarian Aid* (Berlin: Berliner Wissenschaftsverlag, 2004), pp. 111–45

Daniel, Berlingher Remus, "The *Renvoi* in Private International Law" (2013) 3(1) *International Journal of Social Science and Humanity* 66–69

Darcy, Shane, "The Evolution of the Law of Belligerent Reprisals" (2003) 175 *Military Law Review* 184

d'Aspremont, Jean and Elodie Tranchez, "The Quest for a Non-Conflictual Coexistence of International Human Rights Law and Humanitarian Law: Which Role for the Lex Specialis

Principle?" in Robert Kolb and Gloria Gaggioli (eds.), *Research Handbook on Human Rights and Humanitarian Law* (Cheltenham: Edward Elgar, 2013), pp. 223–50

de la Pradelle, Geouffre, "Human Rights and Armed Conflicts: On the 500th Anniversary of the Birth of Las Casas (1474–1974)" (1977) 17(199) *International Review of the Red Cross* 402–6

de Wet, Erika, "The International Constitutional Order" (2006) 55(1) *International and Comparative Law Quarterly* 51–76

de Wijk, Rob, "Hybrid Conflict and the Changing Nature of Actors" in Julian Lindley-French and Yves Boyer (eds.), *The Oxford Handbook of War* (Oxford: Oxford University Press, 2012), pp. 358–72

de Zayas, Alfred, "Human Rights and Humanitarian Law" (1993) 61–62 *Nordic Journal of International Law* 259–61

Dennis, Michael J., "Application of Human Rights Treaties Extraterritorially in Times of Armed Conflict and Military Occupation" (2005) 99(1) *American Journal of International Law* 119–41

"Application of Civil and Political Rights Treaties Extraterritorially during Times of Armed Conflict" (2007) 40(2) *Israel Law Review* 454–502

Dennis, Michael J. and Surena, Andre M., "Application of the International Covenant on Civil and Political Rights in Times of Armed Conflict and Military Occupation: The Gap between Legal Theory and State Practice" (2008) 6 *European Human Rights Law Review* 714–31

Dinstein, Yoram, "The International Law of Inter-State Wars and Human Rights" (1977) 7 *Israel Yearbook of Human Rights* 139–53

Dörmann, Knut, "The Legal Situation of 'Unlawful/Unprivileged Combatants'" (2003) 85(849) *International Review of the Red Cross* 45–74

Dörr, Oliver, "General Rule of Interpretation" in Oliver Dörr and Kirsten Schmalenbach (eds.), *The Vienna Convention on the Law of Treaties: A Commentary* (Heidelberg: Springer, 2012), pp. 521–70

Doswald-Beck, Louise, "The Right to Life in Armed Conflict: Does International Humanitarian Law Provide all the Answers?" (2007) 88(864) *International Review of the Red Cross* 881–904

Doswald-Beck, Louise and Vitè, Sylvain, "International Humanitarian Law and Human Rights Law" (1993) 33(293) *International Review of the Red Cross* 94–119

Downes, Chris, "'Targeted Killings' in an Age of Terror: The Legality of the Yemen Strike" (2004) 9(2) *Journal of Conflict and Security Law* 277–94

Draper, G.I.A.D., "The Relationship between the Human Rights Regime and the Law of Armed Conflict" (1971) 1 *Israel Yearbook of Human Rights* 191–207

"Human Rights and the Law of War" (1972) 12 *Virginia Journal of International Law* 326–42

"Humanitarian Law and Human Rights" in C.F. Forsythe and J.E. Schiller (eds.), *Human Rights: The Cape Town Conference* (Cape Town: Juta, 1979), pp. 193–206

"Humanitarian Law and Human Rights" (1979) *Acta Juridica* 193–206

"Humanitarianism in the Modern Law of Armed Conflict" in Michael A. Meyer (ed.), *Armed Conflict and the New Law*, vol. 1, *Aspects of the 1977 Geneva Protocols and the 1981 Weapons Convention* (London: British Institute of International and Comparative Law, 1989), pp. 3–21

Droege, Cordula, "The Interplay between International Humanitarian Law and International Human Rights Law in Situations of Armed Conflict" (2007) 40(2) *Israel Law Review* 310–55

"Elective Affinities? Human Rights and Humanitarian Law" (2008) 90(871) *International Review of the Red Cross* 501–48

Drzewicki Krzysztof, "The Possible Shape of a Reporting System for International Humanitarian Law: Topics to be Addressed" in Michael Bothe (ed.), *Towards a Better Implementation of International Humanitarian Law, Proceedings of an Expert Meeting Organised by the Advisory Committee on International Humanitarian Law of the German Red Cross, Frankfurt/Main, 28–30 May 1999* (Berlin: Berlin Verlag Arno Spitz, 2001), pp. 73–81

Dugard, John, "Bridging the Gap between Human Rights and Humanitarian Law" (1998) 38(324) *International Review of the Red Cross* 445–53

Eden, Paul and Happold, Matthew, "Symposium: The Relationship between International Humanitarian Law and International Human Rights Law" (2010) 14(3) *Journal of Conflict and Security Law* 441–47

Eide, Asbjorn, Meron, Theodor and Rosas, Allan, "Combating Lawlessness in Gray Zone Conflicts Through Minimum Humanitarian Standards" (1995) 89(1) *American Journal of International Law* 215–23

Feinstein, Barry, "The Applicability of the Regime of Human Rights in Times of Armed Conflict and Particularly to Occupied Territories: The Case of Israel's Security Barrier" (2005) 4(2) *Northwestern Journal of International Human Rights* 238–302

Ferraro, Tristan, "The Law of Occupation and Human Rights Law: Some Selected Issues" in Robert Kolb and Gloria Gaggioli (eds.), *Research Handbook on Human Rights and Humanitarian Law* (Cheltenham: Edward Elgar, 2013), pp. 273–93

Fleck, Dieter, "Humanitarian Protection against Non-State Actors" in Jochen Abr. Frowein, Klaus Scharioth, Ingo Winkelmann and Rüdiger Wolfrum, *Verhandeln für den Frieden – Negotiating for Peace, Liber Amicorum Tono Eitel* (Berlin: Springer, 2003), pp. 69–94

Forsythe, David P., "Human Rights and Internal Conflicts: Trends and Recent Developments" (1982) 12 *California Western International Law Journal* 287–304

"Human Rights and the International Committee of the Red Cross" (1990) 12(2) *Human Rights Quarterly* 265–89

"Choices More Ethical than Legal: The International Committee of the Red Cross and Human Rights" (1993) 7(1) *Ethics and International Affairs* 131–51

"1949 and 1999: Making the Geneva Conventions Relevant After the Cold War" (1999) 81(834) *International Review of the Red Cross* 265–76

Freih, Loubna, "The Role of the United Nations High Commissioner for Human Rights in Armed Conflict Situations" in International Institute of Humanitarian Law (ed.), *Strengthening Measures for the Respect and Implementation of International Humanitarian Law and Other Rules Protecting Human Dignity in Armed Conflict, 28th Round Table on Current Problems of International Humanitarian Law, Sanremo, 2–4 September 2004* (Sanremo: International Institute of Humanitarian Law, 2004), pp. 62–69

Frowein, Jochen Abr., "Die Konstitutionalisierung des Völkerrechts" in Klaus Dicke, Waldemar Hummer, Daniel Girsberger, Katharina Boele-Woelki, Christoph Engel and Jochen Abr. Frowein (eds.), *Völkerrecht und internationales Privatrecht in einem sich globalisierenden System / Public and Private International Law in a Globalizing System. Berichte der deutschen Gesellschaft für Völkerrecht, Band 39* (Karlsruhe: C.F. Müller, 2000), pp. 427–48

Gaggioli, Gloria and Kolb, Robert, "A Right to Life in Armed Conflict? The Contribution of the European Court of Human Rights" (2007) 37 *Israel Yearbook on Human Rights* 115–63

Gallahue, Patrick, "Mexico's 'War on Drugs': Real or Rhetorical Armed Conflict?" (2011) 24(1) *Journal of International Law of Peace and Armed Conflict* 39–45

Gardam, Judith, "The Contribution of the International Court of Justice to International Humanitarian Law" (2001) 14(2) *Leiden Journal of International Law* 349–65

Garraway, Charles H.B., "Occupation Responsibilities and Constraints" in Howard M. Hensel (ed.), *The Legitimate Use of Force: The Just War Tradition and the Customary Law of Armed Conflict* (Aldershot: Ashgate, 2008), pp. 263–82

"'To Kill or not to Kill': Dilemmas in the Use of Force" (2010) 14(3) *Journal of Conflict and Security Law* 499–510

"The International Humanitarian Fact-Finding Commission" in Aldo Zammit Borda (ed.), *International Humanitarian Law and the International Red Cross and Red Crescent Movement* (London: Routledge, 2010), pp. 74–77

Gasser, Hans-Peter, "International Humanitarian Law and Human Rights Law in Non-International Armed Conflict: Joint Venture or Mutual Exclusion?" (2002) 45 *German Yearbook of International Law* 149–65

Gearty, Conor, "The Superpatriotic Fervour of the Moment" (2008) 28(1) *Oxford Journal of Legal Studies* 182–200

Gillard, Emanuela-Chiara, "Reparation for Violations of International Humanitarian Law" (2003) 85(851) *International Review of the Red Cross* 529–54

Gioia, Andrea, "The Role of the European Court of Human Rights in Monitoring Compliance with Humanitarian Law in Armed Conflict" in Orna Ben-Naftali (ed.), *International Humanitarian Law and International Human Rights Law. Pas de Deux* (Oxford: Oxford University Press, 2011), pp. 201–49

Gondek, Michal, "Extraterritorial Application of the European Convention on Human Rights: Territorial Focus in the Age of Globalization?" (2005) 52(3) *Netherlands International Law Review* 349–87

Goodman, Ryan, "Editorial Comment: The Detention of Civilians in Armed Conflict" (2009) 103(1) *American Journal of International Law* 48–74

"The Power to Kill or Capture Enemy Combatant" (2013) 24(3) *European Journal of International Law* 819

Gowlland-Debbas, Vera, "The Right to Life and Genocide: The Court and International Public Policy" in Laurence Boisson de Chazournes and Philippe Sands (eds.), *International Law, the International Court of Justice and Nuclear Weapons* (Cambridge: Cambridge University Press, 1999), pp. 315–37

Gowlland-Debbas, Vera and Gaggioli, Gloria, "The Relationship between International Human Rights Law and Humanitarian Law: An Overview" in Robert Kolb and Gloria Gaggioli (eds.), *Research Handbook on Human Rights and Humanitarian Law* (Cheltenham: Edward Elgar, 2013), pp. 77–103

Graf-Brugère, Anne Laurence, "A *Lex Favorabilis*? Resolving Norm Conflicts between Human Rights Law and Humanitarian Law" in Robert Kolb and Gloria Gaggioli (eds.), *Research Handbook on Human Rights and Humanitarian Law* (Cheltenham: Edward Elgar, 2013), pp. 251–70

Green, Leslie C., "The Contemporary Law of Armed Conflict and the Protection of Human Rights" in Gerald L. Gall (ed.), *Civil Liberties in Canada: Entering the 1980s* (Toronto: Butterworths, 1982), pp. 166–90

"Human Rights and the Law of Armed Conflict" in Leslie C. Green (ed.), *Essays on the Modern Law of War* (Ardsley: Transnational, 1999), pp. 40–58

"Human Rights in Peace and War: An Historical Overview" in Horst Fischer, Ulrike Froissart, Wolff Heinegg von Heintschel and Christian Raap (eds.), *Krisensicherung und Humanitärer Schutz / Crisis Management and Humanitarian Protection, Festschrift für Dieter Fleck* (Berlin: Berliner Wissenschaftsverlag, 2004), pp. 159–94

"Human Rights Law and International Humanitarian Law: A Historical Overview" in Susan C. Breau and Agnieszka Jachec-Neale (eds.), *Testing the Boundaries of International Humanitarian Law* (London: British Institute of International and Comparative Law, 2006), pp. 49–83

Greenwood, Christopher, "The Administration of Occupied Territory in International Law" in Emma Playfair (ed.), *International Law and the Administration of Occupied Territories: Two Decades of Israeli Occupation of the West Bank and Gaza Strip* (Oxford: Clarendon Press, 1992), pp. 241–66

"The Development of International Humanitarian Law by the International Criminal Tribunal for the Former Yugoslavia" (1998) 2 *Max Planck Yearbook of United Nations Law* 97–140

"Rights at the Frontier: Protection of the Individual in Time of War" in Barry A.K. Rider (ed.), *Law at the Centre: The Institute of Advanced Legal Studies at Fifty* (Dordrecht: Kluwer, 1999), pp. 277–93

"Historical Development and Legal Basis" in Dieter Fleck (ed.), *The Handbook of International Humanitarian Law* (Oxford: Oxford University Press, 2008), pp. 1–43

Greig, D.W., "Human Rights and Armed Conflict: Conflicting Views" (1973) *Proceedings of the American Society of International Law* 141–68

Gros Espiell, Héctor, "Humanitarian Law and Human Rights" in Janusz Symonides (ed.), *Human Rights: Concepts and Standards* (Aldershot and Paris: Ashgate and UNESCO, 2000), pp. 345–59

Guilfoyle, Douglas, "The Legal Challenges in Fighting Piracy" in Bibi van Ginkel and Frans-Paul van der Putten (eds.), *The International Response to Somali Piracy: Challenges and Opportunities* (Leiden: Nijhoff, 2010), pp. 127–52

Guillermand, Jean, "The Historical Foundations of Humanitarian Action" in Naorem Sanajaoba (ed.), *A Manual of International Humanitarian Laws* (New Delhi: Regency, 2004), pp. 4–41

Guiora, Amos, "Targeted Killing as Active Self-Defense" (2005) 36(2–3) *Case Western Reserve University Journal of International Law* 319–34

Hadden, Tom and Harvey, Colin, "The Law of Internal Crisis and Conflict: An Outline Prospectus for the Merger of International Human Rights Law, the Law of Armed Conflict, Refugee Law, and the Law on Humanitarian Intervention"(1999) 81(833) *International Review of the Red Cross* 119–33

Hafner-Burton, Emilie M., Helfer, Laurence R. and Fariss, Christopher J., "Emergency and Escape: Explaining Derogations from Human Rights Treaties" (2011) 65 *International Organization* 637–707

Hampson, Françoise, "Fundamental Guarantees" in Elizabeth Wilmshurst and Susan Breau (eds.), *Perspectives on the ICRC Study on Customary International Humanitarian Law* (Cambridge: Cambridge University Press, 2007), pp. 282–301

"The Relationship between International Humanitarian Law and Human Rights Law from the Perspective of a Human Rights Treaty Body" (2008) 90(871) *International Review of the Red Cross* 549–72

Hansen, Michelle, "Preventing the Emasculation of Warfare: Halting the Expansion of Human Rights Law into Armed Conflict" (2007) 194 *Military Law Review* 1

Happold, Matthew, "The Optional Protocol to the Convention on the Rights of Children on the Involvement of Children in Armed Conflict" (2000) 3 *Yearbook of International Humanitarian Law* 77–90

"*Banković* v. *Belgium* and the Territorial Scope of the European Convention on Human Rights" (2003) 3 *Human Rights Law Review* 1

Hayashi, Mika Nishimura, "The Martens Clause and Military Necessity" in Howard M. Hensel (ed.), *The Legitimate Use of Military Force: The Just War Tradition and the Customary Law of Armed Conflict* (Aldershot: Ashgate, 2008), pp. 5–27

Heinegg von Heintschel, Wolff, "Symposium: The Rule of Law in Conflict and Post-Conflict Situations: Factors in War to Peace Transitions" (2004) 27(3) *Harvard Journal of Law and Public Policy* 843–76

Heintze, Hans-Joachim, "Die völkerrechtliche Stellung des Kindes im bewaffneten Konflikt" (1991) 3 *Journal of International Law of Peace and Armed Conflict* 92–98

"The European Court of Human Rights and the Implementation of Human Rights Standards during Armed Conflict" (2002) 45 *German Yearbook of International Law* 789–814

"*Las Palmeras* v. *Bámaca-Velásquez* und *Banković* v. *Loizidou*?" Widersprüchliche Entscheidungen zum Menschenrechtsschutz in bewaffneten Konflikten"(2004) 3 *Journal of International Law of Peace and Armed Conflict* 177–82

"Konsequenzen der Konvergenz von Menschenrechtsschutz und humanitärem Völkerrecht" in Horst Fischer, Ulrike Froissart, Wolff Heinegg von Heintschel and Christian Raap (eds.), *Krisensicherung und humanitärer Schutz / Crisis Management and Humanitarian Protection, Festschrift für Dieter Fleck* (Berlin: Berliner Wissenschaftsverlag, 2004), pp. 243–65

"On the Relationship between Human Rights Law Protection and International Humanitarian Law" (2004) 86 *International Review of the Red Cross* 856

"Convergence between Human Rights Law and International Humanitarian Law and the Consequences for the Implementation" in Hans-Joachim Heintze and Andrej Zwitter (eds.),

International Humanitarian Law and Humanitarian Assistance: A Crosscut through Legal Issues Pertaining to Humanitarianism (Berlin: Springer, 2011), pp. 83–101

"Fortentwicklung des humanitären Völkerrechts durch den Menschenrechtsschutz" in Hans-Joachim Heintze and Knut Ipsen (eds.), *Heutige bewaffnete Konflikte als Herausforderungen an das humanitäre Völkerrecht* (Berlin: Springer, 2011), pp. 163–99

"Theories on the Relationship between International Humanitarian Law and Human Rights Law" in Robert Kolb and Gloria Gaggioli (eds.), *Research Handbook on Human Rights and Humanitarian Law* (Cheltenham: Edward Elgar, 2013), pp. 53–64

Heisbourg, Françoise, "A Surprising Little War: First Lessons of Mali" (2013) 55(2) *Survival: Global Politics and Strategy* 7–18

Henckaerts, Jean-Marie, "The Development of International Humanitarian Law and the Continued Relevance of Custom" in Howard M. Hensel (ed.), *The Legitimate Use of Military Force: The Just War Tradition and the Customary Law of Armed Conflict* (Aldershot: Ashgate, 2008), pp. 118–33

Henckaerts, Jean-Marie and Wiesener, Cornelius, "Human Rights Obligations of Non-State Armed Groups: A Possible Contribution from Customary International Law?" in Robert Kolb and Gloria Gaggioli (eds.), *Research Handbook on Human Rights and Humanitarian Law* (Cheltenham: Edward Elgar, 2013), pp. 146–69

Hensel, Howard M., "The Protection of Cultural Objects during Armed Conflicts" in Howard M. Hensel (ed.), *The Law of Armed Conflict: Constraints on the Contemporary Use of Military Force* (Aldershot: Ashgate, 2006), pp. 40–103

"Anthropocentric Natural Law and Its Implications for International Relations and Armed Conflict" in Howard M. Hensel (ed.), *The Legitimate Use of Military Force: The Just War Tradition and the Customary Law of Armed Conflict* (Aldershot: Ashgate, 2008), pp. 29–62

"The Rejection of Natural Law and Its Implications for International Relations and Armed Conflict" in Howard M. Hensel (ed.), *The Legitimate Use of Military Force: The Just War Tradition and the Customary Law of Armed Conflict* (Aldershot: Ashgate, 2008), pp. 63–96

"Theocentric Natural Law and Just War Doctrine" in Howard M. Hensel (ed.), *The Legitimate Use of Military Force: The Just War Tradition and the Customary Law of Armed Conflict* (Aldershot: Ashgate, 2008), pp. 5–27

Herczegh, Géza, "Some Thoughts on Ideas that Gave Rise to International Humanitarian Law" in Michael N. Schmitt and Leslie C. Green (eds.), *The Law of Armed Conflict: Into the Next Millenium* (Newport, CT: Naval War College, 1998), pp. 293–310

Hewitt, W.E., "Respect for Human Rights in Armed Conflicts" (1971) 4 *New York University Journal of International Law and Politics* 41–65

Hladik, Jan, "Reporting System under the 1954 Convention for the Protection of Cultural Property in the Event of Armed Conflict" (2000) 82(840) *International Review of the Red Cross* 1001–13

Hofmann, Rainer, "Victims of Violations of International Humanitarian Law: Do They Have an Individual Right to Reparation against States under International Law?" in Pierre-Marie Dupuy, Bardo Fassbender, Malcolm N. Shaw and Karl-Peter Sommermann (eds.), *Common Values in International Law, Essays in Honour of Christian Tomuschat* (Kehl: Engel, 2006), pp. 341–59

"Can Victims of Human Rights Violations Claim Damages?" in Thomas Giegerich (ed.), *A Wiser Century? Judicial Dispute Settlement, Disarmament and the Laws of War 100 Years after the Second Hague Peace Conference* (Berlin: Duncker&Humblot, 2009), pp. 322–32

Horowitz, Jonathan, "The Right to Education in Occupied Territories: Making More Room for Human Rights in Occupation Law" (2004) 7 *Yearbook of International Humanitarian Law* 253–77

"Human Rights, Positive Obligations, and Armed Conflict: The Right to Education in Occupied Territories" (2010) 1(2) *International Journal of Humanitarian Legal Studies* 304–28

Iguyovwe, Ruona, "The Interplay between International Humanitarian Law and International Human Rights Law" in Aldo Zammit Borda (ed.), *International Humanitarian Law and the International Red Cross and Red Crescent Movement* (London: Routledge, 2010), pp. 11–51

Imseis, Ardi, "Critical Reflections on the International Humanitarian Law Aspects" (2005) 99(1) *American Journal of International Law* 101–18

Irmscher, Tobias H., "The Legal Framework for the Activities of the United Nations Administration Mission in Kosovo: The Charter, Human Rights, and the Law of Occupation" (2001) 44 *German Yearbook of International Law* 353–95

Iyer, Venkat, "States of Emergency, Human Rights, and International Humanitarian Law" in V.S. Mani (ed.), *Handbook of International Humanitarian Law in South Asia* (New Delhi: Oxford University Press, 2007), pp. 191–202

Jasica, Roman, "Internationales humanitäres Recht und Menschenrechte" (1994) 1 *Journal of International Law of Peace and Armed Conflict* 4–7

Joseph, Sarah, "Scope of Obligations" in Daniel Moeckli, Sangeeta Shah and Sandesh Svikumaran (eds.), *International Human Rights Law* (Oxford: Oxford University Press, 2010), pp. 150–70

Kahn, Paul, "The Paradox of Riskless Warfare" (2002) 22(3) *Philosophy and Public Policy Quarterly* 2–8

Kälin, Walter, "Die Interdependenz von Menschenrechtsschutz und humanitärem Völkerrecht: Lehren aus der Kuwait-Krise" (1993) 3(3) *Schweizerische Zeitschrift für internationales und europäisches Recht* 233–49

"The ICRC's Compilation of the Customary Rules of Humanitarian Law" in Thomas Giegerich (ed.), *A Wiser Century? Judicial Dispute Settlement, Disarmament and the Laws of War 100 Years after the Second Hague Peace Conference* (Berlin: Duncker&Humblot, 2009), pp. 417–28

"Universal Human Rights Bodies and International Humanitarian Law" in Robert Kolb and Gloria Gaggioli (eds.), *Research Handbook on Human Rights and Humanitarian Law* (Cheltenham: Edward Elgar, 2013), pp. 441–65

Kalshoven, Frits, "Applicability of Customary International Law to Non-International Armed Conflicts" in Antonio Cassese (ed.), *Current Problems of International Law, Essays on U.N. Law and on the Law of Armed Conflict* (Milano: Giuffrè, 1975), pp. 276–85

"Human Rights, the Law of Armed Conflicts and Reprisals" (1975) 11(121) *International Review of the Red Cross* 183–92

Karl, Wolfram, "Das humanitäre Völkerrecht auf dem Weg vom Zwischenstaats- zum Weltrecht" in Wolfgang Benedek, Renate Kicker and Hubert Isak (eds.), *Development and Developing International and European Law, Essays in Honour of Konrad Ginther on the Occasion of his 65th Birthday* (Frankfurt/Main: Peter Lang, 1999), pp. 577–93

Kassebaum, David, "A Question of Facts: The Legal Use of Private Security Firms in Bosnia" (2000) 38 *Columbia Journal of Transnational Law* 581–602

Kaye, David, "International Decision (Comment on *Khasyivev and Akayeva* v. *Russia*; *Isayeva, Yusupova and Bazayeva* v. *Russia*; *Isayeva* v. *Russia*)" (2005) 99(4) *American Journal of International Law* 873–81

Kellenberger, Jakob, "Protection Through Complementarity of the Law" in International Institute of Humanitarian Law (ed.), *International Humanitarian Law and Other Legal Regimes: Interplay in Situations of Violence, Challenges and Prospects, 27th Round Table on Current Problems of International Humanitarian Law, Sanremo, 4–6 September 2003* (Sanremo: International Institute of Humanitarian Law, 2003), pp. 9–16

Kelly, Michael J., "Critical Analysis of the International Court of Justice Ruling on Israel's Security Barrier" (2005) 29(1) *Fordham International Law Journal* 181–228

Kennedy, Paul and Andreopoulos, George J., "The Laws of War: Some Concluding Reflections" in Michael Howard, George J. Andreopoulos and Mark R. Shulman (eds.), *The Laws of War: Constraints on Warfare in the Western World* (New Haven, CT: Yale University Press, 1994), pp. 214–26

Kleffner, Jann K., "The Applicability of International Humanitarian Law to Organized Armed Groups" (2011) 93(882) *International Review of the Red Cross* 446–61

Kleffner, Jann and Zegveld, Liesbeth, "Establishing an Individual Complaints Procedure for Violations of International Humanitarian Law" (2000) 3 *Yearbook of International Humanitarian Law* 384–401

Kolb, Robert, "Human Rights Law and International Humanitarian Law between 1945 and the Aftermath of the Teheran Conference of 1968" in Robert Kolb and Gloria Gaggioli (eds.), *Research Handbook on Human Rights and Humanitarian Law* (Cheltenham: Edward Elgar, 2013), pp. 35–52.

Kolb, Robert, "Origin of the Twin Terms *Jus ad Bellum / Jus in Bello*" (1997) 37 320 *International Review of the Red Cross* 553–62

"The Relationship between International Humanitarian Law and International Human Rights Law: A Brief History of the 1948 Universal Declaration of Human Rights and the 1949 Geneva Conventions" (1998) 38(324) *International Review of the Red Cross* 409–19

Koller, David S., "The Moral Imperative: Toward a Human-Rights Based Law of War" (2005) 46(1) *Harvard International Law Journal* 231–64

Kombos, Costas and Hadjisolomou, Maria, "Human Rights and Humanitarian Law: A Dichotomy Transcended?" (2006) 10(1) *Mediterranean Journal of Human Rights* 113–32

Koroteev, Kiril, "Legal Remedies for Human Rights Violations in the Armed Conflict in Chechnya: The Approach of the European Court of Human Rights in Context" (2010) 1(2) *Journal of International Humanitarian Legal Studies* 275–303

Kosirnik, René, "The 1977 Protocols: A Landmark in the Development of International Humanitarian Law" in Naorem Sanajaoba (ed.), *A Manual of International Humanitarian Laws* (New Delhi: Regency, 2004), pp. 68–88

Koskenniemi, Martti, "The Legacy of the Nineteenth Century" in David Armstrong (ed.), *Routledge Handbook of International Law* (London: Routledge, 2009), pp. 141–53

Koutroulis, Vaios, "The Application of International Humanitarian Law and International Human Rights Law in Situation of Prolonged Occupation: Only a Matter of Time?" (2012) 94(885) *International Review of the Red Cross* 165–205

Kracht, Uwe, "Human Rights and Humanitarian Norms: The Right to Food in Armed Conflict" in Morten Bergsmo (ed.), *Human Rights and Criminal Justice for the Downtrodden, Essays in Honour of Asbjorn Eide* (Leiden: Nijhoff, 2003), pp. 261–92

Krähenmann, Sandra, "Positive Obligations in Human Rights Law During Armed Conflicts" in Robert Kolb and Gloria Gaggioli (eds.), *Research Handbook on Human Rights and Humanitarian Law* (Cheltenham: Edward Elgar, 2013), pp. 170–87

Kranz, Jerzy, "Die völkerrechtliche Verantwortlichkeit für die Anwendung militärischer Gewalt" (2010) 48(3) *Zeitschrift für ausländisches öffentliches Recht und Völkerrecht* 281–337

Krasner, Stephen D., "Structural Causes and Regime Consequences: Regimes as Intervening Variables" in Stephen D. Krasner (ed.), *International Regimes* (Ithaca, NY: Cornell University Press, 1983), pp. 1–22

Kretzmer, David, "Targeted Killing of Suspected Terrorists: Extra-Judicial Execution or Legitimate Means of Defence?" (2005) 16(2) *European Journal of International Law* 171–212

Krieger, Heike, "Die Verantwortlichkeit Deutschlands nach der EMRK für seine Streitkräfte im Auslandseinsatz" (2002) 62 *Zeitschrift für ausländisches öffentliches Recht und Völkerrecht* 669–702

"A Conflict of Norms: The Relationship between Humanitarian Law and Human Rights Law in the ICRC Customary Law Study (2006) 11(2) *Journal of Conflict and Security Law* 265–91

Künnemann, Rolf, "Extraterritorial Application of the International Covenant on Economic, Social and Cultural Rights" in Fons Coomans and Menno T. Kamminga (eds.), *Extraterritorial Application of Human Rights Treaties* (Antwerp: Intersentia, 2004), pp. 199–231

Lauterpacht, Hersch, "The Problem of the Revision of the Law of War" (1952) 29 *British Yearbook of International Law* 360–82

Lawson, Rick, "Life After Banković : On the Extraterritorial Application of the European Convention on Human Rights" in Fons Coomans and Menno T. Kamminga (eds.), *Extraterritorial Application of Human Rights Treaties* (Antwerp: Intersentia, 2004), pp. 83–123

Leach, Philip, "The Chechen Conflict: Analysing the Oversight of the European Court of Human Rights" (2008) 6 *European Human Rights Law Review* 732–61

Lenzerini, Federico and Francioni, Francesco, "The Role of Human Rights in the Regulation of Private Military and Security Companies" in Francesco Francioni and Natalino Ronzitti (eds.), *War by Contract: Human Rights, Humanitarian Law, and Private Contractors* (Oxford: Oxford University Press, 2011), pp. 55–79

Levie, Howard, "History of the Law of War on Land" (2000) 82(838) *International Review of the Red Cross* 339–50

Lewis, David A.G., "The Protection of Civilian Educational Institutions during the Active Hostilities of International Armed Conflict in International Humanitarian Law" in Jonas Grimheden and Rolf Ring (eds.), *Human Rights Law: From Dissemination to Application, Essays in Honour of Göran Melander* (Leiden: Nijhoff, 2006), pp. 99–118

Linde, Hansjoachim, "Überlegungen zu den Menschenrechten und zum humanitären Völkerrecht" (1996) 2 *Journal of International Law of Peace and Armed Conflict* 96–98

Lindroos, Anja, "Addressing Norm Conflicts in a Fragmented Legal System: The Doctrine of *Lex Specialis*" (2005) 74 *Nordic Journal of International Law* 27–66

Lubell, Noam, "Challenges in Applying Human Rights Law to Armed Conflict" (2005) 87(860) *International Review of the Red Cross* 737–54

"Parallel Application of International Humanitarian Law and International Human Rights Law: An Examination of the Debate" (2007) 40(2) *Israel Yearbook of Human Rights* 648–60

"Human Rights in Military Occupation" (2012) 94(885) *International Review of the Red Cross* 317–37

MacBride, Sean, "Human Rights in Armed Conflicts: The Inter-Relationship between the Humanitarian Laws and the Law of Human Rights" (1970) 9(2) *Review of Penal Military Law and the Law of Armed Conflict* 373–91

Manby, Bronwen, "Civil and Political Rights in the African Charter on Human and Peoples' Rights: Articles 1–7" in Malcolm Evans and Rachel Murray (eds.), *The African Charter of Human and Peoples' Rights: The System in Practice, 1986–2006* (2nd edn., Cambridge: Cambridge University Press, 2008), pp. 171–212

Mansson, Katarina, "Implementing the Concept of Protection of Civilians in the Light of International Humanitarian Law and Human Rights Law: The Case of MONUC" in Roberta Arnold and Noelle Quénivet, *International Humanitarian Law and Human Rights Law: Towards a Merger in International Law* (Leiden: Nijhoff, 2008), pp. 525–90

Martin, Fanny, "Application du droit international humanitaire par la Cour interaméricaine des droits de l'hommes" (2001) 83(844) *Revue international de la Croix-Rouge* 1037–66

Martin, Francisco Forrest, "Using International Human Rights Law for Establishing a Unified Use of Force Rule in the Law of Armed Conflict" (2001) 64 *Sasketchewan Law Review* 347–96

Maus, Sylvia, "Human Rights in Peacekeeping Missions: A Framework for Humanitarian Obligations?" in Hans-Joachim Heintze and Andrej Zwitter (eds.), *International Humanitarian Law and Humanitarian Assistance: A Crosscut through Legal Issues Pertaining to Humanitarianism* (Berlin: Springer, 2011), pp. 104–28

McCarthy, Conor, "Human Rights and the Laws of War under the American Convention on Human Rights" (2008) 6 *European Human Rights Law Review* 762–80

"Legal Conclusion or Interpretative Process? *Lex Specialis* and the Application of International Human Rights Standards" in Roberta Arnold and Noelle Quénivet (eds.), *International Humanitarian Law and Human Rights Law: Towards a Merger in International Law* (Leiden: Nijhoff, 2008), pp. 102–18

"Legal Reasoning and the Applicability of International Human Rights Standards during Military Occupation" in Roberta Arnold and Noelle Quénivet (eds.), *International Humanitarian Law and Human Rights Law: Towards a Merger in International Law* (Leiden: Nijhoff, 2008), pp. 122–32

McCormack, Timothy, "The Importance of Effective Multilateral Enforcement of International Humanitarian Law" in Liesbeth Lijnzaad, Johanna van Sambeek and Bahia Tahzib-Lie (eds.), *Making the Voice of Humanity Heard, Essays on Humanitarian Assistance and International*

Humanitarian Law in Honour of HRH Princess Margriet of the Netherlands (Leiden: Nijhoff, 2004), pp. 319–38

McCoubrey, Hilaire, "The Protection of Creed and Opinion in the Laws of Armed Conflict" (2000) 5(2) *Journal of Conflict and Security Law* 135–55

McDonald, Avril, "Ghosts in the Machine: Some Legal Issues Concerning US Military Contractors in Iraq" in Michael N. Schmitt and Jelena Pejic (eds.), *International Law and Armed Conflict: Exploring the Faultlines* (Leiden: Nijhoff, 2007), pp. 357–402

McGoldrick, Dominic, "Extraterritorial Application of the International Covenant on Civil and Political Rights" in Fons Coomans and Menno T. Kamminga (eds.), *Extraterritorial Application of Human Rights Treaties* (Antwerp: Intersentia, 2004), pp. 41–72

"The Interface between Public Emergency Powers and International Law" (2004) 2(2) *International Journal of Constitutional Law* 380

"Human Rights and Humanitarian Law in the UK Courts" (2007) 40(2) *Israel Law Review* 527–62

McLaughlin, Rob, "The Law of Armed Conflict and International Human Rights Law: Some Paradigmatic Differences and Operational Implications" (2010) 13 *Yearbook of International Humanitarian Law* 213–43

Mégret, Frédéric, "Nature of Obligations" in Daniel Moeckli, Sangeeta Shah and Sandesh Sivakumaran (eds.), *International Human Rights Law* (Oxford: Oxford University Press, 2010), pp. 124–49

Melander, Goran, "International Humanitarian Law and Human Rights" (1985) 29 *Scandinavian Studies in Law* 137–48

Melzer, Nils, "Bolstering the Protection of Civilians in Armed Conflict" in Antonio Cassese (ed.), *Realizing Utopia: The Future of International Law* (Oxford: Oxford University Press, 2012), pp. 508–18

Meriboute, Zidane, "Humanitarian Rules and Sanctions in the Major Philosophical and Religious Traditions" in Liesbeth Lijnzaad, Johanna van Sambeek and Bahia Tahzib-Lie (eds.), *Making the Voice of Humanity Heard, Essays on Humanitarian Assistance and International Humanitarian Law in Honour of HRH Princess Margriet of the Netherlands* (Leiden: Nijhoff, 2004), pp. 365–84

Meron, Theodor, "On the Inadequate Reach of Humanitarian and Human Rights Law and the Need for a New Instrument" (1983) 77(3) *American Journal of International Law* 589–606

"Human Rights in Time of Peace and in Time of Armed Strife: Selected Problems" in Thomas Buergenthal (ed.), *Contemporary Issues in International Law* (Kehl: Engel, 1984), pp. 1–21

"Towards a Humanitarian Declaration on Internal Strife" (1984) 78(4) *American Journal of International Law* 859–68

"Draft Model Declaration on Internal Strife" (1988) 28(262) *International Review of the Red Cross* 59–76

"On Custom and the Antecedents of the Marten's Clause in Medieval and Renaissance Ordinances of War" in Ulrich Beyerlin (ed.), *Recht zwischen Umbruch und Bewahrung. Festschrift für Rudolf Bernhardt* (Berlin: Springer, 1995), pp. 173–78

"Convergence of International Humanitarian and Human Rights Law" in Daniel Warner (ed.), *Human Rights and Humanitarian Law: The Quest for Universality* (The Hague: Nijhoff, 1997), pp. 97–105

"Francis Lieber's Code and Principles of Humanity" in Jonathan I. Charney, Donald K. Anton and Mary Ellen O'Connell (eds.), *Politics, Values and Functions: International Law in the 21st Century, Essays in Honour of Professor Louis Henkin* (The Hague: Nijhoff, 1997), pp. 249–60

"Common Rights of Mankind in Gentili, Grotius and Suárez" in Theodor Meron (ed.), *War Crimes Law Comes of Age* (Oxford: Clarendon, 1998), pp. 122–30

"Contemporary Conflicts and Minimum Humanitarian Standards" in Karel Wellens (ed.), *International Law: Theory and Practice, Essays in Honour of Eric Suy* (The Hague: Nijhoff, 1998), pp. 623–28

"The Humanization of Humanitarian Law" (2000) 94(2) *American Journal of International Law* 239–78

"The Martens Clause, Principles of Humanity, and Dictates of Public Conscience" (2000) 94(1) *American Journal of International Law* 78–89

Meron, Theodor and Rosas, Allan, "A Declaration of Minimum Humanitarian Standards" (1991) 85(2) *American Journal of International Law* 375–81

Meyrowitz, Henri, "Le droit de la guerre et les droits de l'homme" (1972) 88 *Revue de droit militaire et de droit de la guerre* 1059–1105

Milanovic, Marko, "Lessons for Human Rights and Humanitarian Law in the War on Terror: Comparing Hamdan and the Israeli *Targeted Killings* Case" (2007) 89(866) *International Review of the Red Cross* 373–93

"From Compromise to Principle: Clarifying the Concept of State Jurisdiction in Human Rights Treaties" (2008) 8 *Human Rights Law Review* 411–48

"A Norm Conflict Perspective on the Relationship between International Humanitarian Law and Human Rights Law" (2009) 14(3) *Journal of Conflict and Security Law* 459–83

"Norm Conflicts, International Humanitarian Law and Human Rights Law" in Orna Ben-Naftali (ed.), *International Humanitarian and International Human Rights Law* (Oxford: Oxford University Press, 2011), pp. 95–125

"Al-Skeini and Al-Jedda in Strasbourg" (2012) 23 *European Journal of International Law* 121–39

Milanovic, Marko and Papić, Tatjana, "As Bad as It Gets: The European Court of Human Rights' *Behrami and Saramati* Decision and General International Law" (2008) 58(2) *International and Comparative Law Quarterly* 267–96

Miller, Sarah, "Revisiting Extraterritorial Jurisdiction: A Territorial Justification for Extraterritorial Jurisdiction under the European Convention" (2009) 20(4) *European Journal of International Law* 1233–46

Moir, Lindsay, "Decommissioned? International Humanitarian Law and the Inter-American Human Rights System" (2003) 25(1) *Human Rights Quarterly* 182–212

"Towards the Unification of International Humanitarian Law" in Richard Burchill, Nigel D. White and Justin Morris (eds.), *International Conflict and Security Law, Essays in Memory of Hilaire McCoubrey* (Cambridge: Cambridge University Press, 2005), pp. 108–28

"The European Court of Human Rights and International Humanitarian Law" in Robert Kolb and Gloria Gaggioli (eds.), *Research Handbook on Human Rights and Humanitarian Law* (Cheltenham: Edward Elgar, 2013), pp. 480–502

Mokhtar, Aly, "Will This Mummification Saga Come to an End? The International Fact-Finding Commission: Article 90 of Protocol 1" (2003) 22(2) *Penn State International Law Review* 243–311

Morsink, Johannes, "World War Two and the Universal Declaration" (1993) 15(2) *Human Rights Quarterly* 357–405

Murray, Rachel, "Evidence and Fact-Finding by the African Commission" in Malcolm Evans and Rachel Murray (eds.), *The African Charter of Human and Peoples' Rights: The System in Practice, 1986–2006* (2nd edn., Cambridge: Cambridge University Press, 2008), pp. 139–70

Naert Frederik, "The European Court of Human Rights' *Al-Jedda* and *Al-Skeini* Judgments: An Introduction and Some Reflections" (2011) 50(3–4) *Military Law and the Law of War Review* 315–20

Nambiar, Satis, "Applicability of International Humanitarian Law to United Nations Peace Operations" in V.S. Mani (ed.), *Handbook of International Humanitarian Law* (New Delhi: Oxford University Press, 2007), pp. 217–30

Ní Aoláin, Fionnuala, "The Individual Rights of Access to Justice in Times of Crisis: Emergencies, Armed Conflict and Terrorism" in Francesco Francioni (ed.), *Access to Justice as a Human Right* (Oxford: Oxford University Press, 2007), pp. 57–93

Nirmal, V.S., "International Humanitarian Law in Ancient India" in V.S. Mani (ed.), *Handbook of International Humanitarian Law* (New Delhi: Oxford University Press, 2007), pp. 25–38

O'Boyle, Michael, "The European Convention on Human Rights and Extraterritorial Jurisdiction: A Comment on 'Life After Banković'" in Fons Coomans and Menno T. Kamminga (eds.), *Extraterritorial Application of Human Rights Treaties* (Antwerp: Intersentia, 2004), pp. 125–39

O'Flaherty, Michael, "Human Rights Monitoring and Armed Conflict: Challenges for the UN" (2004) 3 *Disarmament Forum* 17–57

O'Keefe, Roger, "Legal Consequences of the Construction of a Wall in the Occupied Palestinian Territory: A Commentary" (2004) 37 *Revue Belge de Droit International* 92–154

Ober, Josiah, "Classic Greek Times" in Michael Howard, George J. Andreopoulos and Mark R. Shulman (eds.), *The Laws of War: Constraints on Warfare in the Western World* (New Haven, CT: Yale University Press, 1994), pp. 12–27

Oberleitner, Gerd, "Human Security - A Challenge to International Law?" (2005) 11(2) *Global Governance* 185–203

"Human Security" in David P. Forsythe, *Encyclopedia of Human Rights* (Oxford: Oxford University Press, 2009), vol. 2, pp. 486–93

Odello, Marco, "Fundamental Standards of Humanity: A Common Language of International Humanitarian and Human Rights Law" in Roberta Arnold and Noelle Quénivet (eds.), *International Humanitarian Law and Human Rights Law: Towards a Merger in International Law* (Leiden: Nijhoff, 2008), pp. 15–56

Oeter, Stefan, "Collateral Damages: Military Necessity and the Right to Life" in Christian Tomuschat, Evelyne Lagrange and Stefan Oeter (eds.), *The Right to Life* (Leiden: Nijhoff, 2010), pp. 167–93

Ogata, Sadako, "Human Rights, Humanitarian Law and Refugee Protection" in Daniel Warner (ed.), *Human Rights and Humanitarian Law: The Quest for Universality* (The Hague: Nijhoff, 1997), pp. 135–41

Orakhelashvili, Alexander, "Legal Consequences of the Construction of a Wall in the Occupied Palestinian Territory: Opinion and Reaction" (2006) 11(1) *Journal of Conflict and Security Law* 119–39

"Legal Stability and Claims of Change: The International Court's Treatment of *Jus Ad Bellum* and *Jus in Bello*" (2006) 75(3–4) *Nordic Journal of International Law* 371–407

"The Interaction between Human Rights and Humanitarian Law: Fragmentation, Conflict, Parallelism, or Convergence?" (2008) 19(1) *European Journal of International Law* 162–82

Parker, Geoffrey, "Early Modern Europe" in Michael Howard, George J. Andreopoulos and Mark R. Shulman (eds.), *The Laws of War: Constraints on Warfare in the Western World* (New Haven, CT: Yale University Press, 1994)

Parks, W. Hays, "Part IX of the ICRC "Direct Participation in Hostilities" Study: No Mandate, No Expertice, and Legally Incorrect" (2010) 42(3) *New York University Journal of International Law and Politics* 769–830

Partsch, Karl-Josef, "Menschenrechte und Rotkreuz-Grundsätze. Justitiartagung 1973" in Wolfgang Voit (ed.), *Völkerrechtliche Beiträge der Tagungen der Justitiare und Konventionsbeauftragten des deutschen Roten Kreuzes 1957–1989* (Bochum: Universitätsverlag Dr. N. Brockmeyer, 1995), pp. 199–217

"Human Rights and Humanitarian Law" in Rudolf Bernhardt (ed.), *Encyclopedia of Public International Law* (Amsterdam: Elsevier, 1995), pp. 910–12

Patrnogic, Jovan, "Human Rights, Humanitarian Law and Refugee Law: Interdependence and Harmonization" in Fernando Ainsa (ed.), *Human Rights at the Dawn of the of the Twenty-First Century, Karel Vasak Amicorum Liber* (Brussels: Bruylant, 1999), pp. 1105–13

Paulus, Andreas, "*Jus Cogens* in a Time of Hegemony and Fragmentation: An Attempt at a Re-appraisal" (2005) 74 *Nordic Journal of International Law* 297–334

"The Protection of Human Rights in Internal Armed Conflict in Europe: Remarks on the *Isayeva* Decisions of the European Court of Human Rights" (2006) *Uppsala Yearbook of East European Law* 61–80

"The Use of Force in Occupied Territories: The Applicable Legal Framework" in *Appendix to the Expert Meeting: Occupation and Other Forms of Administration of Foreign Territory* (Geneva: International Committee of the Red Cross, 2012), pp. 131–44

Paulus, Andreas and Vashakmadze, Mindia, "Asymmetrical War and the Notion of Armed Conflict: a Tentative Conceptualization" (2009) 91(873) *International Review of the Red Cross* 95–125

Pejic, Jelena, "Non-discrimination in Armed Conflict" (2001) 83(841) *International Review of the Red Cross* 183–94

"Procedural Principles and Safeguards for Internment/Administrative Detention in Armed Conflict and Other Situations of Violence" in Larry Maybee and Benarji Chakka (eds.), *Custom as a Source of International Humanitarian Law* (Geneva: International Committee of the Red Cross and Asian African Legal Consultative Organisation, 2005), pp. 197–219

"The European Court of Human Rights' *Al-Jedda* Judgment: The Oversight of International Humanitarian Law" (2012) 93(838) *International Review of the Red Cross* 837–51

Percy, Sarah, "Morality and Regulation" in Simon Chesterman (ed.), *From Mercenaries to Market: The Rise and Regulation of Private Military Companies* (Oxford: Oxford University Press, 2009), pp. 11–28

Perry, Michael S., "Worker and Trade Union Rights of Palestinian Arabs from the Occupied Palestinian Territories" (1993) 23 *Israel Yearbook on Human Rights* 27–52

Peschardt Pedersen, Marten, "Territorial Jurisdiction in Article 1 of the European Convention on Human Rights" (2004) 73(3) *Nordic Journal of International Law* 279–328

Peters, Anne, "Humanity as the Alpha and Omega of Sovereignty" (2009) 20(3) *European Journal of International Law* 513–44

Pfanner, Toni, "Various Mechanisms and Approaches for Implementing International Humanitarian Law and Protecting and Assisting War Victims" (2009) 91(874) *International Review of the Red Cross* 279–328

Pinzauti, Giulia, "The European Court of Human Rights' Incidental Application of International Criminal and Humanitarian Law: A Critical Discussion of *Kononov* v. *Latvia*" (2008) 6(5) *Journal of International Criminal Justice* 1043–60

"Good Time for a Change: Recognizing Individuals' Rights under the Rules of International Humanitarian Law on the Conduct of Hostilities" in Antonio Cassese (ed.), *Realizing Utopia: The Future of International Law* (Oxford: Oxford University Press, 2012), pp. 571–82

Pokempner, Dinah, "Recognizing and Furthering the Role of NGOs in International Humanitarian Law" in International Institute of Humanitarian Law (ed.), *Strengthening Measures for the Respect and Implementation of International Humanitarian Law and Other Rules Protecting Human Dignity in Armed Conflict, 28th Round Table on Current Problems of International Humanitarian Law, Sanremo, 2–4 September 2004* (Sanremo: International Institute of Humanitarian Law, 2004), pp. 47–50

Popovski, Vesselin, "Protection of Children in International Humanitarian Law and Human Rights Law" in Roberta Arnold and Noelle Quénivet (eds.), *International Humanitarian Law and Human Rights Law: Towards a Merger in International Law* (Leiden: Nijhoff, 2008), pp. 383–402

Post, H.H.G., "Some Curiosities in the Sources of the Law of Armed Conflict" in L.A.N.M. Barnhoorn and Karel Wellens (eds.), *Diversity in Secondary Rules and the Unity of International Law* (The Hague: Nijhoff, 1995), pp. 83–117

Prud'homme, Nancy, "*Lex Specialis*: Oversimplifying a More Complex and Multifaceted Relationship?" (2007) 40(2) *Israel Law Review* 357–93

Quénivet, Noelle, "The *Vavarin* Case: The Legal Standing of Individuals as Subjects of International Law" (2004) 3(2) *Journal of Military Ethics* 181–87

"*Isayeva* v. *Russian Federation* and *Isayeva, Yusupova and Bazayeva* v. *Russian Federation*: Targeting Rules According to Article 2 of the European Convention on Human Rights" (2005) 3 *Journal of International Law of Peace and Armed Conflict* 219

"Introduction: The History of the Relationship between International Humanitarian Law and Human Rights Law" in Roberta Arnold and Noelle Quénivet (eds.), *International Humanitarian Law and Human Rights Law: Towards a Merger in International Law* (Leiden: Nijhoff, 2008), pp. 1–12

"The Right to Life in International Humanitarian Law and Human Rights Law" in Roberta Arnold and Noelle Quénivet (eds.), *International Humanitarian Law and Human Rights Law: Towards a Merger in International Law* (Leiden: Nijhoff, 2008), pp. 331–53.

Quénivet, Noelle and Arnold, Roberta, "Conclusions" in Noelle Quénivet and Roberta Arnold (eds.), *International Humanitarian Law and Human Rights Law: Towards a Merger in International Law*" (Leiden: Nijhoff, 2008), pp. 591–92

Quentin-Baxter, Robert, "Human Rights and Humanitarian Law: Confluence of Conflict?" (1985) 9 *Australian Yearbook of International Law* 94–112

Quigley, John, "Trade Unions and War: The Right to Organize under Belligerent Occupation" (1990) 13(2) *Hastings International and Comparative Law Review* 241–66

Radsan, Afsheen and Murphy, Richard, "Measure Twice, Shoot Once: Higher Care for CIA Targeted Killing" (2011) 4 *University of Illinois Law Review* 1201–42

Ratner, Steven, "Foreign Occupation and International Territorial Administration: The Challenges of Convergence" (2005) 16(4) *European Journal of International Law* 695–719

Reidy, Aisling, Hampson, Françoise and Boyle, Kevin, "Gross Violations of Human Rights: Invoking the European Convention on Human Rights in the Case of Turkey" (1997) 15(2) *Netherlands Quarterly of Human Rights* 161–73

"The Approach of the European Commission and Court of Human Rights to International Humanitarian Law" (1998) 80(324) *International Review of the Red Cross* 513

Reimann, Heinrich B., "Menschenrechtsstandards in bewaffneten Konflikten" in Christophe Swinarski (ed.), *Studies and Essays on International Humanitarian Law and Red Cross Principles in Honour of Jean Pictet* (The Hague: Nijhoff, 1984), pp. 772–82

Reisman, W. Michael, "Sovereignty and Human Rights in Contemporary International Law" (1990) 84(4) *American Journal of International Law* 866–76

Remans, Wilfried, "The Granting of Observer Status by the General Assembly of the United Nations to the International Federation of the Red Cross and Red Crescent Societies" in Karel Wellens (ed.), *International Law: Theory and Practice, Essays in Honour of Eric Suy* (The Hague: Nijhoff, 1998), pp. 347–62

Ricca, Michaela, "Human Rights and the UN Special Rapporteurs' System: Tendencies in Reporting on Conflict Areas" (2002) 15(3) *Journal of International Law of Peace and Armed Conflict* 165–74

Risius, Gordon and Meyer, Michael A., "The Protection of Prisoners of War Against Insults and Public Curiosity" (1993) 33(295) *International Review of the Red Cross* 288–99

Roberts, Adam, "Humanitarian Law and Human Rights" in Christophe Swinarski (ed.), *Studies and Essays on International Humanitarian Law and Red Cross Principles in Honour of Jean Pictet* (The Hague: Nijhoff, 1984), pp. 793–802

"Land Warfare, From Hague to Nuremberg" in Michael Howard, George J. Andreopoulos and Mark R. Shulman (eds.), *The Laws of War: Constraints on Warfare in the Western World* (New Haven, CT: Yale University Press, 1994), pp. 116–39

"Transformative Military Occupation: Applying the Laws of War and Human Rights" in Michael N. Schmitt and Jelena Pejic (eds.), *International Law and Armed Conflict: Exploring the Faultlines* (Leiden: Nijhoff, 2007), pp. 439–95

Robertson, Arthur Henry, "Human Rights as the Basis of International Humanitarian Law" in Institute of International Humanitarian Law (ed.), *Proceedings of the International Conference on Humanitarian Law* (Sanremo: Institute of International Humanitarian Law, 1970), pp. 55–76

Robinson, Darryl and Oosterveld, Valerie, "The Evolution of Humanitarian Law" in Rob McRae and Don Hubert (eds.), *Human Security and the New Diplomacy: Protecting People, Promoting Peace* (Montreal: McGill-Queen's University Press, 2001), pp. 161–69

Rodley, Nigel S., "Integrity of the Person" in Daniel Moeckli, Sangeeta Shah and Sandesh Sivakumaran (eds.), *International Human Rights Law* (Oxford: Oxford University Press, 2010), pp. 209–32

Rogers, A.P.V., "The Principle of Proportionality" in Howard M. Hensel (ed.), *The Legitimate Use of Military Force: The Just War Tradition and the Customary Law of Armed Conflict* (Aldershot: Ashgate, 2008), pp. 189–218

Rogers, Felicity, "Australia's Human Rights Obligations and Australian Defence Force Operations" (1999) 18(1) *University of Tasmania Law Review* 1–10

Rona, Gabor, "Interesting Times for International Humanitarian Law: Challenges from the 'War on Terror'" (2003) 2 *Fletcher Forum of World Affairs* 55–74

Rondeau, Sophie, "Participation of Armed Groups in the Development of the Law Applicable to Armed Conflicts" (2011) 93(883) *International Review of the Red Cross* 649–72

Ronzitti, Natalino, "Access to Justice and Compensation for Violations of the Law of War" in Francesco Francioni (ed.), *Access to Justice as a Human Right* (Oxford: Oxford University Press, 2002), pp. 95–119

Rosas, Allan, "Human Rights at Risk in Situations of Internal Violence and Public Emergency" in Asbjorn Eide and Jan Helgesen (eds.), *The Future of Human Rights Protection in a Changing World: Fifty Years since the Four Freedoms Address, Essays in Honour of Torkel Opsahl* (Oslo: Norwegian University Press, 1991), pp. 165–81

Rothenberg, Gunther, "The Age of Napoleon" in Michael Howard, George J. Andreopoulos and Mark R. Shulman (eds.), *The Laws of War: Constraints on Warfare in the Western World* (New Haven, CT: Yale University Press, 1994), pp. 86–97

Rowe, Peter, "The Application of the European Convention on Human Rights during an Armed Conflict" in Richard Burchill, Nigel D. White and Justin Morris (eds.), *International Conflict and Security Law, Essays in Memory of Hilaire McCoubrey* (Cambridge: Cambridge University Press, 2005), pp. 185–208

"Non-international Armed Conflict and the European Court of Human Rights: Chechnya from 1999" (2007) 4 *New Zealand Yearbook of International Law* 205–26

Ruys, Tim and Verhoeven, Sten, "*DRC* v. *Uganda*: The Applicability of International Humanitarian Law and Human Rights Law in Occupied Territories" in Roberta Arnold and Noelle Quénivet (eds.), *International Humanitarian Law and Human Rights Law: Towards a Merger in International Law* (Leiden: Nijhoff, 2008), pp. 156–95

Rwelamira, Medard R., "Human Rights and International Humanitarian Law: The Link or Common Ground Revisited" (1992) 3(3) *Stellenbosch Law Review* 329–48

Ryniker, Anne, "Respect du droit international humanitaire par les forces des Nations Unies" (1999) 81(836) *Revue International de la Croix-Rouge* 795–805

Salado-Osuna, Ana, "The Victims of Human Rights Violations in Armed Conflicts: The Right to Justice, Truth and Compensation" in Pablo Antonio Fernández-Sánchez (ed.), *The New Challenges of Humanitarian Law in Armed Conflicts* (Leiden: Brill, 2005), pp. 315–41

Sandoz, Yves, "Le demi-siècle des Conventions de Genève" (1999) 81(834) *International Review of the Red Cross* 241–63

Sarkin, Jeremy, "The Historical Origins, Convergence and Interrelationship of International Human Rights Law, International Humanitarian Law, International Criminal Law and Public International Law and their Application since the Nineteenth Century" (2007) 1(2) *Human Rights and International Legal Discourse* 125–72

Sassòli, Marco, "Legislation and Maintenance of Public Order and Civil Life by Occupying Powers" (2005) 16(4) *European Journal of International Law* 661–94

"Terrorism and War" (2006) 4(5) *Journal of International Criminal Justice* 956–81

"The Implementation of International Humanitarian Law: Current and Inherent Challenges" (2007) 10 *Yearbook of International Humanitarian Law* 45–73

"Taking Armed Groups Seriously: Ways to Improve Their Compliance with International Humanitarian Law" (2010) 1(1) *International Journal of Humanitarian Legal Studies* 5–51

"The Role of Human Rights and International Humanitarian Law in New Types of Armed Conflicts" in Orna Ben-Naftali (ed.), *International Humanitarian and International Human Rights Law* (Oxford: Oxford University Press, 2011), pp. 34–94

Sassòli, Marco and Olson, Laura M., "The Relationship between International Humanitarian Law and Human Rights Law Where it Matters: Admissible Killing and Internment of Fighters in Non-international Armed Conflicts" (2008) 90(871) *International Review of the Red Cross* 599–627

Sayapin, Sergey, "The International Committee of the Red Cross and International Human Rights Law" (2009) 9(1) *Human Rights Law Review* 95–126

Schabas, William, "The United Nations High Commissioner for Human Rights and International Humanitarian Law" in International Institute of Humanitarian Law (ed.), *Strengthening Measures for the Respect and Implementation of International Humanitarian Law and Other Rules Protecting Human Dignity in Armed Conflict, 28th Round Table on Current Problems of International Humanitarian Law, Sanremo, 2-4 September 2004* (Sanremo: International Institute of Humanitarian Law, 2004), pp. 196–203

"*Lex Specialis*? Belts and Suspenders? The Parallel Operation of Human Rights Law and the Law of Armed Conflict, and the Conundrum of *Jus ad Bellum*" (2007) 40(2) *Israel Law Review* 592–613

Schaefer, Max, "*Al-Skeini* and the Elusive Parameters of Extraterritorial Jurisdiction" (2011) 16 *European Human Rights Law Review* 566–81

Scheinin, Martin, "Extraterritorial Effect of the International Covenant on Civil and Political Rights" in Fons Coomans and Menno T. Kamminga (eds.), *Extraterritorial Application of Human Rights Treaties* (Antwerp: Intersentia, 2004), pp. 73–81

Schindler, Dietrich, "Das humanitäre Kriegsrecht im Rahmen der internationalen Garantie der Menschenrechte" in *Deutsche Gesellschaft für die Vereinten Nationen* (ed.), *Internationales Kolloquium über Menschenrechte* (Berlin: Deutsche Gesellschaft für die Vereinten Nationen, 1968), pp. 40–54

"The International Committee of the Red Cross and Human Rights" (1979) 19 *International Review of the Red Cross* 3–14

"Human Rights and Humanitarian Law: Interrelationship of the Laws" (1982) 31(4) *American University Law Review* 935–77

"International Humanitarian Law: Its Remarkable Development and Its Persistent Violation" (2003) 5 *Journal of the History of International Law* 165–88

"J.C. Bluntschli's Contribution to the Law of War" in Marcelo G. Kohen (ed.), *Promoting Justice, Human Rights and Conflict Resolution through International Law, Liber Amicorum Lucius Caflisch* (Leiden: Nijhoff, 2007), pp. 437–54

Schmahl, Stefanie, "Der Menschenrechtsschutz in Friedenszeiten im Vergleich zum Menschenrechtsschutz im Krieg" in Jana Hasse, Erwin Müller and Patricia Schneider (eds.), *Humanitäres Völkerrecht: politische, rechtliche und strafgerichtliche Dimensionen* (Baden-Baden: Nomos, 2001), pp. 41–77

Schmalenbach, Kirsten, "Das moderne Recht der Okkupation – ein Instrument des Regimewechsels?" in Hans-Joachim Heintze and Knut Ipsen (eds.), *Heutige bewaffnete Konflikte als Herausforderungen an das humanitäre Völkerrecht* (Berlin: Springer, 2011), pp. 113–31

Schmalenbach, Kirsten, "Application of Successive Treaties in relation to the Same Subject Matter in Oliver Dörr and Kirsten Schmalenbach (eds.), *The Vienna Convention on the Law of Treaties: A Commentary* (Heidelberg: Springer, 2012), pp. 505–18

Schmalenbach, Kirsten, "Der Rechtsstaat und sein Henker: Gezieltes Töten als Mittel der Terrorbekämpfung" (2012) 60 *Jahrbuch des Öffentlichen Rechts der Gegenwart* 251–64

Schmitt, Michael N., "Targeted Killings and International Law: Law Enforcement, Self-defense and Armed Conflict" in Roberta Arnold and Noelle Quénivet (eds.), *International Humanitarian Law and Human Rights Law: Towards a Merger in International Law* (Leiden: Nijhoff, 2008), pp. 525–53

Schöndorf, Roy S., "Extra-State Armed Conflicts: Is There a Need for a New Legal Regime?" (2004) 37(1) *New York University Journal of International Law and Politics* 1–78

Schwager, Elke, "Reparation for Individual Victims of Armed Conflict" in Robert Kolb and Gloria Gaggioli (eds.), *Research Handbook on Human Rights and Humanitarian Law* (Cheltenham: Edward Elgar, 2013), pp. 628–59

Scobbie, Iain, "Principle or Pragmatics? The Relationship between Human Rights Law and the Law of Armed Conflict" (2009) 14(3) *Journal of Conflict and Security Law* 449–57

Selesky, Harold E., "Colonial America" in Michael Howard, George J. Andreopoulos and Mark R. Shulman (eds.), *The Laws of War: Constraints on Warfare in the Western World* (New Haven, CT: Yale University Press, 1994), pp. 59–84

Shelton, Dinah, "Normative Hierarchy in International Law" (2006) 100(2) *American Journal of International Law* 291–323

Shraga, Daphne, "UN Peacekeeping Operations: Applicability of International Humanitarian Law and Responsibility for Operations-Related Damage" (2000) 94(2) *American Journal of International Law* 406–12

Sidoti, Chris, "Role of the High Commissioner for Human Rights in Armed Conflict Situations" in International Institute of Humanitarian Law (ed.), *Strengthening Measures for the Respect and Implementation of International Humanitarian Law and Other Rules Protecting Human Dignity in Armed Conflict, 28th Round Table on Current Problems of International Humanitarian Law, Sanremo, 2–4 September 2004* (Sanremo: International Institute of Humanitarian Law, 2004), pp. 139–41

Simma, Bruno and Pulkowski, Dirk, "Of Planets and the Universe: Self-Contained Regimes in International Law" (2003) 17(3) *European Journal of International Law* 483–529

Sivakumaran, Sandesh, "Binding Armed Opposition Groups" (2006) 55 *International and Comparative Law Quarterly* 369–94

"International Humanitarian Law" in Daniel Moeckli, Sangeeta Shah and Sandesh Sivakumaran (eds.), *International Human Rights Law* (Oxford: Oxford University Press, 2010), pp. 521–39

"Re-envisaging the International Law of Armed Conflict: A Rejoinder to Gabriella Blum" (2011) 22(1) *European Journal of International Law* 273–75

Slim, Habib, "Les moyens de mise en oeuvre du droit international humanitaire: rôle des organisations non gouvernementales" in International Institute of Humanitarian Law (ed.), *Strengthening Measures for the Respect and Implementation of International Humanitarian Law and Other Rules Protecting Human Dignity in Armed Conflict, 28th Round Table on Current Problems of International Humanitarian Law, Sanremo, 2–4 September 2004* (Sanremo: International Institute of Humanitarian Law, 2004), pp. 75–80

Solf, W.A., "Human Rights in Armed Conflict: Some Observations on the Relationship of Human Rights Law to the Law of Armed Conflict" in Henry Hyunwook Han (ed.), *World in Transition: Challenges to Human Rights, Development and World Order* (Washington, DC: University Press of America, 1979), pp. 41–53

"Problems with the Application of Norms Governing Interstate Armed Conflicts to Non-International Armed Conflicts" (1983) 13 *Georgia Journal of International and Comparative Law* 291–301

Sommaruga, Cornelio, "Respect for International Humanitarian Law: ICRC Review of Five Years of Activity (1987–1991)" (1992) 32(286) *International Review of the Red Cross* 74–93

"Humanitarian Law and Human Rights in the Legal Arsenal of the ICRC" in Daniel Warner (ed.), *Human Rights and Humanitarian Law: The Quest for Universality* (The Hague: Nijhoff, 1997), pp. 125–33

Spieker, Heike, "The Possible Shape of a Reporting System for International Humanitarian Law: Composition and Status of an Evaluating Body" in Michael Bothe (ed.), *Towards a Better Implementation of International Humanitarian Law, Proceedings of an Expert Meeting Organised by the Advisory Committee on International Humanitarian Law of the German Red Cross, Frankfurt/Main, 28–30 May 1999* (Berlin: Berlin Verlag Arno Spitz, 2001), pp. 83–103

Stacey, Robert C., "Age of Chivalry" in Michael Howard, George J. Andreopoulos and Mark R. Shulman (eds.), *The Laws of War: Constraints on Warfare in the Western World* (New Haven, CT: Yale University Press, 1994), pp. 27–39

Starck, Christian, "The Religious and Philosophical Background of Human Dignity and its Place in Modern Constitutions" in David Kretzmer and Eckart Klein (eds.), *The Concept of Human Dignity in Human Rights Discourse* (The Hague: Kluwer, 2002), pp. 179–94

Stein, Torsten, "Comment to Hans-Peter Gasser, International Humanitarian Law and Human Rights Law in Non-international Armed Conflict: Joint Venture or Mutual Exclusion" (2002) 45 *German Yearbook of International Law* 163

Sundberg, Ulrika, "The Role of the United Nations Commission on Human Rights in Armed Conflict Situations" in International Institute of Humanitarian Law (ed.), *Strengthening Measures for the Respect and Implementation of International Humanitarian Law and Other Rules Protecting Human Dignity in Armed Conflict, 28th Round Table on Current Problems of International Humanitarian Law, Sanremo, 2–4 September 2004* (Sanremo: International Institute of Humanitarian Law, 2004), pp. 28–35

Sunga, Lyal S., "The Special Procedures of the UN Commission on Human Rights: Should They Be Scrapped?" in Gudmundur Alfredsson, Jonas Grimheden, Bertrand Ramcharan and Alfred de Zayas (eds.), *International Human Rights Monitoring Mechanisms, Essays in Honour of Jakob Th. Möller* (The Hague: Nijhoff, 2001), pp. 233–77

Suter, Keith D., "An Enquiry into the Meaning of the Phrase '"Human Rights in Armed Conflict"'" (1976) 15(3–4) *Revue de droit pénal militaire et de droit de la guerre* 393–430

Svensson-McCarthy, Anna-Lena, "Minimum Humanitarian Standards: From Cape Town towards the Future" (1994) 53 *Review of the International Commission of Jurists* 1–29

Syquia, Enrique P., "Dr Jean Pictet and International Humanitarian Law" in Christophe Swinarski (ed.), *Studies and Essays on International Humanitarian Law and Red Cross Principles in Honour of Jean Pictet* (The Hague: Nijhoff, 1984), pp. 521–57

Tavernier, Paul, "Le recours á la force par la police" in Christian Tomuschat, Evelyne Lagrange and Stefan Oeter (eds.), *The Right to Life* (Leiden: Nijhoff, 2010), pp. 41–66

Tawil, Sobhi, "International Humanitarian Law and Basic Education" (2000) 82(840) *International Review of the Red Cross* 581–97

Taylor, A.J.P., "War and Peace" (1980) 2(19) *London Review of Books* 3–6

Techera, Erika J., "Protection of Cultural Heritage in Times of Armed Conflict: The International Legal Framework Revisited" (2007) 4(1) *Macquarie Journal of International and Comparative Environmental Law* 1–20

Tehindrazanarivelo, Djacoba Liva, "The African Union and International Humanitarian Law" in Robert Kolb and Gloria Gaggioli (eds.), *Research Handbook on Human Rights and Humanitarian Law* (Cheltenham: Edward Elgar, 2013), pp. 503–30

Teubner, Gunther and Fischer-Lescano, Andreas, "Regime-Collisions: The Vain Search for Legal Unity in the Fragmentation of Global Law" (2004) 25(4) *Michigan Journal of International Law* 999–1046

Thürer, Daniel, "International Humanitarian Law as a Core of a 'Constitutional System' of Public International Law?" in Stefania Baldini and Guido Ravasi (eds.), *Humanitarian Action and State Sovereignty, International Congress on the Occasion of its 30th Anniversary, San Remo*, 31 August – 2 September 2000 (Sanremo: International Institute of Humanitarian Law, 2003), pp. 46–58

"International Humanitarian Law: Essence and Perspectives" (2007) 2 *Schweizerische Zeitschrift für internationales und öffentliches Recht* 1–8

Ticehurst, Rupert, "The Martens Clause and the Laws of Armed Conflict" in Naorem Sanajaoba (ed.), *A Manual of International Humanitarian Laws* (New Delhi: Regency, 2004), pp. 312–22

Tobin, John, "Seeking Clarity in Relation to the Principle of Complementarity: Reflections on the Recent Contributions of Some International Bodies" (2007) 8(2) *Melbourne Journal of International Law* 356–72

Tomuschat, Christian, "The Applicability of Human Rights Law to Insurgent Movements" in Horst Fischer, Ulrike Froissart, Wolff Heinegg von Heintschel and Christian Raap, *Krisensicherung und humanitärer Schutz / Crisis Management and Humanitarian Protection. Festschrift für Dieter Fleck* (Berlin: Berliner Wissenschaftsverlag, 2004), pp. 573–91

"Reparation in Favour of Individual Victims of Gross Violations of Human Rights and International Humanitarian Law" in Marcelo G. Kohen (ed.), *Promoting Justice, Human Rights and Conflict Resolution Through International Law, Liber Amicorum Lucius Caflisch* (Leiden: Nijhoff, 2007), pp. 569–90

"The Right to Life: Legal and Political Foundations" in Christian Tomuschat, Evelyne Lagrange and Stefan Oeter (eds.), *The Right to Life* (Leiden: Nijhoff, 2010), pp. 3–18

"Human Rights and International Humanitarian Law" (2010) 21(1) *European Journal of International Law* 15

Tondini, Matteo, "Putting an End to Human Rights Violations by Proxy: Accountability of International Organisations and Member States in the Framework of Jus Post Bellum" in Carsten Stahn and Jann K. Kleffner (eds.), *Jus Post Bellum: Towards a Law of Transition from Conflict to Peace* (The Hague: T.M.C. Asser, 2008), pp. 167–212

Tripodi, Paolo and Wolfendale, Jessica, "Introduction" in Paolo Tripodi and Jessica Wolfendale (eds.), *New Wars and New Soldiers* (Aldershot: Ashgate, 2011), pp. 1–12

Tryggestad, Torunn L., "Trick or Treat? The UN and Implementation of Security Council Resolution 1325 on Women, Peace, and Security" (2009) 15(4) *Global Governance* 539–57

Turns, David, "At the 'Vanishing Point' of International Humanitarian Law: Methods and Means of Warfare in Non-International Armed Conflicts" (2002) 45 *German Yearbook of International Law* 115–48

van Boven, Theo, "Reliance on Norms of Humanitarian Law by United Nations' Organs" in Astrid J.M. Delissen and Gerard J. Tanja (eds.), *Humanitarian Law of Armed Conflict: Challenges Ahead, Essays in Honour of Frits Kalshoven* (Dordrecht: Nijhoff, 1991), pp. 495–512

van Hegelsom, Gert-Jan F., "The Law of Armed Conflict and UN Peace-Keeping and Peace-Enforcing Operations" (1993) 6 *Hague Yearbook of International Law* 45–58

Verdirame, Guglielmo, "Human Rights in Wartime: A Framework for Analysis" (2008) 6 *European Human Rights Law Review* 689–705

Veuthey, Michel, "Public Conscience in International Humanitarian Law Today" in Horst Fischer, Ulrike Froissart, Wolff Heinegg von Heintschel and Christian Raap (eds.), *Krisensicherung und Humanitärer Schutz / Crisis Management and Humanitarian Protection. Festschrift für Dieter Fleck* (Berlin: Berliner Wissenschaftsverlag, 2004), pp. 611–42

"Implementing International Humanitarian Law: Old and New Ways" in Bertrand Ramcharan (ed.), *Human Rights Protection in the Field* (Leiden: Nijhoff, 2006), pp. 87–117

Vigny, Jean-Daniel and Thompson, Cecilia, "Fundamental Standards of Humanity: What Future?" (2002) 20(2) *Netherlands Quarterly of Human Rights* 185–99

Vité, Sylvain, "The Interrelation of the Law of Occupation and Economic, Social and Cultural Rights: The Examples of Food, Health and Property" (2008) 90(871) *International Review of the Red Cross* 629–51

"Typology of Armed Conflicts in International Humanitarian Law: Legal Concepts and Actual Situations" (2009) 91(873) *International Review of the Red Cross* 69–94

von Glahn, Gerhard, "The Protection of Human Rights in Time of Armed Conflict" (1971) 1 *Israel Yearbook of Human Rights* 208–27

Vranes, Erich, "*Lex Superior, lex specialis, lex posterior* – zur Rechtsnatur der 'Konfliktlösungsregeln'" (2005) 65 *Zeitschrift für ausländisches öffentliches Recht und Völkerrecht* 391–406

"The Definition of 'Norm-Conflict' in International Law and Legal Theory" (2006) 17(2) *European Journal of International Law* 395–418

Vrdoljak, Ana Filipa, "Cultural Heritage in Human Rights and Humanitarian Law" in Orna Ben-Naftali (ed.), *International Humanitarian and International Human Rights Law* (Oxford: Oxford University Press, 2011), pp. 251–302

Walker, Philip James, "Iraq and Occupation" in David Wippman and Matthew Evangelista (eds.), *New Wars, New Laws?: Applying Laws of War in 21st Century Conflicts* (Ardsley: Transnational, 2005), pp. 259–88

Walsh, Brian and Peleg, Ilan, "Human Rights under Military Occupation: The Need for Expansion" (1998) 2 *International Journal of Human Rights* 62–78

Watkin, Kenneth, "Assessing Proportionality: Moral Complexity and Legal Rules" (2005) 8 *Yearbook of International Humanitarian Law* 3–53

"21st Century Conflict and International Humanitarian Law: Status Quo or Change?" in Michael N. Schmitt and Jelena Pejic (eds.), *International Law and Armed Conflict: Exploring the Faultlines* (Leiden: Nijhoff, 2007), pp. 295–96

Weeramantry, C.G., "Buddhism and Humanitarian Law" in V.S. Mani (ed.), *Handbook of International Humanitarian Law* (New Delhi: Oxford University Press, 2007), pp. 1–13

Weissbrodt, David, "The Role of International Organizations in the Implementation of Human Rights and Humanitarian Law in Situations of Armed Conflict" (1988) 21 *Vanderbilt Journal of Transnational Law* 327–61

"The Approach of the Committee on the Elimination of Racial Discrimination to Interpreting and Applying International Humanitarian Law" (2010) 19 *Minnesota Journal of International Law* 2

"The Role of the Human Rights Committee in Interpreting and Developing Humanitarian Law" (2010) 31(4) *Pennsylvania Journal of International Law* 1185–237

Weissbrodt, David, Hansen, Joseph C. and Nesbitt, Nathaniel H., "The Role of the Committee on the Rights of the Child in Interpreting and Developing International Humanitarian Law" (2011) 24 *Harvard Human Rights Journal* 115–53

White, Nigel D., "Regulatory Initiatives at the International Level" in Christine Bakker and Mirko Sossai (eds.), *Multilevel Regulation of Military and Security Contractors: The Interplay between International, European and Domestic Norms* (Hart: Oxford, 2012), pp. 11–30

Wieruszewski, Roman, "Application of International Humanitarian Law and Human Rights: Individual Complaints" in Frits Kalshoven and Yves Sandoz (eds.), *Implementation of International Humanitarian Law* (Dordrecht: Nijhoff, 1989), pp. 442–58

Wilde, Ralphe, "Legal 'Black Hole'? Extraterritorial State Action and International Treaty Law on Civil and Political Rights" (2005) 26 *Michigan Journal of International Law* 739–806

"Triggering State Obligations Extraterritorially: The Spatial Test in Certain Human Rights Treaties" (2007) 40(2) *Israel Law Review* 503–26

"Are Human Rights Norms Part of the *Jus Post Bellum*, and Should They Be?" in Carsten Stahn and Jann K. Kleffner (eds.), *Jus Post Bellum: Towards a Law of Transition from Conflict to Peace* (The Hague: T.M.C. Asser, 2008), pp. 163–86

Wolfrum, Rüdiger and Philipp, Christiane E., "The Status of the Taliban: Their Obligations and Rights under International Law" (2002) 6(1) *Max Planck Yearbook of United Nations Law* 559–97

Xu, Ji, "The Evolution of International Laws of War" (2008) 2 *Chinese Journal of International Politics* 171

Zegveld, Liesbeth, "Remedies for Victims of Violations of International Humanitarian Law" (2003) 85(851) *International Review of the Red Cross* 497–526

"The Inter-American Commission on Human Rights and International Humanitarian Law: A Comment on the Tablada Case" (1998) 38(324) *International Review of the Red Cross* 505–11

Zemmali, Ameur, "The Right to Water in Times of Armed Conflict" in Liesbeth Lijnzaad, Johanna van Sambeek and Bahia Tahzib-Lie (eds.), *Making the Voice of Humanity Heard, Essays on Humanitarian Assistance and International Humanitarian Law in Honour of HRH Princess Margriet of the Netherlands* (Leiden: Nijhoff, 2004), pp. 307–18

Zwanenburg, Marten, "The Law of Occupation Revisited: The Beginning of an Occupation" (2007) 10 *Yearbook of International Humanitarian Law* 99–130

Working papers, online publications and conference documents

Bennett, Richard, *Asserting the Presence of the State, One Step at a Time - Rio de Janeiro, Brazil, 2008–2010, Policy Note*, Innovations for Successful Societies (Princeton, NJ: Princeton University Press, 2011), available at www.princeton.edu/successfulsocieties/content/focusareas/PL/policy notes/view.xml?id=139

Boon, Kristen E., *The Future of the Law of Occupation* (2009), available at http://papers.ssrn.com/sol3/papers.cfm?abstract_id=1464443

Cerone, John, *Out of Bounds? Considering the Reach of International Human Rights Law*, New York University School of Law Centre for Human Rights and Global Justice Working Paper No. 5 (2006), available at www.chrgj.org/publications/docs/wp/WPS_NYU_CHRGJ_Cerone_Final.pdf

Chapman, Peter F., "Ensuring Respect: United Nations Compliance with International Humanitarian Law" (2009) 17(1) *Human Rights Brief* 2, available at www.wcl.american.edu/hrbrief/17/1chapman.pdf

Clapham, Andrew, "Rights and Responsibilities: A Legal Perspective" in Oliver Jütersonke and Keith Krause (eds.), *From Rights to Responsibilities: Rethinking Interventions for Humanitarian Purposes*, PSIS Special Study No. 7 (Geneva: Programme for Strategic and International Security Studies, 2006), pp. 61–85

Crawford, Emily, *Road to Nowhere? The Future for the Declaration on Fundamental Standards of Humanity*, Sydney Law School Legal Studies Research Paper No. 12/02 (2012), available at http://works.bepress.com/emily_crawford/2

Doswald-Beck, Louise, "Background Paper" in University Centre for International Humanitarian Law, *Expert Meeting on the Supervision of the Lawfulness of Detention during Armed Conflict* (2004), available at www.geneva-academy.ch/docs/expert-meetings/2004/4rapport_detention.pdf

Fuentes, Carlos Iván, *The Applicability of International Humanitarian Law to Situations of Urban Violence: Are Cities Turning into War Zones?*, McGill University Centre for Human Rights and Legal Pluralism Working Paper (26 February 2008), http://ssrn.com/abstract=1134123

Geneva Academy of International Humanitarian Law and Human Rights, *The UN Human Rights Council: Commissions of Inquiry Conference Brief* (December 2011), available at www.geneva-academy.ch/docs/news/HR-council-inquiry-conference-brief.pdf

Hafner, Gerald, *Risks Ensuing from Fragmentation of International Law, Report of the International Law Commission*, Annex 321, UN GAOR, 55th Session, Supplement No. 10, UN Doc. A/55/10 (27 September 2000)

Hampson, Françoise and Salama, Ibrahim, *Relationship between Human Rights Law and International Humanitarian Law*, Working Paper of the UN Sub-commission on the Promotion and Protection of Human Rights, UN Doc. E/CN.4/2005/14 (21 June 2005)

Jensen, Eric Talbot, "The Future of the Law of Armed Conflict: Ostriches, Butterflies, and Nanobots," http://ssrn.com/abstract=2237509

Lempinen, Miko and Scheinin, Martin, *The New Human Rights Council: The First Two Years, Substantive Report of the Workshop Organized by the European University Institute, Istituto Affari Internazionali, and the Institute for Human Rights at Abo Akademi University, European University Institute, 7–8 November 2007* (Abo: Abo Akademi Institute, 2007), available at www.eui.eu/Documents/DepartmentsCentres/AcademyofEuropeanLaw/Projects/HRCReport.pdf

Lodgaard, Sverre, *Human Security: Concept and Operationalization* (2007), available at www.cpdsindia.org/conceptandoperationalization.htm

Ohlin, Jens David, *The Capture-Kill Debate: Lost Legislative History or Revisionist History?*, Cornell Legal Studies Research Paper (8 March 2013), available at http://papers.ssrn.com/sol3/papers.cfm?abstract_id=2230486

Paulus, Andreas, "The Use of Force in Occupied Territories: The Applicable Legal Framework" in *Expert Meeting: Occupation and Other Forms of Administration of Foreign Territory* (Geneva: International Committee of the Red Cross, 2012), Appendix

Ramcharan, Bertrand, *The United Nations High Commissioner for Human Rights and International Humanitarian Law, Program on Humanitarian Policy and Conflict Research*, Harvard University Occasional Paper Series No. 3 (2005)

Rosas, Alan, "The Interrelationship between Human Rights and International Humanitarian Law" in College of Europe and International Committee of the Red Cross (eds.), *Current Challenges in*

International Humanitarian Law. Proceedings of the Bruges Colloquium, 27–28 October 2000 (Bruges: College of Europe and International Committee of the Red Cross, 2001)

Scheinin, Martin, *Fundamental Standards of Humanity*, Background Paper to the International Expert Meeting, Stockholm, 22–24 February 2000, UN Doc. E/CN.4/2000/145 (4 April 2000)

Turku/Abo Declaration of Minimum Humanitarian Standards (1990), International Council on Human Rights Policy Working Paper (2006), available at www.ichrp.org/files/papers/91/120B_-_Turku-Abo_Declaration_of_Minimum_Humanitarian_Standards_Scheinin__Martin__2005.pdf

Sperotto, Federico, *Violations of Human Rights during Military Operations in Chechnya* (2008), available at http://papers.ssrn.com/sol3/papers.cfm?abstract_id=1081199

"Counter-Insurgency, Human Rights, and the Law of Armed Conflict" (2009) 17(1) *Human Rights Brief* 19, available at http://www.wcl.american.edu/hrbrief/17/1sperotto.pdf

Vité, Sylvain, "The Interrelationship between the Law of Occupation and Economic, Social and Cultural Rights: The Examples of Food and Health" in *Appendix to the Expert Meeting: Occupation and Other Forms of Administration of Foreign Territory* (Geneva: International Committee of the Red Cross, 2012)

Documents and reports

United Nations

Basic Principles and Guidelines on the Right to a Remedy and Reparation for Victims of Gross Violations of International Human Rights Law and Serious Violations of International Humanitarian Law, UN Doc. GA/Res. 60/147 (16 December 2005)

Cairo Declaration on Human Rights in Islam, UN Doc. A/CONF.157/PC/62/Add.18 (9 June 1993)

Declaration of Minimum Humanitarian Standards, UN Doc. E/CN.4/Sub.2/1991/55, reprinted in (1991) 31(282) *International Review of the Red Cross* 330

Final Report of the High-Level Fact-Finding Mission to Beit Hanoun, UN Doc. A/HRC/9/26 (1 September 2008)

Guiding Principles on Internal Displacement, UN Doc. E/CN.4/1998/53, Add. 2 (17 April 1998)

Human Rights Council, *Report of the Working Group of the Universal Periodic Review: Pakistan*, UN Doc. A/HRC/8/42 (4 June 2008)

Report of the Working Group of the Universal Periodic Review: Afghanistan, UN Doc. A/HRC/12/9 (20 July 2009)

Report of the Working Group of the Universal Periodic Review: Democratic Republic of the Congo, UN Doc. A/HRC/13/8 (4 January 2010)

Report of the Working Group of the Universal Periodic Review: Côte d'Ivoire, UN Doc. A/HRC/13/9 (5 January 2010)

Report of the Working Group of the Universal Periodic Review: Israel, UN Doc. A/HRC/10/76 (8 January 2010)

Report of the Working Group of the Universal Periodic Review: United States of America, UN Doc. A/HRC/16/11 (4 January 2011)

Report of the Working Group of the Universal Periodic Review: Somalia, UN Doc. A/HRC/18/6 (11 July 2011)

Joint Declaration of the Independent Experts Responsible for the Special Procedures for the Protection of Human Rights, UN Doc. A/CONF.157/9 (18 June 1993)

Montreux Document on Pertinent International Legal Obligations and Good Practices for States related to Operations of Private Military and Security Companies during Armed Conflict, UN Doc. A/63/467 and S/2008/636 (6 October 2008), Annex

Norms on the Responsibilities of Transnational Corporations and Other Business Enterprises with regard to Human Rights, UN Doc. E/CN.4/Sub.2/2003/12/Rev.2 (2003)

Report of the Commission of Inquiry on Lebanon, UN Doc. A/HRC/3/2 (23 November 2006)

Report of the Fact-Finding Mission headed by the Special Rapporteur on the Situation of Human Rights in the Palestinian Occupied Territories, UN Doc. A/HRC/4/116 (20 December 2006)

Report of the Fact-Finding Mission headed by the Special Rapporteur on the Situation of Human Rights in the Palestinian Occupied Territories, UN Doc. A/HRC/5/11 (8 June 2007)

Report of the High-Level Mission on the Situation of Human Rights in Darfur, UN Doc. A/HRC/4/80 (9 March 2007)

Report of the Independent International Commission of Inquiry on the Syrian Arab Republic, UN Doc. A/HRC/21/50 (16 August 2012)

Report of the Independent International Fact-finding Mission to Investigate the Implications of the Israeli Settlements on the Civil, Political, Economic, Social and Cultural Rights of the Palestinian People throughout the Occupied Palestinian Territory, including East Jerusalem, UN Doc. A/HRC/22/63 (7 February 2013)

Report of the International Commission of Inquiry to Investigate the Facts and Circumstances Surrounding the Allegations of Serious Abuses and Violations of Human Rights Committed in Côte d'Ivoire following the Presidential Election of 28 November 2010, UN Doc. A/HRC/17/48 (14 June 2011)

Report of the International Fact-Finding Mission to Investigate Violations of International Law, including International Humanitarian and Human Rights Law, Resulting from the Israeli Attacks on the Flotilla of Ships Carrying Humanitarian Assistance, UN Doc. A/HRC/15/21 (27 September 2010)

Report of the Secretary-General on Fundamental Standards of Humanity, E/CN.4/1999/92 (18 December 1999)

Report of the Secretary-General on Fundamental Standards of Humanity, UN Doc. E/CN.4/2000/94 (27 December 2000)

Report of the Secretary-General on Fundamental Standards of Humanity, UN Doc. E/CN.4/2006/87 (3 March 2006)

Report of the Secretary-General on Fundamental Standards of Humanity, UN Doc. A/HRC/7/62 (12 March 2008)

Report of the Secretary-General on Fundamental Standards of Humanity, UN Doc. A/HRC/8/14 (28 May 2008)

Report of the Secretary-General on Minimum Humanitarian Standards, UN Doc. E/CN.4/1998/87 (5 January 1998)

Report of the Secretary-General on Respect for Human Rights in Armed Conflict, UN Doc. A/7720 (20 November 1969)

Report of the Secretary-General on Respect for Human Rights in Armed Conflicts, UN Doc. A/8052 (18 September 1970)

Report of the Secretary-General to the Security Council on the Protection of Civilians in Armed Conflict, UN Doc. S/1999/957 (8 December 1999)

Report of the Secretary-General to the Security Council on the Protection of Civilians in Armed Conflict, UN Doc. S/2009/277 (29 May 2009)

Report of the Secretary-General on We, the Peoples: The Role of the United Nations in the Twenty-First Century, UN Doc. A/54/2000 (27 March 2000)

Report of the Study Group of the International Law Commission, finalized by Martii Koskenniemi, Fragmentation of International Law: Difficulties Arising from the Diversification and Expansion of International Law, UN Doc. A/CN.4/L.682 (13 April 2006)

Report of the United Nations Fact-Finding Mission on the Gaza Conflict, UN Doc. A/HRC/12/48 (23 September 2009)

Report of the United Nations High Commissioner for Human Rights on the Outcome of the Expert Consultation on the Issue of Protecting the Human Rights of Civilians in Armed Conflict, UN Doc. A/HRC/11/31 (4 June 2009)

Report of the United Nations High Commissioner for Human Rights on the Outcome of the Expert Consultation on the Issue of Protecting the Human Rights of Civilians in Armed Conflict, UN Doc. A/HRC/14/40 (2 June 2010)

Report of the United Nations High Commissioner for Human Rights on the Situation of Human Rights in Côte d'Ivoire, UN Doc. A/HRC/17/49 (14 June 2011)

Report of the United Nations Independent Commission of Inquiry on Libya, UN Doc. A/HR/19/68 (2 March 2012)

Report on the Technical Assistance to the Government of the Democratic Republic of the Congo and Urgent Examination of the Situation in the East of the Country, UN Doc. A/HRC/10/59 (5 March 2009)

Siracusa Principles on the Limitation and Derogation of Provisions in the International Covenant on Civil and Political Rights, UN Doc. E/CN.4/1984/4 (29 September 1984), Annex

Special Rapporteur on Extrajudicial, Summary or Arbitrary Executions, Philip Alston, Special Rapporteur on the Right of Everyone to the Enjoyment of the Highest Attainable Standard of Physical and Mental Health, Paul Hunt, Representative of the Secretary-General on Human Rights of Internally Displaced Persons, Walter Kälin, and Special Rapporteur on Adequate Housing as a Component of the Right to an Adequate Standard of Living, Miloon Kothari, *Report on the Mission to Lebanon and Israel*, UN Doc. A/HRC/2/7 (2 October 2006)

Special Rapporteur on the Question of Torture, Nigel S. Rodley, and the Special Rapporteur on Extrajudicial, Summary or Arbitrary Executions, Bacre Waly Ndiaye, *Joint Report on the Mission to Colombia*, UN Doc. E/CN.4/1995/111 (16 January 1995)

Sub-Commission on the Promotion and Protection of Human Rights, *Study of Implications for Human Rights of Recent Developments concerning Situations Known as States of Siege or Emergency*, UN Doc. E/CN.4/Sub.2/1982/15 (27 July 1982)

United Nations Peacekeeping Operations: Principles and Guidelines (New York: United Nations, 2008)

Vienna Declaration and Programme of Action, UN Doc. A/CONF.157/23 (12 July 1993)

Other bodies

Food and Agricultural Organisation, *Voluntary Guidelines to Support the Progressive Realization of the Right to Adequate Food in the Context of National Food Security* (23 November 2004), available at ftp://ftp.fao.org/docrep/fao/009/y7937e/y7937e00.pdf

Institute of International Law, *Manual of the Laws of War on Land* (Oxford: IIL, 9 September 1880)

International Committee of the Red Cross, *Final Record of the Diplomatic Conference of Geneva of 1949* (1963) *Judicial Guarantees*, DOCT/34-1985/5 (8 July 1985)

Detention Conditions, DOCT/50-1988/5 (1 May 1993)

Situations of Internal Violence, DOCT /4-1993/1 (1 May 1993)

Judicial Proceedings in Situations of Detention and Imprisonment, DOCT/56-1996/1 (29 May 1996)

Disappeared Persons, DOCT/28-2003/5 (8 May 2003)

Improving Compliance with International Humanitarian Law, ICRC Expert Seminar (Geneva: ICRC, October 2003)

Demarches in Case of Violations of International Humanitarian Law and other Fundamental Protective Rules, DOCT/15-2005/10 (11 April 2005)

The Invocation of International Human Rights Law by the International Committee of the Red Cross, DOCT/63-2006/1 (25 August 2006)

Interpretative Guidance on the Notion of Direct Participation in Hostilities under International Humanitarian Law, adopted by the Assembly of the International Committee of the Red Cross (26 February 2009)

International Humanitarian Law and the Challenges of Contemporary Armed Conflicts, Report to the 31st International Conference of the Red Cross and Red Crescent (2011)

Expert Meeting on the Law of Occupation and Other Forms of Administration of Territory (2012)

International Council for Human Rights Policy, *Ends and Means: Human Rights Approaches to Armed Groups* (Geneva: International Council for Human Rights Policy, 2000), available at www.ichrp.org/paper_files/105_p_01.pdf

International Human Rights Law Institute, *Chicago Principles on Post-Conflict Justice* (2007)

International Law Association, *The Paris Minimum Standards of Human Rights Norms in a State of Emergency*, reprinted in (1985) 79(4) *American Journal of International Law* 1072

Ministry of Foreign Affairs of Denmark, *Copenhagen Process on the Handling of Detainees in International Military Operations* (2000), available at http://um.dk/en/politics-and-diplomacy/copenhagen-process-on-the-handling-of-detainees-in-international-military-operations

Office of the High Commissioner for Human Rights, *International Humanitarian Law and Human Rights Law*, Fact Sheet No. 13 (Geneva: United Nations, 1991)

Enforced or Involuntary Disappearances, Fact Sheet No. 6 (Rev.3) (Geneva: United Nations, 2009)

International Legal Protection of Human Rights in Armed Conflict (New York and Geneva: United Nations, 2011)

"Strategic Management Plan," www.ohchr.org/Documents/Press/SMP2010-2011.pdf

United Nations Development Programme, *Human Development Report 1994: New Dimensions of Human Security* (1994), available at http://hdr.undp.org/reports/global/1994/en

United States Defence Department, *Working Group Report on Detainee Interrogations in the Global War on Terrorism: Assessment of Legal Historical, Policy, and Operational Considerations* (6 March 2003), available at www.antiwar.com/news/?articleid=2776

UPR Info, *Universal Periodic Review: On the Road to Implementation* (2012), available at www.upr-info.org/IMG/pdf/2012_on_the_road_to_implementation.pdf

INDEX